THE MOVIE QUOTE BOOK

THE MOVIE QUOTE BOOK

HARRY HAUN

BONANZA BOOKS • NEW YORK

This 1986 edition is published by Bonanza Books,
distributed by Crown Publishers, Inc., by arrangement with
Harper & Row Publishers, Inc.

Printed and Bound in the United States of America

Library of Congress Cataloging-in-Publication Data
Main entry under title:

The Movie quote book.

  1. Quotations, English. 2. Moving-pictures—
Miscellanea. I. Haun, Harry.
PN6083.M75 1986   791.43   85-30883
ISBN 0-517-60360-8

Designed by C. Linda Dingler

h g f e d c b a

This book is for Valerie Ross, Shirley Kaplan, and Monty Arnold—all of whom supported and sustained me during this project—and it is for The World's Greatest Movie Fan, wherever he is . . . .

CONTENTS

x   CONTENTS

INTRODUCTION

The talkies were about two reels old when they got off their first understatement—Al Jolson assuring the folks, between songs, "You ain't heard nothin' yet." And indeed they hadn't. The mechanical miracle of sound synchronized roughly (very roughly in the beginning) with silent-screen images carried the medium a giant step forward.

Not everyone saw *The Jazz Singer* as a revolutionary turn of the corner. Louella O. Parsons predicted a quick demise for talkies, and Cedric Belfrage went into immediate mourning that the "international language" of silent movies was over. "Here we finally come to a language which could be shown everywhere, and which everyone could understand," he grieved, "and we were just blowing it up."

Sound had indeed exploded on the screen, and Hollywood was never the same again. In the first reverberations of the talkies, everything changed. Stars secure in their galaxy suddenly and unceremoniously fell from favor, to be replaced by stage-trained performers. A literacy much larger and more complex than the occasional title card soon followed suit.

Purists will still tell you that movies are a visual medium and that talk subtracted more than it added to the art form. But evidence to the contrary is a trifle overwhelming, and there is little doubt that the dimension of dialogue has greatly increased the broad base appeal of movies.

Screenwriters have historically been the low men on the totem pole in the Hollywood hierarchy—this, despite the fact that the foundation of any film is its script—and, if their work shows up on the screen at all, it is indirectly through the interplay of directors and actors. "Audiences don't know somebody sits down and writes a picture," observed the cynical screenwriter in *Sunset Boulevard*. "They think the actors make it up as they go along."

By design and by nature, screenwriting remains an unsung art form—the best screenplays, some contend, don't even call attention to themselves—yet this vastly unappreciated literature often reaches beyond the screen into the consciousness of the audience. I am constantly amazed, watching "The Late Show," at how many Joseph Cotten lines have slipped into my normal speech habits.

Favorite lines cling to the mind—not always accurately, either. Bogart never said "Play it again, Sam," Boyer never said "Come with me to the Casbah," and Mae West never said "Come up and see me sometime." These are misquoted myths.

Movies still talk—but with markedly less literary merit and eloquence. Cinema does something else now. Character studies are more pastel, and the accompanying dialogue lacks the primal directness of old.

This book celebrates a time when movies had something to say—and what was said was worth remembering, worth holding on to. I would like to acknowledge the valuable assistance of Judith M. Kass, John Cocchi, Larry Ashmead, James Ross, James Delson, Jamie Mendlovitz, and Andy Graham in the preparation of this material. The book is meant to be a tribute to the unsung heroes who inspired it in the first place.

THE MOVIE QUOTE BOOK

ACCURACY

1.

"I'm the most widely misquoted man in America. When my friends do it, I resent it. From Sergeants McAvity and Schultz, I should find it intolerable."

—Clifton Webb establishing his elitism early on in Otto Preminger's *Laura*
(Screenplay by Jay Dratler, Samuel Hoffenstein and Betty Reinhardt; based on the novel by Vera Caspary)

2.

"Fred C. Dobbs don't say nuthin' he don't mean."

—Humphrey Bogart pretending to be a man of his word in John Huston's *The Treasure of the Sierra Madre*
(Screenplay by John Huston; based on the novel by B. Traven)

3.

"I heard a scream, and I didn't know if it was me who screamed or not—if it was *I* or not."

—Olivia De Havilland getting grammatical about her madness in Anatole Litvak's *The Snake Pit*
(Screenplay by Frank Partos and Millen Brand; based on the novel by Mary Jane Ward)

ACTION

1.

"There are two kinds of people: Those who don't do what they want to do, so they write down in a diary about what they haven't done, and those who haven't time to write about it, because they're out doing it."

—Charles Coburn preaching action to Jean Arthur in George Stevens's *The More the Merrier*
(Screenplay by Richard Flournoy and Lewis R. Foster; based on a story by Robert Russell and Frank Ross)

2.

"Kathy and Harry and Jane and all of them— they scold Bilbo twice a year and think they've fought the good fight for democracy in this country. They haven't got the guts to take the step from talking to action. One little action on one little front. Sure, I know it's not the whole answer, but it's got to start somewhere. And it's got to be with action—not pamphlets, not even with your series. It's got to be with people— nice people, rich people, poor people, big and little people. It's got to be quick."

—Celeste Holm pep-talking to Gregory Peck about the prejudices that spread from a lack of commitment in Elia Kazan's *Gentleman's Agreement*
(Screenplay by Moss Hart; based on the novel by Laura Z. Hobson)

3.

"Today democracy, liberty and equality are words to fool the people. No nation can progress with such ideas. They stand in the way of action. Therefore, we frankly abolish them."

—Henry Daniell laying down the new order of things in Charles Chaplin's *The Great Dictator*
(Original Screenplay by Charles Chaplin)

ALSO SEE: Apathy-2; Love-15.

ACTORS

1.

"I try to be careful, Mr. Dodd, but being an actor's wife is not the easiest of jobs. If I tell him he's magnificent, he says I'm not being honest —if I tell him he's not magnificent, he says I don't love him."

—Grace Kelly explaining to William Holden her marital dilemma with Bing Crosby in George Seaton's *The Country Girl*
(Screenplay by George Seaton; based on the play by Clifford Odets)

2.

"What he did to Shakespeare, we are doing now to Poland."

—Nazi colonel Sig Ruman critiquing Jack Benny's acting in Ernst Lubitsch's *To Be or Not To Be*
(Screenplay by Edwin Justus Mayer; based on an original story by Ernst Lubitsch and Melchior Lengyel)

3.

"Miss Caswell is an actress, a graduate of the Copacabana School of Dramatic Arts."

—George Sanders introducing his protégée (Marilyn Monroe) to Bette Davis in Joseph L. Mankiewicz's *All About Eve*
(Screenplay by Joseph L. Mankiewicz; based on "The Wisdom of Eve," a radio play and short story by Mary Orr)

4.

"How do you know who's an actress and who isn't? You're an actress if you're acting. But you can't just walk up and down a room and act. Without that job and those lines to say, an actress is just like any ordinary girl trying not to look as scared as she feels."

—Andrea Leeds revealing the panic of unemployment to Katharine Hepburn in Gregory La Cava's *Stage Door*
(Screenplay by Morrie Ryskind and Anthony Veiller; based on the play by Edna Ferber and George S. Kaufman)

5.

"As an actor, no one could touch him. As a human being, no one wanted to touch him."

—Walter Matthau characterizing George Burns in Herbert Ross's *The Sunshine Boys*
(Screenplay by Neil Simon; based on his play)

6.

(a) "Have you lost your mind? How can you 'kill the actors'? What do you mean 'kill the actors'? Actors are not animals. They're human beings."

   (b) "They are? Have you ever eaten with one?"

—(a) Gene Wilder and, grudgingly, (b) Zero Mostel trying to dissuade deranged playwright Kenneth Mars from a cast execution in Mel Brooks's *The Producers*
(Original Screenplay by Mel Brooks)

ALSO SEE: Applause; Movies; Star; Theater; Aging-4; Differences-5; Excuses-6; Heart-24; Names-27; Past-2; Past-7; Past-8; Pep Talks-6; Sex-7; Sin-4; Strength-4; Talent-3; Thieves-7.

ADOLESCENCE

1.

"Adolescence! What is adolescence? Adolescence is a time when people worry about things there's no need to worry about."

—Heinz Rühmann consoling Gila Golan in Stanley Kramer's *Ship of Fools*
(Screenplay by Abby Mann; based on the novel by Katherine Anne Porter)

2.

"Susan's growing pains are rapidly becoming a major disease."

—Myrna Loy fretting to Rudy Vallee about her sister (Shirley Temple) in Irving Reis's *The Bachelor and the Bobby-Soxer*
(Original Screenplay by Sidney Sheldon)

3.

"I was never to see her again. Nor was I ever to learn what became of her. We were different then. Kids were different. It took us longer to understand the things we felt. Life is made up of small comings and goings, and, for everything we take with us, there is something that we leave behind. In the summer of '42: we raided the Coast Guard station four times; we saw five movies and had nine days of rain; Benjie broke his watch; Oscy gave up the harmonica; and, in a very special way, I lost Hermie—forever."

—Robert Mulligan, as the never-seen narrator (a grown-up version of Gary Grimes), reflecting on his graduation from Hermie to Herman in the last lines of Robert Mulligan's *Summer of '42*
(Original Screenplay by Herman Raucher)

ADULTERY

1.

"I know, Buddy-boy, I know. But those things don't always run on schedule—like a Greyhound bus."

—David Lewis explaining his prolonged affairs in Jack Lemmon's pad in Billy Wilder's *The Apartment*

(Original Screenplay by Billy Wilder and I. A. L. Diamond)

2.

"You mustn't think too harshly of my secretaries. They were kind and understanding when I came to the office after a hard day at home."

—Claude Rains giving Bette Davis full credit for his infidelity in Vincent Sherman's *Mr. Skeffington*
(Screenplay by Julius J. Epstein and Philip G. Epstein; based on the story by "Elizabeth")

3.

"Get out, go anywhere you want, go to a hotel, go live with her, but don't come back! Because, after 25 years of building a home and raising a family and all the senseless pain that we have inflicted on each other, I'm damned if I'm going to stand here and have you tell me you're in love with somebody else! Because this isn't a convention weekend with your secretary, is it? Or—or some broad that you picked up after three belts of booze. This is your great winter romance, isn't it? Your last roar of passion before you settle into your emeritus years. Is that what's left for me? Is that my share? She gets the winter passion, and I get the dotage? What am I supposed to do? Am I supposed to sit at home knitting and purling while you slink back like some penitent drunk? I'm your wife, damn it! And, if you can't work up a winter passion for me, the least I require is respect and allegiance! I hurt! Don't you understand that? I hurt badly!"

—Beatrice Straight kicking out her unfaithful hubby (William Holden) in Sidney Lumet's *Network*
(Original Screenplay by Paddy Chayefsky)

4.

"What most wives fail to realize is that their husbands' philandering has nothing whatever to do with them."

—John Halliday crediting Mary Nash at least with understanding in George Cukor's *The Philadelphia Story*
(Screenplay by Donald Ogden Stewart; based on the play by Philip Barry)
                    and (almost verbatim)

—Sidney Blackmer dittoing Margalo Gillmore in the remake, Charles Walters's *High Society*
(Screenplay by John Patrick; based on THE PHILADELPHIA STORY, *a screenplay by Donald Ogden Stewart and play by Philip Barry)*

5.

"I was down on my knees asking his forgiveness because I asked him to marry me. Down on my knees! How dare he make love to me and not be a married man!"

—Ingrid Bergman discovering that Cary Grant is not the married man he pretended to be in Stanley Donen's *Indiscreet*
(Screenplay by Norman Krasna; based on his play, KIND SIR)

6.

"You, Bernice, and I are, three of us, in a boat. Now, it's my boat, and it's your lake, but Bernice has the oars."

—Gig Young telling his mistress (Anne Jackson) that his wife (Cloris Leachman) has the upper oar in Cy Howard's *Lovers and Other Strangers*
(Screenplay by Renee Taylor, Joseph Bologna, and David Z. Goodman; based on the play by Renee Taylor and Joseph Bologna)

7.

(a) "You know, Emma, there are three kinds of deceived husbands in the world: first are those who were born to be deceived; second who do not know; and third who do not care. I've been wondering for some time now which of the three I should be myself."

(b) "Have you forgotten the fourth kind, William? The kind that is hard and empty and gives nothing? You married me because you wanted a new ornament for your house, like that painting or that statue or vase. As far as you're concerned, I'm just as ornamental and just as dead."

(a) "But, my dear, how can you call my statues dead? When I'm alone and rather tired, think what it means to me to have my statues with me, to know that they will always be lovely, will never grow old and never walk out with sailors."

—(a) Alan Mowbray confronting (b) Vivien Leigh about her affair with Laurence Olivier in Alexander Korda's *That Hamilton Woman*
(Original Screenplay by Walter Reisch and R. C. Sherriff)

8.

"We women are so much more sensible! When *we* tire of ourselves, we change the way we do our hair, or hire a new cook. Or redecorate the house. I suppose a man could do over his office, but he never thinks of anything so simple. No, dear, a man has only one escape from his old self—to see a different self in the mirror of some woman's eyes."

—Lucile Watson consoling Norma Shearer in George Cukor's *The Women*
(Screenplay by Anita Loos and Jane Murfin; based on the play by Clare Boothe)

ALSO SEE: Fidelity; Awards-2; Feelings-4; Gigolo-7; Headlines-11; Honor-1; Loneliness-9; Manners-5; Stimulating-4; Timing-1; Understand-3; Wrong-6.

ADVERTISING SLOGANS

1.

"If you can't sleep at night, it isn't the coffee—it's the bunk."

—Dick Powell quoting his winning coffee-jingle in Preston Sturges's *Christmas in July*
(Original Screenplay by Preston Sturges)

2.

"If you ain't eating Wham, you ain't eating ham."

—Louise Beavers, a Wham ham-happy maid, accidentally signaling an advertising campaign for her employer (Cary Grant) in H. C. Potter's *Mr. Blandings Builds His Dream House*
(Screenplay by Norman Panama and Melvin Frank; based on the novel by Eric Hodgins)

ADVICE

1.

"Plastics."

—Walter Brooke pointing the way of the future to title-player Dustin Hoffman in Mike Nichols's *The Graduate*
(Screenplay by Calder Willingham and Buck Henry; based on the novel by Charles Webb)

2.

"Box it."

—Ned Sparks telling Claudette Colbert what she can do with her pancake recipe to make a fortune in John Stahl's *Imitation of Life*
(Screenplay by William Hurlbut; based on the novel by Fannie Hurst)

3.

"Hindley, why don't you hit yourself over the head with a hammer the instant you get up in the morning? . . . If you hit yourself hard enough, you will remain unconscious the whole day and achieve virtually the same results you would from a whole gallon of spirits—with much less wear and tear on the kidneys."

—Donald Crisp cynically dispensing medical advice to alcoholic Hugh Williams in William Wyler's *Wuthering Heights*
(Screenplay by Ben Hecht and Charles MacArthur; based on the novel by Emily Brontë)

4.

"Veda's been here for about a month now, Mildred, and I think I know the best way to handle her. Let me give you a little advice: if you want her to do anything for you, just hit her in the head first."

—Jack Carson counseling Joan Crawford about Ann Blyth in Michael Curtiz's *Mildred Pierce*
(Screenplay by Ranald MacDougall; based on the novel by James M. Cain)

5.

"I'm going to give you a piece of advice, Karl: when they let you free again, get out of New York. You butcher one more patient, and, law or no law, I'll find you. I'll put a bullet in the back of your head, and I'll drop your body in the East River. And I'll go home, and I'll sleep sweetly."

—Police detective Kirk Douglas threatening abortionist George Macready in William Wyler's *Detective Story*
(Screenplay by Philip Yordan and Robert Wyler; based on the play by Sidney Kingsley)

6.
"Sing out, Louise. Sing out."

—Rosalind Russell coaching from the sidelines as the ultimate of stage mothers in Mervyn LeRoy's *Gypsy*
(Screenplay by Leonard Spigelgass; based on the musical play by Arthur Laurents and memoirs of Gypsy Rose Lee)

7.
"It's not that I'm prudish. It's just that my mother told me never to enter any man's room in months ending in 'R.' "

—Irene Dunne dodging an amorous Charles Boyer in Leo McCarey's *Love Affair*
(Screenplay by Delmer Daves and Donald Ogden Stewart; based on an original story by Mildred Cram and Leo McCarey)
                    and (almost verbatim)

—Deborah Kerr dittoing Cary Grant in the remake, Leo McCarey's *An Affair to Remember*
(Screenplay by Delmer Daves and Leo McCarey; based on an original story by Mildred Cram and Leo McCarey)

8.
"When I graduate from college, I'm going to go to New York and write novels that'll shock people right out of their senses. I'm never going to fall in love. Not me. I'm not going to live in some jerkwater town and marry some ornery guy and raise a lot of grimy kids—but just because I'm a dope doesn't mean you have to be."

—Susan Strasberg advising her sister (Kim Novak) to run off with William Holden in Joshua Logan's *Picnic*
(Screenplay by Daniel Taradash; based on the play by William Inge)

9.
"Oh, and one more piece of motherly advice. Don't confide in your girlfriends. . . . If you let them advise you, they'll see to it in the name of friendship that you lose your husband and your home."

—Lucile Watson counseling her daughter (Norma Shearer) in George Cukor's *The Women*
(Screenplay by Anita Loos and Jane Murfin; based on the play by Clare Boothe)

ALSO SEE: Available-1; Class-7; Doctors-2; Fingers-4; Macho-3; Macho-21; Stupid-5; Success-3; Wives-11; Youth-1; Youth-2.

AGING

1.
"The name is Smollett, William G. Colonel, United States Army, retired—retired, I might add, by virtue of certain fatuous opinions held by the War Department which judge a man's usefulness neither by his experience nor his ability but by the number of years since he was weaned!"

—Monty Woolley introducing himself as a testy senior citizen to Claudette Colbert in John Cromwell's *Since You Went Away*
(Screenplay by David O. Selznick; adaptation by Margaret Buell Wilder; based on her book of letters)

2.
"Remember, I—I did make a home for you once, and I'll do it again—only you've *got* to let me have my fling now! Because you're simply rushing at old age, Sam, and I'm not ready for that yet."

—Ruth Chatterton reaching a parting of the ways with her husband (Walter Huston) in William Wyler's *Dodsworth*
(Screenplay by Sidney Howard; based on his play and the novel by Sinclair Lewis)

3.
"These are the worst years, I tell you. It's gonna

happen to you. I—I'm afraid to look inna mirror. I'm afraid I'm going to see an old lady with white hair, just like the old ladies inna park—little bundles in a black shawl waiting for the coffin. I'm 56 years old. And what am I to do with myself? I got strength in my hands. I wanna clean. I—I wanna cook. I wanna make dinner for my children. Am I an old dog to lay near the fire till my eyes close? These are terrible years, Theresa! Terrible years!"

—Augusta Ciolli warning her sister (Esther Minciotti) of a grim future in Delbert Mann's *Marty*
(*Screenplay by Paddy Chayefsky; based on his teleplay*)

4.
"I'm just telling you the truth. You know, you never were an actor. You did have looks, but they're gone now. You don't have to take my word for it. Just look in any mirror. They don't lie. Take a good look. Look at those pouches under your eyes. Look at those creases. You sag like an old woman. Get a load of yourself."

—Lee Tracy telling off John Barrymore in George Cukor's *Dinner at Eight*
(*Screenplay by Frances Marion and Herman J. Mankiewicz; based on the play by George S. Kaufman and Edna Ferber*)

5.
"A cultivated woman—a woman of breeding and intelligence—can enrich a man's life immeasurably. I have those things to offer, and time doesn't take them away. Physical beauty is passing—a transitory possession—but beauty of the mind, richness of the spirit, tenderness of the heart—I have all those things—aren't taken away but grow! Increase with the years!"

—Vivien Leigh making an argument (to herself) for inner beauty in Elia Kazan's *A Streetcar Named Desire*
(*Screenplay by Tennessee Williams; adaptation by Oscar Saul; based on the play by Tennessee Williams*)

6.
"You are not young, Mrs. Treadwell. You have

not been young for years. Behind those old eyes you hide a 16-year-old heart."

—Vivien Leigh scrutinizing the mirror in Stanley Kramer's *Ship of Fools*
(*Screenplay by Abby Mann; based on the novel by Katherine Anne Porter*)

7.
"I've aged, Sidney. There are new lines in my face. I look like a brand-new, steel-belted radial tire."

—Maggie Smith scrutinizing the mirror in Herbert Ross's *California Suite*
(*Screenplay by Neil Simon; based on his play*)

8.
"Yes, I can see the makeup now all right. The lines that weren't there before. The beginning. And there'll be more and more and then, one day, this face will begin to decay and there'll be nothing left to make a man grovel."

—Burt Lancaster scrutinizing Rita Hayworth in Delbert Mann's *Separate Tables*
(*Screenplay by Terence Rattigan and John Gay; based on the play by Terence Rattigan*)

9.
"Norma, you're a woman of 50. Now, grow up! There's nothing tragic about being 50—not unless you try to be 25."

—William Holden trying to get Gloria Swanson to act her age in Billy Wilder's *Sunset Boulevard*
(*Original Screenplay by Charles Brackett, Billy Wilder and D. M. Marshman Jr.*)

10.
"Fifty—the old age of youth, the youth of old age."

—William Powell characterizing his awkward age in Irving Pichel's *Mr. Peabody and the Mermaid*
(*Screenplay by Nunnally Johnson; based on PEABODY'S MERMAID, a novel by Guy Jones and Constance Jones*)

11.
"It *was* me, eight years ago. A fella in the states saw that picture. He wrote me. I was lonely so

I answered. There were a lot of letters—beautiful letters—and then last month I agreed to marry him. I never got around to telling him the picture was eight years old. I don't want to bore you with my troubles. That dream kept me sane for a long time. I know I'm a—a mess. I'm so much older than he thinks I am. Oh, if I could just see him and leave without meeting him."

—Jan Sterling bracing for rejection in William A. Wellman's *The High and the Mighty*
(Screenplay by Ernest K. Gann; based on his novel)

12.
"Anyway, I'd be too old for you. 'Cold are the hands of time that creep along relentlessly, destroying slowly but without pity that which yesterday was young. Alone, our memories resist this disintegration and grow more lovely with the passing years.' That's hard to say with false teeth."

—Robert Dudley rattling on to a total stranger (Claudette Colbert) in Preston Sturges's *The Palm Beach Story*
(Original Screenplay by Preston Sturges)

13.
"Remarkable old girl, Lady Millicent. We used to have great times together. Deauville, back in the '20s. I persuaded her to go in swimming at 70. I watched her frolicking in the surf and had sad thoughts about the impermanence of beauty."

—Charles Laughton boring his dinner guests in Alfred Hitchcock's *The Paradine Case*
(Screenplay by David O. Selznick; adaptation by Alma Reville and James Bridie; based on the novel by Robert Hichens)

14.
"Well, at least age does give tone to certain things—violins, old wine, old friends to drink it with."

—Edith Evans defending maturity to Felix Aylmer in Ronald Neame's *The Chalk Garden*
(Screenplay by John Michael Hayes; based on the play by Enid Bagnold)

15.
"At 21 or 22, so many things appear solid, permanent, untenable, which, at 40, seems nothing but disappearing mire. Forty can't tell 20 about this. Twenty can find that only by getting to be 40."

—Joseph Cotten writing Dolores Costello about her son (Tim Holt) in Orson Welles's *The Magnificent Ambersons*
(Screenplay by Orson Welles; based on the novel by Booth Tarkington)

16.
"Do you know what I think when I see a pretty girl? . . . 'Oh, to be 80 again.'"

—Louis Calhern playing the foxy grandpa in John Sturges's *The Magnificent Yankee*
(Screenplay by Emmett Lavery; based on his play and MR. JUSTICE HOLMES, the biography by Francis Biddle)

ALSO SEE: Blood-4; Choice-11; Disease-1; Fake-3; Greetings-7; Home-4; Hope-1; Looks-1; Men-3; Money-6; Passion-3; Platonic Relationships-1; Pretense-5; Proposals-14; Seasons-6; Tired-1.

ALONE

1.
"I want to be alone."

—Greta Garbo dismissing John Barrymore in Edmund Goulding's *Grand Hotel*
(Screenplay by William A. Drake; based on the play and novel by Vicki Baum)

2.
"Go to bed, little father. We want to be alone."

—Greta Garbo dismissing Melvyn Douglas's butler (Richard Carle) in Ernst Lubitsch's *Ninotchka*
(Screenplay by Charles Brackett, Billy Wilder and Walter Reisch; based on an original story by Melchior Lengyel)

3.
(a) "What touches you? What warms you?

Every man has a dream. What do you dream about? What—what do you need? You don't need anything, do you? People love an idea just to cling to them. You poor slob! You're all alone. When you go to your grave, there won't be anybody to pull the grass up over your head. Nobody to mourn you. Nobody to give a damn. You're all alone."

(b) "You're wrong, Henry. You'll be there. You're the type. Who else would defend my right to be lonely?"

—(a) Spencer Tracy and (b) Gene Kelly parting in the last lines of Stanley Kramer's *Inherit the Wind* *(Screenplay by Nathan E. Douglas and Harold Jacob Smith; based on the play by Jerome Lawrence and Robert E. Lee)*

4.
"I don't want to die alone."

—Richard Todd finally articulating his true feelings in Vincent Sherman's *The Hasty Heart* *(Screenplay by Ranald MacDougall; based on the play by John Patrick)*

5.
"Must I carry the weight—the agony—of the world alone?"

—Bette Davis feeling the loneliness of command as Elizabeth I in Michael Curtiz's *The Private Lives of Elizabeth and Essex* *(Screenplay by Norman Reilly Raine and Aeneas MacKenzie; based on ELIZABETH THE QUEEN, a play by Maxwell Anderson)*

6.
"It's hard to believe, but you can be more lonely in New York than this hotel. Even with their separate tables, they can talk back and forth. But being alone in a crowd is worse. It's more painful, more frightening—oh so frightening, so frightening. I'm an awful coward, you see. I—I've never been able to face anything alone."

—Rita Hayworth confessing her fear of loneliness to her ex (Burt Lancaster) in Delbert Mann's *Separate Tables* *(Screenplay by Terence Rattigan and John Gay; based on the play by Terence Rattigan)*

7.
"You just haven't managed to grow up, Mrs. Treadwell of Murray Hill, Virginia. You can paint your toenails green. You know how it ends, don't you? Alone—sitting in a cafe, with a paid escort."

—Vivien Leigh talking to her mirror in Stanley Kramer's *Ship of Fools* *(Screenplay by Abby Mann; based on the novel by Katherine Anne Porter)*

8.
"I don't like to be alone at night. I guess everybody in the world has a time they don't like. With me, it's right before I go to sleep. Now, it's going to be for always—all the rest of my life."

—Bette Davis preparing for life without Paul Lukas in Herman Shumlin's *Watch on the Rhine* *(Screenplay by Dashiell Hammett; additional scenes and dialogue by Lillian Hellman; based on her play)*

9.
"Georgia, I have to be alone tonight. After a picture is finished, something happens to me. The feeling of letdown, emptiness. It's bad. It gets worse. I can't help it."

—Kirk Douglas explaining his post-premiere slump to Lana Turner in Vincente Minnelli's *The Bad and the Beautiful* *(Screenplay by Charles Schnee; based on "Memorial to a Bad Man" and "Of Good and Evil," two short stories by George Bradshaw)*

10.
"If there's anything worse than a woman living alone, it's a woman saying she likes it."

—Thelma Ritter begging to differ with Doris Day in Michael Gordon's *Pillow Talk* *(Screenplay by Stanley Shapiro and Maurice Richlin; based on a story by Russell Rouse and Clarence Greene)*

ALSO SEE: Loneliness; Convictions-1; Elephants-2; Guilty-2; Hands-3; Lies-23; Mothers-9; Pride-4; Proposals-10; Talent-3; Wish-6.

ALWAYS

1.
"Always? That's a dreadful word. It makes me shudder to hear it. Women are so fond of using it, and they spoil every romance by trying to make it last forever."

—George Sanders preaching short-term promiscuity in Albert Lewin's *The Picture of Dorian Gray*
(Screenplay by Albert Lewin; based on the novel by Oscar Wilde)

2.
"I always look well when I'm near death."

—Greta Garbo flicking off a compliment in George Cukor's *Camille*
(Screenplay by Zoe Akins, Frances Marion and James Hilton; based on LA DAME AUX CAMELIAS, a play and novel by Alexandre Dumas)

3.
"I always gagged on that silver spoon."

—Orson Welles putting down his wealth in Orson Welles's *Citizen Kane*
(Original Screenplay by Herman J. Mankiewicz and Orson Welles)

4.
"I always get the fuzzy end of the lollipop."

—Marilyn Monroe admitting a history of bad luck to Tony Curtis in Billy Wilder's *Some Like It Hot*
(Screenplay by Billy Wilder and I. A. L. Diamond; suggested by a story by R. Thoeren and M. Logan)

5.
"I've always been a liar."

—Mary Astor speaking the truth, for a change, to Humphrey Bogart in John Huston's *The Maltese Falcon*
(Screenplay by John Huston; based on the novel by Dashiell Hammett)

6.
"The cops always like to solve murders done with my gun."

—Dick Powell telling Anne Shirley why the police have to be brought into the case in Edward Dmytryk's *Murder, My Sweet*
(Screenplay by John Paxton; based on FAREWELL, MY LOVELY, a novel by Raymond Chandler)

ALSO SEE: Alone-8; Coward-6; Diamonds-1; Disease-7; Drink Excuses-1; Drink Excuses-4; Exchanges-16; Eyes-6; Hanging-5; Head-2; Heart-6; Heart-14; Heaven-7; Help-1; Hero-4; Honest-3; Horses-1; Kindness-6; Kiss-14; Laugh-3; Love-41; Manners-1; Men-9; Paris-2; Pleasures-3; Prayers-1; Prison-6; Producers-1; Run-4; Sayings-6; Self-Perception-11; Static-6; Translations-6; Understand-3; Wish-1.

AMATEUR

1.
"He was doubled up on his face. In that bag-of-old-clothes position that always means the same thing. He had been killed by an amateur. Or by somebody who wanted it to look like an amateur job. Nobody else would hit a man that many times with a sap."

—Dick Powell uncovering a corpse in Edward Dymtryk's *Murder, My Sweet*
(Screenplay by John Paxton; based on FAREWELL, MY LOVELY, a novel by Raymond Chandler)

2.
"They talk about flat-footed policemen. May the saints protect us from the gifted amateur!"

—John Williams getting elitist about being a professional policeman in Alfred Hitchcock's *Dial M for Murder*
(Screenplay by Frederick Knott; based on his play)

3.
" 'Miss Susan Alexander, a pretty but hopelessly incompetent amateur, last night opened the new Chicago Opera House in a performance of'—I still can't pronounce that name, Mr. Kane. 'Her singing, happily, is no concern of this department. Of her acting, it is absolutely impossible to—' "

—Everett Sloane reading to Orson Welles the review of Dorothy Comingore that Joseph Cotten wrote before passing out in a drunken stupor in Orson Welles's *Citizen Kane*

(Original Screenplay by Herman J. Mankiewicz and Orson Welles)

4.

"I have no great respect for psychiatry—and great contempt for meddling amateurs who go around practicing it."

—Edmund Gwenn telling off Porter Hall in George Seaton's *Miracle on 34th Street*
(Screenplay by George Seaton; based on an original story by Valentine Davis)

ALSO SEE: Fools-2.

ANGEL

1.

"I'm going to find me an angel. I'm going to find me a real hootenanny of an angel. If she gives me any trouble, she's going to find herself with them little old wings just pinned right to the ground."

—Don Murray setting his sights for a mate in Joshua Logan's *Bus Stop*
(Screenplay by George Axelrod; based on the play by William Inge)

2.

"Well, you look about like the kind of angel I'd get. Sort of a fallen angel, aren't you? What happened to your wings?"

—James Stewart berating his heavenly messenger (Henry Travers) in Frank Capra's *It's a Wonderful Life*
(Screenplay by Albert Hackett, Frances Goodrich and Frank Capra; based on "The Greatest Gift," a short story by Philip Van Doren Stern)

3.

"Yes, angel, I'm gonna send you over."

—Humphrey Bogart telling Mary Astor that he's turning her in in John Huston's *The Maltese Falcon*
(Screenplay by John Huston; based on the novel by Dashiell Hammett)

4.

"You can't pin sergeant's stripes on an archangel."

—Millard Mitchell addressing his soldiers about a Congressional committee arriving to investigate morals in postwar Germany in Billy Wilder's *A Foreign Affair*
(Screenplay by Charles Brackett, Billy Wilder and Richard L. Breen; adaptation by Robert Harari; based on an original story by David Shaw)

ALSO SEE: Fights-9; Heaven-6; Sounds-2; Trust and Distrust-9; Truth-5.

ANIMALS

1.

"He's like an animal. He has an animal's habits. There's even something subhuman about him. Thousands of years have passed him right by, and there he is! Stanley Kowalski, survivor of the Stone Age, bearing the raw meat home from the kill in the jungle! And you—you here waiting for him. Maybe he'll strike you or maybe grunt and kiss you, that's if kisses have been discovered yet!"

—Vivien Leigh warning Kim Hunter about Marlon Brando in Elia Kazan's *A Streetcar Named Desire*
(Screenplay by Tennessee Williams; adaptation by Oscar Saul; based on the play by Tennessee Williams)

2.

"People! Animals are not like that. They're always cleaning themselves. Did you ever see pigeons? Well, he's always picking on himself and his friends. They're always picking bugs out of their hair all the time. Monkeys, too—except they do something out in the open that I don't go for."

—Helena Kallianiotes railing about human filth in Bob Rafelson's *Five Easy Pieces*
(Screenplay by Adrien Joyce; based on a story by Bob Rafelson and Adrien Joyce)

ALSO SEE: Dogs; Elephants; Horses; Actors-6; Automobiles-3; Eat-1; Imagination-1; Loneliness-4; Men-6; Men-12; Moon-6; Moon-7; Music-8; Orders-5; Remember-3; Sex Appeal-3; Sounds-3; Stomach-1; Taste-2; Why-2.

APATHY

1.

"I'm through with the Movement long since. I saw that if men wanted to be saved from themselves that would mean they'd have to give up greed, and they wouldn't pay that price for liberty, so I said to the world, 'God bless all here, and may the best man win—and die of gluttony!' I took a seat in the grandstand of philosophical detachment to fall asleep observing the cannibals do their death dance."

—Robert Ryan playing the burned-out firebrand to his bartender (Tom Pedi) in John Frankenheimer's *The Iceman Cometh*
(Screenplay based on the play by Eugene O'Neill; text edited by Thomas Quinn Curtiss)

2.

"Addie said there were people who ate the earth and people who stood around and watched them do it. And just now Uncle Ben said the same thing. Really the same thing. Well, tell him for me, Mama, I'm not going to watch you do it. Tell him I'll be fighting as hard as he is, someplace where people don't stand around and watch."

—Teresa Wright quoting her maid (Jessica Grayson) and her uncle (Charles Dingle) defiantly to her mother (Bette Davis) in William Wyler's *The Little Foxes*
(Screenplay by Lillian Hellman; additional scenes and dialogue by Arthur Kober, Dorothy Parker and Alan Campbell; based on the play by Lillian Hellman)

ALSO SEE: Fights-6; Letters-7; People-3; Silence-2.

APOLOGY

1.

"Pres, I can't believe it's you here. I dreamed about it so long—a lifetime. No. Longer than that. I put on this white dress for you—to help me tell you how humbly I ask you to forgive me."

—Bette Davis welcoming Henry Fonda back into her life after scandalizing him by wearing red to a formal ball in William Wyler's *Jezebel*
(Screenplay by Clements Ripley, Abem Finkel and John Huston; based on the play by Owen Davis, Sr.)

2.

"I—I can only think of one apology: will you marry me? I've arranged for a divorce. Wait for me, and, in time, I'll make you forget every word I uttered last night."

—Laurence Harvey proposing as an apology to Elizabeth Taylor in Daniel Mann's *Butterfield 8*
(Screenplay by Charles Schnee and John Michael Hayes; based on the novel by John O'Hara)

3.

"Miss Dobie, there's no way I can take back what I've done to you, but what little I can do—a public apology, the damage suit to be paid in full, of course, and whatever else you will be kind enough to take from me . . ."

—Alma Kruger trying to make amends for ruining Miriam Hopkins's schoolteaching career in William Wyler's *These Three*
(Screenplay by Lillian Hellman; based on her play, THE CHILDREN'S HOUR)
                    and (almost verbatim)

—Fay Bainter dittoing to Shirley MacLaine in the remake, William Wyler's *The Children's Hour*
(Screenplay by John Michael Hayes; adaptation by Lillian Hellman; based on her play)

4.

"What did you get? You got no apology from me, which you didn't accept."

—George Burns pointing out that Walter Matthau rejected an apology that wasn't even offered in Herbert Ross's *The Sunshine Boys*
(Screenplay by Neil Simon; based on his play)

5.

"I know it's considered noble to accept apologies, but I'm afraid I'm not the noble type."

—Joan Crawford playing it cold with Jan Sterling in Joseph Pevney's *Female on the Beach*
(Screenplay by Robert Hill and Richard Alan

Simmons; based on THE BESIEGED HEART, *a play by Robert Hill)*

ALSO SEE: Frigidity-3; Genius-1; Intelligence-3; Talk-12; Weakness-5.

APPEARANCES

1.

"At our last meeting, I died. It alters the appearance."

—Deborah Kerr confronting the judge who had once sentenced her to death (Felix Aylmer) in Ronald Neame's *The Chalk Garden*
(Screenplay by John Michael Hayes; based on the play by Enid Bagnold)

2.

"You might, from your appearance, be the wife of Lucifer, yet you shall not get the better of me. I'm an Englishwoman. I'm your match!"

—Edna May Oliver squaring off against Blanche Yurka in Jack Conway's *A Tale of Two Cities*
(Screenplay by W. P. Lipscomb and S. N. Behrman; based on the novel by Charles Dickens)

3.

"That's the wife of the Austrian critic. She always looks like she's been out in the rain feeding the poultry."

—Clifton Webb pointing out one of his less-desirable party guests to Kurt Kreuger in Henry Hathaway's *The Dark Corner*
(Screenplay by Jay Dratler and Bernard C. Schoenfeld; based on the novel by Leo Rosten)

4.

"I guess you are sort of attractive, in a corn-fed sort of way. You can find yourself a poor girl falling for you if—well, if you threw in a set of dishes."

—Bette Davis flirting with Richard Travis in William Keighley's *The Man Who Came to Dinner*
(Screenplay by Julius J. Epstein and Philip G. Epstein; based on the play by George S. Kaufman and Moss Hart)

5.

"Thanks for the compliment, but I know how I look. This is the way I look when I'm sober. It's enough to make a person drink, wouldn't you say?"

—Lee Remick being realistic with Jack Lemmon in Blake Edwards's *Days of Wine and Roses*
(Screenplay by J. P. Miller; based on his teleplay)

6.

"Yes, I love him. I love those hick shirts he wears with the boiled cuffs and the way he always has his vest buttoned wrong. He looks like a giraffe, and I love him. I love him because he's the kind of a guy who gets drunk on a glass of buttermilk, and I love the way he blushes right up over his ears. I love him because he doesn't know how to kiss—the jerk! I love him, Joe. That's what I'm trying to tell ya."

—Barbara Stanwyck rhapsodizing about Gary Cooper to Dana Andrews in Howard Hawks's *Ball of Fire*
(Screenplay by Charles Brackett and Billy Wilder; based on "From A to Z," an original story by Thomas Monroe and Billy Wilder)

7.

"Sure, I like him. I like the way he looks, as if he's got something to say but he won't say it. I like the way he tucks his thumbs into his belt. But that doesn't mean I want you to go out and lassoo [sic] him for me."

—Katharine Hepburn rhapsodizing about Wendell Corey to her family in Joseph Anthony's *The Rainmaker*
(Screenplay by N. Richard Nash; based on his play)

ALSO SEE: Angel-2; Choice-1; Prison-5; Producers-1; Relatives-2; Static-3; Women-14.

APPLAUSE

1.

"So little. So little, did you say? Why, if there's nothing else—there's applause. I've listened, from backstage, to people applaud. It's like—like waves of love coming over the footlights and wrapping you up. Imagine. To know, every night, that different hundreds of people love you. They smile. Their eyes shine. You've pleased them. They want you. You belong. Just that alone is worth anything."

—Anne Baxter tipping what makes her tick in Joseph L. Mankiewicz's *All About Eve*
(Screenplay by Joseph L. Mankiewicz; based on "The Wisdom of Eve," a radio play and short story by Mary Orr)

2.
"Danny, I know Peggy, and I—I certainly know you. Well, I can't exactly explain this to you, but—but call it applause, call it ambition, call it whatever you like, but it'd take a lot more than a man to come between you two. You see, Danny, when she rubs her eyes open in the morning, she sees her name up in bright lights—Peggy Nash, Dancer—and all day long she keeps moving those lights around to different theaters and different cities. At night, she goes to sleep with the music of applause in her ears. And, Danny, she can't see you and she can't hear you because she's blinded by those lights and deafened by that applause."

—Arthur Kennedy telling James Cagney about Ann Sheridan's true love in Anatole Litvak's *City for Conquest*
(Screenplay by John Wexley; based on the novel by Aben Kandel)

3.
"For the first time in my life, people cheering for *me*. Were you deaf? Didn't you hear 'em? We're not hitchhiking any more. We're riding."

—Kirk Douglas dying as he hallucinates about his first flush of prizefighting fame in Mark Robson's *Champion*
(Screenplay by Carl Foreman; based on the short story by Ring Lardner)

4.
"Now when the Reverend Mr. Playfair, good man that he is, comes down, I wants yez all to cheer like Protestants."

—Ward Bond instructing his Catholic congregation to extend their applause ecumenically to vicar Arthur Shields in John Ford's *The Quiet Man*
(Screenplay by Frank S. Nugent; based on "Green Rushes," a short story by Maurice Walsh)

ALSO SEE: Curtain Speeches-3.

ARMY

1.
"The Army is always the same. The sun and the moon change, but the Army knows no seasons."

—John Wayne mustering a stiff upper lip about his retirement in John Ford's *She Wore a Yellow Ribbon*
(Screenplay by Frank S. Nugent and Laurence Stallings; based on "The Big Hunt" and "War Party," two short stories by James Warner Bellah)

2.
"What do you want to go back to the Army for? What did the Army ever do for you besides treat you like dirt and give you one awful going-over and get your friend killed? What do you want to go back to the Army for?"

—Donna Reed trying to keep Montgomery Clift AWOL in Fred Zinnemann's *From Here to Eternity*
(Screenplay by Daniel Taradash; based on the novel by James Jones)

3.
"They aren't forgotten because they haven't died. They're living, right out there—Collingwood and the rest—and they'll keep on living as long as the regiment lives. The pay is $13 a month. The diet, beans and eggs—may be horsemeat before this campaign is over. They fight over cards or rot-gut whiskey but share the last drop in their canteens. The faces may change. Names. But they're there. They're the regiment—the regular Army—now and 50 years from now."

—John Wayne eulogizing his fallen cavalrymen in John Ford's *Fort Apache*
(Screenplay by Frank S. Nugent; based on "Massacre," a story by James Warner Bellah)

ALSO SEE: Aging-1; Angel-4; Heart-4; Love Objects-1; Money-11; Signs-3; Together-12; Truth-3.

ARROGANCE

1.
"You come to my office today like George God. Everybody's supposed to come up and audition for Human Being in front of you."

—Martin Balsam telling Jason Robards to bring it down a notch or two in Fred Coe's *A Thousand Clowns*
(Screenplay by Herb Gardner; based on his play)

2.
"I'm not a man that people overlook."

—Clifton Webb understating the case in Edmund Goulding's *The Razor's Edge*
(Screenplay by Lamar Trotti; based on the novel by W. Somerset Maugham)

3.
"He's convinced that the world is headed for mass suicide and nothing is of importance anymore except to himself. His arrogance has become unbearable. He cares nothing for happiness or success. He'd jump off a cliff if he didn't have to climb it first. What is there to do when a man deliberately works against himself and knows that he is doing it? He knows it at the moment of the act. It is an instance of premeditated disaster. He deliberately foments ill will among his fellows and gets a kind of drunken elation out of it."

—Robert Montgomery analyzing himself to John Payne in Claude Binyon's *The Saxon Charm*
(Screenplay by Claude Binyon; based on the novel by Frederic Wakeman)

ALSO SEE: Horses-3.

AUTOMOBILES

1.
"Why didn't you take *all* your clothes off? You could have stopped *40* cars."

—Clark Gable resenting the fact that Claudette Colbert used her legs instead of her thumb to hitch a ride in Frank Capra's *It Happened One Night*
(Screenplay by Robert Riskin; based on "Night Bus," a short story by Samuel Hopkins Adams)

2.
"I said, 'Automobiles are a useless nuisance.' They'll never amount to anything but a nuisance. They had no business to be invented."

—Tim Holt triggering an argumentative dinner conversation in Orson Welles's *The Magnificent Ambersons*
(Screenplay by Orson Welles; based on the novel by Booth Tarkington)

3.
"These days, a man doesn't know whether he's driving a car or an animal. Mustangs. Jaguars. Cougars. Pintos. Silly!"

—Art Carney commenting on the times in Paul Mazursky's *Harry and Tonto*
(Original Screenplay by Paul Mazursky and Josh Greenfeld)

4.
"Hark! I think I hear the master's kiddie-car. I hope the drawbridge is down."

—Dorothy Malone announcing the late arrival of her brother (Robert Stack) for dinner in Douglas Sirk's *Written on the Wind*
(Screenplay by George Zuckerman; based on the novel by Robert Wilder)

ALSO SEE: Detectives-3; First Lines-6; Frigidity-4; Honor-8; Insults-9; Mad Acts-5; Progress-3.

AVAILABLE

1.

"Available? You're like an old coat that's hanging in his closet. Every time he reaches in, there you are. Don't be there once."

—Joan Blondell advising Katharine Hepburn to play harder-to-get with Gig Young in Walter Lang's *Desk Set*
(Screenplay by Phoebe Ephron and Henry Ephron; based on THE DESK SET, a play by William Marchant)

2.

"Comes New Year's Eve, everybody starts arranging parties. I'm the guy they got to dig up a date for."

—Ernest Borgnine hating his prolonged bachelorhood in Delbert Mann's *Marty*
(Screenplay by Paddy Chayefsky; based on his teleplay)

3.

"She's got something, Dutch. She's very good in this picture. She's going to attract a lot of attention. She's got what I call, er—it's a quality of availability. She's not particularly pretty. It's —a warmth some women have. It makes every man in the audience think he can make her if he only knew her."

—Bert Freed explaining Kim Stanley's screen appeal to her husband (Lloyd Bridges) in John Cromwell's *The Goddess*
(Original Screenplay by Paddy Chayefsky)

4.

"I'm willing to deal with the available world. I don't choose to shape it up with the lip. There's the people who spill things, and there's the people who get spilled on, and I don't choose to notice the stains. I got a wife. I have children. And business, like they say, is business. I'm not an exceptional man so it's possible for me to state the things the way they are. I'm lucky. I'm gifted. I have a talent for surrender."

—Martin Balsam singing the praise of conformity to his nonconformist brother (Jason Robards) in Fred Coe's *A Thousand Clowns*
(Screenplay by Herb Gardner; based on his play)

AWAKENINGS

1.

"Oh, My God! Someone's been sleeping in my dress."

—Beatrice Arthur, an alcoholic actress, rising groggily out of Lucille Ball's bathtub in Gene Saks's *Mame*
(Screenplay by Paul Zindel; based on the musical play by Jerome Lawrence, Robert E. Lee and Jerry Herman and AUNTIE MAME, a play by Jerome Lawrence and Robert E. Lee and novel by Patrick Dennis)

2.

(a) "This is Miss Judith Traherne of the sleepy Trahernes."

(b) "Is it now? Well, this is Mr. Michael O'Leary of the wide-awake O'Learys."

—(a) Bette Davis waking to a business call from her Irish horse trainer, (b) Humphrey Bogart, in Edmund Goulding's *Dark Victory*
(Screenplay by Casey Robinson; based on the play by George Brewer, Jr. and Bertram Block)

3.

(a) "What time is it?"

(b) "It's the right time, honey."

—(b) Robert Preston arising more aroused than his wife, (a) Dorothy McGuire, in Delbert Mann's *The Dark at the Top of the Stairs*
(Screenplay by Irving Ravetch and Harriet Frank, Jr.; based on the play by William Inge)

4.

"Every morning you come in yelling 'Rise and Shine!' 'Rise and Shine!' I think, 'How lucky dead people are!' But I get up. I go!"

—Arthur Kennedy telling his mother (Gertrude Lawrence) that his factory life has no shine to it in Irving Rapper's *The Glass Menagerie*
(Screenplay by Tennessee Williams and Peter Berneis; based on the play by Tennessee Williams)

5.

"Wake up, you country stewpot! . . . Rouse yourself from this pastoral torpor!"

—Edith Evans shrilly sounding the alarm for her soused brother (Hugh Griffith) in Tony Richardson's *Tom Jones*

(Screenplay by John Osborne; based on the novel by Henry Fielding)

AWARDS

1.
"The Sarah Siddons Award for Distinguished Achievement is perhaps unknown to you. It has been spared the sensational and commercial publicity that attends such questionable 'honors' as the Nobel Prize—and those awards presented annually by that film society."

—George Sanders setting the stage for award giving in the first lines of Joseph L. Mankiewicz's *All About Eve*
(Screenplay by Joseph L. Mankiewicz; based on "The Wisdom of Eve," a radio play and short story by Mary Orr)

2.
"You know, the first man that can think up a good explanation how he can be in love with his wife *and* another woman is going to win that prize they're always giving out in Sweden!"

—Mary Cecil suggesting a Nobel Prize for an ignoble purpose in George Cukor's *The Women*
(Screenplay by Anita Loos and Jane Murfin; based on the play by Clare Boothe)

3.
(a) "Look, sweetheart, I can drink you under any goddamn table you want so don't worry about me."

   (b) "I gave you the prize years ago, Martha. There isn't any abomination award going that you haven't won."

—(a) Elizabeth Taylor playing Can-You-Bottom-This? with (b) Richard Burton in Mike Nichols's *Who's Afraid of Virginia Woolf?*
(Screenplay by Ernest Lehman; based on the play by Edward Albee)

4.
"And now, ladies and gentlemen, I come to the final award: The Challenge Cup, given for the best rose—the best rose grown in the village during the past year. The first prize, the Silver Cup, goes to—goes to Mr. James Ballard, our popular stationmaster. The second prize, the Certificate of Merit, goes to me. All right! This is the first time a rose other than the Beldon Rose has won the Cup since the Shows began. I won't say I'm not disappointed—we Beldons are not used to competitors—in the old days, we just lopped off their heads—can't do that nowadays—more's the pity! But if I had to lose, there's no man I'd sooner lose to than James Ballard because he's a man of spirit. And I like a man of spirit!"

—Dame May Whitty lying graciously, allowing Henry Travers to win the award actually voted to her, in William Wyler's *Mrs. Miniver*
(Screenplay by Arthur Wimperis, George Froeschel, James Hilton and Claudine West; based on the novel by Jan Struther)

5.
"I looked down from our bridge and saw our captain's palm tree! Our trophy for superior achievement! The Admiral John J. Finchley Award for delivering more toothpaste and toilet paper than any other Navy cargo ship in the safe area of the Pacific."

—Henry Fonda citing the cross he bears in John Ford and Mervyn LeRoy's *Mister Roberts*
(Screenplay by Frank S. Nugent and Joshua Logan; based on the play by Thomas Heggen and Joshua Logan and novel by Thomas Heggen)

6.
" 'Order of the Palm. To Lt. (j.g.) Douglas Roberts for action against the enemy, above and beyond the call of duty.' "

—William Powell reading the crew's award to Henry Fonda for destroying the booby-prize above (Awards-5) in John Ford and Mervyn LeRoy's *Mister Roberts*
(Screenplay by Frank S. Nugent and Joshua Logan; based on the play by Thomas Heggen and Joshua Logan and novel by Thomas Heggen)

ALSO SEE: Courage-1; Drunken Rantings-2; Exchanges-14; Heart-14; Questions-5.

BAD

1.
"A week? Are you kidding? This play has got to close on page four."

—Zero Mostel discovering a play which is *that bad* in Mel Brooks's *The Producers*
(Original Screenplay by Mel Brooks)

2.
"I will tell you about Mrs. Paradine. She's bad, bad to the bone. If ever there was an evil woman, she is one."

—Louis Jourdan bad-mouthing Valli to her duped defense attorney (Gregory Peck) in Alfred Hitchcock's *The Paradine Case*
(Screenplay by David O. Selznick; adaptation by Alma Reville and James Bridie; based on the novel by Robert Hichens)

3.
"That doesn't necessarily mean she's bad. Quite a number of respectable citizens get drunk and do silly things. They're bad habits, like biting one's nails, but I don't know that they're worse than that. I call a person bad who lies and cheats and is unkind."

—Herbert Marshall redefining the adjective for Gene Tierney, in defense of an alcoholic Anne Baxter, in Edmund Goulding's *The Razor's Edge*
(Screenplay by Lamar Trotti; based on the novel by W. Somerset Maugham)

ALSO SEE: Good and Bad; Actors-2; Alone-9; Crazy-9; Detectives-2; Dying Words-19; Mad Act-12; Manners-8; Names-23; Proposals-6; Similarities-5; Sin-2; Smell-5; Smell-6.

BATHROOM

1.
"Where is the little comrade's room?"

—Cyd Charisse, a Russian in Paris, asking for the bathroom in Fred Astaire's apartment in Rouben Mamoulian's *Silk Stockings*
(Screenplay by Leonard Gershe and Leonard Spigelgass; based on the musical play by George S. Kaufman, Leueen MacGrath and Abe Burrows

and *NINOTCHKA, a screenplay by Charles Brackett, Billy Wilder and Walter Reisch and original story by Melchior Lengyel)*

2.
"Martha, will you show her where we keep the, er, euphemism?"

—Richard Burton cuing Elizabeth Taylor to escort Sandy Dennis to the bathroom in Mike Nichols's *Who's Afraid of Virginia Woolf?*
(Screenplay by Ernest Lehman; based on the play by Edward Albee)

3.
"I just don't understand it, Daddy. This little baby has to go winky-tink all the time."

—Madeline Kahn baby-talking about her bladder to Ryan O'Neal in Peter Bogdanovich's *Paper Moon*
(Screenplay by Alvin Sargent; based on ADDIE PRAY, a novel by Joe David Brown)

4.
"You just took a little rest-stop that wasn't on the schedule."

—Jon Voight kidding a dying Dustin Hoffman about a kidney mishap during their long bus ride to Miami in John Schlesinger's *Midnight Cowboy*
(Screenplay by Waldo Salt; based on the novel by James Leo Herlihy)

5.
"I mean, any gentleman with the slightest chic would give a girl a $50-bill for the powder room."

—Audrey Hepburn defining the class and income of her dates in Blake Edwards's *Breakfast at Tiffany's*
(Screenplay by George Axelrod; based on the novella by Truman Capote)

6.
"And *another* thing, I think this bathroom is perfectly ridiculous! Good night, Crystal."

—Virginia Weidler leaving Joan Crawford to boil in a bubble bath in George Cukor's *The Women*
(Screenplay by Anita Loos and Jane Murfin; based on the play by Clare Boothe)

ALSO SEE: Sex-6.

BEAUTIFUL

1.

"Once in her life, every woman should have that said to her. I thank you for being the one who said it to me."

—Ingrid Bergman appreciating Curt Jurgens's compliment in Mark Robson's *The Inn of the Sixth Happiness*
(Screenplay by Isobel Lennart; based on THE SMALL WOMAN, *a book by Alan Burgess)*

2.

"Job says that a woman is beautiful only when she is loved."

—Bette Davis quoting Claude Rains in Vincent Sherman's *Mr. Skeffington*
(Screenplay by Julius J. Epstein and Philip G. Epstein; based on the story by "Elizabeth")

3.

"One day that looking glass'll be the man who loves you. It'll be his eyes maybe. And you'll look in that mirror, and you'll be more than pretty. You'll be beautiful."

—Burt Lancaster talking Katharine Hepburn into a beautiful state in Joseph Anthony's *The Rainmaker*
(Screenplay by N. Richard Nash; based on his play)

4.

"Oh, Mark, we both know that even the fat, ugly people of this world believe that being in love makes them beautiful and justifies everything."

—Jennifer Jones reminding William Holden in Henry King's *Love Is a Many-Splendored Thing*
(Screenplay by John Patrick; based on A MANY-SPLENDORED THING, a novel by Han Suyin)

5.

"When I get through with you, you'll look like —well, what do you call beautiful? A tree? You'll look like a tree."

—Fred Astaire convincing Audrey Hepburn to pose for his camera in Stanley Donen's *Funny Face*
(Original Screenplay by Leonard Gershe)

6.

(a) "You're the most beautiful plank in your husband's platform."
   (b) "That's a heck of a thing to call a woman."

—(b) Katharine Hepburn taking exception to the compliment from (a) Adolphe Menjou in Frank Capra's *State of the Union*
(Screenplay by Anthony Veiller and Myles Connolly; based on the play by Howard Lindsay and Russel Crouse)

7.

"You should attack my guards more often. Battle seems to become you. You grow more beautiful each time I see you."

—Rex Harrison charming a belligerent Elizabeth Taylor in Joseph L. Mankiewicz's *Cleopatra*
(Screenplay by Joseph L. Mankiewicz, Ranald MacDougall and Sidney Buchman; based upon histories by Plutarch, Suetonius and Appian and THE LIFE AND TIMES OF CLEOPATRA, *a book by C. M. Franzero)*

8.

"You're the most beautiful woman I've ever seen, which doesn't say much for you."

—Groucho Marx qualifying his ardor in Victor Heerman's *Animal Crackers*
(Screenplay by Morrie Ryskind; based on the musical play by George S. Kaufman and Morrie Ryskind)

9.

"People who are very beautiful make their own laws."

—Vivien Leigh discussing Warren Beatty with Lotte Lenya in Jose Quintero's *The Roman Spring of Mrs. Stone*
(Screenplay by Gavin Lambert; based on the novel by Tennessee Williams)

ALSO SEE: Beauty; Eyes-11; Help-2; Home-8; Memory-4; Painting-6; Paris-3; Prison-2; Proposals-12; Propositions-24; Remember-5; Star-9; Ugly-2; Wealth-8.

BEAUTY

1.

"Isn't it odd how women of our age suddenly start looking for beauty in—well, in our male partners?"

—Coral Browne making an observation to Vivien Leigh in Jose Quintero's *The Roman Spring of Mrs. Stone*
(Screenplay by Gavin Lambert; based on the novel by Tennessee Williams)

2.
(a) "No more tears."
     (b) "I told you that's what beauty does to me."

—(b) Deborah Kerr responding to her first kiss from (a) Cary Grant in Leo McCarey's *An Affair To Remember*
(Screenplay by Delmer Daves and Leo McCarey; based on an original story by Mildred Cram and Leo McCarey)

3.

"I'd never met such a pretty girl, and I guess I'm just sensitive because real—real beauty makes me want to gag."

—Woody Allen encountering Janet Margolin in Woody Allen's *Take the Money and Run*
(Original Screenplay by Woody Allen and Mickey Rose)

ALSO SEE: Beautiful; Aging-5; Compliments-5; Diamonds-3; Directors-1; Eulogies-1; Faces-4; Paris-1; Progress-3; Seasons-2.

BED

1.

"When a marriage goes on the rocks, the rocks are there—right there."

—Judith Anderson slapping the bed to make her point to her daughter-in-law (Elizabeth Taylor) in Richard Brooks's *Cat on a Hot Tin Roof*
(Screenplay by Richard Brooks and James Poe; based on the play by Tennessee Williams)

2.

"I say, marriage with Max is not exactly a bed of roses, is it?"

—George Sanders cheerfully acknowledging the marital woes of Joan Fontaine in Alfred Hitchcock's *Rebecca*
(Screenplay by Robert E. Sherwood and Joan Harrison; adaptation by Philip MacDonald and Michael Hogan; based on the novel by Daphne du Maurier)

ALSO SEE: Furnishings-3; History-1; Past-4.

BELIEFS

1.

"I'm defending the 40 years I've lived with this man and watched him carry the burdens of people like you. If he's been wrong, at least he's stood for something. What do you stand for? Do you believe in Bertram Cates? I believe in my husband. What do you believe in?"

—Florence Eldridge defending Fredric March and challenging Donna Anderson's belief in Dick York in Stanley Kramer's *Inherit the Wind*
(Screenplay by Nathan E. Douglas and Harold Jacob Smith; based on the play by Jerome Lawrence and Robert E. Lee)

2.

"I believe in Rhett Butler. He's the only cause I know. The rest doesn't mean much to me."

—Clark Gable dodging the Civil War talk in Victor Fleming's *Gone With the Wind*
(Screenplay by Sidney Howard; based on the novel by Margaret Mitchell)

3.

"We didn't exactly believe your story, Miss O'Shaughnessy. We believed your $200. . . . You paid us more than if you'd been telling us the truth and enough more to make it all right."

—Humphrey Bogart calling Mary Astor a liar in John Huston's *The Maltese Falcon*

(Screenplay by John Huston; based on the novel by Dashiell Hammett)

4.

"I believe in the human heart now only as a doctor."

—Jennifer Jones graduating from romantic to realistic in Henry King's *Love Is a Many-Splendored Thing*
(Screenplay by John Patrick; based on A MANY-SPLENDORED THING, a novel by Han Suyin)

5.

"Lizzie, I'm sad about you. You don't believe in nothin', not even in yourself. You don't even believe you're a woman—and, if you don't, you're not."

—Burt Lancaster attacking the doubts of Katharine Hepburn in Joseph Anthony's *The Rainmaker*
(Screenplay by N. Richard Nash; based on his play)

6.

"I believe, Sandy—I believe I am past my prime. I had reckoned on my prime lasting till I was at least 50."

—Maggie Smith feeling her defeat in Ronald Neame's *The Prime of Miss Jean Brodie*
(Screenplay by Jay Presson Allen; based on her play and the novel by Muriel Spark)

7.

"A man fights for what he believes in, Fernando."

—Gary Cooper explaining his presence in the Spanish Civil War in Sam Wood's *For Whom the Bell Tolls*
(Screenplay by Dudley Nicholas; based on the novel by Ernest Hemingway)

8.

"I believe there are two things necessary to salvation. . . . Money and gunpowder."

—Robert Morley lecturing Rex Harrison in Gabriel Pascal's *Major Barbara*
(Screenplay by George Bernard Shaw; based on his play)

ALSO SEE: Convictions; Faith; Good-11; Good and Bad-4; Honest-7; Identity Crisis-4; Mad Acts-4; Progress-7; Prologues-7; Proposals-12; Questions-17; Religions-4; Run-1.

BETRAYAL

1.

"Let me tell you what stooling is. Stooling is when you rat on your friends, the guys you're with."

—Rod Steiger explaining the basics to his brother (Marlon Brando) in Elia Kazan's *On the Waterfront*
(Original Screenplay by Budd Schulberg; based on "Crime on the Waterfront," nonfiction articles by Malcolm Johnson)

2.

"Sorta rough, one American squealing on another American. Then again, Cookie, maybe that stoolie's not an American at all. Maybe he's a German the Krauts planted in this barracks. They do that sometimes. They put an agent in on us, a trained specialist. Lots of loose information floating around a prison camp—not just whether somebody's trying to escape—what outfit we were with, where we were stationed, how our radar operates. Could be, couldn't it?"

—William Holden theorizing aloud—and correctly—to Gil Stratton Jr. in Billy Wilder's *Stalag 17*
(Screenplay by Billy Wilder and Edwin Blum; based on the play by Donald Bevan and Edmund Trzcinski)

3.

"If you want to sell your services, I'm not willing to be the price. I loved him. You loved him. What good have we done him? Love! Look at yourself. They have a name for faces like that."

—Valli realizing that Joseph Cotten is betraying a mutual friend (Orson Welles) to get her safely out of Vienna in Carol Reed's *The Third Man*
(Original Screenplay by Graham Greene)

4.

"Where is he? Where'd he go? I'm asking you

where's that squealing son of yours? You think a squealer can get away from me? Huh? You know what I do with squealers? I let 'em have it in the belly so they can roll around for a long time thinking it over."

—Richard Widmark terrorizing a wheelchaired Mildred Dunnock in Henry Hathaway's *Kiss of Death*
(Screenplay by Ben Hecht and Charles Lederer; based on a story by Eleazar Lipsky)

5.
"You know where I was going, Johnny? Right down to the district attorney. Yes, I was, Johnny. I—I was going to turn the key on you. I was going to sing—sing and yodel and blow a loud whistle. I was going to sing the whole beautiful opera—about poor old Lew Rankin and those two impetuous Maletti brothers, may their souls rest in cement. I was going to be the troubadour of all the Eager folk songs, Johnny. And then I was going to blow my brains out."

—Van Heflin confessing a weak moment to his best friend (Robert Taylor) in Mervyn LeRoy's *Johnny Eager*
(Screenplay by John Lee Mahin and James Edward Grant; based on a story by James Edward Grant)

6.
"If you'll be kind enough to glance between my shoulder blades, Mr. and Mrs. Gubbins, you'll find there a knife buried to the hilt. On its handle are your initials."

—Jack Carson chastising James Mason and Judy Garland for getting married without a studio publicist in attendance in George Cukor's *A Star Is Born*
(Screenplay by Moss Hart; based on a screenplay by Dorothy Parker, Alan Campbell and Robert Carson and original story by William A. Wellman and Robert Carson)
and (almost verbatim)

—Lionel Stander dittoing Fredric March and Janet Gaynor in the original, William A. Wellman's *A Star Is Born*
(Screenplay by Dorothy Parker, Alan Campbell and Robert Carson; based on an original story by William A. Wellman and Robert Carson)

7.
"I didn't betray you. I simply put a stop to you."

—Pamela Franklin standing up to Maggie Smith in Ronald Neame's *The Prime of Miss Jean Brodie*
(Screenplay by Jay Presson Allen; based on her play and the novel by Muriel Spark)

8.
"You must feel pretty good, Mr. Higgins. You'll probably get a raise after they fire all these poor people—you Benedict Arnold-in-sheep's clothing!"

—Jean Arthur snarling at Charles Coburn for being a department-store spy in Sam Wood's *The Devil and Miss Jones*
(Original Screenplay by Norman Krasna)

ALSO SEE: Crazy-8; Fools-7; Names-25; Never-3; Soul-6; Swear-2.

BIG

1.
"I *am* big. It's the *pictures* that got small."

—Gloria Swanson bristling at being told she used to be big in pictures in Billy Wilder's *Sunset Boulevard*
(Original Screenplay by Charles Brackett, Billy Wilder and D. M. Marshman Jr.)

2.
"There's nothing to square. You're my pal. You're smart, too. I didn't know how smart until I saw you in court. You fooled me, and that takes a big man. Yeah, a big man."

—Richard Widmark dispensing some smiling menace toward Victor Mature in Henry Hathaway's *Kiss of Death*
(Screenplay by Ben Hecht and Charles Lederer; based on a story by Eleazar Lipsky)

3.
"Big Daddy! Now what makes him so big? His big heart? His big belly? Or his big money?"

—Paul Newman pondering the possibilities about his father (Burl Ives) in Richard Brooks's *Cat on a Hot Tin Roof*

(Screenplay by Richard Brooks and James Poe; based on the play by Tennessee Williams)

ALSO SEE: Heart-3; Heart-4; Heart-5; Hero-1; Newspapering-10; Oops!-2.

BIRDS

1.
"He's up on the roof with his birds. He keeps birds. Dirty, disgusting, filthy, lice-ridden birds. You used to be able to sit out on the stoop like a person. Not any more. No, sir. Birds! You get my drift?"

—Madlyn Gates directing Zero Mostel and Gene Wilder to Kenneth Mars in Mel Brooks's *The Producers*
(Original Screenplay by Mel Brooks)

2.
"Let's talk about the black bird."

—Humphrey Bogart getting down to business with Sydney Greenstreet in John Huston's *The Maltese Falcon*
(Screenplay by John Huston; based on the novel by Dashiell Hammett)

3.
"Look, when I say I want a whole floor, I don't want one wing and I don't want two wings. I want the whole bird."

—Broderick Crawford berating a hotel official in George Cukor's *Born Yesterday*
(Screenplay by Albert Mannheimer; based on the play by Garson Kanin)

4.
"I don't know how fast he moves, but it takes an early bird to get the best of a worm like me."

—Tony Randall mangling metaphors in his haste to head off a romantic rival in Michael Gordon's *Pillow Talk*
(Screenplay by Stanley Shapiro and Maurice Richlin; based on a story by Russell Rouse and Clarence Greene)

ALSO SEE: Eat-3; Eyes-18; Faces-11; Hero-2; Macho-9; Progress-2.

BIRTH

1.
"I don't know nothin' about birthin' babies."

—Butterfly McQueen bowing out as Olivia De Havilland's midwife in Victor Fleming's *Gone With the Wind*
(Screenplay by Sidney Howard; based on the novel by Margaret Mitchell)

2.
"I—I was born backwards. That is why I work in Africa as missionary, teaching little brown babies more backward than myself."

—Ingrid Bergman indicating a very early professional calling in Sidney Lumet's *Murder on the Orient Express*
(Screenplay by Paul Dehn; based on the novel by Agatha Christie)

3.
"He's very progressive. He has all sorts of ideas about artificial insemination and all that sort of thing. He breeds all over the world."

—Debbie Reynolds telling her father (Fred Astaire) about her fiancé (Tab Hunter) in George Seaton's *The Pleasure of His Company*
(Screenplay by Samuel A. Taylor; based on the play by Samuel A. Taylor and Cornelia Otis Skinner)

4.
"I haven't given you my present yet, but I will now. I have an announcement to make . . . an announcement of life beginning. A child is coming, sired by Brick out of Maggie the Cat. I have Brick's child in my body, and that is my present to you."

—Elizabeth Taylor brightening Burl Ives's birthday with the lie that she'll make him a grandfather in Richard Brooks's *Cat on a Hot Tin Roof*
(Screenplay by Richard Brooks and James Poe; based on the play by Tennessee Williams)

5.
(a) "I'm afraid I was born a hundred years before my time."
   (b) "I was born 10 days ahead of mine."

—(b) Cecilia Parker proving to be a more literal thinker than (a) Eric Linden in Clarence Brown's *Ah, Wilderness!*
(Screenplay by Albert Hackett and Frances Goodrich; based on the play by Eugene O'Neill)

6.

"Hand me that section, will ya? I want to see if anyone I know is being born today. Hey, listen to this: Born today to Mr. and Mrs. Charles J. Pendergast, a son. Mrs. Pendergast, the former Constance Milligan, is doing nicely. Mr. Pendergast is doing all right, too. He gets $8,600 a year. The baby arrived three minutes ahead of schedule, so Mr. Pendergast refused delivery."

—Charles Coburn teasing Jean Arthur about her stuffed-shirt fiancé (Richard Gaines) in George Stevens's *The More the Merrier*
(Screenplay by Richard Flournoy and Lewis R. Foster; based on a story by Robert Russell and Frank Ross)

7.

"Eddie, you're a born loser."

—George C. Scott sizing up Paul Newman in Robert Rossen's *The Hustler*
(Screenplay by Sidney Carroll and Robert Rossen; based on the novel by Walter Tevis)

8.

"How do you get a guy to be a Geek? Is that the only one? I mean, is a guy born that way?"

—Tyrone Power shuddering over a repulsive carnival act which he eventually inherits in Edmund Goulding's *Nightmare Alley*
(Screenplay by Jules Furthman; based on the novel by William Lindsay Gresham)

9.

"I suppose it'd been better if I'd never been born at all."

—James Stewart wishing himself into quite a fantasy in Frank Capra's *It's a Wonderful Life*
(Screenplay by Albert Hackett, Frances Goodrich and Frank Capra; based on "The Greatest Gift," a short story by Philip Van Doren Stern)

ALSO SEE: Genius-4; Happiness-2; Headlines-2; Men-5; Sounds-3; Wish-7.

BIRTHDAYS

1.

"Irving R. Feldman's birthday is my own personal National Holiday. I did not open it up for the public. He is proprietor of perhaps the most distinguished Kosher Delicatessen in our neighborhood, and, as such, I hold the day of his birth in reverence."

—Jason Robards explaining why he's not job hunting in Fred Coe's *A Thousand Clowns*
(Screenplay by Herb Gardner; based on his play)

2.

"I'll have a word with you. I didn't understand you. I didn't understand myself. You done a thing that numbs my belly. No man in all my life before give me things before or a kind word or a kick. Forgot it was my birthday. I wouldn't have remembered if it weren't for you. I thank you, one and all."

—Richard Todd thanking his fellow hospital patients for the surprise birthday party in Vincent Sherman's *The Hasty Heart*
(Screenplay by Ranald MacDougall; based on the play by John Patrick)

3.

"Bejeeses, I'm no good at speeches. All I can say is thanks to everybody again for remembering me on my birthday. Only don't think, because I'm 60, I'll be a bigger damned-fool easy mark than ever."

—Fredric March going from thanks to tirade before the bar customers marking his birthday in John Frankenheimer's *The Iceman Cometh*
(Screenplay based on the play by Eugene O'Neill; text edited by Thomas Quinn Curtiss)

4.

"I'm crying because I'm happy. I've had my moment in the theater, and I think Terry deserves her chance. If you say anything to her, that won't get the part for me, will it? There's going to be other parts in other plays. This is my birthday, and I'm going to be happy. The devil with the theater!"

—Andrea Leeds trying to be big about losing a role to Katharine Hepburn in Gregory La Cava's *Stage Door*
(Screenplay by Morrie Ryskind and Anthony Veiller; based on the play by Edna Ferber and George S. Kaufman)

5.
"Yeah, I *am* running, running from lies, lies like birthday congratulations and many happy returns of the day when there won't be any—"

—Paul Newman blurting out to Burl Ives that Ives is dying in Richard Brooks's *Cat on a Hot Tin Roof*
(Screenplay by Richard Brooks and James Poe; based on the play by Tennessee Williams)

BLOOD

1.
"Aye, it was Moby Dick that tore my soul and body until they bled into each other."

—Gregory Peck revealing the depth of his wound—and obsession—in John Huston's *Moby Dick*
(Screenplay by Ray Bradbury and John Huston; based on the novel by Herman Melville)

2.
"How is it that you cannot stand the sight of blood on anyone except me?"

—Gregory Peck questioning Lauren Bacall's qualified squeamishness in Vincente Minnelli's *Designing Woman*
(Original Screenplay by George Wells; based on a suggestion by Helen Rose)

3.
"It's like any other business, only here the blood shows."

—Kirk Douglas explaining boxing to his brother (Arthur Kennedy) in Mark Robson's *Champion*
(Screenplay by Carl Foreman; based on the short story by Ring Lardner)

4.
"My blood *circulates*. I'm not saying everywhere, but it circulates."

—George Burns defending his health to the equally ancient Walter Matthau in Herbert Ross's *The Sunshine Boys*
(Screenplay by Neil Simon; based on his play)

5.
"My blood has gone down to my hip pockets to count my money."

—Bob Hope explaining his paleness in a tense situation in Frank Tashlin's *Son of Paleface*
(Original Screenplay by Frank Tashlin, Robert L. Welch and Joseph Quillan)

ALSO SEE: Passion-1; Pep Talks-8.

BODY

1.
"Why didn't you get a job? You look perfectly able-bodied to me—if I may use the word 'bodied.' "

—Joseph Cotten coming on in his coy way to Claudette Colbert in John Cromwell's *Since You Went Away*
(Screenplay by David O. Selznick; adaptation by Margaret Buell Wilder; based on her book of letters)

2.
"Oh, don't be so fussy. Your body! After all, what is it? Just a physical covering, that's all—worth chemically 32 cents."

—Edward Everett Horton minimizing Robert Montgomery's bodiless state in Alexander Hall's *Here Comes Mr. Jordan*
(Screenplay by Sidney Buchman and Seton I. Miller; based on HEAVEN CAN WAIT, a play by Harry Segall)

3.
"A gladiator is like a stallion. You'll be pampered. You'll be oiled, bathed, shaved, massaged, taught to use your head. A good body with a dull brain is as cheap as life itself."

—Peter Ustinov addressing the new recruits at his gladiator school in Stanley Kubrick's *Spartacus*

BOOKS 25

(Screenplay by Dalton Trumbo; based on the novel by Howard Fast)

4.

"A starved body has a skinny soul."

—Marlon Brando accepting a cup of chocolate during his formal courting of Jean Peters in Elia Kazan's *Viva Zapata!*
(Original Screenplay by John Steinbeck)

5.

"If you take my heart by surprise, the rest of my body has the right to follow."

—Albert Finney responding enthusiastically to Joan Greenwood's forwardness in Tony Richardson's *Tom Jones*
(Screenplay by John Osborne; based on the novel by Henry Fielding)

6.

"What's the matter with you? You got any idea how many times you can get hit in the stomach in a four-round bout? You know, the human body wasn't made for the sole benefit of the fight game. You hit a man in the head hard enough and long enough or just once, and you can either scramble his brains or maybe kill him. And for what? To fill a hall? To win bets for somebody you don't even know? What does it prove? Is that a way to make a living?"

—Paul Stewart trying to talk Kirk Douglas out of a boxing career in Mark Robson's *Champion*
(Screenplay by Carl Foreman; based on the short story by Ring Lardner)

ALSO SEE: Blood-1; Guilty-5; Heart-1; Heart-12; Life and Death-1; Men-8; Neck-3; Prayers-2; Propositions-19; Snake-5; Soul-11; Soul-12; Success-6; Talk-9.

BOOKS

1.

"A book to me means love because when you give a book about a romantic place it's like saying that all the days of your life should be as romantic as Spain and surrounded by a cover of happiness."

—Diane Keaton citing one of the things her husband (Joseph Hindy) did right in Cy Howard's *Lovers and Other Strangers*
(Screenplay by Renee Taylor, Joseph Bologna and David Z. Goodman; based on the play by Renee Taylor and Joseph Bologna)

2.

"You only gave me books with the word Death in the title."

—Diane Keaton underlining the limits of Woody Allen's generosity in Woody Allen's *Annie Hall*
(Original Screenplay by Woody Allen and Marshall Brickman)

3.

"I used to go with a girl who read books. She joined the Book of the Month Club, and they had her reading books all the time. She had no more finished one than they'd shoot her another."

—William Holden recalling a literate girlfriend in Joshua Logan's *Picnic*
(Screenplay by Daniel Taradash; based on the play by William Inge)

4.

"I'm tired of pretending to write this dumb book about my maverick days in the great early years of television. Every goddamn executive fired from a network in the last 20 years has written this dumb book about the great early years of television. And nobody wants the dumb, damn, goddamn book about the early years of television."

—William Holden growing frustrated over his writer pose in Sidney Lumet's *Network*
(Original Screenplay by Paddy Chayefsky)

5.

"Expert! I'm going to write a book about it. Call it *The Hitch-hiker's Hail.*"

—Clark Gable boasting to Claudette Colbert about his hitch-hiking prowess in Frank Capra's *It Happened One Night*

(Screenplay by Robert Riskin; based on "Night Bus," a short story by Samuel Hopkins Adams)

6.

"I want to look somebody up. Does this office have a copy of *Who's Still Who*?"

—George Tobias indirectly commenting on the quick changes-of-command in the Soviet Union in Rouben Mamoulian's *Silk Stockings*
(Screenplay by Leonard Gershe and Leonard Spigelgass; based on the musical play by George S. Kaufman, Leueen MacGrath and Abe Burrows and NINOTCHKA, a screenplay by Charles Brackett, Billy Wilder and Walter Reisch and original story by Melchior Lengyel)

7.

"Go in and read the life of Florence Nightingale and learn how unfitted you are for your chosen profession."

—Monty Woolley insulting his nurse (Mary Wickes) in William Keighley's *The Man Who Came to Dinner*
(Screenplay by Julius J. Epstein and Philip G. Epstein; based on the play by George S. Kaufman and Moss Hart)

8.

"A lot of people think I am just a stooge for you. They don't know I am a modern Boswell, meticulously recording for posterity the doings of a unique individual—an individual out of the days of the Medicis—and I'm your Boswell. The story of Johnny Eager. The next 40 generations will find it required reading along with the words of Machiavelli."

—Van Heflin drunkenly defending his stooge status to Robert Taylor in Mervyn LeRoy's *Johnny Eager*
(Screenplay by John Lee Mahin and James Edward Grant; based on a story by James Edward Grant)

9.

"He's been reading *God's Little Acre* for over a year now! He's underlined every erotic passage and added exclamation points—and after a certain pornographic climax, he's inserted the words 'well written.'"

—Henry Fonda criticizing Jack Lemmon's reading habits in John Ford and Mervyn LeRoy's *Mister Roberts*
(Screenplay by Frank S. Nugent and Joshua Logan; based on the play by Thomas Heggen and Joshua Logan and novel by Thomas Heggen)

10.

"I have no intention of leaving. I'm going to stay here, and I'm going to help rebuild the library. And if anybody ever again tries to remove a book from it, he'll have to do it over my dead body."

—Bette Davis rising from the ashes of a censorship row and library-burning in Daniel Taradash's *Storm Center*
(Original Screenplay by Daniel Taradash and Elick Moll)

ALSO SEE: Disease-8; Feelings-8; Free-3; Hunger-2; Live-1; Professions-13; Sex-5; Snake-6.

BOREDOM

1.

"If I don't get out of here, I'll just die! Living here is like waiting for the funeral to begin. No, it's like waiting in the coffin for them to carry you out!"

—Bette Davis taking a dim view of small town life in King Vidor's *Beyond the Forest*
(Screenplay by Lenore Coffee; based on the novel by Stuart Engstrand)

2.

"One has to be as rich as you, Gaston, to be bored at Monte Carlo."

—Hermione Gingold commenting on Louis Jourdan's jaded elitism in Vincente Minnelli's *Gigi*
(Screenplay by Alan Jay Lerner; based on the novel by Colette)

3.

" 'I've discovered, Doc, that the unseen enemy of this war is the boredom that eventually becomes a faith and, therefore, a terrible sort of suicide—and I know now that the ones who refuse to surrender to it are the strongest of all.' "

—Jack Lemmon reading Henry Fonda's letter to William Powell and the crew in John Ford and Mervyn LeRoy's *Mister Roberts*
(Screenplay by Frank S. Nugent and Joshua Logan; based on the play by Thomas Heggen and Joshua Logan and novel by Thomas Heggen)

4.
"I'm afraid of nothing, except being bored."

—Greta Garbo articulating her free-spirit credo to Robert Taylor in George Cukor's *Camille*
(Screenplay by Zoe Akins, Frances Marion and James Hilton; based on LA DAME AUX CAMELIAS, a play and novel by Alexandre Dumas)

5.
"You must watch yourself, Mr. Kane. I'm telling you this for your own benefit, but you have the makings of an outstanding bore."

—Otto Kruger dodging Robert Cummings's persistent questions in Alfred Hitchcock's *Saboteur*
(Original Screenplay by Peter Viertel, Joan Harrison and Dorothy Parker)

6.
"How would you like to join The Kyle Hadley Society for the Prevention of Boredom?"

—Robert Stack (as one Kyle Hadley) coming on to Lauren Bacall in Douglas Sirk's *Written on the Wind*
(Screenplay by George Zuckerman; based on the novel by Robert Wilder)

7.
"Men are usually so bored with virgins. I'm so glad you're not."

—Maggie McNamara doing wide-eyed innocence in Otto Preminger's *The Moon Is Blue*
(Screenplay by F. Hugh Herbert; based on his play)

ALSO SEE: Business-5; Fun-4; Fun-5; Kiss-14; Life-4; Plans-1; Propositions-24; War-2.

BOTTLE

1.
"Freedom! Free after 2,000 years! Two thousand years ago King Sodiman, master of all Indians, imprisoned me within that bottle. Ha ha ha! For me, this is the first moment of my new freedom. For you—ha ha ha—for you, this is the last moment of your life."

—Rex Ingram materializing out of a bottle and menacing his liberator (Sabu) in Ludwig Berger, Tim Whelan and Michael Powell's *The Thief of Bagdad*
(Screenplay and dialogue by Miles Malleson; based on a scenario by Lajos Biro)

2.
(a) "She's really got it."
   (b) "She's got what?"
   (a) "I don't know, but if we could bottle it we could make a fortune."

—(a) Bob Hope drooling about Jane Russell to (b) Paul E. Burns in Frank Tashlin's *Son of Paleface*
(Original Screenplay by Frank Tashlin, Robert L. Welch and Joseph Quillan)

3.
"Jonathan is more than a man. He's an experience—and he's habit-forming. If they could ever bottle him, he'd outsell ginger ale."

—Barry Sullivan characterizing Kirk Douglas to Dick Powell in Vincente Minnelli's *The Bad and the Beautiful*
(Screenplay by Charles Schnee; based on "Memorial to a Bad Man" and "Of Good and Evil," two short stories by George Bradshaw)

BOXING

1.
"This is the only sport in the world where two guys get paid for doing something they'd be arrested for if they got drunk and did it for nothing."

—Paul Stewart characterizing the sport Kirk Douglas wants to take up in Mark Robson's *Champion*
(Screenplay by Carl Foreman; based on the short story by Ring Lardner)

2.

"Now the four most valuable punches, it says here, are—now let me show you—the straight left, the right cross, the left hook and a right uppercut. See?"

—Nun Ingrid Bergman demonstrating by-the-book boxing to young Dickie Tyler in Leo McCarey's *The Bells of St. Mary's*
(Screenplay by Dudley Nichols; based on an original story by Leo McCarey)

3.

"You just couldn't play it smart, could you? All ya had to do was box. But no, not you, you hard-head! Funny thing is that there ain't gonna be any boxing championships this year —what's the matter with you guys? Ain't you ever seen a dead man? Let's get this body out of here. We ain't got all night."

—Burt Lancaster grieving over the corpse of Montgomery Clift in Fred Zinnemann's *From Here to Eternity*
(Screenplay by Daniel Taradash; based on the novel by James Jones)

4.

"George, tell 'em about the boxing match *we* had."

—Elizabeth Taylor goading another marital horror story out of Richard Burton in Mike Nichols's *Who's Afraid of Virginia Woolf?*
(Screenplay by Ernest Lehman; based on the play by Edward Albee)

5.

"You remember that night in the Garden? You came down to my dressing room and said, 'Kid, this ain't your night. We're going for the price on Wilson.' You remember that? 'This ain't your night.' My night! I coulda taken Wilson apart! So what happens? He gets the title shot outdoors in the ball park—and whadda I get? A one-way ticket to Palookaville. You was my brother, Charley. You shoulda looked out for me a little bit. You shoulda taken care of me— just a little bit, that's all—so I wouldn't have to take them dives for the short-end money."

—Marlon Brando accusing his brother (Rod Steiger) of betrayal in Elia Kazan's *On the Waterfront* *(Original Screenplay by Budd Schulberg; based on "Crime on the Waterfront," nonfiction articles by Malcolm Johnson)*

ALSO SEE: Bums-2; Eulogies-8; Pleasures-1.

BRAVADO

1.

"Doesn't scare me a bit. Tough sergeants just roll off my knife."

—Martin Milner talking tough before meeting John Wayne in Allan Dwan's *Sands of Iwo Jima* *(Screenplay by Harry Brown and James Edward Grant; based on a story by Harry Brown)*

2.

(a) "Don't big empty houses scare you?"
   (b) "Not me. I used to be in vaudeville."

—(b) Bob Hope refusing to let (a) Nydia Westman spook him in Elliott Nugent's *The Cat and the Canary* *(Screenplay by Walter De Leon and Lynn Starling; based on the play by John Willard)*

BREASTS

1.

"You can't show your bosom 'fore three o'-clock."

—Hattie McDaniel instructing Vivien Leigh in proper attire in Victor Fleming's *Gone With the Wind* *(Screenplay by Sidney Howard; based on the novel by Margaret Mitchell)*

2.

"Now you've done it! Now you have done it! . . . You tore off one of my chests."

—Jack Lemmon informing Tony Curtis the rough-housing has got to stop in their delicate (i.e., drag) condition in Billy Wilder's *Some Like It Hot* *(Screenplay by Billy Wilder and I. A. L. Diamond; suggested by a story by R. Thoeren and M. Logan)*

3.

"Good heavens, Agnes! You have a bust. Where you been hiding it all these years?"

—Lucille Ball preparing to glamorize a frumpy Jane Connell in Gene Saks's *Mame*
(Screenplay by Paul Zindel; based on the musical play by Jerome Lawrence, Robert E. Lee and Jerry Herman and AUNTIE MAME, a play by Jerome Lawrence and Robert E. Lee and novel by Patrick Dennis)

and (almost verbatim)

—Rosalind Russell dittoing Peggy Cass in the original, Morton DaCosta's *Auntie Mame*
(Screenplay by Betty Comden and Adolph Green; based on the play by Jerome Lawrence and Robert E. Lee and novel by Patrick Dennis)

ALSO SEE: Women-10.

BUMS

1.

"I walked by the Union Square Bar. I was going to go in. Then I saw myself—my reflection in the window—and I thought, 'I wonder who that bum is.' And then I saw it was me. Now look at me. I'm a bum. Look at me. Look at you. You're a bum. Look at you. And look at us. Look at us. C'mon, look at us. See? A couple of bums."

—Jack Lemmon forcing Lee Remick to a harsh look in the mirror in Blake Edwards's *Days of Wine and Roses*
(Screenplay by J. P. Miller; based on his teleplay)

2.

"I coulda had class! I coulda been a contender! I coulda been somebody! Instead of a bum which is what I am! Let's face it. It was you, Charley!"

—Marlon Brando blaming his brother (Rod Steiger) for an abortive boxing career in Elia Kazan's *On the Waterfront*
(Original Screenplay by Budd Schulberg; based on "Crime on the Waterfront," nonfiction articles by Malcolm Johnson)

3.

"What's the use, baby? I'm a bum. She saw through me like an x-ray machine. There's no place in the world for a guy like me."

—William Holden agreeing with Rosalind Russell's negative evaluation in Joshua Logan's *Picnic*
(Screenplay by Daniel Taradash; based on the play by William Inge)

4.

"Just one more word: if I ever run into any of you bums on a street corner, just let's pretend we never met before."

—William Holden bolting from his prison camp with a parting shot at his barracks buddies in Billy Wilder's *Stalag 17*
(Screenplay by Billy Wilder and Edwin Blum; based on the play by Donald Bevan and Edward Trzcinski)

ALSO SEE: Thieves-6.

BUSINESS

1.

"Well, from all I've heard about heaven, it seems to be a pretty unbusinesslike place. They could probably use a good man like me."

—William Powell advancing a different slant on the hereafter in Michael Curtiz's *Life With Father*
(Screenplay by Donald Ogden Stewart; based on the play by Howard Lindsay and Russel Crouse and stories by Clarence Day, Jr.)

2.

(a) "Convenient the door being open when you didn't have a key."

　(b) "Yeah, wasn't it? By the way, how did you happen to have one?"

　(a) "It any of your business?"

　(b) "I could make it my business."

　(a) "I could make your business mine."

　(b) "You wouldn't like it. The pay's too small."

—(a) John Ridgely meeting (b) Humphrey Bogart in Howard Hawks's *The Big Sleep*

(Screenplay by William Faulkner, Leigh Brackett and Jules Furthman; based on the novel by Raymond Chandler)

3.
"You'll excuse me, gentlemen. Your business is politics. Mine is running a saloon."

—Humphrey Bogart ducking a political conversation in Michael Curtiz's *Casablanca*
(Screenplay by Julius J. Epstein, Philip G. Epstein and Howard Koch; based on EVERYBODY COMES TO RICK'S, a play by Murray Burnett and Joan Alison)

4.
(a) "Why? Why should you carry other people's bags?"
    (b) "Well, that's my business, Madame."
    (a) "That's no business. That's social injustice."
    (b) "That depends on the tip."

—Greta Garbo preaching to a porter (George Davis) in Ernst Lubitsch's *Ninotchka*
(Screenplay by Charles Brackett, Billy Wilder and Walter Reisch; based on an original story by Melchior Lengyel)
            and (almost verbatim)

—Cyd Charisse dittoing to Peter Camlin in the remake, Rouben Mamoulian's *Silk Stockings*
(Screenplay by Leonard Gershe and Leonard Spigelgass; based on the musical play by George S. Kaufman, Leueen MacGrath and Abe Burrows and NINOTCHKA, a screenplay by Charles Brackett, Billy Wilder and Walter Reisch and original story by Melchior Lengyel)

5.
"Television is not the truth. Television is a goddamn amusement park. Television is a circus, a carnival, a traveling troupe of acrobats, storytellers, dancers, singers, jugglers, sideshow freaks, lion tamers and football players. We're in the boredom-killing business."

—Peter Finch ranting on the tube in Sidney Lumet's *Network*
(Original Screenplay by Paddy Chayefsky)

ALSO SEE: Body-1; Changes-3; Detectives-1; Detectives-2; Gigolo-6; Hanging-1; Politics-2; Professions-10; Professions-12; Selfish-4; Taste-2; Television-1; Time-9; Toasts-14.

BUTTERFLIES

1.
"You miserable, cowardly, wretched little caterpillar! Don't you ever want to become a butterfly? Don't you want to spread your wings and flap your way to glory?"

—Zero Mostel inspiring Gene Wilder to live dangerously in Mel Brooks's *The Producers*
(Original Screenplay by Mel Brooks)

2.
"Well, there's nothing else I can say, except that I'm glad before our marriage you showed yourself up in your true colors. You're just a butterfly."

—Virginia Walker breaking her engagement to Cary Grant in Howard Hawks's *Bringing Up Baby*
(Screenplay by Dudley Nichols and Hagar Wilde; based on a story by Hagar Wilde)

ALSO SEE: Wealth-8.

CALLINGS

1.
"Call me Ishmael."

—Richard Basehart beginning his narration with the first line of John Huston's *Moby Dick*
(Screenplay by Ray Bradbury and John Huston; based on the novel by Herman Melville)

2.
"Call me sausage."

—Joyce Grenfell informing Lloyd Lamble in Frank Launder's *Blue Murder at St. Trinian's*
(Screenplay by Frank Launder, Val Valentine and Sidney Gilliat; inspired by the cartoon drawings of Ronald Searle)

3.
"So they call me Concentration Camp Ehrhardt?"

—Sig Ruman, or Jack Benny imitating Sig Ruman, in Ernst Lubitsch's *To Be or Not To Be*
(Screenplay by Edwin Justus Mayer; based on an original story by Ernst Lubitsch and Melchior Lengyel)

4.
"Don't ever again, as long as you live, dare to call me uncle. By no stretch of the imagination could I possibly be a relative of yours. My name is Mr. Belvedere. Is that clear?"

—Clifton Webb shooting flames at young Anthony Sydes in Walter Lang's *Sitting Pretty*
(Screenplay by F. Hugh Herbert; based on the novel by Gwen Davenport)

5.
"They have given you a new title, Divinity: incendiary."

—Leo Genn reporting the shouts of the burned-out mob to Nero (Peter Ustinov) in Mervyn LeRoy's *Quo Vadis*
(Screenplay by John Lee Mahin, S. N. Behrman and Sonya Levien; based on the novel by Henryk Sienkiewicz)

6.
"You call that a marriage? It was a frame-up. The two of 'em cooked it up."

—Kirk Douglas protesting his shotgun marriage to Ruth Roman in Mark Robson's *Champion*
(Screenplay by Carl Foreman; based on the short story by Ring Lardner)

7.
"You call her a child, Laura Belle? Under that heathen blanket, there's a full-blossomed woman fit for the devil to drive men crazy."

—Revivalist preacher Walter Huston drinking in Jennifer Jones in King Vidor's *Duel in the Sun*
(Screenplay by David O. Selznick; adaptation by Oliver H. P. Garrett; based on the novel by Niven Busch)

8.
"You know the terrible thing, Fred darling. I *am* still Lulamae, 14 years old and stealing turkey eggs and running through the briar patch —except now I call it having the 'mean reds.' "

—Audrey Hepburn pretending to herself (and George Peppard) that some of her rustic innocence has survived Manhattan life in Blake Edwards's *Breakfast at Tiffany's*
(Screenplay by George Axelrod; based on the novella by Truman Capote)

9.
"The management insists. If we let you guys go home alone, a lot of you don't go home. You just hit the nearest bar and bounce right back again. What we call the quick ricochet."

—Frank Faylen going over the alcoholic-ward rules with Ray Milland in Billy Wilder's *The Lost Weekend*
(Screenplay by Charles Brackett and Billy Wilder; based on the novel by Charles R. Jackson)

10.
(a) "It's bizarre. Eight years with the National Theater, two Pinter plays, nine Shakespeare, three Shaw—and I finally get nominated for a nauseating little comedy."

  (b) "That's why they call it Hollywood."

—(a) Maggie Smith and (b) Michael Caine musing over her Oscar nomination in Herbert Ross's *California Suite*
(Screenplay by Neil Simon; based on his play)

ALSO SEE: Cruel-1; Friends-9; Home-9; Honest-4; Insults-1; Party-2; Prejudice-4; Progress-4; Selfish-1; Smile-1; Smile-2; Thieves-5.

CAMERAS

1.
"He's a bit old-fashioned. He thinks these things will steal his virtue. He thinks you're kind of a thief."

—Peter O'Toole explaining why Anthony Quinn smashed Arthur Kennedy's cameras in David Lean's *Lawrence of Arabia*
(Screenplay by Robert Bolt; based on THE SEVEN PILLARS OF WISDOM, the autobiography of T. E. Lawrence, and other works by and about T. E. Lawrence)

2.
"They say he ain't scared of nothing. If he

wants the picture of a lion, he just goes up to him and says, 'Look pleasant.' ''

—A bystander characterizing fearless filmmaker Robert Armstrong at the outset of Merian C. Cooper and Ernest B. Schoedsack's *King Kong*
(Screenplay by James Creelman and Ruth Rose; based on an original story by Merian C. Cooper and Edgar Wallace)

3.
"So they were turning, after all—those cameras. Life, which can be strangely merciful, had taken pity on Norma Desmond. The dream she had clung to so desperately had enfolded her."

—William Holden setting up Gloria Swanson's mad exit in Billy Wilder's *Sunset Boulevard*
(Original Screenplay by Charles Brackett, Billy Wilder and D. M. Marshman, Jr.)

ALSO SEE: Mad Act-2.

CHAMPAGNE

1.
"There comes a time in every woman's life when the only thing that helps is a glass of champagne."

—Bette Davis pausing in her wars with Miriam Hopkins in Vincent Sherman's *Old Acquaintance*
(Screenplay by John Van Druten and Lenore Coffee; based on the play by John Van Druten)

2.
"Pink champagne—that's the kind of life we've both been used to. It might be a little difficult to—do you like beer?"

—Deborah Kerr pledging with Cary Grant to give up their rich lovers in Leo McCarey's *An Affair To Remember*
(Screenplay by Delmer Daves and Leo McCarey; based on an original story by Mildred Cram and Leo McCarey)
                    and (almost verbatim)

—Irene Dunne dittoing with Charles Boyer in the original, Leo McCarey's *Love Affair*
(Screenplay by Delmer Daves and Donald Ogden

Stewart; based on an original story by Mildred Cram and Leo McCarey)

3.
(a) "Beer?"
    (b) "Yeah, if we're all out of champagne."

—(a) Connie Gilchrist playing hostess and (b) Thelma Ritter pretending pretense in Joseph L. Mankiewicz's *A Letter to Three Wives*
(Screenplay by Joseph L. Mankiewicz; adaptation by Vera Caspary; based on "One of Our Hearts," a short story by John Klempner)

4.
"Champagne is a great levelerer—leveler. It makes you my equal."

—James Stewart drunkenly greeting a sober Cary Grant in George Cukor's *The Philadelphia Story*
(Screenplay by Donald Ogden Stewart; based on the play by Philip Barry)
                    and (almost verbatim)

—Frank Sinatra dittoing Bing Crosby in the remake, Charles Walters's *High Society*
(Screenplay by John Patrick; based on THE PHILADELPHIA STORY, a screenplay by Donald Ogden Stewart and play by Philip Barry)

5.
"I have made a discovery: champagne is more fun to drink than goat's milk."

—Cyd Charisse, a Russian in Paris, warming to the ways of the West in Rouben Mamoulian's *Silk Stockings*
(Screenplay by Leonard Gershe and Leonard Spigelgass; based on the musical play by George S. Kaufman, Leueen MacGrath and Abe Burrows and NINOTCHKA, a screenplay by Charles Brackett, Billy Wilder and Walter Reisch and original story by Melchior Lengyel)

ALSO SEE: Drink-5; Moon-3.

CHAMPION

1.
"Even I wanted to be one once. I was going to panic New York with dance and song. So,

I end up with featured billing in a Bronx cabaret."

—Bette Davis talking to another champion hopeful (Wayne Morris) in Michael Curtiz's *Kid Galahad*
(Screenplay by Seton I. Miller; based on the novel by Francis Wallace)

2.
"My number finally came up too, didn't it? And Emma. Once wasn't enough for you. You couldn't let her live and be happy, could you? Why did you do it? Because you were bored? Did you have to prove to yourself you're really the champion?"

—Arthur Kennedy fighting with his brother (Kirk Douglas) over Ruth Roman in Mark Robson's *Champion*
(Screenplay by Carl Foreman; based on the short story by Ring Lardner)

3.
"Did I say killer? I meant champion. I get my boxing terms mixed."

—George Sanders having Anne Baxter's number right the first time in Joseph L. Mankiewicz's *All About Eve*
(Screenplay by Joseph L. Mankiewicz; based on "The Wisdom of Eve," a radio play and short story by Mary Orr)

ALSO SEE: Eulogies-4.

CHANGES

1.
"I am not only walking out on this case, Mr. Whiteside, I am leaving the nursing profession. I became a nurse because all my life, ever since I was a little girl, I was filled with the idea of serving a suffering humanity. After one month with you, Mr. Whiteside, I'm going to work in a munitions factory. From now on, anything I can do to help exterminate the human race will fill me with the greatest of pleasure."

—Mary Wickes telling off Monty Woolley in William Keighley's *The Man Who Came to Dinner*
(Screenplay by Julius J. Epstein and Philip G. Epstein; based on the play by George S. Kaufman and Moss Hart)

2.
"Wilkins, after all these years, are you trying to be funny?"

—Billie Burke suspecting her butler (Alan Mowbray) of comedy in Norman Z. McLeod's *Topper*
(Screenplay by Jack Jevne, Eric Hatch and Eddie Moran; based on the novel by Thorne Smith)

3.
"Kay, my father's way of doing things is over. It's finished. Even he knows that. I mean, in five years the Corleone family is going to be completely legitimate. Trust me—that's all I can tell you about my business."

—Al Pacino requesting patience and trust from Diane Keaton in Francis Ford Coppola's *The Godfather*
(Screenplay by Mario Puzo and Francis Ford Coppola; based on the novel by Mario Puzo)

4.
"Seven years ago, I made the most perfect marriage ever devised by man, heaven or radio. My wife was an independent, understanding woman. We thought the same thing about everything, from baseball to Brahms. In those seven years, I was never contemptuous of you. I was proud. But when that drooling pap began to change you, when your independence turned to fear, when I watched you snivel and grovel around those two walking commercials, I didn't like it—and I don't like it! I don't want to be married to Linda Gray, Brenda Brown or even Myrtle Tippet. I want my own wife back!"

—Kirk Douglas confronting his radio-writer wife (Ann Sothern) in Joseph L. Mankiewicz's *A Letter to Three Wives*
(Screenplay by Joseph L. Mankiewicz; adaptation by Vera Caspary; based on "One of Our Hearts," a short story by John Klempner)

5.
"Laura considered me the wisest, the wittiest, the most interesting man she'd ever met. I was

in complete accord with her on that point. She thought me also the kindest, the gentlest, the most sympathetic man in the world. McPherson, you won't understand this, but I tried to become the kindest, the gentlest, the most sympathetic man in the world."

—Clifton Webb admitting to Dana Andrews the mellowing influence of Gene Tierney in Otto Preminger's *Laura*
(Screenplay by Jay Dratler, Samuel Hoffenstein and Betty Reinhardt; based on the novel by Vera Caspary)

ALSO SEE: Aging-15; Christmas-1; Help-2; Moon-6; Moon-7; Prayers-11; Progress-3; Promiscuity-1; Screenplays-1; Sin-4; Smell-16; Soul-7; Spinsters-3; Static-4; Static-5; Static-6; Static-7; Static-11; Strength-8; Wives-2.

CHARACTER

1.
"Madam, *I* am the character of my home."

—William Powell responding indignantly to an employment-office inquiry about the character of his home in Michael Curtiz's *Life with Father*
(Screenplay by Donald Ogden Stewart; based on the play by Howard Lindsay and Russel Crouse and stories by Clarence Day, Jr.)

2.
"By gad, sir, you *are* a character, that you are."

—Sydney Greenstreet complimenting (in his cryptic fashion) Humphrey Bogart in John Huston's *The Maltese Falcon*
(Screenplay by John Huston; based on the novel by Dashiell Hammett)

3.
"Well, it's not easy for a man of my strong character to admit he might have blundered. I'm not what you think I am, Sister."

—Richard Todd acknowledging the errors of his ways to Patricia Neal in Vincent Sherman's *The Hasty Heart*
(Screenplay by Ranald MacDougall; based on the play by John Patrick)

4.
"How can I lose? Twelve ball. How can I lose? Because you were right. It's not enough that you just have talent. You gotta have character, too. Four ball. Yeah, I sure got character now. I picked it up in a hotel room in Louisville."

—Paul Newman, on a pool-shooting winning-streak, blaming his ex-mentor (George C. Scott) for Piper Laurie's Louisville suicide in Robert Rossen's *The Hustler*
(Screenplay by Sidney Carroll and Robert Rossen; based on the novel by Walter Tevis)

5.
(a) "Are you a man of good character where women are concerned?"
    (b) "Have you ever known a man of good character where women are concerned?"

—(a) Scott Sunderland and (b) Leslie Howard displaying opposite views of the opposite sex in Anthony Asquith and Leslie Howard's *Pygmalion*
(Screenplay by George Bernard Shaw; adaptation by W. P. Lipscomb, Cecil Lewis and Ian Dalrymple; based on the play by George Bernard Shaw)
                and (almost verbatim)

—(a) Wilfrid Hyde-White and (b) Rex Harrison dittoing in the remake, George Cukor's *My Fair Lady*
(Screenplay by Alan Jay Lerner; based on his musical play and PYGMALION, *a screenplay and play by George Bernard Shaw)*

6.
"I can afford a blemish on my character but not on my clothes."

—Vincent Price removing a stain on his suit during a party scene in Otto Preminger's *Laura*
(Screenplay by Jay Dratler, Samuel Hoffenstein and Betty Reinhardt; based on the novel by Vera Caspary)

ALSO SEE: Decency-1; Differences-8; Faces-5; Laugh-5; New York-3; Parents-1; Pretense-7; Responsibility-3.

CHILDREN

1.
"Children are life renewing itself, Captain Butler. And when life does that, danger seems very unimportant."

—Olivia De Havilland minimizing, to Clark Gable, the hazards of having children in Victor Fleming's *Gone With the Wind*
(*Screenplay by Sidney Howard; based on the novel by Margaret Mitchell*)

2.
"Personally, Veda's convinced me that alligators have the right idea. They eat their young."

—Eve Arden berating Ann Blyth to Joan Crawford in Michael Curtiz's *Mildred Pierce*
(*Screenplay by Ranald MacDougall; based on the novel by James M. Cain*)

3.
"If I was married to you three years, you'd have the living proof. You'd have three kids already and the fourth in the oven."

—Burl Ives making a lustful aside to his childless daughter-in-law (Elizabeth Taylor) in Richard Brooks's *Cat on a Hot Tin Roof*
(*Screenplay by Richard Brooks and James Poe; based on the play by Tennessee Williams*)

4.
"I always thought I could give them life like a present, all wrapped in white with every promise of happiness. . . . All I can promise them is life itself."

—Dorothy McGuire accepting the limits of her protectiveness in Delbert Mann's *The Dark at the Top of the Stairs*
(*Screenplay by Irving Ravetch and Harriet Frank, Jr.; based on the play by William Inge*)

5.
"My home is hell. We've got a 23-year-old boy. I threw him out of the house last year. Shaggy-haired Maoist! I don't know where he is—presumably building bombs in basements as an expression of his universal brotherhood. We've got a 17-year-old daughter who's had two abortions in two years. Got arrested last week at a rock festival for pushing drugs. They let her go. A typical affluent American family. I don't mean to be facile about this. I blame myself for those two useless young people. I never exercised parental authority. I'm no good at that."

—George C. Scott lamenting his parental blunders in Arthur Hiller's *The Hospital*
(*Original Screenplay by Paddy Chayefsky*)

6.
"Well, Vashti, all you can do is raise them. You can't live their lives for them."

—Elizabeth Taylor playing Modern Mom on the phone to Jane Withers in George Stevens's *Giant*
(*Screenplay by Fred Guiol and Ivan Moffat; based on the novel by Edna Ferber*)

7.
"The Von Trapp children don't play. They march."

—Norma Varden indicating the stern upbringing of Julie Andrews's new charges in Robert Wise's *The Sound of Music*
(*Screenplay by Ernest Lehman; based on the musical play by Howard Lindsay and Russel Crouse and THE TRAPP FAMILY SINGERS, a book by Maria Augusta Von Trapp*)

8.
"Well, there won't ever be no patter of little feet in my house—unless I was to rent some mice."

—Peggy Lee resigning herself to a childless fate in Jack Webb's *Pete Kelly's Blues*
(*Original Screenplay by Richard L. Breen*)

ALSO SEE: Daughters; Sons; Fathers-7; Land-1; Lies-2; Neck-3; Pity-2; Pride-10; Signs-6; Understand-4; Whistle-2.

CHIN

1.
"Oh, I think it's a dream on you. You know, it —it does something to your face. It—it gives you a chin."

—Claudette Colbert complimenting (sort of) Mary Astor's choice of hats in Mitchell Leisen's *Midnight* (*Screenplay by Charles Brackett and Billy Wilder; based on a story by Edwin Justus Mayer and Franz Schulz*)

2.

"If you've got anything on your chest besides your chin, you'd better get it off."

—Walter Matthau wrangling with a woebegone Jack Lemmon in Gene Saks's *The Odd Couple* (*Screenplay by Neil Simon; based on his play*)

3.

"I'll have my double chins in privacy."

—Marie Dressler sidestepping Lionel Barrymore's suggestion of a stage comeback in George Cukor's *Dinner at Eight* (*Screenplay by Frances Marion and Herman J. Mankiewicz; based on the play by George S. Kaufman and Edna Ferber*)

4.

"Now, Bertha, I'd like to give you some encouragement, but all I can say is 'Chins up.'"

—Charles Coburn struggling to be positive with Spring Byington in Ernst Lubitsch's *Heaven Can Wait* (*Screenplay by Samson Raphaelson; based on BIRTHDAY, a play by Lazlo Bus-Fekete*)

CHOICE

1.

"Not much meat on her, but what's there is cherce."

—Spencer Tracy complimenting Katharine Hepburn's physical appearance in George Cukor's *Pat and Mike* (*Original screenplay by Ruth Gordon and Garson Kanin*)

2.

"Mr. President, we are rapidly approaching a moment of truth both for ourselves as human beings and for the life of our nation. Now truth is not always a pleasant thing, but it is necessary now to make a choice, to choose between two admittedly regrettable, but nevertheless, distinguishable, post-war environments. One where you got 20 million people killed, and the other where you got 150 million people killed."

—George C. Scott presenting Peter Sellers with a helluvah choice in Stanley Kubrick's *Dr. Strangelove or: How I Learned To Stop Worrying and Love the Bomb* (*Screenplay by Stanley Kubrick, Terry Southern and Peter George; based on RED ALERT, a novel by Peter George*)

3.

"It is this or that—all the universe or nothing. Which shall it be, Passworthy? Which shall it be? Which shall it be?"

—Raymond Massey pondering the future with Edward Chapman in the last lines of William Cameron Menzies's *Things To Come* (*Screenplay by H. G. Wells; based on his novel, THE SHAPE OF THINGS TO COME*)

4.

"I aim to kill you in one minute, Ned, or see you hang in Fort Smith at Judge Parker's convenience. Which will it be?"

—John Wayne squaring off against Robert Duvall in Henry Hathaway's *True Grit* (*Screenplay by Marguerite Roberts; based on the novel by Charles Portis*)

5.

"Your Honor, we request an immediate ruling from this court: is there or is there not a Santa Claus?"

—Jerome Cowan seeking clarification from Gene Lockhart in George Seaton's *Miracle on 34th Street* (*Screenplay by George Seaton; based on an original story by Valentine Davis*)

6.

"Am I a king or a breeding bull?"

—Charles Laughton feeling pressure to produce a male heir in Alexander Korda's *The Private Life of Henry VIII* (*Original Screenplay by Lajos Biro and Arthur Wimperis*)

7.

"Are you a critic or a wife?"

—William Holden questioning Grace Kelly's treatment of Bing Crosby in George Seaton's *The Country Girl*
(Screenplay by George Seaton; based on the play by Clifford Odets)

8.

"A teacher or a leader? The dangerous Miss Brodie and her troops! Well, where you lead, I cannot follow."

—Robert Stephens walking out on Maggie Smith in Ronald Neame's *The Prime of Miss Jean Brodie*
(Screenplay by Jay Presson Allen; based on her play and the novel by Muriel Spark)

9.

"I've no earthly reason to think I can trust you, and, if I do this and get away with it, you'll have something on me that you can use whenever you want to. Since I've got something on you, I couldn't be sure that you wouldn't put a hole in me some day. All those are on one side. At least some of them are unimportant—I won't argue about that—but look at the *number* of them. And what have we got on the other side? All we've got is that maybe you love me and maybe I love you."

—Humphrey Bogart sizing up his situation with Mary Astor in John Huston's *The Maltese Falcon*
(Screenplay by John Huston; based on the novel by Dashiell Hammett)

10.

"Well, there's not much to choose between you two, is there? When you're together, you slash each other to pieces, and, when you're apart, you slash yourselves to pieces. All told, it's quite a problem."

—Wendy Hiller summing up the no-win dilemma of her lover (Burt Lancaster) and his ex (Rita Hayworth) in Delbert Mann's *Separate Tables*
(Screenplay by Terence Rattigan and John Gay; based on the play by Terence Rattigan)

11.

"Christine, I've reached that realistic age when I have to choose between having fun and a heart attack."

—Joseph Cotten leveling with Jacqueline Bisset in Jerry Paris's *The Grasshopper*
(Screenplay by Jerry Belson and Garry Marshall; based on THE PASSING OF EVIL, a novel by Mark McShane)

12.

"I got brown sandwiches and green sandwiches. . . . It's either very new cheese or very old meat."

—Walter Matthau announcing the menu to his poker cronies in Gene Saks's *The Odd Couple*
(Screenplay by Neil Simon; based on his play)

ALSO SEE: Diamonds-3; Duty-2; Hunger-8; Men-12; New York-4; Proposals-4; Propositions-8; Questions-9; Sensible-2; War-5; Why-9.

CHRISTMAS

1.

"Oh, Christmas isn't just a day. It's a frame of mind. And that's what's been changing. That's why I'm glad I'm here. Maybe I can do something about it. And I'm glad I met you and your daughter. You two are a test case for me."

—Edmund Gwenn laying his Kris Kringle cards on the table to Maureen O'Hara in George Seaton's *Miracle on 34th Street*
(Screenplay by George Seaton; based on an original story by Valentine Davis)

2.

"Nasty weather we're having, eh? And I so much hoped we could give you a white Christmas, just like the ones you used to know. Aren't those the words that clever little man wrote—you know, the one who stole his name from our capital, that something-or-other Berlin?"

—Otto Preminger taunting his American POWs in Billy Wilder's *Stalag 17*
(Screenplay by Billy Wilder and Edwin Blum; based on the play by Donald Bevan and Edmund Trzcinski)

ALSO SEE: Dictation-4; Drink-6; Telephone Scenes-13.

CHURCH

1.
"Vinnie, if there's one place the church should leave alone, it's a man's soul."

—William Powell putting up his own special argument to the religious pleadings of his wife (Irene Dunne) in Michael Curtiz's *Life With Father*
(Screenplay by Donald Ogden Stewart; based on the play by Howard Lindsay and Russel Crouse and stories by Clarence Day, Jr.)

2.
"I don't go to church. Kneeling bags my nylons."

—Jan Sterling telling Kirk Douglas she's not the religious type in Billy Wilder's *The Big Carnival*
(Original Screenplay by Billy Wilder, Lesser Samuels and Walter Newman)

3.
(a) "It's quiet."
     (b) "Yeah. Like a church. Church of the Good Hustler."

—(a) Myron McCormick and (b) Paul Newman entering a pool hall in Robert Rossen's *The Hustler*
(Screenplay by Sidney Carroll and Robert Rossen; based on the novel by Walter Tevis)

ALSO SEE: Legs-6; Money-10.

CIGARETTE

1.
"I feel a lot better, too. Matter of fact, I never felt so good in my life. How about a cigarette?"

—John Wayne relaxing after taking Iwo Jima and preparing to light up as a sniper's bullet kills him in Allan Dwan's *Sands of Iwo Jima*
(Screenplay by Harry Brown and James Edward Grant; based on a story by Harry Brown)

2.
"Shall we just have a cigarette on it?"

—Paul Henreid sealing his love pact with Bette Davis with his famous two-cigarette trick in Irving Rapper's *Now, Voyager*
(Screenplay by Casey Robinson; based on the novel by Olive Higgins Prouty)

3.
"My sister, Elaine, arrived here one day with two suitcases, a hat box, a blue parakeet, a dead goldfish and a five-year-old child. A few days later she went downstairs to buy a pack of filter-tip cigarettes. Six years later she returned for the suitcases and the hat box. Now, the parakeet I'd given away. The goldfish I had long since flushed down the toilet. And the five-year-old child had, with very little effort, become six years older. Now, when Elaine returned for her luggage, I reminded her of the child and the pack of filter-tip cigarettes. And then, I don't know—I slapped my sister. Sister cried at some length and then proceeded calmly, briefly to explain to me her well-practiced theory on the meaning of life—a philosophy falling somewhere to the left of Whoopee. Well, that was almost a year ago, and I still got Nick."

—Jason Robards explaining his surrogate fatherhood in Fred Coe's *A Thousand Clowns*
(Screenplay by Herb Gardner; based on his play)

4.
"May you smoke? What's that supposed to be —homage to a lady?"

—Grace Kelly sneering at William Holden's sudden politeness in George Seaton's *The Country Girl*
(Screenplay by George Seaton; based on the play by Clifford Odets)

5.
"You may smoke, too. I can still enjoy the smell of it. Nice state of affairs when a man has to indulge his vices by proxy."

—Charles Waldron permitting Humphrey Bogart to smoke in Howard Hawks's *The Big Sleep*
(Screenplay by William Faulkner, Leigh Brackett

and Jules Furthman; based on the novel by Raymond Chandler)

CLASS

1.

"This is your neighbor speaking. I'm sure I speak for all of us when I say that something must be done about your garbage cans in the alley here. *It is definitely second-rate garbage!* Now, by next week, I want to see a better class of garbage. I want to see champagne bottles and caviar cans. I'm sure you're all behind me on this, so let's snap it up and get on the ball."

—Jason Robards yelling out his window to no one in particular in Fred Coe's *A Thousand Clowns*
(Screenplay by Herb Gardner; based on his play)

2.

"The prettiest sight in this fine pretty world is the privileged class enjoying its privileges."

—James Stewart making a snooty observation to Katharine Hepburn in George Cukor's *The Philadelphia Story*
(Screenplay by Donald Ogden Stewart; based on the play by Philip Barry)
and (almost verbatim)

—Celeste Holm dittoing to Frank Sinatra in the remake, Charles Walters's *High Society*
(Screenplay by John Patrick; based on THE PHILADELPHIA STORY, a screenplay by Donald Ogden Stewart and play by Philip Barry)

3.

"Hi, sister—all alone? My name's Shapeley. Might as well get acquainted. It's gonna be a long trip—gets tiresome later on. Specially for somebody like you. You look like you got class. Yes sir, with a capital K. I'm the guy that knows class when he sees it, believe you me. Ask any of the boys. They'll tell you. Shapeley sure knows how to pick 'em. Yessir!"

—Roscoe Karns misreading the aloofness of his bus-seat partner (Claudette Colbert) in Frank Capra's *It Happened One Night*
(Screenplay by Robert Riskin; based on "Night Bus," a short story by Samuel Hopkins Adams)

4.

"She looks tolerable enough, but I'm in no humor tonight to give consequence to the middle classes at play."

—Laurence Olivier passing up a chance to meet Greer Garson in Robert Z. Leonard's *Pride and Prejudice*
(Screenplay by Aldous Huxley and Jane Murfin; based on the play by Helen Jerome and novel by Jane Austen)

5.

"Lora May looks good with Brad. Looks like class. But it's him, not her. If she's dancing with a tramp, she'd look like a tramp. Got no class of her own. I like class. You like class?"

—Paul Douglas complimenting Jeffrey Lynn at the expense of Linda Darnell in Joseph L. Mankiewicz's *A Letter to Three Wives*
(Screenplay by Joseph L. Mankiewicz; adaptation by Vera Caspary; based on "One of Our Hearts," a short story by John Klempner)

6.

"I have no curiosity about the working classes."

—Gladys Cooper cutting short Cathleen Nesbitt's gibberish in Delbert Mann's *Separate Tables*
(Screenplay by Terence Rattigan and John Gay; based on the play by Terence Rattigan)

7.

"It doesn't matter who gives them as long as you never wear anything second-rate. Wait for the first-class jewels, Gigi. Hold on to your ideals."

—Isabel Jeans counseling Leslie Caron in courtesan ways in Vincente Minnelli's *Gigi*
(Screenplay by Alan Jay Lerner; based on the novel by Colette)

ALSO SEE: Bums-2; Home-7; Ignorance-1; Incompatibility-4; Prison-6; Propositions-22.

CLEAN

1.

"Ah, it's a great thing to have a lady aboard with clean habits. It sets a man a good example. A man alone, he gets to living like a hog. Then, too, with me, it's always 'Put things off. Never do today what you can put off till tomorrow.' But with you: business before pleasure every time. Do all your personal laundry, make yourself spic and span, get all the mending out of the way and then—and only then—sit down to a nice quiet hour with the Good Book. I tell you, it's a model—like an inspiration. Why, I ain't had this old engine so clean in years, inside and out. Just look at her, Miss. She actually practically sparkles. Myself, too. Guess you ain't never had a look at me without my whiskers and all cleaned up. I bet you wouldn't hardly recognize me, that much of a change."

—Humphrey Bogart warming to Katharine Hepburn in John Huston's *The African Queen*
(Screenplay by James Agee and John Huston; based on the novel by C. S. Forester)

2.

"I ain't dirty. I washed my face and hands before I come, I did."

—Wendy Hiller assuring Leslie Howard in Anthony Asquith and Leslie Howard's *Pygmalion*
(Screenplay by George Bernard Shaw; adaptation by W. P. Lipscomb, Cecil Lewis and Ian Dalrymple; based on the play by George Bernard Shaw)

and

—Audrey Hepburn dittoing Rex Harrison in the remake, George Cukor's *My Fair Lady*
(Screenplay by Alan Jay Lerner; based on his play and PYGMALION, a screenplay and play by George Bernard Shaw)

ALSO SEE: Animals-2; Macho-9; People-6; Sex-6.

COMEBACK

1.

"I hate that word. It's *return*—a return to the millions of people who've never forgiven me for deserting the screen."

—Gloria Swanson correcting William Holden's tactless wording in Billy Wilder's *Sunset Boulevard*
(Original Screenplay by Charles Brackett, Billy Wilder and D. M. Marshman Jr.)

2.

"I'm making a comeback, ya know."

—Mickey Shaughnessy, as a punchy prizefighter, reprising his pet expression for the last line of Vincente Minnelli's *Designing Woman*
(Original Screenplay by George Wells; based on a suggestion by Helen Rose)

COMMUNICATION

1.

"Are you sure you were talking about waterskiing? From where I sat, it looked like you were conjugating some irregular verbs."

—Grace Kelly teasing Cary Grant about his attentions to Brigitte Auber in Alfred Hitchcock's *To Catch a Thief*
(Screenplay by John Michael Hayes; based on the novel by David Dodge)

2.

"Mr. Allen, this may come as a shock to you, but there are some men who don't end every sentence with a proposition."

—Doris Day telling off Rock Hudson in Michael Gordon's *Pillow Talk*
(Screenplay by Stanley Shapiro and Maurice Richlin; based on a story by Russell Rouse and Clarence Greene)

3.

(a) "Mr. Kralik, it's true we're in the same room, but we're not in the same planet."

(b) "Why, Miss Novak, I—although I'm the victim of your remark, I—I can't help but admiring the exquisite way you have of expressing yourself. You certainly know how to put a man in his planet."

—(b) James Stewart warming to (a) Margaret Sullavan in Ernst Lubitsch's *The Shop Around the Corner*
(Screenplay by Samson Raphaelson; based on PARFUMERIE, *a play by Miklos Laszlo)*

4.
"That is an emotional and ill-considered figure of speech. If I *were* 'the last man on earth' and there were a million women left, you'd be fighting tooth and claw with every single one of 'em for the privilege of becoming my mate. You'd be panting to repopulate the world."

—David Niven telling Maggie McNamara to reconsider her phraseology in Otto Preminger's *The Moon Is Blue*
(Screenplay by F. Hugh Herbert; based on his play)

5.
"Well, 'very nice' is hardly the phrase to describe two bodies locked in heavenly transport. You wouldn't chisel 'very nice' in granite under Rodin's 'The Kiss.' 'Very nice' is when you receive a get-well card from your butcher or the television repairman. That's 'very nice.' But, for what we just did, the operational comments range from 'lousy' to 'sensational' to 'rockets went off' or 'the earth moved.' "

—George Segal feeling sexually unappreciated by Glenda Jackson in Melvin Frank's *A Touch of Class*
(Original Screenplay by Melvin Frank and Jack Rose)

6.
"Ladies and gentlemen, when something like this happens to you and you try to tell how you feel about it, you find that, out of all the words in the world, there are only two that really mean anything—*thank you.*"

—Janet Gaynor accepting her Oscar in William A. Wellman's *A Star Is Born*
(Screenplay by Dorothy Parker, Alan Campbell and Robert Carson; based on an original story by William A. Wellman and Robert Carson)
and (similarly)

—Judy Garland dittoing in George Cukor's *A Star Is Born*
(Screenplay by Moss Hart; based on a screenplay by Dorothy Parker, Alan Campbell and Robert Carson and original story by William A. Wellman and Robert Carson)

7.
"Mrs. Robinson, do you think we could say a few words to each other first this time?"

—Dustin Hoffman trying to get a little depth into his affair with Anne Bancroft in Mike Nichols's *The Graduate*
(Screenplay by Calder Willingham and Buck Henry; based on the novel by Charles Webb)

8.
"How long does it take to tell a woman, 'My wife's come back'? I can say it in two seconds. 'My-wife's-come-back.' You've had two days."

—Irene Dunne urging Cary Grant to break the news to his new bride (Gail Patrick) in Garson Kanin's *My Favorite Wife*
(Screenplay by Bella Spewack and Samuel Spewack; based on a story by Bella Spewack, Samuel Spewack and Leo McCarey)

9.
"Elaine communicates with my brother and myself almost entirely by rumor."

—Jason Robards allowing that he's not really close with his sister in Fred Coe's *A Thousand Clowns*
(Screenplay by Herb Gardner; based on his play)

10.
"I seem to have offended your light of love by using a polysyllabic word."

—Van Heflin offering a highbrow apology to Robert Taylor in Mervyn LeRoy's *Johnny Eager*
(Screenplay by John Lee Mahin and James Edward Grant; based on a story by James Edward Grant)

11.
"My dear Mr. Marlowe, I notice in you an unpleasant tendency toward abrupt transitions. A characteristic of your generation, but in this

case, I must ask you to follow some sort of logical progression."

—Otto Kruger criticizing Dick Powell's blunt banter in Edward Dmytryk's *Murder, My Sweet*
(Screenplay by John Paxton; based on FAREWELL, MY LOVELY, a novel by Raymond Chandler)

12.
"I don't understand this conversation at all. How drunk am I?"

—Paul Douglas missing the intrigues going on around him in Joseph L. Mankiewicz's *A Letter to Three Wives*
(Screenplay by Joseph L. Mankiewicz; adaptation by Vera Caspary; based on "One of Our Hearts," a short story by John Klempner)

13.
"Clear? Huh! Why, a four-year-old child can understand this report. Run out and find me a four-year-old child. I can't make head or tail out of it."

—Groucho Marx dressing down his Minister of Finance (William Worthington) in Leo McCarey's *Duck Soup*
(Screenplay by Bert Kalmar and Harry Ruby; additional dialogue by Arthur Sheekman and Nat Perrin)

ALSO SEE: Talk; Compliments-9; Failure-2; Sounds-1; Swear-4.

COMPLIMENTS

1.
"There's a magnificence in you, Tracy . . . the magnificence that comes out of your eyes and your voice and the way you stand there and the way that you walk. You're lit from within, Tracy. You've got fires banked down in you, hearth fires and holocausts. . . . You're made out of flesh and blood. That's the blank, unholy surprise of it! Why, you're the Golden Girl, Tracy —full of life and warmth and delight."

—James Stewart wooing Katharine Hepburn in George Cukor's *The Philadelphia Story*

(Screenplay by Donald Ogden Stewart; based on the play by Philip Barry)
and (similarly)

—Frank Sinatra dittoing Grace Kelly in the remake, Charles Walters's *High Society*
(Screenplay by John Patrick; based on THE PHILADELPHIA STORY, a screenplay by Donald Ogden Stewart and play by Philip Barry)

2.
"I'm not very impressionable, Mildred. I lost my awe of women at an early age. But, ever since that first day you came here, I've thought of nothing but of what I'd say to you when we met again. And now I can't say anything. You take my breath away."

—Zachary Scott rushing Joan Crawford in Michael Curtiz's *Mildred Pierce*
(Screenplay by Ranald MacDougall; based on the novel by James M. Cain)

3.
"Behold she stands with her gown hung loose. Framed is her face in golden tresses, reflecting the milk-white beauty of her shoulders. So it was that Venus stood before Mars, welcoming her lover. Nothing do I see that is not perfection."

—Robert Taylor greeting Deborah Kerr in Mervyn LeRoy's *Quo Vadis*
(Screenplay by John Lee Mahin, S. N. Behrman and Sonya Levien; based on the novel by Henryk Sienkiewicz)

4.
(a) "Oh, your Excellency!"
    (b) "You're not so bad yourself."

—(a) Margaret Dumont and (b) Groucho Marx exchanging greetings in Leo McCarey's *Duck Soup*
(Screenplay by Bert Kalmar and Harry Ruby; additional dialogue by Arthur Sheekman and Nat Perrin)

5.
"Whether by nature or by art, you never make a gesture without imparting beauty to it."

—Herbert Marshall complimenting Gene Tierney in Edmund Goulding's *The Razor's Edge*

(Screenplay by Lamar Trotti; based on the novel by W. Somerset Maugham)

6.

"Well, even as I looked at her, I thought, She's good, but what are they all—what are all the women in the world—compared to Anne?"

—Joseph Cotten trying to wear down Claudette Colbert's just-friends edict in John Cromwell's *Since You Went Away*
(Screenplay by David O. Selznick; adaptation by Margaret Buell Wilder; based on her book of letters)

7.

"With a binding like you've got, people are going to want to know what's in the book."

—Gene Kelly sparking Leslie Caron in Vincente Minnelli's *An American in Paris*
(Original Screenplay by Alan Jay Lerner)

8.

"You're pretty enough for all normal purposes."

—Beulah Bondi allaying the fears of her daughter (Martha Scott) about looks with a minimal compliment in Sam Wood's *Our Town*
(Screenplay by Thornton Wilder, Frank Craven and Harry Chandlee; based on the play by Thornton Wilder)

9.

(a) "I don't go in for that stuff."
  (b) "What stuff?"
  (a) "Compliments to women about their looks. I never met a dame yet that didn't know if she was good-looking or not without being told. And there are some of them that give themselves credit for more than they've got. I once went out with a dame who told me, 'I'm the glamorous type.' She says, 'I am the glamorous type.' I said, 'So what?' "
  (b) "And what did she say then?"
  (a) "She didn't say nothing. I shut her up like a clam."
  (b) "Did it end the romance?"
  (a) "Well, it ended the conversation, that was all."

—(a) Marlon Brando telling (b) Vivien Leigh not to expect any flattery from him in Elia Kazan's *A Streetcar Named Desire*
(Screenplay by Tennessee Williams; adaptation by Oscar Saul; based on the play by Tennessee Williams)

ALSO SEE: Flattery; Appearances-5; Decency-1; Games-8; Gentle-3; Letters-13; Names-4.

COMPROMISE

1.

"This is a man's world, Jeff, and you got to check your ideals outside the door like you do your rubbers. Thirty years ago I had your ideals, too. I was *you*. I had to make the same decision you were asked to make today. And I made it. I compromised—yes! So that all those years I could sit in that Senate and serve the people in a thousand honest ways! You've got to face facts, Jeff. I've served our state well, haven't I? We have the lowest unemployment and the highest Federal grants. But, well, I had to compromise. I had to play ball. You can't count on people voting. Half the time they don't vote anymore. That's how states and empires have been built since time began. Don't you understand?"

—Claude Rains passing along his brand of political realities to James Stewart in Frank Capra's *Mr. Smith Goes to Washington*
(Screenplay by Sidney Buchman; based on "The Gentleman From Montana," a story by Lewis R. Foster)

2.

"How do you compromise? I hate softness. My mother was soft. It killed her. I don't believe in turning the other cheek. You ask me to compromise on this kid. Who's he? Now—right now—I'm faced with a problem of my own, Lou, that's ripping my guts out, and I can't compromise on that, so what do I do?"

—Kirk Douglas confessing his inflexibility to fellow detective William Bendix in William Wyler's *Detective Story*

(Screenplay by Philip Yordan and Robert Wyler; based on the play by Sidney Kingsley)

CONFESSIONS

1.
"'Twas I informed on your son, Mrs. McPhillip. Forgive me."

—Victor McLaglen admitting his skulduggery to Una O'Connor in John Ford's *The Informer*
(Screenplay by Dudley Nichols; based on the novel by Liam O'Flaherty)

2.
"What does it matter now? Andre's dead. The man I love is dead. I thought about it day and night, but I didn't know how. I wanted to do it so that we would be free so that Andre and I could go away and live together as we should. But Andre wouldn't help me. He had his honor."

—Valli admitting murder on the witness stand when she learns of Louis Jourdan's suicide in Alfred Hitchcock's *The Paradine Case*
(Screenplay by David O. Selznick; adaptation by Alma Reville and James Bridie; based on the novel by Robert Hichens)

3.
"This fairy hired me to exchange a necklace for cash for a friend of his. We drove out to the woods. I shot him. I buried the 15 grand. I drove my car back to his place, walked 15 miles back to the woods, knocked myself in the head and then I called the police."

—Robert Mitchum telling the police exactly what they want to hear in Dick Richards's *Farewell, My Lovely*
(Screenplay by David Zelag Goodman; based on the novel by Raymond Chandler)

4.
"Ninotchka, let me confess something. Never did I dream I could feel like this toward a sergeant."

—Melvyn Douglas romancing Greta Garbo in Ernst Lubitsch's *Ninotchka*

(Screenplay by Charles Brackett, Billy Wilder and Walter Reisch; based on an original story by Melchior Lengyel)

5.
"I am married to an American agent."

—Claude Rains telling his mother (Madame Konstantin) about the spy in their house (Ingrid Bergman) in Alfred Hitchcock's *Notorious*
(Original Screenplay by Ben Hecht)

6.
"Every word of what that boy said is the truth! Every word about Taylor and me and graft and the rotten political corruption of our state. Every word of it is true. I'm not fit for office! I'm not fit for any place of honor or trust in this land!"

—Claude Rains agreeing with James Stewart's accusations in Frank Capra's *Mr. Smith Goes to Washington*
(Screenplay by Sidney Buchman; based on "The Gentleman From Montana," a story by Lewis R. Foster)

7.
(a) "I—I peel labels."
   (b) "We all peel labels."

—(a) Sandy Dennis confessing a minor compulsion which (b) Richard Burton interprets in a larger sense in Mike Nichols's *Who's Afraid of Virginia Woolf?*
(Screenplay by Ernest Lehman; based on the play by Edward Albee)

ALSO SEE: Conscience-5; Dictation-5; Heart-17; Murder-6; Murder-7; Murder-11; Murder-12; Trouble-5.

CONFLICT

1.
" 'The love impulse in man frequently reveals itself in terms of conflict.' "

—Katharine Hepburn explaining chaos by quoting psychiatrist Fritz Feld to Cary Grant in Howard Hawks's *Bringing Up Baby*
(Screenplay by Dudley Nichols and Hagar Wilde; based on a story by Hagar Wilde)

2.

"Well, we Texans like a little vinegar in our greens, honey. Gives 'em flavor."

—Rock Hudson giving Elizabeth Taylor a vote in their marriage in George Stevens's *Giant*
(Screenplay by Fred Guiol and Ivan Moffat; based on the novel by Edna Ferber)

3.

"I'm not *living* with you. We occupy the same cage, that's all."

—Elizabeth Taylor characterizing her marriage to Paul Newman in Richard Brooks's *Cat on a Hot Tin Roof*
(Screenplay by Richard Brooks and James Poe; based on the play by Tennessee Williams)

4.

"When we were married, Babe, the Justice of the Peace said something about 'for richer, for poorer, for better, for worse.' Remember? Well, this is the worse."

—Dana Andrews warring with his wife (Virginia Mayo) in William Wyler's *The Best Years of Our Lives*
(Screenplay by Robert E. Sherwood; based on GLORY FOR ME, a verse novel by MacKinlay Kantor)

5.

"Seems we've been at cross purposes, doesn't it?"

—Clark Gable leaving Vivien Leigh just when she realizes that she really loves him in Victor Fleming's *Gone With the Wind*
(Screenplay by Sidney Howard; based on the novel by Margaret Mitchell)

ALSO SEE: Mind-12; Peace-4.

CONSCIENCE

1.

"France is once again today a land of reason and benevolence because one of her sons through an immense work and a great action gave rise to a new order of things based on justice and the rights common to all men! Let's not pity him because he suffered and endured. Let us envy him! Let us envy him because his great heart won him the proudest of destinies. He was a moment in the conscience of man."

—Morris Carnovsky eulogizing Paul Muni in the last lines of William Dieterle's *The Life of Emile Zola*
(Screenplay by Heinz Herald, Geza Herczeg and Norman Reilly Raine; based on a story by Heinz Herald and Geza Herczeg)

2.

"I don't want to be the conscience of the world. I don't want to be the conscience of anybody."

—Marlon Brando declining leadership in Elia Kazan's *Viva Zapata!*
(Original Screenplay by John Steinbeck)

3.

"That's a neat trick, having a clear conscience when you work as a doctor on a ship which has 300 people living in an open deck."

—Simone Signoret challenging Oskar Werner in Stanley Kramer's *Ship of Fools*
(Screenplay by Abby Mann; based on the novel by Katherine Anne Porter)

4.

"What do you got in place of a conscience? Don't answer. I know: a lawyer."

—Kirk Douglas sneering at criminal George Macready in William Wyler's *Detective Story*
(Screenplay by Philip Yordan and Robert Wyler; based on the play by Sidney Kingsley)

5.

"The communication is not hand-written. It is formed by letters cut from the newspaper and pasted together to spell words. It is, ladies and gentlemen, the confession of a tortured conscience."

—Walter Abel introducing as evidence a letter written supposedly by a lynch-mob member but actually by its intended victim (Spencer Tracy) in Fritz Lang's *Fury*
(Screenplay by Bartlett Cormack and Fritz Lang; based on an original story by Norman Krasna)

ALSO SEE: Hunger-5; Letters-11; Toasts-12.

CONVICTIONS

1.

"When a man kills, it's the one act he does totally alone. The world isn't with him. Therefore, his convictions must be tremendous. I admire people with convictions."

—John Mills making an offbeat observation to Deborah Kerr in Ronald Neame's *The Chalk Garden*
(Screenplay by John Michael Hayes; based on the play by Enid Bagnold)

2.

"I like my convictions undiluted, same as I do my bourbon."

—George Brent being the hard-lined Southerner in William Wyler's *Jezebel*
(Screenplay by Clements Ripley, Abem Finkel and John Huston; based on the play by Owen Davis, Sr.)

3.

"I have no conviction, if that's what you mean. I blow with the wind, and the prevailing wind happens to be from Vichy."

—Claude Rains explaining his adaptable politics to Conrad Veidt in Michael Curtiz's *Casablanca*
(Screenplay by Julius J. Epstein, Philip G. Epstein and Howard Koch; based on EVERYBODY COMES TO RICK'S, a play by Murray Burnett and Joan Alison)

ALSO SEE: Beliefs.

(Screenplay by Frank S. Nugent and Joshua Logan; based on the play by Thomas Heggen and Joshua Logan and novel by Thomas Heggen)

2.

"In a world full of frightened people, he likes courage wherever he find it—even in a rude and angry woman."

—Peter Chong translating Robert Donat to Ingrid Bergman in Mark Robson's *The Inn of the Sixth Happiness*
(Screenplay by Isobel Lennart; based on THE SMALL WOMAN, a book by Alan Burgess)

3.

"What good is courage if you have no head?"

—Katina Paxinou arguing against foolhardy heroics in Sam Wood's *For Whom the Bell Tolls*
(Screenplay by Dudley Nichols; based on the novel by Ernest Hemingway)

4.

"With enough courage, you can do without a reputation."

—Clark Gable dancing with a fretful, freshly widowed Vivien Leigh in Victor Fleming's *Gone With the Wind*
(Screenplay by Sidney Howard; based on the novel by Margaret Mitchell)

ALSO SEE: Crazy-18; Dark-5; Hands-4; Life-13; Life and Death-15; Prayers-11; Sayings-3; Youth-2.

COURAGE

1.

" 'Right now, I'm looking at something that's hanging over my desk: a preposterous hunk of brass attached to the most bilious piece of ribbon I've ever seen. I'd rather have it than the Congressional Medal of Honor. It tells me what I'll always be proudest of—that, at a time in the world when courage counted most, I lived among 62 brave men.' "

—Jack Lemmon reading a letter from Henry Fonda to the crew in John Ford and Mervyn LeRoy's *Mister Roberts*

COURTROOM LINES

1.

"Your Honor, every one of these letters is addressed to Santa Claus. The post office has delivered them. Therefore, the post office department—a branch of the federal government—recognizes this man, Kris Kringle, to be the one and only Santa Claus."

—John Payne proving there *is* a Santa Claus in George Seaton's *Miracle on 34th Street*
(Screenplay by George Seaton; based on an original story by Valentine Davis)

2.

"Mr. Deeds, there has been a great deal of damaging testimony against you. Your behavior, to say the least, has been most strange. But, in the opinion of the court, you are not only sane but you're the sanest man that ever walked into this courtroom."

—H. B. Warner making his ruling on Gary Cooper in Frank Capra's *Mr. Deeds Goes to Town*
(Screenplay by Robert Riskin; based on "Opera Hat," a short story by Clarence Budington Kelland)

3.

"Not only is an innocent man crying out for justice, but more—much more! A great nation is in desperate danger of forfeiting her honor! So do not take upon yourself a fault, the burden of which you will forever bear in history! A judicial blunder has been committed. The condemnation of an innocent man induced the acquittal of a guilty man, and now today you are asked to condemn me because I rebelled on seeing our country embarked on this terrible course."

—Paul Muni pleading Joseph Schildkraut's case in William Dieterle's *The Life of Emile Zola*
(Screenplay by Heinz Herald, Geza Herczeg and Norman Reilly Raine; based on a story by Heinz Herald and Geza Herczeg)

4.

"The Gospel According to Brady! God speaks to Brady, and Brady tells the world! Brady, Brady, Brady Almighty! . . . Suppose that a lesser human being—suppose a Cates or a Darwin—had the audacity to think that God might whisper to him, that unBrady thought might still be holy. Must a man go to prison because he differs with the self-appointed prophet? Extend the testaments! Let's have a Book of Brady. We shall hatch the Pentateuch and slip you in neatly between Numbers and Deuteronomy."

—Spencer Tracy attacking Fredric March's smug piety in Stanley Kramer's *Inherit the Wind*
(Screenplay by Nathan E. Douglas and Harold Jacob Smith; based on the play by Jerome Lawrence and Robert E. Lee)

5.

"May it please the court, I submit that my entire line of defense is based upon the proposition that persons of the female sex should be dealt with, before the law, as the equals of persons of the male sex. I submit that I cannot hope to argue this line before minds hostile to and prejudiced against the female sex."

—Katharine Hepburn taking a feminist stance in her defense of a spouse-shooting Judy Holliday in George Cukor's *Adam's Rib*
(Original Screenplay by Ruth Gordon and Garson Kanin)

6.

"I've talked with the prisoner. He's a friend of Lily Langtry's. It stands to reason no friend of Lily Langtry goes around stealing horses—leastways, there's a reasonable doubt."

—Walter Brennan making his ruling on Gary Cooper in William Wyler's *The Westerner*
(Screenplay by Jo Swerling and Niven Busch; based on a story by Stuart N. Lake)

7.

"But she is legally dead, Your Honor! You declared her legally dead yourself in this very courtroom. Your decision is on file."

—Cary Grant appealing to Granville Bates to get out of a bigamy bind in Garson Kanin's *My Favorite Wife*
(Screenplay by Bella Spewack and Samuel Spewack; based on a story by Bella Spewack, Samuel Spewack and Leo McCarey)

ALSO SEE: Choice-5; Life and Death-12; Life and Death-13; Mad Act-3; Mad Act-4; Mad Act-5; Mothers-5; Swear-3.

COWARD

1.

" 'At the fatal stroke of 11 P.M., Rocky was led through the little green door of death. No sooner had he entered the death chamber than he tore himself from the guard's grasp and flung himself on the floor, screaming for mercy. Then, as they dragged him to the electric chair, he clawed wildly at the concrete floor with agonized shrieks. In contrast to his former heroics, Rocky Sullivan died a coward.' "

—Billy Halop reading the newspaper account of James Cagney's deliberately unheroic death in Michael Curtiz's *Angels With Dirty Faces*
(Screenplay by John Wexley and Warren Duff; based on an original story by Rowland Brown)

2.
"Try to remember that, though ignorance becomes a Southern gentleman, cowardice does not."

—Fredric March advising his son (Dan Duryea) in Michael Gordon's *Another Part of the Forest*
(Screenplay by Vladimir Pozner; based on the play by Lillian Hellman)

3.
"Miss Cooper, the plain fact is that I'm far too much of a coward to stay on here now."

—David Niven declining Wendy Hiller's invitation to remain at her hotel despite the scandal that has made him an unwelcome guest in Delbert Mann's *Separate Tables*
(Screenplay by Terence Rattigan and John Gay; based on the play by Terence Rattigan)

4.
(a) "Just how big a coward are you?"
     (b) "Well, I was captain of the Olympic team."

—(a) Roy Rogers and (b) Bob Hope bantering during a shootout with bad guys in Frank Tashlin's *Son of Paleface*
(Original Screenplay by Frank Tashlin, Robert L. Welch and Joseph Quillan)

5.
"I'd punch you right in the nose if I wasn't afraid you'd break my jaw."

—Don Beddoe leaving Cary Grant in a huff in Irving Reis's *The Bachelor and the Bobby-Soxer*
(Original Screenplay by Sidney Sheldon)

6.
"That's one of the tragedies of this life—that the men who are most in need of a beating-up are always enormous."

—Rudy Vallee lamenting the fact to Claudette Colbert in Preston Sturges's *The Palm Beach Story*
(Original Screenplay by Preston Sturges)

7.
"'Tis a coward I am, but I will hold your coat."

—Barry Fitzgerald passing to a better man during a mine disaster in John Ford's *How Green Was My Valley*
(Screenplay by Philip Dunne; based on the novel by Richard Llewellyn)

ALSO SEE: Fear; Alone-6; Drink Excuses-12; Duty-1; Fools-8; Football-1; Headlines-5; Honor-8; Pity-4.

CRAZY

1.
"We dislike the use of that word. All people who behave strangely are not insane."

—Fritz Feld explaining the term to Katharine Hepburn (and adding a facial tic of his own) in Howard Hawks's *Bringing Up Baby*
(Screenplay by Dudley Nichols and Hagar Wilde; based on a story by Hagar Wilde)

2.
"It's not nice to call a person 'utsnay' in this place."

—Olivia De Havilland correcting a pig latin-speaking nurse in Anatole Litvak's *The Snake Pit*
(Screenplay by Frank Partos and Millen Brand; based on the novel by Mary Jane Ward)

3.
"We've got to get these guys ashore. They're going Asiatic!"

—Ward Bond pleading for shore leave to Henry Fonda in John Ford and Mervyn LeRoy's *Mister Roberts*
(Screenplay by Frank S. Nugent and Joshua Logan; based on the play by Thomas Heggen and Joshua Logan and novel by Thomas Heggen)

4.

"Remember the precipice? I frightened you, didn't I? You thought I was mad. Perhaps I was. Perhaps I am mad. It wouldn't make for sanity, would it, living with the devil?"

—Laurence Olivier telling Wife Number Two (Joan Fontaine) about Wife Number One in Alfred Hitchcock's *Rebecca*
(Screenplay by Robert E. Sherwood and Joan Harrison; adaptation by Philip MacDonald and Michael Hogan; based on the novel by Daphne du Maurier)

5.

"He's playing Daffodil From Dopeyville."

—William Demarest figuring that Eddie Bracken is feigning insanity in Preston Sturges's *Hail the Conquering Hero*
(Original Screenplay by Preston Sturges)

6.

"Insanity runs in my family. It practically gallops."

—Cary Grant giving Priscilla Lane fair warning in Frank Capra's *Arsenic and Old Lace*
(Screenplay by Julius J. Epstein and Philip G. Epstein; based on the play by Joseph Kesselring)

7.

"When I married, I didn't realize that in the Czerny family there was a streak of, shall we say, eccentricity. And yet I—I had warnings. Why else should his grandfather have sent me, as an engagement present, one roller skate covered with thousand island dressing?"

—Claudette Colbert lying about Don Ameche's family in Mitchell Leisen's *Midnight*
(Screenplay by Charles Brackett and Billy Wilder; based on a story by Edwin Justus Mayer and Franz Schulz)

8.

"If I were not mad, I could have helped you. Whatever you had done, I could have pitied and protected you. But, because I am mad, I hate you. Because I am mad, I have betrayed you. And, because I am mad, I'm rejoicing in my heart without a shred of regret, watching you go with glory in my heart."

—Ingrid Bergman turning at last on the husband who had tried to unhinge her (Charles Boyer) in George Cukor's *Gaslight*
(Screenplay by John Van Druten, Walter Reisch and John L. Balderston; based on ANGEL STREET, a play by Patrick Hamilton)

9.

"We know the air is unfit to breathe, and our food is unfit to eat—and we sit watching our TVs while some local newscaster tells us that today we had 15 homicides and 63 violent crimes, as if that's the way it's supposed to be. We know things are bad. Worse than bad. They're crazy. It's like everything everywhere is going crazy. So we don't go out any more. We sit in the house, and slowly the world we're living in is getting smaller, and all we say is, 'Please, at least leave us alone in our living rooms. Let me have my toaster and my TV and my steel-belted radials, and I won't say anything, just leave us alone!' Well, I'm not going to leave you alone. I want you to get mad."

—Peter Finch preaching discontentment coast to coast in Sidney Lumet's *Network*
(Original Screenplay by Paddy Chayefsky)

10.

"Why, *everybody* in Mandrake Falls is pixilated —except us."

—Margaret Seddon making an exception of herself and her sister (Margaret McWade) in her courtroom testimony in Frank Capra's *Mr. Deeds Goes to Town*
(Screenplay by Robert Riskin; based on "Opera Hat," a short story by Clarence Budington Kelland)

11.

(a) "I know I'm being disrespectful to his honorable body. I know that. I—a guy like me shouldn't be allowed to get in here in the first place. I know that. And I hate to stand here and try your patience like this, but either I'm dead right or I'm crazy."

(b) "You wouldn't care to put that to a vote, would you, Senator?"

—(b) Grant Mitchell interrupting the filibuster of (a) James Stewart in Frank Capra's *Mr. Smith Goes to Washington*
(Screenplay by Sidney Buchman; based on "The Gentleman From Montana," a story by Lewis R. Foster)

12.
"Yeah, well, it was—it was really terrible, you know. I mean, you—you walk in, and right away they say you're crazy, and—and then they start sticking things in your arm. I mean, I mean how do they expect to see you get uncrazy if you—you're asleep all the time?"

—Chris Sarandon vibrating from a bad trip to Bellevue in Sidney Lumet's *Dog Day Afternoon*
(Original Screenplay by Frank Pierson)

13.
"We all have dreams, Mrs. Smith—bad dreams, sometimes—but we wake up, and we say, 'That was a bad dream.' Occasionally, however, we find a patient who can't wake up. He or she lacks insight, the ability to distinguish between what is real and what isn't. Now, that may be true in your case."

—Stanley Ridges telling Joan Crawford gently of her schizophrenia in Curtis Bernhardt's *Possessed*
(Screenplay by Sylvia Richards and Ranald MacDougall; based on ONE MAN'S SECRET, a novelette by Rita Weiman)

14.
"Hysteria is a kind of psychic bellyache, brought on by worry. The victim runs this way and that way to get out from under. He invents escapes. He invents disguises. You've seen the most effective disguise of all. When everything is too bad, he invents a disguise so effective he doesn't know himself. Then, we say the man is crazy."

—Claude Rains explaining psychic disorders to Robert Cummings in Sam Wood's *Kings Row*
(Screenplay by Casey Robinson; based on the novel by Henry Bellamann)

15.
"She was 15 years old, going on 35, Doc, and she told me she was 18, and she was very willing, you know what I mean. Matter of fact, it would have had to take to sewing my pants shut. But, between you and me, I don't think it's crazy at all now. . . . No man alive could resist that, and that's why I got into jail to begin with. And now they tell me I'm crazy over here because I don't sit there like a damn vegetable. Don't make a bit of sense to me. If that's what's being crazy is, then I'm senseless, out of it, gone-down-the-road wacko. But no more no less, that's it."

—Jack Nicholson stating his position to asylum doctor Dean R. Brooks in Miloš Forman's *One Flew Over the Cuckoo's Nest*
(Screenplay by Lawrence Hauben and Bo Goldman; based on the novel by Ken Kesey)

16.
"I'm going crazy. I'm standing here solidly, on my own two hands, and going crazy."

—Katharine Hepburn getting caught up in premarital chaos in George Cukor's *The Philadelphia Story*
(Screenplay by Donald Ogden Stewart; based on the play by Philip Barry)

17.
"I didn't argue with her. You don't yell at a sleepwalker. He may fall and break his neck. That's it. She was still sleepwalking along the giddy heights of a lost career—plain crazy when it came to that one subject: her celluloid self."

—William Holden diagnosing Gloria Swanson correctly in Billy Wilder's *Sunset Boulevard*
(Original Screenplay by Charles Brackett, Billy Wilder and D. M. Marshman, Jr.)

18.
"This is just a game, this war. You and that Colonel Nicholson—you're two of a kind. Crazy with courage. For what! How to die like a gentleman."

—William Holden likening Jack Hawkins to Alec Guinness under a negative heading of Professional Soldier in David Lean's *The Bridge on the River Kwai*

(Screenplay by Pierre Boulle; based on his novel, THE BRIDGE OVER THE RIVER KWAI)

19.

"Anyone who wants to get out of combat isn't really crazy, so I can't ground him."

—Jack Gilford explaining the hitch of Catch-22 to Alan Arkin in Mike Nichols's *Catch-22*
(Screenplay by Buck Henry; based on the novel by Joseph Heller)

ALSO SEE: Deals-1; Free-1; Good and Bad-2; Greetings-1; Money-4; Priorities-2; Spinsters-3; Stupid-2; Tact-3; Television-1.

CROOKED

1.

"Let us be crooked but never common."

—Charles Coburn telling his daughter (Barbara Stanwyck) to con with class in Preston Sturges's *The Lady Eve*
(Screenplay by Preston Sturges; based on a story by Monckton Hoffe)

2.

"They tell me he was so crooked that when he died they had to *screw* him into the ground."

—Bob Hope characterizing his late uncle in Elliott Nugent's *The Cat and the Canary*
(Screenplay by Walter De Leon and Lynn Starling; based on the play by John Willard)

3.

"Don't be too sure I'm as crooked as I'm supposed to be."

—Humphrey Bogart giving Mary Astor fair warning in John Huston's *The Maltese Falcon*
(Screenplay by John Huston; based on the novel by Dashiell Hammett)

4.

"Who are you going to believe—me or those crooked x-rays?"

—Groucho Marx challenging a medical colleague (Charles Trowbridge) in Sam Wood's *A Day at the Races*

(Screenplay by Robert Pirosh, George Seaton and George Oppenheimer; based on a story by Robert Pirosh and George Seaton)

ALSO SEE: Toasts-8.

CRUEL

1.

"You think I do not know that there are people in Rome who call me a matricide, wife-killer, call me a monster, tyrant? There is something they do not realize. A man's acts may be cruel while he himself is not cruel. And there are moments, dear Petronius, when—when the music caresses my soul, I feel as gentle as a child in a cradle. Believe me?"

—Peter Ustinov soliciting sympathy from Leo Genn in Mervyn LeRoy's *Quo Vadis*
(Screenplay by John Lee Mahin, S. N. Behrman and Sonya Levien; based on the novel by Henryk Sienkiewicz)

2.

"Yes, I can be very cruel. I have been taught by masters."

—Olivia De Havilland learning from the meanness of her father (Ralph Richardson) and suitor (Montgomery Clift) in William Wyler's *The Heiress*
(Screenplay by Ruth Goetz and Augustus Goetz; based on their play and WASHINGTON SQUARE, *a novel by Henry James)*

ALSO SEE: Directors-1; Sea-2; Truth-5.

CURSES

1.

"I'm going. I'm going from here and from this cursed country both! . . . But I'll be back in this house one day, Judge Linton, and I'll pay you out. I'll bring this house down in ruins about your heads! That's my curse on you! On all of you!"

—Laurence Olivier making an emotional exit from Cecil Humphreys's fancy-dress party in William Wyler's *Wuthering Heights*
(Screenplay by Ben Hecht and Charles MacArthur; based on the novel by Emily Brontë)

2.
"You shall remain a dog, and you shall walk in the darkness of the blind until I hold her in my arms."

—Conrad Veidt blinding John Justin and turning Sabu into a dog until he possesses June Duprez in Ludwig Berger, Tim Whelan and Michael Powell's *The Thief of Bagdad*
(Screenplay and dialogue by Miles Malleson; based on a scenario by Lajos Biro)

3.
" 'Hurry,' Maitland, is the curse of civilization."

—Edith Evans refusing to be rushed by her butler (John Mills) in Ronald Neame's *The Chalk Garden*
(Screenplay by John Michael Hayes; based on the play by Enid Bagnold)

4.
"Gold don't carry any curse with it. It all depends on whether or not the guy who finds it is the right guy. The way I see it, gold can be as much of a blessing as a curse."

—Humphrey Bogart trying to convince himself as much as Tim Holt in John Huston's *The Treasure of the Sierra Madre*
(Screenplay by John Huston; based on the novel by B. Traven)

ALSO SEE: Jewels-2.

CURTAIN SPEECHES

1.
"Hello, everybody. This is Mrs. Norman Maine."

—Judy Garland meeting her public as a widow rather than as a star in the last lines of George Cukor's *A Star Is Born*
(Screenplay by Moss Hart; based on a screenplay by Dorothy Parker, Alan Campbell and Robert Carson and original story by William A. Wellman and Robert Carson)

and

—Janet Gaynor dittoing in the original, William A. Wellman's *A Star Is Born*
(Screenplay by Dorothy Parker, Alan Campbell and Robert Carson; based on an original story by William A. Wellman and Robert Carson)

2.
"Ladies and gentlemen, I'm sorry to tell you that Miss Page is unable to dance tonight—nor indeed any other night. Nevertheless, we've decided to present 'The Red Shoes.' "

—Anton Walbrook announcing the death of his ballet star (Moira Shearer) to his opening-night audience in Michael Powell and Emeric Pressburger's *The Red Shoes*
(Original Screenplay by Emeric Pressburger; additional dialogue by Keith Winter)

3.
"I suppose that I should thank you on behalf of the company, and I know that I am grateful to you for your applause. But I must tell you that I don't deserve it. I'm not responsible for what happened on this stage tonight. The person you should be applauding died a few hours ago —a young and brilliant actress who could no longer find a spot in the theater. And it was for her more than for anyone else that I was able to go on. And I hope that, wherever she is, she knows and understands and forgives."

—Katharine Hepburn passing the praise along to Andrea Leeds in Gregory La Cava's *Stage Door*
(Screenplay by Morrie Ryskind and Anthony Veiller; based on the play by Edna Ferber and George S. Kaufman)

4.
"My mother thanks you. My father thanks you. My sister thanks you. And I thank you."

—James Cagney signing off as George M. Cohan in Michael Curtiz's *Yankee Doodle Dandy*
(Screenplay by Robert Buckner and Edmund Joseph; based on an original story by Robert Buckner)

5.

"Yes, my brother made music with his fists so that I might make a gentler music—the symphony that you have heard tonight. It is his as much as mine. And so, with deep pride and gratitude, I dedicate this music to my brother, known to most of you as Young Samson."

—Arthur Kennedy thanking James Cagney from the stage in Anatole Litvak's *City for Conquest* *(Screenplay by John Wexley; based on the novel by Aben Kandel)*

DANCE

1.
"May I have this dance, Mother?"

—John Lund acknowledging Olivia De Havilland as his real mother by asking her to dance in the last line of Mitchell Leisen's *To Each His Own* *(Screenplay by Charles Brackett and Jacques Thery; based on an original story by Charles Brackett)*

2.
"Put on the red shoes, Vicky, and dance for us again."

—Anton Walbrook luring his protégée (Moira Shearer) back into the ballet world in Michael Powell and Emeric Pressburger's *The Red Shoes* *(Original Screenplay by Emeric Pressburger; additional dialogue by Keith Winter)*

3.
"I could dance with you until the cows come home. On second thought, I'd rather dance with the cows till you came home."

—Groucho Marx insulting Raquel Torres in Leo McCarey's *Duck Soup* *(Screenplay by Bert Kalmar and Harry Ruby; additional dialogue by Arthur Sheekman and Nat Perrin)*

4.
"Why, Mr. Lincoln, at least you're a man of honor. You said you wanted to dance with me the worst way, and I must say you've kept your word. This is the worst way I've ever seen."

—Marjorie Weaver criticizing her future husband and President (Henry Fonda) in John Ford's *Young Mr. Lincoln* *(Original Screenplay by Lamar Trotti)*

5.
"Oh, I can tell a lot about a man by dancing with him. You know, some boys—well, when they take a girl in their arms to dance, they—well, they make her feel sort of uncomfortable. But, with you, I—I had the feeling you knew exactly what you were doing, and I could follow you every step of the way."

—Kim Novak complimenting William Holden after their "Moonglow" merging in Joshua Logan's *Picnic* *(Screenplay by Daniel Taradash; based on the play by William Inge)*

6.
"Why, Mr. O'Connor, I've always said that dancing was the most civilized form of social intercourse."

—Gertrude Lawrence approving of Kirk Douglas taking her daughter (Jane Wyman) dancing in Irving Rapper's *The Glass Menagerie* *(Screenplay by Tennessee Williams and Peter Berneis; based on the play by Tennessee Williams)*

7.
(a) "Dancing is a charming amusement for young people. In my opinion, uh—it's one of the first refinements of a polished society."

(b) "It has the added advantage, sir, of being one of the first refinements of savages. Every Hottentot can dance."

—(b) Laurence Olivier deflating the lofty sentiment of (a) E. E. Clive in Robert Z. Leonard's *Pride and Prejudice* *(Screenplay by Aldous Huxley and Jane Murfin; based on the play by Helen Jerome and novel by Jane Austen)*

8.
"I danced in my mother's womb."

—Vanessa Redgrave claiming an early calling to dance in Karel Reisz's *Isadora* *(Screenplay by Melvyn Bragg and Clive Exton; additional dialogue by Margaret Drabble;*

adaptation by Melvyn Bragg; based on the books
MY LIFE *by Isadora Duncan and* ISADORA
DUNCAN, AN INTIMATE PORTRAIT *by Sewell*
Stokes)

9.
"I dance like the wind."

—Sandy Dennis flapping about drunkenly in Mike
Nichols's *Who's Afraid of Virginia Woolf?*
(Screenplay by Ernest Lehman; based on the play
by Edward Albee)

10.
"You know, this floor used to be wood, but I
had it changed. Valentino said there's nothing
like tile for the tango."

—Gloria Swanson tossing a film-history footnote to
William Holden in Billy Wilder's *Sunset Boulevard*
(Original Screenplay by Charles Brackett, Billy
Wilder and D. M. Marshman Jr.)

ALSO SEE: Curtain Speeches-2; Good and
Bad-2; Good-byes-9; Happiness-3; Hate-9;
Live-8; Memory-4; Pleasures-6; Politics-1; Pre-
tense-5; Progress-4; Psychiatry-3; Work-7.

DARK

1.
(a) "How do you find your way back in the
dark?"
    (b) "Just head for that big star straight on.
The highway's under it, and it'll take us right
home."

—(a) Marilyn Monroe and (b) Clark Gable heading
home in their last lines on film, the last in John Huston's *The Misfits*
(Screenplay by Arthur Miller; based on his story)

2.
"I like the dark. The dark is comforting to me."

—Vivien Leigh hiding in the shadows, on the brink
of a mental breakdown, in Elia Kazan's *A Streetcar*
Named Desire
(Screenplay by Tennessee Williams; adaptation by
Oscar Saul; based on the play by Tennessee
Williams)

3.
"People who hate the light usually hate the
truth."

—Burt Lancaster confronting his aging ex (Rita Hayworth) in Delbert Mann's *Separate Tables*
(Screenplay by Terence Rattigan and John Gay;
based on the play by Terence Rattigan)

4.
"There goes my last lead. I feel all dead inside.
I'm backed up in a dark corner, and I don't
know who's hitting me."

—Mark Stevens reaching a dead end in his detective
work in Henry Hathaway's *The Dark Corner*
(Screenplay by Jay Dratler and Bernard C.
Schoenfeld; based on the short story by Leo
Rosten)

5.
"Nothing can hurt us now. What we have can't
be destroyed. That's our victory—our victory
over the dark. It is a victory because we're not
afraid."

—Bette Davis accepting death in Edmund Goulding's *Dark Victory*
(Screenplay by Casey Robinson; based on the play
by George Brewer Jr. and Bertram Bloch)

ALSO SEE: Curses-2; Empathy-8; Mad Act-2;
Prayers-1; Strangers-2; Theater-6.

DAUGHTERS

1.
"They're a mess no matter how you look at 'em,
a headache till they get married—*if* they get
married—and, after that, they get worse. . . .
Either they leave their husbands and come
back with four children and move into your
guest room or their husband loses his job and
the whole *caboodle* comes back. Or else
they're so homely you can't get rid of them at
all and they hang around the house like Spanish Moss and shame you into an early grave."

—William Demarest lecturing his daughters (Betty
Hutton and Diana Lynn) in Preston Sturges's *The*
Miracle of Morgan's Creek
(Original Screenplay by Preston Sturges)

2.

"You don't know what it's like being a mother, Ida. Veda's a part of me. Maybe she didn't turn out as well as I'd hoped she would when she was born, but she's still my daughter and I can't forget that. I went away to try. I was so mixed up I didn't know where I was or what I wanted. But now I know. Now I'm sure of one thing at least: I want my daughter back."

—Joan Crawford defending Ann Blyth to Eve Arden in Michael Curtiz's *Mildred Pierce*
(Screenplay by Ranald MacDougall; based on the novel by James M. Cain)

3.

"Alexandra, I've come to the end of my rope. Somewhere, there has got to be what I want, too. Life goes too fast. You can go where you want, do what you want, think what you want. I'd like to keep you with me, but I won't make you stay. No, I won't make you stay."

—Bette Davis reaching the bottom line with her daughter (Teresa Wright) in William Wyler's *The Little Foxes*
(Screenplay by Lillian Hellman; additional scenes and dialogue by Arthur Kober, Dorothy Parker and Alan Campbell; based on the play by Lillian Hellman)

4.

"Would you try to do a man out of the price of his own daughter what he's brought up, he's fed, he's clothed by the sweat of his brow till she's growed big enough to be interesting to you two gentlemen? Well, is five pounds unreasonable? I puts it to you, and I leaves it to you."

—Wilfrid Lawson trying to sell Wendy Hiller to Leslie Howard and Scott Sunderland in Anthony Asquith and Leslie Howard's *Pygmalion*
(Screenplay by George Bernard Shaw; adaptation by W. P. Lipscomb, Cecil Lewis and Ian Dalrymple; based on the play by George Bernard Shaw)
and (almost verbatim)

—Stanley Holloway dittoing Audrey Hepburn to Rex Harrison and Wilfrid Hyde-White in the remake, George Cukor's *My Fair Lady*
(Screenplay by Alan Jay Lerner; based on his
musical play and PYGMALION, *a screenplay and play by George Bernard Shaw)*

5.

"I don't like the idea of you sneaking around corners to see Peggy, taking her love on a bootleg basis. I give you fair warning. I'm going to do everything I can to keep her away from you, to help her forget about you and get married to some decent guy who can make her happy."

—Fredric March warning unhappily married Dana Andrews away from Teresa Wright in William Wyler's *The Best Years of Our Lives*
(Screenplay by Robert E. Sherwood; based on GLORY FOR ME, *a verse novel by MacKinlay Kantor)*

6.

"You stay away from her. I don't hand out my daughter to newlyweds."

—Eddie Albert warning newly married Charles Grodin away from Cybill Shepherd in Elaine May's *The Heartbreak Kid*
(Screenplay by Neil Simon; based on "A Change of Plan," a story by Bruce Jay Friedman)

7.

"She can love whom she pleases, but she must marry the man I choose."

—Hugh Griffith declaring his conditional control of his daughter (Susannah York) in Tony Richardson's *Tom Jones*
(Screenplay by John Osborne; based on the novel by Henry Fielding)

ALSO SEE: Children-5; Fools-10; Spinsters-4.

DEALS

1.

"You gotta take my deal because once in your life you *got* to take a chance on a con man. You gotta take my deal because there's dying cattle that might pick up and live. Because a hundred bucks is only a hundred bucks, but rain in a dry season is a sight to behold! You gotta take my deal because it's gonna be a hot night and the world goes crazy on a hot night and maybe that's what a hot night is for."

—Burt Lancaster making his rainmaking spiel in Joseph Anthony's *The Rainmaker*
(Screenplay by N. Richard Nash; based on his play)

2.
"Tell you what. I got a proposition for you. Now, you sing us your song, and you can have a drink."

—Edward G. Robinson conning "Moanin' Low" out of Claire Trevor in John Huston's *Key Largo*
(Screenplay by Richard Brooks and John Huston; based on the play by Maxwell Anderson)

3.
"I'll tell you what. I'll make you a little bet. Three times 35 is, er, 105. I'll bet you $105,000 you go to sleep before I do."

—Humphrey Bogart betting a whole gold load that Tim Holt can't keep the drop on him in John Huston's *The Treasure of the Sierra Madre*
(Screenplay by John Huston; based on the novel by B. Traven)

ALSO SEE: Foolish-2; Guilty-2; Pretense-8; Success-4; Suicide-11; Wish-3.

DEATH

1.
"When it comes, it must be met beautifully and finely."

—Bette Davis repeating (and trying to believe) Humphrey Bogart's advice in Edmund Goulding's *Dark Victory*
(Screenplay by Casey Robinson; based on the play by George Brewer Jr. and Bertram Bloch)

2.
"When it comes to dying for your country, it's better not to die at all."

—Lew Ayres being realistic about war to a classroom full of potential soldiers in Lewis Milestone's *All Quiet on the Western Front*
(Screenplay by Dell Andrews, Maxwell Anderson

and George Abbott; based on the novel by Erich Maria Remarque)*

3.
"There is nothing wrong with suffering—if you suffer for a purpose. Our revolution didn't abolish danger or death. It simply made danger and death worthwhile."

—Raymond Massey defending the sacrifice that progress requires in William Cameron Menzies's *Things To Come*
(Screenplay by H. G. Wells; based on his novel THE SHAPE OF THINGS TO COME)

4.
"A free man dies, he loses the pleasure of life; a slave loses pain. Death is the only freedom a slave knows. That's why he's not afraid of it. That's why we'll win."

—Kirk Douglas explaining the real thrust of his "slave uprising" to Herbert Lom in Stanley Kubrick's *Spartacus*
(Screenplay by Dalton Trumbo; based on the novel by Howard Fast)

5.
"All of a sudden, it's closer to the end than it is the beginning, and death is suddenly a perceptible thing to me—with definable features."

—William Holden baring his "primal doubts" to Faye Dunaway in Sidney Lumet's *Network*
(Original Screenplay by Paddy Chayefsky)

6.
"Then, last week, as it must to all men, death came to Charles Foster Kane."

—Newsreel narrator concluding the "News of the World" summary of Orson Welles's life in Orson Welles's *Citizen Kane*
(Original Screenplay by Herman J. Mankiewicz and Orson Welles)

7.
"Death ends a life, but it does not end a relationship, which struggles on in the survivor's mind toward some resolution which it may never find."

—Gene Hackman eulogizing Melvyn Douglas in the first and last lines of Gilbert Cates's *I Never Sang for My Father*
(Screenplay by Robert Anderson; based on his play)

8.
"Death's at the bottom of everything, Martins. Leave death to the professionals."

—Trevor Howard telling Joseph Cotten to stop playing amateur detective in Carol Reed's *The Third Man*
(Original Screenplay by Graham Greene)

9.
"Everybody knows everybody is dying. That's why people are as good as they are."

—Michael Moriarty consoling Robert DeNiro in John Hancock's *Bang the Drum Slowly*
(Screenplay by Mark Harris; based on his novel)

ALSO SEE: Dying Words; Life and Death; Always-2; Books-2; Boredom-1; Dark-5; Dignity-2; Dreams-7; Dreams-8; Feelings-6; Firings-2; Headlines-5; Heaven-3; Heaven-4; Men-17; Men-18; Mistakes-7; Priorities-2; Priorities-3; Privacy-3; Regrets-3; Relatives-2; Relatives-4; Repetitions-2; Republicans-1; Signs-2; Silence-1; Smile-8; Sun-1; Sun-5; Talk-6; Telegrams-3; Transitions-1; Trust and Distrust-1; Truth-7; Wants-4; War-7; Water-2; Wives-6; Worry-3.

DECENCY

1.
"Miss Kubelik, one doesn't get to be a second administrative assistant around here unless he's a pretty good judge of character—and, as far as I'm concerned, you're tops. I mean, decency-wise and otherwise-wise."

—Jack Lemmon complimenting Shirley MacLaine in Billy Wilder's *The Apartment*
(Original Screenplay by Billy Wilder and I. A. L. Diamond)

2.
"I caught a slight case of decency. It's gone to my head."

—Jeff Chandler telling his former sponsors (Cecil Kellaway and Natalie Schafer) that he's graduating from gigolo to husband in Joseph Pevney's *Female on the Beach*
(Screenplay by Robert Hill and Richard Alan Simmons; based on THE BESIEGED HEART, a play by Robert Hill)

3.
"I went to visit my wife today because she's in a state of depression, so depressed that my daughter flew all the way from Seattle to be with her. And I feel lousy about that. I feel lousy about the pain that I've caused my wife and my kids. I feel guilty and conscience-stricken and all of those things you think sentimental but which my generation called simple human decency."

—William Holden telling Faye Dunaway where it hurts in Sidney Lumet's *Network*
(Original Screenplay by Paddy Chayefsky)

4.
"I respect anybody who has had to fight and howl for his decency."

—Deborah Kerr consoling Richard Burton in John Huston's *The Night of the Iguana*
(Screenplay by Anthony Veiller and John Huston; based on the play by Tennessee Williams)

ALSO SEE: Wives-8.

DEFENSE

1.
"If Ernst Janning is to be found guilty, certain implications must arise. A judge does not make the law. He carries out the laws of his country. The statement, 'My country—right or wrong,' was expressed by a great American patriot. It is no less true for a German patriot. Should Ernst Janning have carried out the laws of his country? Or should he have refused to carry them out and become a traitor? This is the crux of the issue at the bottom of this trial. The defense is as dedicated to finding the responsibility as is the prosecution, for it is not only Ernst Jan-

ning who is on trial here. It's the German people."

—Maximilian Schell stating his case for Burt Lancaster (and the German people) in Stanley Kramer's *Judgment at Nuremberg*
(Screenplay by Abby Mann; based on his teleplay)

2.
"If you convict this boy, you are convicting thousands like him—not criminals, not murderers, just nobodies trying to find a place to hang their hat."

—Moroni Olsen pleading the case (or is it the social cause?) of downtrodden John Garfield in Lewis Seiler's *Dust Be My Destiny*
(Screenplay by Robert Rossen; based on the novel by Jerome Odlum)

3.
"I am supposed to have done something infamous by assisting Stillman, an unregistered man and probably the best man in the world on this type of case. I ask you gentlemen: is it infamous for a doctor to be directly instrumental in saving a human life? Gentlemen, it's high time we started putting our house in order. We're everlastingly saying we'll do things and we don't. Doctors have to live, but they have a responsibility to mankind, too. If we go on trying to make out that everything's right inside the profession and everything's wrong outside, it will be the death of scientific progress. I only ask you to remember the words of our own Hippocratic oath: 'Into whatsoever houses I shall enter, I will work for the benefit of the sick, holding aloof from all wrong and corruption.' How many of us remember that? How many of us practice that? I have made mistakes —mistakes I bitterly regret—but Stillman isn't one of them. And, if, by what has been called my infamous conduct, I have done anything however small to benefit humanity, I am more than proud, gentlemen—I am profoundly grateful. Thank you, gentlemen, for letting me speak."

—Robert Donat defending Percy Parsons to medical colleagues in the last lines of King Vidor's *The Citadel*

(Screenplay by Ian Dalrymple, Frank Wead and Elizabeth Hill; additional dialogue by Emlyn Williams; based on the novel by A. J. Cronin)

ALSO SEE: Alone-3; Beliefs-1; Courtroom Lines-5; Duty-4; Fights-7; Politics-4.

DEMOCRATS

1.
"Why did God make so many dumb fools and Democrats?"

—William Powell blowing off steam in Michael Curtiz's *Life With Father*
(Screenplay by Donald Ogden Stewart; based on the play by Howard Lindsay and Russel Crouse and stories by Clarence Day, Jr.)

2.
"Forty-two percent of all liberals are queer. That's a fact. The Wallace people took a poll."

—Peter Boyle flicking off some hard-hat facts and figures in John Avildsen's *Joe*
(Original Screenplay by Norman Wexler)

3.
"When it comes to women, you're a true democrat."

—Humphrey Bogart politely calling Claude Rains promiscuous in Michael Curtiz's *Casablanca*
(Screenplay by Julius J. Epstein, Philip G. Epstein, and Howard Koch; based on EVERYBODY COMES TO RICK'S, a play by Murray Burnett and Joan Alison)

4.
"Some people are Democrats by choice, some by necessity. You, by necessity."

—Fredric March berating his son (Dan Duryea) for associating with a dance-hall girl (Dona Drake) in Michael Gordon's *Another Part of the Forest*
(Screenplay by Vladimir Pozner; based on the play by Lillian Hellman)

5.
(a) "It's worse than horrible, because a zombie has no will of his own. You see them sometimes walking around blindly, with dead eyes, follow-

ing orders, not knowing what they do, not car-
ing."
    (b) "You mean like Democrats?"

—(b) Bob Hope shattering the spook story (a) Richard
Carlson is telling in George Marshall's *The Ghost
Breakers*
*(Screenplay by Walter DeLeon; based on THE
GHOST BREAKER, a play by Paul Dickey and
Charles W. Goddard)*

ALSO SEE: Indecision-3.

DESPERATE

1.
"The truth is something desperate, and Maggie's got it. Believe me, it is desperate, and she
has got it."

—Paul Newman championing Elizabeth Taylor in
Richard Brooks's *Cat on a Hot Tin Roof*
*(Screenplay by Richard Brooks and James Poe;
based on the play by Tennessee Williams)*

2.
" 'Most men lead lives of quiet desperation.' I
can't take 'quiet desperation.' "

—Ray Milland shunning the idea of an ordinary nine-
to-five job in Billy Wilder's *The Lost Weekend*
*(Screenplay by Charles Brackett and Billy Wilder;
based on the novel by Charles R. Jackson)*

ALSO SEE: Legs-2; Letters-2; Never-11; Party-7.

DETECTIVES

1.
"I'd like to know who besides me might have
killed Marriott. He gave me a hundred bucks to
take care of him, and I didn't. I'm just a small
businessman in a very messy business, but I like
to follow through on a sale."

—Dick Powell explaining honor among detectives to
Anne Shirley in Edward Dmytryk's *Murder, My
Sweet*
*(Screenplay by John Paxton; based on FAREWELL,
MY LOVELY, a novel by Raymond Chandler)*

2.
"When a man's partner's killed, he's supposed to do something about it. It doesn't
make any difference what you thought of
him. He was your partner, and you're supposed to do something about it. As it happens, we're in the detective business. Well,
when one of your organization gets killed,
it's—it's bad business to let the killer get
away with it. Bad all around. Bad for every
detective everywhere."

—Humphrey Bogart explaining honor among detectives to Mary Astor in John Huston's *The Maltese
Falcon*
*(Screenplay by John Huston; based on the novel
by Dashiell Hammett)*

3.
"You know, Mrs. Beragon, being a detective is
like—well, like making an automobile. You just
take all the pieces and put them together one
by one. First thing you know, you've got an
automobile—or a murderer."

—Moroni Olsen explaining the mechanics of his
work to Joan Crawford in Michael Curtiz's *Mildred
Pierce*
*(Screenplay by Ranald MacDougall; based on the
novel by James M. Cain)*

4.
"So you're a private detective. I didn't know
they existed, except in books—or else they
were greasy little men snooping around hotel
corridors. My, you're a mess, aren't you?"

—Lauren Bacall ritzing Humphrey Bogart in Howard Hawks's *The Big Sleep*
*(Screenplay by William Faulkner, Leigh Brackett
and Jules Furthman; based on the novel by
Raymond Chandler)*

ALSO SEE: Soul-16; Tired-1; Why-10.

DIAMONDS

1.
"I always say a kiss on the hand might feel very
good, but a diamond tiara lasts forever."

—Marilyn Monroe telling rich Charles Coburn what she always says in Howard Hawks's *Gentlemen Prefer Blondes*
(Screenplay by Charles Lederer; based on the musical play by Joseph Fields and Anita Loos and the novel by Anita Loos)

2.
"Real diamonds! They must be worth their weight in gold. Are you always this generous?"

—Marilyn Monroe thanking Tony Curtis in Billy Wilder's *Some Like It Hot*
(Screenplay by Billy Wilder and I. A. L. Diamond; suggested by a story by R. Thoeren and M. Logan)

3.
"Is this for my beauty and talent—or is it payment in advance?"

—Vanessa Redgrave questioning the motives of Jason Robards's generosity in Karel Reisz's *Isadora*
(Screenplay by Melvyn Bragg and Clive Exton; additional dialogue by Margaret Drabble; adaptation by Melvyn Bragg; based on the books MY LIFE by Isadora Duncan and ISADORA DUNCAN, AN INTIMATE PORTRAIT by Sewell Stokes)

4.
"That's very generous of you, but the diamond was there. I merely supplied a little polish."

—John Barrymore pretending to be modest about directing Carole Lombard in Howard Hawks's *Twentieth Century*
(Screenplay by Ben Hecht and Charles MacArthur; based on their play and NAPOLEON OF BROADWAY, a play by Charles Bruce Milholland)

5.
"A topaz? Among my jewels! Are you mad? It is a yellow diamond."

—Isabel Jeans getting incensed with Leslie Caron in Vincente Minnelli's *Gigi*
(Screenplay by Alan Jay Lerner; based on the novel by Colette)

6.
"Course, personally, I think it a bit tacky to wear diamonds before I'm 40."

—Audrey Hepburn rationalizing a nonbuying spree at Tiffany's in Blake Edwards's *Breakfast at Tiffany's*
(Screenplay by George Axelrod; based on the novella by Truman Capote)

7.
"Sure, we have. Bait by Cartier's! . . . Kidding, my foot! I'm starving! Well, what are you waiting around for? Where's the fish line? . . . I can recommend the bait. I ought to know—I bit on it myself."

—Tallulah Bankhead sacrificing her diamond bracelet to fish for food in Alfred Hitchcock's *Lifeboat*
(Screenplay by Jo Swerling; based on the story by John Steinbeck)

ALSO SEE: Jewels; Exchanges-11; Good-13; Jewels-2; Rejection-13.

DICTATION

1.
" 'Chapter one, page one. Well, Lindsay, this isn't so difficult. Patrick, get me another drink. Let me see, where was I? What are you writing?' "

—Peggy Cass reading back the beginnings of Rosalind Russell's autobiography in Morton DaCosta's *Auntie Mame*
(Screenplay by Betty Comden and Adolph Green; based on the play by Jerome Lawrence and Robert E. Lee and novel by Patrick Dennis)

2.
"Flora, take a letter. 'To whom it may concern: Mr. Vadas has been in the employ of Matuschek and Company for the last two years, during which time he has been very efficient as a stool pigeon, a troublemaker and a rat. . . . And if he doesn't clear out of here, he's going to get a punch in the nose. Yours very truly, Alfred Kralik, Manager of Matuschek and Company.' "

—James Stewart dismissing Joseph Schildkraut by dictating a letter of "recommendation" to Sara Haden in Ernst Lubitsch's *The Shop Around the Corner*

(Screenplay by Samson Raphaelson; based on PARFUMERIE, a play by Miklos Laszlo)

3.

"Lettie, take an editorial. 'To the Women of America'—no, make it 'To Women Everywhere: Banish the black, burn the blue and bury the beige. From now on, girls, think pink!'"

—Kay Thompson dictating a song lead-in to Ruta Lee in Stanley Donen's *Funny Face*
(Original Screenplay by Leonard Gershe)

4.

"Take a sermon. 'Tonight, I want to tell you the story of an empty stocking. Once upon a midnight clear, there was a child's cry. A blazing star hung over a stable, and wise men came with birthday gifts.' Have you got that? Good. 'We haven't forgotten that night down the centuries. We celebrate it with stars hung on Christmas trees and the cry of bells and gifts— especially with gifts. We buy them and wrap them and put them under the tree. You give me a tie. I give you a book. Aunt Martha always wanted an orange squeezer. Uncle Harry could use a new pipe. Oh, we forget nobody, adult or child. All the stockings are filled—all, that is, except one. . . .'"

—Cary Grant dictating David Niven's Christmas sermon to a magically unmanned typewriter in Henry Koster's *The Bishop's Wife*
(Screenplay by Robert E. Sherwood and Leonardo Bercovici; based on the novel by Robert Nathan)

5.

"Office memorandum. 'Walter Neff to Barton Keyes, Claims Manager, Los Angeles, July 16, 1938. Dear Keyes: I suppose you'll call this a confession when you hear it. Well, I don't like the word "confession." I just want to set you right about something you couldn't see because it was smack up against your nose. You think you're such a hot potato as a Claims Manager; such a wolf on a phony claim. Maybe you are. But let's take a look at that Dietrichson claim, Accident and Double Indemnity. You were pretty good in there for a while, Keyes. You said it wasn't an accident. Check. You said

it wasn't suicide. Check. You said it was murder. Check. You thought you had it cold, didn't you? All wrapped up in tissue paper with pink ribbons around it. It was perfect—except it wasn't, because you made one mistake. Just one little mistake. When it came to picking the killer, you picked the wrong guy. You want to know who killed Dietrichson? Hold tight to that cheap cigar of yours, Keyes. *I* killed Dietrichson—me, Walter Neff, insurance salesman, 35 years old, unmarried, no visible scars. Until a while ago, that is. Yes, I killed him. I killed him for money and for a woman. I didn't get the money, and I didn't get the woman. Pretty, isn't it?'"

—Fred MacMurray confessing murder to his boss (Edward G. Robinson) via the office dictaphone in Billy Wilder's *Double Indemnity*
(Screenplay by Billy Wilder and Raymond Chandler; based on the novel by James M. Cain)

6.

"'To my darling wife, Leon, whom I love more than any man has loved another man in all eternity, I leave $2,700 borrowed from a $10,000 life-insurance policy to be used for your sex-change operation. If there is any money left over, I want it to go to you at my first—at the first anniversary of my death, at my grave. To my wife—to my sweet wife, Angela, $5,000 from the same policy. You are the only woman that I ever loved and I repledge my love to you in this sad moment. Oh, to little Kenny and Timmy, I hope you remember me. Timmy, you are the little man of the family now, and I hope you look after them for me. To my mother, I ask forgiveness. You— you don't understand the things I said and did, but I'm me, and I'm different from you. I want a military funeral, and I'm entitled to have one, free of charge. God—God bless you and watch over you till we are joined in the hereafter.'"

—Al Pacino dictating his last will and testament to one of his bank hostages (Penny Allen) in Sidney Lumet's *Dog Day Afternoon*
(Original Screenplay by Frank Pierson)

7.

" 'It has occurred to us that, if there should be several pairs of young male elephants turned loose in forest of America, we are of opinion that, after a while, they will increase in number.' "

—Yul Brynner making a biological blunder as he dictates to Deborah Kerr a letter to Abraham Lincoln in Walter Lang's *The King and I*
(Screenplay by Ernest Lehman; based on the musical play by Oscar Hammerstein II and ANNA AND THE KING OF SIAM, a book by Margaret Landon)

and (almost verbatim)

—Rex Harrison dittoing to Irene Dunne in the original, John Cromwell's *Anna and the King of Siam*
(Screenplay by Talbot Jennings and Sally Benson; based on the book by Margaret Landon)

8.

"Take this down. 'Next Friday evening at the Oliver Jordans, dinner at eight.' Me, eating with Lord and Lady Ferncliffe!—well, you don't have to write that down, stupid!"

—Jean Harlow making note of a social engagement via her slow-witted maid (Hilda Vaughn) in George Cukor's *Dinner at Eight*
(Screenplay by Frances Marion and Herman J. Mankiewicz; based on the play by George S. Kaufman and Edna Ferber)

DIFFERENCES

1.

"Princess, the great difference between people in this world is not between the rich and the poor or the good and the evil. The big difference between people are the ones who have had pleasure in love and those who haven't."

—Paul Newman telling Geraldine Page how sex really separates people in Richard Brooks's *Sweet Bird of Youth*
(Screenplay by Richard Brooks; based on the play by Tennessee Williams)

2.
(a) *"Vive la difference!"*
   (b) "Which means?"

(a) "Which means: Hurray for that little difference!"

—(a) Spencer Tracy and (b) Katharine Hepburn going into a finale clinch in the last lines of George Cukor's *Adam's Rib*
(Original Screenplay by Ruth Gordon and Garson Kanin)

3.

"The only difference between a caprice and a lifelong passion is that the caprice lasts a little longer."

—George Sanders plainly preferring the short-term romance in Albert Lewin's *The Picture of Dorian Gray*
(Screenplay by Albert Lewin; based on the novel by Oscar Wilde)

4.

"The only difference in men is the color of their neckties."

—Helen Broderick writing off the gender in Mark Sandrich's *Top Hat*
(Screenplay by Dwight Taylor and Allan Scott; adaptation by Karl Noti; based on THE GIRL WHO DARED, a play by Alexander Farago and Aladar Laszlo)

5.

"And that's the difference between us, Mr. Dodd. You want him to become the actor he once was. I'm his wife! I want him just once more as the man he once was—able to stand on his own two feet and face responsibility. And—and you don't do that by bending the truth!"

—Grace Kelly confronting William Holden about Bing Crosby in George Seaton's *The Country Girl*
(Screenplay by George Seaton; based on the play by Clifford Odets)

6.

"Ain't much difference between kidnapping and marrying. You get snatched from your parents—but, in marriage, nobody offers a reward."

—Harry Davenport consoling Bette Davis, who has been kidnapped on her way to the altar, in William Keighley's *The Bride Came C.O.D.*

(Screenplay by Julius J. Epstein and Philip G. Epstein; based on a story by Kenneth Earl and M. M. Musselman)

7.

"I'm talking about the difference in mind and spirit. You could marry Mac the night watchman, I'd cheer for you. Kittredge is not for you."

—Cary Grant trying to talk his ex (Katharine Hepburn) out of marrying John Howard in George Cukor's *The Philadelphia Story*
(Screenplay by Donald Ogden Stewart; based on the play by Philip Barry)

8.

"Have a drink—just a little one to lessen the difference in our characters."

—Noel Coward smoothly leading Julie Haydon to ruin in Ben Hecht and Charles MacArthur's *The Scoundrel*
(Original screenplay by Ben Hecht and Charles MacArthur)

9.

"We all come from our own little planets. That's why we're all different. That's what makes life interesting."

—Cary Grant defending individuality to Loretta Young in Henry Koster's *The Bishop's Wife*
(Screenplay by Robert E. Sherwood and Leonardo Bercovici; based on the novel by Robert Nathan)

10.

"This boy is on trial for the act of murder—not the thought of murder. Between the idea and the deed, there's a world of difference. And if you find this boy guilty in desire but not guilty in deed, then he must walk out of this courtroom as free as you or I. However, since the prosecutor lacked evidence, he's given you prejudice; lacking facts, he's given you fantasy. Of all the witnesses he's paraded before you, not one actually saw what happened. I will now call to the stand an eyewitness—the only eyewitness—the only one who knows the truth, the whole truth. George Eastman, will you please take the stand?"

—Fred Clark bringing an accused Montgomery Clift to the witness stand with a drum-roll in George Stevens's *A Place in the Sun*
(Screenplay by Michael Wilson and Harry Brown; based on AN AMERICAN TRAGEDY, a play by Patrick Kearney and novel by Theodore Dreiser)

ALSO SEE: Hunger-4; Looks-3; Loves-35; Men-7; Men-11; Men-12; Money-14; Prayers-11; Pretense-5; Sensible-4; Sin-4; Static-5; Static-11.

DIGNITY

1.

"In Rome, dignity shortens life even more surely than disease."

—Charles Laughton cautioning Peter Ustinov about the dangers of a new-found dignity in Stanley Kubrick's *Spartacus*
(Screenplay by Dalton Trumbo; based on the novel by Howard Fast)

2.

(a) "To me, there's something so unrefined about excessive laughter."

(b) "Oh, if you want to be really refined, you have to be dead. There's no one as dignified as a mummy."

—(b) Greer Garson rattling the stiff-backed (a) Frieda Inescort in Robert Z. Leonard's *Pride and Prejudice*
(Screenplay by Aldous Huxley and Jane Murfin; based on the play by Helen Jerome and novel by Jane Austen)

ALSO SEE: Drink Excuses-6; Women-8.

DIRECTORS

1.

"Tonight's merely the beginning. You're at the foot of a golden stair. Lily Garland, I'm going to take you by this little hand higher and further than any woman in the theater has ever gone before. The beauty and glamour that were mine for a little while during those rehearsals when you thought I was so cruel now belong to the world forever and evermore."

—John Barrymore giving his direction due credit for Carole Lombard's acting success in Howard Hawks's *Twentieth Century*
(Screenplay by Ben Hecht and Charles MacArthur; based on their play and NAPOLEON OF BROADWAY, a play by Charles Bruce Milholland)

2.

"Congratulate Walter on his sets, Lucien on her costumes and Boris on his score—and tell the director he should have his head examined. He shouldn't have shot the picture; he should have shot himself."

—Kirk Douglas damning his own direction in Vincente Minnelli's *The Bad and the Beautiful*
(Screenplay by Charles Schnee; based on "Memorial to a Bad Man" and "Of Good and Evil," two short stories by George Bradshaw)

3.

"He stinks! He's perhaps the worst director that ever lived. He's the only director whose plays close on the first day of rehearsal."

—Zero Mostel filling Gene Wilder in on the (dis)credits of Christopher Hewitt in Mel Brooks's *The Producers*
(Original Screenplay by Mel Brooks)

ALSO SEE: Diamonds-4; Humility-2; Imagination-2.

DISCIPLINE

1.

"The last mass trials were a great success. There are going to be fewer but better Russians."

—Greta Garbo bringing the "good" news to her frivolous comrades in Paris in Ernst Lubitsch's *Ninotchka*
(Screenplay by Charles Brackett, Billy Wilder and Walter Reisch; based on an original story by Melchior Lengyel)

2.

"There's one thing I do know—what this family

needs is discipline. I've been a pretty patient man—but when people start riding horses up the front steps and parking them in the library, that's going a little bit too far."

—Eugene Pallette reading the riot act to his madcap clan in Gregory La Cava's *My Man Godfrey*
(Screenplay by Morrie Ryskind, Eric Hatch and Gregory La Cava; based on TEN ELEVEN FIFTH, a novel by Eric Hatch)

3.

"Dreaming won't get you to Damascus, sir, but discipline will."

—Anthony Quayle war-counseling Alec Guinness in David Lean's *Lawrence of Arabia*
(Screenplay by Robert Bolt; based on THE SEVEN PILLARS OF WISDOM, the autobiography of T. E. Lawrence, and other works by and about T. E. Lawrence)

ALSO SEE: Snake-3.

DISEASE

1.

"Just old age. It's the only disease, Mr. Thompson, that you don't look forward to being cured of."

—Everett Sloane considering the alternative in Orson Welles's *Citizen Kane*
(Original Screenplay by Herman J. Mankiewicz and Orson Welles)

2.

"You're in the green years, Robbie. You suffer the critical disease of being young. The Lord deliver me from ever having to go through that again!"

—Charles Coburn diagnosing his great-grandson (Tom Drake) in Victor Saville's *The Green Years*
(Screenplay by Robert Ardrey and Sonya Levien; based on the novel by A. J. Cronin)

3.

"Delirium is a disease of the night."

—Frank Faylen speaking from the experience of an alcoholic-ward night-nurse in Billy Wilder's *The Lost Weekend*

(Screenplay by Charles Brackett and Billy Wilder; based on the novel by Charles R. Jackson)

4.

"I bet she won't live through the night. She has four fatal diseases."

—Margaret O'Brien fretting about her doll to Chill Wills in Vincente Minnelli's *Meet Me in St. Louis*
(Screenplay by Irving Brecher and Fred F. Finklehoffe; based on the stories and novel by Sally Benson)

5.

"Oh, brother! I'm so smart it's a disease!"

—Jack Carson realizing that Joan Crawford has just framed him for Zachary Scott's murder in Michael Curtiz's *Mildred Pierce*
(Screenplay by Ranald MacDougall; based on the novel by James M. Cain)

6.

"Such a pretty name for a disease. Sounds like a rare flower, doesn't it? Late-blooming dementia praecox."

—Katharine Hepburn making a poetic observation in Joseph L. Mankiewicz's *Suddenly, Last Summer*
(Screenplay by Gore Vidal and Tennessee Williams; based on the one-act play by Tennessee Williams)

7.

"After every first dress rehearsal, I always sit in a draft hoping to catch pneumonia—it never works. Oh, for the peaceful quiet of an oxygen tent."

—William Holden entering rehearsals nervously in George Seaton's *The Country Girl*
(Screenplay by George Seaton; based on the play by Clifford Odets)

8.

"I attract some very rare diseases on cargo days. That day when they knew you had five ships to load, I was greeted with six more cases of beriberi—double beriberi this time. So help me, I'm going down to the ship's library and throw that old copy of *Moby Dick* overboard!"

—William Powell noting a medical phenomenon to Henry Fonda in John Ford and Mervyn LeRoy's *Mister Roberts*
(Screenplay by Frank S. Nugent and Joshua Logan; based on the play by Thomas Heggen and Joshua Logan and novel by Thomas Heggen)

ALSO SEE: Dignity-1; Failure-3; Jealous-1; Love-13; Love-14; Prejudice-1; Royalty-6.

DISHONEST

1.

"These girls in love never realize they should be honestly dishonest instead of being dishonestly honest."

—Clifton Webb making a fine point with fellow bachelor Louis Jourdan in Jean Negulesco's *Three Coins in the Fountain*
(Screenplay by John Patrick; based on the novel by John H. Secondari)

2.

(a) "It's simply a matter of creative accounting. Let's assume just for the moment that you are a dishonest man."
    (b) "Assume away."
    (a) "It's very easy. You simply raise more money than you really need."

—(a) Gene Wilder telling (b) Zero Mostel how to turn flops into hits in Mel Brooks's *The Producers*
(Original Screenplay by Mel Brooks)

ALSO SEE: Money-2; Normal-1; Peace-3; Tact-2.

DISMISSALS

1.

"I'm a man of one word: scram!"

—Groucho Marx dispatching Louis Calhern in Leo McCarey's *Duck Soup*
(Screenplay by Bert Kalmar and Harry Ruby; additional dialogue by Arthur Sheekman and Nat Perrin)

2.

"It should take you exactly four seconds to

get from here to that door. I'll give you two."

—Audrey Hepburn sending away George Peppard in Blake Edwards's *Breakfast at Tiffany's*
(Screenplay by George Axelrod; based on the novella by Truman Capote)

3.
(a) "Would you do me a favor, Harry?"
  (b) "What?"
  (a) "Drop dead!"

—(a) Judy Holliday walking out on (b) Broderick Crawford in George Cukor's *Born Yesterday*
(Screenplay by Albert Mannheimer; based on the play by Garson Kanin)

4.
"All right, get lost. Take a couple of Drop Dead pills."

—Detective Kirk Douglas dismissing Gladys George, an eyewitness he believes has been bribed, in William Wyler's *Detective Story*
(Screenplay by Philip Yordan and Robert Wyler; based on the play by Sidney Kingsley)

5.
"Get out, Veda. Get your things out of this house right now before I throw them into the street and you with them. Get out before I kill you."

—Joan Crawford kicking out Ann Blyth in Michael Curtiz's *Mildred Pierce*
(Screenplay by Ranald MacDougall; based on the novel by James M. Cain)

6.
"And now will you all leave quietly, or must I ask Miss Cutler to pass among you with a baseball bat?"

—Monty Woolley waving away lesser mortals in his usual polite manner in William Keighley's *The Man Who Came to Dinner*
(Screenplay by Julius J. Epstein and Philip G. Epstein; based on the play by George S. Kaufman and Moss Hart)

ALSO SEE: Never-8; Parents-3.

DIVORCE

1.
"I thought it would bring him back to me. I was sure it would bring him back to me."

—Luise Rainer making a major miscalculation about William Powell in Robert Z. Leonard's *The Great Ziegfeld*
(Original Screenplay by William Anthony McGuire)

2.
"My way, your marriage may not last till death —but it's fun while it hangs together."

—Mary Boland rejoicing in the divorcee's life in George Cukor's *The Women*
(Screenplay by Anita Loos and Jane Murfin; based on the play by Clare Boothe)

3.
"When you've been married to a woman for 12 years, you don't just sit down at the breakfast table and say 'Pass the sugar—and I want a divorce.' It's not that easy."

—Fred MacMurray stalling his mistress (Shirley MacLaine) in Billy Wilder's *The Apartment*
(Original Screenplay by Billy Wilder and I. A. L. Diamond)

4.
"I swear, if you existed, I'd divorce you."

—Elizabeth Taylor berating her spineless spouse (Richard Burton) in Mike Nichols's *Who's Afraid of Virginia Woolf?*
(Screenplay by Ernest Lehman; based on the play by Edward Albee)

ALSO SEE: Apology-2; Foolish-2; Good-8; Love-52; Toasts-7; Wrong-6.

DOCTORS

1.
"Eight days ago you showed up half-stoned for a simple nephrectomy, botched it, put the patient in failure and damn near killed him. Then —pausing only to send in your bill—you flew

off on the Wings of Man to an island of sun in Montego Bay. This is the third time in two years we've had to patch up your patients. The other two died. You're greedy, unfeeling, inept, indifferent, self-inflating and unconscionably profitable. Aside from that, I have nothing against you. I'm sure you play a helluva game of golf."

—George C. Scott dragging Richard Dysart over the coals in Arthur Hiller's *The Hospital*
(Original Screenplay by Paddy Chayefsky)

2.
"You young men—Doctors and Scientists of the future. Do not let yourselves be tainted by a barren skepticism, nor discouraged by the sadness of certain hours that creep over nations. Do not become angry at your opponents. For no scientific theory has ever been accepted without opposition. Live in a serene peace of libraries and laboratories. Say to yourselves first: 'What have I done for my instruction?' and as you gradually advance: 'What am I accomplishing?' until the time comes when you may have the immense happiness of thinking that you've contributed in some way to the welfare and progress of mankind."

—Paul Muni inspiring doctors in the last lines of William Dieterle's *The Story of Louis Pasteur*
(Screenplay by Sheridan Gibney and Pierre Collings; based on an original story by Sheridan Gibney and Pierre Collings)

3.
"Thank God, I'm a doctor!"

—Robert Donat beaming after a difficult delivery in King Vidor's *The Citadel*
(Screenplay by Ian Dalrymple, Frank Wead and Elizabeth Hill; additional dialogue by Emlyn Williams; based on the novel by A. J. Cronin)

4.
"I remember this house when it rang with laughter and love. Goodbye, Mrs. Heathcliff. Ask your husband to call another doctor in future. Whoever dwells in this house is beyond my healing arts."

—Donald Crisp making his last housecall on Laurence Olivier and Geraldine Fitzgerald in William Wyler's *Wuthering Heights*
(Screenplay by Ben Hecht and Charles MacArthur; based on the novel by Emily Brontë)

5.
"Dr. Bradley is the greatest living argument for mercy killings."

—Monty Woolley berating his country doctor (George Barbier) in William Keighley's *The Man Who Came to Dinner*
(Screenplay by Julius J. Epstein and Philip G. Epstein; based on the play by George S. Kaufman and Moss Hart)

ALSO SEE: Beliefs-4; Defense-3; Dreams-8; Heart-1; Humility-3; Murder-10; Murder-11; Murder-12; Psychiatry-7; Sensible-4; Soul-10.

DOGS

1.
"Dogs like us, we ain't such dogs as we think we are."

—Ernest Borgnine trying to make Betsy Blair feel better in Delbert Mann's *Marty*
(Screenplay by Paddy Chayefsky; based on his teleplay)

2.
"There's a name for you ladies, but it isn't used in high society—outside of a kennel."

—Joan Crawford making a tart exit in George Cukor's *The Women*
(Screenplay by Anita Loos and Jane Murfin; based on the play by Clare Boothe)

3.
"I guess I'm the bitch with too many pups."

—Pat Quinn tiring of her earth-mother role in Arthur Penn's *Alice's Restaurant*
(Screenplay by Venable Herndon and Arthur Penn; based on "The Alice's Restaurant Massacree," a song by Arlo Guthrie)

4.

"I don't think Little Sheba's ever coming back, Doc. I ain't going to call her anymore."

—Shirley Booth surrendering her favorite illusion at the end of Daniel Mann's *Come Back, Little Sheba*
(Screenplay by Ketti Frings; based on the play by William Inge)

5.

"Have we been trailing Firefly? Why, my partner—he's got a nose just like a bloodhound. . . . The rest of his face don't look so good either."

—Chico Marx describing Harpo Marx to Louis Calhern in Leo McCarey's *Duck Soup*
(Screenplay by Bert Kalmar and Harry Ruby; additional dialogue by Arthur Sheekman and Nat Perrin)

6.

"He has every characteristic of a dog except loyalty."

—Henry Fonda sizing up a political figure in Franklin Schaffner's *The Best Man*
(Screenplay by Gore Vidal; based on his play)

ALSO SEE: Curses-2; Dreams-4; Eulogies-11; Fathers-3; Macho-19; Money-1; Names-2; Professions-11; Strange-7; Strange-8; Whistle-2.

DOMESTICITY

1.

"I learned something today, and it's that—well, there comes a time in a man's life when he's got to quit rolling around like a pinball. Maybe a—a little town like this is it, a place to settle down where people are easy-going and sincere."

—William Holden falling for small-town Kansas in Joshua Logan's *Picnic*
(Screenplay by Daniel Taradash; based on the play by William Inge)

2.

"Underneath this haunted, driven shell of a man, there lives a warm homebody who likes to watch TV and chew cashews while the woman he loves is finishing a good novel."

—Alan Bates rejoicing in his relationship with Jill Clayburgh in Paul Mazursky's *An Unmarried Woman*
(Original Screenplay by Paul Mazursky)

DON'T

1.

"Don't quibble, Sibyl."

—Robert Montgomery arguing with Una Merkel in Sidney Franklin's *Private Lives*
(Screenplay by Hans Kraly, Richard Schayer and Claudine West; based on the play by Noel Coward)

2.

"Don't teeter, Topper."

—Cary Grant cautioning Roland Young in Norman Z. McLeod's *Topper*
(Screenplay by Jack Jevne, Eric Hatch and Eddie Moran; based on the novel by Thorne Smith)

3.

"Don't cry. The damned don't cry."

—Michael Redgrave mixing sympathy and insult in Dudley Nichols's *Mourning Becomes Electra*
(Screenplay by Dudley Nichols; based on the play by Eugene O'Neill)

4.

"And don't pout. If you wanna fight, we'll fight. But don't pout. Fighting, I win. Pouting, you win."

—Walter Matthau raging at Jack Lemmon in Gene Saks's *The Odd Couple*
(Screenplay by Neil Simon; based on his play)

5.

"Don't you shush me! You've been shushing me for 22 months! Now, you've shushed your last shush."

—Jean Arthur writing fini to her fiancé (Richard Gaines) in George Stevens's *The More the Merrier*

(Screenplay by Richard Flournoy and Lewis R. Foster; based on a story by Robert Russell and Frank Ross)

6.
"I don't bray!"

—Elizabeth Taylor braying at Richard Burton in Mike Nichols's *Who's Afraid of Virginia Woolf?* *(Screenplay by Ernest Lehman; based on the play by Edward Albee)*

7.
"I don't provoke."

—Akim Tamiroff refusing to be forced into an argument in Sam Wood's *For Whom the Bell Tolls* *(Screenplay by Dudley Nichols; based on the novel by Ernest Hemingway)*

8.
"Women! They get stirred up, and then they try to get you stirred up, too. But don't you let them do it, Clarence. Don't you let them do it. Now if you can keep reason and logic in the argument—well, a man can hold his own, of course—but if they can switch you, pretty soon the argument's about whether you love them or not. I swear, I don't know how they do it. But don't you let them, Clarence. Don't you let them."

—William Powell counseling his first-born (James Lydon) in Michael Curtiz's *Life With Father* *(Screenplay by Donald Ogden Stewart; based on the play by Howard Lindsay and Russel Crouse and stories by Clarence Day, Jr.)*

9.
"Don't make an issue of my womanhood."

—Greta Garbo cooling Sig Ruman, Felix Bressart and Alexander Granach with a just-Russian-business attitude in Ernst Lubitsch's *Ninotchka* *(Screenplay by Charles Brackett, Billy Wilder and Walter Reisch; based on an original story by Melchior Lengyel)*
and
—Cyd Charisse dittoing Fred Astaire in the remake, Rouben Mamoulian's *Silk Stockings* *(Screenplay by Leonard Gershe and Leonard Spigelgass; based on the musical play by George S. Kaufman, Leueen MacGrath and Abe Burrows and NINOTCHKA, a screenplay by Charles Brackett, Billy Wilder and Walter Reisch and original story by Melchior Lengyel)*

10.
"And, for security reasons, don't call me comrade."

—Alan Napier cautioning a fellow subversive (Gayne Whitman) in Edward Ludwig's *Big Jim McLain* *(Screenplay by James Edward Grant, Richard English and Eric Taylor; based on a story by Richard English)*

11.
"Fredo, you're my only brother and I love you, but don't ever take sides with anyone against the family again. Ever."

—Al Pacino warning John Cazale in Francis Ford Coppola's *The Godfather* *(Screenplay by Mario Puzo and Francis Ford Coppola; based on the novel by Mario Puzo)*

12.
"Don't think too hard, Robert. You might hurt yourself."

—Victor Moore cautioning his son (Ray Mayer) not to strain for wit in Leo McCarey's *Make Way for Tomorrow* *(Screenplay by Vina Delmar; based on the play by Helen Leary and Nolan Leary and THE YEARS ARE SO LONG, a novel by Josephine Lawrence)*

13.
"Don't drop into the chair. Insinuate yourself."

—Isabel Jeans teaching Leslie Caron to sit in Vincente Minnelli's *Gigi* *(Screenplay by Alan Jay Lerner; based on the novel by Colette)*

14.
"Go out then, Mama. Don't look back or you'll turn into a pillar of salt and he'll sell you—$8 a pound."

—Edmond O'Brien reminding Florence Eldridge of Fredric March's old Civil War crime in Michael Gordon's *Another Part of the Forest*

(Screenplay by Vladimir Pozner; based on the play by Lillian Hellman)

15.
"Go on, Owen. Tell her I'm dying—and don't overact."

—John Barrymore sending Roscoe Karns to bait a trap for Carole Lombard in Howard Hawks's *Twentieth Century*
(Screenplay by Ben Hecht and Charles MacArthur; based on their play and NAPOLEON OF BROADWAY, a play by Charles Bruce Milholland)

ALSO SEE: Crooked-3; Doctors-2; Guilty-7; Happiness-1; Heaven-9; Kiss-21; Lies-4; Live-3; Never-4; Public Relations-3; Repetitions-1; Republicans-2; Respect-3; Sayings-1; Sayings-4; Success-3; Suicide-5; Wants-6; Weakness-5.

DREAMS

1.
"Last night I dreamt I went to Manderley again."

—Joan Fontaine recalling her former home in the first line of Alfred Hitchcock's *Rebecca*
(Screenplay by Robert E. Sherwood and Joan Harrison; adaptation by Philip MacDonald and Michael Hogan; based on the novel by Daphne du Maurier)

2.
(a) "It's heavy. What is it?"
  (b) "The, er, stuff that dreams are made of."
  (a) "Huh?"

—(a) Ward Bond and (b) Humphrey Bogart discussing the title objet d'art in the last lines of John Huston's *The Maltese Falcon*
(Screenplay by John Huston; based on the novel by Dashiell Hammett)

3.
"The old man was dreaming about the lions."

—Spencer Tracy ending his narration gently with the last line of John Sturges's *The Old Man and the Sea*

(Screenplay by Peter Viertel; based on the novel by Ernest Hemingway)

4.
"I dreamt about Little Sheba again last night, Doc. . . . It was just as real. I put her on a leash to take her downtown to do some shopping, and everybody in the street turned around to look at her, and I was so proud. And then we started to walk, and the blocks started going by so fast poor Little Sheba couldn't keep up with me. And suddenly I looked around, and she was gone. Ain't that funny? I looked everywhere for her, but I couldn't find her. I stood there feeling kind of afraid. Do you suppose that means anything, Doc?"

—Shirley Booth relaying a dream about her dog to Burt Lancaster in Daniel Mann's *Come Back, Little Sheba*
(Screenplay by Ketti Frings; based on the play by William Inge)

5.
"You think all dreams have to be your kind—golden fleece and thunder on the mountain—but there are other dreams, Starbuck, little quiet ones that come to a woman when she's shining the silverware and putting mothflakes in the closet."

—Katharine Hepburn scaling down her dream world for Burt Lancaster in Joseph Anthony's *The Rainmaker*
(Screenplay by N. Richard Nash; based on his play)

6.
"Haven't I been trying to tell ya? That, until ya have my dowry, ya haven't got any bit of me—me—myself. I'll still be dreamin' amongst the things that are my own—as if I had never met you. There's 300 years of happy dreamin' in those dreams of mine, and—I want them! I want my dream."

—Maureen O'Hara laying down the law to her groom (John Wayne) in John Ford's *The Quiet Man*
(Screenplay by Frank S. Nugent; based on "Green Rushes," a short story by Maurice Walsh)

7.

"There was a dream I used to have about you and I. It was always the same. I'd be told that you were dead, and I would run crying into the street. Someone would stop and ask, 'Why are you crying?' And I would say, 'Because my father is dead, and he never said he loved me.'"

—Martin Sheen confronting Jack Albertson in Ulu Grosbard's *The Subject Was Roses*
(Screenplay by Frank D. Gilroy; based on his play)

8.

"When I had my heart attack, there was a dream I had. You can talk about death. I've seen it many times as a doctor, but you never know what it's like until it almost happens to you. I dreamed I had already died. I dreamed I was in a box. The sweat broke out all over my body. I wanted to cry out, 'I can't be dead—I haven't lived!'"

—Oskar Werner confessing a nightmare to his captain (Charles Korvin) in Stanley Kramer's *Ship of Fools*
(Screenplay by Abby Mann; based on the novel by Katherine Anne Porter)

9.

"Come on, Nat. Join me—one little jigger of dreams, huh?"

—Ray Milland seeking a little drinking companionship from his bartender (Howard da Silva) in Billy Wilder's *The Lost Weekend*
(Screenplay by Charles Brackett and Billy Wilder; based on the novel by Charles R. Jackson)

10.

"A salesman's got to dream, boy. It comes with the territory."

—Royal Beal passing his lifestyle credo along to Fredric March in Laslo Benedek's *Death of a Salesman*
(Screenplay by Stanley Roberts; based on the play by Arthur Miller)

ALSO SEE: Alone-3; Cameras-3; Crazy-13; Discipline-3; Dying Words-31; Faith-2; Fathers-4; Heaven-6; Home-8; Identity Crisis-4; Letters-6; Prologues-1; Prologues-2; Star-9; Timing-4; Truth-7.

DRESS

1.

"That's quite a dress you almost have on."

—Gene Kelly complimenting Nina Foch's one-shoulder gown in Vincente Minnelli's *An American in Paris*
(Original Screenplay by Alan Jay Lerner)

2.

"How did you get into that dress—with a spray gun?"

—Bob Hope commenting on Dorothy Lamour's tight-fitting outfit in Norman Z. McLeod's *Road to Rio*
(Original Screenplay by Edmund Beloin and Jack Rose)

3.

"Sure a pretty dress ya got covering ya."

—Spencer Tracy complimenting Katharine Hepburn's attire (after a fashion) in George Cukor's *Pat and Mike*
(Original Screenplay by Ruth Gordon and Garson Kanin)

4.

"I hate this dress. My husband says I look as though I were going to sing in it."

—Phyllis Povah being specific about her discomfort in George Cukor's *The Women*
(Screenplay by Anita Loos and Jane Murfin; based on the play by Clare Boothe)

5.

"Osgood, I can't get married in your mother's dress. That—she and I, we are not built the same way."

—Jack Lemmon trying gently to break the news he's a man to his fiancé (Joe E. Brown) in Billy Wilder's *Some Like It Hot*
(Screenplay by Billy Wilder and I. A. L. Diamond; suggested by a story by R. Thoeren and M. Logan)

6.

"Child, you're out of your mind. You can't wear red to the Olympus Ball."

—Fay Bainter warning Bette Davis to wear white in William Wyler's *Jezebel*
(*Screenplay by Clements Ripley, Abem Finkel and John Huston; based on the play by Owen Davis Sr.*)

7.

"This is very unusual. I've never been alone with a man before—even with my dress on. With my dress off, it's *most* unusual."

—A drugged Audrey Hepburn settling down innocently for a night in Gregory Peck's apartment in William Wyler's *Roman Holiday*
(*Screenplay by Ian McLellan Hunter and John Dighton; based on an original story by Ian McLellan Hunter*)

8.

"I have heard about your lunch breaks on the set. The only thing you don't do in your dressing room is dress."

—Michael Caine accusing Maggie Smith of infidelity in Herbert Ross's *California Suite*
(*Screenplay by Neil Simon; based on his play*)

ALSO SEE: Apology-1; Awakenings-1; Fashion-2; Tongue-2.

DRINK

1.

"One's too many, and a hundred's not enough."

—Howard da Silva hesitating to serve his steady customer (Ray Milland) in Billy Wilder's *The Lost Weekend*
(*Screenplay by Charles Brackett and Billy Wilder; based on the novel by Charles R. Jackson*)

2.

"Well, there are some people that rarely touch it, but it touches them often."

—Marlon Brando counting his sister-in-law (Vivien Leigh) in that company of secret drinkers in Elia Kazan's *A Streetcar Named Desire*

(*Screenplay by Tennessee Williams; adaptation by Oscar Saul; based on the play by Tennessee Williams*)

3.

"Well, as long as I got a foot, I'll kick booze. And, as long as I got a fist, I'll punch it. And, as long as I got a tooth, I'll bite it. And, when I'm old and gray and toothless and bootless, I'll gum it till I go to heaven and booze goes to hell."

—Burt Lancaster preaching against John Barleycorn in Richard Brooks's *Elmer Gantry*
(*Screenplay by Richard Brooks; based on the novel by Sinclair Lewis*)

4.

"It'll be me or it. One of us has got to go."

—Chill Wills reeling toward the bourbon in George Stevens's *Giant*
(*Screenplay by Fred Guiol and Ivan Moffat; based on the novel by Edna Ferber*)

5.

"Champagne's funny stuff. I'm used to whiskey. Whiskey is a slap on the back, and champagne's heavy mist before my eyes."

—James Stewart explaining the difference to Katharine Hepburn in George Cukor's *The Philadelphia Story*
(*Screenplay by Donald Ogden Stewart; based on the play by Philip Barry*)

6.

"I drink only glug—at Christmastime."

—Loretta Young refusing the bottle (and accompanying advances) of Rhys Williams in H. C. Potter's *The Farmer's Daughter*
(*Screenplay by Allen Rivkin and Laura Kerr; based on HULDA, DAUGHTER OF PARLIAMENT, a play by Juhni Tervataa*)

7.

"None for me, thank you. Alcohol in the middle of the day is exciting when you're 30 but disastrous at 70."

—Felix Aylmer passing on the wine in Ronald Neame's *The Chalk Garden*

(Screenplay by John Michael Hayes; based on the play by Enid Bagnold)

8.

"Excuse me, folks. Somebody must have put alcohol in our liquor."

—Louis Armstrong wisecracking between songs at a speakeasy in Melville Shavelson's *The Five Pennies*
(Screenplay by Jack Rose and Melville Shavelson; based on a story by Robert Smith; suggested by the life of Loring "Red" Nichols)

ALSO SEE: Champagne; Gin; Wine; Differences-8; Dying Words-15; Dying Words-16; Firsts-7; Mellow-2; Mind-2; Never-4; Never-5; Party-7; Propositions-11; Sayings-5; Specializations-1; Talk-4; Trust and Distrust-3; Violence-3; Wine-1.

DRINK EXCUSES

1.

"A lush can always find a reason, if he's thirsty. Listen. If he's happy, he takes a couple of shots to celebrate his happiness. Sad, he needs 'em to drown his sorrow. Low, to pick him up. Excited, to calm him down. Sick, for his health. And healthy, it can't hurt him. So you see, Al, a lush just can't lose."

—James Cagney jawing with the bartender (Morgan Brown) in Gordon Douglas's *Come Fill the Cup*
(Screenplay by Ivan Goff and Ben Roberts; based on the novel by Harlan Ware)

2.

"Oh, I don't know. Just celebrate. One must have some excuse, don't you think? Otherwise, one's just a drunken sot."

—Penelope Dudley Ward proposing a toot with Robert Donat in King Vidor's *The Citadel*
(Screenplay by Ian Dalrymple, Frank Wead and Elizabeth Hill; additional dialogue by Emlyn Williams; based on the novel by A. J. Cronin)

3.

"I envy people who drink. At least they know what to blame everything on."

—Oscar Levant making a wry observation in Jean Negulesco's *Humoresque*
(Screenplay by Clifford Odets and Zachary Gold; based on a short story by Fannie Hurst)

4.

"I always start around noon—in case it gets dark early."

—Peggy Lee boozing by the clock in Jack Webb's *Pete Kelly's Blues*
(Original Screenplay by Richard L. Breen)

5.

"You see, the world looks so dirty to me when I'm not drinking. Joe, remember Fisherman's Wharf? The water when you looked too close? That's the way the world looks to me when I'm not drinking."

—Lee Remick prettifying her surroundings in Blake Edwards's *Days of Wine and Roses*
(Screenplay by J. P. Miller; based on his teleplay)

6.

"You know, as a man gets on in years, he wants to live deeply—a feeling of sad dignity comes upon him, and that's fatal for a comic. It affected my work; I lost contact with the audience; couldn't warm up to them. And that's what started me drinking. I had to have it before I went on. It got so I couldn't be funny without it. The more I drank—it became a vicious circle."

—Charles Chaplin lightening his work load in Charles Chaplin's *Limelight*
(Original Screenplay by Charles Chaplin)

7.

"If you're not careful, you're going to have him full of whiskey before morning. He's getting a cold, and that's a respectable surface reason for any drinker to jump down the well."

—Grace Kelly cautioning William Holden about Bing Crosby's cough medicine in George Seaton's *The Country Girl*
(Screenplay by George Seaton; based on the play by Clifford Odets)

8.

"I only take a drop when I have a cold. Of

course, that cold has been hanging on for years."

—Frank Morgan disbelieving his own medicinal argument in Rouben Mamoulian's *Summer Holiday* *(Screenplay by Irving Brecher and Jean Holloway; based on AH, WILDERNESS!, a screenplay by Albert Hackett and Frances Goodrich and play by Eugene O'Neill)*

9.
"I am drunk. A wise man gets drunk to spend his time with fools."

—Akim Tamiroff berating his associates in Sam Wood's *For Whom the Bell Tolls* *(Screenplay by Dudley Nichols; based on the novel by Ernest Hemingway)*

10.
"You are smug, Mr. Darnay, when you ask why people drink, but I'll tell you: so that they can stand their fellow men better. After a few bottles, I might even like you."

—Ronald Colman deflating Donald Woods in Jack Conway's *A Tale of Two Cities* *(Screenplay by W. P. Lipscomb and S. N. Behrman; based on the novel by Charles Dickens)*

11.
"You're passing the buck. You're passing the buck to things like 'disgust' and 'mendacity.' Now, if you've got to use that kind of language about a thing, it's 90% bull, and I'm not buying any. Now, you started drinking with your friend Skipper's death—now that's the truth, huh?"

—Burl Ives interrogating his alcoholic son (Paul Newman) in Richard Brooks's *Cat on a Hot Tin Roof* *(Screenplay by Richard Brooks and James Poe; based on the play by Tennessee Williams)*

12.
"I know exactly what you're up against, boys. I know you'll turn into such a coward that you'll grab at any lousy excuse not to kill your pipe dreams. And yet, as I said over and over again, it's exactly those damned lying tomorrow dreams that keep you from making peace with

yourselves so you've got to kill them like I did mine."

—Lee Marvin pep-talking a barroom full of rummies in John Frankenheimer's *The Iceman Cometh* *(Screenplay based on the play by Eugene O'Neill; text edited by Thomas Quinn Curtiss)*

13.
"Sure, you got drunk. That's the best excuse in the world for losing. No trouble losing when you got a good excuse. And winning! That can be heavy on your back, too. Like a monkey. You drop that load, too, when you got an excuse. All you gotta do is learn to feel sorry for yourself. One of the best indoor sports: feeling sorry for yourself—a sport enjoyed by all, especially the born losers."

—George C. Scott pep-talking Paul Newman in Robert Rossen's *The Hustler* *(Screenplay by Sidney Carroll and Robert Rossen; based on the novel by Walter Tevis)*

14.
"Listen, I can pick an alky with one eye shut. You're an alky. You'll come back. They all do. Him, for instance. He shows up every month—just like the gas bill. And the one there with the glasses—another repeater. This is his 45th trip. Big executive in the advertising business. Lovely fellow. Been coming here since 1927. Good old prohibition days. Say, you should have seen the joint then. This is nothing. Back then we really had a turnover. Standing room only. Prohibition. That's what started most of these guys off—whoopee!"

—Frank Faylen giving Ray Milland a grim tour of the alcoholic ward in Billy Wilder's *The Lost Weekend* *(Screenplay by Charles Brackett and Billy Wilder; based on the novel by Charles R. Jackson)*

ALSO SEE: Appearances-5; Right-1.

DRINK ORDERS

1.
"Gimme a viskey. Ginger ale on the side. And don' be stingy, ba-bee."

—Greta Garbo addressing bartender Lee Phelps with her first spoken words on film in Clarence Brown's *Anna Christie*
(Screenplay by Frances Marion; based on the play by Eugene O'Neill)

2.
"I'll take lemonade—in a dirty glass."

—Bob Hope adding a note of macho to fit into a rugged Klondike saloon in Hal Walker's *Road to Utopia*
(Original Screenplay by Norman Panama and Melvin Frank)

3.
"Two old-fashioneds for two old-fashioned people."

—Victor Moore ordering drinks for himself and his wife (Beulah Bondi) at their original honeymoon hotel in Leo McCarey's *Make Way for Tomorrow*
(Screenplay by Vina Delmar; based on the play by Helen Leary and Nolan Leary and THE YEARS ARE SO LONG, a novel by Josephine Lawrence)

4.
"Honey, will you get me a Tab? My mouth is so dry they could shoot *Lawrence of Arabia* in it."

—Dyan Cannon requesting relief while sunbathing in Herbert Ross's *The Last of Sheila*
(Original Screenplay by Anthony Perkins and Stephen Sondheim)

5.
"Two bottles of rye! . . . You know what brand, Mr. Brophy. The cheapest. Not a 12-year-old aged-in-the-wood chichi, not for me. Liquor is all one, anyway."

—Ray Milland growling at a liquor-store proprietor (Eddie Laughton) in Billy Wilder's *The Lost Weekend*
(Screenplay by Charles Brackett and Billy Wilder; based on the novel by Charles R. Jackson)

6.
"No tea, Mrs. Morgan. In training, he is. A glass of beer, if you please."

—Barry Fitzgerald accepting Sara Allgood's offer of liquid refreshment for him and boxing coach Rhys Williams in John Ford's *How Green Was My Valley*
(Screenplay by Philip Dunne; based on the novel by Richard Llewellyn)

7.
(a) "Could you be persuaded to have a drink, dear?"
        (b) "Well, maybe just a tiny triple."

—(a) Lucille Ball offering, and (b) Beatrice Arthur accepting, a drink in Gene Saks's *Mame*
(Screenplay by Paul Zindel; based on the musical play by Jerome Lawrence, Robert E. Lee and Jerry Herman and AUNTIE MAME, a play by Jerome Lawrence and Robert E. Lee and novel by Patrick Dennis)

8.
"Martha? Rubbing alcohol for you?"

—Richard Burton replenishing Elizabeth Taylor's drink in Mike Nichols's *Who's Afraid of Virginia Woolf?*
(Screenplay by Ernest Lehman; based on the play by Edward Albee)

ALSO SEE: Dreams-9; Moon-3.

DRUNK

1.
"We have more than a couple of drinks. We get drunk. And we stay drunk most of the time."

—Jack Lemmon forcing Lee Remick to an ugly reality in Blake Edwards's *Days of Wine and Roses*
(Screenplay by J. P. Miller; based on his teleplay)

2.
"What I'm trying to say is, I'm not a drinker— I'm a drunk. They had to put me away once."

—Ray Milland making a grim distinction in Billy Wilder's *The Lost Weekend*
(Screenplay by Charles Brackett and Billy Wilder; based on the novel by Charles R. Jackson)

3.
"Drunk? I'll have you know a Harvard man never resorts to getting a woman drunk—except in emergency, and you, Miss Morrow, are an emergency."

—Nick Adams making an alcoholic pass at Doris Day
in Michael Gordon's *Pillow Talk*
*(Screenplay by Stanley Shapiro and Maurice
Richlin; based on a story by Russell Rouse and
Clarence Greene)*

4.

"One thing I can't stand, it's a dame that's
drunk. Do you know what I mean? They turn
my stomach. No good to themselves or anybody else. She's got the shakes, see, so she has
a drink to get rid of 'em. That one tastes so good
so she has another one. First thing you know,
she's stinko again."

—Edward G. Robinson berating Claire Trevor in
John Huston's *Key Largo*
*(Screenplay by Richard Brooks and John Huston;
based on the play by Maxwell Anderson)*

5.

"You drank everything in this state. Try
Nevada."

—Michael Caine overstating Maggie Smith's alcoholism in Herbert Ross's *California Suite*
(Screenplay by Neil Simon; based on his play)

6.
(a) "Your liver must look like a bomb hit it."
    (b) "Well, you know what I say: 'live and let
liver.' "

—(b) Alan Hale making a bad joke out of the criticism
of (a) Ida Lupino in Raoul Walsh's *They Drive by
Night*
*(Screenplay by Jerry Wald and Richard Macaulay;
based on LONG HAUL, a novel by A. T. Bezzerides)*

ALSO SEE: Communication-12; Drink Excuses-
9; Excuses-2; Goals-4; Last Lines-3; Lies-23;
Lies-24; Life and Death-19; Mad Act-5; Notes-
2; Pain-4; Parting Shots-5; Party-4; Peace-5;
Pep Talks-7; Priorities-3; Run-4; Sayings-6; Self-
Depreciation-1; Telephone Scenes-8; Toasts-
18; Together-8; Truth-6; Understand-4; Water-
2.

DRUNKEN RANTINGS

1.
"Ladies and gentlemen, I'm very happy to be
here. In fact, I'm very happy to be anywhere.
In fact, I'm—I'm very happy. Perhaps it'd be
a good idea if you just put that bottle right
down here in front of me, hmm? It'll save
yourself quite a number of trips. . . . I'm glad
to see you've all pulled through so well. As
Mr., er, Milton so perfectly expressed it, 'Our
country stands today where it stands today,'
wherever that is. And I'm sure you'll all agree
with me if I said that now is the time for all of
us to stop all this nonsense, face facts, get
down to brass tacks, forget about the war and
go fishing. But I'm not going to say it. I'm just
going to sum the whole thing up in one word
—my wife doesn't think I'd better sum it up
in that one word."

—Fredric March addressing postwar bankers in Wil-
liam Wyler's *The Best Years of Our Lives*
*(Screenplay by Robert E. Sherwood; based on
GLORY FOR ME, a verse novel by MacKinlay
Kantor)*

2.
"That's a very pretty speech, my dear. Very
pretty. You said the right thing. I want to be
the very first one to congratulate you on that—
on that valuable little piece of bric-a-brac. Now
I want to make a speech. Gentlemen of the
Academy and fellow suckers, I got one of those
once for a Best Performance. They don't mean
a thing. People get 'em every year. What I
want's a special award—something nobody
else can get. I want a statue for the Worst Performance of the year. In fact, I want three statues for the three worst performances of the
year because I've earned them. And every single one of you that saw those masterpieces of
mine knows that I've earned them."

—Fredric March interrupting the Oscar-acceptance
speech of his wife (Janet Gaynor) in William A. Wellman's *A Star Is Born*
*(Screenplay by Dorothy Parker, Alan Campbell
and Robert Carson; based on an original story by
William A. Wellman and Robert Carson)*

3.

"Congratulations, my dear. I made it just in time, didn't I? May I borrow the end of your speech to make a speech of my own? My method for gaining your attention may seem a little uncon—unconventional, but, er, hard times call for harsh measures. My—I had my speech all prepared, but I—it's gone right out of my head. Let me see—why, it's silly to be so formal, isn't it? I know most of you sitting out there by your first names, don't I? I made a lot o' money for you gentlemen in my time through the years, haven't I? Well, I need a job now. Yeah, that's it. That—that—that—that's the speech. That's the—I need a job. That's what I wanted to say. I—I need a job. It's as simple as that. I—I need a job, that's all. My talents, I might say, are not confined to dramatic parts. I can play comedy, too."

—James Mason interrupting the Oscar-acceptance speech of his wife (Judy Garland) in George Cukor's *A Star Is Born*
(Screenplay by Moss Hart; based on a screenplay by Dorothy Parker, Alan Campbell and Robert Carson and original story by William A. Wellman and Robert Carson)

4.

"I'm drunk. It's a pleasure to stay drunk when your little boy's been killed."

—Eileen Heckart grieving about her son's death in Mervyn LeRoy's *The Bad Seed*
(Screenplay by John Lee Mahin; based on the play by Maxwell Anderson and novel by William March)

5.

"Well, you said yourself you were looking for someone to do dramatic crimitism—er, criticism. I am drunk."

—Joseph Cotten asking, with a drunk-thick tongue, for a transfer to Chicago from his best friend (Orson Welles) in Orson Welles's *Citizen Kane*
(Original Screenplay by Herman J. Mankiewicz and Orson Welles)

6.

"Emperor, I have incurred your displeasure. I shall fall on my sword at the first opportunity."

—Van Heflin mocking humility before Robert Taylor in Mervyn LeRoy's *Johnny Eager*
(Screenplay by John Lee Mahin and James Edward Grant; based on a story by James Edward Grant)

7.

"Perhaps it's for the best, for how can I forget the precepts taught to me at my mother's dying knee when she said, 'Sidney, never marry a woman who drinks.' Too bad. Such a fine woman once, and now a slave to demon rum."

—Wallace Beery making an alcoholic exit, teasing his straitlaced sweetheart (Aline MacMahon), in Clarence Brown's *Ah, Wilderness!*
(Screenplay by Albert Hackett and Frances Goodrich; based on the play by Eugene O'Neill)
and (almost verbatim)

—Frank Morgan dittoing Agnes Moorehead in the remake, Rouben Mamoulian's *Summer Holiday*
(Screenplay by Irving Brecher and Jean Holloway; based on AH, WILDERNESS!, a screenplay by Albert Hackett and Frances Goodrich and play by Eugene O'Neill)

DUTY

1.

"Some of you boys, I know, are wondering whether or not you'll chicken out under fire. Don't worry about it. I can assure you that you will all do your duty. The Nazis are the enemy. Wade into them. Spill *their* blood. Shoot *them* in the belly. When you put your hand into a bunch of goo that a moment before was your best friend's face, you'll know what to do."

—George C. Scott pep-talking to his troops at the outset of Franklin Schaffner's *Patton*
(Original Screenplay by Francis Ford Coppola and Edmund H. North; based on PATTON: ORDEAL AND TRIUMPH, a book by Ladislas Farago, and A SOLDIER'S STORY, a book by Omar N. Bradley)

2.

"These men don't ask for comfort. They don't ask for safety. If they could speak to you, they'd say, 'Let us choose to do our duty willingly, not the choice of a slave but the choice of free Englishmen.' They ask only the freedom that England expects for every man. If one man among you believed that—one man!—he could command the fleets of England. He could sweep the seas for England if he called his men to duty, not by flaying their backs but by lifting their hearts—their hearts, that's all."

—Franchot Tone suggesting in court an alternative to Charles Laughton's cruelty in Frank Lloyd's *Mutiny on the Bounty*
(Screenplay by Talbot Jennings, Jules Furthman and Carey Wilson; based on the novel by Charles Nordhoff and James Norman Hall)

3.

"Mr. Brady, it's the duty of a newspaper to comfort the afflicted and to flick the comfortable."

—Gene Kelly explaining the rules of newspaper conduct to his prime target (Fredric March) in Stanley Kramer's *Inherit the Wind*
(Screenplay by Nathan E. Douglas and Harold Jacob Smith; based on the play by Jerome Lawrence and Robert E. Lee)

4.

"I won't tell you what I personally thought when I read the letter. It's the duty of counsel to defend his client, not to convict her even in his own mind. I don't want you to tell me anything but what is needed to save your neck."

—James Stephenson confessing contempt for his client (Bette Davis) in William Wyler's *The Letter*
(Screenplay by Howard Koch; based on the play and short story by W. Somerset Maugham)

ALSO SEE: Legs-6; Orders-6; Secrets-3; Sensible-4; Silence-2.

DYING WORDS

1.

"Mother of Mercy, is this the end of Rico?"

—Edward G. Robinson gasping out the last line of Mervyn LeRoy's *Little Caesar*
(Screenplay by Francis Edwards Faragoh; based on the novel by W. R. Burnett)

2.

"It is a far, far better thing I do than I have ever done. It is a far, far better rest I go to than I have ever known."

—Ronald Colman meeting his noble end with the last lines of Jack Conway's *A Tale of Two Cities*
(Screenplay by W. P. Lipscomb and S. N. Behrman; based on the novel by Charles Dickens)
and

—Dirk Bogarde dittoing in the remake, Ralph Thomas's *A Tale of Two Cities*
(Screenplay by T. E. B. Clarke; based on the novel by Charles Dickens)

3.

"Perhaps it's better if I live in your heart where the world can't see me. If I am dead, there'll be no stain on our love."

—Greta Garbo dying in Robert Taylor's arms in George Cukor's *Camille*
(Screenplay by Zoe Akins, Frances Marion and James Hilton; based on LA DAME AUX CAMELIAS, a play and novel by Alexandre Dumas)

4.

"Cancel my appointments."

—Sylvia Sidney barking instructions to her daughter (Joanne Woodward) in Gilbert Cates's *Summer Wishes, Winter Dreams*
(Original Screenplay by Stewart Stern)

5.

"How'd you like to make a thousand dollars a day, Mr. Boot? I'm a thousand-dollar-a-day newspaperman. You can have me for nothing."

—Kirk Douglas, mortally wounded, confronting his former employer (Porter Hall) in the last lines of Billy Wilder's *The Big Carnival*

(Original Screenplay by Billy Wilder, Lesser Samuels and Walter Newman)

6.
"I've got to have more steps. I need more steps. I've got to get higher. Higher."

—William Powell hallucinating over his stage glories in the last lines of Robert Z. Leonard's *The Great Ziegfeld*
(Original Screenplay by William Anthony McGuire)

7.
"Hey, Jeff, what's the highest mountain where we're going?"

—Robert Taylor asking Van Heflin about the vacation they were going to take in Mervyn LeRoy's *Johnny Eager*
(Screenplay by John Lee Mahin and James Edward Grant; based on a story by James Edward Grant)

8.
"Made it, Ma. Top of the world!"

—James Cagney shooting it out from the top of a huge oil tank in Raoul Walsh's *White Heat*
(Screenplay by Ivan Goff and Ben Roberts; based on a story by Virginia Kellogg)

9.
"Frankie! Frankie! Your mother forgives me."

—Victor McLaglen dying with an eased conscience in John Ford's *The Informer*
(Screenplay by Dudley Nichols; based on the novel by Liam O'Flaherty)

10.
"After I let you out, I went to a pay phone and put in a call to my mother. I said, 'I'd like to come home for the weekend and talk to you.' She said, 'What about?' I said, 'The end of the world, that's what about.' She said, 'Are you drunk?' I said, 'No, just lonely.' She said, 'Well, honey, I'm going to the Springs, but you can have the apartment. The cook will be there.' I said, 'Thank you, Mother' and hung up. After that, I didn't care where the car went."

—Lee Kinsolving confessing his despair to Shirley Knight in Delbert Mann's *The Dark at the Top of the Stairs*
(Screenplay by Irving Ravetch and Harriet Frank Jr.; based on the play by William Inge)

11.
"Heathcliff, can you see the gray over there where our castle is? I'll wait for you until you come."

—Merle Oberon dying in Laurence Olivier's arms in William Wyler's *Wuthering Heights*
(Screenplay by Ben Hecht and Charles MacArthur; based on the novel by Emily Brontë)

12.
(a) "Don't leave me. I will sell the land."
   (b) "No, I will not allow that—for I must die sometime, but the land is there after me."

—(b) Luise Rainer imploring (a) Paul Muni to keep their property in Sidney Franklin's *The Good Earth*
(Screenplay by Talbot Jennings, Tess Slesinger and Claudine West; based on the novel by Pearl S. Buck)

13.
"You know, they were—they were right, Gabrielle. The stars, I mean. I had to come all this way to find a reason. The Duke understood what it was I wanted. I hope you'll—I hope—."

—Leslie Howard dying from Humphrey Bogart's bullet in Bette Davis's arms in Archie Mayo's *The Petrified Forest*
(Screenplay by Delmer Daves and Charles Kenyon; based on the play by Robert E. Sherwood)

14.
"I'm all for crime, Your Honor. May I propose a toast? Here is to crime."

—Mischa Auer hoisting a glass of poison in René Clair's *And Then There Were None*
(Screenplay by Dudley Nichols; based on TEN LITTLE INDIANS, a play and novel by Agatha Christie)

15.
"Last drink always without water. Is Norwegian custom. True?"

—Oscar Homolka boozing to the end in George Stevens's *I Remember Mama*
(Screenplay by DeWitt Bodeen; based on the play by John Van Druten and "Mama's Bank Account," the stories by Kathryn Forbes)

16.
"One of the gentlemen found time to say, 'How delicious!' "

—Jean Adair recalling a victim of her poisoned elderberry wine in Frank Capra's *Arsenic and Old Lace*
(Screenplay by Julius J. Epstein and Philip G. Epstein; based on the play by Joseph Kesselring)

17.
"It was quite quick and painless. He left us with a smile on his lips. His last words were 'No credit.' "

—Peter Ustinov recounting gleefully the death of a young skinflint (John Baer) in Michael Curtiz's *We're No Angels*
(Screenplay by Ranald MacDougall; based on LA CUISINE DES ANGES, a play by Albert Husson, and MY THREE ANGELS, a Broadway adaptation by Bella Spewack and Samuel Spewack)

18.
(a) "I'm sorry, Pepe. He thought you were going to escape."
    (b) "And so I have, my friend."

—(b) Charles Boyer dying in the arms of (a) detective Joseph Calleia in the last lines of John Cromwell's *Algiers*
(Screenplay by John Howard Lawson and James M. Cain; based on PEPE LE MOKO, a novel by Detective Ashelbe)

19.
"Prew, Prew, listen. Fatso done it, Prew. He liked to whack me in the gut. He asks me if it hurts, and I spit at him like always—only yesterday it was bad. He hit me. He hit me. He hit me. I—I hadda get out, Prew. I hadda get out. . . . They—they gonna send you to the stockade, Prew. . . . Watch out for Fatso. Watch out for Fatso. He'll try to crack you, and, if they put you

in the hole, don't yell. Don't make a sound. You'll still be yelling when they come to take you out. Just lay there. Just lay there, and then be quiet, Prew."

—Frank Sinatra telling Montgomery Clift of Ernest Borgnine's brutality in Fred Zinnemann's *From Here to Eternity*
(Screenplay by Daniel Taradash; based on the novel by James Jones)

20.
"Nothing lost, Mr. Christian."

—Dudley Digges dying in Clark Gable's arms in Frank Lloyd's *Mutiny on the Bounty*
(Screenplay by Talbot Jennings, Jules Furthman and Carey Wilson; based on the novel by Charles Nordhoff and James Norman Hall)

21.
"I am commanded by the king to be brief, and, since I am the king's obedient subject, brief I will be. I die His Majesty's good servant but God's first."

—Paul Scofield reaching the executioner's block in Fred Zinnemann's *A Man for All Seasons*
(Screenplay by Robert Bolt; based on his play)

22.
"Is that 'God Save the King' they're playing? Aye, that's nice of them. Stand up, Robbie. Stand up for both of us."

—Charles Coburn making a last request of his great-grandson (Tom Drake) in Victor Saville's *The Green Years*
(Screenplay by Robert Ardrey and Sonya Levien; based on the novel by A. J. Cronin)

23.
"Take off the red shoes."

—Moira Shearer making a last request of Marius Goring in the last line of Michael Powell and Emeric Pressburger's *The Red Shoes*
(Original Screenplay by Emeric Pressburger; additional dialogue by Keith Winter)

24.
"This is where we change cars, Alvin. The end of the line."

—George Tobias, as a subway guard gone to war, dying in Gary Cooper's arms in Howard Hawks's *Sergeant York*
(Original Screenplay by Abem Finkel, Harry Chandlee, Howard Koch and John Huston; based on WAR DIARY OF SERGEANT YORK and SERGEANT YORK AND HIS PEOPLE, two books by Sam K. Cowan, and SERGEANT YORK—LAST OF THE LONG HUNTERS, a book by Tom Skeyhill)

25.

"And don't you go naming my grandson T. C. It's too big a bag for him to carry. He'll have too much to live up to 'cause there'll never be another like me."

—Walter Huston speaking his last words on film as he dies in Barbara Stanwyck's arms in Anthony Mann's *The Furies*
(Screenplay by Charles Schnee; based on the novel by Niven Busch)

30.

"That you, Martha? . . . I don't want to be disturbed."

—Bette Davis dismissing her maid (Virginia Brissac) to die alone in the last lines of Edmund Goulding's *Dark Victory*
(Screenplay by Casey Robinson; based on the play by George Brewer Jr. and Bertram Bloch)

31.

"How strangely awake I feel, as if living had been just a long dream—someone else's dream, now finished at last—and now will begin a dream of my own which will never end. Antony—Antony will wait."

—Elizabeth Taylor gasping her last in Joseph L. Mankiewicz's *Cleopatra*
(Screenplay by Joseph L. Mankiewicz, Ranald MacDougall and Sidney Buchman; based upon histories by Plutarch, Suetonius and Appian and THE LIFE AND TIMES OF CLEOPATRA, a book by C. M. Franzero)

32.

"Don't pass out, Jordan. Think about America. I can't. Think about Madrid. I can't. Think about Maria. I could do that, all right. No, you fool! You weren't kidding Maria about that talk of 'now.' Now they can't stop us ever. She's going on with me! Yes, by damn!"

—Gary Cooper going out in a blaze of machine-gunned glory, thinking of Ingrid Bergman, in the last lines of Sam Wood's *For Whom the Bell Tolls*
(Screenplay by Dudley Nichols; based on the novel by Ernest Hemingway)

33.

(a) "Pancho Villa spoke for the last time. He said, he said—"
    (b) "Hurry, Johnny. Johnny, what—what were my last words?"
    (a) " 'Goodbye, my Mexico,' said Pancho Villa. 'Forgive me for my crimes. Remember, if I sinned against you, it was because I loved you too much.' "
    (b) " 'Forgive me'? Johnny, what I done wrong?"

—(b) Wallace Beery dying, mystified by the obituary ad-libbed by his war-correspondent friend, (a) Stuart Erwin, in the last lines of Jack Conway's *Viva Villa!*
(Screenplay by Ben Hecht; based on the book by Edgcumb Pinchon and O. B. Stade)

ALSO SEE: Applause-2; Cigarette-1; First Lines-2; First Lines-3; Fools-8; Newspapering-10; Plans-2; Smile-7.

EAT

1.

"Honey, don't push your food with your fingers. If you must push with something, the thing to push with is a crust of bread. And chew your food. Animals have secretions in their stomachs which enable them to digest their food without mastication. Human beings must chew their food before they swallow it down. Come on, chew, chew, chew."

—Gertrude Lawrence lecturing her son (Arthur Kennedy) in Irving Rapper's *The Glass Menagerie*
(Screenplay by Tennessee Williams and Peter Berneis; based on the play by Tennessee Williams)

2.

"Now eat your breakfast, and chew each

mouthful 28 times. Not 20, mind you, or 26, but 28 times."

—Clifton Webb lecturing the children in his care (Larry Olsen, Anthony Sydes, and Roddy McCaskill) in Walter Lang's *Sitting Pretty*
(Screenplay by F. Hugh Herbert; based on the novel by Gwen Davenport)

3.
"If you don't care what folks says about this family, I does. I has told you and told you that you can always tell a lady by the way she eats in front of folks like a bird, and I ain't aiming for you to go to Mr. John Wilkes's and eat like a fieldhand and gobble like a hog."

—Hattie McDaniel dispensing eating etiquette to Vivien Leigh in Victor Fleming's *Gone With the Wind*
(Screenplay by Sidney Howard; based on the novel by Margaret Mitchell)

4.
"I eat like a fool—when I'm in love, I mean. My friends used to tell me they couldn't swallow a morsel, but I eat like a fool."

—Lauren Bacall revealing one of love's little side-effects in Vincente Minnelli's *Designing Woman*
(Original Screenplay by George Welles; based on a suggestion by Helen Rose)

5.
(a) "I regret to say there's a certain peculiar oil in bluefish that invariably poisons me—I can't see what's so darned funny about my being poisoned."
  (b) "Aha! Nat, I suspect—plot. This fish looks blue to me. Very blue. In fact, it looks despondent."

—(b) Wallace Beery teasing (a) Lionel Barrymore for an eating idiosyncrasy in Clarence Brown's *Ah, Wilderness!*
(Screenplay by Albert Hackett and Frances Goodrich; based on the play by Eugene O'Neill)
              and (almost verbatim)

—(b) Frank Morgan dittoing (a) Walter Huston in the remake, Rouben Mamoulian's *Summer Holiday*
(Screenplay by Irving Brecher and Jean Holloway;

based on AH, WILDERNESS!, a screenplay by Albert Hackett and Frances Goodrich and play by Eugene O'Neill)

6.
"Who buys Italian meat anyway? You think my wife buys Italian meat? She goes down to A & P, picks up a lamb chop wrapped in cellophane, opens a can of peas—and that's dinner, boy!"

—Jerry Paris working a grievance against his wife (Karen Steele) into his argument with Ernest Borgnine in Delbert Mann's *Marty*
(Screenplay by Paddy Chayefsky; based on his teleplay)

7.
"Well, Tillie, when the hell are we going to get some dinner?"

—Spencer Tracy signaling his maid (Isabel Sanford) to serve supper with his last words on film—and the last in Stanley Kramer's *Guess Who's Coming to Dinner*
(Original Screenplay by William Rose)

ALSO SEE: Actors-6; Advertising Slogans-2; Hunger-7; Manners-4; Never-15.

ELECTRIC CHAIRS

1.
"They got a little blue chair for little boys and a little pink chair for little gals."

—Henry Jones fatally taunting Patty McCormack in Mervyn LeRoy's *The Bad Seed*
(Screenplay by John Lee Mahin; based on the play by Maxwell Anderson and novel by William March)

2.
"It's like sitting in a barber chair. They're going to ask me, 'You got anything to say?' and I say, 'Sure. Give me a haircut, a shave and a massage —one of those nice new electric massages.' "

—James Cagney practicing his defiant last words on priest Pat O'Brien in Michael Curtiz's *Angels With Dirty Faces*

(Screenplay by John Wexley and Warren Duff; based on an original story by Rowland Brown)

ALSO SEE: Coward-1.

ELEPHANTS

1.

"One morning I shot an elephant in my pajamas. How he got into my pajamas I'll never know."

—Groucho Marx giving his African lecture in Victor Heerman's *Animal Crackers*
(Screenplay by Morrie Ryskind; based on the musical play by George S. Kaufman and Morrie Ryskind)

2.

"Dear New York,

We've had a lot of good times together—you and I—but even the best of times must end, so I have gone to face the end alone—like an elephant."

—Carole Lombard's published adieu to Manhattan in William A. Wellman's *Nothing Sacred*
(Screenplay by Ben Hecht; based on "Letter to the Editor," a short story by James H. Street)

3.

"I'm an elephant, Miss Jones. A veritable elephant. I never forget a good deed done me or an ill one. I consider myself a kind of divine justice. Other people in this world have to forget things. I do not."

—Charles Coburn assuring Jean Arthur he won't forget in Sam Wood's *The Devil and Miss Jones*
(Original Screenplay by Norman Krasna)

4.

"Mr. Dodd, when I was a child we had a town idiot. He kept insisting that elephant tusks came from piano keys—but he had nothing on you!"

—Grace Kelly informing William Holden that he has been duped by her husband (Bing Crosby) in George Seaton's *The Country Girl*

(Screenplay by George Seaton; based on the play by Clifford Odets)

ALSO SEE: Dictation-7; Wish-6.

EMPATHY

1.

"I cry all the time. Any little thing. All my brothers, my brothers-in-law—they're—they're always telling me what a good-hearted guy I am."

—Ernest Borgnine showing a tender side to Betsy Blair in Delbert Mann's *Marty*
(Screenplay by Paddy Chayefsky; based on his teleplay)

2.

"Whenever someone else is crying, I've gotta cry, too. I'm sympathetic. I've got too much of a heart."

—Burt Lancaster showing a tender side to Anna Magnani in Daniel Mann's *The Rose Tattoo*
(Screenplay by Tennessee Williams; adaptation by Hal Kanter; based on the play by Tennessee Williams)

3.

"Can't you read what people are in their faces? You think I'm silly that I call him Sir Tristram, but to me he's like one of King Arthur's knights that we used to read about when we were children, who took the vow of chivalry, to battle against all evil-doers, to defend the right and to protect all women, and to be true in friendship and faithful in love."

—Angela Lansbury wildly misreading Hurd Hatfield in Albert Lewin's *The Picture of Dorian Gray*
(Screenplay by Albert Lewin; based on the novel by Oscar Wilde)

4.

"He's sunk so low—he seems to take pleasure in being mean and brutal—and yet he's more myself than I am. Whatever our souls are made of, his and mine are the same—and Linton's is as different as frost from fire. My one thought

in living is Heathcliff. Ellen, I *am* Heathcliff.
Everything he has suffered, I have suffered.
The little happiness he's ever known, I had too.
Oh, Ellen, if everything in the world died and
Heathcliff remained, life would still be full for
me."

—Merle Oberon confessing to Flora Robson an affinity for Laurence Olivier in William Wyler's *Wuthering Heights*
*(Screenplay by Ben Hecht and Charles MacArthur;
based on the novel by Emily Brontë)*
and (similarly)

—Anna Calder-Marshall dittoing to Judy Cornwell in
the remake, Robert Fuest's *Wuthering Heights*
*(Screenplay by Patrick Tilley; based on the novel
by Emily Brontë)*

5.
"I've had hell inside of me, and I can spot it in
others."

—Lee Marvin confessing to Robert Ryan an affinity
for Jeff Bridges in John Frankenheimer's *The Iceman
Cometh*
*(Screenplay based on the play by Eugene O'Neill;
text edited by Thomas Quinn Curtiss)*

6.
"Hate her? I'm *afraid* for her. More and more,
she's the child I was."

—Deborah Kerr confessing to John Mills an affinity
for Hayley Mills in Ronald Neame's *The Chalk Garden*
*(Screenplay by John Michael Hayes; based on the
play by Enid Bagnold)*

7.
"I know it's harder for you. But now I am you
also. If you go, I go, too. That's the only way I
can go. You're me now. Surely, you must feel
that, Maria. Remember last night? Our time is
now, and it'll never end. You're me now, and
I am you. Now do you understand? Now you
are going. And you're going well and fast and
far, and we'll go to America another time,
Maria. Stand up now and go, and we both go.
Stand up, Maria. Remember you're me, too.
You're all there will ever be of me now. Stand

up. No. Stand up. There's no goodbye, Maria,
because we're not apart. Pilar! No, don't turn
around. Go now. Be strong. Take care of our
life."

—Gary Cooper saying good-bye to Ingrid Bergman
in Sam Wood's *For Whom the Bell Tolls*
*(Screenplay by Dudley Nichols; based on the
novel by Ernest Hemingway)*

8.
"I'll be all around in the dark. I'll be ever'-
where—wherever you can look. Wherever
there's a fight so hungry people can eat, I'll be
there. Wherever there's a cop beatin' up a guy,
I'll be there. I'll be in the way guys yell when
they're mad—an' I'll be in the way kids laugh
when they're hungry an' they know supper's
ready. An' when the people are eatin' the stuff
they raise, livin' in the houses they build—I'll
be there, too."

—Henry Fonda saying goodbye to Jane Darwell in
John Ford's *The Grapes of Wrath*
*(Screenplay by Nunnally Johnson; based on the
novel by John Steinbeck)*

ENEMY

1.
"I always choose my friends for their good
looks and my enemies for their good intellects.
Man cannot be too careful in his choice of enemies."

—George Sanders laying down guidelines in Albert
Lewin's *The Picture of Dorian Gray*
*(Screenplay by Albert Lewin; based on the novel
by Oscar Wilde)*

2.
"Now, there's another thing I want you to remember: I don't want to get any messages saying that we're holding our position. We're not
holding anything. We'll let the Hun do that.
We are advancing constantly, and we're not
interested in holding onto anything—except
the enemy. We're going to hold onto him by
the nose, and we're going to kick him in the ass.

We're going to kick the hell out of him all the time, and we're going to go through him like crap through a goose."

—George C. Scott pep-talking to his troops at the outset of Franklin Schaffner's *Patton*
(*Original Screenplay by Francis Ford Coppola and Edmund H. North; based on* PATTON: ORDEAL AND TRIUMPH, *a book by Ladislas Farago, and* A SOLDIER'S STORY, *a book by Omar N. Bradley*)

3.
"When you jumped in here, you were my enemy—and I was afraid of you. But you're just a man like me, and I killed you. Forgive me, comrade. Say that for me. Say you forgive me! Oh, no, you're dead! You're better off than I am —you're through—they can't do any more to you now. Oh, God! why did they do this to us? We only wanted to live, you and I. Why should they send us out to fight each other? If we threw away these rifles and these uniforms, you could be my brother, just like Kate and Albert. You'll have to forgive me, comrade."

—Lew Ayres pleading with the Frenchman he has killed (Raymond Griffith) in Lewis Milestone's *All Quiet on the Western Front*
(*Screenplay by Dell Andrews, Maxwell Anderson and George Abbott; based on the novel by Erich Maria Remarque*)

4.
"I don't know. Sometimes, a dead man can be a terrible enemy."

—Richard Garrick fearing that assassination has made Marlon Brando a myth in Elia Kazan's *Viva Zapata!*
(*Original Screenplay by John Steinbeck*)

5.
"That's one for the book—your book. Only when you write it, they won't believe it. Our enemy, our prisoner of war. Now, we're his prisoners, and he's gauleiter of the boat, singing German lullabies to us while he rows us to his supply ship and a concentration camp. Tell 'em, Willie. Tell 'em how funny it is."

—John Hodiak getting a perverse laugh out of the fact that a German (Walter Slezak) is steering an American lifeboat in Alfred Hitchcock's *Lifeboat*
(*Screenplay by Jo Swerling; based on the story by John Steinbeck*)

ALSO SEE: Duty-1; Friends-8; Friends-10; Land-4; Static-14; Style-1; Time-4.

EPITAPHS

1.
"This here is William James Joad, dyed of a stroke, old, old man. His fokes bured him because they got no money to pay for funerls. Nobody kilt him. Jus a stroke and he dyed."

—Charley Grapewin's grave marker, written by Henry Fonda on the flyleaf of a Bible, in John Ford's *The Grapes of Wrath*
(*Screenplay by Nunnally Johnson; based on the novel by John Steinbeck*)

2.
" 'The Himmler of the Lower Fifth!' I suppose that will become my epitaph."

—Michael Redgrave acknowledging the hatred of his pupils in Anthony Asquith's *The Browning Version*
(*Screenplay by Terence Rattigan; based on his play*)

3.
"Good grief, look at you. Rittenhouse—C. J. Rittenhouse, self-made man. Made of what? As long as you're sitting there thinking up your last will and testament, I'll write your epitaph for you now—Ritt, he quit! That goes for you, too, Narcissus—it's good thing there's room on that chest of yours for another letter—Q for Quitter."

—Tallulah Bankhead defying the defeatism of Henry Hull and John Hodiak in Alfred Hitchcock's *Lifeboat*
(*Screenplay by Jo Swerling; based on the story by John Steinbeck*)

4.
"That's an epitaph for you: 'Here lies Max Monetti. Period.' "

—Susan Hayward telling off Richard Conte in Joseph L. Mankiewicz's *House of Strangers*
(Screenplay by Philip Yordan; based on the novel by Jerome Weidman)

EULOGIES

1.
"Oh no: it wasn't the airplanes. It was beauty killed the beast."

—Robert Armstrong correcting the cause of Kong's death in the last lines of Merian C. Cooper and Ernest B. Schoedsack's *King Kong*
(Screenplay by James Creelman and Ruth Rose; based on an original story by Merian C. Cooper and Edgar Wallace)

2.
"He used to be a big shot."

—Gladys George grieving over a gunned-down James Cagney in the last line of Raoul Walsh's *The Roaring Twenties*
(Screenplay by Richard Macaulay, Jerry Wald and Robert Rossen; based on a story by Mark Hellinger)

3.
"Cody Jarrett. He finally got to the top of the world—and it blew right up in his face."

—Edmond O'Brien summing up James Cagney, who has just gone out rather spectacularly in an oil-tank shootout, in the last lines of Raoul Walsh's *White Heat*
(Screenplay by Ivan Goff and Ben Roberts; based on a story by Virginia Kellogg)

4.
"This guy could have climbed the highest mountain in the world—if he'd just started up the right one."

—Van Heflin grieving over a gunned-down Robert Taylor in Mervyn LeRoy's *Johnny Eager*
(Screenplay by John Lee Mahin and James Edward Grant; based on a story by James Edward Grant)

5.
"O-Lan, you are the earth."

—Paul Muni eulogizing Luise Rainer in the last line of Sidney Franklin's *The Good Earth*
(Screenplay by Talbot Jennings, Tess Slesinger and Claudine West; based on the novel by Pearl S. Buck)

6.
"You are now in heaven and on earth. Your life begins, oh Bernadette."

—Charles Bickford eulogizing Jennifer Jones in the last lines of Henry King's *The Song of Bernadette*
(Screenplay by George Seaton; based on the novel by Franz Werfel)

7.
"What can you say about a 25-year-old girl who died? That she was beautiful. And brilliant. That she loved Mozart and Bach. And the Beatles. And me."

—Ryan O'Neal lamenting the loss of Ali MacGraw in the first lines of Arthur Hiller's *Love Story*
(Original Screenplay by Erich Segal)

8.
"You want a statement from me, huh? All right, I'll give you a statement. He was a champion. He went out like a champion. He was a credit to the fight game to the very end."

—Arthur Kennedy telling the press what they want to hear about his late brother (Kirk Douglas) in the last lines of Mark Robson's *Champion*
(Screenplay by Carl Foreman; based on the short story by Ring Lardner)

9.
"Yes, it was my privilege to know him and to make him known to the world. He was a poet, a scholar and a mighty warrior. . . . He was also the most shameless exhibitionist since Barnum and Bailey."

—Arthur Kennedy offering two views of Peter O'Toole (one a press statement, and the other a personal aside) in David Lean's *Lawrence of Arabia*
(Screenplay by Robert Bolt; based on THE SEVEN PILLARS OF WISDOM, the autobiography of T. E.

Lawrence, and other works by and about T. E. Lawrence)

10.

"Mr. Kane was a man who got everything he wanted, and then lost it. Maybe Rosebud was something he couldn't get or something he lost. Anyway, it wouldn't have explained anything. I don't think any word can explain a man's life. No, I guess Rosebud is just a piece in a jigsaw puzzle—a missing piece."

—William Alland giving up on the mystery of Orson Welles in Orson Welles's *Citizen Kane*
(Original Screenplay by Herman J. Mankiewicz and Orson Welles)

11.

"Attention must finally be paid to such a man! He's not to be allowed to fall into his grave like an old dog. Attention—attention must be paid!"

—Mildred Dunnock demanding respect for Fredric March at his gravesite in Laslo Benedek's *Death of a Salesman*
(Screenplay by Stanley Roberts; based on the play by Arthur Miller)

12.

"A giant once lived in that body, but Matt Brady got lost because he looked for a god too high up and too far away."

—Spencer Tracy analyzing his late legal adversary (Fredric March) in Stanley Kramer's *Inherit the Wind*
(Screenplay by Nathan E. Douglas and Harold Jacob Smith; based on the play by Jerome Lawrence and Robert E. Lee)

13.

"He was a man of many follies, but he was incapable of meanness. He never bargained with God. He did good things because he enjoyed doing them. Oh, do you think that God, Who understood my great-grandfather, might forgive me for having doubted?"

—Tom Drake renewing his faith as he grieves for

Charles Coburn in Victor Saville's *The Green Years*
(Screenplay by Robert Ardrey and Sonya Levien; based on the novel by A. J. Cronin)

14.

"It's true, boys—every word of it. He died like they said. All right, fellas, let's go and say a prayer for a boy who couldn't run as fast as I could."

—Pat O'Brien allowing young toughs to believe the lie that his old friend (James Cagney) died a coward in the electric chair in the last lines of Michael Curtiz's *Angels With Dirty Faces*
(Screenplay by John Wexley and Warren Duff; based on an original story by Rowland Brown)

15.

"I don't suppose that anybody would think that she was a good person. Strangely enough, she was. On the surface, she was all sex and devil-may-care, yet everything in her was struggling toward respectability. She never gave up trying."

—Laurence Harvey grieving to his wife (Dina Merrill) about his mistress (Elizabeth Taylor) in Daniel Mann's *Butterfield 8*
(Screenplay by Charles Schnee and John Michael Hayes; based on the novel by John O'Hara)

16.

"You look ridiculous in that makeup. Like the caricature of a whore. A little touch of Mommy in the night. Fake Ophelia drowned in a bathtub. I wish you could see yourself. You'd really laugh. You're your mother's masterpiece."

—Marlon Brando addressing the corpse of his suicide-victim wife (Veronica Lazare) in Bernardo Bertolucci's *Last Tango in Paris*
(Original Screenplay by Bernardo Bertolucci and Franco Arcalli)

17.

"It looks like our ancient mariner may have taken a little spill."

—Gig Young covering for Red Buttons' fatal heart attack on the dancefloor in Sydney Pollack's *They Shoot Horses, Don't They?*

18.

"There's very little of importance that anyone can say at a time like this, but I feel that we're burying more than a man. We are burying a phase of American life. In this day of automobiles and airplanes and more conveniences, many of us have forgotten the horse and what he has meant to America. Not so with Peter Goodwin. He loved his horses passionately, with a lifelong devotion, and it was his great privilege—one which all men may envy—to die at the moment of his greatest triumph, with the colors of his beloved Elm Tree once more riding to victory in a Kentucky Derby. I knew him but slightly, but of him I knew much and nothing that did not do him honor. Proud, loyal, jealous of his name and heritage, Peter Goodwin was indeed the grand old man of the American turf."

—Moroni Olsen giving Walter Brennan a grand send-off in the last lines of David Butler's *Kentucky* (*Screenplay by Lamar Trotti and John Taintor Foote; based on THE LOOK OF EAGLES, a novel by John Taintor Foote*)

19.

"He was a natural-born world-shaker."

—George Kennedy praising Paul Newman in the last line of Stuart Rosenberg's *Cool Hand Luke* (*Screenplay by Donn Pearce and Frank Pierson; based on the novel by Donn Pearce*)

20.

"I just want to say that I'm glad that at least before the end he found out what it was like to be a man. The short happy life of Francis Macomber."

—Gregory Peck giving Robert Preston credit for courage in Zoltan Korda's *The Macomber Affair* (*Screenplay by Casey Robinson and Seymour Bennett; adaptation by Seymour Bennett and Frank Arnold; based on "The Short Happy Life of Francis Macomber," a short story by Ernest Hemingway*)

21.

"He was some kind of man. What does it matter what you say about someone?"

—Marlene Dietrich shrugging off a short-and-sweet eulogy for Orson Welles in the last lines of Orson Welles's *Touch of Evil* (*Screenplay by Orson Welles; based on BADGE OF EVIL, a novel by Whit Masterson*)

ALSO SEE: Army-3; Tears-1; Tears-2.

EXCHANGES

1.

(a) "Listen. It's so simple, too. Two fellows meet accidentally, like you and me. No connection between them at all, never saw each other before. Each one has somebody that he'd like to get rid of. So, they swap murders."

(b) "Swap murders?"

(a) "Each fellow does the other fellow's murder. Then, there's nothing to connect them. Each one has murdered a total stranger—like you do my murder, I do yours."

(b) "We're coming into my station."

(a) "For example: your wife, my father. Criss-cross."

—(a) Robert Walker springing his murder scheme on (b) Farley Granger in Alfred Hitchcock's *Strangers on a Train* (*Screenplay by Raymond Chandler and Czenzi Ormonde; adaptation by Whitfield Cook; based on the novel by Patricia Highsmith*)

2.

"One Rocco more or less isn't worth dying for."

—Humphrey Bogart passing on a chance to stand up to Edward G. Robinson in John Huston's *Key Largo* (*Screenplay by Richard Brooks and John Huston; based on the play by Maxwell Anderson*)

3.

"We shot our way out of that town for a dollar's worth of steel holes."

—Strother Martin grousing over a robbery of washers in Sam Peckinpah's *The Wild Bunch* (*Screenplay by Walon Green and Sam Peckinpah; based on a story by Walon Green and Roy N. Sickner*)

4.

"Burn a city in order to create an epic? That's carrying the principle of art for art's sake too far."

—Leo Genn trying to steer Nero (Peter Ustinov) to a more constructive form of songwriting inspiration in Mervyn LeRoy's *Quo Vadis*
(Screenplay by John Lee Mahin, S. N. Behrman and Sonya Levien; based on the novel by Henryk Sienkiewicz)

5.

"Reno's full of women who have their pride, sweetheart—a pretty chilly exchange for the guy you're stuck on."

—Paulette Goddard advising Joan Fontaine to forget pride in George Cukor's *The Women*
(Screenplay by Anita Loos and Jane Murfin; based on the play by Clare Boothe)

6.

"Yes, dear, I know. Now I've got my self-respect—and no husband."

—Mary Nash cheerlessly answering Katharine Hepburn in George Cukor's *The Philadelphia Story*
(Screenplay by Donald Ogden Stewart; based on the play by Philip Barry)
                    and (almost verbatim)

—Margalo Gillmore dittoing Grace Kelly in the remake, Charles Walters's *High Society*
(Screenplay by John Patrick; based on THE PHILADELPHIA STORY, a screenplay by Donald Ogden Stewart and play by Philip Barry)

7.

"Piece by piece, our improvident grandfathers exchanged the land for their epic debauches, to put it mildly, till finally all that was left—and Stella can verify that!—was the house itself and about 20 acres of ground, including a graveyard, to which now all but Stella and I have retreated."

—Vivien Leigh telling her brother-in-law (Marlon Brando) what became of the family estate in Elia Kazan's *A Streetcar Named Desire*
(Screenplay by Tennessee Williams; adaptation by Oscar Saul; based on the play by Tennessee Williams)

8.

"I haven't got the price. Around here, love has a very low cash-surrender value."

—Jan Sterling passing on love in Joseph Pevney's *Female on the Beach*
(Screenplay by Robert Hill and Richard Alan Simmons; based on THE BESIEGED HEART, a play by Robert Hill)

9.

"Once, I told you, if you get what you want, you have to give your heart in exchange, and you said you'd be willing. Remember?"

—May Robson reminding Janet Gaynor in William A. Wellman's *A Star Is Born*
(Screenplay by Dorothy Parker, Alan Campbell and Robert Carson; based on an original story by William A. Wellman and Robert Carson)

10.

"Oh, Cathy, I never broke your heart! You broke it. Cathy, Cathy, you loved me. What right to throw love away for the poor fancy thing you felt for him, for a handful of worldliness? Misery and death and all the evils that God and man could have hammered down would never have parted us. You did that alone. You wandered off like a wanton greedy child to break your heart and mine."

—Laurence Olivier accusing Merle Oberon of selling their love short in William Wyler's *Wuthering Heights*
(Screenplay by Ben Hecht and Charles MacArthur; based on the novel by Emily Brontë)
                    and (similarly)

—Timothy Dalton dittoing Anna Calder-Marshall in the remake, Robert Fuest's *Wuthering Heights*
(Screenplay by Patrick Tilley; based on the novel by Emily Brontë)

(Screenplay by Lamar Trotti; based on the novel by W. Somerset Maugham)

12.
"What's the beef, boys? So I'm trading. Everybody here is trading. So maybe I trade a little sharper. Does that make me a collaborator?"

—William Holden confronting his hostile barracks-buddies in Billy Wilder's *Stalag 17*
(Screenplay by Billy Wilder and Edwin Blum; based on the play by Donald Bevan and Edmund Trzcinski)

13.
"Veda, does a new house mean so much to you that you would trade me for it?"

—Joan Crawford asking a question she doesn't want to hear Ann Blyth answer in Michael Curtiz's *Mildred Pierce*
(Screenplay by Ranald MacDougall; based on the novel by James M. Cain)

14.
"Yes, Jim, Jonathan sure destroyed you. You came out of it with nothing—nothing but a Pulitzer Prize novel and the highest salary of any writer in Hollywood. Look, folks, you've got to give the devil his due. We all owe him something, and you know it, and you've had plenty of years to think it over."

—Walter Pidgeon trying to talk Dick Powell, Barry Sullivan, and Lana Turner into working for Kirk Douglas again in Vincente Minnelli's *The Bad and the Beautiful*
(Screenplay by Charles Schnee; based on "Memorial to a Bad Man" and "Of Good and Evil," two short stories by George Bradshaw)

15.
"You pay your way through life as though every relationship was a tollbooth. Every time you go someplace, you bring something."

—Sylvia Sidney criticizing the empty generosity of her daughter (Joanne Woodward) in Gilbert Cates's *Summer Wishes, Winter Dreams*
(Original Screenplay by Stewart Stern)

16.
"I'm not kind. I'm just tempting you. I never give anything without expecting something in return. Now, I always get paid."

—Clark Gable leveling with Vivien Leigh in Victor Fleming's *Gone With the Wind*
(Screenplay by Sidney Howard; based on the novel by Margaret Mitchell)

17.
"We suffer for what the gods give us, and I'm afraid Dorian Gray will pay for his good looks."

—Lowell Gilmore making an unhappily accurate prediction in Albert Lewin's *The Picture of Dorian Gray*
(Screenplay by Albert Lewin; based on the novel by Oscar Wilde)

ALSO SEE: Adolescence-3; Apathy-1; First Lines-5; Hanging-4; Heart-23; History-6; Life and Death-8; Loneliness-2; Mistakes-4; Parting Shots-3; Party-7; Progress-2; Theater-3; Toasts-6.

EXCUSES

1.
"You know, one's awfully apt to try and excuse one's self sometimes by saying, 'Well, what I do doesn't do anybody else any harm.' But one does, you see. It's not a thought I like very much."

—David Niven sharing an unhappy thought with Wendy Hiller in Delbert Mann's *Separate Tables*
(Screenplay by Terence Rattigan and John Gay; based on the play by Terence Rattigan)

2.
"Mr. Norman Maine, America's Prince Charming, was apprehended driving an ambulance down Wilshire Boulevard—with the siren going full blast. He explained that he was a tree surgeon on a maternity case."

—Lionel Stander telling his studio boss (Adolphe Menjou) about Fredric March's latest alcoholic escapade in William A. Wellman's *A Star Is Born*
(Screenplay by Dorothy Parker, Alan Campbell and Robert Carson; based on an original story by William A. Wellman and Robert Carson)

3.

(a) "John, where did you learn so much about women's clothes?"

(b) "My mother wore women's clothes."

—(b) John Lund concealing his Romeo past from (a) Jean Arthur in Billy Wilder's *A Foreign Affair* *(Screenplay by Charles Brackett, Billy Wilder and Richard L. Breen; adaptation by Robert Harari; based on an original story by David Shaw)*

4.

"Well, now if you're going to shoot me, at—at least be honest about it. You don't give a hoot about Carol and you never have. I'd rather be shot by a jealous woman than a noble one anyway. Now, don't you think we should sit down quietly and think up a little better reason for you to shoot me than that?"

—Van Heflin trying to reason with a pistol-packing Joan Crawford in Curtis Bernhardt's *Possessed* *(Screenplay by Sylvia Richards and Ranald MacDougall; based on ONE MAN'S SECRET, a novelette by Rita Weiman)*

5.

"Politics is a very peculiar thing, Woodrow. If they want you, they want you. They don't need reasons anymore. They find their own reasons. It's just like when a girl wants a man."

—Harry Hayden explaining politics to Eddie Bracken in Preston Sturges's *Hail the Conquering Hero* *(Original Screenplay by Preston Sturges)*

6.

"No, I—I don't have the sentiment on my side. You've got to have a sentimental reason for them to vote for you. Any decent actress can give a good performance, but a dying husband —that would have insured everything!"

—Maggie Smith suggesting lightly to her spouse (Michael Caine) that a husband-sacrifice might improve her Oscar chances in Herbert Ross's *California Suite* *(Screenplay by Neil Simon; based on his play)*

7.

"You will not make me a plank for your politics. I will not be the excuse for any strike."

—Donald Crisp arguing with his mining sons in John Ford's *How Green Was My Valley* *(Screenplay by Philip Dunne; based on the novel by Richard Llewellyn)*

ALSO SEE: Fear-6; Pittsburgh-1; Pittsburgh-2; Water-4.

EYES

1.

"Life with Mary was like being in a phone booth with an open umbrella. No matter which way you turned, you got it in the eye."

—Barry Nelson describing marriage with Debbie Reynolds in Mervyn LeRoy's *Mary, Mary* *(Screenplay by Richard L. Breen; based on the play by Jean Kerr)*

2.

"You're right, of course. I have only one eye. One hot day in August, when Terry was a little boy, he crept into Henry's bedroom and took Henry's air pistol. He ran up to me in the garden. He was so excited that he pressed the trigger with both his little hands. He shouted, 'Bang, you're dead, Mummy!' And he laughed and laughed until he saw the blood spurting out."

—Bette Davis recounting a family tragedy in Roy Ward Baker's *The Anniversary* *(Screenplay by Jimmy Sangster; based on the play by Bill MacIlwraith)*

3.

"All I said was that our son—the apple of our three eyes, Martha being a cyclops—our son is a beanbag."

—Richard Burton discussing his offspring with George Segal in Mike Nichols's *Who's Afraid of Virginia Woolf?* *(Screenplay by Ernest Lehman; based on the play by Edward Albee)*

4.

"She looks like Veronica Lake with two eyes."

—Bob Hope doing a quip characterization in Sidney Lanfield's *Let's Face It*

(Screenplay by Harry Tugend; based on the musical play by Dorothy Fields and Herbert Fields and suggested by the play by Norma Mitchell and Russell G. Medcraft)

5.
(a) "Most girls would give their eyes for a chance to see Monte."
(b) "Wouldn't that rather defeat the purpose?"

—(b) Laurence Olivier challenging the Monte Carlo generalities of (a) Florence Bates in Alfred Hitchcock's *Rebecca*
(Screenplay by Robert E. Sherwood and Joan Harrison; adaptation by Philip MacDonald and Michael Hogan; based on the novel by Daphne du Maurier)

6.
"You see, Ralls, I'm not one of those eye-for-an-eye men. I always take two eyes."

—Luther Adler threatening John Wayne in Edward Ludwig's *Wake of the Red Witch*
(Screenplay by Harry Brown and Kenneth Gamet; based on the novel by Garland Roark)

7.
"Your left eye says yes, and your right eye says no. Fifi, you're cockeyed!"

—Maurice Chevalier getting a double message from Jeanette MacDonald in Ernst Lubitsch's *The Merry Widow*
(Screenplay by Ernest Vajda and Samson Raphaelson; based on Franz Lehar's operetta, libretto by Victor Leon and Leo Stern)

8.
(a) "That color looks wonderful with your eyes."
(b) "Just my right eye. I hate what it does to the left."

—(b) Barbra Streisand qualifying the compliment of (a) Omar Sharif in William Wyler's *Funny Girl*
(Screenplay by Isobel Lennart; based on her musical play)

9.
"Look, when I came here, my eyes were big blue question marks. Now they're big green dollar marks."

—Jean Arthur allowing a loss of idealism along the way in Frank Capra's *Mr. Smith Goes to Washington*
(Screenplay by Sidney Buchman; based on "The Gentleman From Montana," a story by Lewis R. Foster)

10.
"The whites of your eyes are clear. Your cornea is excellent."

—Greta Garbo doing a rather clinical love-scene with Melvyn Douglas in Ernst Lubitsch's *Ninotchka*
(Screenplay by Charles Brackett, Billy Wilder and Walter Reisch; based on an original story by Melchior Lengyel)

11.
"You're a real beautiful woman. It's almost kind of an honor sitting next to you. You just shine in my eyes. That's my true feeling, Roslyn. What makes you so sad? I think you're the saddest girl I ever met."

—Clark Gable complimenting Marilyn Monroe in John Huston's *The Misfits*
(Screenplay by Arthur Miller; based on his story)

12.
"Your eyes! Your eyes! They shine like the pants of a blue serge suit."

—Groucho Marx attempting to compliment Margaret Dumont in Joseph Santley and Robert Florey's *The Cocoanuts*
(Screenplay by Morrie Ryskind; based on the musical play by George S. Kaufman and Morrie Ryskind)

13.
"She's got those eyes that run up and down men like a searchlight."

—Dennie Moore characterizing Joan Crawford in George Cukor's *The Women*
(Screenplay by Anita Loos and Jane Murfin; based on the play by Clare Boothe)

14.
"If I see your eyes, I might forget to be a king."

—Ronald Colman romancing Madeleine Carroll in John Cromwell's *The Prisoner of Zenda* *(Screenplay by Donald Ogden Stewart, John L. Balderston and Wells Root; based on the novel by Anthony Hope)*

15.

"I'm going to hit you hard for trying to sell a man who's on the run. . . . I'm going to hit you hard unless . . . unless you bring him here for me to paint. . . . There'll be something, something in his eyes."

—Robert Newton explaining his interest in fugitive James Mason in Carol Reed's *Odd Man Out* *(Screenplay by F. L. Green and R. C. Sherriff; based on the novel by F. L. Green)*

16.

"Hello, Lily. Gee, you're a sight for sore eyes. And you don't know how sore your eyes can get looking at Waterbury."

—Wallace Beery greeting Aline MacMahon in Clarence Brown's *Ah, Wilderness!* *(Screenplay by Albert Hackett and Frances Goodrich; based on the play by Eugene O'Neill)*

17.

"They get those weak eyes from reading, you know—those long tiny little columns in *The Wall Street Journal*."

—Marilyn Monroe explaining to Tony Curtis her attraction to men who wear glasses in Billy Wilder's *Some Like It Hot* *(Screenplay by Billy Wilder and I. A. L. Diamond; suggested by a story by R. Thoeren and M. Logan)*

18.

"Listen, girl, I can count the great horses I ever saw on the fingers of one hand, and every one of 'em had a look in his eyes—like an eagle. You can't beat a horse with that look. You just can't beat him. And this colt's got it—*the look of eagles!*"

—Walter Brennan tipping the secret of his Derby success to Loretta Young in David Butler's *Kentucky* *(Screenplay by Lamar Trotti and John Taintor Foote; based on THE LOOK OF EAGLES, a novel by John Taintor Foote)*

FACES

1.

"Still wonderful, isn't it? And no dialogue. We didn't need dialogue. We had *faces*. There just aren't any faces like that anymore. Maybe one. Garbo."

—Gloria Swanson going mad on her old movies in Billy Wilder's *Sunset Boulevard* *(Original Screenplay by Charles Brackett, Billy Wilder and D. M. Marshman Jr.)*

2.

"The arrangement of your features is not entirely repulsive to me."

—Cyd Charisse coldly complimenting Fred Astaire in Rouben Mamoulian's *Silk Stockings* *(Screenplay by Leonard Gershe and Leonard Spigelgass; based on the musical play by George S. Kaufman, Leueen MacGrath and Abe Burrows and NINOTCHKA, a screenplay by Charles Brackett, Billy Wilder and Walter Reisch and original story by Melchior Lengyel)*

3.

"McPherson, if you know anything about faces, look at mine. How singularly innocent I look this morning! Have you ever seen such candid eyes?"

—Clifton Webb mustering a pose of innocence for detective Dana Andrews in Otto Preminger's *Laura* *(Screenplay by Jay Dratler, Samuel Hoffenstein and Betty Reinhardt; based on the novel by Vera Caspary)*

4.

"Intellect destroys the beauty in any face."

—George Sanders voting for the superficial in Albert Lewin's *The Picture of Dorian Gray*

(Screenplay by Albert Lewin; based on the novel by Oscar Wilde)

5.
"It's not a pretty face, I grant you, but underneath its flabby exterior is an enormous lack of character."

—Oscar Levant introducing himself at the outset of Vincente Minnelli's *An American in Paris*
(Original Screenplay by Alan Jay Lerner)

6.
"You see her face? A real honest face. Only disgusting thing about her."

—Spencer Tracy sizing up Katharine Hepburn in George Cukor's *Pat and Mike*
(Original Screenplay by Ruth Gordon and Garson Kanin)

7.
"You got a real nice face, you know. Really a nice face."

—Ernest Borgnine complimenting Betsy Blair in Delbert Mann's *Marty*
(Screenplay by Paddy Chayefsky; based on his teleplay)

8.
"Not a beautiful face, but a good face. She's got a face like a Sunday School picnic. You have any idea what kind of face that is, Nulty?"

—Dick Powell describing Anne Shirley to detective Paul Phillips in Edward Dmytryk's *Murder, My Sweet*
(Screenplay by John Paxton; based on FAREWELL, MY LOVELY, a novel by Raymond Chandler)

9.
"I've got a long face, and I poke it where I please. You may think I'm a nuisance."

—Edna May Oliver leveling with Henry Fonda in John Ford's *Drums Along the Mohawk*
(Screenplay by Lamar Trotti and Sonya Levien; based on the novel by Walter D. Edmonds)

10.
"I've got to do something about the way I look.

I mean, a girl just can't go to Sing Sing with a green face."

—Audrey Hepburn fussing over her appearance in Blake Edwards's *Breakfast at Tiffany's*
(Screenplay by George Axelrod; based on the novella by Truman Capote)

11.
"I don't like his face or any part of him. He looks like a Bulgarian bald eagle mourning its first-born."

—Ned Sparks characterizing Guy Kibbee in Lloyd Bacon's *42nd Street*
(Screenplay by Rian James and James Seymour; based on the novel by Bradford Ropes)

ALSO SEE: Aging-7; Aging-8; Betrayal-3; Chin-1; Clean-2; Dogs-5; Empathy-3; Feelings-2; Fools-3; Friends-6; Greed-4; Heart-12; Heaven-5; Looks-1; Memory-7; Selfish-6; Smell-2; Smile-7; Smile-8; Tact-2; Ugly-3; Wealth-6.

FAILURE

1.
"You know, Arnold, you have many successful clients. With all these successful people around, where are all of our new young failures going to come from?"

—Jason Robards rattling his agent-brother (Martin Balsam) with illogic in Fred Coe's *A Thousand Clowns*
(Screenplay by Herb Gardner; based on his play)

2.
"What we've got here is failure to communicate."

—Strother Martin applying brute force to bring Paul Newman in line in Stuart Rosenberg's *Cool Hand Luke*
(Screenplay by Donn Pearce and Frank Pierson; based on the novel by Donn Pearce)

3.
"Failure is a highly contagious disease."

—Paul Newman explaining his run of bad luck to
Shirley Knight in Richard Brooks's *Sweet Bird of
Youth*
*(Screenplay by Richard Brooks; based on the play
by Tennessee Williams)*

4.
"Bloom, look at me. Look at me, Bloom. Bloom,
I'm drowning. Other men have sailed through
life. Bialystock has struck a reef. Bloom, I'm
going under. I'm being sunk by a society that
demands success when all I can offer is failure.
Bloom, I'm reaching out to you. Don't send me
to prison. HELP!"

—Zero Mostel pleading with Gene Wilder in Mel
Brooks's *The Producers*
(Original Screenplay by Mel Brooks)

5.
"They can get awful bent out of shape sometimes, can't they? You know, my wife was so
twisted she once said to me, 'I hope your next
play's a flop—so the whole world can see how
much I love you, even though you're a failure.'"

—William Holden dredging up his own marital hor-
ror-story to console Bing Crosby in George Seaton's
The Country Girl
*(Screenplay by George Seaton; based on the play
by Clifford Odets)*

6.
"You're all flops. I am the Earth Mother, and
you are all flops."

—Elizabeth Taylor berating men generally and
George Segal specifically in Mike Nichols's *Who's
Afraid of Virginia Woolf?*
*(Screenplay by Ernest Lehman; based on the play
by Edward Albee)*

ALSO SEE: Football-1; Letters-9; Love-26; Soul-
11; Success-3.

FAITH

1.
"You don't even know what faith is. Well, I'm
gonna tell you. It's believing you see white
when your eyes tell you black. It's knowing
with your heart."

—Burt Lancaster defining the word for a disbelieving Katharine Hepburn in Joseph Anthony's *The
Rainmaker*
*(Screenplay by N. Richard Nash; based on his
play)*

2.
"You've got no faith in Johnny, have you, Julia?
His little dream may fall flat, you think. Well,
so it may! What if it should? There'll be another. Oh, I've got all the faith in the world in
Johnny. Whatever he does is all right with me.
If he wants to dream for a while, he can dream
for a while. And if he wants to come back and
sell peanuts—oh, how I'll believe in those peanuts!"

—Katharine Hepburn racing after her sister's former
fiancé (Cary Grant) in George Cukor's *Holiday*
*(Screenplay by Donald Ogden Stewart and Sidney
Buchman; based on the play by Philip Barry)*
and (almost verbatim)

—Ann Harding dittoing after Robert Ames in the
original, Edward H. Griffith's *Holiday*
*(Screenplay by Horace Jackson; based on the play
by Philip Barry)*

3.
"Faith is believing in things when common
sense tells you not to."

—Maureen O'Hara defining the word for her daughter (Natalie Wood) in George Seaton's *Miracle on
34th Street*
*(Screenplay by George Seaton; based on an
original story by Valentine Davis)*

ALSO SEE: Boredom-3; Goodbyes-6; Progress-2;
Vanity-1.

FAKE

1.

"Fake! It's a phony! It—it's lead! It's lead! It's a fake!"

—Sydney Greenstreet discovering an imitation of the title objet d'art in John Huston's *The Maltese Falcon*
(Screenplay by John Huston; based on the novel by Dashiell Hammett)

2.

"She's a phony, but she's a *real* phony. Know what I mean, kid?"

—Martin Balsam characterizing Audrey Hepburn to George Peppard in Blake Edwards's *Breakfast at Tiffany's*
(Screenplay by George Axelrod; based on the novella by Truman Capote)

3.

"You been stomping around here in those boots like you owned the place, thinking every woman you saw was going to fall madly in love. Well, here's one woman didn't pay you any mind. Bragging about your father. I bet he wasn't any better than you are. Strutting around here like some crummy Apollo. You think just because you act young that you can come in here and make off with whoever you like. Well, let me tell you something: you're a fake. You're no jive kid. You're just scared to act your age. Buy yourself a mirror sometime and take a look at it. Within a year from now, you'll be counting the gray hairs if you got any left. What'll become of you then? You'll end your life in the gutter, and it'll serve you right. The gutter's where you came from, and the gutter's where you belong."

—Rosalind Russell overkilling William Holden in Joshua Logan's *Picnic*
(Screenplay by Daniel Taradash; based on the play by William Inge)

4.

"I'll tell the world who's a fake! You are! I taught you everything you know. Even your name, Lily Garland—I gave you that. If there's a justice in heaven, Mildred Plotka, you will end up where you belong: in the burlesque house."

—John Barrymore reminding a raging Carole Lombard of her origins in Howard Hawks's *Twentieth Century*
(Screenplay by Ben Hecht and Charles MacArthur; based on their play and NAPOLEON OF BROADWAY, a play by Charles Bruce Milholland)

5.

"Oh, we're both fakers. Isn't faking the essence of acting?"

—Katharine Hepburn leveling with her producer-to-be (Adolphe Menjou) in Gregory La Cava's *Stage Door*
(Screenplay by Morrie Ryskind and Anthony Veiller; based on the play by Edna Ferber and George S. Kaufman)

ALSO SEE: Love-26.

FASHION

1.

"If I live to be 100, I shall never understand how any young man could come to Paris without evening clothes."

—Clifton Webb accenting the frivolous in Edmund Goulding's *The Razor's Edge*
(Screenplay by Lamar Trotti; based on the novel by W. Somerset Maugham)

2.

(a) "They tell me in Paris, if you don't buy your gown from Roberta, you're not dressed at all."

(b) "I see: nude if you don't, and nude if you do."

—(a) Randolph Scott and (b) Fred Astaire dress-shop-talking in William A. Seiter's *Roberta*
(Screenplay by Jane Murfin and Sam Mintz; additional dialogue by Glenn Tryon and Allan Scott; based on the musical play by Jerome Kern and Otto Harbach and GOWNS BY ROBERTA, a novel by Alice Duer Miller)

3.

"Max Bialystock, king of Broadway! Six shows running at once! Lunch at Delmonico's! Two hundred dollar suits! You see this? This once held a pearl as big as your eye! Look at me now! Look at me now! I'm wearing a cardboard belt."

—Zero Mostel bemoaning his bad times in Mel Brooks's *The Producers*
(*Original Screenplay by Mel Brooks*)

4.

"Oh, why not? You may as well go to perdition in ermine. You're sure to come back in rags."

—Katharine Hepburn lending her ermine to Ginger Rogers for a late-night date in Gregory La Cava's *Stage Door*
(*Screenplay by Morrie Ryskind and Anthony Veiller; based on the play by Edna Ferber and George S. Kaufman*)

5.

"You underrate us, Mr. Wickham. Meryton is abreast of everything—everything except insolence and bad manners. Those London fashions we do not admire!"

—Greer Garson defending her small town to Edward Ashley in Robert Z. Leonard's *Pride and Prejudice*
(*Screenplay by Aldous Huxley and Jane Murfin; based on the play by Helen Jerome and novel by Jane Austen*)

ALSO SEE: Sin-4.

FAT

1.

"You and I have a tendency towards corpulence. Corpulence makes a man reasonable, pleasant and phlegmatic. Have you noticed that the nastiest of talents are invariably thin?"

—Charles Laughton commiserating with Peter Ustinov in Stanley Kubrick's *Spartacus*
(*Screenplay by Dalton Trumbo; based on the novel by Howard Fast*)

2.

"Well, come see a fat old man sometime!"

—John Wayne saying goodbye to Kim Darby in the last line of Henry Hathaway's *True Grit*
(*Screenplay by Marguerite Roberts; based on the novel by Charles Portis*)

ALSO SEE: Beautiful-4; Names-26; Remember-6; Talk-3; Ugly-1; Water-7.

FATHERS

1.

"Everything I ever learnt as a small boy came from my father, and I never found anything he ever told me to be wrong or worthless. The simple lessons he taught me are as sharp and clear in my mind as if I'd heard them only yesterday."

—Irving Pichel, as the never-seen narrator (a grown-up version of Roddy McDowall), characterizing Donald Crisp in John Ford's *How Green Was My Valley*
(*Screenplay by Philip Dunne; based on the novel by Richard Llewellyn*)

2.

"My old man spent fourteen hours a day down in that subway. They had to bury him with gloves on."

—Dustin Hoffman telling Jon Voight a family secret in John Schlesinger's *Midnight Cowboy*
(*Screenplay by Waldo Salt; based on the novel by James Leo Herlihy*)

3.

"The letter said: 'Daughter, Read First Kings, Chapter 21, Verse 23.' I looked it up. It said, 'And the dogs of the street shall eat Jezebel.' My old man and his Bible! Tell me, how is it that some people can only find hate in the Bible?"

—Shirley Jones telling Burt Lancaster about her unforgiving father in Richard Brooks's *Elmer Gantry*
(*Screenplay by Richard Brooks; based on the novel by Sinclair Lewis*)

4.

"When I was four years old, my old man ran away. Well, my mother couldn't keep me and Connie both, so I went to the orphanage until I was old enough to go to work. I used to dream about getting rich someday—rich enough to hire a detective to find my father—and—and then I was going to beat his head off. You know, kid stuff."

—Kirk Douglas unburdening some early bitterness in Mark Robson's *Champion*
(Screenplay by Carl Foreman; based on the short story by Ring Lardner)

5.

"Oh, yes. There was also the ever-present smile of my father. He was a telephone man who fell in love with long distance. The last we heard from him was a postcard containing two words —'Hello-Goodbye'—and no address."

—Arthur Kennedy commenting on a photograph of his long-departed father in Irving Rapper's *The Glass Menagerie*
(Screenplay by Tennessee Williams and Peter Berneis; based on the play by Tennessee Williams)

6.

"Old Daddy loved killing Indians. He didn't consider his day complete unless at least one redskin bit the dust. Some of those dopey-looking Indians bit so much dust they had to brush their teeth with a whisk broom."

—Bob Hope letting out a lot of hot air about his Indian-fighting father in Frank Tashlin's *Son of Paleface*
(Original Screenplay by Frank Tashlin, Robert L. Welch and Joseph Quillan)

7.

" 'Anything further, Father?' That can't be right. Isn't it 'Anything farther, further?' The idea! I married your mother because I wanted children. Imagine my disappointment when you arrived!"

—Groucho Marx berating his offspring (Zeppo Marx) in Norman McLeod's *Horse Feathers*
(Screenplay by Bert Kalmar, Harry Ruby, S. J. Perelman and Will B. Johnstone)

8.

"Can't you understand? I never wanted your place or your money. I don't wanna hold anything. All I wanted was a father, not a boss. I wanted you to love me."

—Paul Newman confronting Burl Ives in Richard Brooks's *Cat on a Hot Tin Roof*
(Screenplay by Richard Brooks and James Poe; based on the play by Tennessee Williams)

9.

"He was a sergeant—acting sergeant—acting unpaid sergeant, and do you know what he'd say to me? He'd say, 'Arthur'—he called me Arthur—'Arthur, you are a carbuncle on the behind of humanity.' Carbuncle! I'm a nothing! I'm a nobody!"

—Peter Ustinov learning his self-worth at home in Jules Dassin's *Topkapi*
(Screenplay by Monja Danischewsky; based on THE LIGHT OF DAY, a novel by Eric Ambler)

ALSO SEE: Big-3; Dreams-7; Fidelity-1; Fights-7; Free-2; Illusions-3; Life and Death-19; Life and Death-20; Macho-3; Men-11; Mind-10; Mothers-4; Names-16; Oops!-2; Pretense-1; Questions-4; Secrets-4; Smell-2; Strangers-5; Time-12; Truth-5.

FEAR

1.

"Scared? Me? I'm shaking so hard the water on my knee just splashed."

—Bob Hope admitting a yellow streak in George Marshall's *The Ghost Breakers*
(Screenplay by Walter De Leon; based on THE GHOST BREAKER, a play by Paul Dickey and Charles W. Goddard)

2.

"I get goose pimples. Even my goose pimples have goose pimples."

—Bob Hope admitting a yellow streak—with complications, in Elliott Nugent's *The Cat and the Canary*

(Screenplay by Walter De Leon and Lynn Starling; based on the play by John Willard)

3.

"You too? The ladies of Rome seem to have caught each other's fears this morning, like a head cold. Calpurnia actually pleaded with me not to go to the Senate at all."

—Rex Harrison ignoring Elizabeth Taylor's warning in Joseph L. Mankiewicz's *Cleopatra*
(Screenplay by Joseph L. Mankiewicz, Ranald MacDougall and Sidney Buchman; based upon histories by Plutarch, Suetonius and Appian and THE LIFE AND TIMES OF CLEOPATRA, a book by C. M. Franzero)

4.

"I cough only because I'm a little frightened."

—Ingrid Bergman making the admission that wins her royalty recognition from Helen Hayes in Anatole Litvak's *Anastasia*
(Screenplay by Arthur Laurents; based on the play by Marcelle Maurette and Broadway adaptation by Guy Bolton)

5.

"Do you know what's wrong with you, Miss Whoever-You-Are? You're chicken. You got no guts. You're afraid to stick out your chin and say, 'Okay, life's a fact. People do fall in love. People do belong to each other because that's the only chance anybody's got for real happiness.' You call yourself a free spirit, a wild thing, and you're terrified somebody's going to stick you in a cage. Well, baby, you're already in that cage. You built it yourself, and it's not bound on the west by Tulip, Texas, or on the east by Somaliland. It's wherever you go because no matter where you run you just end up running into yourself."

—George Peppard telling off Audrey Hepburn in Blake Edwards's *Breakfast at Tiffany's*
(Screenplay by George Axelrod; based on the novella by Truman Capote)

6.

"Well, let me tell you, Clara. I think you're kidding yourself. I mean, I used to think about leaving home, you know, and that's what I used to say: 'My mother needs me.' But, when you really come down to it, that ain't it at all. We're just afraid to go out on our own. I—I mean, it's a big step when you go out on your own. And, well, I think you're kidding yourself when you say your father needs you. Actually, you need your father. You know what I mean? Well, you know what I mean."

—Ernest Borgnine advising Betsy Blair in Delbert Mann's *Marty*
(Screenplay by Paddy Chayefsky; based on his teleplay)

7.

"Well, it's just that we're so frightened of other people, and we've somehow managed to forget our fright when we've been in each other's company. Speaking for myself, I'm grateful. I—I always will be."

—David Niven thanking Deborah Kerr for her company in Delbert Mann's *Separate Tables*
(Screenplay by Terence Rattigan and John Gay; based on the play by Terence Rattigan)

8.

"Why do you come here? Why do you dress your hypocrisy in black and parade before your God on Sunday? From love? No, for you've shown that your hearts are too withered to receive the love of your Divine Father. I know why you've come. I've seen it in your faces Sunday after Sunday as I've stood here before you. Fear has brought you here. Horrible, superstitious fear. Fear of divine retribution. A bolt of fire from the skies. The vengeance of the Lord and the justice of God. But you have forgotten the love of Jesus. You disregard His sacrifice. Death, fear, flames, horror and black clothes. Hold your meeting then, but know that, if you do this in the name of God and in the house of God, you blaspheme against Him and His word."

—Walter Pidgeon damning his congregation in John Ford's *How Green Was My Valley*
(Screenplay by Philip Dunne; based on the novel by Richard Llewellyn)

9.
"There was a fever over the land. A fever of disgrace, of indignity, of hunger. We had a democracy, yes, but it was torn by elements within. Above all, there was fear. Fear of today, fear of tomorrow, fear of our neighbors and fear of ourselves. Only when you understand that can you understand what Hitler meant to us."

—Burt Lancaster testifying in Stanley Kramer's *Judgment at Nuremberg*
(Screenplay by Abby Mann; based on his teleplay)

10.
(a) "Who's afraid of Virginia Woolf, Virginia Woolf, Virginia Woolf?"
   (b) "I am, George."
   (a) "Who's afraid of Virginia Woolf?"
   (b) "I am, George. I am."

—(a) Richard Burton and (b) Elizabeth Taylor reaching a peaceful dawn in the last lines of Mike Nichols's *Who's Afraid of Virginia Woolf?*
(Screenplay by Ernest Lehman; based on the play by Edward Albee)

ALSO SEE: Actors-4; Boredom-4; Empathy-6; Feelings-1; Foolish-1; Guilty-4; Guilty-5; Hate-9; Heart-11; Heaven-7; Hypocrisy-2; Intelligence-1; Looks-9; Night-4; Party-3; Similarities-2; Soul-11; Telephone Scenes-8; Weakness-1.

FEELINGS

1.
"The 'blues' are because you're getting fat or maybe it's been raining too long. You're just sad, that's all. The 'mean reds' are horrible. Suddenly you're afraid, and you don't know what you're afraid of. Did you ever get that feeling? . . . Well, when I get it, the only thing that does any good is to jump into a cab and go to Tiffany's. Calms me down right away. The quietness and the proud look of it. Nothing very bad could happen to you there."

—Audrey Hepburn cuing George Peppard to her emotional color-scheme in Blake Edwards's *Breakfast at Tiffany's*
(Screenplay by George Axelrod; based on the novella by Truman Capote)

2.
"Get that look off your face. Who gave you the right to dig into me and turn me inside out and decide what I'm like? How do you know how I feel about you, how deep it goes? Maybe I don't want anybody to own me—you or anybody. Get out. Get out. Get out!"

—Kirk Douglas turning on Lana Turner in Vincente Minnelli's *The Bad and the Beautiful*
(Screenplay by Charles Schnee; based on "Memorial to a Bad Man" and "Of Good and Evil," two short stories by George Bradshaw)

3.
"You know, I have the strangest feeling. I feel as if I were going to see you about five minutes more all the rest of my life. . . . I've never had a feeling like this before. It's just settled, that's all. You're never coming here again. Why, it's all over, isn't it? Why, it's finished, isn't it? Why, yes."

—Katharine Hepburn fancying the finish of her romance with Fred MacMurray in George Stevens's *Alice Adams*
(Screenplay by Dorothy Yost and Mortimer Offner; based on the novel by Booth Tarkington)

4.
(a) "Do you know what I feel like? I feel all the time like a cat on a hot tin roof."
   (b) "Then jump off the roof, Maggie. Jump off it. Now, cats jump off roofs, and they land uninjured. Do it. Jump."
   (a) "Jump where? Into what?"
   (b) "Take a lover."

—(a) Elizabeth Taylor and (b) Paul Newman wrangling in Richard Brooks's *Cat on a Hot Tin Roof*
(Screenplay by Richard Brooks and James Poe; based on the play by Tennessee Williams)

5.

"Let there be killing. All this evening I've had a feeling of destiny closing in."

—Leslie Howard foreshadowing his own death in Archie Mayo's *The Petrified Forest*
(Screenplay by Delmer Daves and Charles Kenyon; based on the play by Robert E. Sherwood)

6.

"You know, you never really feel somebody suffering. You only feel their death."

—Art Carney recalling his late wife in Paul Mazursky's *Harry and Tonto*
(Original Screenplay by Paul Mazursky and Josh Greenfeld)

7.

"I liked you 'cause I thought you had some feeling, but, when you didn't, I liked you even more."

—Mae West leveling with Warren William in Henry Hathaway's *Go West, Young Man*
(Screenplay by Mae West; based on PERSONAL APPEARANCE, a play by Lawrence Riley)

8.

"I read in a book once, to hunt and to conquer, to kill—the savagery of it—brings emotions that are tied in with—well, the feelings that make a man a man and a woman a woman."

—Joan Bennett laying her trap for the great white hunter (Gregory Peck) in Zoltan Korda's *The Macomber Affair*
(Screenplay by Casey Robinson and Seymour Bennett; adaptation by Seymour Bennett and Frank Arnold; based on "The Short Happy Life of Francis Macomber," a short story by Ernest Hemingway)

9.

"Let's just say I'm old enough to know what to do with my young feelings."

—Georges Guetary excusing his graying hair in Vincente Minnelli's *An American in Paris*
(Original Screenplay by Alan Jay Lerner)

ALSO SEE: Alone-9; Dance-5; Decency-3; Fights-11; Frigidity-5; Hunger-2; Knowledge-3; Looks-12; Love-38; Love-50; Patience-3; Proposals-5; Psychiatry-7; Rejection-1; Strange-11; Tired-2; Tongue-1; Translations-1.

FIDELITY

1.

"Mary, in many ways your father was an exceptional man. That, unfortunately, was not one of them."

—Lucile Watson leveling with Norma Shearer in George Cukor's *The Women*
(Screenplay by Anita Loos and Jane Murfin; based on the play by Clare Boothe)

2.

"Your idea of fidelity is not having more than one man in the bed at the same time."

—Dirk Bogarde insulting Julie Christie in John Schlesinger's *Darling*
(Original Screenplay by Frederic Raphael)

3.

(a) "I've loved you as much as I could love, but that wasn't enough. I'm not to blame. We don't make our own hearts."

    (b) "Yes, that's—that's true. You're no more to blame because yours can be faithful only a few weeks than I am because mine will be faithful as long as I live."

—(a) Greta Garbo and (b) Robert Taylor having a lovers' row in George Cukor's *Camille*
(Screenplay by Zoe Akins, Frances Marion and James Hilton; based on LA DAME AUX CAMELIAS, a play and novel by Alexandre Dumas)

4.

"Oh, David, I want a monopoly on you—or whatever it is that people have when they don't want anyone else to have any of you."

—Joan Crawford pleading with Van Heflin in Curtis Bernhardt's *Possessed*
(Screenplay by Sylvia Richards and Ranald

MacDougall; based on ONE MAN'S SECRET, a novelette by Rita Weiman)

ALSO SEE: Indecision-2; Jealous-2; Memory-2.

FIGHTS

1.
"I tell you how it should all be done. Whenever there's a big war coming, you should rope off a big field and sell tickets. And, on the big day, you should take all the kings and cabinets and their generals, put them in the center dressed in their underpants and let them fight it out with clubs. The best country wins."

—Louis Wolheim advancing some German dogface philosophy at the frontlines in Lewis Milestone's *All Quiet on the Western Front*
(Screenplay by Dell Andrews, Maxwell Anderson and George Abbott; based on the novel by Erich Maria Remarque)

2.
"Gentlemen, this is outrageous. I have never heard of such behavior in the War Room before."

—Peter Sellers quelling a high-level one-on-one as Doomsday nears in Stanley Kubrick's *Dr. Strangelove or: How I Learned To Stop Worrying and Love the Bomb*
(Screenplay by Stanley Kubrick, Terry Southern and Peter George; based on RED ALERT, a novel by Peter George)

3.
"Well, a little while ago, six men from your ship broke into the home of the French Colonial Governor and started throwing things through a plate-glass living room window. We found some of the things on the lawn: large world globe, small love seat, lot of books, a bust of Balzac—the French writer. We also found an Army private first class, who was unconscious at the time. He claims they threw him, too."

—Martin Milner breaking the bad news to Henry Fonda in John Ford and Mervyn LeRoy's *Mister Roberts*

(Screenplay by Frank S. Nugent and Joshua Logan; based on the play by Thomas Heggen and Joshua Logan and novel by Thomas Heggen)

4.
"One day when I was about six, my parents had a row, and my mother—she threw a pickled herring at my dad and—and missed. It splattered all against the wall. I took one look at that pickled herring, and that's when I decided to become an abstract expressionist."

—Alan Bates revealing to Jill Clayburgh the spark of his art in Paul Mazursky's *An Unmarried Woman (Original Screenplay by Paul Mazursky)*

5.
"Martha and I are merely exercising, that's all. We're merely walking what's left of our wits. Don't pay any attention."

—Richard Burton minimizing his fights with Elizabeth Taylor to George Segal in Mike Nichols's *Who's Afraid of Virginia Woolf?*
(Screenplay by Ernest Lehman; based on the play by Edward Albee)

6.
"I wish someone loved me enough to hit me. You and Rubin fight. God, I'd like a good fight. Anything'd be better than this nothing."

—Eve Arden complaining to her sister (Dorothy McGuire) about the domestic blahs in Delbert Mann's *The Dark at the Top of the Stairs (Screenplay by Irving Ravetch and Harriet Frank Jr.; based on the play by William Inge)*

7.
"Papa wrote it years ago. Papa said the only men on earth worth their time on earth were the men who would fight for other men. Papa said: 'We have struggled through from darkness. But man moves forward with each day and each hour to a better, freer life. That desire to go forward—that willingness to fight for it—cannot be put in a man. But when it is there—!' "

—Bette Davis grandstanding in Herman Shumlin's *Watch on the Rhine*

(Screenplay by Dashiell Hammett; additional scenes and dialogue by Lillian Hellman; based on her play)

8.
"What is there to fight for? Everything! Life itself! Isn't that enough? To be lived, suffered, enjoyed. What is there to fight for? Life is a beautiful, magnificent thing—even to a jellyfish."

—Charles Chaplin pep-talking a suicidal Claire Bloom in Charles Chaplin's *Limelight*
(Original Screenplay by Charles Chaplin)

9.
"I've never before had to fight an angel, but I suggest you take off your coat and put up your dukes."

—David Niven squaring off against his heavenly helper (Cary Grant) in Henry Koster's *The Bishop's Wife*
(Screenplay by Robert E. Sherwood and Leonardo Bercovici; based on the novel by Robert Nathan)

10.
(a) "I have half a mind to punch you right in the nose, just on general principles."
  (b) "It takes half a mind to resort to such measures."
  (a) "Why you—oh! oh!"
  (b) "I neglected to tell you that in my youth I was quite expert in the art of—of fisticuffs."

—(b) Clifton Webb beating (a) Robert Young to the punch in Walter Lang's *Sitting Pretty*
(Screenplay by F. Hugh Herbert; based on the novel by Gwen Davenport)

11.
"Looks happy, don't he? He just needed exercise. Whenever he gets low in spirits or confused in his mind, he doesn't feel right until he's had a fight. It doesn't matter whether he wins or not. He feels fine again afterward."

—Harry (then Henry) Morgan explaining a knocked-cold Henry Fonda in William A. Wellman's *The Ox-Bow Incident*

(Screenplay by Lamar Trotti; based on the novel by Walter Van Tilburg Clark)

ALSO SEE: Decency-4; Don't-4; Honor-2; Hypocrisy-2; Macho-4; Politics-4; Run-6; Sensible-2; Success-5; War-4.

FINGERNAILS

1.
"I've had two years to grow claws, Mother—jungle red!"

—Norma Shearer racing to a catfight with her "friends" in George Cukor's *The Women*
(Screenplay by Anita Loos and Jane Murfin; based on the play by Clare Boothe)

2.
(a) "I just got your call. I—I was having a manicure."
  (b) "At two o'clock in the morning?"
  (a) "I cannot sleep with long fingernails!"

—(a) Peter Lorre fumbling for an excuse that (b) Jules Munshin doesn't buy in Rouben Mamoulian's *Silk Stockings*
(Screenplay by Leonard Gershe and Leonard Spigelgass; based on the musical play by George S. Kaufman, Leueen MacGrath and Abe Burrows and NINOTCHKA, a screenplay by Charles Brackett, Billy Wilder and Walter Reisch and original story by Melchior Lengyel)

FINGERS

1.
"A sculptor-friend of Auntie Mame's used this room for about six months. A divine man. Such talented fingers, but oh, what he did to my bust."

—Rosalind Russell giving her young nephew (Jan Handzlik) the grand tour of her home in Morton Da Costa's *Auntie Mame*
(Screenplay by Betty Comden and Adolph Green; based on the play by Jerome Lawrence and Robert E. Lee and novel by Patrick Dennis)

2.

"Don't point that finger at me unless you intend to use it."

—Walter Matthau threatening Jack Lemmon in Gene Saks's *The Odd Couple*
(Screenplay by Neil Simon; based on his play)

3.

"You must have a grip on the saucer that is firm but not obviously so. The saucer must seem so much a part of your fingers that one would think it could only be removed by surgery."

—Isabel Jeans teaching Leslie Caron to pour in Vincente Minnelli's *Gigi*
(Screenplay by Alan Jay Lerner; based on the novel by Colette)

4.

"He can look like a hundred people, but one thing he cannot disguise—this: half of his little finger is missing—so if ever you should meet a man with no top joint there, be very careful about that."

—Lucie Mannheim telling Robert Donat how to spot a bad guy in Alfred Hitchcock's *The Thirty-Nine Steps*
(Screenplay by Charles Bennett; dialogue by Ian Hay; continuity by Alma Reville; based on the novel by John Buchan)

FIRINGS

1.

"Sure we're speaking, Jedediah. You're fired."

—Orson Welles canning Joseph Cotten in Orson Welles's *Citizen Kane*
(Original Screenplay by Herman J. Mankiewicz and Orson Welles)

2.

"You can't discharge me. I'm my own master for the first time in my life. You can't discharge me. I'm sick. I'm going to die. Do you understand? I'm going to die, and nobody can do anything to me anymore. Nothing can happen to me anymore. Before I can be discharged, I'll be dead! Ha ha ha ha!"

—Lionel Barrymore getting a grim last laugh on his employer (Wallace Beery) in Edmund Goulding's *Grand Hotel*
(Screenplay by William A. Drake; based on the play and novel by Vicki Baum)

3.

"Now I have some instructions for you: I want you to go straight back to the gallery. Start your motor. When you get to the gallery, tell Jennifer that she will be looking after things temporarily. She's to give me a ring if there's anything she can't deal with herself. Then go into the office and make out a check for cash for the sum of $5,000. Then carefully, but carefully, Hilary, remove absolutely everything that might subsequently remind me that you'd ever been there, including that yellow thing with the blue bulbs which you have such an affection for. Then take the check for $5,000, which I feel you deserve, and get permanently lost. It's not that I don't want to know you, Hilary—although I don't—it's just that I'm afraid we're not really the sort of people that you can afford to be associated with. Don't speak, Hilary. Just go."

—Katharine Hepburn giving the old heave-ho to bigoted Virginia Christine in Stanley Kramer's *Guess Who's Coming to Dinner*
(Original Screenplay by William Rose)

4.

"I've gotten the 'sackaroo' in many ways—but never in rhyme."

—Lionel Stander misinterpreting one of Gary Cooper's poems in Frank Capra's *Mr. Deeds Goes to Town*
(Screenplay by Robert Riskin; based on "Opera Hat," a short story by Clarence Budington Kelland)

5.

"Mr. Ruddy had a mild heart attack and is not taking calls. In his absence, I'm making all network decisions—including one I've been waiting to make a long time: you're fired. I want you out of this building by noon. I'll call the security guards and have you thrown out if you're still here."

—Robert Duvall dispatching William Holden in Sidney Lumet's *Network*
(Original Screenplay by Paddy Chayefsky)

6.
"Out! I close the iron door on you."

—John Barrymore firing Charles Levison (later Charles Lane) with his form of dismissal in Howard Hawks's *Twentieth Century*
(Screenplay by Ben Hecht and Charles MacArthur; based on their play and NAPOLEON OF *BROADWAY, a play by Charles Bruce Milholland)*

7.
"You know what Mr. Kockenlocker is like. He didn't exactly take it lying down when they fired him. He left on very bad terms. They had to take six stitches in Mr. Tuerck alone."

—Alan Bridge informing Eddie Bracken of William Demarest's unemployment fate in Preston Sturges's *The Miracle of Morgan's Creek*
(Original Screenplay by Preston Sturges)

8.
"I'm going to fire some of those people. Gimme the fire bell."

—Groucho Marx manning the hotel desk in Joseph Santley and Robert Florey's *The Cocoanuts*
(Screenplay by Morrie Ryskind; based on the musical play by George S. Kaufman and Morrie Ryskind)

ALSO SEE: Dictation-2.

FIRST LINES

1.
"Hello, gorgeous."

—Barbra Streisand addressing a mirror with her first line on film in William Wyler's *Funny Girl*
(Screenplay by Isobel Lennart; based on her musical play)

2.
"Rosebud!"

—Orson Welles gasping his last at the beginning of Orson Welles's *Citizen Kane*

(Original Screenplay by Herman J. Mankiewicz and Orson Welles)

3.
"Mildred!"

—Zachary Scott gasping his last at the beginning of Michael Curtiz's *Mildred Pierce*
(Screenplay by Ranald MacDougall; based on the novel by James M. Cain)

4.
"I am Matthew Macauley. I have been dead for two years. So much of me is still living that I know now the end is only the beginning. As I look down on my homeland of Ithaca, California, with its cactus, vineyards and orchards, I see that so much of me is still living there—in the places I've been, in the fields and streets and church and most of all in my home where my hopes, my dreams, my ambitions, my beliefs still live in the daily lives of my loved ones."

—Ray Collins opening the narration, from beyond the grave, of Clarence Brown's *The Human Comedy*
(Screenplay by Howard Estabrook; based on an original story by William Saroyan)

5.
"Yes, this is Sunset Boulevard, Los Angeles, California. It's about five o'clock in the morning. That's the homicide squad—complete with detectives and newspapermen. A murder has been reported from one of those great big houses in the ten thousand block. You'll read about it in the late editions, I'm sure. You'll get it over your radio and see it on television because an old-time star is involved—one of the biggest. But before you hear it all distorted and grown out of proportion, before those Hollywood columnists get their hands on it, maybe you'd like to see the facts, the whole truth. If so, you've come to the right party. You see, the body of a young man was found floating in the pool of her mansion—with two shots in his back and one in his stomach. Nobody important, really. Just a movie writer with a coupla 'B' pictures to his credit. The poor dope! He always wanted a pool. Well, in the end, he got

himself a pool—only the price turned out to be a little high."

—William Holden, as the corpse-in-question, providing the opening notes for Billy Wilder's *Sunset Boulevard*
(Original Screenplay by Charles Brackett, Billy Wilder and D. M. Marshman Jr.)

6.
"Hey, boy, what you doin' with my momma's car? Wait there!"

—Faye Dunaway meeting Warren Beatty in mid-car theft in Arthur Penn's *Bonnie and Clyde*
(Original Screenplay by David Newman and Robert Benton)

ALSO SEE: Death-7; Dreams-1; Eulogies-7; Fools-1; Love-31; Memory-1; Sun-1; Tired-1; Violence-3; Work-6.

FIRSTS

1.
"Lizzie, for the first time in my life: rain! Give me my hundred bucks."

—Burt Lancaster rejoicing with Katharine Hepburn in his rainmaking magic in Joseph Anthony's *The Rainmaker*
(Screenplay by N. Richard Nash; based on his play)

2.
"Veda, I think I'm really seeing you for the first time in my life—and you're cheap and horrible."

—Joan Crawford at last getting the message about Ann Blyth in Michael Curtiz's *Mildred Pierce*
(Screenplay by Ranald MacDougall; based on the novel by James M. Cain)

3.
"Did he tell you about the time he overwhelmed a 45-year-old maiden by the simple tactic of being the first man in her life to ask her a direct question?"

—Henry Fonda discussing with William Powell the amorous ways of Jack Lemmon in John Ford and Mervyn LeRoy's *Mister Roberts*
(Screenplay by Frank S. Nugent and Joshua Logan; based on the play by Thomas Heggen and Joshua Logan and novel by Thomas Heggen)

4.
"Look, Jo, one night—well, actually, it was afternoon—I loved him. I'd never really been with a man before. It was the first time. You can remember the second and the third and the fourth time, but there's no time like the first. It's always there."

—Dora Bryan remembering the father of her daughter (Rita Tushingham) in Tony Richardson's *A Taste of Honey*
(Screenplay by Shelagh Delaney and Tony Richardson; based on the play by Shelagh Delaney)

5.
"I told you boys I'm no escape artist, but, for the first time, I like the odds because now I got me a decoy."

—William Holden plotting to bolt from POW camp by using traitor Peter Graves to attract enemy fire in Billy Wilder's *Stalag 17*
(Screenplay by Billy Wilder and Edwin Blum; based on the play by Donald Bevan and Edmund Trzcinski)

6.
"You see, it's the first time I've ever flown, and this morning I had to borrow one of my maid Armstrong's pep-up pills. It pepped me up, all right—but not just up, but all directions."

—Margaret Rutherford explaining her stupor in Anthony Asquith's *The V.I.P.'s*
(Original Screenplay by Terence Rattigan)

7.
"You gave me my first drink, Johnny."

—Claire Trevor reminding Edward G. Robinson who started her drinking in John Huston's *Key Largo*
(Screenplay by Richard Brooks and John Huston; based on the play by Maxwell Anderson)

8.
"Oh, believe me, that's the first time I've ever had a—had a caddy in my hand."

—Barry Fitzgerald insisting he's never played golf before to a doubting Bing Crosby in Leo McCarey's *Going My Way*
(Screenplay by Frank Butler and Frank Cavett; based on an original story by Leo McCarey)

9.
"Nobody laughs at me because I laugh first. At me. Me from Seattle. Me with no education. Me with no talent, as you kept reminding me my whole life. Well, Mama, look at me now. I'm a star. Look. Look how I live. Look at my friends. Look where I'm going. I'm not staying in burlesque. I'm moving—maybe up, maybe down—but wherever it is, I'm enjoying it. I'm having the time of my life because, for the first time, it *is* my life. And I love it. I love every second of it."

—Natalie Wood telling off Rosalind Russell in Mervyn LeRoy's *Gypsy*
(Screenplay by Leonard Spigelgass; based on the musical play by Arthur Laurents and memoirs of Gypsy Rose Lee)

10.
"For the first time in my life, I've tasted life."

—Lionel Barrymore roaring on a champagne toot in Edmund Goulding's *Grand Hotel*
(Screenplay by William A. Drake; based on the play and novel by Vicki Baum)

11.
(a) "I take it—this is your first honeymoon."
  (b) "Yes. I mean, it would be—if it were."

—(a) Gregory Peck and (b) Ingrid Bergman bedding down the first night of their pretend marriage in Alfred Hitchcock's *Spellbound*
(Screenplay by Ben Hecht; adaptation by Angus MacPhail; based on THE HOUSE OF DR. EDWARDES, a novel by Francis Beeding)

12.
"I suppose I was in your way going down the rapids. Then what you said to me back there on the river was a lie about how you never could

have done it alone and how you lost your heart and everything. You liar! Oh, Charlie, we're having our first quarrel!"

—Katharine Hepburn arguing with Humphrey Bogart in John Huston's *The African Queen*
(Screenplay by James Agee and John Huston; based on the novel by C. S. Forester)

ALSO SEE: Applause-2; Dance-7; Names-27.

FLATTERY

1.
"Flattery'll get you anywhere."

—Jane Russell coaxing Elliott Reid in Howard Hawks's *Gentlemen Prefer Blondes*
(Screenplay by Charles Lederer; based on the musical play by Joseph Fields and Anita Loos and novel by Anita Loos)

2.
"Flattery is cheap, Mr. Dodd—how about a little costly truth?"

—Grace Kelly asking for some straight talk from William Holden in George Seaton's *The Country Girl*
(Screenplay by George Seaton; based on the play by Clifford Odets)

3.
"Oh, Lord Dudley, your flattery would turn a young girl's head."

—Rosalind Russell launching into a disastrous stage debut in Morton DaCosta's *Auntie Mame*
(Screenplay by Betty Comden and Adolph Green; based on the play by Jerome Lawrence and Robert E. Lee)

ALSO SEE: Compliments.

FLOOZY

1.
"Mama, face it: I was the slut of all time."

—Elizabeth Taylor confronting Mildred Dunnock in Daniel Mann's *Butterfield 8*

(Screenplay by Charles Schnee and John Michael Hayes; based on the novel by John O'Hara)

2.

"I'm a girl you met at the New Congress Club. That's two steps up from the pavement."

—Donna Reed telling Montgomery Clift she's not the marrying kind in Fred Zinnemann's *From Here to Eternity*
(Screenplay by Daniel Taradash; based on the novel by James Jones)

3.

"Men have paid $200 for me, and here you are, turning down a freebie. You could get a perfectly good dishwasher for that."

—Jane Fonda vamping Donald Sutherland in Alan J. Pakula's *Klute*
(Original Screenplay by Andy Lewis and Dave Lewis)

4.

"Those bits? Three cigarette girls in two whole years! You call that acting? 'Big part coming up. Testing you next week. Won't you come out to dinner?' And the next week never comes. Charlie, they hire girls like me to entertain the visiting exhibitor."

—Shelley Winters lamenting her starlet life in Robert Aldrich's *The Big Knife*
(Screenplay by James Poe; based on the play by Clifford Odets)

5.

"Harry, remember how you used to say life wrote lousy scripts? Even in one of yours, I would have thrown this glass at him. But I'm going home with him, instead. Do you want to know the what-do-you-call-it—motivation? Easy—I'm a frightened tramp."

—Mari Aldon explaining to Humphrey Bogart why she's leaving with Warren Stevens in Joseph L. Mankiewicz's *The Barefoot Contessa*
(Original Screenplay by Joseph L. Mankiewicz)

6.

"She tried to sit on my lap while I was standing up."

—Humphrey Bogart describing Martha Vickers to her father (Charles Waldron) in Howard Hawks's *The Big Sleep*
(Screenplay by William Faulkner, Leigh Brackett and Jules Furthman; based on the novel by Raymond Chandler)

ALSO SEE: Fathers-3; Hair-6; Home-4; Tongue-3.

FLOWERS

1.

"The calla lilies are in bloom again. Such a strange flower, suitable to any occasion. I carried them on my wedding day, and now I place them here in memory of something that has died."

—Katharine Hepburn making her stage entrance in Gregory La Cava's *Stage Door*
(Screenplay by Morrie Ryskind and Anthony Veiller; based on the play by Edna Ferber and George S. Kaufman)

2.

"Every year, in every theater, some young person makes a hit. Sometimes it's a big hit, sometimes a little one. It's a distinct success, but how many of them keep their heads? How many of them work? Youth comes to the fore. Youth has its hour of glory. But too often it's only a morning glory—a flower that fades before the sun is very high."

—C. Aubrey Smith advising Katharine Hepburn after her triumphant Broadway opening in Lowell Sherman's *Morning Glory*
(Screenplay by Howard J. Green; based on the play by Zoe Akins)

3.

"Well, we've been shaken out of the magnolias."

—Lucile Watson vibrating from the preceding drama in her living room in Herman Shumlin's *Watch on the Rhine*
(Screenplay by Dashiell Hammett; additional scenes and dialogue by Lillian Hellman; based on her play)

4.

"The flowers won't grow for me. I tell you, when a flower dies in my garden, it hurts me as if a dear friend had died."

—Edith Evans grieving about her garden to Deborah Kerr in Ronald Neame's *The Chalk Garden*
(Screenplay by John Michael Hayes; based on the play by Enid Bagnold)

5.

"I can't send you flowers, baby, but I can send you."

—Nick Adams panting after Kim Novak in Joshua Logan's *Picnic*
(Screenplay by Daniel Taradash; based on the play by William Inge)

ALSO SEE: Orchids; Roses; Disease-6; Head-5; Lady-1; Self-Depreciation-5; Smell-15.

FOOLISH

1.

"Nellie, they've all been trying to frighten me. They've been trying to frighten me into being sensible, but they can't do it. Not now. Not yet. They've got to let me be as foolish as I want to be. I—I want to ride through the park. I want to—I want to go riding in the country. And I'll buy you a beautiful present. And Mr. Hedges! I'll buy Mr. Hedges a little house. And I'll have rooms full of white orchids. And they've got to tell me I'm much more wonderful than anyone else because, Nellie—Nellie, I'm not afraid. I'm not afraid of being just a morning glory. I'm not afraid. I'm not afraid. I'm not afraid. Why should I be afraid? I'm not afraid."

—Katharine Hepburn soaring after her triumphant Broadway opening in the last lines of Lowell Sherman's *Morning Glory*
(Screenplay by Howard J. Green; based on the play by Zoe Akins)

2.

" 'I'll make a bargain with you,' she said. 'You'd look rather foolish trying to divorce me now after four days of marriage, so I'll play the part of a devoted wife, mistress of your precious Manderley. I'll make it the most famous show place in England if you like—and people will visit us and envy us and say we're the luckiest, happiest couple in the whole country. What a grand joke it will be—what a triumph.' "

—Laurence Olivier quoting Wife Number One to Wife Number Two (Joan Fontaine) in Alfred Hitchcock's *Rebecca*
(Screenplay by Robert E. Sherwood and Joan Harrison; adaptation by Philip MacDonald and Michael Hogan; based on the novel by Daphne du Maurier)

ALSO SEE: Loneliness-9; Pretense-1; Strange-1.

FOOLS

1.

"My name is Karl Glocken, and this is a ship of fools. I'm a fool. You'll meet more fools as we go along. This tub is packed with them. Emancipated ladies and ballplayers. Lovers. Dog lovers. Ladies of joy. Tolerant Jews. Dwarfs. All kinds. And who knows—if you look closely enough—you may even find yourself on board!"

—Michael Dunn providing introductory notes in the first lines of Stanley Kramer's *Ship of Fools*
(Screenplay by Abby Mann; based on the novel by Katherine Anne Porter)

2.

"I'm only a little fool. I'm an amateur at it. You're a professional. You've been shaking your cap and bells all over town."

—Joseph Cotten insulting Trevor Howard in Carol Reed's *The Third Man*
(Original Screenplay by Graham Greene)

3.

"Give thanks to God, Brighton, that when He made you a fool He gave you a fool's face."

—Anthony Quinn insulting Anthony Quayle in David Lean's *Lawrence of Arabia*

(Screenplay by Robert Bolt; based on THE SEVEN PILLARS OF WISDOM, the autobiography of T. E. Lawrence, and other works by and about T. E. Lawrence)

4.

"He picks on me, too. The other day he called me an idiot. What could I do? I said, 'Yes, Mr. Matuschek, I'm an idiot.' I'm no fool."

—Felix Bressart telling James Stewart how to survive the bullying of their boss (Frank Morgan) in Ernst Lubitsch's *The Shop Around the Corner*
(Screenplay by Samson Raphaelson; based on PARFUMERIE, a play by Miklos Laszlo)

5.

"Miss Melly's a fool, but not the kind you think. It's just that there's too much honor in her to ever conceive of dishonor in anyone she loves. And she loves you—though just why she does, I'm sure I don't know."

—Clark Gable defending Olivia De Havilland to Vivien Leigh in Victor Fleming's *Gone With the Wind*
(Screenplay by Sidney Howard; based on the novel by Margaret Mitchell)

6.

"Our hero, alas, was always being exploited by villains like Black George. For a generous man is merely a fool in the eyes of a thief."

—Michael MacLiammoir, the all-seeing but never-seen narrator, making a wry observation about the ungrateful beggar (Wilfrid Lawson) who gets a guinea out of Albert Finney in Tony Richardson's *Tom Jones*
(Screenplay by John Osborne; based on the novel by Henry Fielding)

7.

"Anyone who believes that I'll turn informer for nothing is a fool."

—Peter Ustinov indicating he has his price to Charles Laughton in Stanley Kubrick's *Spartacus*
(Screenplay by Dalton Trumbo; based on the novel by Howard Fast)

8.

"You fool! You cowardly, hysterical fool! You and your—"

—Claude Rains spitting out his last words at his killer (Bette Davis) in Irving Rapper's *Deception*
(Screenplay by John Collier and Joseph Than; based on MONSIEUR LAMBERTHIER, a play by Louis Verneuil)

9.

"Darling, you poor fool, don't you know I'm in love with you?"

—Bette Davis telling George Brent the obvious in Edmund Goulding's *Dark Victory*
(Screenplay by Casey Robinson; based on the play by George Brewer Jr. and Bertram Bloch)

10.

"Why, when Tina said she wanted to come home and stay with me—well, it was like a miracle happening, like having your child, a part of you. And I even allowed myself to indulge in the fantasy that both of us loving her and doing what was best for her together would make her seem actually like our child after a while. But I see no such fantasy has occurred to you. Again, I've been just a big sentimental fool. It's a tendency I have."

—Bette Davis confessing a fantasy to Paul Henreid about his daughter (Janis Wilson) in Irving Rapper's *Now, Voyager*
(Screenplay by Casey Robinson; based on the novel by Olive Higgins Prouty)

11.

"I'll never be a success in the grandstand—or anywhere else! Life is too much for me! I'll be a weak fool, looking with pity at the two sides of everything till the day I die! And may the day come soon!"

—Robert Ryan accepting his failings in John Frankenheimer's *The Iceman Cometh*
(Screenplay based on the play by Eugene O'Neill; text edited by Thomas Quinn Curtiss)

12.

"I don't object to your headline-grabbing and

crying 'wolf' all the time—that's standard stuff in politics—but it disturbs me you take yourself so seriously. It's par for the course, trying to fool the people, but it's downright dangerous when you start fooling yourself."

—Lee Tracy advising Cliff Robertson in Franklin Schaffner's *The Best Man*
(Screenplay by Gore Vidal; based on his play)

13.
"Look closely, Eve. It's time you did. I am Addison DeWitt. I am nobody's fool. Least of all—yours."

—George Sanders refusing to be duped by Anne Baxter in Joseph L. Mankiewicz's *All About Eve*
(Screenplay by Joseph L. Mankiewicz; based on "The Wisdom of Eve," a radio play and short story by Mary Orr)

ALSO SEE: Democrats-1; Drink Excuses-9; Eat-4; Goals-3; Indecision-5; Joke-2; Kiss-14; Proposals-4; Tears-8; Telephone Scenes-7.

FOOTBALL

1.
"You're a sports announcer. Give us a—a running account of the all-American bust. Tell Big Daddy how many times Skipper fumbled and stumbled and fell apart. On offensive, he was useless; on defensive, he was a coward. And it was all over. Chicago, 47. Dixie Stars, 0."

—Elizabeth Taylor goading Paul Newman to tell his father (Burl Ives) of a friend's gridiron failure in Richard Brooks's *Cat on a Hot Tin Roof*
(Screenplay by Richard Brooks and James Poe; based on the play by Tennessee Williams)

2.
(a) "My God! They've shot him!"
    (b) "Hot Lips, you incredible nincompoop! It's the end of the quarter."

—(b) Roger Bowen becoming annoyed at the football naiveté of (a) Sally Kellerman in Robert Altman's *M*A*S*H*

(Screenplay by Ring Lardner, Jr.; based on the novel by Richard Hooker)

ALSO SEE: Pep Talks-1; Pep Talks-2; Responsibility-2; Run-4; Strength-5.

FREE

1.
"I like you too much not to say it: you've got everything, except one thing—madness. A man needs a little madness, or else . . . he never dares cut the rope and be free."

—Anthony Quinn counseling Alan Bates in Michael Cacoyannis's *Zorba the Greek*
(Screenplay by Michael Cacoyannis; based on the novel by Nikos Kazantzakis)

2.
"This is your son. He is free, Spartacus. Free. He's free. He's free. He'll remember you, Spartacus, because I'll tell him. I'll tell him who his father was and what he dreamed of."

—Jean Simmons showing the crucified Kirk Douglas their son in Stanley Kubrick's *Spartacus*
(Screenplay by Dalton Trumbo; based on the novel by Howard Fast)

3.
"You see—you see, boys forget what their country means by just reading 'the land of the free' in history books. When they get to be men, they forget even more. Liberty is too precious a thing to be buried in books, Miss Saunders. Men should hold it up in front of them every single day of their lives and say, 'I'm free—to think and to speak. My ancestors couldn't. I can. And my children will.' "

—James Stewart dazzling Jean Arthur with his idealism in Frank Capra's *Mr. Smith Goes to Washington*
(Screenplay by Sidney Buchman; based on "The Gentleman From Montana," a story by Lewis R. Foster)

4.
"No one in love is free—or wants to be."

—Shirley Knight giving her opinion to Paul Newman in Richard Brooks's *Sweet Bird of Youth*
(Screenplay by Richard Brooks; based on the play by Tennessee Williams)

ALSO SEE: Bottle-1; Floozy-3; Heart-2; Heart-3; Suicide-10; War-10.

FRIENDS

1.
"Louis, I think this is the beginning of a beautiful friendship."

—Humphrey Bogart sauntering off into the night fog with Claude Rains in the last line of Michael Curtiz's *Casablanca*
(Screenplay by Julius J. Epstein, Philip G. Epstein and Howard Koch; based on EVERYBODY COMES TO RICK'S, a play by Murray Burnett and Joan Alison)

2.
"I came into your house, my dear friend, and in your unhappiness you reached out your hand for help and in my loneliness I took it. We have such a friendship that is given to very few."

—Bette Davis making a poignant admission to Charles Boyer in Anatole Litvak's *All This and Heaven, Too*
(Screenplay by Casey Robinson; based on the novel by Rachel Field)

3.
(a) "I do not make friends freely."
    (b) "You don't make friends, period."

—(b) Ronald Reagan agreeing in italics with the admission of (a) Richard Todd in Vincent Sherman's *The Hasty Heart*
(Screenplay by Ranald MacDougall; based on the play by John Patrick)

4.
"You keep me around because even Johnny Eager has to have one friend."

—Van Heflin understanding his place in Robert Taylor's entourage in Mervyn LeRoy's *Johnny Eager*
(Screenplay by John Lee Mahin and James

Edward Grant; based on a story by James Edward Grant)

5.
"I was his oldest friend, and, as far as I was concerned, he behaved like a swine. Not that Charles was ever brutal. He just did brutal things. Maybe I wasn't his friend, but, if I wasn't, he never had one."

—Joseph Cotten reflecting on Orson Welles in Orson Welles's *Citizen Kane*
(Original Screenplay by Herman J. Mankiewicz and Orson Welles)

6.
"Friends, my eye! Listen, I got you out of your jams because it was my job, not because I was your friend. I don't like you. I never did like you. And nothing made me happier than to see all those cute little pranks of yours catch up with you and land you on your celebrated face."

—Jack Carson telling off his former client (James Mason) in George Cukor's *A Star Is Born*
(Screenplay by Moss Hart; based on a screenplay by Dorothy Parker, Alan Campbell and Robert Carson and original story by William A. Wellman and Robert Carson)
            and (almost verbatim)

—Lionel Stander dittoing Fredric March in the original, William A. Wellman's *A Star Is Born*
(Screenplay by Dorothy Parker, Alan Campbell and Robert Carson; based on an original story by William A. Wellman and Robert Carson)

7.
"I'm a friend to no one and to nothing except logic."

—Joseph Wiseman standing alone (proudly) in Elia Kazan's *Viva Zapata!*
(Original Screenplay by John Steinbeck)

8.
"He hasn't an enemy in the world. Only his friends hate him."

—Gene Kelly characterizing Fredric March in Stanley Kramer's *Inherit the Wind*
(Screenplay by Nathan E. Douglas and Harold

Jacob Smith; based on the play by Jerome Lawrence and Robert E. Lee)

9.
"Only my friends call me 'wop.' "

—Frank Sinatra distinguishing between friends and Ernest Borgnine in Fred Zinnemann's *From Here to Eternity*
(Screenplay by Daniel Taradash; based on the novel by James Jones)

10.
"Horror has a face, and you must make a friend of horror. Horror and mortal terror are your friends. If they are not, then they are enemies to be feared. They are truly your enemies."

—Marlon Brando advising Martin Sheen in Francis Ford Coppola's *Apocalypse Now*
(Screenplay by John Milius and Francis Ford Coppola; narration written by Michael Herr)

11.
"This is all I need here: drink and drugs and no friends. I had too many friends."

—Hurd Hatfield going to waste in a tavern in Albert Lewin's *The Picture of Dorian Gray*
(Screenplay by Albert Lewin; based on the novel by Oscar Wilde)

ALSO SEE: Platonic Relationships; Advice-9; Betrayal-1; Enemy-1; Flowers-4; Greetings-7; Letters-1; Letters-4; Loneliness-2; Mothers-10; Pet Expressions-8; Pity-6; Professions-6; Proposals-5; Repetitions-2; Stomach-2; Strange-2; Trust and Distrust-4.

FRIGIDITY

1.
"Every time I get affectionate with you, I feel as if I'm snuggling up to the Taft-Hartley Bill!"

—Robert Montgomery complaining of Bette Davis's coolness in Bretaigne Windust's *June Bride*
(Screenplay by Ranald MacDougall; based on FEATURE FOR JUNE, a play by Eileen Tighe and Graeme Lorimer)

2.
"I am not one of the warm people."

—William Daniels regretting his formality with Jason Robards in Fred Coe's *A Thousand Clowns*
(Screenplay by Herb Gardner; based on his play)

3.
"Oh, Harry, I just want to go around apologizing to everybody. I just want to thank everybody for being so patient with me. Oh, Harry, regret hurts so much. I never could—I never could tell Mama I loved her. I never could tell anybody. I wanted to tell Bobby so bad. I don't want to die without saying it to somebody. Harry, just because I'm not demonstrative, it doesn't mean I don't feel. I just—I can't show anything to the ones that mean the most to me. I'm not cold."

—Joanne Woodward leveling with her husband (Martin Balsam) in Gilbert Cates's *Summer Wishes, Winter Dreams*
(Original Screenplay by Stewart Stern)

4.
"My performances can be quite cold. I had more fun in the backseat of a '39 Ford than I can ever have in the vault at the Chase National Bank."

—Elizabeth Taylor warning Laurence Harvey that his wealth doesn't impress her in Daniel Mann's *Butterfield 8*
(Screenplay by Charles Schnee and John Michael Hayes; based on the novel by John O'Hara)

5.
"I'm not sure she's capable of any real feeling. She's television generation. She learned life from Bugs Bunny."

—William Holden telling his wife (Beatrice Straight) about his mistress (Faye Dunaway) in Sidney Lumet's *Network*
(Original Screenplay by Paddy Chayefsky)

ALSO SEE: Adultery-7.

FUN

1.
" 'I think it would be fun to run a newspaper.' "

—George Coulouris quoting, incredulously, Orson Welles in Orson Welles's *Citizen Kane*
(Original Screenplay by Herman J. Mankiewicz and Orson Welles)

2.
"It is recognized that you have a funny sense of fun."

—Claude Rains marveling at Peter O'Toole's enthusiasm for a desert trek in David Lean's *Lawrence of Arabia*
(Screenplay by Robert Bolt; based on THE SEVEN PILLARS OF WISDOM, the autobiography of T. E. Lawrence, and other works by and about T. E. Lawrence)

3.
"Well, Martha thinks that unless you, as she demurely puts it, 'bust a gut,' you're not amused, you know—unless you're carrying on like a hyena, you're not having any fun."

—Richard Burton claiming a quieter sense of humor than Elizabeth Taylor in Mike Nichols's *Who's Afraid of Virginia Woolf?*
(Screenplay by Ernest Lehman; based on the play by Edward Albee)

4.
"Fun? Listen, getting a clear picture on Channel 2 is not my idea of whoopee."

—Walter Matthau criticizing Jack Lemmon's drab life in Gene Saks's *The Odd Couple*
(Screenplay by Neil Simon; based on his play)

5.
"The only fun I get is feeding the goldfish, and they only eat once a day!"

—Bette Davis complaining of boredom in Archie Mayo's *Bordertown*
(Screenplay by Laird Doyle and Wallace Smith; adaptation by Robert Lord; based on the novel by Carroll Graham)

ALSO SEE: Champagne-5; Choice-11; Divorce-2; Frigidity-4; Hanging-2; Pretense-5; Sex-1; Toasts-18; War-2.

FURNISHINGS

1.
"Early nothing."

—Gloria Grahame critiquing Glenn Ford's living quarters in Fritz Lang's *The Big Heat*
(Screenplay by Sydney Boehm; based on a story by William P. McGivern)

2.
"That's what I like—everything done in contrasting shades of money."

—Bob Hope drinking in George Sanders's luxury apartment in Norman Panama and Melvin Frank's *That Certain Feeling*
(Screenplay by Norman Panama, Melvin Frank, I. A. L. Diamond and William Altman; based on THE KING OF HEARTS, a play by Jean Kerr and Eleanor Brooke)

3.
"You should have seen that man's apartment. He's got it down to a science. He pushes a button, and the couch becomes a bed with baby-blue sheets."

—Doris Day bristling about Rock Hudson's sex-trap pad in Michael Gordon's *Pillow Talk*
(Screenplay by Stanley Shapiro and Maurice Richlin; based on a story by Russell Rouse and Clarence Greene)

FUTURE

1.
(a) "I wish I had your worm's eye view of history. It would certainly make things a lot easier."
    (b) "Oh, oh no. Not with you. Oh, no. You'd —you'd still be spending your time trying to make sense out of what is laughingly referred to as the human race. Why don't you take your

blinders off? Don't you know the future is already obsolete?"

—(b) Gene Kelly advancing some futuristic pessimism to (a) Spencer Tracy in Stanley Kramer's *Inherit the Wind*
(Screenplay by Nathan E. Douglas and Harold Jacob Smith; based on the play by Jerome Lawrence and Robert E. Lee)

2.

"You know something, Phil? I suddenly want to live to be very old. Very. I want to be around to see what happens. The world is stirring in very strange ways. Maybe this is the century for it. Maybe that's why it's so troubled. Other centuries had their driving forces. What will ours have been when men look far back to it one day? Maybe it won't be the American century after all. Or the Russian century. Or the atomic century. Wouldn't it be wonderful, Phil, if it turned out to be everybody's century? When people all over the world—free people —found a way to live together? I'd like to be around to see some of that in the beginning. I may stick around for quite a while."

—Anne Revere advancing some futuristic optimism to Gregory Peck in Elia Kazan's *Gentleman's Agreement*
(Screenplay by Moss Hart; based on the novel by Laura Z. Hobson)

3.

"You know what it will be, don't you, Peggy? It may take us years to get anywhere. Not enough money, no decent place to live. We'll have to work and sweat and get kicked around . . ."

—Dana Andrews promising an uncertain future to Teresa Wright in the last lines of William Wyler's *The Best Years of Our Lives*
(Screenplay by Robert E. Sherwood; based on GLORY FOR ME, a verse novel by MacKinlay Kantor)

4.

"You know, I've always had a great sense of tomorrow. I mean, when I'm dressing or eating or brushing my teeth, at the back of my mind there's something else going on, you know. I find that I'm—I'm thinking about what I'll be doing next Saturday, or next month, or next year. In a vague kind of way, I mean. Well, tonight, before you came, I was aware of something missing. I realized I wasn't thinking of next month or even next Saturday. And when I tried to think of them—nothing came. It sounds absurd, but I find it most disconcerting."

—Claude Rains not realizing that Bette Davis is about to murder him in Irving Rapper's *Deception*
(Screenplay by John Collier and Joseph Than; based on MONSIEUR LAMBERTHIER, a play by Louis Verneuil)

5.

"Mrs. Treadwell, I am only a third-grade officer on a second-rate ship, but it has given me an opportunity to observe people. I have seen women like you before—46-year-old women who are still coquettes. They travel on boats often, and always searching for something. Do you know where that searching ends, Mrs. Treadwell? It ends by sitting in a nightclub with a paid escort who tells you the lies you must hear."

—Werner Klemperer forecasting a grim fate for Vivien Leigh in Stanley Kramer's *Ship of Fools*
(Screenplay by Abby Mann; based on the novel by Katherine Anne Porter)

6.

"So that was once a tree? Hmmm. 'The Petrified Forest,' eh? A suitable haven for me. Well, perhaps that's what I'm destined for—to make an interesting fossil for future study."

—Leslie Howard feeling out of touch with the times in Archie Mayo's *The Petrified Forest*
(Screenplay by Delmer Daves and Charles Kenyon; based on the play by Robert E. Sherwood)

7.

"Perhaps publishing a pro-Nazi paper in the United States isn't the best of occupations. There may be no future in it."

—Erwin Kalser understating the case to George Coulouris in Herman Shumlin's *Watch on the Rhine*
(Screenplay by Dashiell Hammett; additional scenes and dialogue by Lillian Hellman; based on her play)

8.

"What future is there in being a Chinaman? You're born, eat your way through a handful of rice and you die. What a country!"

—Eugene Pallette offending Warner Oland in Josef von Sternberg's *Shanghai Express*
(Screenplay by Jules Furthman; based on a story by Harry Hervey)

9.

"Hannah, can you hear me? Wherever you are, look up, Hannah! The clouds are lifting! The sun is breaking through! We are coming out of the darkness into the light! We are coming into a new world—a kindlier world, where men will rise above their hate and their greed and brutality. Look up! Hannah! The soul of man has been given wings, and at last he is beginning to fly. He is flying into the rainbow—into the light of hope—into the future—the glorious future that belongs to you—to me—and to all of us! Look up! Hannah! Look up!"

—Charles Chaplin grandstanding to Paulette Goddard at the end of Charles Chaplin's *The Great Dictator*
(Original Screenplay by Charles Chaplin)

ALSO SEE: Directors-1; Past-9; Past-10; Spinsters-1; Star-1; Translations-3.

GAMES

1.

"Now that we're through with Humiliate the Host—we're through with that one for this round anyway, and we don't want to play Hump the Hostess yet, not yet—so I know what we do: how about a little round of Get the Guests? How about that? How about a little game of Get the Guests?"

—Richard Burton turning on his guests (George Segal and Sandy Dennis) in Mike Nichols's *Who's Afraid of Virginia Woolf?*
(Screenplay by Ernest Lehman; based on the play by Edward Albee)

2.

"Now I'll be the innocent little milkmaid, and you'll be the naughty stableboy."

—Estelle Winwood proposing to Zero Mostel their next sexual charade in Mel Brooks's *The Producers*
(Original Screenplay by Mel Brooks)

3.

"We were just playing a game called Photography. You turn off the lights and see what develops."

—Barry Coe making light of the heavy smooching party which Lana Turner finds in her home in Mark Robson's *Peyton Place*
(Screenplay by John Michael Hayes; based on the novel by Grace Metalious)

4.

"All right, let's play Twenty Questions. If you answer them correctly, maybe I won't knock your teeth out."

—Mark Stevens giving William Bendix a rough interrogation in Henry Hathaway's *The Dark Corner*
(Screenplay by Jay Dratler and Bernard C. Schoenfeld; based on the short story by Leo Rosten)

5.

"Entertaining the rustics is not as difficult as I feared. Any simple, childish game seems to amuse them excessively."

—Frieda Inescort playing the haughty hostess in Robert Z. Leonard's *Pride and Prejudice*
(Screenplay by Aldous Huxley and Jane Murfin; based on the play by Helen Jerome and novel by Jane Austen)

6.

"Listen, listen, listen. Let's have a game—a little lovely game of Roman Ping-Pong, like two civilized senators. Roman Ping. You're supposed to say 'Roman Pong.' "

—Peter Sellers kidding around with his killer (James Mason) in Stanley Kubrick's *Lolita*
(Screenplay by Vladimir Nabokov; based on his novel)

7.
"Bunny Bixler and I were in the semifinals—the very semifinals, mind you—of the Ping-Pong tournament at the club, and this ghastly thing happened. We were both playing way over our heads, and the score was 29-28. And we had this really terrific volley, and I stepped back to get this really terrific shot, and I stepped on the Ping-Pong ball. Well, I just squashed it to bits. And then Bunny and I and the partners went to the game room to get another Ping-Pong ball, and the closet was locked. Imagine! We had to call the whole thing off. Well, it was ghastly. Well, it was just ghastly."

—Joanna Barnes relaying at length her idea of a funny story in Morton DaCosta's *Auntie Mame*
(Screenplay by Betty Comden and Adolph Green; based on the play by Jerome Lawrence and Robert E. Lee and novel by Patrick Dennis)

8.
(a) "Fat man, you shoot a great game of pool."
(b) "So do you, Fast Eddie."

—(a) Paul Newman and (b) Jackie Gleason swapping compliments in the last lines of Robert Rossen's *The Hustler*
(Screenplay by Sidney Carroll and Robert Rossen; based on the novel by Walter Tevis)

9.
"Good afternoon, gentlemen. . . . What's the name of this game?"

—Kirk Douglas taking his usual place at the poker table in the last line of John Sturges's *Gunfight at the O. K. Corral*
(Screenplay by Leon Uris; suggested by "The Killer," a short story by George Scullin)

ALSO SEE: Gin-1; Propositions-6.

GENIUS

1.
"Dear Petronius, you must forgive me if I seem to have slighted you greatly, but I've been steeped in my genius."

—Peter Ustinov apologizing for his absence to Leo Genn in Mervyn LeRoy's *Quo Vadis*
(Screenplay by John Lee Mahin, S. N. Behrman and Sonya Levien; based on the novel by Henryk Sienkiewicz)

2.
(a) "For my work, I require an atmosphere of spartan simplicity."
      (b) "And may I ask what your profession is?"
(a) "Certainly. I am a genius."

—(a) Clifton Webb answering the babysitting ad of (b) Maureen O'Hara in Walter Lang's *Sitting Pretty*
(Screenplay by F. Hugh Herbert; based on the novel by Gwen Davenport)

3.
"I'm not just talented. I'm geniused."

—Rita Tushingham declaring herself in Tony Richardson's *A Taste of Honey*
(Screenplay by Shelagh Delaney and Tony Richardson; based on the play by Shelagh Delaney)

4.
"You know, Oliver, I sometimes think I was born with a genius, an absolute genius for doing the wrong thing."

—James Mason admitting to Charles Bickford a sense of lifelong bad timing in George Cukor's *A Star Is Born*
(Screenplay by Moss Hart; based on a screenplay by Dorothy Parker, Alan Campbell and Robert Carson and original story by William A. Wellman and Robert Carson)

GENTLE

1.

"Well, this is where you came in. Back at that pool again, the one I always wanted. It's dawn now, and they must have photographed me a thousand times. Then they got a couple of pruning hooks from the garden and fished me out, ever so gently. Funny how gentle people get with you once you're dead. They beached me like a harpooned baby whale and started to check the damage, just for the record."

—William Holden bringing his story up to the post-humous present in Billy Wilder's *Sunset Boulevard (Original Screenplay by Charles Brackett, Billy Wilder and D. M. Marshman Jr.)*

2.

"Millions of years ago, dinosaurs fed on the leaves of those trees. The dinosaurs were vegetarians. That's why they became extinct. They were just too gentle for their size. And then the carnivorous creatures—the ones that eat flesh—the killers—inherited the earth. But, then, they always do, don't they?"

—Katharine Hepburn advancing a grim view of life in Joseph L. Mankiewicz's *Suddenly, Last Summer (Screenplay by Gore Vidal and Tennessee Williams; based on the one-act play by Tennessee Williams)*

3.

"You are gentle, and there's nothing stronger in the world than gentleness."

—Jennifer Jones complimenting William Holden in Henry King's *Love Is a Many-Splendored Thing (Screenplay by John Patrick; based on A MANY-SPLENDORED THING, a novel by Han Suyin)*

ALSO SEE: Cruel-1; Curtain Speeches-5.

GENTLEMAN

1.

"If my wonderful, beautiful, marvelous virtue is still intact, it is no thanks to me, I assure you. It is purely by courtesy of the gentleman from South Bend."

—Grace Kelly giving credit where credit is due (Frank Sinatra) in Charles Walters's *High Society (Screenplay by John Patrick; based on THE PHILADELPHIA STORY, a screenplay by Donald Ogden Stewart and play by Philip Barry)*

2.

"I want you to say, 'Trudy, it's your bounden duty to say goodbye to our boys, to dance with them, to give them something to remember, something to fight for. I won't take no for an answer, so I'll drop you off at the church basement, take in a movie, then pick you up and take you home like a chivalrous gentleman so you won't get in wrong with Papa.' That's what I want you to say."

—Betty Hutton asking a lot of Eddie Bracken in Preston Sturges's *The Miracle of Morgan's Creek (Original Screenplay by Preston Sturges)*

ALSO SEE: Beautiful-5; Coward-2; Jealous-2; Manners-9; Murder-6; Prejudice-2.

GIGOLO

1.

"A gigolo? Why, the nerve! Huh! Who just paid for these teas?"

—Louis Jourdan pretending indignation at the word in Anthony Asquith's *The V.I.P.'s (Original Screenplay by Terence Rattigan)*

2.

"Tell me, when you get married, will you keep your maiden name?"

—Oscar Levant teasing Gene Kelly about having a rich patroness (Nina Foch) in Vincente Minnelli's *An American in Paris (Original Screenplay by Alan Jay Lerner)*

3.

"Well, I'll tell you the truth now. I ain't a real cowboy, but I am one helluvah stud."

—Jon Voight bluntly advertising at a party in John Schlesinger's *Midnight Cowboy (Screenplay by Waldo Salt; based on the novel by James Leo Herlihy)*

4.

"Our hero released from Lady Bellaston a torrent of affection as well as a flood of gifts, which he found suitably embarrassing and quite irresistible."

—Narrator Michael MacLiammoir describing the relationship between Albert Finney and Joan Greenwood in Tony Richardson's *Tom Jones*
(Screenplay by John Osborne; based on the novel by Henry Fielding)

5.

"I do not accept gifts from disapproving gentlemen—especially not disapproving gentlemen who are kept by other ladies. So take it. You should be used to taking money from ladies by now."

—Audrey Hepburn paying George Peppard, with a vengeance, for her own drink in Blake Edwards's *Breakfast at Tiffany's*
(Screenplay by George Axelrod; based on the novella by Truman Capote)

6.

"I won't go on taking tips from you as I used to. Course, if I owned a share in your business . . ."

—Zachary Scott turning his romance with Joan Crawford into a business arrangement in Michael Curtiz's *Mildred Pierce*
(Screenplay by Ranald MacDougall; based on the novel by James M. Cain)

7.

"When an impoverished character, unendowed with any appreciable virtues, succumbs to a rich man's wife, it's to be suspected that his interest is less passionate than pecuniary."

—Clifton Webb worrying his wife (Cathy Downs) about her lover (Kurt Kreuger) in Henry Hathaway's *The Dark Corner*
(Screenplay by Jay Dratler and Bernard C. Schoenfeld; based on the novel by Leo Rosten)

8.

"It's lonely here so she got herself a companion. Very simple set-up. Older woman who's well-to-do and a younger man who's not doing too well. Can you figure it out yourself?"

—William Holden telling Nancy Olson his arrangement with Gloria Swanson in Billy Wilder's *Sunset Boulevard*
(Original Screenplay by Charles Brackett, Billy Wilder and D. M. Marshman Jr.)

9.

"I am not part of your luggage. Whatever I am, I am not part of your luggage."

—Paul Newman drawing the line with his "sponsor" (Geraldine Page) in Richard Brooks's *Sweet Bird of Youth*
(Screenplay by Richard Brooks; based on the play by Tennessee Williams)

GIN

1.

"Gin!"

—Judy Holliday beating Broderick Crawford at gin rummy in George Cukor's *Born Yesterday*
(Screenplay by Albert Mannheimer; based on the play by Garson Kanin)

2.

"Shmooooooooth! Please buy Guzzler's. It comes in 29 sizes. With Guzzler's, you don't need a chaser. Nothing can catch you!"

—Red Skelton sampling the wares he's selling on "The Guzzler's Gin Program" in a George Sidney-directed sketch from Vincente Minnelli's *Ziegfeld Follies*
(Sketch "When Television Comes" by Harry Tugend; based on "Gulper's Gin," a sketch written by Red Skelton and Edna Skelton)

3.

"Gin was mother's milk to her."

—Wendy Hiller horrifying an elite crowd with an inappropriate anecdote about her aunt in Anthony Asquith and Leslie Howard's *Pygmalion*
(Screenplay by George Bernard Shaw; adaptation by W. P. Lipscomb, Cecil Lewis and Ian Dalrymple; based on the play by George Bernard Shaw)

and

—Audrey Hepburn dittoing in the remake, George Cukor's *My Fair Lady*

(Screenplay by Alan Jay Lerner; based on his musical play and PYGMALION, *a screenplay and play by George Bernard Shaw)*

4.
(a) "The air! Isn't it wonderful?"
    (b) "Yeah, it's like—I know you don't approve, but it's like a shot of gin. It makes your blood race, your face numb and your spirits soar."

—(a) Katharine Hepburn and (b) Humphrey Bogart taking in the African air in John Huston's *The African Queen*
(Screenplay by James Agee and John Huston; based on the novel by C. S. Forester)

5.
"Do I breathe gin?"

—Kate Reid making an entrance with a breath check from her brother-in-law (Paul Scofield) in Tony Richardson's *A Delicate Balance*
(Screenplay by Edward Albee; based on his play)

6.
"Have some gin. It's my only weakness."

—Ernest Thesiger admitting his one failing in James Whale's *The Bride of Frankenstein*
(Screenplay by William Hurlbut and John L. Balderston; suggested by FRANKENSTEIN, *a novel by Mary Wollstonecraft Shelley)*
                    and
—Ernest Thesiger dittoing in James Whale's *The Old Dark House*
(Screenplay by Benn W. Levy; additional dialogue by R. C. Sherriff; based on BENIGHTED, *a novel by J. B. Priestley)*

7.
"Get me a bromide. And put some gin in it."

—Mary Boland weeping over losing her husband to Joan Crawford in George Cukor's *The Women*
(Screenplay by Anita Loos and Jane Murfin; based on the play by Clare Boothe)

GOALS

1.
"The aim of life is self-development, to realize one's nature perfectly. That's what we're here for. A man should live out his life fully and completely, give form to every feeling, expression to every thought, reality to every dream. Every impulse that we suppress broods in the mind and poisons us. There's only one way to get rid of a temptation, and that's to yield to it. Resist it, and the soul grows sick with longing for the things it has forbidden to itself. But there's nothing that can cure the soul but the senses, just as there is nothing that can cure the senses but the soul."

—George Sanders making an eloquent case for hedonism in Albert Lewin's *The Picture of Dorian Gray*
(Screenplay by Albert Lewin; based on the novel by Oscar Wilde)

2.
"I'm jes trying to get on without shovin' anybody, that's all."

—Henry Fonda expressing his simple objective in John Ford's *The Grapes of Wrath*
(Screenplay by Nunnally Johnson; based on the novel by John Steinbeck)

3.
"We are the intelligent, civilized people who carry out orders we are given, no matter what they may be. Our biggest mission in life is to avoid being fools, and we wind up being the biggest fools of all."

—Oskar Werner balking at conformity in Stanley Kramer's *Ship of Fools*
(Screenplay by Abby Mann; based on the novel by Katherine Anne Porter)

4.
"Don't waste your pity. They manage to stay drunk and keep their pipe dreams, and that's all they ask out of life. It isn't often that men attain the true goal of their heart's desire."

—Robert Ryan looking on the bright side of the barroom riffraff around him in John Frankenheimer's *The Iceman Cometh*

(Screenplay based on the play by Eugene O'Neill; text edited by Thomas Quinn Curtiss)

5.

"Yes, again—again and again! Remember our aim: 'Find the microbe, kill the microbe.'"

—Paul Muni preaching to his lab workers in William Dieterle's *The Story of Louis Pasteur*
(Screenplay by Sheridan Gibney and Pierre Collings; based on an original story by Sheridan Gibney and Pierre Collings)

ALSO SEE: Wants; Spinsters-5.

GOD

1.

"Oh, Henry, why don't you wake up? Darwin was wrong. Man's still an ape. His creed's still a totem pole. When he first achieved the upright position, he took a look at the stars, thought they were something to eat. When he couldn't reach them, he decided they were groceries belonging to a bigger creature. That's how Jehovah was born."

—Gene Kelly reciting his cynical version of Genesis to Spencer Tracy in Stanley Kramer's *Inherit the Wind*
(Screenplay by Nathan E. Douglas and Harold Jacob Smith; based on the play by Jerome Lawrence and Robert E. Lee)

2.

"I never mentioned God in the nightclub, did I? . . . Have I mentioned Him in this racket? Have you ever heard me do it? C'mon, c'mon, when did I do it? . . . No, I'll say I haven't. I know what I'm doing. I've read the Bible. I can recite the Ten Commandments backwards, and I'll tell you what the Third Commandment is, too: 'Thou shall not take the name of the Lord thy God in vain.' A lot of people think that means swearing, but I'll tell you what it means. It means exactly what you're talking about. I'm not taking any chances, baby. There's nothing to worry about. There's no difference between this and—and mentalism. It's just another angle of show business."

—Tyrone Power defending his dubious act to his wife (Coleen Gray) in Edmund Goulding's *Nightmare Alley*
(Screenplay by Jules Furthman; based on the novel by William Lindsay Gresham)

3.

"I hope you are as wise, as brilliant, a god as they say you are. You Roman generals become divine so quickly. A few victories, a few massacres. Only yesterday Pompey was a god. They murdered him, didn't they?"

—Elizabeth Taylor sizing up Rex Harrison in Joseph L. Mankiewicz's *Cleopatra*
(Screenplay by Joseph L. Mankiewicz, Ranald MacDougall and Sidney Buchman; based upon histories by Plutarch, Suetonius and Appian and THE LIFE AND TIMES OF CLEOPATRA, a book by C. M. Franzero)

4.

"If God ever wanted to be a fish, He'd be a whale. Believe that. He'd be a whale."

—Harry Andrews offering some tavern-house theology in John Huston's *Moby Dick*
(Screenplay by Ray Bradbury and John Huston; based on the novel by Herman Melville)

5.

"Well, man, don't stand there with half the morning gone. Get the rods. Come along, boy. Wasn't it just fine of God to make all the rivers and fill them all with little fishes and then send you and me here to catch them, Andrew? Hmmm?"

—Gregory Peck going fishing with young George Nokes in the last lines of John M. Stahl's *The Keys of the Kingdom*
(Screenplay by Joseph L. Mankiewicz and Nunnally Johnson; based on the novel by A. J. Cronin)

6.

"Answers to questions involving God must be carefully phrased."

—Felix Aylmer being cautious with Deborah Kerr in Ronald Neame's *The Chalk Garden*
(Screenplay by John Michael Hayes; based on the play by Enid Bagnold)

ALSO SEE: Arrogance-1; Courtroom Lines-4; Democrats-1; Dying Words-21; Eulogies-12; Eulogies-13; Fear-8; Fools-3; Hands-9; Hate-3; Human-3; Hunger-1; Joke-3; Newspapering-3; Prologues-7; Rome-1; Rome-2; Sin-1; Specializations-6; Specializations-7; Trouble-12; Truth-1; War-10; Weakness-1.

GOLF

1.
"A golf course is nothing but a poolroom moved outdoors."

—Barry Fitzgerald declining an invitation to hit the links with Bing Crosby and Frank McHugh in Leo McCarey's *Going My Way*
(Screenplay by Frank Butler and Frank Cavett; based on an original story by Leo McCarey)

ALSO SEE: Doctors-1; Firsts-8; Good and Bad-3.

GOOD

1.
"In spite of everything, I still believe that people are really good at heart."

—Millie Perkins reprising a brave optimism in the last line of George Stevens's *The Diary of Anne Frank*
(Screenplay by Albert Hackett and Frances Goodrich; based on their play and the book ANNE FRANK, THE DIARY OF A YOUNG GIRL)

2.
"You're good. You're very good."

—Humphrey Bogart appreciating Mary Astor's sincerity act in John Huston's *The Maltese Falcon*
(Screenplay by John Huston; based on the novel by Dashiell Hammett)

3.
"I'm a good girl, I am."

—Wendy Hiller declaring herself to Leslie Howard in Anthony Asquith and Leslie Howard's *Pygmalion*
(Screenplay by George Bernard Shaw; adaptation by W. P. Lipscomb, Cecil Lewis and Ian Dalrymple; based on the play by George Bernard Shaw)

and

—Audrey Hepburn dittoing to Rex Harrison in the remake, George Cukor's *My Fair Lady*
(Screenplay by Alan Jay Lerner; based on his musical play and PYGMALION, *a screenplay and play by George Bernard Shaw)*

4.
"I'll be a good girl, ma'am. I promise I will. I want to be like you. That's what my father wanted."

—Jennifer Jones making a promise to Lillian Gish in King Vidor's *Duel in the Sun*
(Screenplay by David O. Selznick; adaptation by Oliver H. P. Garrett; based on the novel by Niven Busch)

5.
(a) "Too many girls follow the line of least resistance."
   (b) "Yeah, but a good line is hard to resist."

—(a) Helen Jerome Eddy and (b) Mae West discussing sinners in Raoul Walsh's *Klondike Annie*
(Screenplay and dialogue by Mae West; additional material suggested by Frank Mitchell Dazey; story ingredients by Marion Morgan and George B. Dowell; based on an original story by Mae West)

6.
"Oh, Noah, you're so full of what's right you can't see what's good. It's good for a girl to get married, sure. Maybe you were right when you said she won't ever have it. But she's gotta have something. Lizzie has got to have something—even if it's only one minute with a man talking quiet, his hand touching her face—and, if you go out there and put one little dark shadow over the brightest time of Lizzie's life, I swear I'll come out after you with a whip."

—Cameron Prud'homme defending the affair of his daughter (Katharine Hepburn) and a con man (Burt Lancaster) in Joseph Anthony's *The Rainmaker*
(Screenplay by N. Richard Nash; based on his play)

7.
"You don't like her. My mother don't like her. She's a dog, and I'm a fat, ugly man. Well, all I know is I had a good time last night. I'm going to have a good time tonight. If we have enough good times together, I'm going to get down on my knees. I'm going to beg that girl to marry me. If we make a party on New Year's, I got a date for that party. You don't like her? That's too bad."

—Ernest Borgnine telling off Joe Mantell in Delbert Mann's *Marty*
(Screenplay by Paddy Chayefsky; based on his teleplay)

8.
"That's the only good thing about divorce. You get to sleep with your mother."

—Virginia Weidler finding one silver lining to her parents' parting in George Cukor's *The Women*
(Screenplay by Anita Loos and Jane Murfin; based on the play by Clare Boothe)

9.
(a) "You—you've been here for quite a long time, haven't you?"
(b) "Oh—yes. Yes, ever since I married what's-her-name—er, Martha. Even before that. Forever. Dashed hopes, and good intentions. Good, better, best, bested. How do you like that for a declension, young man?"

—(b) Richard Burton being glib with (a) George Segal in Mike Nichols's *Who's Afraid of Virginia Woolf?*
(Screenplay by Ernest Lehman; based on the play by Edward Albee)

10.
(a) "You're gonna get used to wearing them chains after a while, Luke, but you never stop listening to them clinking because they're

going to remind you of what I been saying—for your own good."
(b) "Wish you'd stop being so good to me, Captain."

—(b) Paul Newman back talking to (a) Strother Martin in Stuart Rosenberg's *Cool Hand Luke*
(Screenplay by Donn Pearce and Frank Pierson; based on the novel by Donn Pearce)

11.
"Oh, the odor of goodness! Give me a drink. You know, we're never going to get anywhere as long as that Zapata's alive. He believes in what he is fighting for."

—Frank Silvera opposing Marlon Brando in Elia Kazan's *Viva Zapata!*
(Original Screenplay by John Steinbeck)

12.
"You see, my dear, goodness is after all the greatest force in the world, and he's got it."

—Herbert Marshall lauding Tyrone Power to Gene Tierney in the last line of Edmund Goulding's *The Razor's Edge*
(Screenplay by Lamar Trotti; based on the novel by W. Somerset Maugham)

13.
(a) "Goodness, what beautiful diamonds!"
(b) "Goodness had nothing to do with it, dearie."

—(b) Mae West qualifying the compliment of a cloakroom girl in Archie Mayo's *Night After Night*
(Screenplay by Vincent Lawrence; additional dialogue by Mae West; based on "Single Night," an original story by Louis Bromfield)

ALSO SEE: Good and Bad; Eulogies-15; Hanging-5; Letters-3; Names-23; Oops!-1; Right-2; Time-10; War-11.

GOOD AND BAD

1.
"You make the same sounds for pain or happiness."

—Walter Matthau criticizing Jack Lemmon's method of communication in Gene Saks's *The Odd Couple*
(Screenplay by Neil Simon; based on his play)

2.

"When my little boy, Dimitri, died, everybody was crying. Me? I got up, and I danced. They said, 'Zorba is mad.' But it was the dancing—only the dancing—that stopped the pain. You see, he was my first. He was only three. When I'm happy, it's the same thing."

—Anthony Quinn advocating dancing as therapy in Michael Cacoyannis's *Zorba the Greek*
(Screenplay by Michael Cacoyannis; based on the novel by Nikos Kazantzakis)

3.

(a) "Do you know the only thing I can think of right now? The only thought that comes into my mind is the way I wash my hair. You see, when anything happens to me good or bad, I make straight for the shampoo bottle. Why would I have to think of that now?"

   (b) "I understand that perfectly. With me, it's golf balls. If I'm happy or if I'm miserable, I—I putt golf balls around the living room. It makes perfect sense."

—(a) Judy Garland and (b) James Mason confessing eccentricities in George Cukor's *A Star Is Born*
(Screenplay by Moss Hart; based on a screenplay by Dorothy Parker, Alan Campbell and Robert Carson and original story by William A. Wellman and Robert Carson)

4.

"Nobody believes good unless they have to, if they've got a chance to believe something bad."

—Diana Lynn advising her older, pregnant sister (Betty Hutton) in Preston Sturges's *The Miracle of Morgan's Creek*
(Original Screenplay by Preston Sturges)

ALSO SEE: Bad; Good; Newspapering-6; Soul-9; Wives-6.

GOOD-BYES

1.

"Ilsa, I'm no good at being noble, but it doesn't take much to see that the problems of three little people don't amount to a hill of beans in this crazy world. Someday you'll understand that. Not now. Here's looking at you, kid."

—Humphrey Bogart sending Ingrid Bergman off with her husband (Paul Henreid)—nobly—in Michael Curtiz's *Casablanca*
(Screenplay by Julius J. Epstein, Philip G. Epstein and Howard Koch; based on EVERYBODY COMES TO RICK'S, a play by Murray Burnett and Joan Alison)

2.

(a) "In case I don't see you again—"
   (b) "What?"
   (a) "Well, anything might happen. The train could jump off the track. If it should happen that I don't see you again, it's been very nice knowing you, Miss Breckenridge."
   (b) "Bark, that's probably the sweetest speech you've ever made to me. And, in case I don't see you—well, I don't know why—I just want to tell you it's been lovely. Every bit of it. The whole 50 years. I'd sooner been your wife, Bark, than any one else on earth."

—(a) Victor Moore and (b) Beulah Bondi parting at the end of Leo McCarey's *Make Way for Tomorrow*
(Screenplay by Vina Delmar; based on the play by Helen Leary and Nolan Leary and THE YEARS ARE SO LONG, a novel by Josephine Lawrence)

3.

"Well, mustn't miss the old train, what, what? I must—I must stop saying 'what.' Cheeriebye. I must stop doing that too, I suppose."

—David Niven stumbling through his good-byes to Wendy Hiller in Delbert Mann's *Separate Tables*
(Screenplay by Terence Rattigan and John Gay; based on the play by Terence Rattigan)

4.

"Well, that's it for tonight, folks. This is Sweet Sue, saying good night, reminding all you daddies out there that every girl in my band is a virtuoso, and I intend to keep it that way."

—Joan Shawlee signing off from the bandstand in Billy Wilder's *Some Like It Hot*
(Screenplay by Billy Wilder and I. A. L. Diamond; suggested by a story by R. Thoeren and M. Logan)

5.
(a) "If you ever need anything, no matter what it is or wherever you happen to be—"
  (b) "Yes, I know. I just dial O for O'Malley."
  (a) "Right."

—(a) Bing Crosby and (b) Ingrid Bergman parting in the last lines of Leo McCarey's *The Bells of St. Mary's*
(Screenplay by Dudley Nichols; based on an original story by Leo McCarey)

6.
"In a little while, we must leave our city—perhaps for years, perhaps forever. For those of us who are old, certainly forever. Elders of Wangcheng, I thank you for your help in this time of trouble, but we were born to our trouble. There is one who has taken it upon herself not from necessity but from love: Jan-Ai. We thank you for those who are not here, for the dead whose children you have taken as your own, for the poor and the sick and the afflicted, for all the people of Wangcheng, for the past and for the future. I honor you for your strength. I wish to share with you the faith from which it comes. . . . It is time to go, old friends. We shall not see each other again, I think. Farewell, Jan-Ai."

—Robert Donat saying good-bye to Ingrid Bergman (and screen audiences) with his final words on film in Mark Robson's *The Inn of the Sixth Happiness*
(Screenplay by Isobel Lennart; based on THE SMALL WOMAN, a book by Alan Burgess)

7.
"So long. So long, you ancient pelican."

—Regis Toomey watching John Wayne saunter off whistling in the last line of William A. Wellman's *The High and the Mighty*
(Screenplay by Ernest K. Gann; based on his novel)

8.
"We're going to miss you, Shirley. Isn't that right, folks? So long, Shirl. But don't despair.

Every heart in this room is with you, and that's what really counts. It's hard on all of us after we've lived all these hours and weeks together to see one of these wonderful, courageous kids fall out. But life goes on. And so does the marathon."

—Gig Young waving Allyn Ann McLerie out of the dance marathon in Sydney Pollack's *They Shoot Horses, Don't They?*
(Screenplay by James Poe and Robert E. Thompson; based on the novel by Horace McCoy)

9.
(a) "I guess this is where the funny man says, 'Shall we dance?' "
  (b) "You are not a funny man, Captain Pringle, but you are quite a dancer. What a waltz we had! Good night."

—(b) Jean Arthur catching (a) John Lund with Marlene Dietrich in Billy Wilder's *A Foreign Affair*
(Screenplay by Charles Brackett, Billy Wilder and Richard L. Breen; adaptation by Robert Harari; based on an original story by David Shaw)

10.
"And it's a happy ending. Wayward husband comes to his senses, returns to his wife with whom he's established a long and sustaining love. Heartless young woman left alone in her arctic desolation. Music up with a swell. Final commercial. And here are a few scenes from next week's show."

—William Holden leaving Faye Dunaway in Sidney Lumet's *Network*
(Original Screenplay by Paddy Chayefsky)

11.
"Remember the blue beetle promised us a long and happy life."

—William Holden leaving Jennifer Jones for death at the front lines in Henry King's *Love Is a Many-Splendored Thing*
(Screenplay by John Patrick; based on A MANY-SPLENDORED THING, a novel by Han Suyin)

12.
"Every time you leave me for a minute, it's like good-bye."

—Elizabeth Taylor parting with Montgomery Clift before his flight from the police in George Stevens's *A Place in the Sun*
(Screenplay by Michael Wilson and Harry Brown; based on AN AMERICAN TRAGEDY, a play by Patrick Kearney and novel by Theodore Dreiser)

ALSO SEE: Empathy-7; Letters-12; Money-8; Moon-5; Pet Expressions-15; Wants-7.

GREED

1.
"Too bad it didn't happen further down the street—in front of the May Company. From *them*, you can collect! Couldn't you have dragged yourself another 20 feet?"

—Shyster lawyer Walter Matthau counseling a client-to-be (Howard McNear) in Billy Wilder's *The Fortune Cookie*
(Original Screenplay by Billy Wilder and I. A. L. Diamond)

2.
"He has grown greedier with the years. The first time he wanted my money. This time he wants my love, too. Well, he came to the wrong house—and he came twice. I shall see he shall never come a third time."

—Olivia De Havilland plotting vengeance on Montgomery Clift in William Wyler's *The Heiress*
(Screenplay by Ruth Goetz and Augustus Goetz; based on their play and WASHINGTON SQUARE, a novel by Henry James)

3.
(a) "I was just thinking what a bonehead play that old jackass made when he put all his goods in our keeping."
(b) "How do you mean?"
(a) "Figured he'd let us do his sweating for him, did he? Well, we'll show him."
(b) "What are you getting at?"
(a) "Well, man, can't you see? It's all ours. We don't go back to Durango at all, savvy? Not at all."
(b) "I don't follow you, Dobbsie."

(a) "Aw, don't be such a sap. Where did you ever grow up? All right, to make it clear to a dumbhead like you: we take all his goods and go straight up north and leave the old jackass flat."

—(a) Humphrey Bogart telling (b) Tim Holt that they're making off with Walter Huston's gold share in John Huston's *The Treasure of the Sierra Madre*
(Screenplay by John Huston; based on the novel by B. Traven)

4.
"He said 595,000 acres, Mama—and you should see the greedy look on your face."

—Elizabeth Taylor teasing her mother (Judith Evelyn) for being impressed with Rock Hudson's wealth in George Stevens's *Giant*
(Screenplay by Fred Guiol and Ivan Moffat; based on the novel by Edna Ferber)

ALSO SEE: Apathy-1; Knowledge-2; Prayers-10; Soul-7; Trouble-8.

GREETINGS

1.
"Good morning, Mr. Beale. They tell me you're a madman."

—Ned Beatty meeting Peter Finch in Sidney Lumet's *Network*
(Original Screenplay by Paddy Chayefsky)

2.
(a) "As chairwoman of the reception committee, I welcome you with open arms."
(b) "Is that so? How late do you stay open?"

—(a) Margaret Dumont and (b) Groucho Marx colliding for the first time in Leo McCarey's *Duck Soup*
(Screenplay by Bert Kalmar and Harry Ruby; additional dialogue by Arthur Sheekman and Nat Perrin)

3.
"Remember me? I'm the fellow you slept on last night."

—Clark Gable greeting his bus-seat partner (Claudette Colbert) in the depot in Frank Capra's *It Happened One Night*
(Screenplay by Robert Riskin; based on "Night Bus," a short story by Samuel Hopkins Adams)

4.
"How dear of you to let me out of jail!"

—Katharine Hepburn thanking Peter O'Toole for the Christmas break from her exile in Anthony Harvey's *The Lion in Winter*
(Screenplay by James Goldman; based on his play)

5.
"Hello, Monkey Face."

—Cary Grant greeting Joan Fontaine with a dubious term of endearment in Alfred Hitchcock's *Suspicion*
(Screenplay by Samson Raphaelson, Joan Harrison and Alma Reville; based on BEFORE THE FACT, a novel by Francis Iles)

6.
"Ah, est Bialystock and Bloom, I presume."

—Christopher Hewitt greeting Zero Mostel and Gene Wilder in poetry in Mel Brooks's *The Producers*
(Original Screenplay by Mel Brooks)

7.
"Vera, my old, old, *old* friend."

—Lucille Ball greeting Beatrice Arthur in Gene Saks's *Mame*
(Screenplay by Paul Zindel; based on the musical play by Jerome Lawrence, Robert E. Lee and Jerry Herman and AUNTIE MAME, a play by Jerome Lawrence and Robert E. Lee and novel by Patrick Dennis)

8.
"Not a brass farthing!"

—Audrey Hepburn, among others, greeting her money-mooching father (Stanley Holloway) in George Cukor's *My Fair Lady*
(Screenplay by Alan Jay Lerner; based on his musical play and PYGMALION, a screenplay and play by George Bernard Shaw)

9.
"Welcome to the Burnside Fireside."

—Rosalind Russell giving a cloyingly cute greeting to Willard Waterman and Lee Patrick in Morton Da Costa's *Auntie Mame*
(Screenplay by Betty Comden and Adolph Green; based on the play by Jerome Lawrence and Robert E. Lee and novel by Patrick Dennis)

10.
"Hello, Devil. Welcome to Hell."

—Gene Kelly welcoming Spencer Tracy to God's country in Stanley Kramer's *Inherit the Wind*
(Screenplay by Nathan E. Douglas and Harold Jacob Smith; based on the play by Jerome Lawrence and Robert E. Lee)

11.
"What have you been doing, standing over a hot resolution all day?"

—Howard St. John greeting a congressman (Larry Oliver) in George Cukor's *Born Yesterday*
(Screenplay by Albert Mannheimer; based on the play by Garson Kanin)

12.
"In college, I majored in geology and anthropology and running out of gas on Bunker Hill. What's your name, honey?"

—Bob Hope coming on strong to Jane Russell in Frank Tashlin's *Son of Paleface*
(Original Screenplay by Frank Tashlin, Robert L. Welch and Joseph Quillan)

13.
"I am Dracula. I bid you welcome."

—Bela Lugosi flashing a dark smile in Tod Browning's *Dracula*
(Screenplay by Garrett Fort; based on the play by Hamilton Deane and John L. Balderston and novel by Bram Stoker)
and

—Frank Langella dittoing in the remake, John Badham's *Dracula*
(Screenplay by W. D. Richter; based on the play by Hamilton Deane and John L. Balderston and novel by Bram Stoker)

ALSO SEE: Class-3; Compliments-4; First Lines-1; Law-1; Narcissism-5; Narcissism-6; Work-7.

GUILTY

1.

"Guilty is what the man says when your luck runs out."

—Franklyn Seales voicing the cynical view of the accused in Harold Becker's *The Onion Field*
(Screenplay by Joseph Wambaugh; based on his book)

2.

"I want to call for a vote. I want you 11 men to vote by secret ballot. I'll abstain. If there are still 11 votes for guilty, I won't stand alone. We'll take in a guilty verdict right now."

—Henry Fonda striking a bargain with his fellow jurors in Sidney Lumet's *Twelve Angry Men*
(Screenplay by Reginald Rose; based on his teleplay)

3.

"We find the defendants incredibly guilty."

—The foreman returning the verdict on Zero Mostel and Gene Wilder in Mel Brooks's *The Producers*
(Original Screenplay by Mel Brooks)

4.

"Mr. President, I stand guilty as framed because Section 40 is graft, and I'm afraid to say so. I'm afraid to tell you that a certain man in my state—a Mr. James Taylor—wanted to put through his dam for his own profit—a man who controls a political machine and controls everything else worth controlling in my state."

—James Stewart rising in the Senate to smite Edward Arnold in Frank Capra's *Mr. Smith Goes to Washington*
(Screenplay by Sidney Buchman; based on "The Gentleman From Montana," a story by Lewis R. Foster)

5.

"If I'd have made love to you, I'd have felt guilty—guilty of desecration. Yes, isn't that funny? I'm more afraid of your soul than you're afraid of my body."

—Laurence Harvey confessing an irony to Geraldine Page in Peter Glenville's *Summer and Smoke*
(Screenplay by James Poe and Meade Roberts; based on the play by Tennessee Williams)

6.

"You insist without proof that you're a murderer. You know what that is, don't you? Whoever you are, it's the guilt complex that speaks for you—a guilt fantasy that goes way back to your childhood."

—Ingrid Bergman advising Gregory Peck in Alfred Hitchcock's *Spellbound*
(Screenplay by Ben Hecht; adaptation by Angus MacPhail; based on THE HOUSE OF DR. EDWARDES, a novel by Francis Beeding)

7.

"Well, guilt is something that I get livid about because it's kind of a man-made emotion. And I would like to see you take a vacation from guilt. Stop feeling guilty for one week. Just—just say, 'Erica, turn off the guilt. Just turn it off. Don't feel guilty.' It doesn't get you anywhere. It really prolongs the agony."

—Penelope Russianoff advising Jill Clayburgh in Paul Mazursky's *An Unmarried Woman*
(Original Screenplay by Paul Mazursky)

ALSO SEE: Differences-10; Pity-1; Repetitions-3; Responsibility-3; Silence-2; Telegrams-4.

GUNS

1.

"Oh, that. That's just part of my clothes. I hardly ever shoot anybody with it."

—Dick Powell relinquishing his gun to gangsters in Edward Dmytryk's *Murder, My Sweet*
(Screenplay by John Paxton; based on FAREWELL, MY LOVELY, a novel by Raymond Chandler)

2.

"My, my, my! Such a lot of guns around town and so few brains. You know, you're the second guy I've met today that seems to think a gat in the hand means the world by the tail. Put it down, Joe."

—Humphrey Bogart trying to get Louis Jean Heydt to drop it in Howard Hawks's *The Big Sleep*
(Screenplay by William Faulkner, Leigh Brackett and Jules Furthman; based on the novel by Raymond Chandler)

3.
"We've got to start thinking beyond our guns. Those days are closing fast."

—William Holden realizing the old outlaw days are numbered in Sam Peckinpah's *The Wild Bunch*
(Screenplay by Walon Green and Sam Peckinpah; based on a story by Walon Green and Roy H. Sickner)

4.
"Out here, due process is a bullet."

—John Wayne explaining the law of the land to David Janssen in John Wayne and Ray Kellogg's *The Green Berets*
(Screenplay by James Lee Barrett; based on the novel by Robin Moore)

5.
"Folks back home used to say I could shoot a rifle before I was weaned. They were exaggerating some."

—Gary Cooper dirt-kicking his sureshot reputation in Howard Hawks's *Sergeant York*
(Original Screenplay by Abem Finkel, Harry Chandlee, Howard Koch and John Huston; based on WAR DIARY OF SERGEANT YORK and SERGEANT YORK AND HIS PEOPLE, two books by Sam K. Cowan, and SERGEANT YORK—LAST OF THE LONG HUNTERS, a book by Tom Skeyhill)

6.
"Oh, it was all instinctive. I didn't even know I'd fired. Then I followed him out to the veranda. He staggered across the porch, grabbed the railing, but it slipped through his hand and he fell down the steps. I don't remember anything more, just the reports one after another till there was a funny little click and the revolver was empty. It was only then I knew what I'd done."

—Bette Davis telling her husband (Herbert Marshall) and her lawyer (James Stephenson) how she killed David Newell in William Wyler's *The Letter*
(Screenplay by Howard Koch; based on the play and short story by W. Somerset Maugham)

7.
"I know what you're thinking. Did he fire six shots or only five? Well, to tell you the truth, in all this excitement I've kinda lost track myself. But being this is a .44 magnum, the most powerful handgun in the world, and would blow your head clean off—you've got to ask yourself one question: do I feel lucky? Well, do ya, punk?"

—Clint Eastwood holding a gun to the temple of a criminal in Don Siegel's *Dirty Harry*
(Screenplay by Harry Julian Fink, R. M. Fink and Dean Riesner; based on a story by Harry Julian Fink and R. M. Fink)

8.
"Everything happens to me. Now, I'm shot by a child."

—Jeff Corey complaining about being wounded by Kim Darby in Henry Hathaway's *True Grit*
(Screenplay by Marguerite Roberts; based on the novel by Charles Portis)

9.
"Owen, I was aiming at myself. He grabbed the gun away from me and shot me. That's the final irony: killed by a lunatic."

—John Barrymore carrying on melodramatically about a flesh wound to his associate (Roscoe Karns) in Howard Hawks's *Twentieth Century*
(Screenplay by Ben Hecht and Charles MacArthur; based on their play and NAPOLEON OF BROADWAY, a play by Charles Bruce Milholland)

10.
"I knew one thing: as soon as anyone said you didn't need a gun, you'd better take one along that worked."

—Robert Mitchum revealing a rule he lives by in Dick Richards's *Farewell, My Lovely*
(Screenplay by David Zelag Goodman; based on the novel by Raymond Chandler)

11.
"We gotta stick together. There's a rope 'round

my neck right now, and they only hang you once. If anybody turns yellow and squeals, my gun's gonna speak its piece."

—Edward G. Robinson warning his gang in Mervyn LeRoy's *Little Caesar*
(*Screenplay by Francis Edwards Faragoh; based on the novel by W. R. Burnett*)

ALSO SEE: Always-6; Lucky-2; Moon-4; Notes-7; Party-7; Threats-1; Tough-1; Why-9.

HAIR

1.
"I'd love to kiss yuh, but I just washed mah ha-yer."

—Bette Davis ducking a clinch in Michael Curtiz's *Cabin in the Cotton*
(*Screenplay by Paul Green; based on the novel by Harry Harrison Kroll*)

2.
"If I kept my hair 'natural' the way you do, I'd be bald."

—Rosalind Russell insulting Coral Browne in Morton Da Costa's *Auntie Mame*
(*Screenplay by Betty Comden and Adolph Green; based on the play by Jerome Lawrence and Robert E. Lee*)

and (almost verbatim)

—Beatrice Arthur dittoing Lucille Ball in the remake, Gene Saks's *Mame*
(*Screenplay by Paul Zindel; based on the musical play by Jerome Lawrence, Robert E. Lee and Jerry Herman and AUNTIE MAME, a play by Jerome Lawrence and Robert E. Lee and novel by Patrick Dennis*)

3.
"Just look at that. They guaranteed me this was going to be a permanent wave. Ain't permanent. Ain't a wave. Ain't nothing. It's just hair —but it's all my own."

—Lee Patrick grousing at her mirror in Anatole Litvak's *City for Conquest*

(*Screenplay by John Wexley; based on the novel by Aben Kandel*)

4.
"A girl can't get married without a permanent. It wouldn't be legal."

—Priscilla Lane explaining to John Garfield why every curl is in place in Michael Curtiz's *Four Daughters*
(*Screenplay by Julius J. Epstein and Lenore Coffee; based on "Sister Act," a short story by Fannie Hurst*)

5.
"Gramp, how many other people in the world have green hair?"

—Dean Stockwell meaning the question literally in Joseph Losey's *The Boy With Green Hair*
(*Screenplay by Ben Barzman and Alfred Lewis Levitt; based on a short story by Betsy Beaton*)

6.
"In my time, women with hair like that didn't come outside in the daylight."

—Elizabeth Patterson commenting on Mae West in Henry Hathaway's *Go West, Young Man*
(*Screenplay by Mae West; based on PERSONAL APPEARANCE, a play by Lawrence Riley*)

7.
"I'm not saying we wouldn't get our hair mussed, but I do say no more than 10 to 20 million killed, top—that is, depending on the break."

—George C. Scott minimizing a Doomsday statistic for Peter Sellers in Stanley Kubrick's *Dr. Strangelove or: How I Learned To Stop Worrying and Love the Bomb*
(*Screenplay by Stanley Kubrick, Terry Southern and Peter George; based on RED ALERT, a novel by Peter George*)

ALSO SEE: Good and Bad-3; Hangover-3; Looks-10; Men-3; Proposals-13; Run-3; Timing-3.

HANDS

1.

"Observe my hands, my dear. I could tear you to pieces with them, and I'd do it if it'd take Ashley out of your mind forever. But it wouldn't, so I'll remove him from your mind forever this way. I'll put my hands so—one on each side of your head—and I'll smash your skull between them like a walnut, and that'll block him out."

—Clark Gable, in a drunken fit of jealousy, menacing Vivien Leigh in Victor Fleming's *Gone With the Wind*
(Screenplay by Sidney Howard; based on the novel by Margaret Mitchell)

2.

"Oh, I know I must be punished, of course, but not on the hands. Please. Not on my hands. Today is the music scholarship, and, if you cane me, if my hands were—oh, please!"

—Ann Todd pleading (in vain) to a cruel headmistress in Compton Bennett's *The Seventh Veil*
(Original Screenplay by Muriel Box and Sydney Box)

3.

"You don't know what it's like to stand out there on that stage all alone, with the whole show on your shoulders. If I'm no good, the show's no good! I've got the future of one hundred people in my hand—this hand! This hand!"

—Bing Crosby feeling the responsibility of a star in George Seaton's *The Country Girl*
(Screenplay by George Seaton; based on the play by Clifford Odets)

4.

"When we go to the guillotine, will you let me hold your hand? It will give me courage, too."

—Isabel Jewell asking Ronald Colman's help for the dark ordeal ahead of them in Jack Conway's *A Tale of Two Cities*
(Screenplay by W. P. Lipscomb and S. N. Behrman; based on the novel by Charles Dickens)

5.

"Here they are. All of them! All papers! I hereby endow you with them! Take them. Peruse them. Commit them to memory, even! I think it's wonderfully fitting that Belle Reve should finally be this bunch of old papers in your big capable hands."

—Vivien Leigh thrusting the remains of her family estate at her brutish brother-in-law (Marlon Brando) in Elia Kazan's *A Streetcar Named Desire*
(Screenplay by Tennessee Williams; adaptation by Oscar Saul; based on the play by Tennessee Williams)

6.

(a) "Barney had about 12 hands, and I didn't like any of 'em."
　(b) "Oh, Barney's all right."
　(a) "Yeah? You didn't have to pass him a hundred times a day. It was like tangling with an octopus."

—(a) Ann Sheridan telling (b) George Raft why she quit her hashhouse job in Raoul Walsh's *They Drive by Night*
(Screenplay by Jerry Wald and Richard Macaulay; based on LONG HAUL, a novel by A. I. Bezzerides)

7.

"Don't you touch me. You keep your paws clean for the undergraduates."

—Richard Burton objecting to Elizabeth Taylor's attention to George Segal in Mike Nichols's *Who's Afraid of Virginia Woolf?*
(Screenplay by Ernest Lehman; based on the play by Edward Albee)

8.

"That's all I've become to you—a pair of dirty hands. Well, have them then. Have them where they belong. It doesn't hurt to strike you."

—Laurence Olivier striking Merle Oberon in William Wyler's *Wuthering Heights*
(Screenplay by Ben Hecht and Charles MacArthur; based on the novel by Emily Brontë)

9.

"Boss, why did God give us hands? To grab. Well, grab!"

—Anthony Quinn encouraging Alan Bates to court Irene Papas in Michael Cacoyannis's *Zorba the Greek* *(Screenplay by Michael Cacoyannis; based on the novel by Nikos Kazantzakis)*

10.

"A hand I could have sat in took hold of my shoulder."

—Robert Mitchum getting a tap from a big-bruiser client (Jack O'Halloran) in Dick Richards's *Farewell, My Lovely* *(Screenplay by David Zelag Goodman; based on the novel by Raymond Chandler)*

11.

"He looked at me. His hands were on her throat, and he was strangling me."

—Patricia Hitchcock feeling strangely strangled by Robert Walker in Alfred Hitchcock's *Strangers on a Train* *(Screenplay by Raymond Chandler and Czenzi Ormonde; adaptation by Whitfield Cook; based on the novel by Patricia Highsmith)*

12.

"Fill your hands, you son of a bitch!"

—John Wayne charging into a showdown with Robert Duvall in Henry Hathaway's *True Grit* *(Screenplay by Marguerite Roberts; based on the novel by Charles Portis)*

ALSO SEE: Clean-2; Crazy-16; Directors-1; Jewels-2; Lady-4; Newspapering-3; Painting-5; Party-2; Pride-1; Snake-1.

HANGING

1.

"Hangin's any man's business that's around."

—Henry Fonda preaching the everyman gospel in William A. Wellman's *The Ox-Bow Incident* *(Screenplay by Lamar Trotti; based on the novel by Walter Van Tilburg Clark)*

2.

"If these boys had more than one life, I'd say, 'Go ahead. Maybe a little hanging mightn't do 'em any harm.' But the sort of hanging you boys'd give 'em would be so—so permanent. Trouble is, when men start taking the law into their own hands, they're just as apt to—in all the confusion and fun—to start hanging somebody who's not a murderer as somebody who is. Then, the next thing you know, they're hanging one another just for fun till it gets to a place a man can't pass a tree or look at a rope without feeling uneasy."

—Henry Fonda lightly dispersing a lynch mob in John Ford's *Young Mr. Lincoln* *(Original Screenplay by Lamar Trotti)*

3.

"I'll plead for you as hard as ever I can. Better than that, I'll come tomorrow morning and cut you down from the tree myself and bury you with grief and respect."

—Edmond O'Brien promising no help to his father (Fredric March) when the lynch mob comes in Michael Gordon's *Another Part of the Forest* *(Screenplay by Vladimir Pozner; based on the play by Lillian Hellman)*

4.

"Hanging'd be a small price to pay for the company of such a charming lady."

—Errol Flynn gallantly informing Basil Rathbone that Olivia De Havilland is worth the risk in Michael Curtiz and William Keighley's *The Adventures of Robin Hood* *(Original Screenplay by Norman Reilly Raine and Seton I. Miller; based on the ancient Robin Hood legends)*

5.

"The chances are you'll get off with life. That means if you're a good girl, you'll be out in 20 years. I'll be waiting for you. If they hang you, I'll always remember you."

—Humphrey Bogart turning in Mary Astor in John Huston's *The Maltese Falcon*

(Screenplay by John Huston; based on the novel by Dashiell Hammett)

6.
(a) "Everything is perfect—except for a couple of details."
  (b) "They *hang* people for a couple of details."

—(a) William Demarest and (b) Eddie Bracken discussing their hero charade in Preston Sturges's *Hail the Conquering Hero*
(Original Screenplay by Preston Sturges)

7.
"Well, I'll hang in the end, but they'll get their money's worth at the trial. You wait."

—Robert Montgomery making a parting promise as police lead him away in Richard Thorpe's *Night Must Fall*
(Screenplay by John Van Druten; based on the play by Emlyn Williams)

8.
"Would you hang us together, please?"

—Katharine Hepburn making a sentimental request of Theodore Bikel, who's preparing to hang her and Humphrey Bogart in John Huston's *The African Queen*
(Screenplay by James Agee and John Huston; based on the novel by C. S. Forester)

ALSO SEE: Choice-4; Guns-11; Letters-10; Letters-11; Life and Death-12; Threats-7.

HANGOVER

1.
"Hazel, you've got what is known in medicine as a hangover."

—Charles Winninger dispensing his medical ruling to Carole Lombard in William A. Wellman's *Nothing Sacred*
(Screenplay by Ben Hecht; based on "Letter to the Editor," a short story by James H. Street)

2.
"Darling, your Auntie Mame is hung!"

—Rosalind Russell receiving a rowdy wake-up call from her young nephew (Jan Handzlik) in Morton Da Costa's *Auntie Mame*
(Screenplay by Betty Comden and Adolph Green; based on the play by Jerome Lawrence and Robert E. Lee)
and (almost verbatim)

—Lucille Ball dittoing from Kirby Furlong in the remake, Gene Saks's *Mame*
(Screenplay by Paul Zindel; based on the musical play by Jerome Lawrence, Robert E. Lee and Jerry Herman and AUNTIE MAME, a play by Jerome Lawrence and Robert E. Lee and novel by Patrick Dennis)

3.
"I've had hangovers before, but this time even my hair hurts."

—Rock Hudson moaning to Tony Randall in Michael Gordon's *Pillow Talk*
(Screenplay by Stanley Shapiro and Maurice Richlin; based on a story by Russell Rouse and Clarence Greene)

4.
"I'm testing the air. I like it, but it doesn't like me."

—James Stewart moving gingerly into the morning in George Cukor's *The Philadelphia Story*
(Screenplay by Donald Ogden Stewart; based on the play by Philip Barry)

ALSO SEE: Idea-1.

HAPPINESS

1.
(a) "These kids today! All they're looking for is happiness!"
  (b) "Don't look for happiness, Richard. It'll only make you miserable."

—(a) Richard Castellano and (b) Beatrice Arthur telling their son (Joseph Hindy) not to expect too much out of life in Cy Howard's *Lovers and Other Strangers*
(Screenplay by Renee Taylor, Joseph Bologna and David Z. Goodman; based on the play by Renee Taylor and Joseph Bologna)

2.

"The happiest days are when babies come."

—Olivia De Havilland rejoicing in an event that eventually means her death in Victor Fleming's *Gone With the Wind*
(Screenplay by Sidney Howard; based on the novel by Margaret Mitchell)

3.

"Happiness is the reward of industry and labor. Dancing is a waste of time."

—Cyd Charisse advancing a philosophy contrary to Fred Astaire's in Rouben Mamoulian's *Silk Stockings*
(Screenplay by Leonard Gershe and Leonard Spigelgass; based on the musical play by George S. Kaufman, Leueen MacGrath and Abe Burrows and NINOTCHKA, a screenplay by Charles Brackett, Billy Wilder and Walter Reisch and original story by Melchior Lengyel)

4.

"Well, Bart, I figure that everyone is entitled to just so much happiness in life. Some get it in the beginning and some in the middle and others at the end. And then there are those that have it spread thin all through the years."

—Beulah Bondi reflecting on her fifty years with Victor Moore in Leo McCarey's *Make Way for Tomorrow*
(Screenplay by Vina Delmar; based on the play by Helen Leary and Nolan Leary and THE YEARS ARE SO LONG, a novel by Josephine Lawrence)

5.

"How can I answer you when I don't know the answer myself? If you say we're happy, let's leave it at that. Happiness is something I know nothing about."

—Laurence Olivier curtly concurring with Joan Fontaine in Alfred Hitchcock's *Rebecca*
(Screenplay by Robert E. Sherwood and Joan Harrison; adaptation by Philip MacDonald and Michael Hogan; based on the novel by Daphne du Maurier)

6.

(a) "The Inn of the Sixth Happiness. Ah! Sounds quite Oriental, doesn't it?

(b) "Yes. Yes. But Yang—Yang said that—that everybody in China wishes you the five happinesses: wealth, longevity, good health, virtue and a—"

(a) "And a peaceful death in old age."

(b) "Yes, but they didn't mention any more. What is the sixth happiness?"

(a) "That you will find out for yourself. Each person decides in his own heart what the sixth happiness is."

—(a) Athene Seyler instructing (b) Ingrid Bergman in Mark Robson's *The Inn of the Sixth Happiness*
(Screenplay by Isobel Lennart; based on THE SMALL WOMAN, a book by Alan Burgess)

ALSO SEE: Good and Bad-1; Good and Bad-2; Mad Act-2; Moon-1; Peace-5; Promiscuity-6; Realities-1; Rules-3; Selfish-6; Stupid-5; Success-1; Tears-6; Telephone Scenes-1; Wants-8; Wealth-8; Work-8.

HATE

1.

"If there's anything in the world I hate, it's leeches—filthy little devils!"

—Humphrey Bogart shuddering as Katharine Hepburn removes leeches from his body in John Huston's *The African Queen*
(Screenplay by James Agee and John Huston; based on the novel by C. S. Forester)

2.

"Norman or Saxon, what's that matter? It's injustice I hate, not the Normans."

—Errol Flynn telling Olivia De Havilland what he stands for in Michael Curtiz and William Keighley's *The Adventures of Robin Hood*
(Original Screenplay by Norman Reilly Raine and Seton I. Miller; based on the ancient Robin Hood legends)

3.

"Why do any of us have to cry? You or me? What have we done? Oh, I hate it! I hate everything! I'd hate God if I could, but there's nothing you can reach!"

—Betty Field breaking into hysteria in Sam Wood's
Kings Row
*(Screenplay by Casey Robinson; based on the
novel by Henry Bellamann)*

4.
"Your eyes are full of hate, Forty-One. That's
good. Hate keeps a man alive. It gives him
strength."

—Jack Hawkins meeting Charlton Heston among the
galley slaves in William Wyler's *Ben-Hur*
*(Screenplay by Karl Tunberg; based on BER-HUR
(A TALE OF THE CHRIST), a novel by General Lew
Wallace)*

5.
"In this house with Heathcliff, nothing can live.
Nothing but hate. I can feel it breathing like
the devil's own breath on me. And you. He
hates you worse than he does me. He loathes
you. Each time you kiss him, his heart breaks
with rage because it's not Cathy."

—Hugh Williams brooding aloud to Geraldine Fitzgerald about Laurence Olivier in William Wyler's
Wuthering Heights
*(Screenplay by Ben Hecht and Charles MacArthur;
based on the novel by Emily Brontë)*

6.
"We hate the people we love because they're
the only ones who can hurt us."

—Samuel S. Hinds counseling Claudette Colbert in
Gregory La Cava's *Private Worlds*
*(Screenplay by Lynn Starling; based on the novel
by Phyllis Bottome)*

7.
"We're not quarreling! We're in complete
agreement! We hate each other!"

—Nanette Fabray yelling at her husband (Oscar Levant) during out-of-town tryouts in Vincente Minnelli's *The Band Wagon*
*(Original Screenplay by Betty Comden and
Adolph Green)*

8.
"Who'd look after her? She'd be alone up
there. The fire would go out. It'd be cold and

damp like a grave. If you love someone, you
don't do that to them—even if you hate them.
Understand, I don't hate her. I hate what she's
become. I hate the illness."

—Anthony Perkins discussing his mother with Janet
Leigh in Alfred Hitchcock's *Psycho*
*(Screenplay by Joseph Stefano; based on the novel
by Robert Bloch)*

9.
"I hate shoes, Mr. Dawes. I wear them to dance
or to show myself, but I feel afraid in shoes and
I feel safe with my feet in the dirt."

—Ava Gardner confessing a private hate to Hum-
phrey Bogart in Joseph L. Mankiewicz's *The Barefoot
Contessa*
(Original Screenplay by Joseph L. Mankiewicz)

10.
"I can't afford to hate anybody. I'm only a pho-
tographer."

—Ruth Hussey passing on the subject in George
Cukor's *The Philadelphia Story*
*(Screenplay by Donald Ogden Stewart; based on
the play by Philip Barry)*

ALSO SEE: Comeback-1; Compromise-2; Crazy-
8; Dark-3; Dress-4; Fathers-3; Friends-8; Heart-
18; Hope-6; Husbands-8; Incompatibility-1;
Love-7; Movies-4; Party-3; Party-6; Prayers-5;
Questions-17; Self-Perception-2; Sons-4; Sun-2;
Trust and Distrust-4; Truth-5; Understand-2;
Wives-8.

HEAD

1.
"I've got it! I've got it! Of course, there is no-
body that's missing. All the information's inside
Memory's head."

—Robert Donat realizing where all the spy secrets
are stored in Alfred Hitchcock's *The Thirty-Nine
Steps*
*(Screenplay by Charles Bennett; dialogue by Ian
Hay; continuity by Alma Reville; based on the
novel by John Buchan)*

2.

"You were right. If your head says one thing and your whole life says another, your head always loses."

—Humphrey Bogart rising to heroism against his better judgment in John Huston's *Key Largo* (*Screenplay by Richard Brooks and John Huston; based on the play by Maxwell Anderson*)

3.

"I don't mind being killed, but I resent hearing it from a character whose head comes to a point."

—Groucho Marx berating his messenger of death (Chico Marx) in Archie Mayo's *A Night in Casablanca* (*Original Screenplay by Joseph Fields and Roland Kibbee*)

4.

"Why should I not give my head to Agrippa? It would be no great loss to me—dying a second time is painless, they say—and it's supposed to be a great advantage to you: a basis, perhaps, of a great new alliance with Rome."

—Richard Burton making the sacrificial gesture to Elizabeth Taylor in Joseph L. Mankiewicz's *Cleopatra* (*Screenplay by Joseph L. Mankiewicz, Ranald MacDougall and Sidney Buchman; based upon histories by Plutarch, Suetonius and Appian and THE LIFE AND TIMES OF CLEOPATRA, a book by C. M. Franzero*)

5.

"You oughta put handles on that skull. Maybe you could grow geraniums in it."

—Henry Fonda berating his bodyguard (William Demarest) in Preston Sturges's *The Lady Eve* (*Screenplay by Preston Sturges; based on the story by Monckton Hoffe*)

ALSO SEE: Advice-3; Advice-4; Headlines-8; Heart-4; Home-8; Mothers-4; Neck-3; Quiet-1; Snake-5.

HEADLINES

1.

"Kris Kringle Krazy?
      Kourt Kase Koming;
      'Kalamity,' Kries Kids"

—Headline summarizing George Seaton's *Miracle on 34th Street* (*Screenplay by George Seaton; based on an original story by Valentine Davis*)

2.

"Six! All Boys! Six!"

—Headline heralding Betty Hutton's title miracle in Preston Sturges's *The Miracle of Morgan's Creek* (*Original Screenplay by Preston Sturges*)

3.

"It's Katie for Congress"

—Headline announcing Loretta Young's political victory in H. C. Potter's *The Farmer's Daughter* (*Screenplay by Allen Rivkin and Laura Kerr; based on HULDA, DAUGHTER OF PARLIAMENT, a play by Juhni Tervataa*)

4.

"Charles Foster Kane Defeated
      Fraud at Polls!"

—Headline, in Orson Welles's paper, announcing his political defeat in Orson Welles's *Citizen Kane* (*Original Screenplay by Herman J. Mankiewicz and Orson Welles*)

5.

"Rocky Dies Yellow;
      Killer Coward at End"

—Headline announcing James Cagney's death in the electric chair in Michael Curtiz's *Angels With Dirty Faces* (*Screenplay by John Wexley and Warren Duff; based on an original story by Rowland Brown*)

6.

"Ex-officer pleads guilty;
      Offense in theatre"

—Headline spelling scandal for David Niven in Delbert Mann's *Separate Tables*

(Screenplay by Terence Rattigan and John Gay; based on the play by Terence Rattigan)

7.
"Tomato's Tomato
      Pinched by Cops"

—Headline announcing Audrey Hepburn's arrest as the moll of Sally Tomato (Alan Reed) in Blake Edwards's *Breakfast at Tiffany's*
(Screenplay by George Axelrod; based on the novella by Truman Capote)

8.
" 'Monkey Trial!' Here's another one: 'Monkey Shines in Hillsboro.' The whole world's laughing at us. Look, from Chicago: 'Heavenly Hillsboro—Does It Have a Hole in Its Head or Its Head in a Hole?' "

—George Dunn reading the bad press his town is getting over its anti-evolution stand in Stanley Kramer's *Inherit the Wind*
(Screenplay by Nathan E. Douglas and Harold Jacob Smith; based on the play by Jerome Lawrence and Robert E. Lee)

9.
"It sure would have made attractive headlines: 'Great Star Kills Herself for Unknown Writer.' "

—William Holden shuddering over Gloria Swanson's suicide attempt in Billy Wilder's *Sunset Boulevard*
(Original Screenplay by Charles Brackett, Billy Wilder and D. M. Marshman Jr.)

10.
"What do you think the newspapers'll say when they find out about this? 'Wife Quits Miracle Worker.' "

—Tyrone Power trying to get a headline hold on his departing wife (Coleen Gray) in Edmund Goulding's *Nightmare Alley*
(Screenplay by Jules Furthman; based on the novel by William Lindsay Gresham)

11.
"I can already see the headline: 'Wife Names Fish.' "

—Clinton Sundberg responding to William Powell's story in Irving Pichel's *Mr. Peabody and the Mermaid*
(Screenplay by Nunnally Johnson; based on PEABODY'S MERMAID, a novel by Guy Jones and Constance Jones)

12.
"Fine thing! Me, known as The Flying Pug. The papers will all say, 'Flying Pug Takes Train.' Fine thing!"

—Robert Montgomery deciding to take a fateful plane trip in Alexander Hall's *Here Comes Mr. Jordan*
(Screenplay by Sidney Buchman and Seton I. Miller; based on HEAVEN CAN WAIT, a play by Harry Segall)

ALSO SEE: Newspapering-8.

HEALTH

1.
"Sometimes I think I'm not as sick as the others. But they say that if you think you're well, then you're really sick. If I say I'm sick, maybe that means I'm well."

—Olivia De Havilland making progress in Anatole Litvak's *The Snake Pit*
(Screenplay by Frank Partos and Millen Brand; based on the novel by Mary Jane Ward)

2.
"I've come to the conclusion that the world would be a healthier place if more people were sick."

—Richard Todd praising his nurse (Patricia Neal) with a touch of irony in Vincent Sherman's *The Hasty Heart*
(Screenplay by Ranald MacDougall; based on the play by John Patrick)

ALSO SEE: Life and Death-5; Taste-1; Toasts-20.

HEART

1.

"Yes, it is an Army document—a medical report—dated Oct. 25, 1942, from a base hospital in Bengazi. It describes, in detail, the degree to which my body was blown apart by an explosion and, with understandable pride, the skill with which they put some of it together again. You understand now why it is so important to me for you to believe that I love you with all my heart. The report will tell you that almost the only undestroyed part of me is my heart. I love you with all of it."

—Rossano Brazzi giving Ava Gardner the bad news on their wedding night in Joseph L. Mankiewicz's *The Barefoot Contessa* *(Original Screenplay by Joseph L. Mankiewicz)*

2.

" *'Straight'?* What's 'straight'? A line can be straight, or a street. But the heart of a human being?"

—Vivien Leigh telling Karl Malden that, in her fashion, she has been "straight" with him in Elia Kazan's *A Streetcar Named Desire* *(Screenplay by Tennessee Williams; adaptation by Oscar Saul; based on the play by Tennessee Williams)*

3.

"Back where I come from, there are men who do nothing all day but good deeds. They are called er, er, er, er, good-deed doers, and their hearts are no bigger than yours. But they have one thing you haven't got: a testimonial. Therefore, in consideration of your kindness, I take pleasure at this time in presenting you with a small token of our esteem and affection. And remember, my sentimental friend, that a heart is not judged by how much you love, but by how much you are loved by others."

—Frank Morgan giving heart to Jack Haley in Victor Fleming's *The Wizard of Oz* *(Screenplay by Noel Langley, Florence Ryerson and Edgar Allan Woolf; adaptation by Noel Langley; based on the novel by L. Frank Baum)*

4.

"Rosie'd give the shirt off her back to anybody. She got a heart as big as her head."

—William Bendix intending to compliment his girlfriend in Alfred Hitchcock's *Lifeboat* *(Screenplay by Jo Swerling; based on the story by John Steinbeck)*

5.

(a) "You got a heart as big—"
        (b) "As big as an artichoke. A leaf for everyone."

—(a) Tyrone Power and (b) Joan Blondell agreeing about her generous spirit in Edmund Goulding's *Nightmare Alley* *(Screenplay by Jules Furthman; based on the novel by William Lindsay Gresham)*

6.

"Well, isn't it enough that you've gathered every other man's heart today? You've always had mine. You cut your teeth on it."

—Leslie Howard treating Vivien Leigh with brotherly regard in Victor Fleming's *Gone With the Wind* *(Screenplay by Sidney Howard; based on the novel by Margaret Mitchell)*

7.

"I hope all your teeth have cavities, and don't forget: abscess makes the heart grow fonder."

—Groucho Marx cracking wise to Chico Marx in Joseph Santley and Robert Florey's *The Cocoanuts* *(Screenplay by Morrie Ryskind; based on the musical play by George S. Kaufman and Morrie Ryskind)*

8.

"A man wants to be met by a generous heart in a woman. An open heart. Honey, never be ashamed to say what you feel. And, if you come to love a man, let him know it. Let him know all about it."

—Robert Preston counseling his daughter (Shirley Knight) in Delbert Mann's *The Dark at the Top of the Stairs* *(Screenplay by Irving Ravetch and Harriet Frank Jr.; based on the play by William Inge)*

9.

"What is essential is invisible to the eye. It's only with the heart that one can see clearly."

—Gene Wilder dispensing advice in Stanley Donen's *The Little Prince*
(Screenplay by Alan Jay Lerner; based on the story by Antoine de Saint Exupéry)

10.

"I am sitting here, Mr. Cook, toying with the idea of removing your heart and stuffing it— like an olive."

—Walter Connolly raging at his reporter (Fredric March) in William A. Wellman's *Nothing Sacred*
(Screenplay by Ben Hecht; based on "Letter to the Editor," a short story by James H. Street)
                and (almost verbatim)

—Fred Clark dittoing at Janet Leigh in the remake, Norman Taurog's *Living It Up*
(Screenplay by Jack Rose and Melville Shavelson; based on HAZEL FLAGG, *a musical play by Ben Hecht,* NOTHING SACRED, *a screenplay by Ben Hecht and "Letter to the Editor," a short story by James H. Street)*

11.

"You know, Jerry, I think, in order to be afraid, you got to have a heart. I don't think I got one. I had that cut out of me a long time ago."

—James Cagney making a cocky confession to his priest (Pat O'Brien) in Michael Curtiz's *Angels With Dirty Faces*
(Screenplay by John Wexley and Warren Duff; based on an original story by Rowland Brown)

12.

"You have a good mind, Tracy. You have a pretty face, a fine disciplined body that does what you tell it. You have everything it takes to make a lovely woman—except the one essential: an understanding heart. Without it, you might just as well be made of bronze."

—Sidney Blackmer telling Grace Kelly what's missing in Charles Walters's *High Society*
(Screenplay by John Patrick; based on THE PHILADELPHIA STORY, *a screenplay by Donald Ogden Stewart and play by Philip Barry)*
                and (almost verbatim)

—John Halliday dittoing Katharine Hepburn in the original, George Cukor's *The Philadelphia Story*
(Screenplay by Donald Ogden Stewart; based on the play by Philip Barry)

13.

"Eastman, that night when you left that dinner party at the house at Bride's Lake to meet Alice Tripp in the bus station, do you remember leaving anything behind you? . . . I'm referring to your heart, Eastman. Did you leave that behind you? Did you, Eastman? Out there on that terrace in the moonlight. You left behind, didn't you, the girl you loved—and, with her, your hopes, your ambitions, your dreams? Didn't you, Eastman? You left behind everything in the world you ever wanted, including the girl you loved. But you planned to return to it, didn't you, Eastman? Answer me!"

—Raymond Burr cross-examining Montgomery Clift in George Stevens's *A Place in the Sun*
(Screenplay by Michael Wilson and Harry Brown; based on AN AMERICAN TRAGEDY, *a play by Patrick Kearney and novel by Theodore Dreiser)*

14.

"Nice speech, Eve. But I wouldn't worry too much about your heart. You can always put that award where your heart ought to be."

—Bette Davis "congratulating" Anne Baxter in Joseph L. Mankiewicz's *All About Eve*
(Screenplay by Joseph L. Mankiewicz; based on "The Wisdom of Eve," a radio play and short story by Mary Orr)

15.

"I think you must have an adding machine for your heart."

—Bette Davis objecting to Paul Muni's indifference to her in Archie Mayo's *Bordertown*
(Screenplay by Laird Doyle and Wallace Smith; adaptation by Robert Lord; based on the novel by Carroll Graham)

16.

"Vera, your heart is from Tiffany's, too."

—Rosalind Russell appreciating the kindness of Coral Browne in Morton DaCosta's *Auntie Mame*

(Screenplay by Betty Comden and Adolph Green; based on the play by Jerome Lawrence and Robert E. Lee)

17.

"With all my heart, I still love the man I killed."

—Bette Davis confessing murder and infidelity to her husband (Herbert Marshall) in William Wyler's *The Letter*
(Screenplay by Howard Koch; based on the play and short story by W. Somerset Maugham)

18.

"I hated Francis. I wanted him dead. Maybe I killed him. If there's such a thing as murder in the heart, there's your certain answer."

—Joan Bennett confessing to Gregory Peck that she may indeed be a murderess in Zoltan Korda's *The Macomber Affair*
(Screenplay by Casey Robinson and Seymour Bennett; adaptation by Seymour Bennett and Frank Arnold; based on "The Short Happy Life of Francis Macomber," a short story by Ernest Hemingway)

19.

(a) "You don't know this man. You know only science. You know his mind, but you don't know his heart."

   (b) "We are speaking of a schizophrenic and not a valentine."

—(a) Ingrid Bergman and (b) Michael Chekhov discussing Gregory Peck in Alfred Hitchcock's *Spellbound*
(Screenplay by Ben Hecht; adaptation by Angus MacPhail; based on THE HOUSE OF DR. EDWARDES, a novel by Francis Beeding)

20.

"Was that cannon fire, or is it my heart pounding?"

—Ingrid Bergman romancing Humphrey Bogart as Germans march into Paris in Michael Curtiz's *Casablanca*
(Screenplay by Julius J. Epstein, Philip G. Epstein and Howard Koch; based on EVERYBODY COMES TO RICK'S, a play by Murray Burnett and Joan Alison)

21.

(a) "When I'm close to you like this, there's a sound in the air like the beating of wings. You know what it is?"
    (b) "No. What?"
    (a) "My heart. Beating like a schoolboy's."
    (b) "Is it? I thought it was mine."

—(a) Zachary Scott and (b) Joan Crawford meeting on the same romantic wavelength in Michael Curtiz's *Mildred Pierce*
(Screenplay by Ranald MacDougall; based on the novel by James M. Cain)

22.

"Now, in studying your basic metabolism, we first listen to your heartbeat. And, if your hearts beat anything but diamonds and clubs, it's because your partner is cheating— or your wife."

—Groucho Marx cracking wise in Norman Z. McLeod's *Horse Feathers*
(Screenplay by Bert Kalmar, Harry Ruby, S. J. Perelman and Will B. Johnstone)

23.

"Oh, don't think it's going to be easy. Nothing you really want is ever given away free. You have to pay for it—and usually with your heart."

—Adolphe Menjou advising his new contract player (Janet Gaynor) in William A. Wellman's *A Star Is Born*
(Screenplay by Dorothy Parker, Alan Campbell and Robert Carson; based on an original story by William A. Wellman and Robert Carson)

24.

"It takes more than greasepaint and footlights to make an actress. It takes heartbreak as well."

—Constance Collier advising Katharine Hepburn in Gregory La Cava's *Stage Door*
(Screenplay by Morrie Ryskind and Anthony Veiller; based on the play by Edna Ferber and George S. Kaufman)

25.

"All right, so I'll go to the Stardust Ballroom. I'll put on a blue suit, and I'll go. And you know

what I'm going to get for my trouble? Heartache. A big night of heartache."

—Ernest Borgnine deciding to go out (against his
better judgment) in Delbert Mann's *Marty*
*(Screenplay by Paddy Chayefsky; based on his
teleplay)*

26.
(a) "I'll sue the airline for this. I'm not supposed to exert myself. The doctor says my
heart—"
    (b) "Your heart is breaking my heart."

—(b) Paul Fix shutting up (a) Sidney Blackmer in
William A. Wellman's *The High and the Mighty*
*(Screenplay by Ernest K. Gann; based on his
novel)*

ALSO SEE: Aging-5; Aging-6; Beliefs-4; Body-5;
Conscience-1; Crazy-8; Duty-2; Dying Words-
3; Empathy-1; Empathy-2; Exchanges-9; Ex-
changes-10; Faith-1; Fidelity-3; Good-byes-8;
Happiness-6; Hate-5; Home-8; Human-4; Let-
ters-4; Letters-5; Letters-12; Lies-6; Lock-3;
Loneliness-2; Loneliness-6; Love-13; Love-25;
Love Objects-4; Lucky-3; Mothers-4; Pain-1;
Pep Talks-8; Pet Expressions-11; Prayers-3;
Psychiatry-7; Public Relations-3; Questions-17;
Rejection-14; Sensible-4; Sin-1; Sounds-1; Sto-
mach-2; Strange-1; Trust and Distrust-7;
Wants-4; Weakness-1; Wish-2; Wives-10.

HEAVEN

1.
"If you're there, Vinnie, I'll manage to get in
some way—even if I have to climb the
fence."

—William Powell reassuring a fretful Irene Dunne in
Michael Curtiz's *Life With Father*
*(Screenplay by Donald Ogden Stewart; based on
the play by Howard Lindsay and Russel Crouse
and stories by Clarence Day, Jr.)*

2.
"I feel like we've died and gone to heaven—
only we had to climb up."

—Mildred Natwick arriving breathlessly at her
daughter's five-flight walk-up apartment in Gene
Saks's *Barefoot in the Park*
(Screenplay by Neil Simon; based on his play)

3.
"And now Major Amberson was engaged in the
profoundest thinking of his life, and he realized
that everything which had worried him or de-
lighted him during his lifetime—all his buying
and building and trading and banking—that it
was all a trifle and a waste beside what concerned him now, for the major knew now that
he had to plan how to enter an unknown country where he was not even sure of being recognized as an Amberson."

—Orson Welles narrating the death of Richard Bennett in Orson Welles's *The Magnificent Ambersons*
*(Screenplay by Orson Welles; based on the novel
by Booth Tarkington)*

4.
"I shall enter the kingdom of heaven with a
letter of introduction from a Prince of the
Church. I fancy all doors will be open to me.
. . . There'll be none of this confounded democracy there. I shall pick and choose my company
as I always have."

—Clifton Webb holding his elitist pose on his deathbed in Edmund Goulding's *The Razor's Edge*
*(Screenplay by Lamar Trotti; based on the novel
by W. Somerset Maugham)*

5.
"Oh dear, oh dear. I have a queer feeling
there's going to be a strange face in heaven in
the morning."

—J. M. Kerrigan being confronted by a brothel
bouncer in John Ford's *The Informer*
*(Screenplay by Dudley Nichols; based on the
novel by Liam O'Flaherty)*

6.
"I don't think I belong in heaven, Ellen. I
dreamt once I was there. I dreamt I went to
heaven and that heaven didn't seem to be
my home and I broke my heart with weeping to come back to earth and the angels

were so angry they flung me out in the middle of the heath on top of Wuthering Heights and I woke up sobbing with joy. That's it, Ellen. I've no more business marrying Edgar Linton than I have of being in heaven."

—Merle Oberon realizing her place on earth in William Wyler's *Wuthering Heights*
(Screenplay by Ben Hecht and Charles MacArthur; based on the novel by Emily Brontë)

7.
(a) "I am so happy it frightens me. I have a feeling that heaven is unfair and is preparing for you and for me a great sadness because we have been given so much."
(b) "Darling, whatever happens, always remember: nothing is fair, nor unfair, under heaven."

—(b) William Holden giving (a) Jennifer Jones fair warning in Henry King's *Love Is a Many-Splendored Thing*
(Screenplay by John Patrick; based on A MANY-SPLENDORED THING, a novel by Han Suyin)

8.
"You've suffered enough, my child, for the heaven of heavens."

—Charles Bickford recognizing Jennifer Jones's ordeal in Henry King's *The Song of Bernadette*
(Screenplay by George Seaton; based on the novel by Franz Werfel)

9.
(a) "How about the top of the Empire State Building?"
(b) "Oh, yes. That's perfect. It's the nearest thing to heaven we have in New York."
(a) "Good. The 102nd floor. And don't forget to take the elevator."

—(a) Cary Grant and (b) Deborah Kerr picking their rendezvous spot in Leo McCarey's *An Affair To Remember*
(Screenplay by Delmer Daves and Leo McCarey; based on an original story by Mildred Cram and Leo McCarey)
and (similarly)

—(a) Charles Boyer and (b) Irene Dunne dittoing in the original, Leo McCarey's *Love Affair*
(Screenplay by Delmer Daves and Donald Ogden Stewart; based on an original story by Mildred Cram and Leo McCarey)

ALSO SEE: Business-1; Loneliness-8; Love-39; Prayers-1; Prayers-5; Prayers-7; Secrets-2; Specializations-6.

HELP

1.
"From what I can see, no matter what system of government we have, there will always be leaders and always be followers. It's like the road out in front of my house. It's on a steep hill. And every day I watch the cars climbing up. Some go lickety-split up that hill on high—some have to shift into second—and some sputter and shake and slip back to the bottom again. Same cars—same gasoline—yet some make it and some don't. And I say the fellas who can make the hill on high should stop once in a while and help those who can't. That's all I'm trying to do with this money. Help the fellas who can't make the hill on high."

—Gary Cooper defending his philanthropy in court in Frank Capra's *Mr. Deeds Goes to Town*
(Screenplay by Robert Riskin; based on "Opera Hat," a short story by Clarence Budington Kelland)

2.
"There's much that *is* horrible in China, as in any country—babies left to die in ditches, the poor preying on the poor, many things—but they'll change. One thing at a time, with the help of the Lord. And that's what we're here for, in this dirty room—to try to help. It's a hard life for a young woman, but it won't seem hard, I promise you, when you're my age and look back. It'll only seem beautiful."

—Athene Seyler pep-talking her new associate (Ingrid Bergman) in Mark Robson's *The Inn of the Sixth Happiness*

(Screenplay by Isobel Lennart; based on THE SMALL WOMAN, a book by Alan Burgess)

3.

"I'll do my best, Mrs. St. Maugham, to help you with your garden—and the child. Their problems are similar."

—Deborah Kerr accepting Edith Evans's position for a governess and gardener in Ronald Neame's *The Chalk Garden*
(Screenplay by John Michael Hayes; based on the play by Enid Bagnold)

4.

"All right, I'll help you. I'll help you for two reasons. . . . The first reason is I'm too young to be sent to jail. The second reason is you've got a lot of animal magnetism."

—George Winslow coming, conditionally, to the aid of a porthole-stuck damsel (Marilyn Monroe) in Howard Hawks's *Gentlemen Prefer Blondes*
(Screenplay by Charles Lederer; based on the musical play by Joseph Fields and Anita Loos and novel by Anita Loos)

5.

"Allow me to assist you from that ludicrous and liquid posture."

—Clifton Webb helping Dorothy McGuire out of a fountain in Jean Negulesco's *Three Coins in the Fountain*
(Screenplay by John Patrick; based on the novel by John H. Secondari)

ALSO SEE: Champagne-1; Failure-4; Humility-4; Kiss-5; Mind-13; People-3; Proposals-10; Telephone Scenes-9.

HERO

1.

"In all that fine riding you used to do, with all that fancy roping and all that glamour stuff you did to dazzle me—oh, it was impressive, but none of it ever made you quite as big a man to me as you were on the floor of Sarge's Hamburger Joint. When you tumbled rearward and landed crashing into that pile of dirty dishes, you were at last my hero. That's what you always wanted to be, you know."

—Elizabeth Taylor telling Rock Hudson how he won the fight in George Stevens's *Giant*
(Screenplay by Fred Guiol and Ivan Moffat; based on the novel by Edna Ferber)

2.

"All everybody else knows is he's a hero. He's got a statue in the park, and the birds sit on it. Except that I ain't got no birds on me, I'm in the same boat."

—William Demarest telling Eddie Bracken about heroes in Preston Sturges's *Hail the Conquering Hero*
(Original Screenplay by Preston Sturges)

3.

"You've been a hero to these kids, and hundreds of others, all through your life—and now you're going to be a glorified hero in death, and I want to prevent that, Rocky. They've got to despise your memory. They've got to be ashamed of you."

—Pat O'Brien asking for a really heroic action from a condemned killer (James Cagney) in Michael Curtiz's *Angels With Dirty Faces*
(Screenplay by John Wexley and Warren Duff; based on an original story by Rowland Brown)

4.

"My villain? My hero, you mean. I always think of my murderers as my heroes."

—Mystery writer Auriol Lee revising the impression of a reader (Joan Fontaine) in Alfred Hitchcock's *Suspicion*
(Screenplay by Samson Raphaelson, Joan Harrison and Alma Reville; based on BEFORE THE FACT, a novel by Francis Iles)

5.

"Oh, Big Daddy, you don't think I ravaged a football hero!"

—Elizabeth Taylor cynically denying to her father-in-law (Burl Ives) an affair with the best friend of her husband (Paul Newman) in Richard Brooks's *Cat on a Hot Tin Roof*

(Screenplay by Richard Brooks and James Poe; based on the play by Tennessee Williams)

6.
"What did you want me to do? Be reasonable. You didn't expect me to give myself up.... 'It's a far, far better thing that I do.' The old limelight. The fall of the curtain. Oh, Holly, you and I aren't heroes. The world doesn't make any heroes."

—Orson Welles leveling with an old friend (Joseph Cotten) in Carol Reed's *The Third Man*
(Original Screenplay by Graham Greene)

7.
"You're learning, Cates. Disillusionment is what little heroes are made of."

—Gene Kelly cynically consoling Dick York in Stanley Kramer's *Inherit the Wind*
(Screenplay by Nathan E. Douglas and Harold Jacob Smith; based on the play by Jerome Lawrence and Robert E. Lee)

ALSO SEE: Human-3; Illusions-5; Sea-2; Static-14.

HISTORY

1.
"Oh, this is one of those days that the pages of history teach us are best spent lying in bed."

—Roland Young coping with a hangover in George Cukor's *The Philadelphia Story*
(Screenplay by Donald Ogden Stewart; based on the play by Philip Barry)
                    and (almost verbatim)

—Louis Calhern dittoing in the remake, Charles Walters's *High Society*
(Screenplay by John Patrick; based on THE PHILADELPHIA STORY, a screenplay by Donald Ogden Stewart and play by Philip Barry)

2.
"He ain't like the other men you done made history of."

—Louise Beavers noting the difference about Cary Grant to Mae West in Lowell Sherman's *She Done Him Wrong*
(Screenplay by Harvey Thew and John Bright; based on DIAMOND LIL, a play by Mae West)

3.
"Kane helped to change the world, but Kane's world now is history, and the great yellow journalist himself lived to be history, outlived his power to make it."

—Newsreel narrator commenting on Orson Welles in Orson Welles's *Citizen Kane*
(Original Screenplay by Herman J. Mankiewicz and Orson Welles)

4.
"You're better than news. You're history."

—War correspondent Stuart Erwin saying good-bye to Wallace Beery in Jack Conway's *Viva Villa!*
(Screenplay by Ben Hecht; based on the book by Edgcumb Pinchon and O. B. Stade)

5.
"Take a good look, my dear. It's a historical moment. You can tell your grandchildren how you watched the Old South disappear one night."

—Clark Gable watching Confederates in retreat as he shepherds Vivien Leigh to safety in Victor Fleming's *Gone With the Wind*
(Screenplay by Sidney Howard; based on the novel by Margaret Mitchell)

6.
"You have often reminded us, Nero, of the judgment of history. What will its verdict be if you punish the innocent and betray your own greatness? Let future ages looking back at this time regard Nero as with wonder and amazement. Let history say, 'Nero, the ruler of the world—Nero, a god—burned Rome because he was as powerful as Jupiter. He loved poetry so much that he sacrificed Rome for a song.' History need not say that the burning of Rome was good, but it must say that it was colossal."

—Leo Genn trying to talk Peter Ustinov out of Christian scapegoats in Mervyn LeRoy's *Quo Vadis*

(*Screenplay by John Lee Mahin, S. N. Behrman and Sonya Levien; based on the novel by Henryk Sienkiewicz*)

ALSO SEE: Free-3; Future-1; Justice-1; Lies-24; Parting Shots-6; Selfish-1.

HOME

1.
"Tara! Home! I'll go home, and I'll think of some way to get him back. After all, tomorrow is another day!"

—Vivien Leigh finding her true direction in the last lines of Victor Fleming's *Gone With the Wind*
(*Screenplay by Sidney Howard; based on the novel by Margaret Mitchell*)

2.
"Oh, but anyway, Toto, we're home! Home! And this is my room—and you're all here! And I'm not going to leave here ever, ever again because I love you all! And—Oh, Auntie Em, there's *no* place like home."

—Judy Garland finding her true place in the last lines of Victor Fleming's *The Wizard of Oz*
(*Screenplay by Noel Langley, Florence Ryerson and Edgar Allan Woolf; adaptation by Noel Langley; based on the novel by L. Frank Baum*)

3.
"I want a home for them where they can stay and where they can learn—a town for boys, governed by boys. It's worth a shot, isn't it?"

—Spencer Tracy pitching his dream to Jonathan Hale in Norman Taurog's *Boys Town*
(*Screenplay by John Meehan and Dore Schary; based on an original story by Dore Schary and Eleanore Griffin*)

4.
"There oughta be a home for dames like me. Yep, they shoulda organized. You know, a house somewhere with—with no mirror in it, far away where we'd never have to look at the young girls. They have homes for unmarried mothers, but everybody forgets about the girls

who—who never quite managed to make things legal. I think I could start one. Yeah, I think I could call it May Holst's Home for Broken-Down Broads."

—Claire Trevor feeling her years in William A. Wellman's *The High and the Mighty*
(*Screenplay by Ernest K. Gann; based on his novel*)

5.
"What a dump!"

—Bette Davis raging at her smalltown Wisconsin home in King Vidor's *Beyond the Forest*
(*Screenplay by Lenore Coffee; based on the novel by Stuart Engstrand*)
                    and

—Elizabeth Taylor quoting Bette Davis in the above in Mike Nichols's *Who's Afraid of Virginia Woolf?*
(*Screenplay by Ernest Lehman; based on the play by Edward Albee*)

6.
"Well, this is what is laughingly known as my apartment."

—Gregory Peck orienting his princess pickup (Audrey Hepburn) in William Wyler's *Roman Holiday*
(*Screenplay by Ian McLellan Hunter and John Dighton; based on an original story by Ian McLellan Hunter*)

7.
"It's a nice building. You get a better class of cockroaches."

—James Earl Jones introducing Diahann Carroll to his apartment in John Berry's *Claudine*
(*Original Screenplay by Tina Pine and Lester Pine*)

8.
"Bill, Muriel and I have found what I'm not ashamed to call our dream house. It's like a fine painting. You buy it with your heart, not your head. You don't ask, 'How much was the paint? How much was the canvas?' You look at her, and you say, 'It's beautiful, and I want it.' And if it costs a few more pennies, you pay it—and gladly—because you love it. And you can't

measure the things you love in dollars and cents. Well, anyway, that's the way I feel about it, and, when I sign those papers on Saturday, I can look the world in the face and say, 'It's mine. My house. My home. My 35 acres.' "

—Cary Grant defending his home purchase to Melvyn Douglas in H. C. Potter's *Mr. Blandings Builds His Dream House*
(Screenplay by Norman Panama and Melvin Frank; based on the novel by Eric Hodgins)

9.
"It's lavish, but I call it home."

—Clifton Webb airily showing off his apartment to Dana Andrews in Otto Preminger's *Laura*
(Screenplay by Jay Dratler, Samuel Hoffenstein and Betty Reinhardt; based on the novel by Vera Caspary)

10.
"We make a home for each other, my grandfather and I. Oh, I don't mean a—a regular home, because I don't regard a home as a—as a place, a building, bricks, wood, stone. I think of a home as something two people have between them in which each can nest, rest, live in emotionally speaking."

—Deborah Kerr speaking to Richard Burton of her life on the road with Cyril Delevanti in John Huston's *The Night of the Iguana*
(Screenplay by Anthony Veiller and John Huston; based on the play by Tennessee Williams)

11.
"That's the Australian word for people like us. A 'sundowner' is someone whose home is where the sun goes down. It's the same as saying someone who doesn't have a home."

—Michael Anderson Jr. acquainting Peter Ustinov with the title term in Fred Zinnemann's *The Sundowners*
(Screenplay by Isobel Lennart; based on the novel by Jon Cleary)

12.
"Where would I go to live? I still know a lot of people around here, Tonto. If you know people, that's home."

—Art Carney facing eviction with his cat in Paul Mazursky's *Harry and Tonto*
(Original Screenplay by Paul Mazursky and Josh Greenfeld)

13.
"You can have any kind of home you want. Why, you can even get stucco. Oh, how you can get stucco!"

—Groucho Marx running an auction in Joseph Santley and Robert Florey's *The Cocoanuts*
(Screenplay by Morrie Ryskind; based on the musical play by George S. Kaufman and Morrie Ryskind)

ALSO SEE: Dark-1; Letters-3; Loneliness-10; Money-4; Orders-10; Painting-1; Pretense-1; Prologues-4; Propositions-1; Secrets-4; Toasts-4; Wealth-5; Wish-2.

HONEST

1.
"When three people come to you with their lives spread out on a table for you to cut to pieces, then the only honest thing to do is to give them one last chance for them to come out alive. We want that last chance. If you're honest, you'll give it to us. Where's Mary?"

—Joel McCrea confronting Alma Kruger about the lie started by her granddaughter, Mary (Bonita Granville), in William Wyler's *These Three*
(Screenplay by Lillian Hellman; based on her play, THE CHILDREN'S HOUR)
and (almost verbatim)

—James Garner dittoing Fay Bainter concerning Karen Balkin in the remake, William Wyler's *The Children's Hour*
(Screenplay by John Michael Hayes; adaptation by Lillian Hellman; based on her play)

2.
"I'm honest because, with you, I think it's the best way to get results."

—Cary Grant affecting candor with Joan Fontaine in Alfred Hitchcock's *Suspicion*
(Screenplay by Samson Raphaelson, Joan Harrison

and Alma Reville; based on BEFORE THE FACT, a
novel by Francis Iles)

3.
"I don't know if you'll understand this, but I've
always looked on myself as an honest man.
You're asking me to do something which is no
better than suborning a witness."

—James Stephenson feeling compromised by the
murderess (Bette Davis) he's defending in court in
William Wyler's *The Letter*
*(Screenplay by Howard Koch; based on the play
and short story by W. Somerset Maugham)*

4.
(a) "Professional people are just a lot of bloody
parasites—doctors, lawyers, parsons. You know
what I mean, Jake? The whole bloody lot of
them. Now, I call myself a tradesman. It's the
only thing left to respect, in my honest opinion.
In my honest opinion, an honest tradesman is
the only thing left to respect. In my honest
opinion."
    (b) "You say that in all honesty, do you?"
    (a) "In all honesty, Jake. In complete
honesty, old boy."

—(a) James Mason boring (b) Peter Finch with
drunken declarations of honesty in Jack Clayton's
The Pumpkin Eater
*(Screenplay by Harold Pinter; based on the novel
by Penelope Mortimer)*

5.
"I wish I had your confidence. I've never been
able to discover an honest warmth in any
woman."

—Leo Genn making a miserable admission to Robert
Taylor in Mervyn LeRoy's *Quo Vadis*
*(Screenplay by John Lee Mahin, S. N. Behrman
and Sonya Levien; based on the novel by Henryk
Sienkiewicz)*

6.
"There's no such thing as total honesty. Not
with men. They're all wrapped up in sexual
ego."

—Kelly Bishop advancing her opinion in Paul Mazursky's *An Unmarried Woman*
(Original Screenplay by Paul Mazursky)

7.
"She's a *real* phony. You know why? Because
she honestly believes all the phony junk that
she believes."

—Martin Balsam explaining Audrey Hepburn to
George Peppard in Blake Edwards's *Breakfast at
Tiffany's*
*(Screenplay by George Axelrod; based on the
novella by Truman Capote)*

8.
"Maybe it's easy for the dying to be honest. I'm
sick of you, sick of this house, sick of my unhappy life with you. I'm sick of your brothers
and their dirty tricks to make a dime. There
must be better ways of getting rich than building sweatshops and pounding the bones of the
town to make dividends for you to spend.
You'll wreck the town, you and your brothers.
You'll wreck the country, you and your kind, if
they let you. But not me, I'll die my own way,
and I'll do it without making the world any
worse. I leave that to you."

—Herbert Marshall confronting Bette Davis in William Wyler's *The Little Foxes*
*(Screenplay by Lillian Hellman; additional scenes
and dialogue by Arthur Kober, Dorothy Parker
and Alan Campbell)*

ALSO SEE: Dishonest-1; Excuses-4; Faces-6;
Lock-4; Love-45; Mind-5; Names-25; Peace-3;
Truth-4.

HONOR

1.
"Lady Nelson! What an honor! They point after
my coach, point up at my windows, point at me
in the streets. There's a coarse joke about me
in the taverns, a foul song about me on the
limehouse barges. Lady Nelson! How funny!
How pitiful! And how proud I might be!"

—Gladys Cooper telling Laurence Olivier how she
has been humiliated by his affair with Vivien Leigh
in Alexander Korda's *That Hamilton Woman*
*(Original Screenplay by Walter Reisch and R. C.
Sherriff)*

2.

"Remember: you're fighting for this woman's honor, which is probably more than she ever did."

—Groucho Marx pausing in the heat of battle to insult Margaret Dumont in Leo McCarey's *Duck Soup*
(Screenplay by Bert Kalmar and Harry Ruby; additional dialogue by Arthur Sheekman and Nat Perrin)

3.

"Oh, Ashley, you should have told me years ago that you loved her, not me, and not left me dangling with your talk of honor."

—Vivien Leigh finally getting Leslie Howard's message as his wife (Olivia De Havilland) lies dying in Victor Fleming's *Gone With the Wind*
(Screenplay by Sidney Howard; based on the novel by Margaret Mitchell)

4.

"You're not going to let a woman have the last word, are you? Where is your sense of honor, your male patriotism?"

—Maurice Chevalier advising Louis Jourdan in Vincente Minnelli's *Gigi*
(Screenplay by Alan Jay Lerner; based on the novel by Colette)

5.

(a) "Colonel Thursday, I gave my word to Cochise. No man is going to make a liar out of me, sir."

    (b) "Your word to a breech-clouted savage, an illiterate uncivilized murderer and treatybreaker. There's no question of honor, sir, between an American officer and Cochise."

—(a) John Wayne and (b) Henry Fonda clashing about Indian policy in John Ford's *Fort Apache*
(Screenplay by Frank S. Nugent; based on "Massacre," a story by James Warner Bellah)

6.

"There may be honor among thieves, but there's none in politicians."

—Peter O'Toole colliding with Claude Rains's foreign policy in David Lean's *Lawrence of Arabia*
(Screenplay by Robert Bolt; based on THE SEVEN PILLARS OF WISDOM, the autobiography of T. E. Lawrence, and other works by and about T. E. Lawrence)

7.

"Then came the scrubbing out in the backyard. It was the duty of my sister, Angharad, to bring the buckets of hot water and cold—and I performed what little tasks I could as my father and brothers scrubbed the coal dust from their backs. Most would come off, but some would stay for life. It is the honorable badge of the coal miner—and I envied it on my father and grown-up brothers. Scrub and scrub, and Mr. Coal would lie there and laugh at you."

—Irving Pichel, as the never-seen narrator (a grown-up version of Roddy McDowall), reminiscing about the nightly washing ritual in John Ford's *How Green Was My Valley*
(Screenplay by Philip Dunne; based on the novel by Richard Llewellyn)

8.

"Dad, I said it was a matter of honor, remember? They called me chicken. You know, chicken? I had to go 'cause if I didn't I'd never be able to face those kids again. I got in one of those cars, and Buzz, that—Buzz, one of those kids—he got in the other car, and we had to drive fast and then jump, see, before the car came to the end of the bluff, and I got out okay, but Buzz didn't and got killed."

—James Dean telling his father (Jim Backus) about Corey Allen's death in Nicholas Ray's *Rebel Without a Cause*
(Screenplay by Stewart Stern; adaptation by Irving Shulman; based on an original story by Nicholas Ray)

ALSO SEE: Confessions-2; Dance-4; Fools-5; Jealous-2; Manners-9; Pretense-8; Professions-4; Run-1.

HOPE

1.

"You know, Chuck, when you're young, you can keep the fires of hope burning bright, but at my age you're lucky if the pilot light doesn't go out."

—Barry Fitzgerald confessing to Bing Crosby a discouragement that comes with age in Leo McCarey's *Going My Way*
(Screenplay by Frank Butler and Frank Cavett; based on an original story by Leo McCarey)

2.

"You called her an old maid. You took away the last little bit of hope she ever had. And, when you left, she took those bedcovers and ran out. I didn't ask where she was going, but I'm glad she went because, if she lost her hope in here, maybe she'll find it out there."

—Cameron Prud'homme telling Lloyd Bridges that Katharine Hepburn has run to the waiting arms of Burt Lancaster in Joseph Anthony's *The Rainmaker*
(Screenplay by N. Richard Nash; based on his play)

3.

"Myrtle Mae, you have a lot to learn—and I hope you never learn it."

—Josephine Hull hoping to keep her daughter (Victoria Horne) sheltered in Henry Koster's *Harvey*
(Screenplay by Mary Chase and Oscar Brodney; based on the play by Mary Chase)

4.

"And you're so full with honest emotion you fall in love every time someone sings a ballad. You're worse than a hopeless romantic. You're a hopeful one. You're the kind of man who would end the world famine problem by having them all eat out, preferably at a good Chinese restaurant."

—Jane Fonda counterpunching her ex (Alan Alda) in Herbert Ross's *California Suite*
(Screenplay by Neil Simon; based on his play)

5.

(a) "You know, don't you, Ann, that we don't have very much hope together?"

   (b) "Have we all that much apart?"

—(b) Rita Hayworth arguing for a reconciliation with her ex, (a) Burt Lancaster, in Delbert Mann's *Separate Tables*
(Screenplay by Terence Rattigan and John Gay; based on the play by Terence Rattigan)

6.

"You know, the guy who kills me, I hope he does it because he hates my guts—not because it's his job."

—Al Pacino hoping not to fall in the line of (somebody else's) duty in Sidney Lumet's *Dog Day Afternoon*
(Original Screenplay by Frank Pierson)

ALSO SEE: Justice-3; Letters-12; Toasts-5; Toasts-6.

HORSES

1.

"People have always scared me a bit, you see. They're so complicated. I suppose that's why I prefer horses."

—May Hallatt revealing her true preference to Wendy Hiller in Delbert Mann's *Separate Tables*
(Screenplay by Terence Rattigan and John Gay; based on the play by Terence Rattigan)

2.

"Apparently, Josefa, you do not know that I am the best judge of horses in the country. You are the only one who does not know this. I was with him for years. I bought every horse in his stable. When I have not helped Don Nacio buy his horses, it's later discovered that they have five legs."

—Marlon Brando boasting a bit to Jean Peters in Elia Kazan's *Viva Zapata!*
(Original Screenplay by John Steinbeck)

3.

"Judah Ben-Hur, my people are praying for a

man who can drive their team to victory over Messala. You could be that man! You could be the one to stamp this Roman's arrogance into the sand of that arena. You've seen my horses. They need only a driver who is worthy of them."

—Hugh Griffith trying to talk Charlton Heston into being his charioteer in William Wyler's *Ben-Hur* (*Screenplay by Karl Tunberg; based on BEN-HUR (A TALE OF THE CHRIST), a novel by General Lew Wallace*)

4.
(a) "Water polo? Isn't that terribly dangerous?"
      (b) "I'll say! I had two ponies drown under me."

—(b) Tony Curtis playing the great sportsman to (a) Marilyn Monroe in Billy Wilder's *Some Like It Hot* (*Screenplay by Billy Wilder and I. A. L. Diamond; suggested by a story by R. Thoeren and M. Logan*)

5.
"It's all right to live on a horse—if it's your own horse."

—Walter Brennan suspecting that Gary Cooper is a horse thief in William Wyler's *The Westerner* (*Screenplay by Jo Swerling and Niven Busch; based on a story by Stuart N. Lake*)

ALSO SEE: Body-3; Courtroom Lines-6; Crazy-6; Discipline-2; Eulogies-18; Eyes-18; Knowledge-3; Proposals-3; Propositions-22; Self-Perception-6; Talk-10; Talk-11.

HOT

1.
"You know, there's nothin' I like better than to meet a high-class mama that can snap 'em back at you. 'Cause the colder they are, the hotter they get, is what I always say. Yessir! When a cold mama gets hot—boy, how she sizzles!"

—Roscoe Karns totally misreading Claudette Colbert's cold-shoulder treatment in Frank Capra's *It Happened One Night* (*Screenplay by Robert Riskin; based on "Night Bus," a short story by Samuel Hopkins Adams*)

2.
"You know, when it's hot like this—you know what I do? I keep my undies in the icebox."

—Marilyn Monroe tipping her summertime secret to Tom Ewell in Billy Wilder's *The Seven Year Itch* (*Screenplay by Billy Wilder and George Axelrod; based on the play by George Axelrod*)

ALSO SEE: Deals-1; Drink Orders-4.

HUMAN

1.
"You'll never be a first-class human being or a first-class woman until you've learned to have some regard for human frailty. It's a pity your own foot can't slip a little sometime, but your sense of inner divinity wouldn't allow that. This goddess must and shall remain intact."

—Cary Grant telling Katharine Hepburn she's too lofty in George Cukor's *The Philadelphia Story* (*Screenplay by Donald Ogden Stewart; based on the play by Philip Barry*)
                  and (almost verbatim)

—Bing Crosby dittoing Grace Kelly in the remake, Charles Walters's *High Society* (*Screenplay by John Patrick; based on THE PHILADELPHIA STORY, a screenplay by Donald Ogden Stewart and play by Philip Barry*)

2.
"I have grown up in a great man's shadow. All my life, I have been a symbol—a symbol of eternal changes—an abstraction. A human being is mortal and changeable, with desires and impulses, hopes and despairs. I'm tired of being a symbol, Chancellor. I long to be a human being. This longing I cannot suppress."

—Greta Garbo complaining to Lewis Stone about the empty life she leads in Rouben Mamoulian's *Queen Christina* (*Screenplay by H. M. Harwood and Salka Viertel; dialogue by S. N. Behrman; based on a story by Salka Viertel and Margaret P. Levino*)

3.
"Heroes, whatever high ideas we may have of

them, are mortal, not divine. We are all as God made us and many of us much worse."

—Narrator Michael MacLiammoir setting the stage for the lusty supper scene between Albert Finney and Joyce Redman in Tony Richardson's *Tom Jones* (*Screenplay by John Osborne; based on the novel by Henry Fielding*)

4.
"You're a clever little man, little master of the universe, but mortals are weak and frail. If their stomach speaks, they forget their brain. If their brain speaks, they forget their hearts. And if their hearts speak—ha ha ha ha ha—if their hearts speak, they forget everything."

—Rex Ingram giving himself an edge on Sabu in Ludwig Berger, Tim Whelan and Michael Powell's *The Thief of Bagdad* (*Screenplay and dialogue by Miles Malleson; based on a scenario by Lajos Biro*)

5.
"Nothing human disgusts me, Mr. Shannon—unless it's unkind or violent."

—Deborah Kerr telling Richard Burton her guidelines in John Huston's *The Night of the Iguana* (*Screenplay by Anthony Veiller and John Huston; based on the play by Tennessee Williams*)

6.
"Oh, I keep forgetting, Gabelle. You're a—you're a humanitarian, aren't you? You think one person is as good as another—a naïve notion so contradicted by the facts."

—Basil Rathbone taunting H. B. Warner in Jack Conway's *A Tale of Two Cities* (*Screenplay by W. P. Lipscomb and S. N. Behrman; based on the novel by Charles Dickens*)

7.
"Why, Miss Hicks, I never knew that schoolteachers were human beings like everybody else. And better, too."

—Mickey Rooney paying Mary Nash a dubious compliment in Clarence Brown's *The Human Comedy* (*Screenplay by Howard Estabrook; based on an original story by William Saroyan*)

8.
"Listen, listen. You're not playing with paper dolls. We're human beings, see? It's our lives you're fooling with. Our lives. That's serious business to us. Can you understand that?"

—Miriam Hopkins confronting Alma Kruger about a damaging lie in William Wyler's *These Three* (*Screenplay by Lillian Hellman; based on her play, THE CHILDREN'S HOUR*)
                      and (almost verbatim)

—Shirley MacLaine dittoing Fay Bainter in the remake, William Wyler's *The Children's Hour* (*Screenplay by John Michael Hayes; adaptation by Lillian Hellman; based on her play*)

9.
"There are some human experiences, Birdie, that do not take place in a vaudeville house—and that even a fifth-rate vaudevillian should understand and respect!"

—Bette Davis criticizing her maid (Thelma Ritter) for callousness toward Anne Baxter in Joseph L. Mankiewicz's *All About Eve* (*Screenplay by Joseph L. Mankiewicz; based on "The Wisdom of Eve," a radio play and short story by Mary Orr*)

ALSO SEE: Arrogance-1; Beliefs-4; Love Objects-4; Mad Act-1; Promiscuity-6; Public Relations-6; Religions-2; Trumpet-3.

HUMILITY

1.
"I think the time has come to shed some of your humility. It's just as false not to blow your horn at all as it is to blow it too loudly."

—George Sanders advising Anne Baxter to cut the false modesty in Joseph L. Mankiewicz's *All About Eve* (*Screenplay by Joseph L. Mankiewicz; based on "The Wisdom of Eve," a radio play and short story by Mary Orr*)

2.
"To direct a picture, a man needs humility. Do you have humility, Mr. Shields?"

—Director Ivan Triesault asking a direct question of his producer-successor (Kirk Douglas) in Vincente Minnelli's *The Bad and the Beautiful*
(Screenplay by Charles Schnee; based on "Memorial to a Bad Man" and "Of Good and Evil," two short stories by George Bradshaw)

3.
"Humility is a virtue, Monsieur, not only in those who suffer, but in those who hope to heal."

—Akim Tamiroff tearing down establishment resistance to Paul Muni in William Dieterle's *The Story of Louis Pasteur*
(Screenplay by Sheridan Gibney and Pierre Collings; based on an original story by Sheridan Gibney and Pierre Collings)

4.
"You know, I had you pegged right from the start: just the spoiled brat of a rich father. The only way you can get anything is to buy it, isn't it? You're in a jam, and all you can think of is your money. It never fails, does it? Ever hear of the word 'Humility'? No, you wouldn't. I guess it never occurred to you to just say, 'Please, mister, I'm in trouble. Will you help me?' No; that'd bring you down off your high horse for a minute."

—Clark Gable telling off Claudette Colbert in Frank Capra's *It Happened One Night*
(Screenplay by Robert Riskin; based on "Night Bus," a short story by Samuel Hopkins Adams)

ALSO SEE: Spinsters-1.

HUNGER

1.
"As God is my witness—as God is my witness—they're not going to lick me! I'm going to live through this, and, when it's all over, I'll never be hungry again—no, nor any of my folks!—if I have to lie, steal, cheat or kill! As God is my witness, I'll never be hungry again."

—Vivien Leigh rising like a phoenix from the ashes of a war-ravaged Tara in Victor Fleming's *Gone With the Wind*
(Screenplay by Sidney Howard; based on the novel by Margaret Mitchell)

2.
"What're you squawking about? When you write your book, it'll make a swell chapter: 'How It Feels To Be Starving—First Person Singular.'"

—John Hodiak snarling at Tallulah Bankhead in Alfred Hitchcock's *Lifeboat*
(Screenplay by Jo Swerling; based on the story by John Steinbeck)

3.
"Hunger is an indulgence with these peasants as gout is with us."

—Basil Rathbone advancing a hissable, elitist view in Jack Conway's *A Tale of Two Cities*
(Screenplay by W. P. Lipscomb and S. N. Behrman; based on the novel by Charles Dickens)

4.
"There's a difference. If you give a hungry man a loaf of bread, that's democracy. If you leave the wrapper on it, it's imperialism."

—Michael Raffetto splitting hairs about postwar politics in Billy Wilder's *A Foreign Affair*
(Screenplay by Charles Brackett, Billy Wilder and Richard L. Breen; adaptation by Robert Harari; based on an original story by David Shaw)

5.
"Hunger has no conscience."

—Sydney Chaplin commenting on his lean-and-hungry period in Charles Chaplin's *Limelight*
(Original Screenplay by Charles Chaplin)

6.
"To raise $100, I would have to sell 13,000 hamburgers between now and six o'clock tonight. Do you know anybody that's *that* hungry?"

—Thelma Ritter responding to the foreclosure of her hamburger joint in Mitchell Leisen's *The Mating Season*
(Screenplay by Charles Brackett, Walter Reisch and Richard L. Breen; suggested by MAGGIE, a play by Caesar Dunn)

7.
"You are like a hungry child who is given ravioli to eat. My dear girl, you are hungry. Eat the ravioli."

—Rossano Brazzi encouraging Katharine Hepburn to give in to her romantic impulses in David Lean's *Summertime*
(Screenplay by David Lean and H. E. Bates; based on THE TIME OF THE CUCKOO, a play by Arthur Laurents)

8.
"You've got ten minutes. You're a hungry little girl. You've been starving all your life. There's a feast out there. The theater is serving you a feast. You can either take it or forever wish you had."

—Henry Fonda pep-talking Susan Strasberg on her opening night in Sidney Lumet's *Stage Struck*
(Screenplay by Ruth Goetz and Augustus Goetz; based on MORNING GLORY, a play by Zoe Akins)

9.
"The English have a great hunger for desolate places. I fear they hunger for Arabia."

—Alec Guinness expressing his distrust to Peter O'Toole in David Lean's *Lawrence of Arabia*
(Screenplay by Robert Bolt; based on THE SEVEN PILLARS OF WISDOM, the autobiography of T. E. Lawrence, and other works by and about T. E. Lawrence)

ALSO SEE: Empathy-8; Introductions-7; Thieves-1.

HUSBANDS

1.
"Toy, he was my first husband—not my Number One husband."

—Lilli Palmer going over a fine point about her ex (Fred Astaire) with her Japanese servant (Harold Fong) in George Seaton's *The Pleasure of His Company*
(Screenplay by Samuel A. Taylor; based on the play by Samuel A. Taylor and Cornelia Otis Skinner)

2.
"Perhaps it offends my vanity to have anyone who was even remotely my wife remarry so obviously beneath her."

—Cary Grant taking exception to Katharine Hepburn's next (John Howard) in George Cukor's *The Philadelphia Story*
(Screenplay by Donald Ogden Stewart; based on the play by Philip Barry)

3.
"I'm more or less particular about whom my wife marries."

—Cary Grant taking exception to Rosalind Russell's next (Ralph Bellamy) in Howard Hawks's *His Girl Friday*
(Screenplay by Charles Lederer; based on THE FRONT PAGE, a play by Ben Hecht and Charles MacArthur)

4.
"Any husband of Constance is a husband of mine, so to speak."

—Michael Chekhov congratulating, nonsensically, Ingrid Bergman on marrying Gregory Peck in Alfred Hitchcock's *Spellbound*
(Screenplay by Ben Hecht; adaptation by Angus MacPhail; based on THE HOUSE OF DR. EDWARDES, a novel by Francis Beeding)

5.
"How wonderful to meet a silent American again! All my husbands were foreigners—and such chatterboxes!"

—Mary Astor zeroing in on Joel McCrea in Preston Sturges's *The Palm Beach Story*
(Original Screenplay by Preston Sturges)

6.
"Is this your year for looking up old husbands?"

—Burt Lancaster greeting his ex (Rita Hayworth) in Delbert Mann's *Separate Tables*
(Screenplay by Terence Rattigan and John Gay; based on the play by Terence Rattigan)

7.
"What did you think I was anyway? A guy that walks into a good-looking dame's front parlor

and says, 'Good afternoon. I sell accident insurance on husbands. Have you got one that's been around too long? One you'd like to turn into a little hard cash? Just give me a smile and I'll help you collect'? Huh! Boy, what a dope you must think I am!"

—Fred MacMurray reacting badly to Barbara Stanwyck's deadly suggestion in Billy Wilder's *Double Indemnity*
(Screenplay by Billy Wilder and Raymond Chandler; based on the novel by James M. Cain)

8.
"I detest mountains. You know, they always remind me of the day that Gustav made me climb to the top of an Alp. Gustav was my third husband. Oh, give Flora another little drinkie, dear. Well, anyhow, there we were, when suddenly it struck me that Gustav had pushed me. I slid halfway down the mountain before I realized that Gustav didn't love me any more. But love takes care of its own, Mrs. Haines. I slid right into the arms of my fourth husband, the Count."

—Mary Boland recalling a husband transition in George Cukor's *The Women*
(Screenplay by Anita Loos and Jane Murfin; based on the play by Clare Boothe)

ALSO SEE: Adultery-7; Animals-1; Jealous-3; Jewels-2; Letters-1; Love-52; Poverty-6; Tact-6; Tact-7; Timing-2; Tired-1; Wives-3.

HYPOCRISY

1.
"I am an informer, not a hypocrite!"

—Gene Lockhart assuring police that he doesn't also play on the team of Pepe le Moko (Charles Boyer) in John Cromwell's *Algiers*
(Screenplay by John Howard Lawson and James M. Cain; based on PEPE LE MOKO, a novel by Detective Ashelbe)

2.
"Okay, I'm a cat, but this is dirty pool. Well, I'm intolerant of hypocrites. That's what I said, Phil

—hypocrites. She'd rather let Dave lose that job than risk a fuss up there. That's it, isn't it? She's afraid. The Kathys everywhere are afraid of getting the gate from their little groups of nice people. They make little clucking sounds of disapproval, but they want you and Uncle John to stand up and yell and take sides and fight. But do they fight? Oh, no!"

—Celeste Holm railing to Gregory Peck about the lack of commitment of his fiancée (Dorothy McGuire) in Elia Kazan's *Gentleman's Agreement*
(Screenplay by Moss Hart; based on the novel by Laura Z. Hobson)

3.
"Everybody in this town hides behind plain wrappers."

—Diane Varsi telling Russ Tamblyn about the two-faced town they live in in Mark Robson's *Peyton Place*
(Screenplay by John Michael Hayes; based on the novel by Grace Metalious)

4.
"I'm the only boss around here, and I built this place with no help from you, and I'll run this place till the day I die. Now is that plain to you, Ida? Is that perfectly clear to you? And I ain't going to die. Ain't nothing wrong with me but a spastic colon—made spastic, I reckon, by all the lies and liars I've had to put up with around here and all the hypocrisy I've had to live with these 40 years I've lived with you."

—Burl Ives telling off Judith Anderson in Richard Brooks's *Cat on a Hot Tin Roof*
(Screenplay by Richard Brooks and James Poe; based on the play by Tennessee Williams)

5.
"Yeah, I think I'd like to be 'an angry prophet denouncing the hypocrisies of our times.'"

—Peter Finch embracing his new on-air image in Sidney Lumet's *Network*
(Original Screenplay by Paddy Chayefsky)

6.
"We had a son, 23 years old. I threw him out of

the house last year. Pioutistic little humbug! He preached universal love, but he despised everyone. He had a blanket contempt for the middle class, even its decency. He detested my mother because she had a petty bourgeois pride in her son, the doctor. I cannot tell you how boorishly he ignored that rather good lady. When she died, he didn't even come to the funeral. He felt the chapel service was a hypocrisy. He told me his generation didn't live with lies. I said, 'Listen: everybody lives with lies.' I—I—I grabbed him by his poncho, and I dragged him the length of our seven-room, despicably affluent, middle-class apartment, and I flung him. Out. I haven't seen him since."

—George C. Scott recalling a home-front war in Arthur Hiller's *The Hospital*
(*Original Screenplay by Paddy Chayefsky*)

ALSO SEE: Fear-8; Parents-4.

IDEA

1.
"I've got a wonderful idea. We can spend the whole day doing things we've never done before. We'll take turns—first something you've never done, then me—course, I can't really think of anything I've never done."

—Audrey Hepburn offering George Peppard a suggestion for the day in Blake Edwards's *Breakfast at Tiffany's*
(*Screenplay by George Axelrod; based on the novella by Truman Capote*)

2.
"Let me just pull something out of a hat here and see if it hops for us."

—Alan Hewitt brainstorming over the phone in glib Madison Avenue jargon in Blake Edwards's *Days of Wine and Roses*
(*Screenplay by J. P. Miller; based on his teleplay*)

3.
"I've spent 20 years—20 years!—watching my friends killed and broken and disgraced and discarded for one single idea: to get our country air power."

—Walter Pidgeon grandstanding to his World War II officers in Sam Wood's *Command Decision*
(*Screenplay by William R. Laidlaw and George Froeschel; based on the play by William Wister Haines*)

4.
"I got home at midnight, intoxicated with an idea, and worked myself into a creative hangover."

—Clifton Webb explaining a writing spree to Dorothy McGuire in Jean Negulesco's *Three Coins in the Fountain*
(*Screenplay by John Patrick; based on the novel by John H. Secondari*)

5.
"That's what my ex-wife used to keep reminding me of. Tearfully. She had a theory that behind every great man there was a great woman. She also was thoroughly convinced that she was great and that all I needed to qualify was guidance on her part. She worked hard at it—too hard."

—William Holden projecting his ex's attitudes onto Grace Kelly in George Seaton's *The Country Girl*
(*Screenplay by George Seaton; based on the play by Clifford Odets*)

6.
"Everything was his idea, except my leaving him."

—Dorothy Comingore telling William Alland of a life ruled by Orson Welles in Orson Welles's *Citizen Kane*
(*Original Screenplay by Herman J. Mankiewicz and Orson Welles*)

7.
"I got no idea of love. I mean, neither of us would know what it was if we saw it coming down the street."

—Paul Newman speaking to, and for, Piper Laurie in Robert Rossen's *The Hustler*

(Screenplay by Sidney Carroll and Robert Rossen; based on the novel by Walter Tevis)

8.

"Okay, sister, but my idea of love is that love isn't ashamed of nothing."

—Paulette Goddard defining the word as "anything goes" in George Cukor's *The Women*
(Screenplay by Anita Loos and Jane Murfin; based on the play by Clare Boothe)

9.

" 'What an absurd idea!' 'What an absurd idea!' Lady, you got ten absurd ideas for my one!"

—Humphrey Bogart butting heads with Katharine Hepburn in John Huston's *The African Queen*
(Screenplay by James Agee and John Huston; based on the novel by C. S. Forester)

ALSO SEE: Alone-3; Birth-3; Differences-10; Fidelity-2; Fun-4; Intelligence-1; Lasts-3; Moon-2; Propositions-11; Telephone Scenes-3; Toasts-12; Work-1.

IDENTITY CRISIS

1.

"I don't know who I am anymore. I don't know what I remember and what I've been told I remember. What is real? Am I?"

—Ingrid Bergman getting lost in Yul Brynner's royalty ruse in Anatole Litvak's *Anastasia*
(Screenplay by Arthur Laurents; based on the play by Marcelle Maurette and Broadway adaptation by Guy Bolton)

2.

"Oh, I—I'm not myself tonight. I don't know who I am. One false move, and I'm yours."

—Groucho Marx romancing Margaret Dumont in Joseph Santley and Robert Florey's *The Cocoanuts*
(Screenplay by Morrie Ryskind; based on the musical play by George S. Kaufman and Morrie Ryskind)

3.

"Matricide is probably the most unbearable crime of all—most unbearable for the son who commits it—so he had to erase the crime, at least in his own mind. He stole her corpse. A weighted coffin was buried. He hid the body in the fruit cellar. He even treated it to keep it as long as it would keep, and that still wasn't enough. She was there, but she was a corpse, so he began to think and speak for her—give her half his life, so to speak. At times, he could be both personalities, carry on conversations. At other times, the mother half took over completely. Now, he was never all Norman, but he was often only Mother."

—Simon Oakland explaining Anthony Perkins at the end of Alfred Hitchcock's *Psycho*
(Screenplay by Joseph Stefano; based on the novel by Robert Bloch)

4.

"We all have our daydreams. Mine has just gone a step further than most people's. Sometimes—sometimes, I even manage to believe in the major myself."

—David Niven admitting to Deborah Kerr that he buys his own make-believe major routine in Delbert Mann's *Separate Tables*
(Screenplay by Terence Rattigan and John Gay; based on the play by Terence Rattigan)

ALSO SEE: Crazy-14; Mind-12.

IF

1.

"If I'd get back my youth, I'd do anything in the world—except get up early, take exercise or be respectable."

—George Sanders lightly lamenting his lost youth in Albert Lewin's *The Picture of Dorian Gray*
(Screenplay by Albert Lewin; based on the novel by Oscar Wilde)

2.

"If I hold you any closer, I'll be in back of you."

—Groucho Marx romancing Esther Muir in Sam Wood's *A Day at the Races*

(Screenplay by Robert Pirosh, George Seaton and George Oppenheimer; based on a story by Robert Pirosh and George Seaton)

3.

"It was Dandy Gow's hope, Robert, that you'd spend the sum wisely on your education. But I seem to mind him saying—oh, sort of after-thought, it was—that if you preferred to invest it in wine, women and song that was your privilege."

—Lumsden Hare relaying Charles Coburn's will instructions to Tom Drake in Victor Saville's *The Green Years*
(Screenplay by Robert Ardrey and Sonya Levien; based on the novel by A. J. Cronin)

4.

"I am going to turn this kid into a decent, God-fearing Christian if I have to break every bone in his body!"

—Fred Clark threatening Jan Handzlik with the good life in Morton DaCosta's *Auntie Mame*
(Screenplay by Betty Comden and Adolph Green; based on the play by Jerome Lawrence and Robert E. Lee and novel by Patrick Dennis)
              and (almost verbatim)

—John McGiver dittoing Kirby Furlong in the remake, Gene Saks's *Mame*
(Screenplay by Paul Zindel; based on the musical play by Jerome Lawrence, Robert E. Lee and Jerry Herman and AUNTIE MAME, a play by Jerome Lawrence and Robert E. Lee and novel by Patrick Dennis)

5.

"If I don't come back with the biggest story you ever handled, you can put me back in short pants and make me marble editor."

—Fredric March promising Walter Connolly a big story on the supposedly doomed Carole Lombard in William A. Wellman's *Nothing Sacred*
(Screenplay by Ben Hecht; based on "Letter to the Editor," a short story by James M. Street)

ALSO SEE: Good-byes-2; Guilty-2; Hunger-1; Kiss-21; Legs-5; Lock-2; Love-41; Memory-4; Orders-7; Prison-6; Tears-6; Together-8; Youth-3.

IGNORANCE

1.

"Porter says Addie Ross has class. And he knows class. Like I know navigation."

—Linda Darnell putting down Paul Douglas in Joseph L. Mankiewicz's *A Letter to Three Wives*
(Screenplay by Joseph L. Mankiewicz; adaptation by Vera Caspary; based on "One of Our Hearts," a short story by John Klempner)

2.

"Can't you understand that, if you take a law like evolution and you make it a crime to teach it in the public schools, tomorrow you can make it a crime to teach it in the private schools? And tomorrow you may make it a crime to read about it? And soon you may ban books and newspapers? And then you may turn Catholic against Protestant and Protestant against Protestant and try to force your own religion upon the mind of man? If you can do one, you can do the other because fanaticism and ignorance is forever busy, and it needs feeding. And soon, Your Honor, with banners flying and with drums beating, we'll be marching backward—backward through the glorious ages of that 16th century when bigots burned the man who dared bring enlightenment and intelligence to the human mind."

—Spencer Tracy telling the judge (Harry Morgan) in Stanley Kramer's *Inherit the Wind*
(Screenplay by Nathan E. Douglas and Harold Jacob Smith; based on the play by Jerome Lawrence and Robert E. Lee)

3.

"Your ignorance, brother, as the great Milton says, almost subdues my patience."

—Edith Evans expressing her exasperation with Hugh Griffith in Tony Richardson's *Tom Jones*
(Screenplay by John Osborne; based on the novel by Henry Fielding)

4.

(a) "Nobody's *born* smart, Billie. You know what the stupidest thing on earth is? An infant."

    (b) "What've you got against babies all of a sudden?"

    (a) "Nothing. I've got nothing against a brain that's three weeks old and empty. But, after it hangs around for 30 years and hasn't absorbed anything, I begin to wonder about it."

    (b) "What makes you think I'm 30?"

—(a) William Holden stating his position to (b) Judy Holliday in George Cukor's *Born Yesterday*
(Screenplay by Albert Mannheimer; based on the play by Garson Kanin)

5.

"Nuts? Nuts, am I? Let me tell you something, my two fine bedfellows. You're so dumb there's nothing to compare you with. You're dumber than the dumbest jackass. Look at each other, will ya? Did ya ever see anything like yourself for being dumb specimens? Ha ha ha ha! Aha ha ha ha ha ha! You're so dumb you don't even see riches you're treading on with your own feet. Ha ha ha ha ha ha!"

—Walter Huston discovering gold under the feet of Humphrey Bogart and Tim Holt in John Huston's *The Treasure of the Sierra Madre*
(Screenplay by John Huston; based on the novel by B. Traven)

6.

"You want to grow up and be dumb like ZaSu Pitts?"

—W. C. Fields wising up Gloria Jean in Eddie Cline's *Never Give a Sucker an Even Break*
(Screenplay by John T. Neville and Prescott Chaplin; based on an original story by Otis Criblecoblis, a.k.a. W. C. Fields)

ALSO SEE: Coward-2; Intelligence-2; Knowledge-5; Producers-2; Strange-9.

ILLUSIONS

1.

"You've taken a new tack, Martha, in the last century or two which is just too much. Too much. I don't mind your dirty underthings in public—well, I do mind, but I've reconciled myself to that—but you've moved bag and baggage into your own fantasy world."

—Richard Burton warring with Elizabeth Taylor in Mike Nichols's *Who's Afraid of Virginia Woolf?*
(Screenplay by Ernest Lehman; based on the play by Edward Albee)

2.

"Doctor, I'm going to tell you something I've never told anyone before—not even Myrtle Mae. Sometimes, I see that big rabbit myself."

—Josephine Hull admitting she shares the fantasy of her brother (James Stewart) in Henry Koster's *Harvey*
(Screenplay by Mary Chase and Oscar Brodney; based on the play by Mary Chase)

3.

"I made you up, didn't I, Eddie? You weren't real. I made you up, like everything else. There was no car crash, Eddie. When I was five, I had polio. I was never an actress. The rich old man is my father. He walked out on us when I was seven. He sends me a check every month. That's how he buys his way out of my life. The men I've known—after they've left, I'd say they weren't real. I made them up. But you, Eddie—I wanted you to be real."

—Piper Laurie adding Paul Newman to her list of illusions in Robert Rossen's *The Hustler*
(Screenplay by Sidney Carroll and Robert Rossen; based on the novel by Walter Tevis)

4.

"What's wrong with romance—and what's wrong with illusions as far as that goes, if you can keep them?"

—Carole Lombard debating the issue with a divorced, disenchanted Katharine Alexander in John Cromwell's *In Name Only*

*(Screenplay by Richard Sherman; based on
MEMORY OF LOVE, a novel by Bessie Breuer)*

5.

"You and Skipper and millions like you are living in a kid's world, playing games, touch-
downs, no worries, no responsibilities. Life
ain't no damn football game. Life ain't just a
bunch of high spots. You're a 30-year-old kid.
Soon, you'll be a 50-year-old kid, pretending to
be in shape when he ain't in it, dreaming and
drinking your life away. Heroes in the real
world live 24 hours a day and not just two hours
in a game. Mendacity! You won't—you won't
live with mendacity! Why, you're an expert at
it!"

—Burl Ives confronting Paul Newman in Richard
Brooks's *Cat on a Hot Tin Roof*
*(Screenplay by Richard Brooks and James Poe;
based on the play by Tennessee Williams)*

ALSO SEE: Macho-19; Mind-2; Night-4; Poets-2.

IMAGINATION

1.

"To me, the imagination is a place all by itself.
A separate country. Now, you've heard of the
French nation, the British nation—well, this is
the imagination. It's a wonderful place. How
would you like to be able to make snowballs in
the summertime, eh? Or drive a great big bus
right down Fifth Avenue? How would you like
to have a ship all to yourself that makes daily
trips to China? Australia? How would you like
to be the Statue of Liberty in the morning and
in the afternoon fly south with a flock of geese?
Very simple. But it takes practice. Now, the
first thing you've got to learn is how to pretend.
And the next time Homer says, 'What kind of
animal are you?'—you tell him you're a monkey."

—Edmund Gwenn opening up new worlds to
Natalie Wood in George Seaton's *Miracle on 34th
Street*
*(Screenplay by George Seaton; based on an
original story by Valentine Davis)*

2.

"Whose imagination, Mr. Shields? Yours or
mine? There is only one answer to that. You see
this picture one way, and I another. It will be
done your way—but not by me and not by any
other director who respects himself. You know
what you have to do, Mr. Shields, so that you
have it exactly as you want it? You must direct
this picture yourself."

—Ivan Triesault passing the director's megaphone to
Kirk Douglas in Vincente Minnelli's *The Bad and the
Beautiful*
*(Screenplay by Charles Schnee; based on
"Memorial to a Bad Man" and "Of Good and
Evil," two short stories by George Bradshaw)*

3.

"It's just my imagination. Some people have
flat feet. Some people have dandruff. I have
this appalling imagination."

—Tom Ewell admitting his malady to Marilyn
Monroe in Billy Wilder's *The Seven Year Itch*
*(Screenplay by Billy Wilder and George Axelrod;
based on the play by George Axelrod)*

INCOMPATIBILITY

1.

"I know now that the love we should have
borne each other has turned into a bitter hatred. And that's all the problem is, not a very
unusual one, I venture to imagine. Nor—nor
half so tragic as you seem to think it: merely the
problem of an unsatisfied wife and a hen-
pecked husband. You'll find it all over the
world. It is usually, I believe, a—a subject for
farce."

—Michael Redgrave explaining his marital maladies
to Nigel Patrick in Anthony Asquith's *The Browning
Version*
*(Screenplay by Terence Rattigan; based on his
play)*

2.

"In some humpty-dumpty way, that was true
love."

—Roscoe Karns characterizing the stormy relationship of John Barrymore and Carole Lombard in Howard Hawks's *Twentieth Century*
(Screenplay by Ben Hecht and Charles MacArthur; based on their play and NAPOLEON OF BROADWAY, a play by Charles Bruce Milholland)

3.
"You know, I liked the Macombers when I first met them, but sometimes when I looked at them I—I felt as though I'd opened the wrong door in a hotel and seen something shameful."

—Reginald Denny characterizing the marriage of Robert Preston and Joan Bennett in Zoltan Korda's *The Macomber Affair*
(Screenplay by Casey Robinson and Seymour Bennett; adaptation by Seymour Bennett and Frank Arnold; based on "The Short Happy Life of Francis Macomber," a short story by Ernest Hemingway)

4.
"What a dope I was! I thought you were class, like a real high note you hit once in a lifetime. That's because I couldn't understand what you were saying half the time. Why, you're like those carnival joints I used to work in—big flash on the outside but on the inside nothing but filth."

—Kirk Douglas finally getting Lauren Bacall's number in Michael Curtiz's *Young Man With a Horn*
(Screenplay by Carl Foreman and Edmund H. North; based on the novel by Dorothy Baker)

5.
(a) "Please, Julia, let's not bicker since there's no love lost between us."
   (b) "That's the tragic part, Richard. There's been so much love between us."

—(a) Clifton Webb and (b) Barbara Stanwyck having a civilized quarrel in Jean Negulesco's *Titanic*
(Original Screenplay by Charles Brackett, Walter Reisch and Richard L. Breen)

ALSO SEE: Idea-5; Love-35; Love-36; Movies-3; Notes-1; Parents-2; Questions-17; Trouble-6; Wives-8; Wrong-6.

INDECISION

1.
"We're back to that, huh? I say to you, 'What do you feel like doing tonight?' And you say back to me, 'I dunno. What do you feel like doing tonight?' Then we wind up sitting around your house with a couple of cans of beer watching the *Hit Parade* on television."

—Joe Mantell grousing to Ernest Borgnine about their usual Saturday night dilemma in Delbert Mann's *Marty*
(Screenplay by Paddy Chayefsky; based on his teleplay)

2.
"Of course, the comic figure in all this is the long-suffering Mr. Wilkes!—Mr. Wilkes who can't be mentally faithful to his wife—and won't be unfaithful to her technically. Why doesn't he make up his mind?"

—Clark Gable raging to Vivien Leigh about his lingering romantic rival (Leslie Howard) in Victor Fleming's *Gone With the Wind*
(Screenplay by Sidney Howard; based on the novel by Margaret Mitchell)

3.
"He'll do or say anything to be loved by all. People like Frank ought to have two votes. Then, they could mark their ballots Democrat and Republican—that way, everyone would love them."

—Grace Kelly explaining Bing Crosby to William Holden in George Seaton's *The Country Girl*
(Screenplay by George Seaton; based on the play by Clifford Odets)

4.
"I did just what she told me. I lived! I've got to find out what to do now."

—Peggy Cass returning disheveled from the hot date prescribed by Rosalind Russell in Morton DaCosta's *Auntie Mame*
(Screenplay by Betty Comden and Adolph Green; based on the play by Jerome Lawrence and Robert E. Lee and novel by Patrick Dennis)

5.

"Well, Ann, I'm still up a tree. Just can't seem to make up my mind what to do. Maybe I ought to take on the law and take my chances. I admit I got a kinda taste for something different than this in my mouth. Still, I don't know. But I feel such a fool setting myself up as knowing so much. Course, I know what you'd say. I been hearing it every day over and over. 'Go on, Abe. Make something of yourself. You got friends. Show 'em what you got in you.' Oh, yes, I know what you'd say. But I don't know. Ann, I'll tell you what I'll do. Let the stick decide. If it falls back toward me, then I'll stay here as I always have. If it falls forward toward you, then it's—well, it's the law. Here goes, Ann."

—Henry Fonda deciding his future at the grave of his sweetheart (Pauline Moore) in John Ford's *Young Mr. Lincoln*
(Original Screenplay by Lamar Trotti)

6.

"I'm an atheist. Besides, I'm superstitious."

—Porter Hall getting testy with priest Bing Crosby in Leo McCarey's *Going My Way*
(Screenplay by Frank Butler and Frank Cavett; based on an original story by Leo McCarey)

ALSO SEE: Pet Expressions-2.

INNOCENT

1.

"At this solemn moment, in the presence of this tribunal which is the representative of human justice, before you gentlemen of the jury, before France, before the whole world—I swear that Dreyfus is innocent! By my 40 years of work, by all that I have won, by all that I have written to spread the spirit of France, I swear that Dreyfus is innocent! May all that melt away!—may my name perish if Dreyfus be not innocent! *He is innocent.*"

—Paul Muni defending Joseph Schildkraut in court in William Dieterle's *The Life of Emile Zola*
(Screenplay by Heinz Herald, Geza Herczeg and Norman Reilly Raine; based on a story by Heinz Herald and Geza Herczeg)

2.

"You make out like every young girl was Jennifer Jones in *The Song of Bernadette.*"

—Shirley Booth correcting Burt Lancaster's impression of Terry Moore in Daniel Mann's *Come Back, Little Sheba*
(Screenplay by Ketti Frings; based on the play by William Inge)

3.

"Baroness, you've got to face facts: sooner or later, the innocence of your daughter cannot be respected if the family is going to continue, you know."

—Burt Lancaster telling Anna Magnani she's too protective of her daughter (Marisa Pavan) in Daniel Mann's *The Rose Tattoo*
(Screenplay by Tennessee Williams; adaptation by Hal Kanter; based on the play by Tennessee Williams)

4.

"Confess it: you've been hermetically sealed most of your life."

—George Brent coming on to Barbara Stanwyck in Curtis Bernhardt's *My Reputation*
(Screenplay by Catherine Turney; based on INSTRUCT MY SORROWS, a novel by Clare Jaynes)

5.

"Barzini's dead. So is Phillip Tattaglia, Moe Greene, Stracci, Cuneo. Today I settled all family business, so don't tell me you're innocent, Carlo. I know what you did. Come on. Don't be afraid, Carlo. Come on. You think I make my sister a widow? I'm godfather to your son, Carlo."

—Al Pacino coaxing a confession for James Caan's death from their brother-in-law (Gianni Russo) in Francis Ford Coppola's *The Godfather*
(Screenplay by Mario Puzo and Francis Ford Coppola; based on the novel by Mario Puzo)

6.

"Don't you know I can see a great deal farther than you can? I can see intangible things. For example, innocence."

—A blind Vaughan Glaser sensing the innocence of fugitive Robert Cummings in Alfred Hitchcock's *Saboteur*
(Original Screenplay by Peter Viertel, Joan Harrison and Dorothy Parker)

ALSO SEE: Courtroom Lines-3; Faces-3; Games-2; History-6; Normal-3; People-3; Priorities-2.

INSULTS

1.

"You, a descendant of generations of inbred, incestuous mental defectives—how dare you call anyone barbarian!"

—Rex Harrison counterattacking Elizabeth Taylor in Joseph L. Mankiewicz's *Cleopatra*
(Screenplay by Joseph L. Mankiewicz, Ranald MacDougall and Sidney Buchman; based upon histories by Plutarch, Suetonius and Appian and THE LIFE AND TIMES OF CLEOPATRA, a book by C. M. Franzero)

2.

"You know what you are, Willie? You're a 73-year-old schmo."

—George Burns summing up Walter Matthau in Herbert Ross's *The Sunshine Boys*
(Screenplay by Neil Simon; based on his play)

3.

"Your best, Mr. Keith, is only a maximum of inefficiency."

—Humphrey Bogart dressing down Robert Francis in Edward Dmytryk's *The Caine Mutiny*
(Screenplay by Stanley Roberts; additional dialogue by Michael Blankfort; based on the novel by Herman Wouk)

4.

"You're not a detective—you're a slot machine—you'd slit your own throat for six bits plus tax."

—Don Douglas calling Dick Powell cheap (very) in Edward Dmytryk's *Murder, My Sweet*
(Screenplay by John Paxton; based on FAREWELL, MY LOVELY, a novel by Raymond Chandler)
and (almost verbatim)

—Harry Dean Stanton dittoing Robert Mitchum in the remake, Dick Richards's *Farewell, My Lovely*
(Screenplay by David Zelag Goodman; based on the novel by Raymond Chandler)

5.

"I don't mind a parasite. I object to a cut-rate one."

—Humphrey Bogart writing off Peter Lorre in Michael Curtiz's *Casablanca*
(Screenplay by Julius J. Epstein, Philip G. Epstein and Howard Koch; based on EVERYBODY COMES TO RICK'S, a play by Murray Burnett and Joan Alison)

6.

"Your husband has a great deal to be modest about."

—Clifton Webb assuring Maureen O'Hara that Robert Young's modesty is well founded in Walter Lang's *Sitting Pretty*
(Screenplay by F. Hugh Herbert; based on the novel by Gwen Davenport)

7.

"There you are, my dear: in a moment of supreme disaster, he's trite."

—Clifton Webb criticizing Gene Tierney's fiancé (Vincent Price) in Otto Preminger's *Laura*
(Screenplay by Jay Dratler, Samuel Hoffenstein and Betty Reinhardt; based on the novel by Vera Caspary)

8.

"Young man, if there is such a thing as a tartuffe, you are just that thing. One more peep out of you, and I'll give you a sound trundling."

—W. C. Fields insulting a prospective son-in-law (James Bush) in George Marshall's *You Can't Cheat an Honest Man*
(Screenplay by George Marion Jr., Richard Mack and Everett Freeman; based on an original story by Charles Bogle, a.k.a. W. C. Fields)

9.
(a) "I think I could fix you up with Mr. Powell's chauffeur. The chauffeur has a very nice car, too."

(b) "Yes, but I understand Mr. Powell's chauffeur doesn't go as far in his car as Mr. Powell does."

(a) "Even a chauffeur has to have an incentive."

(b) "Well, you should know."

—(a) Gail Patrick and (b) Ginger Rogers sparring in Gregory La Cava's *Stage Door*
(Screenplay by Morrie Ryskind and Anthony Veiller; based on the play by Edna Ferber and George S. Kaufman)

ALSO SEE: Joke-4; Likes and Dislikes-5; Party-2; Past-5; Peace-8; Snake-4; Static-8; Talk-3; Vulture-1.

INTELLIGENCE

1.
"In a child's power to master the multiplication table, there is more sanctity than in all your shouted 'amens' and 'holy holys' and 'hosannas.' An idea is a greater monument than a cathedral, and the advance of man's knowledge is a greater miracle than all the sticks turned to snakes or the parting of the waters. But, now, are we to forego all this progress because Mr. Brady now frightens us with a fable?"

—Spencer Tracy putting Darwin's theory ahead of Fredric March's fundamentalist religion in Stanley Kramer's *Inherit the Wind*
(Screenplay by Nathan E. Douglas and Harold Jacob Smith; based on the play by Jerome Lawrence and Robert E. Lee)

2.
"It's sort of a cause. I want everybody to be smart. I want 'em to be as smart as they can be. A world full of ignorant people is too dangerous to live in."

—William Holden explaining his personal crusade to Judy Holliday in George Cukor's *Born Yesterday*

(Screenplay by Albert Mannheimer; based on the play by Garson Kanin)

3.
"I apologize for the intelligence of my remarks, Sir Thomas. I had forgotten that you were a member of Parliament."

—George Sanders insulting Robert Greig by way of an apology in Albert Lewin's *The Picture of Dorian Gray*
(Screenplay by Albert Lewin; based on the novel by Oscar Wilde)

4.
"Let's put aside my personal likes and dislikes, they're not important. I'm willing to admit that, to a majority of my fellow citizens, I'm a slightly comic figure: an educated man."

—Kirk Douglas arguing his brains-over-brawn position in Joseph L. Mankiewicz's *A Letter to Three Wives*
(Screenplay by Joseph L. Mankiewicz; adaptation by Vera Caspary; based on "One of Our Hearts," a short story by John Klempner)

5.
"Ingenuity is never a substitute for intelligence."

—Zachary Scott putting down Sydney Greenstreet in Jean Negulesco's *The Mask of Dimitrios*
(Screenplay by Frank Gruber; based on A COFFIN FOR DIMITRIOS, a novel by Eric Ambler)

ALSO SEE: Disease-5; Faces-4; Ignorance-2; Macho-10; Rejection-14.

INTRODUCTIONS

1.
"Ladies and gentlemen, I'm here tonight to tell you a very strange story—a story so strange that no one will believe it—but, ladies and gentlemen, seeing is believing. And we—my partners and I—have brought back the living proof of our adventure, an adventure in which 12 of our party met horrible deaths. And now, ladies and gentlemen, be-

fore I tell you any more, I'm going to show you the greatest thing your eyes have ever beheld. He was a king in the world he knew, but now he comes to civilization merely a captive—a show to gratify your curiosity. Ladies and gentlemen, look at Kong—the eighth wonder of the world!"

—Robert Armstrong laying it on thick for his first (and last) nighters in Merian C. Cooper and Ernest B. Schoedsack's *King Kong*
(Screenplay by James Creelman and Ruth Rose; based on an original story by Merian C. Cooper and Edgar Wallace)

2.
"Lovely ladies, kind gentlemen, pleased to introduce myself: Sakini by name, interpreter by profession, education by the ancient dictionary, Okinawan by whim of gods."

—Marlon Brando introducing himself to the audience in Daniel Mann's *The Teahouse of the August Moon*
(Screenplay by John Patrick; based on his play and the book by Vern J. Sneider)

3.
"To those of you who do not read, attend the theater, listen to unsponsored radio programs or know anything of the world in which you live—it is perhaps necessary to introduce myself. My name is Addison DeWitt."

—George Sanders introducing himself to the audience in Joseph L. Mankiewicz's *All About Eve*
(Screenplay by Joseph L. Mankiewicz; based on "The Wisdom of Eve," a radio play and short story by Mary Orr)

4.
"I am Tondelayo."

—Hedy Lamarr slinking through bamboo curtains with a sultry introduction in Richard Thorpe's *White Cargo*
(Screenplay by Leon Gordon; based on his play and HELL'S PLAYGROUND, a novel by Ida Vera Simonton)

5.
(a) "You may call me Tanka."

(b) "Tanka?"
(a) "You're welcome."

—(a) Ginger Rogers greeting (b) Fred Astaire in William A. Seiter's *Roberta*
(Screenplay by Jane Murfin and Sam Mintz; additional dialogue by Glenn Tryon and Allan Scott; based on the musical play by Jerome Kern and Otto Harbach and GOWNS BY ROBERTA, a novel by Alice Duer Miller)

6.
"Rita and George—Deborah! Debby, Rita and George Phipps. They were with me the day I swallowed my first worm, and I hope they'll be with me the day I swallow my last."

—Jeffrey Lynn introducing his bride (Jeanne Crain) to Ann Sothern and Kirk Douglas in Joseph L. Mankiewicz's *A Letter to Three Wives*
(Screenplay by Joseph L. Mankiewicz; adaptation by Vera Caspary; based on "One of Our Hearts," a short story by John Klempner)

7.
"Now just behave yourself, you two, and nobody'll get hurt. This is Duke Mantee, the world-famous killer, and he's hungry."

—Joe Sawyer introducing Humphrey Bogart to Bette Davis and Dick Foran in Archie Mayo's *The Petrified Forest*
(Screenplay by Delmer Daves and Charles Kenyon; based on the play by Robert E. Sherwood)

8.
"This aging debutante, Mr. Jefferson, I retain in my employ only because she is the sole support of her two-headed brother."

—Monty Woolley introducing Bette Davis to Richard Travis in William Keighley's *The Man Who Came to Dinner*
(Screenplay by Julius J. Epstein and Philip G. Epstein; based on the play by George S. Kaufman and Moss Hart)

9.
"I now take great pleasure in presenting to you the well-preserved and partially pickled Mrs. Potter."

—Groucho Marx introducing Margaret Dumont in Joseph Santley and Robert Florey's *The Cocoanuts* *(Screenplay by Morrie Ryskind; based on the musical play by George S. Kaufman and Morrie Ryskind)*

ALSO SEE: Actors-3; Fools-1; Greetings-13; Heaven-4; Thieves-1.

JEALOUS

1.
" 'Jealous' is a disease of the flesh."

—Rex Harrison reminding Gene Tierney (rather testily) that he is spirit in Joseph L. Mankiewicz's *The Ghost and Mrs. Muir* *(Screenplay by Philip Dunne; based on THE GHOST OF CAPTAIN GREGG AND MRS. MUIR, a novel by R. A. Dick)*

2.
"Jealous, am I? Yes, I suppose I am—even though I know you've been faithful to me all along. How do I know? Because I know Ashley Wilkes and his honorable breed. They're gentlemen! That's more than I can say for you or for me. We're not gentlemen, and we have no honor, have we?"

—Clark Gable fighting with Vivien Leigh about Leslie Howard in Victor Fleming's *Gone With the Wind* *(Screenplay by Sidney Howard; based on the novel by Margaret Mitchell)*

3.
"I've been listening. All I can hear is a typical suburban husband reacting in a typically stupid and stuffy manner to a typical tempest in a teapot."

—Clifton Webb minimizing Robert Young's jealousy in Walter Lang's *Sitting Pretty* *(Screenplay by F. Hugh Herbert; based on the novel by Gwen Davenport)*

ALSO SEE: Excuses-4.

JEWELS

1.
"Between us all the time were those jewels, like a fire—a fire in my brain that separated us —those jewels which I wanted all my life."

—Charles Boyer explaining why he tried to drive Ingrid Bergman insane in George Cukor's *Gaslight* *(Screenplay by John Van Druten, Walter Reisch, and John L. Balderston; based on ANGEL STREET, a play by Patrick Hamilton)*

2.
(a) "My husband, Mr. Greer, is very wealthy. I have more jewels than I can possibly wear. You, of course, are a charity patient."
   (b) "Oh, no. It so happens that my husband, Mr. Cunningham, is very wealthy. My diamonds simply weight me down."
   (a) "I have the Hope Diamond."
   (b) "I have the Hopeless Emerald. It carries the Cunningham curse. You've probably read about it."
   (a) "Mr. Greer—"
   (b) "Your husband?"
   (a) "Mr. Greer, my husband, considered buying it, but it has a flaw. You see, you can't put an imperfect stone on the most beautiful hands in the world."

—(a) Beulah Bondi and (b) Olivia De Havilland playing a jewelry version of can-you-top-this? in the mental ward in Anatole Litvak's *The Snake Pit* *(Screenplay by Frank Partos and Millen Brand; based on the novel by Mary Jane Ward)*

3.
"Without a knowledge of jewelry, my dear Gigi, a woman is lost."

—Isabel Jeans instructing Leslie Caron in Vincente Minnelli's *Gigi* *(Screenplay by Alan Jay Lerner; based on the novel by Colette)*

ALSO SEE: Diamonds; Class-7; Movies-1.

JOKE

1.

"Aw, laugh, Curtin, old boy, it's a great joke played on us by the Lord or fate or nature, whatever you prefer, but whoever or whatever played it certainly had a sense of humor: the gold has gone back to where we found it."

—Walter Huston encouraging Tim Holt to see the comedy in their final disaster in John Huston's *The Treasure of the Sierra Madre*
(Screenplay by John Huston; based on the novel by B. Traven)

2.

"You never did anything for the sake of anybody but yourself. You enjoy playing with people, making fools of them. That's why you're doing it, as a joke—to prove that you are great and alive and the others are small and dead. Yes, and for money."

—Ingrid Bergman understanding why Yul Brynner likes deception in Anatole Litvak's *Anastasia*
(Screenplay by Arthur Laurents; based on the play by Marcelle Maurette and Broadway adaptation by Guy Bolton)

3.

"Everything you say and do is so true and wonderful, and you make it sound so sacred and holy when all the time it's just a gag with you. You're just laughing your head off at those chumps. Do you think God's going to stand for that? Do you want Him to strike you dead? You can't do it, Stan. Nobody's ever done it! Never!"

—Coleen Gray understanding why Tyrone Power likes deception in Edmund Goulding's *Nightmare Alley*
(Screenplay by Jules Furthman; based on the novel by William Lindsay Gresham)

4.

"You're a joke—a dirty joke, from one end of this town to the other!"

—Laurence Harvey insulting Elizabeth Taylor in Daniel Mann's *Butterfield 8*
(Screenplay by Charles Schnee and John Michael Hayes; based on the novel by John O'Hara)

5.

"You know what your trouble was, Willie? You always took the jokes too seriously. They were just jokes. We did comedy on the stage for 43 years. I don't think you enjoyed it once."

—George Burns leveling with his old partner (Walter Matthau) in Herbert Ross's *The Sunshine Boys*
(Screenplay by Neil Simon; based on his play)

6.

"What I said about having to get out and carry this old boat was meant to be a joke. It don't look like a joke now."

—Humphrey Bogart resigning himself to having to pull his boat through the reeds in John Huston's *The African Queen*
(Screenplay by James Agee and John Huston; based on the novel by C. S. Forester)

ALSO SEE: Honor-1; Names-22; Soul-11.

JUSTICE

1.

"Sign that, and Roman justice will receive a blow from which it may never recover. Condemn these Christians, and you make martyrs of them and ensure their immortality. Condemn them, and, in the eyes of history, you condemn yourself."

—Leo Genn trying to reason Nero (Peter Ustinov) away from disaster in Mervyn LeRoy's *Quo Vadis*
(Screenplay by John Lee Mahin, S. N. Behrman and Sonya Levien; based on the novel by Henryk Sienkiewicz)

2.

"So much for those bandits. You know, you got to hand it to the Mexicans when it comes to swift justice. Once the Federales get their mitts on a criminal, they know just what to do with him. They hand him a shovel, tell him where to dig, and when he's dug deep enough, they tell him to put the shovel down, smoke a cigarette and say his prayers. In another five minutes, he's being covered over with the earth he dug up."

—Bruce Bennett marveling aloud to Tim Holt about the phenomenon in John Huston's *The Treasure of the Sierra Madre*
(Screenplay by John Huston; based on the novel by B. Traven)

3.
"Something had happened. A thing which years ago had been the eagerest hope of many, many good citizens of the town. And now it came at last: George Amberson Minafer had got his comeuppance. He got it three times filled and running over. But those who had so longed for it were not there to see it, and they never knew it. Those who were still living had forgotten all about it and all about him."

—Orson Welles, as narrator, commenting on the fate of the finally and emphatically humbled Tim Holt in Orson Welles's *The Magnificent Ambersons*
(Screenplay by Orson Welles; based on the novel by Booth Tarkington)

ALSO SEE: Elephants-3; Fake-4; Innocent-1; Letters-9; Names-17; Toasts-8.

KINDNESS

1.
"I'd like to see you again very much. The reason I didn't let you kiss me was because I just didn't know how to handle the situation. You're the kindest man I ever met. The reason I tell you this is because I want to see you again very much. I know that when you take me home I'm just going to lie on my bed and think about you. I want very much to see you again."

—Betsy Blair soothing Ernest Borgnine's hurt feelings in Delbert Mann's *Marty*
(Screenplay by Paddy Chayefsky; based on his teleplay)

2.
"I asked you to come out with me because I wanted your company. You've blotted out the past for me more than all the bright lights of Monte Carlo. But if you think I just asked you out of kindness or charity—you can leave the car now and find your own way home. Go on, open the door and get out!"

—Laurence Olivier "romancing" Joan Fontaine in Alfred Hitchcock's *Rebecca*
(Screenplay by Robert E. Sherwood and Joan Harrison; adaptation by Philip MacDonald and Michael Hogan; based on the novel by Daphne du Maurier)

3.
"I wouldn't give you two cents for all your fancy rules if, behind them, they didn't have a little bit of plain, ordinary, everyday kindness and a—a little looking out for the other fella, too."

—James Stewart filibustering in Frank Capra's *Mr. Smith Goes to Washington*
(Screenplay by Sidney Buchman; based on "The Gentleman From Montana," a story by Lewis R. Foster)

4.
"Simple kindness is so rare in this house that it's instantly mistaken for passion."

—John Mills correcting Hayley Mills's impression about his interest in Deborah Kerr in Ronald Neame's *The Chalk Garden*
(Screenplay by John Michael Hayes; based on the play by Enid Bagnold)

5.
"You see: there's not enough kindness in the world."

—Sydney Greenstreet reprising his pet expression to bid good-bye to Peter Lorre in the last line of Jean Negulesco's *The Mask of Dimitrios*
(Screenplay by Frank Gruber; based on A COFFIN FOR DIMITRIOS, a novel by Eric Ambler)

6.
"Confound it, June, when will you learn that I am *always* kind and courteous! Bring this idiot in!"

—Monty Woolley doing his "kind and courteous" for Elisabeth Fraser in William Keighley's *The Man Who Came to Dinner*

(Screenplay by Julius J. Epstein and Philip G. Epstein; based on the play by George S. Kaufman and Moss Hart)

ALSO SEE: Prayers-14; Propositions-3; Smile-7; Strangers-1; Stupid-6.

KISS

1.
"Here's a soldier of the South who loves you, Scarlett, wants to feel your arms around him, wants to carry the memory of your kisses into battle with him. Never mind about loving me. You're a woman sending a soldier to his death with a beautiful memory. Scarlett, kiss me. Kiss me, once."

—Clark Gable leaving Vivien Leigh for war in Victor Fleming's *Gone With the Wind*
(Screenplay by Sidney Howard; based on the novel by Margaret Mitchell)

2.
"I don't know how to kiss, or I would kiss you. Where do the noses go?"

—Ingrid Bergman making a poignant admission to Gary Cooper in Sam Wood's *For Whom the Bell Tolls*
(Screenplay by Dudley Nichols; based on the novel by Ernest Hemingway)

3.
"I don't know why I should act so experienced. It was only my second kiss this year."

—Diane Varsi making a poignant admission to Russ Tamblyn in Mark Robson's *Peyton Place*
(Screenplay by John Michael Hayes; based on the novel by Grace Metalious)

4.
"That was restful. Again."

—Greta Garbo allowing Melvyn Douglas to teach her this western custom in Ernst Lubitsch's *Ninotchka*
(Screenplay by Charles Brackett, Billy Wilder and Walter Reisch; based on an original story by Melchior Lengyel)

and

—Cyd Charisse dittoing Fred Astaire in the remake, Rouben Mamoulian's *Silk Stockings*
(Screenplay by Leonard Gershe and Leonard Spigelgass; based on the musical play by George S. Kaufman, Leueen MacGrath and Abe Burrows and NINOTCHKA, a screenplay by Charles Brackett, Billy Wilder and Walter Reisch and original story by Melchior Lengyel)

5.
"It's even better when you help."

—Lauren Bacall criticizing Humphrey Bogart's passivity in Howard Hawks's *To Have and Have Not*
(Screenplay by Jules Furthman and William Faulkner; based on the novel by Ernest Hemingway)

6.
"When a woman kisses me, Louise, she has to take pot luck."

—Van Heflin cooling it with Joan Crawford in Curtis Bernhardt's *Possessed*
(Screenplay by Sylvia Richards and Ranald MacDougall; based on ONE MAN'S SECRET, a novelette by Rita Weiman)

7.
"Want to kiss me, ducky?"

—A disguised Marlene Dietrich flashing scars to Charles Laughton in Billy Wilder's *Witness for the Prosecution*
(Screenplay by Billy Wilder and Harry Kurnitz; adaptation by Larry Marcus; based on the play and story by Agatha Christie)

8.
"Come on, give your mommy a big sloppy kiss."

—Elizabeth Taylor mother-smothering her husband (Richard Burton) in Mike Nichols's *Who's Afraid of Virginia Woolf?*
(Screenplay by Ernest Lehman; based on the play by Edward Albee)

9.
"Tell Mama. Tell Mama all."

—Elizabeth Taylor romancing Montgomery Clift in George Stevens's *A Place in the Sun*

(Screenplay by Michael Wilson and Harry Brown; based on AN AMERICAN TRAGEDY, a play by Patrick Kearney and novel by Theodore Dreiser)

10.
"Baby, what you do!"

—William Holden responding to Kim Novak in Joshua Logan's *Picnic*
(Screenplay by Daniel Taradash; based on the play by William Inge)

11.
(a) "Where did you learn to kiss like that?"
    (b) "I used to sell kisses for the milk fund."
    (a) "Tomorrow, remind me to send a check for $100,000 to the milk fund."

—(a) Tony Curtis responding to (b) Marilyn Monroe in Billy Wilder's *Some Like It Hot*
(Screenplay by Billy Wilder and I. A. L. Diamond; suggested by a story by R. Thoeren and M. Logan)

12.
"Gil Martin, I'm going to kiss you so I'm going to do it now so's you won't go off with the taste of a widow in your mouth."

—Edna May Oliver sending her employee (Henry Fonda) off to the Revolutionary War in John Ford's *Drums Along the Mohawk*
(Screenplay by Lamar Trotti and Sonya Levien; based on the novel by Walter D. Edmonds)

13.
"Mustard!"

—Bette Davis discovering from a kiss that (1) she isn't trapped in a mine cave-in as she had believed and (2) James Cagney has been sneaking out for food in William Keighley's *The Bride Came C.O.D.*
(Screenplay by Julius J. Epstein and Philip G. Epstein; based on a story by Kenneth Earl and M. M. Musselman)

14.
"You cad! You dirty swine! I never cared for you, not once. I was always making a fool of you. You bored me stiff. I hated you. It made me sick when I had to let you kiss me. I only did it because you begged me. You hounded me. You drove me crazy. And, after you kissed me,

I always used to wipe my mouth—*wipe my mouth*—but I made up for it. For every kiss, I had to laugh."

—Bette Davis berating Leslie Howard in John Cromwell's *Of Human Bondage*
(Screenplay by Lester Cohen; based on the novel by W. Somerset Maugham)

15.
"I will not have my face smeared with lipstick. If you want to kiss me, kiss me on the lips, which is what a merciful providence provided them for."

—Herbert Marshall giving Gene Tierney kissing instructions in Edmund Goulding's *The Razor's Edge*
(Screenplay by Lamar Trotti; based on the novel by W. Somerset Maugham)

16.
"Frankly, my child, I had a sudden, powerful and very ignoble desire to kiss you till your lips were somewhat bruised."

—David Niven confessing a compulsion to Maggie McNamara in Otto Preminger's *The Moon Is Blue*
(Screenplay by F. Hugh Herbert; based on his play)

17.
"What will you give me for a basket of kisses?"

—Patty McCormack playing a kissing game with her parents (Nancy Kelly and William Hopper) in Mervyn LeRoy's *The Bad Seed*
(Screenplay by John Lee Mahin; based on the play by Maxwell Anderson and novel by William March)

18.
"When a clumsy cloud from here meets a fluffy little cloud from there, he billows towards her. She scurries away, and he scuds right up to her. She cries a little, and there you have your shower. He comforts her. They spark. That's the lightning. They kiss. Thunder!"

—Fred Astaire giving Ginger Rogers an amorous weather report in Mark Sandrich's *Top Hat*
(Screenplay by Dwight Taylor and Allan Scott; adaptation by Karl Noti; based on THE GIRL WHO

DARED, a play by Alexander Farago and Aladar Laszlo)

19.

"I don't understand these modern girls. . . . Well, Polly, for instance. Sometimes, she won't let you kiss her at all. But, there's Cynthia. Oh, she'll let you kiss her whenever you want. She doesn't want to swim. She doesn't want to play tennis, go for walks. All she wants to do is kiss you. I'm a nervous wreck!"

—Mickey Rooney having a heart-to-heart with Lewis Stone in George B. Seitz's *Love Finds Andy Hardy* (Screenplay by William Ludwig; based on the stories by Vivien R. Bretherton and characters created by Aurania Rouverol)

20.

"William, that was *not* a preacher's kiss!"

—Susan Hayward registering surprise at the passion of her preacher-husband (William Lundigan) in Henry King's *I'd Climb the Highest Mountain* (Screenplay by Lamar Trotti; based on the novel by Corra Harris)

21.

"I have a message for your wife. Don't wipe it off. If she thinks that's cranberry sauce, tell her she's got cherry pits in her head."

—Marilyn Monroe sending Tom Ewell back to his wife (Evelyn Keyes) with a kiss in Billy Wilder's *The Seven Year Itch* (Screenplay by Billy Wilder and George Axelrod; based on the play by George Axelrod)

22.

"Tom, we ain't the kissin' kind, but . . ."

—Jane Darwell saying good-bye to Henry Fonda in John Ford's *The Grapes of Wrath* (Screenplay by Nunnally Johnson; based on the novel by John Steinbeck)

23.

"Persian good-bye? Why, that ain't nuttin' compared to a Oklahoma hello!"

—Gene Nelson setting out to kiss Gloria Grahame better than Eddie Albert in Fred Zinnemann's *Oklahoma!*

(Screenplay by Sonya Levien and William Ludwig; based on the musical play by Oscar Hammerstein II and GREEN GROW THE LILACS, a play by Lynn Riggs)

ALSO SEE: Appearances-6; Diamonds-1; Hair-1; Hate-5; Kindness-1; Life and Death-9; Pet Expressions-11; Rejection-8; Republicans-2; Time-15; Time-16; Wrong-8.

KNOWLEDGE

1.

"I know. You know I know. I know you know I know. We know Henry knows, and Henry knows we know it. We're a knowledgeable family."

—John Castle discussing court intrigues with his mother (Katharine Hepburn) in Anthony Harvey's *The Lion in Winter* (Screenplay by James Goldman; based on his play)

2.

"I know what gold does to men's souls."

—Walter Huston lecturing on greed in John Huston's *The Treasure of the Sierra Madre* (Screenplay by John Huston; based on the novel by B. Traven)

3.

"Anything can be great. I don't care, bricklaying can be great—if a guy knows, if he knows what he's doing and why, and if he can make it come off. When I'm goin'—I mean, when I'm really goin'—I feel like a—like a jockey must feel. Sitting on his horse, he's got all that speed and that power underneath him, he's comin' into the stretch, the pressure's on him—and he knows. Just feels, when to let it go, how much. 'Cause he's got everything working for him— timing, touch. It's a great feeling, boy—a real great feeling—when you're right and you know you're right. Like all of a sudden, I got oil in my arm. Pool cue's part of me. You know, it's a—pool cue has got nerves in it. It's a piece of wood; it's got nerves in it. You can feel the roll of those balls. You don't have to look. You just know. You make shots that nobody's ever made before. And you play that game the way nobody's ever played it before."

—Paul Newman explaining pool to Piper Laurie in Robert Rossen's *The Hustler*
(Screenplay by Sidney Carroll and Robert Rossen; based on the novel by Walter Tevis)

4.

"Mr. Babcock, knowledge is power!"

—Rosalind Russell defending the martini-mixing prowess of her young nephew (Jan Handzlik) to Fred Clark in Morton DaCosta's *Auntie Mame*
(Screenplay by Betty Comden and Adolph Green; based on the play by Jerome Lawrence and Robert E. Lee and novel by Patrick Dennis)

5.

"Knowledge can be more terrible than ignorance if one can do nothing."

—John Justin feeling unable to rescue June Duprez in Ludwig Berger, Tim Whelan and Michael Powell's *The Thief of Bagdad*
(Screenplay and dialogue by Miles Malleson; based on a scenario by Lajos Biro)

6.

"To hardly know him is to know him well."

—Cary Grant criticizing Katharine Hepburn's fiancé (John Howard) in George Cukor's *The Philadelphia Story*
(Screenplay by Donald Ogden Stewart; based on the play by Philip Barry)

7.

"I do not know what is to happen, darling, but this I do know—life's greatest tragedy is not to be loved. God has been good to us, Suyin."

—William Holden appreciating his affair with Jennifer Jones in Henry King's *Love Is a Many-Splendored Thing*
(Screenplay by John Patrick; based on A MANY-SPLENDORED THING, a novel by Han Suyin)

ALSO SEE: Intelligence; Jewels-3; Oops!-1; Parting Shots-1; Progress-2; Questions-3; Questions-6; Similarities-4; Smell-2; Sun-1; Sun-4; Toasts-8; War-7.

LADY

1.

(a) "We were above that in Covent Garden."

    (b) "What do you mean?"

    (a) "I sold flowers. I didn't sell myself. Now you've made a lady of me, I'm not fit to sell anything else."

—(a) Wendy Hiller putting down (b) Leslie Howard for suggesting that she marry into the upper classes in Anthony Asquith and Leslie Howard's *Pygmalion*
(Screenplay by George Bernard Shaw; adaptation by W. P. Lipscomb, Cecil Lewis and Ian Dalrymple; based on the play by George Bernard Shaw)

and

—(a) Audrey Hepburn dittoing Rex Harrison in the remake, George Cukor's *My Fair Lady*
(Screenplay by Alan Jay Lerner; based on his musical play and PYGMALION, *a screenplay and play by George Bernard Shaw)*

2.

"I'm going to be a lady if it kills me!"

—Jean Harlow clashing with Wallace Beery about class in George Cukor's *Dinner at Eight*
(Screenplay by Frances Marion and Herman J. Mankiewicz; based on the play by George S. Kaufman and Edna Ferber)

3.

"I got a date with a lady. You know what a lady is? Naw, how could you?"

—Kirk Douglas insulting Marilyn Maxwell in Mark Robson's *Champion*
(Screenplay by Carl Foreman; based on the short story by Ring Lardner)

4.

"Look at my hands! Mother always said you could always tell a lady by her hands."

—Evelyn Keyes lamenting her field-hand fate in Victor Fleming's *Gone With the Wind*
(Screenplay by Sidney Howard; based on the novel by Margaret Mitchell)

5.

"Killing a man with a sap's quiet, but it's no work for a lady."

—Dick Powell accusing Claire Trevor of murder in Edward Dmytryk's *Murder, My Sweet*
(*Screenplay by John Paxton; based on* FAREWELL, MY LOVELY, *a novel by Raymond Chandler*)

6.

"Listen, Paolo: there is no such thing as a great American lady. Great ladies do not occur in a nation less than 200 years old."

—Lotte Lenya correcting Warren Beatty's impression about Vivien Leigh in Jose Quintero's *The Roman Spring of Mrs. Stone*
(*Screenplay by Gavin Lambert; based on the novel by Tennessee Williams*)

ALSO SEE: Cigarette-4; Clean-1; Eat-3; Hanging-4; Run-3; Static-12.

LAND

1.

"Before I sell it, I'll feed it to my children."

—Paul Muni holding on to his land at all costs in Sidney Franklin's *The Good Earth*
(*Screenplay by Talbot Jennings, Tess Slesinger and Claudine West; based on the novel by Pearl S. Buck*)

2.

(a) "Do you mean to tell me, Katie Scarlett O'Hara, that Tara—that land doesn't mean anything to you? Why, land is the only thing in the world worth working for, worth fighting for, worth dying for, because it's the only thing that lasts."
  (b) "Oh, Pa. You talk like an Irishman."
  (a) "It's proud I am that I'm Irish, and don't you be forgetting, Missy, that you're half-Irish, too. And, to anyone with a drop of Irish blood in them—why, the land they live on is like their mother. Oh, but there, there. Now, you're just a child. It'll come to you, this love of the land. There's no getting away from it if you're Irish."

—(a) Thomas Mitchell lecturing (b) Vivien Leigh in Victor Fleming's *Gone With the Wind*
(*Screenplay by Sidney Howard; based on the novel by Margaret Mitchell*)

3.

"There's only one thing on this earth more important than money, and that's land. Why, I've heard Luz say it a thousand times. Pa said it, and Bick Benedict says it, and it's true."

—Jane Withers advancing Texas values in George Stevens's *Giant*
(*Screenplay by Fred Guiol and Ivan Moffat; based on the novel by Edna Ferber*)

4.

"This land is yours. You must protect it. It won't be yours long if you don't protect it—if necessary with your lives and your children with their lives. Don't discount your enemies. They will be back. And if your house is burned, build it again. If your corn is destroyed, replant. If your children die, bear more. If they drive you out of the valley, live in the sides of the mountains—but live!"

—Marlon Brando addressing his people in Elia Kazan's *Viva Zapata!*
(*Original Screenplay by John Steinbeck*)

ALSO SEE: Dying Words-12; Exchanges-7; Sea-1; Strength-3.

LAST LINES

1.

"Captain, it is I—Ensign Pulver—and I just threw your stinking palm tree overboard. Now, what's all this crud about no movie tonight?"

—Jack Lemmon rising to his long-overdue showdown with James Cagney in John Ford and Mervyn LeRoy's *Mister Roberts*
(*Screenplay by Frank S. Nugent and Joshua Logan; based on the play by Thomas Heggen and Joshua Logan and novel by Thomas Heggen*)

2.

"Shut up and deal."

—Shirley MacLaine settling down to a card game/ happy ending with Jack Lemmon in Billy Wilder's *The Apartment*
(Original Screenplay by Billy Wilder and I. A. L. Diamond)

3.
"And out there in that great big concrete jungle, I wonder how many others there are like me—poor bedeviled guys on fire with thirst. Such comical figures to the rest of the world as they stagger blindly toward another binge, another bender, another spree."

—Ray Milland pondering the plights of less fortunate alcoholics in Billy Wilder's *The Lost Weekend*
(Screenplay by Charles Brackett and Billy Wilder; based on the novel by Charles R. Jackson)

4.
"Well, nobody's perfect."

—Joe E. Brown responding to the news that his bride-to-be is a man (Jack Lemmon) in Billy Wilder's *Some Like It Hot*
(Screenplay by Billy Wilder and I. A. L. Diamond; suggested by a story by R. Thoeren and M. Logan)

5.
"Where the devil are my slippers, Eliza?"

—Leslie Howard welcoming Wendy Hiller back home in Anthony Asquith and Leslie Howard's *Pygmalion*
(Screenplay by George Bernard Shaw; adaptation by W. P. Lipscomb, Cecil Lewis and Ian Dalrymple; based on the play by George Bernard Shaw)
and (almost verbatim)

—Rex Harrison dittoing Audrey Hepburn in the remake, George Cukor's *My Fair Lady*
(Screenplay by Alan Jay Lerner; based on his musical play and PYGMALION, a screenplay and play by George Bernard Shaw)

6.
"Hello, Clara?"

—Ernest Borgnine forgetting friends and family to phone up Betsy Blair in Delbert Mann's *Marty*
(Screenplay by Paddy Chayefsky; based on his teleplay)

7.
"Hey, Stella! Hey, Stella!"

—Marlon Brando yelling for the return of his wife (Kim Hunter) in Elia Kazan's *A Streetcar Named Desire*
(Screenplay by Tennessee Williams; adaptation by Oscar Saul; based on the play by Tennessee Williams)

8.
"Catherine! Catherine! Catherine! Catherine! Catherine! Catherine! Catherine! Catherine! Catherine! Catherine! Catherine!"

—Montgomery Clift calling for his rejecting fiancée (Olivia De Havilland) on her doorstep in William Wyler's *The Heiress*
(Screenplay by Ruth Goetz and Augustus Goetz; based on their play and WASHINGTON SQUARE, a novel by Henry James)

9.
"She's here, Doctor. Miss Catherine's here."

—Elizabeth Taylor telling Montgomery Clift she has returned to a less painful present in *Suddenly, Last Summer*
(Screenplay by Gore Vidal and Tennessee Williams; based on the one-act play by Tennessee Williams)

10.
"Oh, what times we're going to have! What vistas we're going to explore together! We'll spend the day at an ancient Hindu temple. The headmaster is a very good friend of Auntie Mame's, and perhaps he'll let you ring the temple bells to bring the monks to prayer. And there, on the highest tower, on a clear day, you can see the Taj Mahal. Beyond that is a beautiful city . . ."

—Rosalind Russell scaling her staircase with her grand-nephew (Terry Kelman) in Morton DaCosta's *Auntie Mame*
(Screenplay by Betty Comden and Adolph Green; based on the play by Jerome Lawrence and Robert E. Lee and novel by Patrick Dennis)

11.
(a) "Well, he certainly fooled me. I never

recognized him. Stanton. Stanton the Great."

(b) "How can a guy get so low?"

(a) "He reached too high. Good night, boys. Lock up."

—(a) Roy Roberts explaining to his workmen how Tyrone Power could plummet to sideshow freak in Edmund Goulding's *Nightmare Alley*
(Screenplay by Jules Furthman; based on the novel by William Lindsay Gresham)

12.
"I was to think of these days many times. Of Jem and Dill and Boo Radley and Tom Robinson—and Atticus. He would be in Jem's room all night, and he would be there when Jem waked up in the morning."

—Kim Stanley, as the never-seen narrator (a grownup version of Mary Badham), rounding off her childhood memories in Robert Mulligan's *To Kill a Mockingbird*
(Screenplay by Horton Foote; based on the novel by Harper Lee)

13.
"See that those others are released. We need some fresh air in here. Looks like a nice morning. You can go now. We'll call you when we want you. You know, Mrs. Beragon, there are times when I regret being a policeman."

—Moroni Olsen solving his case and dismissing Joan Crawford in Michael Curtiz's *Mildred Pierce*
(Screenplay by Ranald MacDougall; based on the novel by James M. Cain)

14.
"Rain!"

—Burt Lancaster rejoicing in his miracle in Joseph Anthony's *The Rainmaker*
(Screenplay by N. Richard Nash; based on his play)

15.
"I'm going to be baptized!"

—William Powell surrendering grudgingly to the Christian will of his wife (Irene Dunne) in Michael Curtiz's *Life With Father*
(Screenplay by Donald Ogden Stewart; based on the play by Howard Lindsay and Russel Crouse and stories by Clarence Day, Jr.)

16.
"I now pronounce you men and wives."

—Ian Wolfe performing the finale wedding in Stanley Donen's *Seven Brides for Seven Brothers*
(Screenplay by Albert Hackett, Frances Goodrich and Dorothy Kingsley; based on "The Sobbin' Women," a short story by Stephen Vincent Benét)

17.
"I've just launched Gerald."

—Spencer Tracy informing Katharine Hepburn that he has given Dan Tobin a champagne-bottle "christening" in George Stevens's *Woman of the Year*
(Original Screenplay by Ring Lardner, Jr., and Michael Kanin)

18.
"The Russians are coming! The Russians are coming! The Russians are coming!"

—Ben Blue finally getting into Paul Revere gear (after the Russians have gone) in Norman Jewison's *The Russians Are Coming The Russians Are Coming*
(Screenplay by William Rose; based on THE OFF-ISLANDERS, a novel by Nathaniel Benchley)

19.
"Alex, will you come in please? I wish to talk to you."

—Ivan Triesault paging Claude Rains for an accounting after the escape of two U.S. agents (Cary Grant and Ingrid Bergman) in Alfred Hitchcock's *Notorious*
(Original Screenplay by Ben Hecht)

20.
"He said he wanted his wife to get this letter, didn't he? He said there was nobody to look after the kids, didn't he?"

—Henry Fonda telling Harry (then Henry) Morgan their next move will be to tend to the unfinished business of a lynch-mob victim (Dana Andrews) in William A. Wellman's *The Ox-Bow Incident*
(Screenplay by Lamar Trotti; based on the novel by Walter Van Tilburg Clark)

21.

"Yowsir! Yowsir! Yowsir! Here they are again—these wonderful, wonderful kids, still struggling, still hoping as the clock of fate ticks away. The dance of destiny continues. The marathon goes on and on and on. How long can they last? Let's hear it. C'mon, let's hear it. Let's hear it."

—Gig Young continuing his dance-marathon emceeing in Sydney Pollack's *They Shoot Horses, Don't They?*
(Screenplay by James Poe and Robert E. Thompson; based on the novel by Horace McCoy)

22.

"Oh, I can just hear you saying, 'What has all this to do with us?' Nothing."

—Michael Dunn addressing the camera/audience in Stanley Kramer's *Ship of Fools*
(Screenplay by Abby Mann; based on the novel by Katherine Anne Porter)

23.

"When I was a kid, I couldn't wait to be grown up and they said childhood was the best time of my life and it wasn't. Now I want his company, and people say, 'What's half a loaf? You're well shot of him.' And I say, 'I know that. I miss him, that's all.' They say he'd never have made me happy and I say, 'I am happy, apart from missing him. You might throw me a pill or two for my cough.' All my life I've been looking for someone courageous and resourceful, not like myself, and he's not it. But something. We were something. You've no right to call me to account. I've only come about my cough."

—Peter Finch addressing the camera/audience in John Schlesinger's *Sunday Bloody Sunday*
(Original Screenplay by Penelope Gilliatt)

24.

"Campers! The entertainment committee was quite disappointed in the really poor turnout at this morning's community sing. I mean, where is all that old Camp Chickawattamee spirit? I'm sure I speak for all of us here when I say that I—now, I'd like to say right now that—that—campers, I can't think of anything to say."

—Jason Robards giving up his eccentric ways and returning to the workaday world in Fred Coe's *A Thousand Clowns*
(Screenplay by Herb Gardner; based on his play)

25.

"The drama is done. All have departed away. The great shroud of the sea rolls over the *Pequod,* her crew and Moby Dick. I only am escaped, alone, to tell thee."

—Richard Basehart ending his narration of John Huston's *Moby Dick*
(Screenplay by Ray Bradbury and John Huston; based on the novel by Herman Melville)

26.

(a) "Forgive me, Aunt Marie, but what will you say?"

    (b) "Say? Oh, I will say, 'The play is over. Go home.' "

—(a) Ivan Desny asking (b) Helen Hayes how she will dismiss the dignitaries who have assembled to see Ingrid Bergman accepted as Russian royalty in Anatole Litvak's *Anastasia*
(Screenplay by Arthur Laurents; based on the play by Marcelle Maurette and Broadway adaptation by Guy Bolton)

27.

(a) "Major, the big brass are going to yell their heads off about this, and the Japanese aren't going to like it much either. Have you got anything to say to them, sir?"

    (b) "Yeah. Tell 'em we said sayonara."

—(b) Marlon Brando exiting with Miiko Taka in Joshua Logan's *Sayonara*
(Screenplay by Paul Osborn; based on the novel by James A. Michener)

28.

"Th—that's all, folks!"

—Mel Blanc's Porky Pig voice signing off in Peter Bogdanovich's *What's Up, Doc?*
(Screenplay by Buck Henry, David Newman and Robert Benton; based on a story by Peter Bogdanovich)

LASTS

1.

"This? This is No Chance Saloon, Bedrock Bar, The end of the Line Cafe, The Bottom of the Sea Rathskeller. Don't you notice the beautiful calm in the atmosphere? That's because this is the last harbor. No one here has to worry about where they're going next because they can go no further."

—Robert Ryan orienting new-drunk-in-town Jeff Bridges in John Frankenheimer's *The Iceman Cometh*
(Screenplay based on the play by Eugene O'Neill; text edited by Thomas Quinn Curtiss)

2.

"I adore simple pleasures. They're the last refuge of the complex."

—George Sanders holding court in Albert Lewin's *The Picture of Dorian Gray*
(Screenplay by Albert Lewin; based on the novel by Oscar Wilde)

3.

"Well, you'd better come with me, Duke. I'm planning to be buried in the Petrified Forest. You know, I've been evolving a theory about that that would interest you. It's the graveyard of the civilization that's shot from under us, the world of outmoded ideas. They're all so many stumps in the desert. That's where I belong, and so do you, Duke. You're the last great apostle of rugged individualism."

—Leslie Howard saluting the equally outmoded Humphrey Bogart in Archie Mayo's *The Petrified Forest*
(Screenplay by Delmer Daves and Charles Kenyon; based on the play by Robert E. Sherwood)

4.

"Dolly Messiter! Poor, well-meaning, irritating Dolly Messiter, crashing into those last few precious minutes we had together. She chattered and fussed and I didn't hear what she said. I felt dazed and bewildered."

—Celia Johnson resenting her last moments with Trevor Howard being interrupted by Everley Gregg in David Lean's *Brief Encounter*
(Screenplay by David Lean, Anthony Havelock-Allan and Ronald Neame; based on STILL LIFE, a one-act play by Noel Coward)

LAUGH

1.

"Laugh now, Heathcliff. There's no laughter in hell."

—Hugh Williams pulling a gun on Laurence Olivier in William Wyler's *Wuthering Heights*
(Screenplay by Ben Hecht and Charles MacArthur; based on the novel by Emily Brontë)

2.

"I'll tell you something else: there's a lot to be said for making people laugh. Did you know that's all some people have? It isn't much, but it's better than nothing in this cockeyed caravan. Boy!"

—Joel McCrea summarizing what he's learned in the last lines of Preston Sturges's *Sullivan's Travels*
(Original Screenplay by Preston Sturges)

3.
"That's just it. That's been his downfall, everyone always laughing at him, saying 'He's a case. Oh, he's a caution.' He's gone on. We're all responsible. We're all to blame. All we do is laugh."

—Aline MacMahon finding Wallace Beery sad in his constant clowning in Clarence Brown's *Ah, Wilderness!*
(Screenplay by Albert Hackett and Frances Goodrich; based on the play by Eugene O'Neill)
and (almost verbatim)

—Agnes Moorehead dittoing Frank Morgan in the remake, Rouben Mamoulian's SUMMER HOLIDAY
(Screenplay by Irving Brecher and Jean Holloway; based on AH, WILDERNESS!, a screenplay by Albert Hackett and Frances Goodrich and play by Eugene O'Neill)

4.
"Very funny. Ha, ha, I like an associate of mine to have a sense of humor. A good laugh does more for the stomach muscles than five-minute sitting-up exercises."

—Robert Morley commending Humphrey Bogart's wit in John Huston's *Beat the Devil*
(Screenplay by John Huston and Truman Capote; based on the novel by James Helvick)

5.
"In those early years, the boys used sometimes even to laugh at me. Not with me, of course, never with me, for I have so little sense of humor; but at me, at my little mannerisms and tricks of speech, and that made me very effective. And I remember I used to encourage the boys' laughter by rather overdoing those little mannerisms and tricks of speech for their benefit. Perhaps they didn't like me as a man, but at least they found me funny as a character, and you can teach far

more things by laughter than by earnestness. So, you see, for a time at least, I had quite a few successes as a schoolmaster."

—Michael Redgrave revealing his classroom strategy in Anthony Asquith's *The Browning Version*
(Screenplay by Terence Rattigan; based on his play)

6.
"Miami Beach. That's where you could score. Anybody could score there, even you. In New York, no rich lady with any class at all buys that cowboy crap anymore. They're laughing at you on the street."

—Dustin Hoffman trying to talk his partner (Jon Voight) into a change of locale in John Schlesinger's *Midnight Cowboy*
(Screenplay by Waldo Salt; based on the novel by James Leo Herlihy)

7.
"Now, you've got to tell them not to laugh at me. If they laugh at me, I'll yump in the bay."

—Ellen Corby fearing the reaction of her sisters to her wedding plans in George Stevens's *I Remember Mama*
(Screenplay by DeWitt Bodeen; based on the play by John Van Druten and "Mama's Bank Account," the stories by Kathryn Forbes)

ALSO SEE: Dignity-2; Eyes-2; Firsts-9; Head-8; Joke-3; Kiss-14; Mad Act-5; Sex-1; Soul-11.

LAW

1.
"The law is a jealous mistress and a stern mistress."

—Erskine Sanford grimly greeting his new apprentice (Tim Holt) with an old law-school bromide in Orson Welles's *The Magnificent Ambersons*
(Screenplay by Orson Welles; based on the novel by Booth Tarkington)

2.

(a) "I didn't know you were a lawyer. You're awfully shy for a lawyer."

    (b) "You bet I'm shy. I'm a shyster lawyer."

—(b) Groucho Marx giving (a) Thelma Todd the old runaround in Norman Z. McLeod's *Monkey Business*
(Screenplay by S. J. Perelman and Will B. Johnstone; additional dialogue by Arthur Sheekman)

3.

"Now this is the law of Pancho Villa's court: two for one. Understand? One peon is killed, I kill two majordomos or the best that I can find."

—Wallace Beery laying down his law in Jack Conway's *Viva Villa!*
(Screenplay by Ben Hecht; based on the book by Edgcumb Pinchon and O. B. Stade)

4.

"I say that you cannot administer a wicked law impartially. You can only destroy. You can only punish. I warn you that a wicked law, like cholera, destroys everyone it touches—its upholders as well as its defiers."

—Spencer Tracy fighting for evolution in Stanley Kramer's *Inherit the Wind*
(Screenplay by Nathan E. Douglas and Harold Jacob Smith; based on the play by Jerome Lawrence and Robert E. Lee)

5.

"What kind of law is it that says a man's gotta go against the Book and its teachings?"

—Gary Cooper asking his preacher (Walter Brennan) about the draft in Howard Hawks's *Sergeant York*
(Original Screenplay by Abem Finkel, Harry Chandlee, Howard Koch and John Huston; based on WAR DIARY OF SERGEANT YORK and SERGEANT YORK AND HIS PEOPLE, two books by Sam K. Cowan, and SERGEANT YORK—LAST OF THE LONG HUNTERS, a book by Tom Skeyhill)

6.

"I'll take my chance against the law. You'll take yours against the sea."

—Clark Gable casting Charles Laughton adrift in Frank Lloyd's *Mutiny on the Bounty*
(Screenplay by Talbot Jennings, Jules Furthman and Carey Wilson; based on the novel by Charles Nordhoff and James Norman Hall)

7.

"Whose law? We're on our own here. We can make our own law."

—John Hodiak making a point to his fellow sea-survivors in Alfred Hitchcock's *Lifeboat*
(Screenplay by Jo Swerling; based on the story by John Steinbeck)

ALSO SEE: Beautiful-3; Courtroom Lines-5; Defense-1; Hanging-2; Ignorance-2; Indecision-5; Letters-10; Life and Death-13; Lucky-6; Strength-6; Women-5.

LAZINESS

1.

"Why, Frank Thoreau Pulver! You mean you'd be willing to unglue yourself from that sack for the purpose of doing a favor for someone else?"

—Henry Fonda pretending surprise at Jack Lemmon's sudden industry in John Ford and Mervyn LeRoy's *Mister Roberts*
(Screenplay by Frank S. Nugent and Joshua Logan; based on the play by Thomas Heggen and Joshua Logan and novel by Thomas Heggen)

2.

"You were probably frightened by a callus at an early age."

—Eve Arden excusing Zachary Scott's aversion to work in Michael Curtiz's *Mildred Pierce*
(Screenplay by Ranald MacDougall; based on the novel by James M. Cain)

ALSO SEE: Professions-5; Science-4.

LEGS

1.
"I proved once and for all the limb is mightier than the thumb."

—Claudette Colbert using her legs rather than her thumb to hitch a ride in Frank Capra's *It Happened One Night*
(Screenplay by Robert Riskin; based on "Night Bus," a short story by Samuel Hopkins Adams)

2.
"Harry, we must beware of those men. They're desperate characters. . . . Not one of them looked at my legs."

—Jennifer Jones cautioning Edward Underdown in John Huston's *Beat the Devil*
(Screenplay by John Huston and Truman Capote; based on the novel by James Helvick)

3.
"Young man, let's see your legs. . . . No. No. No. No. New rule tonight: every man here has got to show his legs. . . . Come on, come on, come on. The other one, too."

—Rosalind Russell vamping William Holden in Joshua Logan's *Picnic*
(Screenplay by Daniel Taradash; based on the play by William Inge)

4.
"Where's the rest of me?"

—Ronald Reagan discovering his legs have been amputated in Sam Wood's *Kings Row*
(Screenplay by Casey Robinson; based on the novel by Henry Bellamann)

5.
"What good is a hep cat with one gam missing? If my leg goes, Rosie goes."

—William Bendix facing more than a leg amputation in Alfred Hitchcock's *Lifeboat*
(Screenplay by Jo Swerling; based on the story by John Steinbeck)

6.
"The first duty of these new legs is to get you to Chapel next Sunday."

—Walter Pidgeon inviting the finally ambulatory Roddy McDowall to church in John Ford's *How Green Was My Valley*
(Screenplay by Philip Dunne; based on the novel by Richard Llewellyn)

ALSO SEE: Together-2.

LETTERS

1.
"As you know by now, you'll have to carry on without me from here. It isn't easy to leave a town like our town, to tear myself away from you three dear, dear friends who meant so much to me. And so I consider myself extremely lucky to be able to take with me a sort of memento. Something to remind me always of the town that was my home, and of my three very dearest friends—whom I want never to forget. And I won't. You see, girls, I've run off with one of your husbands."

—Celeste Holm, as the never-seen narrator, breaking the news to Jeanne Crain, Linda Darnell and Ann Sothern in Joseph L. Mankiewicz's *A Letter to Three Wives*
(Screenplay by Joseph L. Mankiewicz; adaptation by Vera Caspary; based on "One of Our Hearts," a short story by John Klempner)

2.
" 'Robert will be away for the night. I absolutely must see you. I am desperate, and, if you don't come, I won't answer for the consequences. Don't drive up.' "

—James Stephenson confronting Bette Davis with the letter she wrote to the man she murdered (David Newell) in William Wyler's *The Letter*
(Screenplay by Howard Koch; based on the play and short story by W. Somerset Maugham)

3.
"I must go home now. I'm sure you'll understand. There is much I have to do. I won't try and explain what happened last night because I know that, in time, you'll find a proper way in which to remember it. What I will do is re-

member you, and I pray that you be spared all senseless tragedies. I wish you good things, Hermie—only good things."

—Jennifer O'Neill leaving Gary Grimes a good-bye note the morning after in Robert Mulligan's *Summer of '42*
(*Original Screenplay by Herman Raucher*)

4.

" 'My heart was trembling as I walked into the post office, and there you were, lying in Box 237. I took you out of your envelope and read you, read you right there. Oh, my dear friend!' "

—James Stewart reading Felix Bressart the latest from an amorous pen pal (Margaret Sullavan) in Ernst Lubitsch's *The Shop Around the Corner*
(*Screenplay by Samson Raphaelson; based on PARFUMERIE, a play by Miklos Laszlo*)
and (almost verbatim)

—Van Johnson dittoing Clinton Sundberg in the remake, Robert Z. Leonard's *In the Good Old Summertime*
(*Screenplay by Albert Hackett, Frances Goodrich and Ivan Tors; based on THE SHOP AROUND THE CORNER, a screenplay by Samson Raphaelson, and PARFUMERIE, a play by Miklos Laszlo*)

5.

"I am writing this you, and I hope that you read it so you'll know. My heart beats like a hammer, and I stutter and I stammer ev'ry time I see you at the picture show. I guess I'm just another fan of yours, and I thought I'd write and tell you so ho! ho! ho! You made me love you. I didn't want to do it. I didn't want to do it. You made me love you. . . ."

—Judy Garland reciting a fan letter to Clark Gable ("Dear Mr. Gable") for a song lead-in in Roy Del Ruth's *Broadway Melody of 1938*
(*Screenplay by Jack McGowan; based on a story by Jack McGowan and Sid Silvers; special lyrics for the song, "You Made Me Love You," by Roger Edens*)

6.

" 'I've had a dream: me. My dream is like a nightmare, Mama. I dreamed I was a very old lady, but I was still doing the same old act. I was

so ashamed of myself. I ran away, Mama—from the act, from you, from your dreams because they only made you happy and I want a dream of my own, my very own. I have to be like you, Mama. I have to fight for it. I started toward my dream three weeks ago in between shows. I— I married—Jerry.' "

—Natalie Wood reading the letter Ann Jillian left Rosalind Russell in Mervyn LeRoy's *Gypsy*
(*Screenplay by Leonard Spigelgass; based on the musical play by Arthur Laurents and memoirs of Gypsy Rose Lee*)

7.

" 'I've been aboard this destroyer for two weeks now, and we've already been through four air attacks. I'm in the war at last, Doc. I've caught up with that task force that passed me by. I'm glad to be here. I had to be here, I guess. But I'm thinking now of you, Doc, and you, Frank, and Dolan, and Dowdy, and Insigna and everybody else on that bucket—all the guys everywhere who sail from Tedium to Apathy and back again, with an occasional side trip to Monotony.' "

—Jack Lemmon reading Henry Fonda's letter to William Powell and the crew in John Ford and Mervyn LeRoy's *Mister Roberts*
(*Screenplay by Frank S. Nugent and Joshua Logan; based on the play by Thomas Heggen and Joshua Logan and novel by Thomas Heggen*)

8.

" 'If it had not been for these things, I might have lived out my life talking at street corners to scorning men. I might have died unmarked, unknown, a failure. Now, we are not a failure. Never in our full life could we hope to do so much work for tolerance, for Justice, for man's understanding of man, as now we do by accident. Our words, our lives, our pain, nothing! The taking of our lives, the lives of a good shoemaker and a poor fish-peddler, all! That last moment belongs to us—that agony is our triumph.' "

—Henry Fonda reading to his class a controversial letter by Bartolomeo Vanzetti in Elliott Nugent's *The Male Animal*

(Screenplay by Julius J. Epstein, Philip G. Epstein and Stephen Morehouse Avery; based on the play by James Thurber and Elliott Nugent)

9.
" 'Mr. Davies will tell you what's happening here tonight. He's a good man, and he's done everything he can for me. I suppose there's some other good men here, too, only they don't seem to realize what they're doing. They're the ones I feel sorry for 'cause it'll be over for me in a little while, but they'll have to go on remembering for the rest of their lives. A man just naturally can't take the law into his own hands and hang people without hurting everybody in the world, 'cause then he's not just breaking one law but all laws.' "

—Henry Fonda reading the letter Dana Andrews wrote home en route to the hanging tree in William A. Wellman's *The Ox-Bow Incident*
(Screenplay by Lamar Trotti; based on the novel by Walter Van Tilburg Clark)

10.
" 'I can't hide the truth any longer. I am a citizen of Sage, who helped clean up the jail mess. In the ashes I found this enclosed ring. Nobody knew it, so I was keeping it for a mement—memento, but it is upsetting my conscience. I don't dare sign this or I would probably get lynched myself.' "

—Walter Abel introducing as evidence in court a letter written by Spencer Tracy (believed killed in a mob-started jail fire) in Fritz Lang's *Fury*
(Screenplay by Bartlett Cormack and Fritz Lang; based on an original story by Norman Krasna)

11.
" 'An extraordinary thing has happened. All our difficulties may soon be solved. Leonard is suspected of murdering the old lady I told you about. His only hope of an alibi depends on me —on me alone. Suppose I testify that he was not at home with me at the time of the murder, that he came home with blood on his sleeves and that he even admitted to me that he killed her. Strange, isn't it? He always said that he would never let me leave him, but now, if this succeeds, he will be leaving me because they

will take him away forever and I shall be free and yours, my beloved. I count the hours until we are together.' "

—Charles Laughton introducing as evidence in court a clever bit of fiction authored by Marlene Dietrich to free Tyrone Power in Billy Wilder's *Witness for the Prosecution*
(Screenplay by Billy Wilder and Harry Kurnitz; adaptation by Larry Marcus; based on the play and story by Agatha Christie)

12.
" 'Goodbye. Remember me as someone you made very happy. I have enjoyed everything. There is only one thing left to enjoy—your river that smiles outside of my window. It is easy to die when the heart is full of gratitude.' "

—Troy Brown reading Walter Connolly the suicide note Carole Lombard wrote to New York City in William A. Wellman's *Nothing Sacred*
(Screenplay by Ben Hecht; based on "Letter to the Editor," a short story by James H. Street)
and (similarly)

—Dabbs Greer dittoing Fred Clark the suicide note Jerry Lewis wrote to New York City in the remake, Norman Taurog's *Living It Up*
(Screenplay by Jack Rose and Melville Shavelson; based on HAZEL FLAGG, a musical play by Ben Hecht, and "Letter to the Editor," a short story by James H. Street)

13.
" '. . . Allow me, in conclusion, to congratulate you warmly on your sexual intercourse as well as your singing.' "

—Celia Johnson reading a letter supposedly written by Maggie Smith to Gordon Jackson but actually written by Pamela Franklin and Diane Grayson in Ronald Neame's *The Prime of Miss Jean Brodie*
(Screenplay by Jay Presson Allen; based on her play and the novel by Muriel Spark)

ALSO SEE: Notes; Aging-11; Courtroom Lines-1; Dictation-2; Duty-4; Elephants-2; Fathers-3; Last Lines-20; Never-12.

LIES

1.

"Martha's lying. I want you to know that right now. Martha is lying. There are very few things that I am certain of anymore, but the one thing —the one thing in this whole stinking world that I am sure of is my partnership, my chromosomological partnership, in the creation of our blond-eyed, blue-haired son!"

—Richard Burton challenging Elizabeth Taylor in Mike Nichols's *Who's Afraid of Virginia Woolf?* *(Screenplay by Ernest Lehman; based on the play by Edward Albee)*

2.

"I didn't lie to Pete. The child is mine. Your part was finished the minute you gave that baby to me. From that day on, I had only one purpose in my life: to make that baby mine and forget you ever existed."

—Bette Davis telling off Mary Astor in Edmund Goulding's *The Great Lie* *(Screenplay by Lenore Coffee; based on JANUARY HEIGHTS, a novel by Polan Banks)*

3.

"If to act out a little lie to save one's mother humiliation was a fault—in other words, if tenderness toward, and consideration of, one's mother was a fault—it was a fault any man might be proud of."

—Harry Hayden defending Eddie Bracken's charade as hero in Preston Sturges's *Hail the Conquering Hero* *(Original Screenplay by Preston Sturges)*

4.

"Did I lie to you? All right, I did. But you learned two things worth more than a dollar bill. Number One: when a man swears on his mother's grave, watch out. My mother is a healthy Republican out in Cooke County. Moral Number Two: don't trust anybody."

—Arthur Kennedy giving advice to the crowd he has just fleeced a dollar a head in Mark Robson's *Trial* *(Screenplay by Don N. Mankiewicz; based on his novel)*

5.

"Course, I lied. How could I have friends? No education. Being as poor as a church mouse, I had no money to squander. And there was always the fact that I was—there, there are a lot of reasons why—so I kept to myself. Thought no one liked me and that there was no one I liked."

—Richard Todd explaining his remoteness in Vincent Sherman's *The Hasty Heart* *(Screenplay by Ranald MacDougall; based on the play by John Patrick)*

6.

(a) "You lied to me, Blanche."

 (b) "Don't say I lied to you."

 (a) "Lies! Lies, inside and out! All lies!"

 (b) "Never inside! I never lied in my heart."

(b) Vivien Leigh pleading trueheartedness to (a) Karl Malden in Elia Kazan's *A Streetcar Named Desire* *(Screenplay by Tennessee Williams; adaptation by Oscar Saul; based on the play by Tennessee Williams)*

7.

"A man who lies cannot love."

—Goldie Hawn giving her opinion in Gene Saks's *Cactus Flower* *(Screenplay by I.A.L. Diamond; based on FLEUR DE CACTUS, a French play by Pierre Barillet and Jean-Pierre Gredy, and Broadway adaptation by Abe Burrows)*

8.

"The only people who make love all the time are liars."

—Louis Jourdan informing Leslie Caron in Vincente Minnelli's *Gigi* *(Screenplay by Alan Jay Lerner; based on the novel by Colette)*

9.

"Why can't women play the game properly? Everyone knows that in love affairs only the man has the right to lie."

—Clifton Webb pretending to console Louis Jourdan in Jean Negulesco's *Three Coins in the Fountain* (*Screenplay by John Patrick; based on the novel by John H. Secondari*)

10.
"There is no sincerity like a woman telling a lie."

—Cecil Parker observing Ingrid Bergman in action in Stanley Donen's *Indiscreet* (*Screenplay by Norman Krasna; based on his play, KIND SIR*)

11.
"You know something, Ann? No one I know of lies with such sincerity."

—Burt Lancaster giving his ex (Rita Hayworth) a dubious compliment in Delbert Mann's *Separate Tables* (*Screenplay by Terence Rattigan and John Gay; based on the play by Terence Rattigan*)

12.
"Any lie will find believers as long as you tell it with force."

—Greta Garbo telling John Gilbert how it's done in Rouben Mamoulian's *Queen Christina* (*Screenplay by H. M. Harwood and Salka Viertel; dialogue by S. N. Behrman; based on a story by Salka Viertel and Margaret P. Levino*)

13.
"People will believe any lie if it is fantastic enough."

—Leo Genn explaining to Robert Taylor why Christians will be believable scapegoats for the burning of Rome in Mervyn LeRoy's *Quo Vadis* (*Screenplay by John Lee Mahin, S. N. Behrman and Sonya Levien; based on the novel by Henryk Sienkiewicz*)

14.
"A lie's a lie, and dressed in white don't help it."

—Marjorie Main snapping at Judy Garland's "little white lie" in Vincente Minnelli's *Meet Me in St. Louis* (*Screenplay by Irving Brecher and Fred F. Finklehoffe; based on the stories and novel by Sally Benson*)

15.
"If we've told lies, you've told half-lies. And a man who tells lies—like me—merely hides the truth, but a man who tells half-lies has forgotten where he put it."

—Claude Rains bringing Peter O'Toole down a notch or two in David Lean's *Lawrence of Arabia* (*Screenplay by Robert Bolt; based on THE SEVEN PILLARS OF WISDOM, the autobiography of T. E. Lawrence, and other works by and about T. E. Lawrence*)

16.
"The state's promise didn't mean anything. It was all lies. They just wanted to get me back so they can have their revenge, to keep me here nine more years. Why, their crimes are worse than mine, worse than anybody's here. They're the ones who should be in jail, not me."

—Paul Muni learning his pardon has been refused in Mervyn LeRoy's *I Am a Fugitive from a Chain Gang* (*Screenplay by Howard J. Green and Brown Holmes; based on the story by Robert E. Burns*)

17.
"You said it yourself, Big Daddy: mendacity is the system we live in."

—Paul Newman quoting Burl Ives's words back to him in Richard Brooks's *Cat on a Hot Tin Roof* (*Screenplay by Richard Brooks and James Poe; based on the play by Tennessee Williams*)

18.
"Want to tell you something, Mary. Everybody lies all the time. Sometimes they have to, and sometimes they don't. I've lied for a lot of different reasons myself. But there never was a time when, if I'd had a second chance, I wouldn't have taken back the lie and told the truth. You're a lucky girl, Mary, because we're giving you that second chance. Were you telling your grandmother the exact truth about—about us this afternoon?"

—Joel McCrea confronting Bonita Granville in William Wyler's *These Three* (*Screenplay by Lillian Hellman; based on her play, THE CHILDREN'S HOUR*)
                    and (almost verbatim)

—James Garner dittoing Karen Balkin in the re-make, William Wyler's *The Children's Hour*
(Screenplay by John Michael Hayes; adaptation by Lillian Hellman; based on her play)

19.
"I've done a lot of lying in my time. I've lied to men who wear belts. I've lied to men who wear suspenders. But I'd never be so stupid as to lie to a man who wears both belt and suspenders."

—Kirk Douglas deciding at a glance that Porter Hall is not a trusting soul in Billy Wilder's *The Big Carnival*
(Original Screenplay by Billy Wilder, Lesser Samuels and Walter Newman)

20.
"If you want to believe other people, you'd better give up lying yourself."

—Claude Rains advising Bette Davis in Irving Rapper's *Deception*
(Screenplay by John Collier and Joseph Than; based on MONSIEUR LAMBERTHIER, a play by Louis Verneuil)

21.
"Now if you want to see old Johnny at his very best, just say something about chairs. He doesn't need more than one second to invent the most howling lie you ever heard. I wouldn't miss this for anything in the world!"

—Nigel Bruce gleefully filling Joan Fontaine with distrust for her husband (Cary Grant) in Alfred Hitchcock's *Suspicion*
(Screenplay by Samson Raphaelson, Joan Harrison and Alma Reville; based on BEFORE THE FACT, a novel by Francis Iles)

22.
"I found out about one lie that you told: there is no such thing as a 'stick bloodhound.' "

—Patty McCormack confronting teaser Henry Jones in Mervyn LeRoy's *The Bad Seed*
(Screenplay by John Lee Mahin; based on the play by Maxwell Anderson and novel by William March)

23.
"I've never had a headache in my life. You

know it as well as I do. I never had a headache, Zan. That's a lie they tell me for me. I drink. All by myself, in my own room, by myself, I drink. And, when they want to hide it, they say, 'Birdie's got a headache.' "

—Patricia Collinge admitting her alcoholism to Teresa Wright in William Wyler's *The Little Foxes*
(Screenplay by Lillian Hellman; additional scenes and dialogue by Arthur Kober, Dorothy Parker and Alan Campbell; based on the play by Lillian Hellman)

24.
"To hell with the truth! The history of the world proves that truth has no bearing on anything. It's the lie of the pipe dream that gives life to the whole misbegotten mad lot of us, drunk or sober."

—Robert Ryan bending the ear of his bartender (Tom Pedi) in John Frankenheimer's *The Iceman Cometh*
(Screenplay based on the play by Eugene O'Neill; text edited by Thomas Quinn Curtiss)

ALSO SEE: Always-5; Bad-3; Beliefs-3; Birthdays-5; Firsts-12; Future-5; Hypocrisy-4; Hypocrisy-6; Illusions-5; Lock-1; Loneliness-5; Oops!-3; Peace-5; Politics-4; Politics-5.

LIFE

1.
"Ah, life and money both behave like loose quicksilver in a nest of cracks. When they're gone, you can't tell where or what the devil you did with them."

—Ray Collins saying good-bye to Tim Holt in Orson Welles's *The Magnificent Ambersons*
(Screenplay by Orson Welles; based on the novel by Booth Tarkington)

2.
"Life is a thief. Sebastian always said, 'Life steals everything.' "

—Katharine Hepburn greeting Montgomery Clift grimly with quotes from her late son in Joseph L. Mankiewicz's *Suddenly, Last Summer*

(Screenplay by Gore Vidal and Tennessee Williams; based on the one-act play by Tennessee Williams)

3.

"He's saying that life is bullshit, and it is, so what are you screaming about?"

—William Holden defending Peter Finch's on-air obscenity in Sidney Lumet's *Network*
(Original Screenplay by Paddy Chayefsky)

4.

"With Her Majesty, life is one eternal glass of milk."

—Martita Hunt having a less-than-exciting time of it waiting on Helen Hayes in Anatole Litvak's *Anastasia*
(Screenplay by Arthur Laurents; based on the play by Marcelle Maurette and Broadway adaptation by Guy Bolton)

5.

"It's a very important moment—a new chapter. In fact, for me, it's the first chapter. For what has my life been up to now? A preface? An empty foreword?"

—Gary Cooper proposing to Barbara Stanwyck in Howard Hawks's *Ball of Fire*
(Screenplay by Charles Brackett and Billy Wilder; based on "From A to Z," an original story by Thomas Monroe and Billy Wilder)

6.

"Well, life is very long and full of salesmanship, Miss Clara. You might buy something yet."

—Paul Newman coming on to spinsterish Joanne Woodward in Martin Ritt's *The Long, Hot Summer*
(Screenplay by Irving Ravetch and Harriet Frank, Jr.; based on THE HAMLET, a novel by William Faulkner, and "Barn Burning" and "The Spotted Horses," two short stories by William Faulkner)

7.

"Life, every now and then, behaves as if it had seen too many bad movies when everything fits too well—the beginning, the middle and the end—from fade in to fade out."

—Humphrey Bogart commenting, off camera, on the story he is narrating in Joseph L. Mankiewicz's *The Barefoot Contessa*
(Original Screenplay by Joseph L. Mankiewicz)

8.

"Life's never quite interesting enough, somehow. You people who come to the movies know that."

—Shirley Booth addressing the camera/audience in Joseph Anthony's *The Matchmaker*
(Screenplay by John Michael Hayes; based on the play by Thornton Wilder)

9.

"I don't have a lifestyle. I have a life."

—Jane Fonda correcting her ex (Alan Alda) in Herbert Ross's *California Suite*
(Screenplay by Neil Simon; based on his play)

10.

"If you want to give me a present, give me a good life. That's something I can value."

—Raymond Massey rejecting James Dean's birthday present of money in Elia Kazan's *East of Eden*
(Screenplay by Paul Osborn; based on the novel by John Steinbeck)

11.

"I have a very pessimistic view of life. You should know this about me if we're going to go out. You know, I—I feel that life is—is divided up into the horrible and the miserable. Those are the two categories, you know. The—the horrible would be like, I don't know, terminal cases, you know, and blind people, crippled. I don't know how they get through life. It's amazing to me. You know, and the miserable is everyone else. That's—that's—so—so—when you feel like—you should be thankful you're miserable because you're very lucky to be miserable."

—Woody Allen giving his gloomy view of things to Diane Keaton in Woody Allen's *Annie Hall*
(Original Screenplay by Woody Allen and Marshall Brickman)

12.

"What do you want a meaning for? Life is a

desire, not a meaning. Desire is the theme of all life! It's what makes a rose want to be a rose and want to grow like that, and a rock want to contain itself and remain like that."

—Charles Chaplin pep-talking, with mime, to a suicidal Claire Bloom in Charles Chaplin's *Limelight* (*Original Screenplay by Charles Chaplin*)

13.

"To life! To the magnificent, dangerous, brief, brief, wonderful life and the courage to live it! You know, Baron, I've only lived last night, but that little while seems longer than all the time that has gone before."

—Lionel Barrymore drinking and talking himself into a faint in Edmund Goulding's *Grand Hotel* (*Screenplay by William A. Drake; based on the play and novel by Vicki Baum*)

ALSO SEE: Life and Death; Live; Adolescence-3; Cameras-3; Champagne-2; Children-1; Children-4; Cigarette-3; Death-4; Eyes-1; Fear-5; Fights-8; Firsts-9; Firsts-10; Goals-1; Goodbyes-8; Head-2; Help-2; Illusions-5; Knowledge-7; Lies-24; Love-18; Love-40; Mad Act-2; Men-19; Nature-2; Never-11; Prayers-1; Prison-3; Privacy-2; Realities-5; Screenplays-3; Self-Perception-11; Similarities-2; Suicide-8; Tired-3; Together-3.

LIFE AND DEATH

1.

"You remember the last time I went up in that plane? Well, something went flooey, and the ship went into a spin, and then one of those guys that goes around collecting people—he pulled a boner. All the time he thought I was dead, I wasn't dead at all. He grabbed me up before my time, and, while I'm arguing with him whether I'm dead or not, you cremate me. Then, they gotta make good. They gotta get me another body. Get it?"

—Robert Montgomery explaining his rather unprecedented predicament to James Gleason in Alexander Hall's *Here Comes Mr. Jordan*

(*Screenplay by Sidney Buchman and Seton I. Miller; based on HEAVEN CAN WAIT, a play by Harry Segall*)

2.

"What can I do, old man? I'm dead, aren't I?"

—Orson Welles preferring to hold on to his official "deceased" status than help his friends in Carol Reed's *The Third Man* (*Original Screenplay by Graham Greene*)

3.

"Now, I may sound like a Bible-beater yelling up a revival at a river-crossing camp-meeting, but that don't change the truth none. There's right, and there's wrong. You gotta do one or the other. You do the one, and you're living. You do the other, and you may be walking around but you're dead as a beaver hat."

—John Wayne voting for right and life in John Wayne's *The Alamo* (*Original Screenplay by James Edward Grant*)

4.

"You're just walkin' around to save funeral expenses."

—Valerie Perrine noting the burned-out condition of her ex (Robert Redford) in Sydney Pollack's *The Electric Horseman* (*Screenplay by Robert Garland; based on a screen story by Paul Gaer and Robert Garland and story by Shelly Burton*)

5.

"No, I'm fine. In fact, considering I've been dead for 16 years, I'm in remarkable health."

—Howard St. John dating his death from the time he sold out to Broderick Crawford in George Cukor's *Born Yesterday* (*Screenplay by Albert Mannheimer; based on the play by Garson Kanin*)

6.

"Yes, it's pleasant to be back again, amongst the living. Hurray!"

—Leslie Howard welcoming an exciting crisis to his otherwise drab life in Archie Mayo's *The Petrified Forest*

(Screenplay by Delmer Daves and Charles
Kenyon; based on the play by Robert E.
Sherwood)

7.
"It's kind of startling to be brought to life twice
—and each time in Warsaw."

—Carole Lombard learning from her doctor in War-
saw, Vermont (Charles Winninger), that she's not ter-
minally ill after all in William A. Wellman's *Nothing
Sacred*
*(Screenplay by Ben Hecht; based on "Letter to the
Editor," a short story by James H. Street)*

8.
"If Cathy died, I might begin to live."

—Geraldine Fitzgerald grieving not at the prospect
of losing a romantic rival (Merle Oberon) in William
Wyler's *Wuthering Heights*
*(Screenplay by Ben Hecht and Charles MacArthur;
based on the novel by Emily Brontë)*

9.
"I was born when you kissed me. I died when
you left me. I lived a few days while you loved
me."

—Screenwriter Humphrey Bogart trying out some of
his movie dialogue on Gloria Grahame in Nicholas
Ray's *In a Lonely Place*
*(Screenplay by Andrew Solt; adaptation by
Edmund H. North; based on the novel by Dorothy
B. Hughes)*

10.
"I love you, June. You're life, and I'm leaving
you."

—David Niven encountering Kim Hunter on his
plane radio just as he is going down in flames in
Michael Powell and Emeric Pressburger's *Stairway
to Heaven*
*(Original Screenplay by Michael Powell and
Emeric Pressburger)*

11.
"She is, as you rightly say, 'out to kill me.' That
is only another fact that I have managed to
face, as indeed I have faced the more important fact, that she succeeded in her purpose
long ago."

—Michael Redgrave acknowledging that he is a casu-
alty of a bad marriage in Anthony Asquith's *The
Browning Version*
*(Screenplay by Terence Rattigan; based on his
play)*

12.
"I plead no mitigating circumstances. They
deserved to die, as I deserve to die, for I
long since killed a person much superior to
either of them: myself. I killed that person
the day I gave my family name to the
woman who became my wife. And since I
believe that punishment should fit the crime,
I suggest that you hang me by the neck until
I'm dead."

—Herbert Marshall pleading guilty to murdering his
wife (Tilly Losch) and her lover (Sidney Blackmer) in
King Vidor's *Duel in the Sun*
*(Screenplay by David O. Selznick; adaptation by
Oliver H. P. Garrett; based on the novel by Niven
Busch)*

13.
"They're murderers. I know the law says
they're not because I'm still alive, but that's not
their fault."

—Spencer Tracy damning the lynch mob that almost
killed him in Fritz Lang's *Fury*
*(Screenplay by Bartlett Cormack and Fritz Lang;
based on an original story by Norman Krasna)*

14.
"Wait till you start tramping around to the
offices looking for a job, and you don't know
agents that'll handle you, sitting in those
anterooms hour after hour and giving your
name to office boys that never even heard of
you. You're through, Renault. You're through
in pictures and plays and vaudeville and
radio and everything. You're a corpse, and
you don't know it. Go get yourself buried."

—Lee Tracy telling off John Barrymore in George
Cukor's *Dinner at Eight*
*(Screenplay by Frances Marion and Herman J.
Mankiewicz; based on the play by George S.
Kaufman and Edna Ferber)*

15.
"The trouble is you *won't* fight! You've given in —continually dwelling on sickness and death! There's something just as inevitable as death, and that's life! Life! Life! Life! Think of the power that's in the universe—moving the earth, growing the trees. And that's the same power within you! If you'll only have courage and the will to use it."

—Charles Chaplin pep-talking the suicidal Claire Bloom in Charles Chaplin's *Limelight*
(Original Screenplay by Charles Chaplin)

16.
"The best of life, Passworthy, lies nearest to the edge of death."

—Raymond Massey telling Edward Chapman that progress requires risks in William Cameron Menzies's *Things To Come*
(Screenplay by H. G. Wells; based on his novel, THE SHAPE OF THINGS TO COME)

17.
"Believe me, if a man doesn't know death, he doesn't know life."

—Lionel Barrymore enjoying what he believes to be his last fling in Edmund Goulding's *Grand Hotel*
(Screenplay by William A. Drake; based on the play and novel by Vicki Baum)

18.
"You know, it's quite possible, Octavian, that, when you die, you will die without ever having been alive."

—Richard Burton addressing Roddy McDowall in Joseph L. Mankiewicz's *Cleopatra*
(Screenplay by Joseph L. Mankiewicz, Ranald MacDougall, and Sidney Buchman; based upon histories by Plutarch, Suetonius, and Appian and THE LIFE AND TIMES OF CLEOPATRA, a book by C. M. Franzero)

19.
"Martha's father expects his staff to come here and grow old and fall in the line of service. One man, a professor of Latin and Elocution, actually fell in the cafeteria line, one lunch. But the old man is not going to fall anywhere. The old man is not going to die. There *are* rumors— which you must not breathe in front of Martha, for she foams at the mouth—that the old man, her father, is over 200 years old. There's probably an irony in there some place, but I'm not drunk enough to figure out what it is."

—Richard Burton telling George Segal what to expect in the employ of Elizabeth Taylor's father in Mike Nichols's *Who's Afraid of Virginia Woolf?* *(Screenplay by Ernest Lehman; based on the play by Edward Albee)*

20.
"Men like my father cannot die. They are with me still—real in memory as they were in flesh —beloving and beloved forever."

—Irving Pichel, as the never-seen narrator (a grown-up version of Roddy McDowall), clinging to memories of his father and family in John Ford's *How Green Was My Valley*
(Screenplay by Philip Dunne; based on the novel by Richard Llewellyn)

21.
"Oh, by the way, how was my funeral?"

—Irene Dunne questioning Ann Shoemaker after returning to civilization in Garson Kanin's *My Favorite Wife*
(Screenplay by Bella Spewack and Samuel Spewack; based on a story by Bella Spewack, Samuel Spewack and Leo McCarey)

ALSO SEE: Appearances-1; Courtroom Lines-7; Dreams-8; First Lines-4; Gentle-1; Head-4; Love-15; Mistakes-2; Prayers-13; Regrets-4; Suicide-1; Suicide-11; Trouble-1; War-6; Wisdom-2.

LIKES AND DISLIKES

1.
"I don't like lobsters. I have a long list of dislikes. It's getting longer."

—Joan Crawford playing it cold with Jeff Chandler in Joseph Pevney's *Female on the Beach*

(Screenplay by Robert Hill and Richard Alan Simmons; based on THE BESIEGED HEART, a play by Robert Hill)

2.
"There are moments when I don't positively dislike you, and sometimes I think you're rather sweet."

—Gene Tierney playing it warm with Herbert Marshall in Edmund Goulding's *The Razor's Edge*
(Screenplay by Lamar Trotti; based on the novel by W. Somerset Maugham)

3.
"I don't like boat whistles."

—Maria Ouspenskaya hating the signal for good-byes in Leo McCarey's *Love Affair*
(Screenplay by Delmer Daves and Donald Ogden Stewart; based on an original story by Mildred Cram and Leo McCarey)
and
—Cathleen Nesbitt dittoing in the remake, Leo McCarey's *An Affair To Remember*
(Screenplay by Delmer Daves and Leo McCarey; based on an original story by Mildred Cram and Leo McCarey)

4.
"There's something about working the streets I like. It's the tramp in me, I suppose."

—Charles Chaplin discussing his street entertaining with Nigel Bruce and Sydney Chaplin in Charles Chaplin's *Limelight*
(Original Screenplay by Charles Chaplin)

5.
"I do not like to be interrupted in the middle of an insult."

—Charles Laughton telling Charles Coburn to butt out in Alfred Hitchcock's *The Paradine Case*
(Screenplay by David O. Selznick; adaptation by Alma Reville and James Bridie; based on the novel by Robert Hichens)

6.
"I can't stand a naked light bulb any more than I can a rude remark or a vulgar action."

—Vivien Leigh putting on airs of gentility for a potential beau (Karl Malden) in Elia Kazan's *A Streetcar Named Desire*
(Screenplay by Tennessee Williams; adaptation by Oscar Saul; based on the play by Tennessee Williams)

ALSO SEE: Alone-8; Alone-10; Friends-6; Lasts-2; Movies-3; Violence-6.

LIVE

1.
(a) "Agnes, where is your spine? Here you've been taking my dictation for weeks, and you don't get the message of my book: Live! That's the message!"
    (b) "Live?"
    (a) "Yes! Life is a banquet, and most poor suckers are starving to death!"

—(a) Rosalind Russell inspiring (b) Peggy Cass to break loose and live it up in Morton DaCosta's *Auntie Mame*
(Screenplay by Betty Comden and Adolph Green; based on the play by Jerome Lawrence and Robert E. Lee and novel by Patrick Dennis)
            and (almost verbatim)
—(a) Lucille Ball dittoing (b) Jane Connell in the remake, Gene Saks's *Mame*
(Screenplay by Paul Zindel; based on the musical play by Jerome Lawrence, Robert E. Lee and Jerry Herman and AUNTIE MAME, a play by Jerome Lawrence and Robert E. Lee, and novel by Patrick Dennis)

2.
"Gimme an L! Gimme an I! Gimme a V! Gimme an E! L-I-V-E! Live! Otherwise, you got nothing to talk about in the locker room."

—Ruth Gordon passing the joie-de-vivre message along to Bud Cort in Hal Ashby's *Harold and Maude*
(Original Screenplay by Colin Higgins)

3.
"What the gods give, they quickly take away. Time is jealous of you, Mr. Gray. Don't squander the gold of your days. Live. Let noth-

ing be lost upon you. Be afraid of nothing. There's such a little time that your youth will last. You can never get it back."

—George Sanders spurring Hurd Hatfield onward in Albert Lewin's *The Picture of Dorian Gray*
(Screenplay by Albert Lewin; based on the novel by Oscar Wilde)

4.
"You live it up. You kick up your heels. You grab everything you can get. You light the candle from one end to the other, like they say— and then, one day, you too can be the proud proprietor of a very heavily mortgaged roadside brothel."

—Kay Medford spurring Elizabeth Taylor onward (for what good it'll do) in Daniel Mann's *Butterfield 8*
(Screenplay by Charles Schnee and John Michael Hayes; based on the novel by John O'Hara)

5.
"Fanny cannot live by oxygen alone. She must be surrounded by men."

—Claude Rains being philosophical about his wife's persistent suitors in Vincent Sherman's *Mr. Skeffington*
(Screenplay by Julius J. Epstein and Philip G. Epstein; based on the story by "Elizabeth")

6.
"That's where I live—on stage."

—Barbra Streisand preferring to live as a performer in William Wyler's *Funny Girl*
(Screenplay by Isobel Lennart; based on her musical play)

7.
"I somehow feel most alive when I'm singing."

—Judy Garland preferring to live as a performer in George Cukor's *A Star Is Born*
(Screenplay by Moss Hart; based on a screenplay by Dorothy Parker, Alan Campbell and Robert Carson and original story by William A. Wellman and Robert Carson)

8.
"To dance is to live."

—Vanessa Redgrave preferring to live as a performer in Karel Reisz's *Isadora*
(Screenplay by Melvyn Bragg and Clive Exton; additional dialogue by Margaret Drabble; adaptation by Melvyn Bragg; based on the books, MY LIFE by Isadora Duncan and ISADORA DUNCAN, AN INTIMATE PORTRAIT by Sewell Stokes)

9.
"A life that is planned is a closed life, my friend. It can be endured, perhaps. It cannot be lived."

—Robert Donat advising Curt Jurgens in Mark Robson's *The Inn of the Sixth Happiness*
(Screenplay by Isobel Lennart; based on THE SMALL WOMAN, a book by Alan Burgess)

10.
"Happy the man and happy he alone,
He who can call today his own,
He who secure within can say:
Tomorrow do thy worst! For I have lived today."

—Michael MacLiammoir narrating a happy ending, in rhyme, in the last lines of Tony Richardson's *Tom Jones*
(Screenplay by John Osborne; based on the novel by Henry Fielding)

ALSO SEE: Life; Life and Death; Indecision-4; Land-4; Nature-2; Prayers-10; Priorities-8; Trumpet-3.

LOCK

1.
"Maggie, we're through with lies and liars in this house. Lock the door."

—Paul Newman reconciling with Elizabeth Taylor in the last lines of Richard Brooks's *Cat on a Hot Tin Roof*
(Screenplay by Richard Brooks and James Poe; based on the play by Tennessee Williams)

2.
"Why bother? If I wanted to come in, no lock could keep me out."

—Clark Gable making his point by breaking down Vivien Leigh's door in Victor Fleming's *Gone With the Wind*
(Screenplay by Sidney Howard; based on the novel by Margaret Mitchell)

3.
"There'll be no locks or bolts between us, Mary Kate—except those in your own mercenary little heart."

—John Wayne making his point by breaking down Maureen O'Hara's door in John Ford's *The Quiet Man*
(Screenplay by Frank S. Nugent; based on "Green Rushes," a short story by Maurice Walsh)

4.
(a) "I don't care much for locks."
    (b) "Nevertheless, they're the principal reason for whatever honesty still exists in our society today."

—(b) John Mills displaying less trust in his fellow man than (a) Deborah Kerr in Ronald Neame's *The Chalk Garden*
(Screenplay by John Michael Hayes; based on the play by Enid Bagnold)

ALSO SEE: Sex-6; Strange-1; Trust and Distrust-5.

LONELINESS

1.
"Forty-nine thousand acres of nothing but scenery and statues. I'm lonesome."

—Dorothy Comingore complaining to Orson Welles about the lonely life at Xanadu in Orson Welles's *Citizen Kane*
(Original Screenplay by Herman J. Mankiewicz and Orson Welles)

2.
"Isn't loneliness a small price to pay for power, Sire? Am I to understand that the master of Europe who can command a million men to die for him cannot command one of them to be his friend? Why don't you issue an order, Sire, abolishing your loneliness? . . . You say you're lonely. Where would you receive a friend? In your heart? But it's too full of yourself. In your mind? It's too full of the world—and your desires are unworthy of friendship. You will always be lonely, Sire, but you will bear it. You're pitiless enough, even to yourself."

—Greta Garbo telling off Napoleon (Charles Boyer) in Clarence Brown's *Conquest*
(Screenplay by Samuel Hoffenstein, Salka Viertel and S. N. Behrman; based on PANI WALEWSKA, a play by Helen Jerome and novel by Waclaw Gasiorowski)

3.
"You see me surrounded by thousands of subjects, and yet I'm lonely, Marquis. I'm lonely."

—Tallulah Bankhead laying it on thick as Catherine the Great in Otto Preminger's *A Royal Scandal*
(Screenplay by Edwin Justus Mayer; adaptation by Bruno Frank; based on THE CZARINA, a play by Lajos Biro and Melchior Lengyel)

4.
"They call me a great man, but it's the loneliest animal in the world."

—Claude Rains playing for sympathy from Bette Davis in Irving Rapper's *Deception*
(Screenplay by John Collier and Joseph Than; based on MONSIEUR LAMBERTHIER, a play by Louis Verneuil)

5.
"Nobody ever lies about being lonely."

—Montgomery Clift advancing his theory in Fred Zinnemann's *From Here to Eternity*
(Screenplay by Daniel Taradash; based on the novel by James Jones)

6.
"Well, we movie stars get the glory. I guess we have to take the little heartaches that go with it. People think we lead lives of glamour and romance, but we're really lonely—terribly lonely."

—Gene Kelly feeding a line of malarkey to the airwaves in Gene Kelly and Stanley Donen's *Singin' in the Rain*

(Original Screenplay by Adolph Green and Betty Comden)

7.

"I know all about loneliness—only I don't whine about it."

—Anthony Quinn walking out on Kirk Douglas in Vincente Minnelli's *Lust for Life*
(Screenplay by Norman Corwin; based on the novel by Irving Stone)

8.

"I just couldn't go to heaven without Clare. Why, I get lonesome for him even when I go to Ohio."

—Irene Dunne demonstrating the extent of her marital togetherness with William Powell in Michael Curtiz's *Life With Father*
(Screenplay by Donald Ogden Stewart; based on the play by Howard Lindsay and Russel Crouse and stories by Clarence Day, Jr.)

9.

"This is my home. You're my husband. And my children are upstairs in bed. I'm a happily married woman—or, rather, I was until a few weeks ago. This is my whole world, and it's enough—or, rather, it was until a few weeks ago. But, oh, Fred, I've been so foolish. I've fallen in love. I'm a lonely woman. I didn't think such violent things could happen to lonely people."

—Celia Johnson thinking to herself of her predicament in David Lean's *Brief Encounter*
(Screenplay by David Lean, Anthony Havelock-Allan and Ronald Neame; based on STILL LIFE, a one-act play by Noel Coward)

10.

"I want to come home. I know what you're thinking about me. A lot's happened. Lots of detours. There were plenty of 'em, but they were nothing. I never looked at them. They had no identity. I never gave anything out of myself to them. I thought they'd help me from being so lonely, but I was just as lonely because love is the only thing that keeps you from being lonely—and I didn't have that."

—Lee Remick pleading for a reconciliation with Jack Lemmon in Blake Edwards's *Days of Wine and Roses*
(Screenplay by J. P. Miller; based on his teleplay)

11.

"You know, my first husband used to tell me about how lonely he felt. Now, I know what he meant. It's like the whole world's off someplace else, like an echo."

—Kim Stanley finding it lonely at the top in John Cromwell's *The Goddess*
(Original Screenplay by Paddy Chayefsky)

12.

"Young lady, I know what Bert is going through. It's the loneliest feeling in the world. It's like walking down an empty street and listening to your own footsteps. But all you have to do is to knock on any door and say, 'If you let me in, I'll live the way you want me to live and I'll think the way you want me to think.' And all the blinds'll go up and all the doors'll open and you'll never be lonely ever again."

—Spencer Tracy telling Donna Anderson what her fiancé (Dick York) is standing up for in Stanley Kramer's *Inherit the Wind*
(Screenplay by Nathan E. Douglas and Harold Jacob Smith; based on the play by Jerome Lawrence and Robert E. Lee)

13.

"No, Ben. You'll always be busy. You'll have to be busy because you're a lonely man. All your life you're going to be lonely. An empty man."

—Florence Eldridge telling off her son (Edmond O'Brien) in Michael Gordon's *Another Part of the Forest*
(Screenplay by Vladimir Pozner; based on the play by Lillian Hellman)

14.

"I should think that loneliness would be unknown to a lovely woman."

—José Ferrer passing a compliment in John Huston's *Moulin Rouge*
(Screenplay by Anthony Veiller and John Huston; based on the novel by Pierre La Mure)

15.

"A great many mistakes are made in the name of loneliness."

—William Holden explaining to Jennifer Jones his bad marriage in Henry King's *Love Is a Many-Splendored Thing*
(Screenplay by John Patrick; based on A MANY-SPLENDORED THING, a novel by Han Suyin)

16.

"Well, you couldn't expect a moustache to go around by itself. Don't you think a moustache gets lonely, Captain?"

—Groucho Marx confounding Ben Taggart in Norman Z. McLeod's *Monkey Business*
(Screenplay by S. J. Perelman and Will B. Johnstone; additional dialogue by Arthur Sheekman)

ALSO SEE: Alone; Dying Words-10; Friends-2; Gigolo-8; Love-6.

LOOKS

1.

"Look at my face. Wouldn't you walk away? I'm so much older than my years have made me. Look at my face carefully as he'll do. You'll see how very old I am. I'm beat. I'll make a swell-looking bride. The beat bride."

—Jan Sterling removing her makeup and asking for an opinion from Paul Kelly in William A. Wellman's *The High and the Mighty*
(Screenplay by Ernest K. Gann; based on his novel)

2.

"I'm tired. I'm sick. Can you see it? Look at me good. You've been looking at me like I used to be."

—Claire Trevor telling Humphrey Bogart to look again in William Wyler's *Dead End*
(Screenplay by Lillian Hellman; based on the play by Sidney Kingsley)

3.

"Look at me. Look at me hard. I'm the same man I was yesterday. That's true, isn't it? Why should you be so astonished, Miss Wales? You still can't believe that anybody would give up the glory of being a Christian for even eight weeks, can you? That's what's eating you, isn't it? Now, if I tell you that that's anti-Semitism —your feeling that being Christian is better than being Jewish—you're going to tell me that I'm heckling you again or that I'm twisting your words around or that it's just facing facts, as someone else said to me yesterday. Face me now, Miss Wales. C'mon, look at me. Same face, same eyes, same nose, same suit, same everything. Here, take my hand. Feel it. Same flesh as yours, isn't it? No different today than it was yesterday, Miss Wales. The only thing that's different is the word Christian."

—Gregory Peck calling June Havoc on her prejudice in Elia Kazan's *Gentleman's Agreement*
(Screenplay by Moss Hart; based on the novel by Laura Z. Hobson)

4.

"I guess, when you're used to standing on the outside looking in, you can see a lot of things other people can't."

—John Garfield making an outsider's observation to Priscilla Lane about her family in Michael Curtiz's *Four Daughters*
(Screenplay by Julius J. Epstein and Lenore Coffee; based on "Sister Act," a short story by Fannie Hurst)

5.

(a) "I just can't go back being on the outside of people's lives, looking in."

   (b) "Louise, we're all on the outside of other people's lives, looking in. You wouldn't like being on the inside of my life, anyway. There's—there's nothing there but a few mathematical equations and lot of question marks."

—(b) Van Heflin cooling it with a clinging (a) Joan Crawford in Curtis Bernhardt's *Possessed*
(Screenplay by Sylvia Richards and Ranald MacDougall; based on ONE MAN'S SECRET, a novelette by Rita Weiman)

6.

"It's gone forever, that funny young lost look I loved. It won't ever come back. I killed that when I told you about Rebecca. It's gone. In a few hours, you've grown so much older."

—Laurence Olivier becoming melancholy about Joan Fontaine's sudden maturity in Alfred Hitchcock's *Rebecca*
(Screenplay by Robert E. Sherwood and Joan Harrison; adaptation by Philip MacDonald and Michael Hogan; based on the novel by Daphne du Maurier)

7.

"No, your look is cordial—not connubial. I've married you, Fanny, but I haven't won you."

—Claude Rains making a realistic post-marital appraisal of Bette Davis in Vincent Sherman's *Mr. Skeffington*
(Screenplay by Julius J. Epstein and Philip G. Epstein; based on the story by "Elizabeth")

8.

"And the way you're looking at me, is that the way you look at a man you've just beaten? As if you had just taken his money and now you want his pride?"

—Piper Laurie conceding to George C. Scott in their private battle for Paul Newman's priorities in Robert Rossen's *The Hustler*
(Screenplay by Sidney Carroll and Robert Rossen; based on the novel by Walter Tevis)

9.

"You're slipping, Red. I used to be frightened of that look—the withering glance of the goddess."

—Cary Grant telling Katharine Hepburn he's worked up an immunity to her frostbite in George Cukor's *The Philadelphia Story*
(Screenplay by Donald Ogden Stewart; based on the play by Philip Barry)
            and (almost verbatim)
—Bing Crosby dittoing Grace Kelly in the remake, Charles Walters's *High Society*
(Screenplay by John Patrick; based on THE PHILADELPHIA STORY, a screenplay by Donald Ogden Stewart and play by Philip Barry)

10.

"Her hair was the color of gold in old paintings. She had a full set of curves which nobody had been able to improve on. She was giving me the kind of look I could feel in my hip pocket."

—Robert Mitchum picking up Charlotte Rampling's vibes at first glance in Dick Richards's *Farewell, My Lovely*
(Screenplay by David Zelag Goodman; based on the novel by Raymond Chandler)

11.

"He looks as if he knows what I look like without my shimmy."

—Viven Leigh noticing Clark Gable noticing at their first encounter in Victor Fleming's *Gone With the Wind*
(Screenplay by Sidney Howard; based on the novel by Margaret Mitchell)

12.

(a) "Two people look at each other, and they see something way deep inside that nobody else can, and that's it. I wouldn't be surprised if the greatest love affair in the world was between a Chinaman wearing a pigtail and a girl who's missing two front teeth, if you could measure it. If they feel it, they feel it."
    (b) "Do you?"
    (a) "Not the way you see in the movies or hear in those songs, you know, about 'the touch of your hand,' 'you set me on fire.' I guess I'm not the combustible type."

—(a) Jean Arthur explaining love to (b) Charles Coburn in Sam Wood's *The Devil and Miss Jones*
(Original Screenplay by Norman Krasna)

13.

"Hey—do you mind if I take just one more look?"

—Fredric March leaving Janet Gaynor with his pet expression (his last words before a suicidal swim in the ocean) in William A. Wellman's *A Star Is Born*
(Screenplay by Dorothy Parker, Alan Campbell and Robert Carson; based on an original story by William A. Wellman and Robert Carson)
            and (almost verbatim)

—James Mason dittoing Judy Garland in the remake, George Cukor's *A Star Is Born*
(Screenplay by Moss Hart; based on a screenplay by Dorothy Parker, Alan Campbell and Robert Carson and original story by William A. Wellman and Robert Carson)

ALSO SEE: Eyes-18; Firsts-9; Greed-4; Hands-11; History-5; Water-1.

LOS ANGELES

1.
"I don't want to live in a city where the only cultural advantage is that you can make a right turn on a red light."

—Woody Allen plainly preferring Manhattan in Woody Allen's *Annie Hall*
(Original Screenplay by Woody Allen and Marshall Brickman)

2.
"It's like paradise, with a lobotomy."

—Jane Fonda playing it true to form as a New Yorker grudgingly gone West in Herbert Ross's *California Suite*
(Screenplay by Neil Simon; based on his play)

LOVE

1.
"It's the old, old story: 'Boy Meets Girl'—Romeo and Juliet—Minneapolis and St. Paul!"

—Groucho Marx declaring himself, in his fashion, to Margaret Dumont in Sam Wood's *A Day at the Races*
(Screenplay by Robert Pirosh, George Seaton and George Oppenheimer; based on a story by Robert Pirosh and George Seaton)

2.
"Love means never having to say you're sorry."

—Ryan O'Neal quoting his late wife (Ali MacGraw) to his father (Ray Milland) in the last line of Arthur Hiller's *Love Story*
(Original Screenplay by Erich Segal)
and

—Barbra Streisand throwing the line back to Ryan O'Neal (who replies: "That's the dumbest thing I ever heard") at the end of Peter Bogdanovich's *What's Up, Doc?*
(Screenplay by Buck Henry, David Newman and Robert Benton; based on a story by Peter Bogdanovich)

3.
"Love is a miracle. It's like a birthmark. You can't hide it."

—George Segal offering a joyful definition in Paul Mazursky's *Blume in Love*
(Original Screenplay by Paul Mazursky)

4.
"Love, my dear Gigi, is a thing of beauty like a work of art. And, like a work of art, it is created by artists. The greater the artist, the greater the art."

—Isabel Jeans instructing Leslie Caron in the art in Vincente Minnelli's *Gigi*
(Screenplay by Alan Jay Lerner; based on the novel by Colette)

5.
"And what is love? Love is the morning and the evening star."

—Burt Lancaster breaking into gospel stride in Richard Brooks's *Elmer Gantry*
(Screenplay by Richard Brooks; based on the novel by Sinclair Lewis)

6.
"I love you now; in half an hour, I'll wonder how I ever got into this. You have a passion for respectability, and I have a horror of loneliness—that's love."

—Steven Hill being candid with Kim Stanley on their wedding day in John Cromwell's *The Goddess*
(Original Screenplay by Paddy Chayefsky)

7.
"Is that what love is? Using people? And maybe that's what hate is—not being able to use people."

—Elizabeth Taylor arriving at a twisted definition in Joseph L. Mankiewicz's *Suddenly, Last Summer* (*Screenplay by Gore Vidal and Tennessee Williams; based on the one-act play by Tennessee Williams*)

8.

"Maybe love is like luck. You have to go all the way to find it."

—Robert Mitchum considering the possibilities in Jacques Tourneur's *Out of the Past* (*Screenplay by Geoffrey Homes; based on his novel, BUILD MY GALLOWS HIGH*)

9.

"Scientists can write all the books they like about love being a trap of nature. I remember reading that—that it's biology and the chemistry inside of her that fools her. But all that scientists are going to convince are other scientists, not women in love."

—Jean Arthur putting heart over head in Sam Wood's *The Devil and Miss Jones* (*Original Screenplay by Norman Krasna*)

10.

"Why must you bring in wrong values? Love is a romantic designation for a most ordinary biological—or, shall we say, chemical?—process. A lot of nonsense is talked and written about it."

—Greta Garbo cooling off Melvyn Douglas in Ernst Lubitsch's *Ninotchka* (*Screenplay by Charles Brackett, Billy Wilder and Walter Reisch; based on an original story by Melchior Lengyel*)

11.

"But, George, I've heard you say love is largely nonsense."

—Richard Haydn noting a mellowed Ronald Colman in Joseph L. Mankiewicz's *The Late George Apley* (*Screenplay by Philip Dunne; based on the play by John P. Marquand and George S. Kaufman and novel by John P. Marquand*)

12.

"Georgia, love is for the very young."

—Kirk Douglas telling Lana Turner he's too old for that sort of thing in Vincente Minnelli's *The Bad and the Beautiful* (*Screenplay by Charles Schnee; based on "Memorial to a Bad Man" and "Of Good and Evil," two short stories by George Bradshaw*)

13.

"Love is not the exclusive province of adolescence, my dear. It's a heart ailment that strikes all age groups. Like my love for you. My love for you is the only malady I've contracted since the usual childhood diseases, and it's incurable."

—Clifton Webb confessing love for his unfaithful wife (Cathy Downs) in Henry Hathaway's *The Dark Corner* (*Screenplay by Jay Dratler and Bernard C. Schoenfeld; based on the novel by Leo Rosten*)

14.

"Love is like the measles. You only get it once. The older you are, the tougher it goes."

—Howard Keel explaining love to his brothers in Stanley Donen's *Seven Brides for Seven Brothers* (*Screenplay by Albert Hackett, Frances Goodrich and Dorothy Kingsley; based on "The Sobbin' Women," a short story by Stephen Vincent Benét*)

15.

"Love is eternal. It has been the strongest motivation for human action throughout centuries. Love is stronger than life. It reaches beyond the dark shadow of death."

—Clifton Webb curling the airwaves on the subject in Otto Preminger's *Laura* (*Screenplay by Jay Dratler, Samuel Hoffenstein and Betty Reinhardt; based on the novel by Vera Caspary*)

16.

"Now, I know you still love me—and it won't die, what's between us. Do what you will. Ignore it. Neglect it. Starve it. It's stronger than both of us together."

—Paul Henreid pledging devotion to Bette Davis in Irving Rapper's *Now, Voyager*

(Screenplay by Casey Robinson; based on the novel by Olive Higgins Prouty)

17.
"I wish I could dismiss it like that, but I can't. When I love a woman, I'm an Oriental. It never goes. It never dies."

—John Barrymore laying it on thick to Carole Lombard in Howard Hawks's *Twentieth Century*
(Screenplay by Ben Hecht and Charles MacArthur; based on their play and NAPOLEON OF BROADWAY, a play by Charles Bruce Milholland)

18.
"Really foolish, vulgar, a clown—but not to me. To me, he was a man like a rock. Nothing could shake his love. It was from him that I learned what love really was, not a frail little fancy to be smashed and broken by pride and vanity and self-pity—that's for children, that's for high school kids—but a rock as strong as life itself, indestructible and determined."

—Bette Davis praising her husband (Keenan Wynn) to Gary Merrill in Jean Negulesco's *Phone Call From a Stranger*
(Screenplay by Nunnally Johnson; based on a novella by I. A. R. Wylie)

19.
(a) "No one has ever loved you as I love you."
    (b) "That may be true, but what can I do about it?"

—(b) Greta Garbo pretending to be light about the love of (a) Robert Taylor in George Cukor's *Camille*
(Screenplay by Zoë Akins, Frances Marion and James Hilton; based on LA DAME AUX CAMÉLIAS, a play and novel by Alexandre Dumas)

20.
"Love isn't something you can put on or take off like an overcoat, you know."

—Arthur Kennedy talking to Ruth Roman about resuming her marriage to his brother (Kirk Douglas) in Mark Robson's *Champion*
(Screenplay by Carl Foreman; based on the short story by Ring Lardner)

21.
"Oh, of course. Everybody on this ship is in love. Love me whether or not I love you. Love me whether I am fit to love. Love me whether I am able to love. Even if there is no such thing as love. Love me."

—Vivien Leigh letting her bitterness show in Stanley Kramer's *Ship of Fools*
(Screenplay by Abby Mann; based on the novel by Katherine Anne Porter)

22.
"If the rest of one's life were only a—a few days or a few hours, would that be enough to justify love?"

—Fredric March posing the question to Gail Patrick in Mitchell Leisen's *Death Takes a Holiday*
(Screenplay by Maxwell Anderson and Gladys Lehman; based on the play by Alberto Casella)

23.
"If you love a person, you can forgive anything."

—Herbert Marshall setting himself up for an acid test from his faithless, murdering wife (Bette Davis) in William Wyler's *The Letter*
(Screenplay by Howard Koch; based on the play and short story by W. Somerset Maugham)

24.
"The master must not be loved—never loved. Give yourself to love, and you give yourself to forgetfulness—what you are and who you are and what you want."

—Elizabeth Taylor raging on the subject to Richard Burton in Joseph L. Mankiewicz's *Cleopatra*
(Screenplay by Joseph L. Mankiewicz, Ranald MacDougall and Sidney Buchman; based upon histories by Plutarch, Suetonius and Appian and THE LIFE AND TIMES OF CLEOPATRA, a book by C. M. Franzero)

25.
"It's a mistake you always made, Doc, trying to love a wild thing. You were always lugging home wild things. Once, it was a hawk with a broken wing, and—and that time it was a full-grown wildcat with a broken leg. Remember? . . . You mustn't give your heart to a wild thing. The more you do, the stronger they get until

they're strong enough to run into the woods or fly into a tree and then to a higher tree and then to the sky."

—Audrey Hepburn rejecting her Texas past and Buddy Ebsen in Blake Edwards's *Breakfast at Tiffany's*
(Screenplay by George Axelrod; based on the novella by Truman Capote)

26.
"Oh, no—no, you want him wholly and utterly dependent. You realized long ago, with all your fine background and breeding, you were a failure—but it gave you a reason for being, a feeling of power to control and manipulate someone else's life. And, worst of all, you do it in the name of love. You're as phoney to me as an opera soprano."

—William Holden telling off Grace Kelly in George Seaton's *The Country Girl*
(Screenplay by George Seaton; based on the play by Clifford Odets)

27.
"The same old John, throwing out the same old cascade of truths, half truths and distortions. But human nature isn't as simple as you make it, John. You've left out the most important fact of all. You see, you're the only person in the world I've ever really been fond of. Notice how tactfully I leave out the word love."

—Rita Hayworth complimenting her ex (Burt Lancaster) in Delbert Mann's *Separate Tables*
(Screenplay by Terence Rattigan and John Gay; based on the play by Terence Rattigan)

28.
"You don't know what love means. To you, it's just another four-letter word."

—Paul Newman confronting his father (Burl Ives) in Richard Brooks's *Cat on a Hot Tin Roof*
(Screenplay by Richard Brooks and James Poe; based on the play by Tennessee Williams)

29.
(a) "Mack, you ever been in love?"
  (b) "No. I been a bartender all my life."

—(b) J. Farrell MacDonald ducking the question of (a) Henry Fonda in John Ford's *My Darling Clementine*
(Screenplay by Samuel G. Engel and Winston Miller; based on a story by Sam Hellman and WYATT EARP, FRONTIER MARSHAL, *a book by Stuart N. Lake)*

30.
(a) "You ever been in love, Hornbeck?"
  (b) "Only with the sound of my own words, thank God."

—(b) Gene Kelly ducking the question of (a) Spencer Tracy in Stanley Kramer's *Inherit the Wind*
(Screenplay by Nathan E. Douglas and Harold Jacob Smith; based on the play by Jerome Lawrence and Robert E. Lee)

31.
(a) "If you had the choice—"
  (b) "Yeah?"
  (a) "Would you rather love a girl or have her love you?"

—(a) Jack Nicholson posing a hypothetical question to (b) Arthur Garfunkel in the first lines of Mike Nichols's *Carnal Knowledge*
(Original Screenplay by Jules Feiffer)

32.
"Adoring someone is certainly better than being adored. Being adored is a nuisance. You'll discover, Dorian, that women treat us just as humanity treats its gods: they worship us but keep bothering us to do something for them."

—George Sanders counseling Hurd Hatfield in Albert Lewin's *The Picture of Dorian Gray*
(Screenplay by Albert Lewin; based on the novel by Oscar Wilde)

33.
"I don't want to be worshiped. I want to be loved."

—Katharine Hepburn telling her fiancé (John Howard) that he's got it wrong in George Cukor's *The Philadelphia Story*
(Screenplay by Donald Ogden Stewart; based on the play by Philip Barry)
and

—Grace Kelly dittoing John Lund in the remake, Charles Walters's *High Society*
(Screenplay by John Patrick; based on THE PHILADELPHIA STORY, a screenplay by Donald Ogden Stewart and play by Philip Barry)

34.
"You know, you'd soon get tired of a man who had nothing else to do but to worship you. That's a dull kind of love, Gabrielle. It's the kind of love that makes people old, too soon."

—Leslie Howard cooling off Bette Davis in Archie Mayo's *The Petrified Forest*
(Screenplay by Delmer Daves and Charles Kenyon; based on the play by Robert E. Sherwood)

35.
"How could I help loving you—you who have all the passion for life that I lack? But that kind of love isn't enough to make a successful marriage for two people who are as different as we are."

—Leslie Howard cooling off Vivien Leigh in Victor Fleming's *Gone With the Wind*
(Screenplay by Sidney Howard; based on the novel by Margaret Mitchell)

36.
"Two kinds of love, hers and mine, worlds apart, as I know now, though when I married her I did not think they were incompatible. Nor, I suppose, did she. In those days I—I had not thought that her kind of love, that the kind of love she requires and which I had seemed unable to give her, was so important that its absence would drive out the other kind of love, the kind of love I required and—and which I had thought in my folly was by far the greater part of love."

—Michael Redgrave explaining his marital maladies to Nigel Patrick in Anthony Asquith's *The Browning Version*
(Screenplay by Terence Rattigan; based on his play)

37.
"You know, I don't believe Clare has come right out and told me he loves me since we've been married. Course, I know he does because I keep reminding him of it. You have to keep reminding them, Cora."

—Irene Dunne revealing a marital secret to ZaSu Pitts in Michael Curtiz's *Life With Father*
(Screenplay by Donald Ogden Stewart; based on the play by Howard Lindsay and Russel Crouse and stories by Clarence Day, Jr.)

38.
"Mrs. Prentiss says that, like her husband, I'm a burnt-out old shell of a man who cannot even remember what it's like to love a woman the way her son loves my daughter. And, strange as it seems, that's the first statement made to me all day with which I am prepared to take issue because I think you're wrong. You're as wrong as you can be. I admit that I hadn't considered it—hadn't even thought about it—but I know exactly how he feels about her, and there is nothing—absolutely nothing—that your son feels for my daughter that I didn't feel for Christina. Old, yes. Burnt-out, certainly. But I can tell you. The memories are still there—clear, intact, indestructible—and they'll be there if I live to be 110."

—Spencer Tracy restating his love for Katharine Hepburn in Stanley Kramer's *Guess Who's Coming to Dinner*
(Original Screenplay by William Rose)

39.
"I believe that love cannot be bought except with love, and he who has a good wife wears heaven in his hat."

—Marlon Brando inventing amorous sayings for his formal courtship of Jean Peters in Elia Kazan's *Viva Zapata!*
(Original Screenplay by John Steinbeck)

40.
"He married for love. Love. That's why he did everything. That's why he went into politics. It seems we weren't enough. He wanted all the voters to love him, too. All he really wanted out of life was love. That's Charlie's story—how he

lost it. You see, he just didn't have any to give. Oh, he loved Charlie Kane, of course. Yeah. Very dearly. And his mother. I guess he always loved her."

—Joseph Cotten explaining Orson Welles to William Alland in Orson Welles's *Citizen Kane*
(Original Screenplay by Herman J. Mankiewicz and Orson Welles)

41.
"Listen to me. I'm no good—I never pretended to be—but I love you. I'm a hustler—I've always been one—but I love you. I may be the thief of the world, but with you I've always been on the level. You've done a lot of talking about love. I never mentioned it before, but I guess you get the general idea. If you want to walk out on that, it's okay with me."

—Tyrone Power pleading with his wife (Coleen Gray) in Edmund Goulding's *Nightmare Alley*
(Screenplay by Jules Furthman; based on the novel by William Lindsay Gresham)

42.
"I want to crawl to her feet—whimper to be forgiven for loving her, for needing her more than my own life, for belonging to her more than my own soul."

—Laurence Olivier regretting his love for Merle Oberon in William Wyler's *Wuthering Heights*
(Screenplay by Ben Hecht and Charles MacArthur; based on the novel by Emily Brontë)

43.
"I just want you to love me, primal doubts and all."

—William Holden telling Faye Dunaway the bottom line in Sidney Lumet's *Network*
(Original Screenplay by Paddy Chayefsky)

44.
"Just say you love me. You don't have to mean it."

—Carolyn Jones trying to find love with a pickup (Don Murray) in Delbert Mann's *The Bachelor Party*
(Screenplay by Paddy Chayefsky; based on his teleplay)

45.
"I think a state of love exists between us. That's the most honest way I can describe it."

—Leo Genn playing it cautious in Anthony Pelissier's *Personal Affair*
(Screenplay by Lesley Storm; based on THE DAY'S MISCHIEF, a play by Lesley Storm)

46.
"Do you think that you are Providence that you can ordain love?"

—Pamela Franklin telling off Maggie Smith in Ronald Neame's *The Prime of Miss Jean Brodie*
(Screenplay by Jay Presson Allen; based on her play and the novel by Muriel Spark)

47.
"I love you. I've loved you since the first moment I saw you. I guess maybe I even loved you even before I saw you."

—Montgomery Clift admitting his love for Elizabeth Taylor in George Stevens's *A Place in the Sun*
(Screenplay by Michael Wilson and Harry Brown; based on AN AMERICAN TRAGEDY, a play by Patrick Kearney and novel by Theodore Dreiser)

48.
"It's all a question of climate. You cannot serenade a woman in a snowstorm. All the graces in the art of love—elaborate approaches that will make the game of love amusing—can only be practiced in those countries that quiver in the heat of the sun."

—John Gilbert educating Greta Garbo in Rouben Mamoulian's *Queen Christina*
(Screenplay by H. M. Harwood and Salka Viertel; dialogue by S. N. Behrman; based on a story by Salka Viertel and Margaret P. Levino)

49.
"For heaven be thanked,
We live in such an age
When no man dies for love
Except upon the stage."

—Michael MacLiammoir, as narrator, adding rhyme to another close call for Albert Finney in Tony Richardson's *Tom Jones*

(Screenplay by John Osborne; based on the novel by Henry Fielding)

50.

"I'd almost forgotten about it, but, when I was in high school, I thought I was just one of those cold people who would never love anyone. I just—some people have the capacity, and I guess I didn't. It just wasn't in me. And, when I fell in love with this guy, it was just—I mean, it meant so much to me. It meant that I was a real person. I wasn't just a machine. I had really incredibly deep emotions, and I didn't know I could feel that strongly about anybody. . . . I'll never forget it. I was using a part of me—I still had a part of me that I'd never felt before, and the best part, too: my capacity to love somebody."

—"David" discussing his awakening to homosexual love in Mariposa Film Group's *Word Is Out*
(A documentary directed by Peter Adair, Nancy Adair, Veronica Selver, Andrew Brown, Robert Epstein and Lucy Massie Phenix)

51.

"We have not missed, you and I—we have not missed that many-splendored thing."

—William Holden echoing in his posthumous letters his love for Jennifer Jones in the last line of Henry King's *Love Is a Many-Splendored Thing*
(Screenplay by John Patrick based on A MANY-SPLENDORED THING, *a novel by Han Suyin)*

52.

"Cheer up, cherie. Wait till you've lost as many husbands as I have. Married, divorced, married, divorced. Ah, l'amour, l'amour. That's French for love."

—Mary Boland wistfully resigning herself to love's merry-go-round in George Cukor's *The Women*
(Screenplay by Anita Loos and Jane Murfin; based on the play by Clare Boothe)

ALSO SEE: Love Objects; Advice-8; Appearances-6; Applause-1; Beautiful-4; Betrayal-3; Books-1; Choice-9; Conflict-1; Daughters-7; Differences-1; Dreams-7; Dying Words-3; Exchanges-8; Fear-5; Fear-8; Fools-9; Free-4; Good-byes-6; Greed-2; Hate-6; Hate-8; Heart-1; Heart-3; Heart-17; Home-8; Honor-3; Husbands-8; Idea-7; Idea-8; Incompatibility-1; Incompatibility-2; Incompatibility-5; Indecision-3; Kiss-1; Knowledge-7; Land-2; Lies-7; Lies-8; Lies-9; Life and Death-9; Life and Death-10; Loneliness-9; Loneliness-10; Looks-12; Macho-19; Marriage-10; Men-11; Money-4; Money-5; Names-3; Names-27; Narcissism-1; Narcissism-2; Never-3; Painting-6; Peace-1; Pep Talks-2; Poets-2; Poverty-4; Prayers-7; Pride-3; Prologues-5; Proposals-5; Propositions-15; Propositions-16; Questions-17; Rejection-8; Rejection-16; Seasons-1; Seasons-2; Self-Perception-2; Sex-6; Similarities-5; Sons-4; Specializations-4; Specializations-6; Specializations-8; Strangers-4; Strength-6; Suicide-3; Suicide-12; Tact-6; Theater-4; Time-15; Time-17; Toasts-15; Trouble-5; Trust and Distrust-6; Wants-6; Wants-7; Window-6; Wives-8; Women-6; Women-8; Women-9; Wrong-7.

LOVE OBJECTS

1.

"I love the Army. A man loves a thing, that don't mean it's got to love him back. . . . You love a thing, you gotta be grateful. See, I left home when I was 17. Both my folks is dead, and I don't belong no place—till I entered the Army. If it weren't for the Army, I wouldn't have learned how to bugle. . . . I play the bugle well."

—Montgomery Clift explaining his commitment in Fred Zinnemann's *From Here to Eternity*
(Screenplay by Daniel Taradash; based on the novel by James Jones)

2.

"Yes, there is something—something you love better than me, though you may not know it: Tara."

—Leslie Howard telling Vivien Leigh where her heart lies in Victor Fleming's *Gone With the Wind*
(Screenplay by Sidney Howard; based on the novel by Margaret Mitchell)

3.
"You want to know what's wrong with our waterfront? It's the love of a lousy buck. It's making the love of the lousy buck, the cushy job, more important than the love of man! It's forgetting every fellow down here is your brother in Christ."

—Karl Malden preaching to longshoremen in Elia Kazan's *On the Waterfront*
(*Original Screenplay by Budd Schulberg; based on "Crime on the Waterfront," nonfiction articles by Malcolm Johnson*)

4.
"I love the Cornbelt Loan and Trust Company. There are some who say that the old bank is suffering from hardening of the arteries and of the heart. I refuse to listen to such radical talk. I say that our bank is alive. It's generous. It's human. And we're going to have such a line of customers seeking—and getting—small loans that people will think we're gambling with the depositors' money. And we will be. We will be gambling on the future of this country."

—Fredric March leading his fellow bankers to a big change in postwar policy in William Wyler's *The Best Years of Our Lives*
(*Screenplay by Robert E. Sherwood; based on GLORY FOR ME, a verse novel by MacKinlay Kantor*)

ALSO SEE: Love.

LUCKY

1.
"People all say that I've had a bad break, but today—today I consider myself the luckiest man on the face of the earth."

—Gary Cooper saying good-bye to baseball in Sam Wood's *The Pride of the Yankees*
(*Screenplay by Herman J. Mankiewicz and Jo Swerling; based on an original story by Paul Gallico*)

2.
"I know him. Well. I shot him in the lip last August over at Winding Stair Mountains. He was lucky that day, all right. My shooting was off."

—John Wayne recalling one that got away in Henry Hathaway's *True Grit*
(*Screenplay by Marguerite Roberts; based on the novel by Charles Portis*)

3.
"As for you, my galvanized friend, you want a heart. You don't know how lucky you are not to have one. Hearts will never be practical until they can be made unbreakable."

—Frank Morgan telling Jack Haley to consider the advantages of being heartless in Victor Fleming's *The Wizard of Oz*
(*Screenplay by Noel Langley, Florence Ryerson and Edgar Allan Woolf; adaptation by Noel Langley; based on the novel by L. Frank Baum*)

4.
"You know what luck is? Luck is believing you're lucky, that's all."

—Marlon Brando boasting to his poker cronies in Elia Kazan's *A Streetcar Named Desire*
(*Screenplay by Tennessee Williams; adaptation by Oscar Saul; based on the play by Tennessee Williams*)

5.
"Nothing can happen to me when I got my lucky saxophone."

—Robert Montgomery assuring Edward Everett Horton and Claude Rains that he couldn't be dead in Alexander Hall's *Here Comes Mr. Jordan*
(*Screenplay by Sidney Buchman and Seton I. Miller; based on HEAVEN CAN WAIT, a play by Harry Segall*)

6.
(a) "My ancestors came over on the Mayflower."
    (b) "You're lucky. Now they have immigration laws."

—(b) Mae West insulting (a) Almira Sessions in Gregory Ratoff's *The Heat's On*

(Original Screenplay by Fitzroy Davis, George S. George and Fred Schiller)

ALSO SEE: Available-4; Awakenings-4; Guilty-1; Guns-7; Hope-1; Letters-1; Lies-18; Life-11; Love-8; Mad Act-11; Vulture-2; Wives-8.

MACHO

1.
"I won't need that. He's a *young* lion."

—Victor Mature spurning the spear offered by Hedy Lamarr in Cecil B. DeMille's *Samson and Delilah* *(Screenplay by Jesse Lasky Jr. and Fredric M. Frank from original treatments by Harold Lamb and Vladimir Jabotinsky; based on the history of Samson and Delilah in the Holy Bible, Judges 13–16)*

2.
"Let's just get something straight right off the top, babe, huh? I don't get involved with my women. I'm a short-termed guy. I don't fall in love. I don't want to get married. The only thing you can count on me for is sex. I am what I am. I make no bones about it."

—Cliff Gorman setting the ground rules before going to bed with Jill Clayburgh in Paul Mazursky's *An Unmarried Woman* *(Original Screenplay by Paul Mazursky)*

3.
"He used to sit down on the bed at night, and I'd tug 'em off, and he'd say, 'Son, the man of the house has got to have a pair of boots because he's got to do a lot of kicking.' Then he'd say, 'Son, there'll be times when the only thing you got to be proud of is the fact that you're a man, so wear your boots so people know you're coming and keep your fists doubled up so they know you mean business when you get there.' My old man, he was a corker!"

—William Holden telling what he learned from his father in Joshua Logan's *Picnic* *(Screenplay by Daniel Taradash; based on the play by William Inge)*

4.
(a) "Naturally, I like to see a man who can take care of himself. On the outside, it's—it's a man's world."
    (b) "How are they doing, Father?"
    (a) "They're not doing too good, but you know what I mean. There are some times a man has to fight his way through."
    (b) "Wouldn't it be better to—to think your way through?"

—(a) Bing Crosby and (b) Ingrid Bergman debating the meaning of manhood in Leo McCarey's *The Bells of St. Mary's* *(Screenplay by Dudley Nichols; based on an original story by Leo McCarey)*

5.
"It's a man's world. Yeah. See something you want, go after it. Get it. That's nature. Why we're made strong and women weak. Strong conquer, provide for the weak. That's what a man's for. Teach our kids more of that, be more men."

—Paul Douglas gruffly giving his world view in Joseph L. Mankiewicz's *A Letter to Three Wives* *(Screenplay by Joseph L. Mankiewicz; adaptation by Vera Caspary; based on "One of Our Hearts," a short story by John Klempner)*

6.
"Oh, darling, I'm almost sorry for you, having such a nice quiet peaceful time when things were really happening, but that's what men are for, isn't it—to go out and do things while you womenfolk look after the house?"

—Walter Pidgeon returning from Dunkirk heroics, unaware that his wife (Greer Garson) has single-handedly captured a downed Nazi flyer (Helmut Dantine), in William Wyler's *Mrs. Miniver* *(Screenplay by Arthur Wimperis, George Froeschel, James Hilton and Claudine West; based on the novel by Jan Struther)*

7.
"You see, Clarence, we men have to run this world, and it's not an easy job. It takes work, and it takes thinking. A man has to reason things out. Now, you take a woman. A woman

thinks—no, I'm wrong right there—a woman doesn't think at all. She gets stirred up."

—William Powell having a father-and-son talk with James Lydon in Michael Curtiz's *Life With Father*
(Screenplay by Donald Ogden Stewart; based on the play by Howard Lindsay and Russel Crouse and stories by Clarence Day, Jr.)

8.
"Women should not think at all. They are not equal to it."

—Robert Bice telling his brother (Turhan Bey) about women in Jack Conway and Harold S. Bucquet's *Dragon Seed*
(Screenplay by Marguerite Roberts and Jane Murfin; based on the novel by Pearl S. Buck)

9.
"Women should be kept illiterate and clean, like canaries."

—Roscoe Karns advancing his opinion in George Stevens's *Woman of the Year*
(Original Screenplay by Ring Lardner, Jr., and Michael Kanin)

10.
"Queen Cleopatra is widely read, well versed in the natural sciences and mathematics. She speaks seven languages proficiently. Were she not a woman, one would consider her to be an intellectual."

—Andrew Keir characterizing Elizabeth Taylor for Rex Harrison in Joseph L. Mankiewicz's *Cleopatra*
(Screenplay by Joseph L. Mankiewicz, Ranald MacDougall and Sidney Buchman; based upon histories by Plutarch, Suetonius and Appian and THE LIFE AND TIMES OF CLEOPATRA, a book by C. M. Franzero)

11.
"Dear Poppaea, one woman should never judge another. She hasn't the glands for it."

—Peter Ustinov overriding Patricia Laffan's opinion of Deborah Kerr in Mervyn LeRoy's *Quo Vadis*
(Screenplay by John Lee Mahin, S. N. Behrman and Sonya Levien; based on the novel by Henryk Sienkiewicz)

12.
"She shouldn't try to be top man. She's not built for it. She's flying in the face of nature."

—Ray Milland criticizing Ginger Rogers's careerism in Mitchell Leisen's *Lady in the Dark*
(Screenplay by Albert Hackett and Frances Goodrich; based on the play by Moss Hart)

13.
"I'm analyzing women at present. The subject is less difficult than I was led to believe. Women represent the triumph of matter over mind just as men represent the triumph of the mind over morals."

—George Sanders advancing some slanted generalizations in Albert Lewin's *The Picture of Dorian Gray*
(Screenplay by Albert Lewin; based on the novel by Oscar Wilde)

14.
"Oh, it's incredible, utterly incredible. Perched up on that pinnacle of masculine ego, looking down at poor, weak, defenseless females—and pitying them because they don't have beards."

—Bette Davis tearing into Robert Montgomery in Bretaigne Windust's *June Bride*
(Screenplay by Ranald MacDougall; based on FEATURE FOR JUNE, a play by Eileen Tighe and Graeme Lorimer)

15.
(a) "Wilson, you don't know what it does to a man's ego to be constantly reminded that he's married to a beautiful woman."
  (b) "Usually what it does to yours, darling, air does to a balloon."

—(b) Joan Bennett deflating (a) Robert Preston in front of his African guide (Gregory Peck) in Zoltan Korda's *The Macomber Affair*
(Screenplay by Casey Robinson and Seymour Bennett; adaptation by Seymour Bennett and Frank Arnold; based on "The Short Happy Life of Francis Macomber," a short story by Ernest Hemingway)

16.
" 'Men's stuff'? Lord have mercy! Get out my

spinning wheel, girls. I'll join the harem section in a minute."

—Elizabeth Taylor ridiculing the after-dinner husbands-huddle that excludes her in George Stevens's *Giant*
(Screenplay by Fred Guiol and Ivan Moffat; based on the novel by Edna Ferber)

17.
"It's not that easy, Scarlett. You've turned me out while you've chased Ashley Wilkes, while you've dreamed of Ashley Wilkes. This is one night you're not turning me out."

—Clark Gable taking his wife (Vivien Leigh) by force in Victor Fleming's *Gone With the Wind*
(Screenplay by Sidney Howard; based on the novel by Margaret Mitchell)

18.
"Certain women should be struck regularly, like gongs."

—Robert Montgomery advancing his opinion in Sidney Franklin's *Private Lives*
(Screenplay by Hans Kraly, Richard Schayer and Claudine West; based on the play by Noel Coward)

19.
"Women are strange little beasts. You can treat them like dogs, you can beat them until your arm aches—and still they love you. Of course, it's an absurd illusion that they have souls."

—George Sanders hewing the hard line in Albert Lewin's *The Moon and Sixpence*
(Screenplay by Albert Lewin; based on the novel by W. Somerset Maugham)

20.
"I never hit a woman in my life till I met you."

—Harry Guardino giving his wife (Anne Meara) a dubious distinction in Cy Howard's *Lovers and Other Strangers*
(Screenplay by Renee Taylor, Joseph Bologna and David Z. Goodman; based on the play by Renee Taylor and Joseph Bologna)

21.
"If you was my girl and took the words out of my mouth like that, I'd give you somethin' you'd feel hurtin', I would. You take my tip, mate. Stop her jaw or you'll die afore your time. Wore out, that's what you'll be. Wore out."

—Robert Newton telling Rex Harrison how to handle Wendy Hiller in Gabriel Pascal's *Major Barbara*
(Screenplay by George Bernard Shaw; based on his play)

ALSO SEE: Men; Drink Orders-2; Fake-3; Names-8; Never-9; Together-7.

MAD ACT

1.
"I don't know what to do about the depression and the inflation and the Russians and the crime in the street. All I know is that first you've got to get mad. You've got to say, 'I'm a human being, goddammit! My life has value!' So I want you to get up now. I want all of you to get up out of your chairs. I want you to get up right now and go to the window, open it and stick your head out and yell, 'I'm as mad as hell, and I'm not going to take this anymore!' "

—Peter Finch raging on national television in Sidney Lumet's *Network*
(Original Screenplay by Paddy Chayefsky)

2.
"I can't go on with the scene. I'm too happy! Mr. DeMille, do you mind if I say a few words? Thank you. I just want to tell you all how happy I am to be back in the studio, making a picture again! You don't know how much I've missed all of you. And I promise you I'll never desert you again because after *Salome* we'll make another picture and another picture! You see, this is my life. It always will be! There's nothing else —just us—and the cameras—and those wonderful people out there in the dark. All right, Mr. DeMille, I'm ready for my closeup."

—Gloria Swanson descending a staircase into madness in the last lines of Billy Wilder's *Sunset Boulevard*

(Original Screenplay by Charles Brackett, Billy Wilder and D. M. Marshman Jr.)

3.

"Ah, but the strawberries! That's—that's where I had them. They laughed and made jokes, but I proved beyond a shadow of a doubt, and with geometric logic, that a duplicate key to the wardroom icebox did exist. And I'd have produced that key if they hadn't have pulled the Caine out of action. I know now they were out to protect some fellow officer."

—Humphrey Bogart blowing his case on the witness stand in Edward Dmytryk's *The Caine Mutiny*
(Screenplay by Stanley Roberts; additional dialogue by Michael Blankfort; based on the novel by Herman Wouk)

4.

"All of you know what I stand for—what I believe! I believe in the truth of the Book of Genesis! Exodus! Leviticus! Numbers! Deuteronomy! Joshua! Judges! Ruth! First Samuel! Second Samuel! First Kings! Second Kings! Isaiah! Jeremiah! Lamentations! Ezekiel!—".

—Fredric March losing his cool (but not his case) on the witness stand in Stanley Kramer's *Inherit the Wind*
(Screenplay by Nathan E. Douglas and Harold Jacob Smith; based on the play by Jerome Lawrence and Robert E. Lee)

5.

"He was laughing. Yes, he—he was laughing. He kissed me when he was drunk. Yes, he kissed me when he was drunk. So I got a new car. Yes, I—I got a new car, and I bought some new clothes. Yes, pretty. And he—he used to tell terrible jokes, and he'd laugh at them. He was always laughing. Then, I saw him lying there, drunk, and I heard the motor running. Then, I saw the doors, and I heard the motor. I saw the doors. The doors made me do it. Yes, the doors made me do it. The doors made me do it. The doors made me do it."

—Ida Lupino becoming unhinged on the witness stand, admitting that she let close the electronic garage doors which caused the asphyxiation of her drunken husband (Alan Hale), in Raoul Walsh's *They Drive by Night*
(Screenplay by Jerry Wald and Richard Macaulay; based on LONG HAUL, a novel by A. I. Bezzerides)

6.

"Doors will open beyond which I shall catch a glimpse of the unknown. Let it be wonderful or let it be awful so long as it is uncommon! And now, behold, dear Petronius: my new Rome, to rise in gleaming white beauty, master gem of the world's crown. It shall have a new name: Neropolis. City of Nero."

—Peter Ustinov announcing plans to burn Rome and build his own city in its place in Mervyn LeRoy's *Quo Vadis*
(Screenplay by John Lee Mahin, S. N. Behrman and Sonya Levien; based on the novel by Henryk Sienkiewicz)

7.

"What's that light? There's somebody out there holding a flashlight. Somebody's watching. They've got no call to watch. I'm the one that watches. I'll tell 'em. *I'm the one that watches!* Eyes. Eyes. Hundreds of eyes. Back of each tree. Thousands of eyes. What's that? Like the sound of a big wall falling over into the sea. Everything's slipping out from under me. Can't you feel it? Starting in slow and then hundreds of miles an hour. There's a wind in my ears—a terrible rushin' wind. Everything's going past me like telegraph poles. Everything's going backward. Everything I've ever seen, faster and faster back to the day I was born. I can see it coming, the day I was born."

—Robert Montgomery sensing (correctly) the police closing in on him in Richard Thorpe's *Night Must Fall*
(Screenplay by John Van Druten; based on the play by Emlyn Williams)

8.

"I can no longer sit back and allow Communist infiltration, Communist indoctrination, Communist subversion and the international Communist conspiracy to sap and impurify all of our precious bodily fluids."

—Sterling Hayden explaining why he triggered World War III in Stanley Kubrick's *Dr. Strangelove or: How I Learned To Stop Worrying and Love the Bomb*
(Screenplay by Stanley Kubrick, Terry Southern and Peter George; based on RED ALERT, *a novel by Peter George)*

9.

"The best part of myself, that's what you are. Do you think I'm going to leave it to the vulgar pawing of a second-rate detective who thinks you're a dame? Do you think I could bear the thought of him holding you in his arms, kissing you, loving you?"

—Clifton Webb wielding a shotgun at Gene Tierney in Otto Preminger's *Laura*
(Screenplay by Jay Dratler, Samuel Hoffenstein and Betty Reinhardt; based on the novel by Vera Caspary)

10.

"I'm sorry. I don't like people touching my blue blanket. It's not important. It's a minor compulsion. I can deal with it if I want to. It's just that I've had it ever since I was a baby, and I find it very comforting."

—Gene Wilder apologizing for his hysteria to Zero Mostel in Mel Brooks's *The Producers*
(Original Screenplay by Mel Brooks)

11.

"Oh, Sebastian. What a lovely summer it's been. Just the two of us. Sebastian and Violet. Violet and Sebastian. Just the way it's always going to be. Oh, we are lucky, my darling, to have one another and need no one else ever."

—Katharine Hepburn retreating into a fantasy with her late son in Joseph L. Mankiewicz's *Suddenly, Last Summer*
(Screenplay by Gore Vidal and Tennessee Williams; based on the one-act play by Tennessee Williams)

12.

"It's sad when a mother has to speak the words that condemn her own son, but I couldn't allow them to believe that I would commit murder. They'll put him away now, as I should have years ago. He was always *bad*, and in the end he intended to tell them I killed those girls and that man, as if I could do anything except just sit and stare like one of his stuffed birds. Well, they know I can't even move a finger—and I won't. I'll just sit here and be quiet, just in case they do suspect me. They're probably watching me. Well, let them. Let them see what kind of a person I am. I'm not even going to swat that fly. I hope they *are* watching. They'll see. They'll see and they'll know and they'll say, 'Why, she wouldn't even harm a fly.' "

—Anthony Perkins assuming his mother's personality in the last lines of Alfred Hitchcock's *Psycho*
(Screenplay by Joseph Stefano; based on the novel by Robert Bloch)

MANNERS

1.

"I've always been a man of the world. There's no reason why I should forget my manners as I am leaving it."

—Clifton Webb dictating his party regrets on his deathbed in Edmund Goulding's *The Razor's Edge*
(Screenplay by Lamar Trotti; based on the novel by W. Somerset Maugham)

2.

"Chivalry is not only dead, it's decomposed."

—Rudy Vallee lamenting the lack of manners in the world to Claudette Colbert in Preston Sturges's *The Palm Beach Story*
(Original Screenplay by Preston Sturges)

3.

"Well, there's plenty to complain about! The way that they throw food at you here—there's no grace, no courtesy. This city used to be a lovely place to live, just lovely. Everybody had time for everybody else. You'd go to a fine restaurant, and the maitre d' would say, 'Mrs. Pritchett, how nice to see you' and kiss my hand."

—Sylvia Sidney lamenting the lack of manners in the world to Joanne Woodward in Gilbert Cates's *Summer Wishes, Winter Dreams*
(Original Screenplay by Stewart Stern)

4.
"You eat terrible. You got no manners. Taking your shoes off—that's another thing—picking your teeth. You're just not couth!"

—Judy Holliday telling off Broderick Crawford in George Cukor's *Born Yesterday*
(Screenplay by Albert Mannheimer; based on the play by Garson Kanin)

5.
"Bad table manners, my dear Gigi, have broken up more households than infidelity."

—Isabel Jeans advising Leslie Caron in Vincente Minnelli's *Gigi*
(Screenplay by Alan Jay Lerner; based on the novel by Colette)

6.
"Easy now, easy now. Is this a courtin' or a donnybrook? Have the good manners not to hit the man until he's your husband—and entitled to hit you back."

—Barry Fitzgerald refereeing the courtship of John Wayne and Maureen O'Hara in John Ford's *The Quiet Man*
(Screenplay by Frank S. Nugent; based on "Green Rushes," a short story by Maurice Walsh)

7.
"Young woman, either you have been raised in some incredibly rustic community where good manners aren't known or you suffer from the common feminine delusion that the mere fact of being a woman exempts you from the rules of civilized conduct. Possibly both."

—Clifton Webb resisting Gene Tierney's pushiness at their first meeting in Otto Preminger's *Laura*
(Screenplay by Jay Dratler, Samuel Hoffenstein and Betty Reinhardt; based on the novel by Vera Caspary)

8.
"I don't mind if you don't like my manners. I don't like 'em myself. They're pretty bad. I grieve over them long winter evenings."

—Humphrey Bogart sparring with Lauren Bacall in Howard Hawks's *The Big Sleep*
(Screenplay by William Faulkner, Leigh Brackett and Jules Furthman; based on the novel by Raymond Chandler)

9.
"All right, Phil. Mind your manners. Be a little gentleman. Don't let the flag touch the ground. This sort of honorableness gets me sick."

—Celeste Holm puncturing Gregory Peck's polite act in Elia Kazan's *Gentleman's Agreement*
(Screenplay by Moss Hart; based on the novel by Laura Z. Hobson)

10.
"You lose your manners when you're poor."

—Betsy Blair apologizing to Fredric March in Michael Gordon's *Another Part of the Forest*
(Screenplay by Vladimir Pozner; based on the play by Lillian Hellman)

11.
"With Major Lawrence, mercy is a passion. With me, it is merely good manners. You may judge which motive is the more reliable."

—Alec Guinness being interviewed by Arthur Kennedy about Peter O'Toole in David Lean's *Lawrence of Arabia*
(Screenplay by Robert Bolt; based on THE SEVEN PILLARS OF WISDOM, the autobiography of T. E. Lawrence, and other works by and about T. E. Lawrence)

12.
"We are not questioning your authority, sir, but, if manners prevent our speaking the truth, we will be without manners."

—John Loder standing up to his father (Donald Crisp) on the issue of a mine strike in John Ford's *How Green Was My Valley*
(Screenplay by Philip Dunne; based on the novel by Richard Llewellyn)

ALSO SEE: Breasts-1; Fashion-5; Static-6.

MARRIAGE

1.

"Marriage is like a dull meal, with the dessert at the beginning."

—José Ferrer providing a cynical definition of the word in John Huston's *Moulin Rouge*
(Screenplay by Anthony Veiller and John Huston; based on the novel by Pierre La Mure)

2.

"Getting married is serious business. It's kinda formal, like funerals or playing stud poker."

—William Gargan explaining matrimony to Charles Laughton in Garson Kanin's *They Knew What They Wanted*
(Screenplay by Robert Audrey; based on the play by Sidney Howard)

3.

"It is a deadly cancer in the body politic, and I will have it out!"

—Robert Shaw, as Henry VIII, demanding that his Lord Chancellor (Paul Scofield) grant him a divorce from the barren Catherine of Aragon in Fred Zinnemann's *A Man for All Seasons*
(Screenplay by Robert Bolt; based on his play)

4.

"Allie and I are united in the holy bonds of politics."

—Bob Hope explaining his public marriage in Melville Shavelson's *Beau James*
(Screenplay by Jack Rose and Melville Shavelson; based on the biography by Gene Fowler)

5.

"Yes, he married you. He married you to get past that gate—for the same reason that I married my little American, and with the same ring. Just take a look inside at the engraving: 'To Toots, For Keeps.'"

—Paulette Goddard disenchanting Olivia De Havilland about Charles Boyer in Mitchell Leisen's *Hold Back the Dawn*
(Screenplay by Charles Brackett and Billy Wilder; based on the novel by Ketti Frings)

6.

"Anybody could make a case—and a helluvah good case—against your getting married. The arguments are so obvious that nobody has to make them, but you're two wonderful people who happened to fall in love and happen to have a pigmentation problem. And I think that now, no matter what kind of a case some bastard could make against your getting married, there would be only one thing worse—and that would be if, knowing what you two are, knowing what you two have and knowing what you two feel, you didn't get married."

—Spencer Tracy giving his blessing to the marriage of his daughter (Katharine Houghton) and Sidney Poitier in Stanley Kramer's *Guess Who's Coming to Dinner*
(Original Screenplay by William Rose)

7.

"Make him feel important. If you do that, you'll have a happy and wonderful marriage—like two out of every ten couples."

—Mildred Natwick advising Jane Fonda about Robert Redford in Gene Saks's *Barefoot in the Park*
(Screenplay by Neil Simon; based on his play)

8.

"Oh, so you are married! Well, then, there is nothing so nice as a new marriage. No psychosis yet. No regressions. No deep complexes. I congratulate you. I hope you have babies and not phobias."

—Michael Chekhov extending somewhat clinical congratulations to Ingrid Bergman and Gregory Peck in Alfred Hitchcock's *Spellbound*
(Screenplay by Ben Hecht; adaptation by Angus MacPhail; based on THE HOUSE OF DR. EDWARDES, a novel by Francis Beeding)

9.

"You're my woman of the century. I always felt that you were *above* marriage."

—Katharine Hepburn complimenting Fay Bainter in George Stevens's *Woman of the Year*
(Original Screenplay by Ring Lardner, Jr., and Michael Kanin)

10.

"But, ma'am, you know how them big, strong, red-headed men are: they just got to get to the point. So we got married, ma'am. Natcheraly, I ain't had no chance to think about love since."

—Marjorie Main recalling her courtship in George Cukor's *The Women*
(Screenplay by Anita Loos and Jane Murfin; based on the play by Clare Boothe)

11.

"You married? Me neither. Everybody tells you, 'Why don't you get married? You should be married.' My mother. My father. My sister. 'Try and get married.' As if I didn't want to get married! Where do you find a man? You get me a man, and I'll marry him—anything, as long as it's got pants."

—Lee Grant lamenting her spinsterhood in William Wyler's *Detective Story*
(Screenplay by Philip Yordan and Robert Wyler; based on the play by Sidney Kingsley)

12.

"Listen, Ange. I been looking for a girl every Saturday night of my life. I'm 34 years old. I'm just tired of looking, that's all. I'd like to find a girl. Everybody's always telling me, 'Get married, get married, get married!' Don't you think I want to get married? I want to get married. Everybody drives me crazy."

—Ernest Borgnine lamenting his bachelorhood in Delbert Mann's *Marty*
(Screenplay by Paddy Chayefsky; based on his teleplay)

13.

"Marriage is not forbidden to us, but, instead of getting married at once, it sometimes happens we get married at last."

—Isabel Jeans preparing Leslie Caron for the life of a courtesan in Vincente Minnelli's *Gigi*
(Screenplay by Alan Jay Lerner; based on the novel by Colette)

14.

"Well, what difference does it make who you marry—so long as he's a Southerner and thinks like you?"

—Thomas Mitchell qualifying the open field for a son-in-law in Victor Fleming's *Gone With the Wind*
(Screenplay by Sidney Howard; based on the novel by Margaret Mitchell)

15.

"You know, I'm not sure if I dig the whole marriage scene. I mean, yeah, it's all right for some people, I guess, but I don't know if it's today—I mean, you know what I mean 'today.' Today! Today is—is—to live. Free. Man. Woman. Love. Oh, you don't need a diploma, do you? Ha-ha-ha!"

—Bob Dishy printing big for his date (Marian Hailey) that he's not the marrying kind in Cy Howard's *Lovers and Other Strangers*
(Screenplay by Renee Taylor, Joseph Bologna and David Z. Goodman; based on the play by Renee Taylor and Joseph Bologna)

16.

"Jonathan, before a man gets married, he's a—he's like a tree in the forest. He—he stands there independent, an entity unto himself. And then he's chopped down. His branches are cut off, and he's stripped of his bark, and he's thrown into the river with the rest of the logs. Then this tree is taken to the mill. Now, when it comes out, it's no longer a tree. It's a vanity table, a breakfast nook, a baby crib and the newspaper that lines the family garbage can."

—Rock Hudson explaining his bachelorhood to Tony Randall in Michael Gordon's *Pillow Talk*
(Screenplay by Stanley Shapiro and Maurice Richlin; based on a story by Russell Rouse and Clarence Greene)

17.

"The responsibility for recording a marriage has always been up to the woman; if it wasn't for her, marriage would have disappeared long since. No man is going to jeopardize his present or poison his future with a lot of little brats hollering around the house unless he's forced to. It's up to the woman to knock him down, hog-tie him and drag him in front of two witnesses immediately if not sooner."

—Alan Bridge explaining marital responsibility to Betty Hutton and Diana Lynn in Preston Sturges's *The Miracle of Morgan's Creek*
(Original Screenplay by Preston Sturges)

ALSO SEE: Proposals; Wedding; Bed-1; Bed-2; Callings-6; Changes-4; Daughters-7; Differences-6; Divorce-2; Hair-4; Love-35; Love-36; Love-37; Moon-4; Never-6; Never-13; Passion-4; People-4; Pittsburgh-1; Promiscuity-3; Questions-17; Rejection-5; Sex-6; Silence-4; Spinsters-5; Strangers-4; Stupid-3; Stupid-4; Stupid-6; Tact-6; Tact-7; Time-12; Timing-2.

MELLOW

1.
"You know, I don't think I could take a mellow evening because I—I don't respond well to mellow. You know what I mean? I have a tendency to—if I get too mellow, I ripen and then rot."

—Woody Allen passing on a pot party in Woody Allen's *Annie Hall*
(Original Screenplay by Woody Allen and Marshall Brickman)

2.
"It's cyanide cut with carbolic acid to give it a mellow flavor."

—Robert Ryan telling Jeff Bridges about the rot-gut whiskey served at Fredric March's bar in John Frankenheimer's *The Iceman Cometh*
(Screenplay based on the play by Eugene O'Neill; text edited by Thomas Quinn Curtiss)

MEMORY

1.
"I am packing my belongings in the shawl my mother used to wear when she went to the market, and I am going from my valley. And this time I shall never return. I am leaving behind me my 50 years of memory. Memory! Strange that the mind will forget so much of what only this moment is passed and yet hold clear and bright the memory of what happened years ago, of the men and women long since dead. Yet who shall say what is real and what is not? Can I believe my friends all gone, when their voices are still a glory in my ears? No, and I will stand to say no, and no again. For they remain a living truth within my mind."

—Irving Pichel, as the never-seen narrator (a grown-up version of Roddy McDowall), setting off memories with the first lines of John Ford's *How Green Was My Valley*
(Screenplay by Philip Dunne; based on the novel by Richard Llewellyn)

2.
"I didn't go to the moon. I went much further. I followed my father's footsteps, attempting to find in motion what was really lost in space. I traveled around a great deal. I would have stopped, but I was pursued by something. It always came upon me unawares, taking me altogether by surprise. Perhaps it was a—a familiar bit of music. Perhaps it was only a piece of transparent glass. Then, all at once, my sister touched my shoulder. I turned around and—and looked into her eyes. Oh, Laura, I tried to leave you behind me, but I'm—I am more faithful than I intended to be."

—Arthur Kennedy remembering Jane Wyman in Irving Rapper's *The Glass Menagerie*
(Screenplay by Tennessee Williams and Peter Berneis; based on the play by Tennessee Williams)

3.
"A fellow will remember a lot of things you wouldn't think he remembers. You take me. One day, back in 1896, I was crossing over to Jersey on the ferry, and, as we pulled out, there was another ferry pulling in, and on it there was a girl waiting to get off. A white dress she had on. She was carrying a white parasol. I only saw her for one second. She didn't see me at all, but I'll bet a month hasn't gone by since that I haven't thought of that girl."

—Everett Sloane recalling an ancient image to William Alland in Orson Welles's *Citizen Kane*
(Original Screenplay by Herman J. Mankiewicz and Orson Welles)

4.
"Once I stood where we're standing now to say good-bye to a pretty girl—only it was in the old station before this was built. We called it the 'depot.' We knew we wouldn't see each other again for almost a year. I thought I couldn't live through it, and she stood there crying—don't even know where she lives now, or if she *is* living. If she ever thinks of me, she probably imagines I'm still dancing in the ballroom of the Amberson Mansion. She probably thinks of the Mansion as still beautiful—still the finest house in town."

—Ray Collins recalling an ancient love as he says good-bye to his nephew (Tim Holt) in Orson Welles's *The Magnificent Ambersons*
(Screenplay by Orson Welles; based on the novel by Booth Tarkington)

5.
"She is playing solitaire with her memories."

—Martita Hunt telling Yul Brynner how a lonely Helen Hayes occupies herself in Anatole Litvak's *Anastasia*
(Screenplay by Arthur Laurents; based on the play by Marcelle Maurette and Broadway adaptation by Guy Bolton)

6.
"They can't censor our memories, can they?"

—Felix Bressart consoling Greta Garbo for her Soviet-censored love letter from Paris in Ernst Lubitsch's *Ninotchka*
(Screenplay by Charles Brackett, Billy Wilder and Walter Reisch; based on an original story by Melchior Lengyel)
                    and (almost verbatim)

—Jules Munshin dittoing Cyd Charisse in the remake, Rouben Mamoulian's *Silk Stockings*
(Screenplay by Leonard Gershe and Leonard Spigelgass; based on the musical play by George S. Kaufman, Leueen MacGrath and Abe Burrows and NINOTCHKA, a screenplay by Charles Brackett,
Billy Wilder and Walter Reisch, and original story by Melchior Lengyel)

7.
"I'm trying to memorize your face. I'm trying to memorize everything about you so that, no matter what happens, I won't forget you."

—Robert Montgomery urgently drinking in Evelyn Keyes in Alexander Hall's *Here Comes Mr. Jordan*
(Screenplay by Sidney Buchman and Seton I. Miller; based on HEAVEN CAN WAIT, a play by Harry Segall)

8.
"I have been memorizing this room. In the future, in my memory, I shall live a great deal in this room."

—Greta Garbo surveying the scene of her affair with John Gilbert in Rouben Mamoulian's *Queen Christina*
(Screenplay by H. M. Harwood and Salka Viertel; dialogue by S. N. Behrman; based on a story by Salka Viertel and Margaret P. Levino)

ALSO SEE: Remember; Aging-12; Head-1; Kiss-1; Last Lines-12; Life and Death-20; Love-38; Seasons-3.

MEN

1.
"There are no great men, buster. There are only men."

—Elaine Stewart harboring no illusions in Vincente Minnelli's *The Bad and the Beautiful*
(Screenplay by Charles Schnee; based on "Memorial to a Bad Man" and "Of Good and Evil," two short stories by George Bradshaw)

2.
"Oh, men! I never yet met one of them who didn't have the instincts of a heel. Sometimes I wish I could get along without them."

—Eve Arden harboring no illusions (but a little hope) in Michael Curtiz's *Mildred Pierce*
(Screenplay by Ranald MacDougall; based on the novel by James M. Cain)

3.

"Men don't get smarter when they grow older. They just lose their hair."

—Claudette Colbert telling her husband (Joel McCrea) what she has to look forward to in Preston Sturges's *The Palm Beach Story*
(Original Screenplay by Preston Sturges)

4.

"I have heard that the Christians teach you to love your neighbor, and, as I see what men are, I cannot for the life of me love my brother."

—Leo Genn explaining why he doesn't qualify as a Christian in Mervyn LeRoy's *Quo Vadis*
(Screenplay by John Lee Mahin, S. N. Behrman and Sonya Levien; based on the novel by Henryk Sienkiewicz)

5.

"Jack, there's something on everybody. Man is conceived in sin and born in corruption."

—Broderick Crawford passing along a negative view of his fellow man to John Ireland in Robert Rossen's *All the King's Men*
(Screenplay by Robert Rossen; based on the novel by Robert Penn Warren)

6.

"Man is the only animal that blushes—or needs to."

—Fredric March dispensing a famous Twainism in Irving Rapper's *The Adventures of Mark Twain*
(Screenplay by Alan LeMay; additional dialogue by Harry Chandlee; adaptation by Alan LeMay and Harold M. Sherman; based on MARK TWAIN, a play by Harold M. Sherman, and works owned or controlled by the Mark Twain Company)

7.

"Perhaps you're interested in how a man undresses. You know, there's a funny thing about that. Quite a study in psychology. No two men do it alike. You know, I once knew a man who kept his hat on until he was completely undressed. Yes! Now he made a picture! Years later, his secret came out. He wore a toupee. Yeah! You know, I have a method all my own. If you'll notice, the coat came first—then the tie—then the shirt—now, according to Hoyle, after that the pants should be next. Here's where I'm different. I go for the shoes next. First the right, then the left. After that, it's every man for himself."

—Clark Gable stripping to scare Claudette Colbert over to her side of their motel room in Frank Capra's *It Happened One Night*
(Screenplay by Robert Riskin; based on "Night Bus," a short story by Samuel Hopkins Adams)

8.

"Laura, you have one tragic weakness. For you, a lean, strong body is the measure of a man—and you always get hurt."

—Clifton Webb advising Gene Tierney in Otto Preminger's *Laura*
(Screenplay by Jay Dratler, Samuel Hoffenstein and Betty Reinhardt; based on the novel by Vera Caspary)

9.

"You like to get hurt. Always picking the wrong guy. It's a sickness with a lot of women. Always looking for a new way to get hurt by a new man. Get smart: there hasn't been a new man since Adam."

—Richard Conte confronting Susan Hayward in Joseph L. Mankiewicz's *House of Strangers*
(Screenplay by Philip Yordan; based on the novel by Jerome Weidman)

10.

"If there's one thing I know, it's men. I ought to. It's been my life's work."

—Marie Dressler counseling Madge Evans in George Cukor's *Dinner at Eight*
(Screenplay by Frances Marion and Herman J. Mankiewicz; based on the play by George S. Kaufman and Edna Ferber)

11.

"Dad, you're my father. I'm your son. I love you. I always have, and I always will. But you think of yourself as a colored man. I think of myself as a man."

—Sidney Poitier telling Roy Glenn how they differ in Stanley Kramer's *Guess Who's Coming to Dinner* (*Original Screenplay by William Rose*)

12.
"I tried to believe it was born in me and that I couldn't help it, but that's not so. Man has a choice. You used to say that was where we differed from an animal. See, I remember. 'Man has a choice, and it's—the, the choice is what makes him a man,' see? You see, I do remember."

—James Dean reconciling with his father (Raymond Massey) in Elia Kazan's *East of Eden* (*Screenplay by Paul Osborn; based on the novel by John Steinbeck*)

13.
"Frank, you asked me what I thought of you. Well, I'll tell you. The day you finish one thing you started out to do, the day you actually put those marbles in the Captain's overhead and then have the guts to knock on his door and say, 'Captain, I put those marbles there'—that's the day I'll have some respect for you. That's the day I'll look up to you as a man. Okay?"

—Henry Fonda defining manhood to Jack Lemmon in John Ford and Mervyn LeRoy's *Mister Roberts* (*Screenplay by Frank S. Nugent and Joshua Logan; based on the play by Thomas Heggen and Joshua Logan and novel by Thomas Heggen*)

14.
"A man should be what he can do."

—Montgomery Clift explaining why he's a soldier in Fred Zinnemann's *From Here to Eternity* (*Screenplay by Daniel Taradash; based on the novel by James Jones*)

15.
"A man ought to do what he thinks is right."

—John Wayne advancing his credo in John Farrow's *Hondo* (*Screenplay by James Edward Grant; based on "The Gift of Cochise," a short story by Louis L'Amour*)

16.
"Man is not made for defeat. Man can be destroyed but not defeated."

—Spencer Tracy expressing man's unconquerable spirit in John Sturges's *The Old Man and the Sea* (*Screenplay by Peter Viertel; based on the novel by Ernest Hemingway*)

17.
"I wish I had been born a man. . . . The concerns are so simple: money and death. Making ends meet until they meet—the end, if they do."

—Katharine Hepburn thinking aloud to her daughter (Lee Remick) in Tony Richardson's *A Delicate Balance* (*Screenplay by Edward Albee; based on his play*)

18.
(a) "It is written that there are only two perfectly good men—one dead, the other unborn."
    (b) "Which are you?"

—(b) Mae West considering the source, (a) Harold Huber, in Raoul Walsh's *Klondike Annie* (*Screenplay and dialogue by Mae West; additional material suggested by Frank Mitchell Dazey; story ingredients by Marion Morgan and George B. Dowell; based on an original story by Mae West*)

19.
"It's not the men in my life, but the life in my men."

—Mae West rephrasing a reporter's questions in Wesley Ruggles's *I'm No Angel* (*Screenplay and dialogue by Mae West; story suggestions by Lowell Brentano; continuity by Harlan Thompson*)

ALSO SEE: Macho; Clean-1; Differences-4; Differences-5; Eulogies-20; Future-1; Honest-6; Lies-9; Live-5; Platonic Relationships-2; Poverty-3; Prayers-4; Promiscuity-5; Proposals-12; Questions-8; Run-2; Sea-1; Sex-4; Strength-8; Stupid-4; Together-2; Truth-2; Why-6; Why-7; Why-8; Women-2; Women-3; Women-4; Women-5; Women-7; Women-10.

MIND

1.

"She tries to read my mind, and, if she can't read my mind, she reads my mail."

—Walter Slezak characterizing Ginger Rogers in Leo McCarey's *Once Upon a Honeymoon* (*Screenplay by Sheridan Gibney; based on an original story by Leo McCarey*)

2.

"It shrinks my liver, doesn't it, Nat? It pickles my kidneys, yeah. But what does it do to my mind? It tosses the sandbags overboard so the balloon can soar. Suddenly, I'm above the ordinary. I'm competent, supremely competent. I'm walking a tightrope over Niagara Falls. I'm one of the great ones. I'm Michelangelo, moulding the beard of Moses. I'm Van Gogh, painting pure sunlight. I'm Horowitz, playing the Emperor Concerto. I'm John Barrymore before the movies got him by the throat. I'm Jesse James and his two brothers—all three of them. I'm W. Shakespeare. And out there it's not Third Avenue any longer—it's the Nile, Nat—the Nile—and down it moves the barge of Cleopatra."

—Ray Milland waxing eloquent to his bartender (Howard da Silva) about the benefits of booze in Billy Wilder's *The Lost Weekend* (*Screenplay by Charles Brackett and Billy Wilder; based on the novel by Charles W. Jackson*)

3.

"Boston's not just a city. It's a state of mind. You can't move away from a state of mind."

—Ronald Colman arguing that environment is everything in Joseph L. Mankiewicz's *The Late George Apley* (*Screenplay by Philip Dunne; based on the play by John P. Marquand and George S. Kaufman and novel by John P. Marquand*)

4.

(a) "You're a Texan now."
   (b) "Is that a state of mind?"

—(a) Rock Hudson expecting behavior changes in his bride, (b) Elizabeth Taylor, in George Stevens's *Giant* (*Screenplay by Fred Guiol and Ivan Moffat; based on the novel by Edna Ferber*)

5.

"God, I can just hear the quips flying when you and 'the second best mind since Adlai Stevenson' get together, sitting there freezing under a blanket at the Washington Redskins games, playing anagrams with the names of all the Polish players. Your mind clicks off bric-a-brac so goddamn fast it never has a chance for an honest emotion or thought ever to get through."

—Alan Alda criticizing his ex (Jane Fonda) in Herbert Ross's *California Suite* (*Screenplay by Neil Simon; based on his play*)

6.

"Every time I've heard your mind click click click click. Is she? Isn't she? Is she? Isn't she? Very—very unattractive of you, and very noisy."

—Ingrid Bergman expressing her discomfort with a suspicious suitor (Ivan Desny) in Anatole Litvak's *Anastasia* (*Screenplay by Arthur Laurents; based on the play by Marcelle Maurette and Broadway adaptation by Guy Bolton*)

7.

"He's using his brain, is he, Hal? Look at him. Clickety clickety click. I can see it perking."

—Humphrey Bogart cautioning his brother (Dewey Martin) about the intelligence of their hostage (Fredric March) in William Wyler's *The Desperate Hours* (*Screenplay by Joseph Hayes; based on his play and novel*)

8.

"Huw is a scholar. Why take brains down a coal mine?"

—Donald Crisp debating with Sara Allgood the future of their youngest (Roddy McDowall) in John Ford's *How Green Was My Valley* (*Screenplay by Philip Dunne; based on the novel by Richard Llewellyn*)

9.

"Now there's a guy who never goes out of a girl's mind. He just stays there like a heavy meal."

—Veda Ann Borg swooning after Cary Grant in Irving Reis's *The Bachelor and the Bobby-Soxer*
(Original Screenplay by Sidney Sheldon)

10.

"If you don't mind my mentioning it, Father, I think you have a mind like a swamp."

—Diana Lynn criticizing the sternness of William Demarest in Preston Sturges's *The Miracle of Morgan's Creek*
(Original Screenplay by Preston Sturges)

11.

"What is there for you to say? We both know that the mind of a woman in love is operating on the lowest level of the intellect."

—Michael Chekhov accusing Ingrid Bergman of a blurred professional view of her patient-lover (Gregory Peck) in Alfred Hitchcock's *Spellbound*
(Screenplay by Ben Hecht; adaptation by Angus MacPhail; based on THE HOUSE OF DR. EDWARDES, a novel by Francis Beeding)

12.

"You see, when the mind houses two personalities, there's always a conflict. A battle. In Norman's case, the battle is over—and the dominant personality has won."

—Simon Oakland explaining Anthony Perkins at the end of Alfred Hitchcock's *Psycho*
(Screenplay by Joseph Stefano; based on the novel by Robert Bloch)

13.

"Dr. Kendal, a surgeon doesn't operate without first taking off the patient's clothes—or nor do we with the mind. You know what Staples says? The human mind is like Salome at the beginning of her dance, hidden from the outside world by seven veils—veils of reserve, shyness, fear. Now, with friends, the average person will drop first one veil, then another—maybe three or four altogether.

With a lover, she will take off five or even six. But never the seventh. Never. You see, the human mind likes to cover its nakedness, too, and keep its private thoughts to itself. Salome dropped her seventh veil of her own free will, but you will never get the human mind to do that. And that is why I use narcosis. Five minutes under narcosis, and down comes the seventh veil and we can see what is actually going on behind it. Then, we can really help."

—Herbert Lom explaining his planned treatment for Ann Todd in Compton Bennett's *The Seventh Veil*
(Original Screenplay by Muriel Box and Sydney Box)

14.

"Trouble is, Ann, when I'm standing up, my mind's lying down. When I'm lying down, my mind's standing—course, allowing I got a mind."

—Henry Fonda joshing with Pauline Moore in John Ford's *Young Mr. Lincoln*
(Original Screenplay by Lamar Trotti)

15.

(a) "It would be a terrific innovation if you could get your mind to stretch a little further than the next wisecrack."

(b) "You know, I tried that once, but it didn't snap back into place."

—(b) Eve Arden firing back at (a) Katharine Hepburn in Gregory La Cava's *Stage Door*
(Screenplay by Morrie Ryskind and Anthony Veiller; based on the play by Edna Ferber and George S. Kaufman)

16.

"What you want to do is to forget all about it. Just make your mind a complete blank. You know? Watch me. You can't go wrong."

—Michael Redgrave humoring the hysterical Margaret Lockwood in Alfred Hitchcock's *The Lady Vanishes*
(Screenplay by Sidney Gilliat and Frank Launder; based on THE WHEEL SPINS, a novel by Ethel Lina White)

17.

"I'm glad it's off my mind at last."

—Wylie Watson dying in peace, having just spilled the spy secret stored in his brain, in the last line of Alfred Hitchcock's *The Thirty-Nine Steps* (*Screenplay by Charles Bennett; dialogue by Ian Hay; continuity by Alma Reville; based on the novel by John Buchan*)

ALSO SEE: Body-3; Christmas-1; Differences-7; Fights-10; Hands-1; Heart-12; Heart-19; Human-4; Ignorance-2; Macho-13; Memory-1; Painting-4; Prayers-2; Prayers-3; Psychiatry-7; Rome-1; Smell-2; Soul-4; Stupid-2; Why-1.

MISTAKES

1.

"When I was new on this job, we brought in two boys caught stealing from a car. They looked like babies. They cried. I let them go. Two nights later—two nights!—one of them held up a butcher in Harlem and shot him through the head and killed him. Yes, I made a mistake—and I'm not going to make it again."

—Kirk Douglas explaining his hard line in William Wyler's *Detective Story* (*Screenplay by Philip Yordan and Robert Wyler; based on the play by Sidney Kingsley*)

2.

"It's all been a mistake, Bessie. I'm not a ghost, really."

—Gene Tierney calming her hysterical maid (Dorothy Adams) in Otto Preminger's *Laura* (*Screenplay by Jay Dratler, Samuel Hoffenstein and Betty Reinhardt; based on the novel by Vera Caspary*)

3.

"Oh, Jo, why can't you learn from my mistakes? It takes half your lifetime to learn from your own."

—Dora Bryan trying to head off trouble for her daughter (Rita Tushingham) in Tony Richardson's *A Taste of Honey*

(*Screenplay by Shelagh Delaney and Tony Richardson; based on the play by Shelagh Delaney*)

4.

"To regain one's youth, you must bear to repeat one's follies."

—George Sanders revealing his version of the secret of youth in Albert Lewin's *The Picture of Dorian Gray* (*Screenplay by Albert Lewin; based on the novel by Oscar Wilde*)

5.

"I should have anticipated this. Twenty years ago, I made the pardonable mistake of thinking I could civilize a girl who bought her hats out of a Sears Roebuck catalog."

—Clifton Webb learning that his wife (Barbara Stanwyck) is leaving him in Jean Negulesco's *Titanic* (*Original Screenplay by Charles Brackett, Walter Reisch and Richard L. Breen*)

6.

"So this is where the loser tells the winner she's making a terrible mistake. On the way out, think of something original, will you?"

—Joan Crawford growling at Jan Sterling over Jeff Chandler in Joseph Pevney's *Female on the Beach* (*Screenplay by Robert Hill and Richard Alan Simmons; based on THE BESIEGED HEART, a play by Robert Hill*)

7.

"A lot of guys make mistakes, I guess, but every one we make, a whole stack of chips goes with it. We make a mistake, and some guy don't walk away—forevermore, he don't walk away."

—John Wayne lecturing Forrest Tucker in Allan Dwan's *Sands of Iwo Jima* (*Screenplay by Harry Brown and James Edward Grant; based on a story by Harry Brown*)

ALSO SEE: Wrong; Kindness-4; Life and Death-1; Loneliness-15; Love-25; Suicide-8.

MONEY

1.

"Look down there. Would you really feel any pity if one of those dots stopped moving forever? If I offered you 20,000 pounds for every dot that stopped, would you really, old man, tell me to keep my money or would you calculate how many dots you could afford to spare? Free of income tax, old man, free of income tax—it's the only way to save money nowadays."

—Orson Welles tempting Joseph Cotten during their Ferris-wheel ride in Carol Reed's *The Third Man* (*Original Screenplay by Graham Greene*)

2.

"Bloom, do me a favor. Move a few decimal points around. You can do it. You're an accountant. You're in a noble profession. The word count is part of your title."

—Zero Mostel pleading for some shady accounting from Gene Wilder in Mel Brooks's *The Producers* (*Original Screenplay by Mel Brooks*)

3.

"I've just been going over last month's bills, and I find that you people have confused me with the treasury department."

—Eugene Pallette discussing the family finances with his scatterbrained clan in Gregory La Cava's *My Man Godfrey* (*Screenplay by Morrie Ryskind, Eric Hatch and Gregory La Cava; based on TEN ELEVEN FIFTH, a novel by Eric Hatch*)

4.

"Anybody who builds a house today is crazy. The minute you start, they put you on the list —the All-American Sucker list. You start out to build a home, and you wind up in the poor house. And, if it can happen to me, what about the fellows who aren't making $15,000 a year? What about the kids who just got married and want a home of their own? It's a conspiracy, I tell you—a conspiracy against every boy and girl who were ever in love."

—Cary Grant raging over expenses in H. C. Potter's *Mr. Blandings Builds His Dream House* (*Screenplay by Norman Panama and Melvin Frank; based on the novel by Eric Hodgins*)

5.

"It costs money to love. If *he* loved you, why didn't he take you out of this hole? A girl as beautiful as you should have the best—jewels, furs, a fine apartment. I'll get 'em for you!"

—Zachary Scott promising Faye Emerson better things in Jean Negulesco's *The Mask of Dimitrios* (*Screenplay by Frank Gruber; based on A COFFIN FOR DIMITRIOS, a novel by Eric Ambler*)

6.

"You can be young without money, but you can't be old without it."

—Elizabeth Taylor being wistfully philosophic with her husband (Paul Newman) in Richard Brooks's *Cat on a Hot Tin Roof* (*Screenplay by Richard Brooks and James Poe; based on the play by Tennessee Williams*)

7.

(a) "Money isn't all, you know, Jett."
    (b) "Not when you got it."

—(a) Elizabeth Taylor and (b) James Dean discussing the subject from different sides of the economic fence in George Stevens's *Giant* (*Screenplay by Fred Guiol and Ivan Moffat; based on the novel by Edna Ferber*)

8.

"Money talks, they say. All it ever said to me was 'good-bye.'"

—Cary Grant being flip about finances in Clifford Odets's *None But the Lonely Heart* (*Screenplay by Clifford Odets; based on the novel by Richard Llewellyn*)

9.

"We had some money put aside for a rainy day, but we didn't know it was going to get this wet."

—Jane Connell presenting a Christmas present of money which she and George Chiang saved for their

suddenly impoverished employer (Lucille Ball) in Gene Saks's *Mame*
(Screenplay by Paul Zindel; based on the musical play by Jerome Lawrence, Robert E. Lee and Jerry Herman and AUNTIE MAME, a play by Jerome Lawrence and Robert Lee and novel by Patrick Dennis)

10.
(a) "Son, never loan money to a church. As soon as you start to close in on them, everybody thinks you're a heel."
  (b) "Well, aren't you?"
  (a) "Yes."

—(a) Gene Lockhart and (b) James Brown coming up with opposing opinions about Barry Fitzgerald's church in Leo McCarey's *Going My Way*
(Screenplay by Frank Butler and Frank Cavett; based on an original story by Leo McCarey)

11.
"I want to tell you all that the reason for my success as a sergeant is due primarily to my previous training in the Cornbelt Loan & Trust Company. The knowledge I acquired in the good old bank I applied to my problems in the infantry. For instance, one day in Okinawa, a major comes up to me, and he says, 'Stephenson, you see that hill?' 'Yes, sir, I see it.' 'All right,' he said, 'you and your platoon will attack said hill and take it.' So I said to the major, 'But that operation involves considerable risk. We haven't sufficient collateral.' 'I'm aware of that,' said the major, 'but the fact remains that there is the hill and you are the guys who are going to take it.' So I said to him, 'I'm sorry, Major. No collateral, no hill.' So we didn't take the hill, and we lost the war."

—Fredric March springing a cynical anecdote on his banking associates in William Wyler's *The Best Years of Our Lives*
(Screenplay by Robert E. Sherwood; based on GLORY FOR ME, a verse novel by MacKinlay Kantor)

12.
(a) "I haven't touched a cent of this money, Colonel. Now, now it's all banked in the name of the Tobiki Co-Operative Company. You see, everybody in the village—they're—they're all partners, don't you see? You know? You know, share and share alike."
  (b) "That's communism!"

—(b) Paul Ford fuming at the brand of capitalism which (a) Glenn Ford has brought to postwar Okinawans in Daniel Mann's *The Teahouse of the August Moon*
(Screenplay by John Patrick; based on his play and the book by Vern J. Sneider)

13.
"Ah, this is beginning to make sense—in a screwy sort of way. I get dragged in and get money shoved at me. I get pushed out and get money shoved at me. Everybody pushes me in, and everybody pushes me out. Nobody wants me to do anything. Okay. Put a check in the mail. I cost a lot not to do anything. I get restless. Throw in a trip to Mexico."

—Dick Powell agreeing to play (for pay) the detective nobody wants in Edward Dmytryk's *Murder, My Sweet*
(Screenplay by John Paxton; based on FAREWELL, MY LOVELY, a novel by Raymond Chandler)

14.
"Money seems to have lost its value these days. With $200,000 my grandfather cornered the wheat market and started a panic in Omaha. Today, you can't even frighten songwriters with it."

—Tony Randall nudging a Broadway score out of Rock Hudson in Michael Gordon's *Pillow Talk*
(Screenplay by Stanley Shapiro and Maurice Richlin; based on a story by Russell Rouse and Clarence Greene)

15.
"Sentiment has no cash value."

—John Baer being the dry-eyed skinflint in Michael Curtiz's *We're No Angels*
(Screenplay by Ranald MacDougall; based on LA CUISINE DES ANGES, a play by Albert Husson, and MY THREE ANGELS, a Broadway adaptation by Bella Spewack and Samuel Spewack)

16.
"The sentiment comes easily at 50 cents a word."

—Clifton Webb explaining his prime mover as a writer in Otto Preminger's *Laura*
(Screenplay by Jay Dratler, Samuel Hoffenstein and Betty Reinhardt; based on the novel by Vera Caspary)

17.
"Imagine! Charging $1.20 just to ride to the top of an old building."

—Maggie McNamara carping about the Empire State Building fare in the last line of Otto Preminger's *The Moon Is Blue*
(Screenplay by F. Hugh Herbert; based on his play)

18.
"You're right, Mr. Thatcher. I did lose a million dollars last year. I expect to lose a million dollars this year. I expect to lose a million dollars next year. You know, Mr. Thatcher, at the rate of a million dollars a year, I'll have to close this place—in 60 years."

—Orson Welles remaining a newspaper publisher, against the advice of George Coulouris, in Orson Welles's *Citizen Kane*
(Original Screenplay by Herman J. Mankiewicz and Orson Welles)

ALSO SEE: Poverty; Wealth; Beliefs-3; Blood-5; Dying Words-5; Eyes-9; Floozy-3; Furnishings-2; Gigolo-5; Help-1; Home-8; Humility-4; Land-3; Life-1; Looks-8; Love Objects-4; Men-17; Never-11; Pretense-2; Pride-9; Secrets-3; Sin-5; Smell-11; Soul-1; Spiders-3; Static-12; Success-2; Success-3; Toasts-14; Window-6.

MOOD-BREAKERS

1.
"What a story! Everything but the bloodhounds snappin' at her rear end!"

—Thelma Ritter reacting glibly to Anne Baxter's tale of woe in Joseph L. Mankiewicz's *All About Eve*

(Screenplay by Joseph L. Mankiewicz; based on "The Wisdom of Eve," a radio play and short story by Mary Orr)

2.
"Who writes your material for you? Charles Dickens?"

—Jason Robards countering the news that he must surrender his nephew (Barry Gordon) for adoption in Fred Coe's *A Thousand Clowns*
(Screenplay by Herb Gardner; based on his play)

3.
"Tell me, did you write the song, 'I'll Never Smile Again'?"

—Cary Grant breaking the ice with Deborah Kerr in Leo McCarey's *An Affair To Remember*
(Screenplay by Delmer Daves and Leo McCarey; based on an original story by Mildred Cram and Leo McCarey)

MOON

1.
(a) "And will you be happy, Charlotte?"
    (b) "Oh, Jerry, don't let's ask for the moon. We have the stars."

—(a) Paul Henreid and (b) Bette Davis reaching a romantic understanding in the last lines of Irving Rapper's *Now, Voyager*
(Screenplay by Casey Robinson; based on the novel by Olive Higgins Prouty)

2.
"What is it you want, Mary? What do you want? You—you want the moon? Just say the word, and I'll throw a lasso around it and pull it down. Hey, that's a pretty good idea. I'll give you the moon, Mary."

—James Stewart sweet-talking Donna Reed in Frank Capra's *It's a Wonderful Life*
(Screenplay by Albert Hackett, Frances Goodrich and Frank Capra; based on "The Greatest Gift," a short story by Philip Van Doren Stern)

3.
"It must be a marvelous supper. We may not

eat it, but it must be marvelous. And, waiter, you see that moon? I want to see that moon in the champagne."

—Herbert Marshall giving supper instructions in Ernst Lubitsch's *Trouble in Paradise*
(Screenplay by Grover Jones and Samson Raphaelson; based on THE HONEST FINDER, a play by Laszlo Aladar)

4.
"I wanted to marry her when I saw the moonlight shining on the barrel of her father's shotgun."

—Eddie Albert citing his sudden matrimonial incentive in Fred Zinnemann's *Oklahoma!*
(Screenplay by Sonya Levien and William Ludwig; based on the musical play by Oscar Hammerstein II and GREEN GROW THE LILACS, a play by Lynn Riggs)

5.
"I'm really awfully glad you came, and I'm not going to say good-bye to you here in the moonlight. It would just be too touching."

—Elizabeth Taylor saying good night to Rock Hudson in George Stevens's *Giant*
(Screenplay by Fred Guiol and Ivan Moffat; based on the novel by Edna Ferber)

6.
"Even the man who is pure in heart
And says his prayers by night
May become a wolf when the wolf bane blooms
And the moon is full and bright."

—Maria Ouspenskaya chanting away in George Waggner's *The Wolf Man*
(Screenplay by Kurt Siodmak and Gordon Kahn; based on a story by Kurt Siodmak)

7.
(a) "You don't understand. Every night, when the moon is full, I turn into a wolf."
   (b) "You and 50 million other guys!"

—(b) Lou Costello misreading the admission of (a) Lon Chaney, Jr., in Charles T. Barton's *Abbott and Costello Meet Frankenstein*
(Original Screenplay by Robert Lees, Frederic I. Rinaldo and John Grant)

8.
"Just think—tonight, tonight when the moon is sneaking around the clouds, I'll be sneaking around you. I'll meet you tonight under the moon. Oh, I can see you now—you and the moon. You wear a necktie so I'll know you."

—Groucho Marx romancing Margaret Dumont in Joseph Santley and Robert Florey's *The Cocoanuts*
(Screenplay by Morrie Ryskind; based on the musical play by George S. Kaufman and Morrie Ryskind)

ALSO SEE: Memory-2; Prologues-5; Propositions-5; Rejection-8; Sleep-1.

MOTHERS

1.
"My mother—a waitress!"

—Ann Blyth gasping at the truth about Joan Crawford in Michael Curtiz's *Mildred Pierce*
(Screenplay by Ranald MacDougall; based on the novel by James M. Cain)

2.
"As for you, Mother, I love you very much—but my address is Paris, France."

—Audrey Dalton choosing her father (Clifton Webb) and Europe over her mother (Barbara Stanwyck) and the U.S. in Jean Negulesco's *Titanic*
(Original Screenplay by Charles Brackett, Walter Reisch and Richard L. Breen)

3.
"You mustn't kid Mother, dear. I was a married woman before you were born."

—Lucile Watson counseling Norma Shearer in George Cukor's *The Women*
(Screenplay by Anita Loos and Jane Murfin; based on the play by Clare Boothe)

4.
"If my father was the head of our house, my mother was its heart."

—Irving Pichel, as the never-seen narrator (a grown-up version of Roddy McDowall), recalling

Sara Allgood in John Ford's *How Green Was My Valley*
(Screenplay by Philip Dunne; based on the novel by Richard Llewellyn)

5.
"My mother—what you say about her—she was a woman, a servant-woman who worked hard. She was a hard-working woman, and it is not fair—not fair—what you say. Here. I want to show you—I have her pic—her picture. I would like you looked at it. I would like you to judge. I want that you tell me. Was she feebleminded? My mother. Was she feebleminded?"

—Montgomery Clift pleading on the witness stand in Stanley Kramer's *Judgment at Nuremberg*
(Screenplay by Abby Mann; based on his teleplay)

6.
"My mother's a Jezebel. She's so overloaded with sex that it sparkles! She's golden and striped like something in the jungle!"

—Hayley Mills characterizing Elizabeth Sellars to Deborah Kerr in Ronald Neame's *The Chalk Garden*
(Screenplay by John Michael Hayes; based on the play by Enid Bagnold)

7.
"I put a crimp in her career. It slows her down, having a growing boy around the house, but that's all right because she gives me two big weeks a year at home—Christmas and Easter— plus an autographed picture of herself for my birthday, signed 'Sincerely, Gertrude Vanderhof.' It comes out of the studio mailing room. It seems they've got me mixed up with one of her fans."

—Lee Kinsolving telling Shirley Knight about his movie-star mom in Delbert Mann's *The Dark at the Top of the Stairs*
(Screenplay by Irving Ravetch and Harriet Frank, Jr.; based on the play by William Inge)

8.
"Tonight she belongs to me! Tonight I want her to call me mother!"

—Bette Davis planning to claim her now-grown illegitimate daughter (Jane Bryan) in Edmund Goulding's *The Old Maid*
(Screenplay by Casey Robinson; based on the play by Zoë Akins and novel by Edith Wharton)

9.
"You've been alone so much, Belinda, but you're not going to be alone anymore. You're going to be a mother."

—Lew Ayres breaking the news to Jane Wyman in Jean Negulesco's *Johnny Belinda*
(Screenplay by Irmgard Von Cube and Allen Vincent; based on the play by Elmer Harris)

10.
"A boy's best friend is his mother."

—Anthony Perkins advancing his opinion to Janet Leigh in Alfred Hitchcock's *Psycho*
(Screenplay by Joseph Stefano; based on the novel by Robert Bloch)

ALSO SEE: Advice-7; Advice-9; Compromise-2; Dance-8; Daughters-2; Dictation-6; Dress-5; Drunken Rantings-7; Dying Words-8; Dying Words-9; Dying Words-10; Excuses-3; Good-8; Hate-8; Identity Crisis-3; Lady-4; Land-2; Letters-6; Lies-3; Mad Act-12; Names-11; Public Relations-4; Remember-1; Smell-2; Sons-1; Sons-3; Soul-15; Spinsters-7; Telegrams-4.

MOVIES

1.
"Those movies you were in! It's sacrilege, throwing you away on things like that. When I left that movie house, I felt some magnificent ruby had been thrown into a platter of lard. You set yourself back ten years—but we can mend all that. You'll be greater than ever, Lily Garland!"

—John Barrymore luring Carole Lombard off the screen and back to the stage in Howard Hawks's *Twentieth Century*
(Screenplay by Ben Hecht and Charles MacArthur; based on their play and NAPOLEON OF BROADWAY, a play by Charles Bruce Milholland)

2.

"Oh, boys, I've had it! I've really had it. *The Girl From the Sleepy Lagoon, The Cowboy and the Mermaid, Neptune's Mother.* I never got a chance to dry off. No, from now on, I am just going to swim socially."

—Janis Paige telling the press she's through with underwater musicals in Rouben Mamoulian's *Silk Stockings*
(Screenplay by Leonard Gershe and Leonard Spigelgass; based on the musical play by George S. Kaufman, Leueen MacGrath and Abe Burrows and NINOTCHKA, a screenplay by Charles Brackett, Billy Wilder and Walter Reisch, and original story by Melchior Lengyel)

3.

"I don't like the way this script of ours is turning out. It's turning into a seedy little drama. Middle-aged man leaves wife and family for young heartless woman, goes to pot. *The Blue Angel* with Marlene Dietrich and Emil Jannings. I—I don't like it."

—Faye Dunaway complaining about her affair with William Holden in Sidney Lumet's *Network*
(Original Screenplay by Paddy Chayefsky)

4.

"Ed hates anything that keeps him from going to the movies every night. I guess I'm what you call a Garbo widow."

—Louise Closser Hale characterizing her husband (Grant Mitchell) to Billie Burke in George Cukor's *Dinner at Eight*
(Screenplay by Frances Marion and Herman J. Mankiewicz; based on the play by George S. Kaufman and Edna Ferber)

ALSO SEE: Screenplays; Big-1; Directors-2; Drink Orders-4; Innocent-2; Last Lines-1; Life-7; Life-8; Mad Act-2; Pity-8; Producers-2; Sex-6; Together-5; Wrong-4.

MURDER

1.

"I can't get you out of this, Veda."

—Joan Crawford confronting Ann Blyth over Zachary Scott's corpse in Michael Curtiz's *Mildred Pierce*
(Screenplay by Ranald MacDougall; based on the novel by James M. Cain)

2.

"Well, I guess I've done murder. Oh, I won't think about that now. I'll think about that tomorrow."

—Vivien Leigh pondering the Yankee looter (Paul Hurst) she has gunned down in Victor Fleming's *Gone With the Wind*
(Screenplay by Sidney Howard; based on the novel by Margaret Mitchell)

3.

"We'll start with a few murders—big man, little man—just to show we make no distinction."

—Claude Rains plotting his mayhem democratically in James Whale's *The Invisible Man*
(Screenplay by R. C. Sherriff; based on the novel by H. G. Wells)

4.

"Well, what would you fellas say to an assassination? I think I can get the Mao Tse-tung people to kill Beale for us as one of his shows. In fact, it'd make a helluvah kickoff show for the season. We're facing heavy opposition on the other networks for Wednesday nights, and 'The Mao Tse-tung Hour' could use a sensational opener. It could be done right on camera in the studio. We ought to get a fantastic look-in audience for the assassination of Howard Beale as our opening show."

—Faye Dunaway "booking" Peter Finch's murder in Sidney Lumet's *Network*
(Original Screenplay by Paddy Chayefsky)

5.

"Young lady, there's no overlooking the fact that murder is at our doorstep, so I wish you wouldn't drag it into the living room."

—Leo G. Carroll objecting to the enthusiasm of his daughter (Patricia Hitchcock) about Laura Elliot's murder in Alfred Hitchcock's *Strangers on a Train* *(Screenplay by Raymond Chandler and Czenzi Ormonde; adaptation by Whitfield Cook; based on the novel by Patricia Highsmith)*

6.
"If it wasn't for me, you'd still be rolling drunks at the Silver Slipper. I made you rich. I put those swell clothes on your back. Now, just because you got your neck washed, you think you're a gentleman. No one can make you that. You're riffraff, and so am I. You belong to me, and you'll stay with me. You bet you're going to stay with me because I'm holding on to you. Why, I committed murder to get you."

—Bette Davis confessing the extent of her love for Paul Muni in Archie Mayo's *Bordertown* *(Screenplay by Laird Doyle and Wallace Smith; adaptation by Robert Lord; based on the novel by Carroll Graham)*

7.
"If it weren't for me, you'd still be kicking trucks up and down the coast. I get Ed to take you off the road. I put that clean collar around your dirty neck. I put those creases in your pants. I'm the one that put the money in your pocket. What makes you think you can walk out on me? . . . Well, you're not getting out. You belong with me, and you're going to stay with me. And, if you don't like it now, you'll learn to like it—only you're not going off and marrying that cheap redhead. . . . She hasn't any right to you. You're mine, and I'm hanging on to you. I committed murder to get you. Understand? Murder!"

—Ida Lupino confessing the extent of her love for George Raft in Raoul Walsh's *They Drive by Night* *(Screenplay by Jerry Wald and Richard Macaulay; based on LONG HAUL, a novel by A. I. Bezzerides)*

8.
"People don't commit murder on credit."

—Ray Milland explaining how he couldn't have hired a wife-killer in Alfred Hitchcock's *Dial M for Murder* *(Screenplay by Frederick Knott; based on his play)*

9.
"People don't kill reasonably. They kill unreasonably, passionately."

—Deborah Kerr speaking from personal experience to John Mills in Ronald Neame's *The Chalk Garden* *(Screenplay by John Michael Hayes; based on the play by Enid Bagnold)*

10.
"This wasn't surgery. It was murder."

—Robert Donat blaming Cecil Parker for fatally blundering Ralph Richardson's operation in King Vidor's *The Citadel* *(Screenplay by Ian Dalrymple, Frank Wead and Elizabeth Hill; additional dialogue by Emlyn Williams; based on the novel by A. J. Cronin)*

11.
"She will be removed from the hospital there and operated on. Unfortunately, the operation will not be successful. Oh, I should perhaps have explained. The operation will be performed by me."

—Paul Lukas showing his hand to Michael Redgrave and Margaret Lockwood in *The Lady Vanishes* *(Screenplay by Sidney Gilliat and Frank Launder; based on THE WHEEL SPINS, a novel by Ethel Lina White)*

12.
"You're an excellent analyst, Dr. Petersen. But a rather stupid woman. What did you think I'd do—when you told me all this? Congratulate you? You forget—in your imbecilic devotion to your patient—that the punishment for two murders is the same as for one."

—Leo G. Carroll showing his hand to Ingrid Bergman in Alfred Hitchcock's *Spellbound* *(Screenplay by Ben Hecht; adaptation by Angus MacPhail; based on THE HOUSE OF DR. EDWARDES, a novel by Francis Beeding)*

ALSO SEE: Always-6; Amateur-1; Detectives-1; Detectives-2; Detectives-3; Dictation-5; Differences-10; Exchanges-1; First Lines-5; Heart-17; Heart-18; Identity Crisis-3; Lady-5; Letters-12; Mad Act-12; Mistakes-1; People-4; Privacy-3; Questions-2; Right-5; Telephone

Scenes-11; Trouble-5; Unfeeling-2; Violence-6; Why-10.

MUSIC

1.
"Music opens up new worlds for me, draws back the veil from new delights. I can see Olympus, and a breeze blows on me from the olive fields. And in those moments I, a god, feel as diminutive as dust."

—Peter Ustinov parading his artistic pretenses in Mervyn LeRoy's *Quo Vadis*
(Screenplay by John Lee Mahin, S. N. Behrman and Sonya Levien; based on the novel by Henryk Sienkiewicz)

2.
(a) "What's that?"
  (b) "Sounds to me like mice."
  (a) "Mice? Mice don't play music."
  (b) "No? How about the old maestro?"

—(a) Margaret Dumont and (b) Groucho Marx responding to a radio blasting a Sousa march in Leo McCarey's *Duck Soup*
(Screenplay by Bert Kalmar and Harry Ruby; additional dialogue by Arthur Sheekman and Nat Perrin)

3.
"You brought music back into the house. I'd forgotten."

—Christopher Plummer thanking Julie Andrews in Robert Wise's *The Sound of Music*
(Screenplay by Ernest Lehman; based on the musical play by Howard Lindsay and Russel Crouse and THE TRAPP FAMILY SINGERS, a book by Maria Augusta Trapp)

4.
"Music is essential for parades."

—Cyd Charisse allowing that music has its place in Rouben Mamoulian's *Silk Stockings*
(Screenplay by Leonard Gershe and Leonard Spigelgass; based on the musical play by George S. Kaufman, Leueen MacGrath and Abe Burrows and NINOTCHKA, a screenplay by Charles Brackett, Billy Wilder and Walter Reisch, and original story by Melchior Lengyel)

5.
"The German people love to sing, no matter what the situation."

—Marlene Dietrich making a nationalistic observation to Spencer Tracy in Stanley Kramer's *Judgment at Nuremberg*
(Screenplay by Abby Mann; based on his teleplay)

6.
"For me, a little German music goes a long way."

—Simone Signoret admitting a low threshold to Oskar Werner in Stanley Kramer's *Ship of Fools*
(Screenplay by Abby Mann; based on the novel by Katherine Anne Porter)

7.
"Someone would strike up a song, and the valley would ring with the sound of many voices —for singing is in my people as sight is in the eye."

—Irving Pichel, as the never-seen narrator (a grown-up version of Roddy McDowall) reminiscing in John Ford's *How Green Was My Valley*
(Screenplay by Philip Dunne; based on the novel by Richard Llewellyn)

8.
"Listen to them. Children of the night. What music they make."

—Bela Lugosi admiring the howls of wolves in Tod Browning's *Dracula*
(Screenplay by Garrett Fort; based on the play by Hamilton Deane and John L. Balderston and novel by Bram Stoker)
                    and
—Frank Langella dittoing in the remake, John Badham's *Dracula*
(Screenplay by W. D. Richter; based on the play by Hamilton Deane and John L. Balderston and novel by Bram Stoker)

ALSO SEE: Cruel-1; Curtain Speeches-5; Pleasures-6; Priorities-6; Religions-3.

NAMES

1.

"From now on, they'll spell mutiny with my name."

—Clark Gable accepting his place in history in Frank Lloyd's *Mutiny on the Bounty*
(Screenplay by Talbot Jennings, Jules Furthman and Carey Wilson; based on the novel by Charles Nordhoff and James Norman Hall)

2.

"There is no escape from the *Caine,* save death. We're all doing penance, sentenced to an outcast ship, manned by outcasts, and named after the greatest outcast of them all."

—Fred MacMurray preaching dissension in Edward Dmytryk's *The Caine Mutiny*
(Screenplay by Stanley Roberts; additional dialogue by Michael Blankfort; based on the novel by Herman Wouk)

3.

"The Venus flytrap—a devouring organism, aptly named for the goddess of love."

—Katharine Hepburn advancing her dark view of love while giving Montgomery Clift a tour of her garden in Joseph L. Mankiewicz's *Suddenly, Last Summer*
(Screenplay by Gore Vidal and Tennessee Williams; based on the one-act play by Tennessee Williams)

4.

(a) "Rose?"
  (b) "How did you know my name?"
  (a) "What other name could it be?"

—(a) Ben Cooper meeting and flattering (b) Marisa Pavan in Daniel Mann's *The Rose Tattoo*
(Screenplay by Tennessee Williams; adaptation by Hal Kanter; based on the play by Tennessee Williams)

5.

"Oh, stop calling me Lorene. My name's Alma. . . . Yes, Alma Burke. . . . Mrs. Kipfer picked Lorene out of a perfume ad. She thought it sounded French."

—Donna Reed leveling with Montgomery Clift in Fred Zinnemann's *From Here to Eternity*
(Screenplay by Daniel Taradash; based on the novel by James Jones)

6.

"It's a French name. It means woods, and Blanche means white, so the two together means white woods. Like an orchard in spring. You can remember it by that, if you care to."

—Vivien Leigh playing the coquette for Karl Malden in Elia Kazan's *A Streetcar Named Desire*
(Screenplay by Tennessee Williams; adaptation by Oscar Saul; based on the play by Tennessee Williams)

7.

"Do you know what Quick means in this country? Hellfire. Ashes and char. Flames follow that man around like a dog. He's a barn burner!"

—Orson Welles spreading the word about Paul Newman in Martin Ritt's *The Long, Hot Summer*
(Screenplay by Irving Ravetch and Harriet Frank Jr.; based on THE HAMLET, a novel by William Faulkner, and "Barn Burning" and "The Spotted Horses," two short stories by William Faulkner)

8.

"You know what name I was born with? Smith. Smith, for the love of Mike, Smith. Now, what kind of name is that for a fella like me? I need a name with the whole sky in it and the power of a man. Star—buck. Now, there's a name, and it's mine!"

—Burt Lancaster explaining his name creation to Katharine Hepburn in Joseph Anthony's *The Rainmaker*
(Screenplay by N. Richard Nash; based on his play)

9.

"Physical ed? Who's he?"

—Spencer Tracy misreading Katharine Hepburn's credentials in George Cukor's *Pat and Mike*
(Original Screenplay by Ruth Gordon and Garson Kanin)

10.

(a) "Hey, Jenny, you won't laugh?"

(b) "What?"

(a) "I'm actually getting to like the name Bozo."

(b) "For what?"

(a) "For our kid, dammit. Our huge and bruising All-Ivy tackle."

(b) "Bozo Barrett?"

(a) "Jenny, it's the name of a real Harvard superjock."

(b) "You would actually call our soon-to-be-conceived offspring Bozo?"

(a) "Only if he's a boy."

—(a) Ryan O'Neal and (b) Ali MacGraw battling about names for their first-born in Arthur Hiller's *Love Story*
(*Original Screenplay by Erich Segal*)

11.

"I wonder how a mother could call a boy Florenz."

—Kay Medford pondering the cross Walter Pidgeon has borne in William Wyler's *Funny Girl*
(*Screenplay by Isobel Lennart; based on her musical play*)

12.

"I made a deal with him when he was six, up to which time he was known rather casually as Chubby, that he could use whatever name he wished, for however long he wished until his 13th birthday at which time he'd have to pick a name he liked permanently. Now, he went through a long period of dogs' names, when he was little, 'King' and 'Rover' having a real vogue there for a while. For three months, he referred to himself as 'Big Sam,' then there was Little Max, Snoopy, Chip, Rock, Rex, Mike, Martin, Lamont, Chev—Chevrolet, Woodrow, Lefty, The Phantom. He received his library card last year in the name of Rafael Sabatini; his cub scout membership lists him as Dr. Morris Fishbein. 'Nick' seems to be the one that'll stick."

—Jason Robards reciting the name history of his nephew (Barry Gordon) in Fred Coe's *A Thousand Clowns*
(*Screenplay by Herb Gardner; based on his play*)

13.

"You must have been born with that name. You couldn't have made it up."

—James Mason responding to meeting Esther Blodgett (Judy Garland) in George Cukor's *A Star Is Born*
(*Screenplay by Moss Hart; based on a screenplay by Dorothy Parker, Alan Campbell and Robert Carson and original story by William A. Wellman and Robert Carson*)

14.

"Madame A. Anderson. The least real thing about me is my legal reality."

—Ingrid Bergman musing over her forged passport in Anatole Litvak's *Anastasia*
(*Screenplay by Arthur Laurents; based on the play by Marcelle Maurette and Broadway adaptation by Guy Bolton*)

15.

"Please don't call me Mr. de Winter. I have a very impressive array of first names: George Fortescue Maximilian. But you needn't bother with them all at once. My family call me Maxim."

—Laurence Olivier struggling to be unstuffy with Joan Fontaine in Alfred Hitchcock's *Rebecca*
(*Screenplay by Robert E. Sherwood and Joan Harrison; adaptation by Philip MacDonald and Michael Hogan; based on the novel by Daphne du Maurier*)

16.

(a) "You collect shells?"

(b) "Yes. So did my father and my grandfather. You might say we had a passion for shells. That's why we named the oil company after it."

(a) "Shell Oil?"

(b) "Please, no names. Just call me Junior."

—(b) Tony Curtis coming on rich to (a) Marilyn Monroe in Billy Wilder's *Some Like It Hot*
(*Screenplay by Billy Wilder and I.A.L. Diamond; suggested by a story by R. Thoeren and M. Logan*)

17.

(a) "And I shall call you Lucia."

(b) "My name is Lucy."

(a) "It doesn't do you justice, my dear. Women named Lucy are always being imposed upon, but Lucia! Now, there's a name for an Amazon, for a queen."

—(a) Rex Harrison renaming (b) Gene Tierney in Joseph L. Mankiewicz's *The Ghost and Mrs. Muir* (*Screenplay by Philip Dunne; based on* THE GHOST OF CAPTAIN GREGG AND MRS. MUIR, *a novel by R. A. Dick*)

18.
"Philip Marlowe—name for a duke. You're just a nice mug."

—Claire Trevor confronting Dick Powell in Edward Dmytryk's *Murder, My Sweet* (*Screenplay by John Paxton; based on* FAREWELL, MY LOVELY, *a novel by Raymond Chandler*)

19.
"Ma'am, I sure like that name—Clementine."

—Henry Fonda bidding good-bye to Cathy Downs in the last line of John Ford's *My Darling Clementine* (*Screenplay by Samuel G. Engel and Winston Miller; based on a story by Sam Hellman and* WYATT EARP, FRONTIER MARSHAL, *a book by Stuart N. Lake*)

20.
"Shapeley's the name, and that's the way I like 'em."

—Roscoe Karns coming on too strong to Claudette Colbert in Frank Capra's *It Happened One Night* (*Screenplay by Robert Riskin; based on "Night Bus," a short story by Samuel Hopkins Adams*)

21.
"Whenever I run across a funny name, I like to poke around for a rhyme. Don't you?"

—Gary Cooper explaining his eccentricity to Lionel Stander in Frank Capra's *Mr. Deeds Goes to Town* (*Screenplay by Robert Riskin; based on "Opera Hat," a short story by Clarence Budington Kelland*)

22.
"Why do you always make jokes about my name? In Chile, the name of O'Hara is—is a tip-top name. Many Germans in Chile have become to be called O'Hara."

—Peter Lorre getting defensive with Humphrey Bogart in John Huston's *Beat the Devil* (*Screenplay by John Huston and Truman Capote; based on the novel by James Helvick*)

23.
"Good name! Look, nobody has a good name in a bad house. Nobody has a good name in a silly house, either."

—Ray Collins shrugging off Tim Holt's fear of gossip in Orson Welles's *The Magnificent Ambersons* (*Screenplay by Orson Welles; based on the novel by Booth Tarkington*)

24.
"Robert E. Lee Prewitt. Isn't that a silly old name?"

—Donna Reed lamenting Montgomery Clift to Deborah Kerr in the last lines of Fred Zinnemann's *From Here to Eternity* (*Screenplay by Daniel Taradash; based on the novel by James Jones*)

25.
"Honest, sensible, sober, harmless Holly Martins. Holly—what a silly name. You must feel very proud to be a police informer."

—Valli ridiculing Joseph Cotten for betraying a mutual friend (Orson Welles) in Carol Reed's *The Third Man* (*Original Screenplay by Graham Greene*)

26.
"May I call you Christine? Oh, I'm quite aware you come from a high level of society. You probably made a debut, all that. I always considered Christine a gentle name. Hortense sounds fat. Hortense! 'My girl Hortense,' they used to say to me, 'hasn't got much sense. Put her name on the privy fence.'"

—Eileen Heckart boozily getting chummy with Nancy Kelly in Mervyn LeRoy's *The Bad Seed* (*Screenplay by John Lee Mahin; based on the play by Maxwell Anderson and novel by William March*)

27.

"I hope you're going to tell me your name. I want you to be my first friend in New York. Mine's Eva Lovelace. It's partly made up and partly real. It was Ada Love. Love is my family name. I added the 'lace.' Do you like it, or would you prefer something shorter? A shorter name would be more convenient on a sign. Still, 'Eva Lovelace in *Camille*,' for instance, or 'Eva Lovelace in *Romeo and Juliet*' sounds very distinguished, doesn't it?"

—Katharine Hepburn meeting C. Aubrey Smith in Lowell Sherman's *Morning Glory*
(Screenplay by Howard J. Green; based on the play by Zoë Akins)

ALSO SEE: Introductions; Fake-4; Mad Act-6; Promiscuity-1.

NARCISSISM

1.

"Hey, don't knock masturbation. It's sex with someone I love."

—Woody Allen doing one of his campus comedy routines in Woody Allen's *Annie Hall*
(Original Screenplay by Woody Allen and Marshall Brickman)

2.

"It would take a great woman to make Crassus fall out of love with himself."

—Charles Laughton questioning Jean Simmons's powers on Laurence Olivier in Stanley Kubrick's *Spartacus*
(Screenplay by Dalton Trumbo; based on the novel by Howard Fast)

3.

"Not interested in yourself? You're fascinated, Red. You're far and away your favorite person in the world."

—Cary Grant telling Katharine Hepburn not to pretend otherwise in George Cukor's *The Philadelphia Story*
(Screenplay by Donald Ogden Stewart; based on the play by Philip Barry)

4.

"In my case, self-absorption is completely justified. I have never discovered any other subject quite so worthy of my attention."

—Clifton Webb being shamelessly candid about it in Otto Preminger's *Laura*
(Screenplay by Jay Dratler, Samuel Hoffenstein and Betty Reinhardt; based on the novel by Vera Caspary)

5.

"Easy, folks. It's only me. *Only me?* That's the understatement of the year."

—Bob Hope making his entrance out West in Frank Tashlin's *Son of Paleface*
(Original Screenplay by Frank Tashlin, Robert L. Welch and Joseph Quillan)

6.

"Don't tell me how you are, Sherry. I want none of the tiresome details. I've very little time, and so the conversation will be entirely about me, and I shall love it. Shall I tell you how I glittered through the South Seas like a silver scimitar, or would you rather hear how I finished a three-act play with one hand and made love to a maharaja's daughter with the other?"

—Reginald Gardiner making his entrance on Monty Woolley's turf in William Keighley's *The Man Who Came to Dinner*
(Screenplay by Julius J. Epstein and Philip G. Epstein; based on the play by George S. Kaufman and Moss Hart)

7.

"You've been all over the world, and you've met all kinds of people—but you never write about them. You only write about yourself. You think this whole war's a show put on for you to cover like a Broadway play, and, if enough people die before the last act, maybe you might give it four stars."

—John Hodiak criticizing Tallulah Bankhead's first-person-first brand of journalism in Alfred Hitchcock's *Lifeboat*
(Screenplay by Jo Swerling; based on the story by John Steinbeck)

8.

"Your love affair with yourself has reached heroic proportions. It doesn't seem to leave much room for me. Are you sure you can get along without somebody to help you admire yourself?"

—Joan Crawford telling off Van Heflin in Curtis Bernhardt's *Possessed*
(Screenplay by Sylvia Richards and Ranald MacDougall; based on ONE MAN'S SECRET, a novelette by Rita Weiman)

ALSO SEE: Changes-5; Love-30.

NATURE

1.

"Nature, Mr. Allnut, is what we are put into this world to rise above."

—Katharine Hepburn putting Humphrey Bogart in his place in John Huston's *The African Queen*
(Screenplay by James Agee and John Huston; based on the novel by C. S. Forester)

2.

"Do I know human nature? Look, didn't I say that fella Quick was made for my Clara? Am I going to be a grandfather? I am! Ah, Minnie, it sure is good to be alive this summer evening— yeah, alive with friends and family and a big healthy woman to love you. Come on. I like life, Minnie. Yeah! I like it so much I might just live forever."

—Orson Welles savoring life in the last lines of Martin Ritt's *The Long, Hot Summer*
(Screenplay by Irving Ravetch and Harriet Frank, Jr.; based on THE HAMLET, a novel by William Faulkner, and "Barn Burning" and "The Spotted Horses," two short stories by William Faulkner)

3.

"Nature's far too subtle to repeat herself."

—Paul Muni making an observation at the microscope in William Dieterle's *The Story of Louis Pasteur*
(Screenplay by Sheridan Gibney and Pierre

Collings; based on an original story by Sheridan Gibney and Pierre Collings)

4.

"That's my nature, Godfrey. I never say anything behind your back that I wouldn't say in public."

—Alice Brady explaining her ways to William Powell in Gregory La Cava's *My Man Godfrey*
(Screenplay by Morrie Ryskind, Eric Hatch and Gregory La Cava; based on TEN ELEVEN FIFTH, a novel by Eric Hatch)

5.

"I have an extravagant nature. Surely you've discovered that about me by now."

—Vanessa Redgrave understating her case in Karel Reisz's *Isadora*
(Screenplay by Melvyn Bragg and Clive Exton; additional dialogue by Margaret Drabble; adaptation by Melvyn Bragg; based on the books MY LIFE by Isadora Duncan and ISADORA DUNCAN, AN INTIMATE PORTRAIT by Sewell Stokes)

ALSO SEE: Love-9; Love-27; Macho-5; Macho-12; Promiscuity-3; Static-6.

NECK

1.

"I stick my neck out for nobody. I'm the only cause I'm interested in."

—Humphrey Bogart ducking World War II intrigues in Michael Curtiz's *Casablanca*
(Screenplay by Julius J. Epstein, Philip G. Epstein and Howard Koch; based on EVERYBODY COMES TO RICK'S, a play by Murray Burnett and Joan Alison)

2.

"Well, if you get a good break, you'll be out of Tehachapi in 20 years and you can come back to me then. I hope they don't hang you, precious, by that sweet neck."

—Humphrey Bogart turning in Mary Astor in John Huston's *The Maltese Falcon*

(Screenplay by John Huston; based on the novel by Dashiell Hammett)

3.
(a) "Now, why did you call Gooper's kiddies no-neck monsters?"
    (b) "Because your brother's children got no necks, that's why. . . . Their fat little heads sit on their fat little bodies without a bit of connection."

—(b) Elizabeth Taylor explaining to (a) Paul Newman her insult in Richard Brooks's *Cat on a Hot Tin Roof*
(Screenplay by Richard Brooks and James Poe; based on the play by Tennessee Williams)

ALSO SEE: Duty-4; Guns-11; Quiet-3.

NEVER

1.
"You know, Sherry, you have one great advantage over everyone else in the world. You've never had to meet Sheridan Whiteside."

—Bette Davis pointing up the importance of being Sheridan Whiteside (Monty Woolley) in William Keighley's *The Man Who Came to Dinner*
(Screenplay by Julius J. Epstein and Philip G. Epstein; based on the play by George S. Kaufman and Moss Hart)

2.
"And remember, never let those ruby slippers off your feet for a moment, or you'll be at the mercy of the Wicked Witch of the West."

—Billie Burke warning Judy Garland about Margaret Hamilton in Victor Fleming's *The Wizard of Oz*
(Screenplay by Noel Langley, Florence Ryerson and Edgar Allan Woolf; adaptation by Noel Langley, based on the novel by L. Frank Baum)

3.
"Never trust or love anyone so much you can't betray him."

—Montagu Love, as Henry VIII, giving his son, Prince Edward (Bobby Mauch), a rule to rule by in William Keighley's *The Prince and the Pauper*

(Screenplay by Laird Doyle; based on the novel by Mark Twain)

4.
"Don't forget the old proverb, Doctor: never trust a man who doesn't drink."

—Barry Fitzgerald cautioning Walter Huston in René Clair's *And Then There Were None*
(Screenplay by Dudley Nichols; based on TEN LITTLE INDIANS, a play and novel by Agatha Christie)

5.
"Never mix, never worry."

—Elizabeth Taylor recycling Sandy Dennis's drinking rule in Mike Nichols's *Who's Afraid of Virginia Woolf?*
(Screenplay by Ernest Lehman; based on the play by Edward Albee)

6.
"Mike and I are still together, of course. We never argue anymore, and, when we do, it never lasts more than a week or two. We're really very happily married."

—Lauren Bacall summing up life with Gregory Peck in Vincente Minnelli's *Designing Woman*
(Original Screenplay by George Wells; based on a suggestion by Helen Rose)

7.
"Here, take my handkerchief. Never at any crisis of your life have I known you to have a handkerchief."

—Clark Gable leaving a weeping Vivien Leigh a parting gift in Victor Fleming's *Gone With the Wind*
(Screenplay by Sidney Howard; based on the novel by Margaret Mitchell)

8.
"Go, and never darken my towels again!"

—Groucho Marx dismissing Louis Calhern in Leo McCarey's *Duck Soup*
(Screenplay by Bert Kalmar and Harry Ruby; additional dialogue by Arthur Sheekman and Nat Perrin)

9.

"Laddie, I've never gone any place peacefully in my life."

—Victor McLaglen launching into a platoon of cavalrymen dispatched to arrest him for boozing in John Ford's *She Wore a Yellow Ribbon*
(Screenplay by Frank S. Nugent and Laurence Stallings; based on "The Big Hunt" and "War Party," two short stories by James Warner Bellah)

10.

"In my country, General, they say, 'Never blow a bridge until you come to it.'"

—Gary Cooper proposing to take his participation in the Spanish Civil War one step at a time in Sam Wood's *For Whom the Bell Tolls*
(Screenplay by Dudley Nichols; based on the novel by Ernest Hemingway)

11.

"I never lose. You see, poker is played by desperate men who cherish money. I don't lose because I have nothing to lose—including my life."

—Kirk Douglas explaining his gambling confidence to Burt Lancaster in John Sturges's *Gunfight at the O. K. Corral*
(Screenplay by Leon Uris; suggested by "The Killer," a short story by George Scullin)

12.

"I never answer letters from large organizations."

—Jason Robards priding himself on an idiosyncrasy in Fred Coe's *A Thousand Clowns*
(Screenplay by Herb Gardner; based on his play)

13.

"I never dated Carlo. I married him. I never dated him."

—Beatrice Arthur correcting Lucille Ball in Gene Saks's *Mame*
(Screenplay by Paul Zindel; based on the musical play by Jerome Lawrence, Robert E. Lee and Jerry Herman and AUNTIE MAME, a play by Jerome Lawrence and Robert E. Lee and novel by Patrick Dennis)

14.

"And another thing. Please promise me never to wear black satin or pearls, or to be 36 years old."

—Laurence Olivier telling Joan Fontaine to revise her idea of chic in Alfred Hitchcock's *Rebecca*
(Screenplay by Robert E. Sherwood and Joan Harrison; adaptation by Philip MacDonald and Michael Hogan; based on the novel by Daphne du Maurier)

15.

"Mrs. King, throughout this grisly meal your son has been pelting me with cereal. I have taught him an object lesson, and, as you will observe, he doesn't like it. I guarantee that he will never throw cereal at me or anyone else again. Ever."

—Clifton Webb explaining to Maureen O'Hara why a bowl of cereal has been dumped on the head of her youngest (Roddy McCaskill) in Walter Lang's *Sitting Pretty*
(Screenplay by F. Hugh Herbert; based on the novel by Gwen Davenport)

16.

"I'll never forget the way you looked going over the falls—head up, chin out, hair blowing in the wind—the living picture of a heroine!"

—Humphrey Bogart complimenting Katharine Hepburn's courage in John Huston's *The African Queen*
(Screenplay by James Agee and John Huston; based on the novel by C. S. Forester)

17.

"Never say never."

—Paul Newman refusing to take "never" for an answer from Joanne Woodward in Martin Ritt's *The Long, Hot Summer*
(Screenplay by Irving Ravetch and Harriet Frank, Jr.; based on THE HAMLET, a novel by William Faulkner, and "Barn Burning" and "The Spotted Horses," two short stories by William Faulkner)

ALSO SEE: Confessions-4; Disease-7; Drunk-3; Drunken Rantings-7; Dying Words-25; Exchanges-16; Fashion-1; Fights-9; Firings-4; Fools-11; Friends-6; Frigidity-3; Heart-8; Honest-5; Hope-3; Human-7; Humility-4; Hunger-1; Idea-1; Intelligence-5; Joke-2; Joke-3; Kiss-14; Last Lines-11; Lies-6; Lies-18; Lies-23; Loneliness-10; Love-17; Love-50; Macho-20; Mind-5; Mind-9; Narcissism-4; Narcissism-7; Nature-4; Newspapering-1; Oops!-1; Paris-3; Past-6; Pep Talks-7; Plans-1; Poets-3; Pretense-7; Producers-2; Producers-4; Professions-13; Progress-1; Promiscuity-5; Proposals-6; Proposals-9; Psychiatry-4; Regrets-1; Rejection-16; Remember-5; Respect-3; Rules-5; Run-7; Sayings-5; Sex-6; Silence-1; Static-4; Static-12; Static-13; Stimulating-1; Stimulating-2; Suicide-2; Swear-3; Talk-5; Time-4; Tongue-2; Trust and Distrust-8; Understand-7; Understand-8; War-4; War-11; Water-9; Wine-1; Wish-2; Wish-7; Women-9; Work-1.

NEW YORK

1.
"New York is not the center of the goddamn universe. I grant you it's an exciting, vibrant, stimulating, fabulous city, but it is not Mecca. It just smells like it."

—Alan Alda attacking the East Coast elitism of his ex (Jane Fonda) in Herbert Ross's *California Suite*
(Screenplay by Neil Simon; based on his play)

2.
"You know what's wrong with New Mexico, Mr. Wendel? Too much outdoors. Give me those eight spindly trees in front of Rockefeller Center any day. That's enough outdoors for me. No subways smelling sweet and sour. What do you use for noise around here? No beautiful roar of eight million ants fighting, cursing, loving. No shows. No *South Pacific*. No chic little dames across a crowded bar. And, worst of all, Herbie, no 80th floor to jump from when you feel like it."

—Kirk Douglas feeling the wide open spaces in Billy Wilder's *The Big Carnival*
(Original Screenplay by Billy Wilder, Lesser Samuels and Walter Newman)

3.
"Jan, if you marry him, you'll have to live out there. Look at that. New York! People jostling, shoving, struggling, milling, fighting for their lives—and you're part of it. In Texas, there's nothing but a bunch of prairie dogs and stuff. And even the air out there—there's nothing in it but air. New York, you got air you can sink your teeth into. It has character. Jan, you can't live in Texas."

—Tony Randall trying to dissuade Doris Day from a bad move in Michael Gordon's *Pillow Talk*
(Screenplay by Stanley Shapiro and Maurice Richlin; based on a story by Russell Rouse and Clarence Greene)

4.
"Which would you prefer: New York or Manderley?"

—Laurence Olivier proposing as Joan Fontaine departs for New York in Alfred Hitchcock's *Rebecca*
(Screenplay by Robert E. Sherwood and Joan Harrison; adaptation by Philip MacDonald and Michael Hogan; based on the novel by Daphne du Maurier)

ALSO SEE: Advice-8; Alone-6; Elephants-2; Heaven-9; Laugh-6; Parting Shots-8; Success-4; Television-3.

NEWSPAPERING

1.
"You never pushed a noun against a verb except to blow up something."

—Spencer Tracy defining Gene Kelly's approach to newspapering in Stanley Kramer's *Inherit the Wind*
(Screenplay by Nathan E. Douglas and Harold Jacob Smith; based on the play by Jerome Lawrence and Robert E. Lee)

2.
(a) "You're not going to use the story?"
    (b) "No, sir. As our late and great editor, Dutton Peabody, used to say: 'It ain't news. This is the West. When the legend becomes a fact, print the legend.' "

—(b) Newspaper reporter Carleton Young quoting Edmond O'Brien to (a) James Stewart as assurance that the identity of the title character will remain a secret in John Ford's *The Man Who Shot Liberty Valance*
(Screenplay by James Warner Bellah and Willis Goldbeck; based on the short story by Dorothy M. Johnson)

3.
"I'll tell you briefly what I think of newspapermen: the hand of God reaching down into the mire couldn't elevate one of them to the depths of degradation—not by a million miles."

—Charles Winninger greeting newspaperman Fredric March in William A. Wellman's *Nothing Sacred*
(Screenplay by Ben Hecht; based on "Letter to the Editor," a short story by James H. Street)

4.
"When it comes to newspapermen, give me a reformed lush every time. Your solid citizen writes the facts and watches the clock. The ex-dipso lets himself go. Work takes the place of liquor. He's dedicated, Julian."

—James Cagney suggesting an off-beat hiring practice to Larry Keating in Gordon Douglas's *Come Fill the Cup*
(Screenplay by Ivan Goff and Ben Roberts; based on the novel by Harlan Ware)

5.
"I don't know how to run a newspaper, Mr. Thatcher. I just try everything I can think of."

—Orson Welles gleefully leveling with his financial advisor (George Coulouris) in Orson Welles's *Citizen Kane*
(Original Screenplay by Herman J. Mankiewicz and Orson Welles)

6.
"Me? I didn't go to any college, but I know what makes a good story because, before I ever worked on a paper, I sold 'em on a street corner. You know the first thing I found out? Bad news sells best because good news is no news."

—Kirk Douglas teaching journalism to Robert Arthur in Billy Wilder's *The Big Carnival*

(Original Screenplay by Billy Wilder, Lesser Samuels and Walter Newman)

7.
"You know, it's too bad I'm not covering this dinner of yours tonight because I've got an angle that would really be sensational: the outstanding woman of the year isn't a woman at all."

—Spencer Tracy berating his award-winning wife (Katharine Hepburn) in George Stevens's *Woman of the Year*
(Original Screenplay by Ring Lardner, Jr., and Michael Kanin)

8.
"Here was an item *everybody* could have some fun with. The heartless so-and-sos! What would they do to Norma? Even if she got away with it in court—crime of passion, temporary insanity—those headlines would kill her: 'Forgotten Star a Slayer,' 'Aging Actress,' 'Yesterday's Glamour Queen' . . ."

—William Holden anticipating the press slaughter of Gloria Swanson in Billy Wilder's *Sunset Boulevard*
(Original Screenplay by Charles Brackett, Billy Wilder and D. M. Marshman, Jr.)

9.
"She's the star reporter on the *Mail!* Every time you opened your kisser, you gave her another story. She's the dame who slapped that moniker on you! Cinderella Man! You've been making love to a double dose of cyanide."

—Lionel Stander informing Gary Cooper of Jean Arthur in Frank Capra's *Mr. Deeds Goes to Town*
(Screenplay by Robert Riskin; based on "Opera Hat," a short story by Clarence Budington Kelland)

10.
(a) "I hear about big men, what they say when they die. You write something very big about me."

(b) "I'll write—I—I'll write about how Pancho Villa died with the medal that had once been given him for the rescue of Mexico still around his neck."

(a) "And the ring Mr. Madero gave me. You write that, too?"

(b) "I'll throw that in for good measure."

(a) "What else, Johnny? I like to hear."

(b) "Well, I'll—I'll—the peons! From near and far, from north and south, the peons who had loved him came to see him as he lay. They gathered in size, the tattered multitudes kneeling reverently in the streets. And then, once again, the thrilling strains of 'La Cucaracha' rang out on the night air."

—(b) Stuart Erwin ad-libbing an obituary for the dying (a) Wallace Beery in Jack Conway's *Viva Villa!*
(Screenplay by Ben Hecht; based on the book by Edgcumb Pinchon and O. B. Stade)

11.
"The mule trains pass through here. They stay the night at the inns and then go on their way. These muleteers are the newspapers of North China. If we can make one of them listen to us —and believe—we've reached more people than there are in Wangcheng."

—Athene Seyler telling Ingrid Bergman how to spread God's word in North China in Mark Robson's *The Inn of the Sixth Happiness*
(Screenplay by Isobel Lennart; based on THE SMALL WOMAN, a book by Alan Burgess)

12.
"I never did like the idea of sitting on a newspaper. I did it once, and all the headlines came off on my white pants. On the level! It actually happened. Nobody bought a paper that day. They just followed me around all over town and read the news on the seat of my pants."

—Clark Gable explaining why he transferred a bundle of newspapers from his bus seat to the street in Frank Capra's *It Happened One Night*
(Screenplay by Robert Riskin; based on "Night Bus," a short story by Samuel Hopkins Adams)

ALSO SEE: Headlines; Duty-3; Dying Words-5; Fun-1; Future-7; If-5; Professions-1; Smell-8; Static-15; Telegrams-2; Telephone Scenes-11; Telephone Scenes-12.

NIGHT

1.
"Fasten your seatbelts. It's going to be a bumpy night."

—Bette Davis bracing for a rocky party in Joseph L. Mankiewicz's *All About Eve*
(Screenplay by Joseph L. Mankiewicz; based on "The Wisdom of Eve," a radio play and short story by Mary Orr)

2.
"Jim, do you think the end of the world will come at nighttime?"

—Sal Mineo wondering aloud to James Dean in Nicholas Ray's *Rebel Without a Cause*
(Screenplay by Stewart Stern; adaptation by Irving Shulman; based on an original story by Nicholas Ray)

3.
(a) "The night is young."

(b) "The night is $2,000 old."

—(b) George C. Scott packing in his pool player (Paul Newman) after a long night of losing to (a) Murray Hamilton in a game of billiards in Robert Rossen's *The Hustler*
(Screenplay by Sidney Carroll and Robert Rossen; based on the novel by Walter Tevis)

4.
"Listen to me. I thought I was frightened the other day, but today when I—when I saw the light beginning to fail and night coming nearer and nearer, I felt my fingertips getting cold and I knew for the first time what real terror was. I'm not a fool, and I'm not hysterical. Well, I can't tell anymore what—what are real things and what aren't. Day is over, and the past is all about us. Anything can happen. Auntie, you shouldn't stay in this house tonight either."

—Rosalind Russell warning Dame May Whitty in Richard Thorpe's *Night Must Fall*
(Screenplay by John Van Druten; based on the play by Emlyn Williams)

5.
"Look at that sunset, Howard. . . . It's like the

daytime didn't want to end, isn't it? It's like the daytime's going to put up a big scrap, set the world on fire to keep the nighttime from creeping on."

—Rosalind Russell watching the sunset with Arthur O'Connell in Joshua Logan's *Picnic*
(Screenplay by Daniel Taradash; based on the play by William Inge)

6.

"In the morning when the sun rises, sometimes it's hard to believe there ever was a night. You'll find that, too."

—Joseph Cotten consoling Ingrid Bergman after her ordeal with Charles Boyer in George Cukor's *Gaslight*
(Screenplay by John Van Druten, Walter Reisch and John L. Balderston; based on ANGEL STREET, a play by Patrick Hamilton)

ALSO SEE: Alone-8; Disease-3; Music-8; Propositions-6; Realities-5; Theater-6.

NORMAL

1.

"He's contemptible, dishonest, selfish, deceitful, vicious—and yet he's out there, and I'm in here. He's called normal, and I'm not. If that's normal, I don't want it."

—Edmund Gwenn complaining about the twitchy fink who had him institutionalized (Porter Hall) in George Seaton's *Miracle on 34th Street*
(Screenplay by George Seaton; based on an original story by Valentine Davis)

2.

"She cut off her nipples with garden shears. You call that normal?"

—Elizabeth Taylor being bluntly direct with Brian Keith about his wife (Julie Harris) in John Huston's *Reflections in a Golden Eye*
(Screenplay by Chapman Mortimer and Gladys Hall; based on the novel by Carson McCullers)

3.

"I'm not being precocious. I'm just a normal 15-year-old girl. Actually, I'm not normal. I'm still a virgin."

—Lisa Lucas going for the shock effects in front of the date (Alan Bates) of her mother (Jill Clayburgh) in Paul Mazursky's *An Unmarried Woman*
(Original Screenplay by Paul Mazursky)

ALSO SEE: Compliments-8.

NOSE

1.

"People all over the world have noses. To prove that point, all you have to do is look around the room. There—there are noses—there are noses all over the place. The nose is one of the funniest parts of the human face, and it's also a source of embarrassment. Some people talk through them. Most people snore through them. Some people get punched in them. A handful whistle and sing through them, generally the amateurs on the radio programs. Noses have been bitten by mad dogs and movie actors in passionate love scenes. Doors have been slammed on them, and they've been caught in eggbeaters and electric fans. The true purpose of the nose is to smell what's in the air. Some people sniff with the nose at other people's ideas. One of the most important things about the nose is that it makes trouble, causes wars, breaks up old friendships and wrecks many happy homes. Now may I go to the track meet, Miss Hicks?"

—Mickey Rooney improvising an ode to the nose to get out of class in Clarence Brown's *The Human Comedy*
(Screenplay by Howard Estabrook; based on an original story by William Saroyan)

2.

"Mom's got a good nose for people. You get one, standing—year in, year out—behind a hamburger stand."

—John Lund introducing Thelma Ritter in Mitchell Leisen's *The Mating Season*

(Screenplay by Charles Brackett, Walter Reisch and Richard L. Breen; suggested by MAGGIE, a play by Caesar Dunn)

3.

"There's some things that are private, Mr. Dingle, and—and, when people go poking their nose in, it's just too much, that's all! And you have a very long nose, Mr. Dingle."

—Jean Arthur objecting to Charles Coburn's nosiness in George Stevens's *The More the Merrier*
(Screenplay by Richard Flournoy and Lewis R. Foster; based on a story by Robert Russell and Frank Ross)

4.

"Listen, partner. You may not like my nose, but I do. I always wear it out in the open where if anybody wants to take a sock at it they can do it."

—Clark Gable squaring off with an equally argumentative Ward Bond in Frank Capra's *It Happened One Night*
(Screenplay by Robert Riskin; based on "Night Bus," a short story by Samuel Hopkins Adams)

ALSO SEE: Dogs-5; Kiss-2; Prison-1; Quiet-3; Sayings-1.

NOTES

1.

"I can't take it anymore, Felix; I'm crackin' up. Everything you do irritates me. And, when you're not here, the things I know you're gonna do when you come in irritate me. You leave me little notes on my pillow. I told you 158 times I cannot stand little notes on my pillow. 'We are all out of corn flakes. F. U.' It took me three hours to figure out F. U. was Felix Ungar. It's not your fault, Felix; it's a rotten combination, that's all."

—Walter Matthau reaching the end of the road with his roommate (Jack Lemmon) in Gene Saks's *The Odd Couple*
(Screenplay by Neil Simon; based on his play)

2.

"Do you understand that? I'll read it to you: 'This is to certify that Ben Chenkin is suffering from the effects of overindulgence in malt liquor but is perfectly fit to work.' "

—Robert Donat refusing to give his medical okay to a malingering Francis L. Sullivan in King Vidor's *The Citadel*
(Screenplay by Ian Dalrymple, Frank Wead and Elizabeth Hill; additional dialogue by Emlyn Williams; based on the novel by A. J. Cronin)

3.

"Don't bother to read the note. I'll tell you what it says: 'Eleven roses, and the twelfth is you.' "

—Gail Patrick reciting from memory the stock love note accompanying flowers which her ex-beau (Adolphe Menjou) has sent his current favorite (Ginger Rogers) in Gregory La Cava's *Stage Door*
(Screenplay by Morrie Ryskind and Anthony Veiller; based on the play by Edna Ferber and George S. Kaufman)

4.

"Now is the time for all good men to come to the aid of V. Cunningham."

—Olivia De Havilland typing out a cry for help inside a mental asylum in Anatole Litvak's *The Snake Pit*
(Screenplay by Frank Partos and Millen Brand; based on the novel by Mary Jane Ward)

5.

"Now is the time for all good men to come to the aid of Johnny Sykes. Now is the time for all good men to come to the aid of Johnny Sykes. Now is the time for all good men to come to the aid of Johnny Sykes."

—Stuart Erwin pretending to write up the exploits of Pancho Villa (Wallace Beery) with armed bandidos on all sides in Jack Conway's *Viva Villa!*
(Screenplay by Ben Hecht; based on the book by Edgcumb Pinchon and O. B. Stade)

6.

"To Captain Brittles,
    From C Troop.
    Lest We Forget"

—Inscription of John Wayne's Army-retirement watch in John Ford's *She Wore a Yellow Ribbon*
(Screenplay by Frank S. Nugent and Laurence Stallings; based on "The Big Hunt" and "War Party," short stories by James Warner Bellah)

7.
"Please put $15,000 into this bag and act naturally. I am pointing a gun at you."

—Woody Allen's illegible robbery note which none of the bank tellers can decipher in Woody Allen's *Take the Money and Run*
(Original Screenplay by Woody Allen and Mickey Rose)

8.
"Darling Toby,
    It's a lovely story, but it hasn't got an ending. It would be marvelous with an ending."

—Leslie Caron leaving Tom Bell for good with a critique of his first finished story in the last lines of Bryan Forbes's *The L-Shaped Room*
(Screenplay by Bryan Forbes; based on the novel by Lynne Reid Banks)

ALSO SEE: Letters; Fathers-5.

NURSES

1.
"If you nurse as good as your sense of humor, I won't make it to Thursday."

—Walter Matthau grousing at Rosetta LeNoire in Herbert Ross's *The Sunshine Boys*
(Screenplay by Neil Simon; based on his play)

2.
"If Florence Nightingale had ever nursed *you*, Mr. Whiteside, she would have married Jack the Ripper instead of founding the Red Cross. Good day."

—Mary Wickes walking out on her cranky patient (Monty Woolley)—forgetting apparently that Clara Barton founded the Red Cross—in William Keighley's *The Man Who Came to Dinner*
(Screenplay by Julius J. Epstein and Philip G.

Epstein; based on the play by George S. Kaufman and Moss Hart)

ALSO SEE: Books-7; Changes-1; Poverty-4.

OOPS!

1.
"I knew Edwardes only slightly. I never really liked him, but he was a good man, in a way, I suppose."

—Leo G. Carroll identifying himself as a killer with a slip of the tongue to Ingrid Bergman in Alfred Hitchcock's *Spellbound*
(Screenplay by Ben Hecht; adaptation by Angus MacPhail; based on THE HOUSE OF DR. EDWARDES, a novel by Francis Beeding)

2.
'He's a big boy, isn't he? Spitting image of his father."

—Stephen McNally letting it slip to Charles Bickford that he fathered the latter's grandchild in Jean Negulesco's *Johnny Belinda*
(Screenplay by Irmgard Von Cube and Allen Vincent; based on the play by Elmer Harris)

3.
"San Francisco has no Shubert Theater. You've never been to San Francisco! That was a stupid lie, easy to expose, not worthy of you."

—George Sanders confronting Anne Baxter about her fabricated past in Joseph L. Mankiewicz's *All About Eve*
(Screenplay by Joseph L. Mankiewicz; based on "The Wisdom of Eve," a radio play and short story by Mary Orr)

ORCHIDS

1.
"You are the only woman I know who can wear an orchid. Generally, it's the orchid that wears the woman."

—Alexander Knox passing a classy compliment in Henry King's *Wilson*
(Original Screenplay by Lamar Trotti)

2.
(a) "You like orchids?"
  (b) "Not particularly."
  (a) "Nasty things! Their flesh is too much like the flesh of men. Their perfume has the rotten sweetness of corruption."

—(a) Charles Waldron and (b) Humphrey Bogart having a hothouse discussion in Howard Hawks's *The Big Sleep*
(Screenplay by William Faulkner, Leigh Brackett and Jules Furthman; based on the novel by Raymond Chandler)

ALSO SEE: Relatives-6; Self-Depreciation-5.

ORDERS

1.
"Beulah, peel me a grape."

—Mae West instructing Gertrude Howard in Wesley Ruggles's *I'm No Angel*
(Screenplay and dialogue by Mae West; story suggestions by Lowell Brentano; continuity by Harlan Thompson)

2.
(a) "Of all the gin joints in all the towns in all the world, she walks into mine! What's that you're playing?"
  (b) "Oh, just a little something of my own."
  (a) "Well, stop it. You know what I want to hear."
  (b) "No, I don't."
  (a) "You played it for her, and you can play it for me."
  (b) "Well, I don't think I can remember it."
  (a) "If she can stand it, I can. Play it."
  (b) "Yes sir, boss."

—(a) Humphrey Bogart requesting "As Time Goes By" from Sam the piano player, (b) Dooley Wilson, in Michael Curtiz's *Casablanca*
(Screenplay by Julius J. Epstein, Philip G. Epstein and Howard Koch; based on EVERYBODY COMES

TO RICK'S, a play by Murray Burnett and Joan Alison)

3.
"I think I'll have a large order of 'prognosis negative.'"

—Bette Davis informing her doctor-fiancé (George Brent), with her meal order, that she has seen his negative medical report on her in Edmund Goulding's *Dark Victory*
(Screenplay by Casey Robinson; based on the play by George Brewer, Jr. and Bertram Bloch)

4.
". . . now all you have to do is hold the chicken, bring me the toast, give me a check for the chicken-salad sandwich—and you haven't broken any rules."

—Jack Nicholson going to elaborate lengths just to get a simple side-order of toast from a rule-bound waitress (Lorna Thayer) in Bob Rafelson's *Five Easy Pieces*
(Screenplay by Adrien Joyce; based on a story by Bob Rafelson and Adrien Joyce)

5.
"Noah, I want to build me a boat, and I want you to call it de 'Ark.' I want you to take two of every kind of animal and bird dere is in de country. I want you to take seeds an' sprouts an' put dem on dat Ark, because I'm gonter make a storm dat'll sink everythin' from a hencoop to a barn. Dey ain't a ship on de sea dat'll be able to fight dat tempest. Dey all got to go. Everythin'. Everythin' in dis pretty worl' I made, except one thing, Noah. You an' yo' fam'ly an' de things I said is going to ride dat storm in de Ark."

—Rex Ingram giving Eddie "Rochester" Anderson sailing orders in Marc Connelly and William Keighley's *The Green Pastures*
(Screenplay by Marc Connelly and Sheridan Gibney; based on the play by Marc Connelly and suggested by the sketches in OL' MAN ADAM AN' HIS CHILLUN, a novel by Roark Bradford)

6.
"The ship's company will remember that I am

your captain, your judge and your jury. You do your duty, and we may get along. Whatever happens, you'll do your duty."

—Charles Laughton setting his collision course in Frank Lloyd's *Mutiny on the Bounty*
(Screenplay by Talbot Jennings, Jules Furthman and Carey Wilson; based on the novel by Charles Nordhoff and James Norman Hall)

7.
"Mr. Maryk, you may tell the crew for me there are four ways of doing things on board my ship: the right way, the wrong way, the Navy way—and my way. If they do things my way, we'll get along."

—Humphrey Bogart setting his collision course in Edward Dmytryk's *The Caine Mutiny*
(Screenplay by Stanley Roberts; additional dialogue by Michael Blankfort; based on the novel by Herman Wouk)

8.
"I want that man put on report. I don't want no one on deck without a shirt. Is that clearly understood?"

—James Cagney running a tidy, if unhappy, ship in John Ford and Mervyn LeRoy's *Mister Roberts*
(Screenplay by Frank S. Nugent and Joshua Logan; based on the play by Thomas Heggen and Joshua Logan and novel by Thomas Heggen)

9.
"It's a white whale. Skin your eyes for him."

—Gregory Peck telling his crew what to look for in John Huston's *Moby Dick*
(Screenplay by Ray Bradbury and John Huston; based on the novel by Herman Melville)

10.
"Then close your eyes and tap your heels together three times. And think to yourself 'There's no place like home.'"

—Billie Burke telling Judy Garland how to get from Oz to Kansas in Victor Fleming's *The Wizard of Oz*
(Screenplay by Noel Langley, Florence Ryerson and Edgar Allan Woolf; adaptation by Noel Langley; based on the novel by L. Frank Baum)

ALSO SEE: Propositions-13; Water-6.

PAIN

1.
"You don't get to be good-hearted by accident. If you've been kicked around long enough, you get to be a—a real professor of pain."

—Ernest Borgnine consoling Betsy Blair in Delbert Mann's *Marty*
(Screenplay by Paddy Chayefsky; based on his teleplay)
                    and
—Barry Miller performing the above scene from *Marty* in Alan Parker's *Fame*
(Original Screenplay by Christopher Gore)

2.
"I can stand anything but pain."

—Oscar Levant admitting his weakness to Fred Astaire and Nanette Fabray in Vincente Minnelli's *The Band Wagon*
(Original Screenplay by Betty Comden and Adolph Green)

3.
"They're not going to torture me. It hurts."

—Bob Hope meeting a crisis in various shades of yellow in Hal Walker's *Road to Bali*
(Screenplay by Frank Butler, Hal Kanter and William Morrow; based on an original story by Frank Butler and Harry Tugend)

4.
"Mister Maine is feeling no pain."

—Judy Garland sizing up a drunken James Mason at first glance in George Cukor's *A Star Is Born*
(Screenplay by Moss Hart; based on a screenplay by Dorothy Parker, Alan Campbell and Robert Carson and original story by William A. Wellman and Robert Carson)

ALSO SEE: Adultery-3; Death-4; Good and Bad-1; Good and Bad-2; Rejection-1; Truth-7.

PAINTING

1.
"For a painter, the mecca of the world for study, for inspiration and for living is here

on this star called Paris. Just look at it. No wonder so many artists have come here and called it home. Brother, if you can't paint in Paris, you'd better give up and marry the boss's daughter."

—Gene Kelly setting the scene for Vincente Minnelli's *An American in Paris*
(Original Screenplay by Alan Jay Lerner)

2.
"Of course, as far as I'm concerned, art is just a guy's name."

—Rock Hudson pleading ignorance to painter Otto Kruger in Douglas Sirk's *Magnificent Obsession*
(Screenplay by Robert Blees; adaptation by Wells Root; based on a screenplay by George O'Neill, Sarah Y. Mason and Victor Heerman and novel by Lloyd C. Douglas)

3.
(a) "What I see when I look at your work is just you paint too fast."
   (b) "You look too fast."

—(a) Anthony Quinn attacking, and (b) Kirk Douglas defending, the latter's paintings in Vincente Minnelli's *Lust for Life*
(Screenplay by Norman Corwin; based on the novel by Irving Stone)

4.
"What it is, actually, it's a pictorial representation of the order of Martha's mind."

—Richard Burton insulting his wife (Elizabeth Taylor) by way of explaining a way-out painting to George Segal in Mike Nichols's *Who's Afraid of Virginia Woolf?*
(Screenplay by Ernest Lehman; based on the play by Edward Albee)

5.
"Whenever Dorian poses for me, it seems as if a power outside myself is guiding my hand. It's as if the painting had a life of its own, independent of me."

—Lowell Gilmore guessing correctly about his mysterious model (Hurd Hatfield) in Albert Lewin's *The Picture of Dorian Gray*
(Screenplay by Albert Lewin; based on the novel by Oscar Wilde)

6.
"You are the most beautiful woman I've ever painted—not because you're beautiful but because I'm in love with you, hopelessly in love with you."

—Albert Lieven falling for his model (Ann Todd) in Compton Bennett's *The Seventh Veil*
(Original Screenplay by Muriel Box and Sydney Box)

7.
"I found the portrait long before I met Mari, and I worshiped it. When I did meet her, it was as if I'd always known her and wanted her."

—Clifton Webb allowing that a painting led him to his wife (Cathy Downs) in Henry Hathaway's *The Dark Corner*
(Screenplay by Jay Dratler and Bernard C. Schoenfeld; based on the short story by Leo Rosten)

ALSO SEE: Eyes-15; Fights-4; Home-8; Paris-3; Party-3; Peace-1; Pleasures-5; Walk-2.

PARENTS

1.
"Suppose your parents *are* unhappy—it's good for them. It develops their characters. Now look at *me*. I left home at the age of four, and I haven't been back since. They can hear me on the radio, and that's enough for them."

—Monty Woolley advising elopement for Elisabeth Fraser in William Keighley's *The Man Who Came to Dinner*
(Screenplay by Julius J. Epstein and Philip G. Epstein; based on the play by George S. Kaufman and Moss Hart)

2.
"His mother and father together are like a bad car-wreck."

—Chris Sarandon characterizing Al Pacino's home-life in Sidney Lumet's *Dog Day Afternoon*
(Original Screenplay by Frank Pierson)

3.

"There'll be $1,000 on that table for you by six in the morning. Get on the early train. Send a Christmas card each year to an aging parent who now wishes you to stop talking."

—Fredric March sending his son (Dan Duryea) packing in Michael Gordon's *Another Part of the Forest* *(Screenplay by Vladimir Pozner; based on the play by Lillian Hellman)*

4.

"If I seem a bit sinister as a parent, Mr. Marlowe, it's because my hold on life is too slight to include any Victorian hypocrisy. I need hardly add that any man who has lived as I have and who indulges for the first time in parenthood at my age deserves all he gets."

—Charles Waldron leveling with Humphrey Bogart in Howard Hawks's *The Big Sleep* *(Screenplay by William Faulkner, Leigh Brackett and Jules Furthman; based on the novel by Raymond Chandler)*

ALSO SEE: Fathers; Mothers; Children-5; Fights-4; Self-Perception-11.

PARIS

1.

"I do not deny its beauty, but it's a waste of electricity."

—Greta Garbo drinking in The City of Light in Ernst Lubitsch's *Ninotchka* *(Screenplay by Charles Brackett, Billy Wilder and Walter Reisch; based on an original story by Melchior Lengyel)*

2.

"We'll always have Paris. We didn't have it. We'd—we'd lost it until you came to Casablanca. We got it back last night."

—Humphrey Bogart telling Ingrid Bergman to be content with memories in Michael Curtiz's *Casablanca* *(Screenplay by Julius J. Epstein, Philip G. Epstein and Howard Koch; based on EVERYBODY COMES*

TO RICK'S, a play by Murray Burnett and Joan Alison)

3.

(a) "Paris has ways of making people forget."

(b) "Paris? No, not this city. It's too real and too beautiful. It never lets you forget anything. It reaches in and opens you wide, and you stay that way. I know. I came to Paris to study and to paint because Utrillo did and Lautrec did and Rouault did. I loved what they created, and I thought something would happen to me, too. Well, it happened all right. Now, what have I got left? Paris. Maybe that's enough for some, but it isn't for me anymore because the more beautiful everything is, the more it will hurt without you."

—(a) Leslie Caron and (b) Gene Kelly parting in Vincente Minnelli's *An American in Paris* *(Original Screenplay by Alan Jay Lerner)*

4.

"You know what you are to me? Paris. That's you. Paris. . . . a spring morning in Paris."

—Charles Boyer romancing Hedy Lamarr in John Cromwell's *Algiers* *(Screenplay by John Howard Lawson and James M. Cain; based on PEPE LE MOKO, a novel by Detective Ashelbe)*

ALSO SEE: Fashion-1; Fashion-2; Mothers-2; Painting-1; Prologues-3; Talent-1; Telephone Scenes-1; Time-15.

PARTING SHOTS

1.

"Damn Mrs. Pearce! And damn the coffee! And damn you! And damn my own folly in having lavished hard-earned knowledge and the treasure of my regard and intimacy on a heartless guttersnipe!"

—Leslie Howard telling off Wendy Hiller in Anthony Asquith and Leslie Howard's *Pygmalion* *(Screenplay by George Bernard Shaw; adaptation by W. P. Lipscomb, Cecil Lewis and Ian*

Dalrymple; based on the play by George Bernard
Shaw)

and (almost verbatim)

—Rex Harrison dittoing Audrey Hepburn in the remake, George Cukor's *My Fair Lady*
(*Screenplay by Alan Jay Lerner; based on his
musical play and* PYGMALION, *a screenplay and
play by George Bernard Shaw*)

2.
"Frankly, my dear, I don't give a damn."

—Clark Gable walking out on Vivien Leigh in Victor
Fleming's *Gone With the Wind*
(*Screenplay by Sidney Howard; based on the novel
by Margaret Mitchell*)

3.
"I always knew that someday we'd come to this
particular moment in the scheme of things.
You want Veda and your business and a nice
quiet life, and the price of all that is me. Well,
you can go back to making your pies now, Mildred. We're through."

—Zachary Scott walking out on Joan Crawford in
Michael Curtiz's *Mildred Pierce*
(*Screenplay by Ranald MacDougall; based on the
novel by James M. Cain*)

4.
"You ain't even worth hitting. Jett, you want to
know something true: you're through."

—Rock Hudson deciding not to dirty his hands by
fighting James Dean in George Stevens's *Giant*
(*Screenplay by Fred Guiol and Ivan Moffat; based
on the novel by Edna Ferber*)

5.
"You're drunk, and your last penny is spent,
and I have no further use for you, Mr. Gypo
Nolan, ipso facto."

—J. M. Kerrigan telling off Victor McLaglen in John
Ford's *The Informer*
(*Screenplay by Dudley Nichols; based on the
novel by Liam O'Flaherty*)

6.
"Very well. I hope you'll never regret what
promises to be a disgustingly earthy relation-

ship. My congratulations, Mr. McPherson. Listen to my broadcast in 15 minutes. I'm discussing great lovers of history."

—Clifton Webb leaving Gene Tierney to Dana Andrews in Otto Preminger's *Laura*
(*Screenplay by Jay Dratler, Samuel Hoffenstein
and Betty Reinhardt; based on the novel by Vera
Caspary*)

7.
"For four years, I've invited the guests and
bought the favors and provided the entertainment and cleaned up the dirt and paid off the
waiters and paid off the cops and paid off the
papers and paid off the guests, and now it's
Good Night, Ladies, The Party's Over—I've
Had a Lovely Evening, But I Must Be Going."

—Edmond O'Brien telling off his boss (Warren Stevens) in Joseph L. Mankiewicz's *The Barefoot Contessa*
(*Original Screenplay by Joseph L. Mankiewicz*)

8.
"If you ever come to New York, Doctor, try
and find me."

—Monty Woolley bidding bye to a bore (George Bar-
bier) in William Keighley's *The Man Who Came to
Dinner*
(*Screenplay by Julius J. Epstein and Philip G.
Epstein; based on the play by George S. Kaufman
and Moss Hart*)

ALSO SEE: Beautiful-6; Bums-4; Butterflies-2;
Curses-1; Dogs-2; Life and Death-14; Peace-1;
Suicide-12.

PARTY

1.
"Darling, I was afraid you might be angry or
resent my coming here, but—but I had to take
that chance. Why, right in the middle of everything, suddenly I knew one thing so clearly: the
party's where you are."

—Lana Turner leaving her premiere party to be
alone with Kirk Douglas (who isn't alone) in Vincente
Minnelli's *The Bad and the Beautiful*

(Screenplay by Charles Schnee; based on "Memorial to a Bad Man" and "Of Good and Evil," two short stories by George Bradshaw)

2.

"You call this a party? The beer is warm, the women are cold, and I'm hot under the collar. In fact, a more poisonous little barbecue I've never attended."

—Groucho Marx insulting his host (Rockliffe Fellowes) in Norman Z. McLeod's *Monkey Business*
(Screenplay by S. J. Perelman and Will B. Johnstone; additional dialogue by Arthur Sheekman)

3.

"You know, whenever you put about 50 artists together in one room, you get a—a really pleasant combination of gossip, paranoia, envy, fear, trembling, hatred, lust and pretense. It's, er, wonderful."

—Alan Bates interpreting the immediate surroundings for Jill Clayburgh in Paul Mazursky's *An Unmarried Woman*
(Original Screenplay by Paul Mazursky)

4.

"You know, I've been to so many wonderful parties here, Mame. Now, I'm going to find out how they all ended."

—Alcoholic actress Coral Browne scanning the galleys of Rosalind Russell's autobiography in Morton DaCosta's *Auntie Mame*
(Screenplay by Betty Comden and Adolph Green; based on the play by Jerome Lawrence and Robert E. Lee and novel by Patrick Dennis)

5.

"It's a nauseating mixture of Park Avenue and Broadway. It proves I'm a liberal."

—Clifton Webb characterizing his party to Constance Collier in Henry Hathaway's *The Dark Corner*
(Screenplay by Jay Dratler and Bernard Schoenfeld; based on the short story by Leo Rosten)

6.

"I'll pray for rain as I have never prayed before. The old—witch! She'd never have got anywhere if it hadn't been for me. Now, she doesn't invite me to the greatest party of her career. Fireworks, my dear fellow! There are going to be fireworks! Oh, it's so unkind! I hate them! I hate them all!"

—Clifton Webb smarting from Cobina Wright, Sr.'s snubbing as he lies dying in Edmund Goulding's *The Razor's Edge*
(Screenplay by Lamar Trotti; based on the novel by W. Somerset Maugham)

7.

(a) "So when they parked in front of this tourist cabin, I said, 'Okay, girls, if I gotta pay for the ride, this is the easiest way I know.' So we got busy—on the martinis. Gee, they musta thought I was Superman."

(b) "Nothing like that ever happens to me."

(a) "So then I said, 'Okay, girls, party's over. Let's get going.' And one of 'em sticks a gun right in my back, and she says, '*This* party's going on till *we* say it's over, buck!' You'd have thought she was Humphrey Bogart."

(b) "Now, wait a minute now. Then what?"

(a) "Well, so finally I passed out, and, when I woke up, the dames were gone and so was my two hundred bucks. I went to the police, and they wouldn't believe me. They said my story was wishful thinking. How do you like that? I'm telling you, Benson, women are getting desperate."

—(a) William Holden spinning a wild yarn to (b) Cliff Robertson in Joshua Logan's *Picnic*
(Screenplay by Daniel Taradash; based on the play by William Inge)

ALSO SEE: Regrets-3.

PASSION

1.

"I can feel the hot blood pounding through your varicose veins."

—Jimmy Durante meeting Mary Wickes for the first time in William Keighley's *The Man Who Came to Dinner*
(Screenplay by Julius J. Epstein and Philip G. Epstein; based on the play by George S. Kaufman and Moss Hart)

2.
"Ninotchka, why do doves bill and coo? Why do snails, the coldest of all creatures, circle interminably around each other? Why do moths fly hundreds of miles to find their mates? Why do flowers slowly open their petals? Oh, Ninotchka, Ninotchka, surely you feel some slight symptom of the divine passion—a general warmth in the palms of your hands, a strange heaviness in your limbs, a burning of the lips that isn't thirst but something a thousand times more tantalizing, more exalting, than thirst?"

—Melvyn Douglas vamping Greta Garbo in Ernst Lubitsch's *Ninotchka*
(Screenplay by Charles Brackett, Billy Wilder and Walter Reisch; based on an original story by Melchior Lengyel)

3.
"The possibility of arousing unsuspected passion at my age would be not only disturbing but rather miraculous."

—Clifton Webb being distantly romantic with Dorothy McGuire in Jean Negulesco's *Three Coins in the Fountain*
(Screenplay by John Patrick; based on the novel by John H. Secondari)

4.
"I was married for nine years. Eight of those years were very passionate. But—well, passion's a mild word for it really. It's—well, it was more like war."

—Alan Bates describing his married life to Jill Clayburgh in Paul Mazursky's *An Unmarried Woman*
(Original Screenplay by Paul Mazursky)

ALSO SEE: Adultery-3; Differences-3; Gigolo-7; Kindness-4; Love-6; Love-35; Manners-11; Murder-9; Names-16; Poverty-4.

PAST

1.
"The past is a foreign country. They do things differently there."

—Michael Redgrave setting off memories in the first line of Joseph Losey's *The Go-Between*
(Screenplay by Harold Pinter; based on the novel by L. P. Hartley)

2.
"We're like two junkies getting a fix from the past—you with your war and me with my farm."

—Joanne Woodward talking truth to her husband (Martin Balsam) in Gilbert Cates's *Summer Wishes, Winter Dreams*
(Original Screenplay by Stewart Stern)

3.
"You know, Richie, the best thing about the past is you figure out what it was that could have made you happy."

—Richard Castellano advising his son (Joseph Hindy) in Cy Howard's *Lovers and Other Strangers*
(Screenplay by Renee Taylor, Joseph Bologna and David Z. Goodman; based on the play by Renee Taylor and Joseph Bologna)

4.
"There it was again—that room of hers, all satin and ruffles. And that bed, like a gilded rowboat. The perfect setting for a silent movie queen. Poor devil—still waving proudly to a parade which had long since passed her by."

—William Holden pitying Gloria Swanson in Billy Wilder's *Sunset Boulevard*
(Original Screenplay by Charles Brackett, Billy Wilder and D. M. Marshman, Jr.)

5.
"I've had my fill of the smug condescension of you worn-out pretenders, parading on the ruins of your past glories."

—Rex Harrison telling off Elizabeth Taylor in Joseph L. Mankiewicz's *Cleopatra*

(Screenplay by Joseph L. Mankiewicz, Ranald MacDougall and Sidney Buchman; based upon histories by Plutarch, Suetonius and Appian and THE LIFE AND TIMES OF CLEOPATRA, a book by C. M. Franzero)

6.

"Look at them, all these poor tragic people. The South sinking to its knees. It'll never rise again. The cause! The cause of living in the past is dying right in front of us."

—Clark Gable becoming enraged by the Gettysburg death roll in Victor Fleming's *Gone With the Wind* *(Screenplay by Sidney Howard; based on the novel by Margaret Mitchell)*

7.

"*In* vaudeville? I *was* vaudeville. You should see my scrapbook."

—Kay Medford boasting to Laurence Harvey and Elizabeth Taylor in Daniel Mann's *Butterfield 8* *(Screenplay by Charles Schnee and John Michael Hayes; based on the novel by John O'Hara)*

8.

"You remember Dunlap and Rosita? Well, he used to go around with Rosita. And Rosita wore a little black velvet ribbon on her neck, and she tied it very tight because she was skinny. She wanted her cheeks to puff up, but she tied it so tight it affected her hearing. She couldn't hear the music. . . ."

—George Burns reminiscing with his old vaudeville partner (Walter Matthau) in the last lines of Herbert Ross's *The Sunshine Boys* *(Screenplay by Neil Simon; based on his play)*

9.

"I am the past. I like it. It's sweet and familiar, and the present is cold and foreign, and the future—fortunately, I don't need to concern myself with that. But you do. It's yours."

—Helen Hayes contrasting herself with Ingrid Bergman in Anatole Litvak's *Anastasia* *(Screenplay by Arthur Laurents; based on the play by Marcelle Maurette and Broadway adaptation by Guy Bolton)*

10.

"But, darling, we won't have to worry about our future if you're willing to raffle off your past."

—Melvyn Douglas trying to talk Ina Claire into publishing her memoirs in Ernst Lubitsch's *Ninotchka* *(Screenplay by Charles Brackett, Billy Wilder and Walter Reisch; based on an original story by Melchior Lengyel)*

ALSO SEE: Fashion-3; Future-6; Lasts-3; Manners-2; Manners-3; Memory-4; Money-14; Prologues-1.

PATIENCE

1.

"With your permission, my President, we make our tortillas out of corn, not patience—and patience will not cross an armed and guarded fence. To do as you suggest, to verify those boundaries, we need your authority to cross that fence."

—Marlon Brando being respectfully dissonant toward Porfirio Diaz (Fay Roope) in Elia Kazan's *Viva Zapata!* *(Original Screenplay by John Steinbeck)*

2.

"We got a little Spanish peasants proverb: with the rich and mighty, always a little patience."

—James Stewart enlightening Katharine Hepburn in George Cukor's *The Philadelphia Story* *(Screenplay by Donald Ogden Stewart; based on the play by Philip Barry)*
          and (almost verbatim)

—Frank Sinatra dittoing Celeste Holm in the remake, Charles Walters's *High Society* *(Screenplay by John Patrick; based on THE PHILADELPHIA STORY, a screenplay by Donald Ogden Stewart and play by Philip Barry)*

3.

"Being with you is wonderful, Baby. You make me feel important—no—you make me feel patient."

—William Holden recognizing Kim Novak's calming influence in Joshua Logan's *Picnic*
(Screenplay by Daniel Taradash; based on the play by William Inge)

ALSO SEE: Crazy-11; Discipline-2; Frigidity-3; Ignorance-3.

PEACE

1.
"In Italy, for 30 years under the Borgias, they had warfare, terror, murder and bloodshed, but they produced Michelangelo, Leonardo da Vinci and the Renaissance. In Switzerland, they had brotherly love; they had 500 years of democracy and peace—and what did that produce? The cuckoo clock. So long, Holly."

—Orson Welles showing where his sympathies are as he leaves Joseph Cotten in Carol Reed's *The Third Man*
(Original Screenplay by Graham Greene)

2.
"Most of the miseries of the world were caused by wars. And, when the wars were over, no one ever knew what they were about."

—Leslie Howard trying to cool off a roomful of Southern hotheads in Victor Fleming's *Gone With the Wind*
(Screenplay by Sidney Howard; based on the novel by Margaret Mitchell)

3.
(a) "I've been fighting so long I don't understand peace."
  (b) "Peace is the hard problem. Any man can be honest in war, but peace—! I often wonder how a man can stay honest under the pressure of peace."

—(a) Marlon Brando and (b) Harold Gordon having a restless break from war in Elia Kazan's *Viva Zapata!*
(Original Screenplay by John Steinbeck)

4.
"Now, now, now. We're all sort of fellow travelers in a mighty small boat on a mighty big ocean. And the more we quarrel and criticize and misunderstand each other, the bigger the ocean gets and the smaller the boat."

—Henry Hull playing the peacemaker in Alfred Hitchcock's *Lifeboat*
(Screenplay by Jo Swerling; based on the story by John Steinbeck)

5.
"You don't think I'd come around here peddling any brand of temperance bunk, do you? Just 'cause I quit the stuff don't mean I'm going prohibition. I'm not that ungrateful. It's given me too many good times. So, if anybody wants to get drunk—if that's the only way they can be happy and feel at peace with themselves—why the hell shouldn't they? Don't I know that game from soup to nuts? I wrote the book. The only reason I quit is—well, I finally had the guts to face myself and throw overboard that damned lying pipe dream that was making me miserable and do what I had to do for the happiness of all concerned. Then all at once, I was at peace with myself, and I didn't need the booze any more."

—Lee Marvin preaching to the barflies in John Frankenheimer's *The Iceman Cometh*
(Screenplay based on the play by Eugene O'Neill; text edited by Thomas Quinn Curtiss)

7.
"I've learned in Tobiki the wisdom of gracious acceptance. You see, I don't want to be a world leader. I've made peace with myself somewhere between my ambitions and my limitations. . . . It's a step backward in the right direction."

—Glenn Ford proclaiming his self-awareness to Marlon Brando in Daniel Mann's *The Teahouse of the August Moon*
(Screenplay by John Patrick; based on his play and the book by Vern J. Sneider)

8.
"Peace on you, too, brother!"

—Bruce Dern greeting, upon his return from Vietnam, an antiwar demonstrator in Hal Ashby's *Coming Home*
(*Screenplay by Waldo Salt and Robert C. Jones; based on a story by Nancy Dowd*)

ALSO SEE: Pep Talks-6; Progress-3.

PEOPLE

1.
"Rich fellas come up, an' they die, an' their kids ain't no good, an' they die out. But we keep a-comin'. We're the people that live. Can't wipe us out. Can't lick us. We'll go on forever, Pa, because we're the people."

—Jane Darwell showing spunk and spirit in the last lines of John Ford's *The Grapes of Wrath*
(*Screenplay by Nunnally Johnson; based on the novel by John Steinbeck*)

2.
"There you are, Norton! The people! Try and lick that!"

—James Gleason telling off Edward Arnold in the last lines of Frank Capra's *Meet John Doe*
(*Screenplay by Robert Riskin; based on a story by Richard Connell and Robert Presnell, Sr.*)

3.
(a) "You really do think I'm an anti-Semite."
   (b) "No, I don't, Kathy."
   (a) "You do. You've thought it secretly for a long time."
   (b) "No. It's just that I've come to see that lots of nice people who aren't—people who despise it and detest it and deplore it and protest their own innocence—help it along and then wonder why it grows, people who'd never beat up a Jew or yell 'kike' at a child, people who think that anti-Semitism is something away off in some dark crackpot place with low-class morons. That's the biggest discovery I've made about this whole business, Kathy: the good people, the nice people."

—(b) Gregory Peck telling (a) Dorothy McGuire about the prejudice in passivity in Elia Kazan's *Gentleman's Agreement*
(*Screenplay by Moss Hart; based on the novel by Laura Z. Hobson*)

4.
"So it's your opinion that nice people never murder their husbands. . . . It's amazing how 11 years of wedlock with the greatest realist in the country haven't altered a single one of your lovely delusions about nice people."

—Gregory Peck teasing his wife (Ann Todd) about his next client (Valli) in Alfred Hitchcock's *The Paradine Case*
(*Screenplay by David O. Selznick; adaptation by Alma Reville and James Bridie; based on the novel by Robert Hichens*)

5.
"A strong man makes a weak people. A strong people don't need a strong man."

—Marlon Brando telling Jean Peters why his country no longer needs him in Elia Kazan's *Viva Zapata!*
(*Original Screenplay by John Steinbeck*)

6.
"It's just filthy. People are filthy. I think that's the biggest thing that's wrong with people. I think they wouldn't be as violent if they were clean because they wouldn't have anybody to pick on."

—Helena Kallianiotes launching into an ecology tirade in Bob Rafelson's *Five Easy Pieces*
(*Screenplay by Adrien Joyce; based on a story by Bob Rafelson and Adrien Joyce*)

ALSO SEE: Action-2; Future-5; Good-1; Home-12; Horses-1; Joke-2; Laugh-2; Music-7; Nose-2; Past-6; Priorities-4; Priorities-5; Priorities-8; Producers-4; Psychiatry-1; Secrets-3; Soul-12; Star-3; Strange-11; Strength-8; Truth-1; War-10.

PEP TALKS

1.

"I'm going to tell you something I've kept to myself for years. None of you ever knew George Gipp. He was long before your time, but you all know what a tradition he is at Notre Dame. And the last thing he said to me, 'Rock,' he said, 'some time when the team is up against it and the breaks are beating the boys, tell them to go out there with all they got and win just one for the Gipper. I don't know where I'll be then, Rock,' he said, 'but I'll know about it, and I'll be happy.'"

—Pat O'Brien quoting Ronald Reagan to a losing team at half time in Lloyd Bacon's *Knute Rockne—All American*
(Original Screenplay by Robert Buckner; based on the private papers of Mrs. Knute Rockne and reports of Knute Rockne's associates and intimate friends)

2.

"Jesus had guts! He wasn't afraid of the whole Roman army. Think that quarterback's hot stuff? Well, let me tell you, Jesus would have made the best little All-American quarterback in the history of football. Jesus was a real fighter—the best little scrapper, pound for pound, that you ever saw. And why, gentlemen? Love! Jesus had love in both fists!"

—Burt Lancaster preaching up a storm in a speakeasy in Richard Brooks's *Elmer Gantry*
(Screenplay by Richard Brooks; based on the novel by Sinclair Lewis)

3.

"The *Torrin* has been in one scrap after another, but, even when we've had men killed, the majority survived and brought the old ship back. Now she lies in 1,500 fathoms and with her more than half our shipmates. If they had to die, what a grand way to go! And now they lie all together with the ship we loved, and they're in very good company. We've lost her, but they're still with her. There may be less than half the *Torrin* left, but I feel that we'll all take up the battle with even stronger heart.

Each of us knows twice as much about fighting, and each of us has twice as good a reason to fight. You will all be sent to replace men who've been killed in other ships, and, the next time you're in action, remember the *Torrin!* I should like to add that there isn't one of you that I wouldn't be proud and honored to serve with again."

—Noel Coward saying good-bye to his surviving crew in Noel Coward and David Lean's *In Which We Serve*
(Original Screenplay by Noel Coward)

4.

"I've called you here as freeborn Englishmen, loyal to our king. While he reigned over us, we lived in peace. But since Prince John has seized the regency, Guy of Gisbourne and the rest of his traitors have murdered and pillaged. You've all suffered from their cruelty—the ear loppings, the beatings, the blindings with hot irons, the burning of our farms and homes, the mistreatment of our women. It's time we put an end to this! Now, this forest is wide. It can shelter and clothe and feed a band of good, determined men—good swordsmen, good archers, good fighters. Men, if you're willing to fight for our people, I want you! Are you with me?"

—Errol Flynn recruiting merry men in Michael Curtiz and William Keighley's *The Adventures of Robin Hood*
(Original Screenplay by Norman Reilly Raine and Seton I. Miller; based on the ancient Robin Hood legends)

5.

"Fie upon it, have more resolution. Are you frightened by the word rape? All women love a man of spirit. Remember the story of the Sabine ladies. I believe they made tolerably good wives afterwards."

—Joan Greenwood encouraging David Tomlinson in his pursuit of Susannah York in Tony Richardson's *Tom Jones*
(Screenplay by John Osborne; based on the novel by Henry Fielding)

6.

"Very well then, think of Kaye. Are you going to let her down? You've *got* to give the performance she wanted you to give. Then, perhaps, wherever she is, it might bring her peace."

—Constance Collier pointing Katharine Hepburn toward the stage after Andrea Leeds's suicide in Gregory La Cava's *Stage Door*
(Screenplay by Morrie Ryskind and Anthony Veiller; based on the play by Edna Ferber and George S. Kaufman)

7.

"Sympathy? That's not what you're getting from me, baby. You don't deserve it. You're a great monument to Norman Maine, you are. He was a drunk, and he wasted his life, but he loved you. And he took enormous pride in the one thing in his life that wasn't a waste, you. His love for you and your success. That was the one thing in his life that wasn't a waste. And he knew it. Maybe he was wrong to do what he did, I don't know. But he didn't want to destroy that, destroy the only thing he took pride in. And now you're doing the one thing he was terrified of, you're wiping it out! You're tossing aside the one thing he had left. You're tossing it right back into the ocean after 'im. You're the only thing that remains of him now. And if you just kick it away, it's like he never existed, like there never was a Norman Maine at all."

—Tommy Noonan pointing Judy Garland toward the stage after James Mason's suicide in George Cukor's *A Star Is Born*
(Screenplay by Moss Hart; based on a screenplay by Dorothy Parker, Alan Campbell and Robert Carson and original story by William A. Wellman and Robert Carson)

8.

"You know, Esther, there'll always be a wilderness to conquer. Maybe Hollywood's your wilderness now. From all I hear, it sounds like it. And, if you've got one drop of my blood in your veins, you won't let Mattie or any of her kind break your heart. You'll go right out there and break it yourself. That's your right!"

—May Robson pointing her granddaughter (Janet Gaynor) toward Hollywood in William A. Wellman's *A Star Is Born*
(Screenplay by Dorothy Parker, Alan Campbell and Robert Carson; based on an original story by William A. Wellman and Robert Carson)

ALSO SEE: Hunger-8; Life and Death-15; Mad Act-1; Sounds-1; Star-1; Work-7.

PET EXPRESSIONS

1.
"I'll think about it tomorrow."

—Vivien Leigh pushing away unpleasant thoughts in Victor Fleming's *Gone With the Wind*
(Screenplay by Sidney Howard; based on the novel by Margaret Mitchell)

2.
(a) "What do you feel like doing tonight?"
   (b) "I don't know, Ange. What do *you* feel like doing?"

—(a) Joe Mantell and (b) Ernest Borgnine running in circles in Delbert Mann's *Marty*
(Screenplay by Paddy Chayefsky; based on his teleplay)

3.
"So what's the story?"

—Richard Castellano asking for info in Cy Howard's *Lovers and Other Strangers*
(Screenplay by Renee Taylor, Joseph Bologna and David Z. Goodman; based on the play by Renee Taylor and Joseph Bologna)

4.
"I haven't the foggiest."

—Alec Guinness confessing bafflement in David Lean's *The Bridge on the River Kwai*
(Screenplay by Pierre Boulle; based on his novel, THE BRIDGE OVER THE RIVER KWAI)

5.
"Whaddaya hear? Whaddaya say?"

—James Cagney giving his zippy greeting in Michael Curtiz's *Angels With Dirty Faces*

(Screenplay by John Wexley and Warren Duff;
based on an original story by Rowland
Brown)

6.
" 'Damn the torpedoes! Full speed ahead!' "

—Charles Coburn meeting crises by quoting Admiral Farragut in George Stevens's *The More the Merrier*
(Screenplay by Richard Flournoy and Lewis R.
Foster; based on a story by Robert Russell and
Frank Ross)

7.
"Ods zodikins!"

—Hugh Griffith swearing in Tony Richardson's *Tom Jones*
(Screenplay by John Osborne; based on the novel
by Henry Fielding)

8.
"Some of my best friends are . . ."

—Tallulah Bankhead beginning sentences like a much-traveled know-it-all in Alfred Hitchcock's *Lifeboat*
(Screenplay by Jo Swerling; based on the story by
John Steinbeck)

9.
"Et cetera, et cetera, et cetera."

—Yul Brynner being officious in Walter Lang's *The King and I*
(Screenplay by Ernest Lehman; based on the
musical play by Oscar Hammerstein II and ANNA
AND THE KING OF SIAM, a book by Margaret
Landon)

10.
"That's my rulin'."

—Walter Brennan issuing judgments in William Wyler's *The Westerner*
(Screenplay by Jo Swerling and Niven Busch;
based on a story by Stuart N. Lake)

11.
"Cross my heart, and kiss my elbow."

—Audrey Hepburn promising the truth in Blake Edwards's *Breakfast at Tiffany's*

(Screenplay by George Axelrod; based on the
novella by Truman Capote)

12.
"Wuz you ever bit by a dead bee?"

—Walter Brennan tossing off a nonsensical question (which Lauren Bacall subsequently adopts) in Howard Hawks's *To Have and Have Not*
(Screenplay by Jules Furthman and William
Faulkner; based on the novel by Ernest
Hemingway)

13.
"Yowsir! Yowsir! Yowsir!"

—Gig Young emceeing a dance marathon in Sydney Pollack's *They Shoot Horses, Don't They?*
(Screenplay by James Poe and Robert E.
Thompson; based on the novel by Horace McCoy)

14.
"Oh, Gad!"

—William Powell roaring dissatisfaction in Michael Curtiz's *Life With Father*
(Screenplay by Donald Ogden Stewart; based on
the play by Howard Lindsay and Russel Crouse
and stories by Clarence Day, Jr.)

15.
"Cheeriebye."

—David Niven making chipper exits in Delbert Mann's *Separate Tables*
(Screenplay by Terence Rattigan and John Gay;
based on the play by Terence Rattigan)

ALSO SEE: Good-3; Good-byes-3; Kindness-5;
Looks-13; Love-5.

PIANO

1.
"Making love to the piano—one of my more attractive minor accomplishments."

—Van Heflin treating Joan Crawford to Schumann in Curtis Bernhardt's *Possessed*
(Screenplay by Sylvia Richards and Ranald
MacDougall; based on ONE MAN'S SECRET, a
novelette by Rita Weiman)

2.

(a) "It's about time the piano realized it has not written the concerto!"

(b) "And you, I take it, are the Paderewski who plays his concerto on me, the piano?"

—(a) Author (Hugh Marlowe) and (b) actress (Bette Davis) arguing over text and interpretation in Joseph L. Mankiewicz's *All About Eve*
(Screenplay by Joseph L. Mankiewicz; based on "The Wisdom of Eve," a radio play and short story by Mary Orr)

ALSO SEE: Elephants-4; Hands-2; Translations-4.

PITTSBURGH

1.

(a) "Why did you two ever get married?"

(b) "Ahh, I don't know. It was raining, and we were in Pittsburgh . . ."

—(a) Barbara Stanwyck wondering and (b) Helen Broderick replying in Leigh Jason's *The Bride Walks Out*
(Screenplay by P. J. Wolfson and Philip G. Epstein; based on a story by Howard Emmett Rogers)

2.

(a) "Oh, she's not English, darling. She's from Pittsburgh."

(b) "She sounded English."

(a) "Well, when you're from Pittsburgh, you have to do something."

—(a) Rosalind Russell telling (b) Jan Handzlik about her actress-friend, Coral Browne, in Morton DaCosta's *Auntie Mame*
(Screenplay by Betty Comden and Adolph Green; based on the play by Jerome Lawrence and Robert E. Lee and novel by Patrick Dennis)
            and (almost verbatim)

—(a) Lucille Ball dittoing (b) Kirby Furlong about Beatrice Arthur in the remake, Gene Saks's *Mame*
(Screenplay by Paul Zindel; based on the musical play by Jerome Lawrence, Robert E. Lee and Jerry Herman and AUNTIE MAME, a play by Jerome Lawrence and Robert E. Lee and novel by Patrick Dennis)

PITY

1.

"Of course, I have pity. But now that I've seen the light, it's not my old kind of pity—the kind yours is. The kind that lets itself off easy by encouraging some poor guy to go on kidding himself with a lie. The kind that leaves the poor slob worse off because he feels guiltier than ever. The kind that makes his lying hopes nag at him and reproach him until he's a rotten skunk in his own eyes. No, sir. The kind of pity I feel now is after final results that really helped save the poor guy, make him contented with what he is and quit battling himself so he can find peace for the rest of his life."

—Lee Marvin informing Robert Ryan of a finer kind of pity in John Frankenheimer's *The Iceman Cometh*
(Screenplay based on the play by Eugene O'Neill; text edited by Thomas Quinn Curtiss)

2.

"It seems funny to say, but I don't like you, Benjamin. I don't like any of my children. I just feel sorry for you."

—Florence Eldridge telling off Edmond O'Brien in Michael Gordon's *Another Part of the Forest*
(Screenplay by Vladimir Pozner; based on the play by Lillian Hellman)

3.

"Now don't misunderstand me. I do not hold your frivolity against you. As basic material, you may not be bad, but you are the unfortunate product of a doomed culture. I feel very sorry for you."

—Greta Garbo high-hatting Melvyn Douglas in Ernst Lubitsch's *Ninotchka*
(Screenplay by Charles Brackett, Billy Wilder and Walter Reisch; based on an original story by Melchior Lengyel)
            and (almost verbatim)

—Cyd Charisse dittoing Fred Astaire in the remake, Rouben Mamoulian's *Silk Stockings*
(Screenplay by Leonard Gershe and Leonard Spigelgass; based on the musical play by George S. Kaufman, Leueen MacGrath and Abe Burrows and NINOTCHKA, a screenplay by Charles Brackett,

Billy Wilder and Walter Reisch and original story by Melchior Lengyel)

4.
"Ooooh! Coward yourself! You ain't no lady. No, Miss. That's what my poor old mother would say to you if my poor old mother was to hear you. Whose boat is this anyway? I asked you on board 'cause I was sorry for you on account of you losing your brother and all. What you get for feeling sorry for people! Well, I ain't sorry no more, you crazy, psalm-singin', skinny old maid!"

—Humphrey Bogart turning on Katharine Hepburn in John Huston's *The African Queen*
(Screenplay by James Agee and John Huston; based on the novel by C. S. Forester)

5.
"I do pity her! Who needs pity more than a woman who's sinned?"

—Ethel Barrymore confessing sympathy for a murderess (Valli) in Alfred Hitchcock's *The Paradine Case*
(Screenplay by David O. Selznick; adaptation by Alma Reville and James Bridie; based on the novel by Robert Hichens)

6.
"But you tricked and cheated me. You didn't give me friendship. You gave me pity."

—Richard Todd turning on his friends in Vincent Sherman's *The Hasty Heart*
(Screenplay by Ranald MacDougall; based on the play by John Patrick)

7.
"Why are you nervous? This isn't 'Have-a-gimp-over-for-dinner night,' is it? You're not one of *those* weirdos."

—Jon Voight questioning the motives of Jane Fonda's dinner invitation in Hal Ashby's *Coming Home*
(Screenplay by Waldo Salt and Robert C. Jones; based on a story by Nancy Dowd)

8.
(a) "Didn't you just love the picture? I did. But I just felt so sorry for the creature at the end."

(b) "Sorry for the creature? What did you want? Him to marry the girl?"
(a) "He was kinda scary-looking, but he wasn't really all bad. I think he just craved a little affection—you know, a sense of being loved and needed and wanted."

—(a) Marilyn Monroe surprising (b) Tom Ewell with sympathy for *The Creature From the Black Lagoon* in Billy Wilder's *The Seven Year Itch*
(Screenplay by Billy Wilder and George Axelrod; based on the play by George Axelrod)

ALSO SEE: Cameras-3; Crazy-8; Drink Excuses-13; Fools-11; Goals-4; Human-1; Letters-10; Macho-14; Money-1; Producers-2; Spinsters-1; Together-2; Together-3.

PLANS

1.
"Doc, he lies in his sack all day long, bores me silly with great moronic plots against the captain. He's never carried out one of them."

—Henry Fonda criticizing Jack Lemmon to William Powell in John Ford and Mervyn LeRoy's *Mister Roberts*
(Screenplay by Frank S. Nugent and Joshua Logan; based on the play by Thomas Heggen and Joshua Logan and novel by Thomas Heggen)

2.
"You should be grateful to me for having the foresight to think ahead. To survive one must have a plan. But there's nothing to worry about. Soon we will reach the supply ship, and then we'll all have food and water. Too bad Schmidt couldn't have waited."

—Walter Slezak inciting his fellow survivors to murder him with what proves to be his last words in Alfred Hitchcock's *Lifeboat*
(Screenplay by Jo Swerling; based on the story by John Steinbeck)

3.
"See, this is a floor plan of the apartment. Here's my room; here's your room; here's the bathroom, and here's the kitchen. Now, my alarm goes off at seven o'clock, and we both get

up. At 7:01, I enter the bathroom; then you go down to get the milk, and by 7:05 you've started the coffee. One minute later I leave the bathroom, and then after that you take your bath. Now, that's when I've started to dress. Three minutes later I'm having my coffee, and a minute after that, at 7:12, you should leave the bathroom. At 7:13 I put on my eggs, and I leave to finish dressing. Then you put on your shoes and take off my eggs at 7:16. At 7:17 you start to shave. At 7:18 I eat my eggs, and at 7:21 I'm in the bathroom fixing my hair, and at 7:24 you're in the kitchen putting on your eggs. At 7:25 you make your bed. At 7:26 I make my bed. Then, while you're eating your eggs, I take out the papers and cans. At 7:29 you're washing the dishes. At 7:30 we're all finished. You see? It's really very simple."

—Jean Arthur posting the morning schedule for her new boarder (Charles Coburn) in George Stevens's *The More the Merrier*
(Screenplay by Richard Flournoy and Lewis R. Foster; based on a story by Robert Russell and Frank Ross)

4.
"Bloom, worlds are turned on such thoughts. Don't you see, Bloom, darling Bloom, glorious Bloom? It's so simple. Step one: you find the worst play in the world, a surefire flop. Step two: I raise a million bucks. There are a lot of little old ladies in the world. Step three: you go back to work on the books, only list the backers one for the government and one for us. You can do it, Bloom. You're a wizard. Step four: we open on Broadway, and, before you can say step five, we close on Broadway. Step six: we take our million bucks, and we fly to Rio de Janeiro. Rio, Rio-by-the-sea-o . . ."

—Zero Mostel plotting to turn a dishonest million with Gene Wilder in Mel Brooks's *The Producers*
(Original Screenplay by Mel Brooks)

ALSO SEE: Exchanges-1; Rejection-5; Stupid-3.

PLATONIC RELATIONSHIPS

1.
"I've arrived at the age where a platonic friendship can be sustained on the highest moral plane."

—Charles Chaplin playing harmless to Claire Bloom in Charles Chaplin's *Limelight*
(Original Screenplay by Charles Chaplin)

2.
"When men get around me, they get allergic to wedding rings. You know, 'Big sister type. Good old Ida. You can talk it over with her man to man.' I'm getting awfully tired of men talking to me man to man."

—Eve Arden complaining to Joan Crawford in Michael Curtiz's *Mildred Pierce*
(Screenplay by Ranald MacDougall; based on the novel by James M. Cain)

PLEASURES

1.
"There are certain pleasures you get, little— little jabs of pleasure when—when a swordfish takes the hook or—or—or when you watch a great fighter getting ready for the kill, see?"

—James Mason telling Judy Garland how she sings in George Cukor's *A Star Is Born*
(Screenplay by Moss Hart; based on a screenplay by Dorothy Parker, Alan Campbell and Robert Carson and original story by William A. Wellman and Robert Carson)

2.
"No civilized man ever regrets a pleasure, and no uncivilized man ever knows what the pleasure is."

—George Sanders holding court in Albert Lewin's *The Picture of Dorian Gray*
(Screenplay by Albert Lewin; based on the novel by Oscar Wilde)

3.
"It's always a pleasure to watch the rich enjoy the comforts of the poor."

—Hermione Gingold welcoming to her home a wealthy guest (Louis Jourdan) in Vincente Minnelli's *Gigi*
(Screenplay by Alan Jay Lerner; based on the novel by Colette)

4.
"The joy of giving is indeed a pleasure—especially when you get rid of something you don't want."

—Barry Fitzgerald refining the rule somewhat for Bing Crosby in Leo McCarey's *Going My Way*
(Screenplay by Frank Butler and Frank Cavett; based on an original story by Leo McCarey)

5.
"The enjoyment of art is the only remaining ecstasy that's neither immoral nor illegal."

—Clifton Webb making a brittle observation to Constance Collier in Henry Hathaway's *The Dark Corner*
(Screenplay by Jay Dratler and Bernard C. Schoenfeld; based on the short story by Leo Rosten)

6.
"Look, I know perfectly well the pleasures of music and dancing, but pleasure itself is an indulgence. Only by denying selfish interests can one properly serve the state."

—Cyd Charisse hewing the hard Communist line with frivolous Fred Astaire in Rouben Mamoulian's *Silk Stockings*
(Screenplay by Leonard Gershe and Leonard Spigelgass; based on the musical play by George S. Kaufman, Leueen MacGrath and Abe Burrows and NINOTCHKA, a screenplay by Charles Brackett, Billy Wilder and Walter Reisch and original story by Melchior Lengyel)

ALSO SEE: Differences-1; Empathy-4; Lasts-2; Secrets-3; Women-2.

POETS

1.
"Strictly speaking, his life was his occupation. Yes, yes, Sebastian was a poet. That's what I meant when I said his life was his work because the work of a poet is the life of a poet, and, vice versa, the life of a poet is the work of a poet. I mean, you can't separate them. I mean, a poet's life is his work, and his work is his life in a special sense."

—Katharine Hepburn going mad on the subject of her son the poet in Joseph L. Mankiewicz's *Suddenly, Last Summer*
(Screenplay by Gore Vidal and Tennessee Williams; based on the one-act play by Tennessee Williams)

2.
(a) "I think that the greatest harm done the human race has been done by the poets."
    (b) "Oh, poets are dull boys, most of them —but not especially fiendish."
    (a) "Well, they keep filling people's heads with delusions about love. Writing about it as if it were a symphony orchestra, flights of angels."
    (b) "Which it isn't—eh?"
    (a) "Of course not. People 'fall in love'—as they put it—because they respond to certain hair coloring, or vocal tones, or mannerisms that remind them of their parents."

—(a) Ingrid Bergman falling in love with (b) Gregory Peck in Alfred Hitchcock's *Spellbound*
(Screenplay by Ben Hecht; adaptation by Angus MacPhail; based on THE HOUSE OF DR. EDWARDES, a novel by Francis Beeding)

3.
"You're right. My concentration does not burn enough. Do you know why? I've never seen a burning city. You said once, 'Suffer an experience to recreate it.'"

—Peter Ustinov getting the idea that the burning of Rome might improve his poetry in Mervyn LeRoy's *Quo Vadis*
(Screenplay by John Lee Mahin, S. N. Behrman and Sonya Levien; based on the novel by Henryk Sienkiewicz)

4.
"It is easy to understand why the most beautiful poems about England in the spring

were written by poets living in Italy at the time."

—George Sanders greeting Gene Tierney in a London downpour in Joseph L. Mankiewicz's *The Ghost and Mrs. Muir*
(Screenplay by Philip Dunne; based on THE GHOST OF CAPTAIN GREGG AND MRS. MUIR, a novel by R. A. Dick)

ALSO SEE: Names-21; Tears-2; Telegrams-2; Toasts-4; Toasts-18.

POLITICS

1.
"Gentlemen and fellow citizens, I presume you all know who I am. I'm plain Abraham Lincoln. I've been solicited by many friends to become a candidate for the legislature. My politics are short and sweet, like the old woman's dance. I'm in favor of a national bank, an internal improvement system and a high protective tariff. These are my sentiments and political principles. If elected, I shall be thankful. If not, it'll be all the same."

—Henry Fonda laying it all out there in John Ford's *Young Mr. Lincoln*
(Original Screenplay by Lamar Trotti)

2.
"Now don't you be so stiff-necked about it. Politics is a practical profession. If a criminal has what you want, you do business with him."

—Charles Laughton telling Julius Caesar (John Gavin) how the game is played in Stanley Kubrick's *Spartacus*
(Screenplay by Dalton Trumbo; based on the novel by Howard Fast)

3.
"Politics? You couldn't get into politics. You couldn't get in anywhere. You couldn't even get into the men's room at the Astor."

—Jean Harlow berating her husband (Wallace Beery) in George Cukor's *Dinner at Eight*
(Screenplay by Frances Marion and Herman J.

Mankiewicz; based on the play by George S. Kaufman and Edna Ferber)

4.
"I guess this is just another lost cause, Mr. Paine. All you people don't know about lost causes. Mr. Paine does. He said once they were the only causes worth fighting for, and he fought for them once, for the only reason that any man ever fights for them. Because of just one plain, simple rule, 'love thy neighbor,' and, in this world today, full of hatred, a man who knows that one rule has a great trust. You know that rule, Mr. Paine, and I loved you for it, just as my father did. And you know that you fight for the lost causes harder than for any others. Yes, you even die for them, like a man we both knew, Mr. Paine. You think I'm licked. You all think I'm licked. Well, I'm not licked and I'm going to stay right here and fight for this lost cause even if this room gets filled with lies like these, and the Taylors and all their armies come marching into this place. Somebody'll listen to me. Some—"

—James Stewart filibustering till he faints in Frank Capra's *Mr. Smith Goes to Washington*
(Screenplay by Sidney Buchman; based on "The Gentleman From Montana," a story by Lewis R. Foster)

5.
"Those ain't lies. Those are campaign promises. They expect 'em."

—William Demarest defending Eddie Bracken's hero charade in Preston Sturges's *Hail the Conquering Hero*
(Original Screenplay by Preston Sturges)

ALSO SEE: Excuses-5; Excuses-7; Fools-12; Honor-6; Hunger-4; Love-40; Marriage-3; Marriage-4; Specializations-3; Theater-5; Truth-4.

POVERTY

1.
"Look, I fought as long and as hard as you did. Every day you fought, I fought. I'm a general.

Look, look, here's my pay—a little dust. I can't even buy a bottle of tequila."

—Anthony Quinn confronting his brother (Marlon Brando) in Elia Kazan's *Viva Zapata!*
(Original Screenplay by John Steinbeck)

2.

"Oh, I realize it's a penny here and a penny there, but look at me: I've worked myself up from nothing to a state of extreme poverty."

—Groucho Marx trying to get a job out of Rockliffe Fellowes in Norman Z. McLeod's *Monkey Business*
(Screenplay by S. J. Perelman and Will B. Johnstone; additional dialogue by Arthur Sheekman)

3.

"I'm one of the undeserving poor, that's what I am. Now think what that means to a man. It means he's up against middle-class morality all the time. If there's anything going and I puts in for a bit of it, it's always the same story: you're undeserving so you can't have it. But my needs is as great as the most deserving widow's that ever got money out of six different charities in one week for the death of the same husband. I don't need less than a deserving man. I need more. I don't eat less hearty than he does, and I drink—oh, a lot more."

—Stanley Holloway telling Rex Harrison and Wilfrid Hyde-White about poverty's curse in George Cukor's *My Fair Lady*
(Screenplay by Alan Jay Lerner; based on his musical play and PYGMALION, a screenplay and play by George Bernard Shaw)
                and (almost verbatim)

—Wilfrid Lawson dittoing Leslie Howard and Scott Sunderland in the original, Anthony Asquith and Leslie Howard's *Pygmalion*
(Screenplay by George Bernard Shaw; adaptation by W. P. Lipscomb, Cecil Lewis and Ian Dalrymple; based on the play by George Bernard Shaw)

4.

"Have you ever been in love with poverty like St. Francis? Have you ever been in love with dirt like St. Simeon? Have you ever been

in love with disease and suffering like our nurses and philanthropists? Such passions are unnatural. This love of the common people may please an earl's granddaughter and a university professor, but I've been a poor man and a common man, and it has no romance for me. Leave it to the poor to pretend that poverty is a blessing. We know better than that. We three must stand together above the common people and help their children climb up beside us. Barbara must belong to us, not to the Salvation Army."

—Robert Morley lecturing Rex Harrison about Wendy Hiller in Gabriel Pascal's *Major Barbara*
(Screenplay by George Bernard Shaw; based on his play)

5.

"Leo, he who hesitates is poor."

—Zero Mostel pressuring Gene Wilder to be his partner-in-crime in Mel Brooks's *The Producers*
(Original Screenplay by Mel Brooks)

6.

"I once was so poor I didn't know where my next husband was coming from."

—Mae West telling her maid (Louise Beavers) how bad it can get in Lowell Sherman's *She Done Him Wrong*
(Screenplay by Harvey Thew and John Bright; based on DIAMOND LIL, a play by Mae West)

ALSO SEE: Manners-10; Pleasures-3; Wants-4.

PRAYERS

1.

"What do they know of Heaven or Hell, Cathy, who know nothing of life? Oh, they're praying for you, Cathy. I'll pray one prayer with them. I repeat till my tongue stiffens: 'Catherine Earnshaw, may you not rest so long as I live on. I killed you. Haunt me then! Haunt your murderer! I know that ghosts have wandered on the earth. Be with me always—take any form—drive me mad! Only do not leave me in this dark alone where I cannot find you. I cannot live without my life. I cannot die without my soul.' "

—Laurence Olivier grieving over the dead Merle Oberon in William Wyler's *Wuthering Heights* (*Screenplay by Ben Hecht and Charles MacArthur; based on the novel by Emily Brontë*) and (similarly)

—Timothy Dalton dittoing at the grave of Anna Calder-Marshall in the remake, Robert Fuest's *Wuthering Heights* (*Screenplay by Patrick Tilley; based on the novel by Emily Brontë*)

2.
"By prayer, I don't mean shouting and mumbling and wallowing like a hog in religious sentiment. Prayer is only another name for good, clean, direct thinking. When you pray, think. Think well what you're saying, and make your thoughts into things that are solid. In that way, your prayer will have strength, and that strength will become a part of you in body, mind and spirit."

—Walter Pidgeon instructing Roddy McDowall in John Ford's *How Green Was My Valley* (*Screenplay by Philip Dunne; based on the novel by Richard Llewellyn*)

3.
"Let us pray: Most High, Thou hast led our feeble steps to this far young city. Thou hast put into the hearts and minds of the people here to feed and clothe me and mine. Thou hast given us evidence tonight of their bounty, and we thank Thee that Thou, in Thy infinite wisdom, have given me but one child to feed and one wife to clothe."

—Walter Huston shaming his penny-pinching congregation in Clarence Brown's *Of Human Hearts* (*Screenplay by Bradbury Foote; based on "Benefits Forgot," a story by Honore Morrow*)

4.
"Oh, Lord, have mercy on all men—young and old alike—who gaze upon this, Thy regained servant. Amen."

—Walter Huston praying over his sultry convert (Jennifer Jones) in King Vidor's *Duel in the Sun* (*Screenplay by David O. Selznick; adaptation by Oliver H. P. Garrett; based on the novel by Niven Busch*)

5.
"Oh, God, I've tried to storm the gates of heaven by sacrificing myself. I know now that we must be chosen, that we must be graced as You have graced this child. God, forgive me. I have persecuted one. I did not believe her because I was filled with hate and envy. God, help me to serve this chosen soul for the rest of my days. God help me. God help me."

—Gladys Cooper requesting forgiveness for her harsh treatment of Jennifer Jones in Henry King's *The Song of Bernadette* (*Screenplay by George Seaton; based on the novel by Franz Werfel*)

6.
"Lord, You sure knowed what You was doin' when You brung me to this very cell at this very time. A man with $10,000 hid somewheres, and a widder in the makin'.' "

—Robert Mitchum plotting skulduggery from having Peter Graves for a short-termed cellmate in Charles Laughton's *The Night of the Hunter* (*Screenplay by James Agee; based on the novel by Davis Grubb*)

7.
"Dear God, we've come to the end of our journey. In a little while, we will stand before You. I pray for You to be merciful. Judge us not for our weakness but for our love, and open the doors of heaven for Charlie and me."

—Katharine Hepburn praying herself and Humphrey Bogart out of a crisis in John Huston's *The African Queen* (*Screenplay by James Agee and John Huston; based on the novel by C. S. Forester*)

8.
"Our Father Who art in heaven, please don't shovel the dirt in yet—not when they're still alive."

—Gary Cooper praying himself out of a dark hour in World War II in Cecil B. DeMille's *The Story of Dr. Wassell*
(Screenplay by Alan LeMay and Charles Bennett; based on the short story by James Hilton and nonfiction account by Commander Corydon M. Wassell)

9.
"Well, I—I suppose any prayer would do. Let's see now. 'The Lord is my shepherd; I shall not want. He maketh me to lie down in green pastures; He, er, He, er—' "

—Henry Hull forgetting Psalm 23 during the burial-at-sea of Heather Angel's baby in Alfred Hitchcock's *Lifeboat*
(Screenplay by Jo Swerling; based on the story by John Steinbeck)

10.
"Get me back. Get me back. I don't care what happens to me. Get me back to my wife and kids. Help me, Clarence. Please. Please. I wanna live again. I wanna live again. I wanna live again. Please, God, let me live again."

—James Stewart taking back the wish that he'd never been born in Frank Capra's *It's a Wonderful Life*
(Screenplay by Albert Hackett, Frances Goodrich and Frank Capra; based on "The Greatest Gift," a short story by Philip Van Doren Stern)

11.
(a) "Say your prayer for me, Daddy. I love to hear it."
   (b) " 'God, grant me the serenity to accept the things I cannot change, courage to change the things I can and wisdom always to know the difference.' "

—(b) Burt Lancaster praying the alcoholic's prayer for (a) Shirley Booth in Daniel Mann's *Come Back, Little Sheba*
(Screenplay by Ketti Frings; based on the play by William Inge)

12.
"Hey, Old Man, You home tonight?"

—Paul Newman launching informally into prayer in Stuart Rosenberg's *Cool Hand Luke*

(Screenplay by Donn Pearce and Frank Pierson; based on the novel by Donn Pearce)

13.
"This here ol' man jus' lived a life an' jus' died out of it. I don't know whether he was good or bad, an' it don't matter much. Heard a fella say a poem once, an' he says, 'All that lives is holy.' But I wouldn't pray for jus' a ol' man that's dead, because he's awright. If I was to pray, I'd pray for the folks that's alive an' don't know which way to turn. Grampa here, he ain't got no more trouble like that. He's got his job all cut out for 'im—so cover 'im up an' let 'im get to it."

—John Carradine saying a few words over the grave of Charley Grapewin in John Ford's *The Grapes of Wrath*
(Screenplay by Nunnally Johnson; based on the novel by John Steinbeck)

14.
"Well, Sir, here we are again. We had a little trouble, but that's not Your fault. You spread the milk of human kindness—and, if some of it gets curdled, that's *our* look out. Anyway, things have turned out fine. Alice is going to marry Tony. The Kirbys are going to live with us for a while. And everybody on the block is happy. We've all got our health—and, as far as anything else is concerned, we leave it up to You. Thank You."

—Lionel Barrymore windily returning thanks in the last lines of Frank Capra's *You Can't Take It With You*
(Screenplay by Robert Riskin; based on the play by George S. Kaufman and Moss Hart)

15.
"Much obliged, Lord. Looks like the Tuckers are going to make it after all. Amen."

—Zachary Scott returning thanks in Jean Renoir's *The Southerner*
(Screenplay by Jean Renoir; adaptation by Hugo Butler; based on HOLD AUTUMN IN YOUR HAND, a novel by George Sessions Perry)

ALSO SEE: Eulogies-14; Respect-3.

PREJUDICE

1.

"We're the victims of a foul disease called social prejudice, my child. . . . These dear ladies of the Law and Order League are scouring out the dregs of the town. Come on—be a proud, glorified dreg like me."

—Thomas Mitchell helping Claire Trevor make a graceful exit from town in John Ford's *Stagecoach (Screenplay by Dudley Nichols; based on "Stage to Lordsburg," a short story by Ernest Haycox)*

2.

"It's detestable, but that's the way it is. It's even worse in New Canaan. There, nobody can sell or rent to a Jew. And, even in Darien where Jane's house is and my house is, there's sort of a gentleman's agreement when you—"

—Dorothy McGuire being casual about Connecticut prejudice in Elia Kazan's *Gentleman's Agreement (Screenplay by Moss Hart; based on the novel by Laura Z. Hobson)*

3.

"Why, we don't think a thing of a person's being Jewish, do we, Morris?"

—Eve Arden getting her husband (Frank Overton) to help her hide her prejudice in Delbert Mann's *The Dark at the Top of the Stairs (Screenplay by Irving Ravetch and Harriet Frank, Jr.; based on the play by William Inge)*

4.

"You ought to disqualify yourself for incompetence. You're a frightened little man, selling out his own people for a fancy title and a black gown. They may call you Judge to your face, but they got better words for you behind your back. You're a handkerchief head! You're an Uncle Tom!"

—Arthur Kennedy attacking Juano Hernandez in order to provoke a mistrial in Mark Robson's *Trial (Screenplay by Don M. Mankiewicz; based on his novel)*

ALSO SEE: Future-8; Looks-3; People-3; Pride-5.

PRETENSE

1.

"Here's the foolish little house where I live. It is a queer little place, but, you know, my father is so attached to it that the family has just about given up hope of getting him to build a real house farther up. You know, he doesn't mind us being extravagant about anything else, but he won't let us change one single thing about his precious little old house. Well, adieu."

—Katharine Hepburn apologizing for her home to a potential beau (Fred MacMurray) in George Stevens's *Alice Adams (Screenplay by Dorothy Yost and Mortimer Offner; based on the novel by Booth Tarkington)*

2.

"With this money, I can get away from you. . . . From you and your chickens and your pies and your kitchens and everything that smells of grease. I can get away from this shack with its cheap furniture and this town and its dollar days and its women that wear uniforms and its men that wear overalls."

—Ann Blyth making her exit speech to her mother (Joan Crawford) in Michael Curtiz's *Mildred Pierce (Screenplay by Ranald MacDougall; based on the novel by James M. Cain)*

3.

"You won't need much of anybody's help. You're good. It's chiefly your eyes, I think, and that throb you get in your voice when you say things like 'Be generous, Mr. Spade.' "

—Humphrey Bogart calling Mary Astor's act in John Huston's *The Maltese Falcon (Screenplay by John Huston; based on the novel by Dashiell Hammett)*

4.

"Harry's the greatest kidder in this dump—and that's saying something! Look how he's kidded himself for 20 years."

—Lee Marvin dubbing Fredric March the most self-deluded of the surrounding barflies in John Frankenheimer's *The Iceman Cometh*

*(Screenplay based on the play by Eugene O'Neill;
text edited by Thomas Quinn Curtiss)*

5.
"When you're 17 and the world's beautiful, facing facts is just as slick fun as dancing or going to parties, but when you're 70—well, you don't care about dancing, you don't think about parties anymore, and about the only fun you have left is pretending that there ain't any facts to face. So would you mind if I just kind of went on pretending?"

—Beulah Bondi leveling with her granddaughter (Barbara Read) in Leo McCarey's *Make Way for Tomorrow*
*(Screenplay by Vina Delmar; based on the
play by Helen Leary and Nolan Leary and THE
YEARS ARE SO LONG, a novel by Josephine
Lawrence)*

6.
"Maybe you think it's improper for an old man to have a young, desirable wife. I've played a little game with myself. I—I've pretended that she would have become my wife, even if I'd been unable to give her wealth. I've enjoyed pretending that. It's given me great happiness."

—Miles Mander admitting his pretense about Claire Trevor to Dick Powell in Edward Dmytryk's *Murder, My Sweet*
*(Screenplay by John Paxton; based on FAREWELL,
MY LOVELY, a novel by Raymond Chandler)*

7.
"I never believe in making pretenses. Lots of men who have separated from their wives simply let it be understood that they're not married. I believe, in this day and age, that a man can have his home on the one hand and still live his own life—that is, any man of character."

—Adolphe Menjou pretending to be married in Gregory La Cava's *Stage Door*
*(Screenplay by Morrie Ryskind and Anthony
Veiller; based on the play by Edna Ferber and
George S. Kaufman)*

8.
(a) "Since I have no intention of getting married, I feel honor-bound to declare myself at the beginning."
(b) "What? Before the favor?"
(a) "Certainly before the favor. That's where the honor comes in. Now, how do I declare myself? By saying 'I will never marry'? What woman really believes that? If anything, it's a challenge to them."
(b) "Well, what do you do?"
(a) "Well, I say, 'I *am* married. I'm married, and I can't get a divorce.' Now, our position is clear. There can't be any misunderstanding later."

—(a) Cary Grant explaining his bachelor strategy to (b) Cecil Parker in Stanley Donen's *Indiscreet*
*(Screenplay by Norman Krasna; based on his play,
KIND SIR)*

9.
"We keep up a front for everyone else. Why can't we do it for ourselves?"

—Michael Caine struggling to keep his marital act going with Maggie Smith in Herbert Ross's *California Suite*
(Screenplay by Neil Simon; based on his play)

ALSO SEE: Foolish-2; Imagination-1; Party-3; Poverty-4.

PRIDE

1.
"The girl who said 'no,' she doesn't exist anymore. She died last summer—suffocated from the smoke—something on fire inside of her, and she doesn't live now, but she left me her ring, you see, and she said to me when she slipped this ring on my finger, 'Remember I died empty-handed so make sure that your hands have something in them.' I said, 'What about pride?' And she said, 'Forget about pride whenever it stands between you and what you must have!'"

—Geraldine Page offering herself, too late, to Laurence Harvey in Peter Glenville's *Summer and Smoke*
(Screenplay by James Poe and Meade Roberts; based on the play by Tennessee Williams)

2.
"Pride! I ran out of that a long time ago. I just want to be a woman."

—Katharine Hepburn dropping pretenses in Joseph Anthony's *The Rainmaker*
(Screenplay by N. Richard Nash; based on his play)

3.
"No pride at all! That's a luxury a woman in love can't afford."

—Norma Shearer racing to the waiting arms of her ex in the last lines of George Cukor's *The Women*
(Screenplay by Anita Loos and Jane Murfin; based on the play by Clare Boothe)

4.
"Emily, I'm going out looking for my pride—alone. When I find it, if you're here, I'll come back, and we'll see if it'll have any value to either of us."

—Laurence Harvey leaving his wife (Dina Merrill) after the death of his mistress (Elizabeth Taylor) in the last lines of Daniel Mann's *Butterfield 8*
(Screenplay by Charles Schnee and John Michael Hayes; based on the novel by John O'Hara)

5.
(a) "You're very puzzling, Mr. Darcy. At this moment, it's difficult to believe that you're so proud."
   (b) "At this moment, it's difficult to believe that you're so prejudiced. Shall we not call it quits and start again?"

—(a) Greer Garson and (b) Laurence Olivier warming to each other in Robert Z. Leonard's *Pride and Prejudice*
(Screenplay by Aldous Huxley and Jane Murfin; based on the play by Helen Jerome and novel by Jane Austen)

6.
"He just swallowed his pride. It'll take him a moment or two to digest it."

—Patricia Neal explaining a suddenly humbled Richard Todd in Vincent Sherman's *The Hasty Heart*
(Screenplay by Ranald MacDougall; based on the play by John Patrick)

7.
"We fellas have those offices high up there so that we can catch the wind and go with it, however it blows. But I have nothing to apologize for. I take pride. I am the best possible Arnold Burns."

—Martin Balsam defending the conformist's life to his eccentric brother (Jason Robards) in Fred Coe's *A Thousand Clowns*
(Screenplay by Herb Gardner; based on his play)

8.
"Great stars have great pride."

—Gloria Swanson making a pitiful admission to William Holden in Billy Wilder's *Sunset Boulevard*
(Original Screenplay by Charles Brackett, Billy Wilder and D. M. Marshman, Jr.)

9.
"I can't afford you, Mildred. You have money, and I haven't. All I have is pride and the name, and I can't sell either."

—Zachary Scott deal-making with Joan Crawford in Michael Curtiz's *Mildred Pierce*
(Screenplay by Ranald MacDougall; based on the novel by James M. Cain)

10.
"There's only one thing holding him to you, Maggie, and that's *my* baby. Why, I'd be too proud to hold a man with another woman's child!"

—Mary Astor warring with Bette Davis over George Brent in Edmund Goulding's *The Great Lie*
(Screenplay by Lenore Coffee; based on JANUARY HEIGHTS, a novel by Polan Banks)

11.
"Understand me, gentlemen. I am not a marti-

net, but I do want to take pride in my command. We here have little chance for glory or advancement. While some of our brother officers are leading their well-publicized campaigns against the great Indian nations—the Sioux and the Cheyenne—we are asked to ward off the gnat stings and fleabites of a few cowardly digger Indians."

—Henry Fonda assuming command in John Ford's *Fort Apache*
(Screenplay by Frank S. Nugent; based on "Massacre," a story by James Warner Bellah)

12.
"Men, I won't be going out with ya. I won't be here when ya return. Wish I could. But I know your performance under your new commander will make me proud of ya, as I've always been proud of ya."

—John Wayne relinquishing command in John Ford's *She Wore a Yellow Ribbon*
(Screenplay by Frank S. Nugent and Laurence Stallings; based on "The Big Hunt" and "War Party," two short stories by James Warner Bellah)

13.
"Did I forget to tell you I'm proud?"

—Grace Kelly telling off William Holden in George Seaton's *The Country Girl*
(Screenplay by George Seaton; based on the play by Clifford Odets)

ALSO SEE: Changes-4; Conscience-1; Courage-1; Curtain Speeches-5; Exchanges-5; Land-2; Lies-3; Looks-8; Love-18; Names-25; Pep Talks-7; Prejudice-1; Thieves-6; Violence-5; Work-2.

PRIORITIES

1.
"I'm tired of playing second fiddle to the ghost of Beethoven."

—Joan Crawford complaining about taking a backseat to the career of her violinist-protégé (John Garfield) in Jean Negulesco's *Humoresque*

(Screenplay by Clifford Odets and Zachary Gold; based on a short story by Fannie Hurst)

2.
(a) "There are worse things than chastity, Mr. Shannon."
 (b) "Yes: lunacy and death."

—(a) Deborah Kerr and (b) Richard Burton reaching relative accord in John Huston's *The Night of the Iguana*
(Screenplay by Anthony Veiller and John Huston; based on the play by Tennessee Williams)

3.
"It's just that I'd rather have you drunk than dead."

—Jane Wyman settling for the happier alternative for Ray Milland in Billy Wilder's *The Lost Weekend*
(Screenplay by Charles Brackett and Billy Wilder; based on the novel by Charles R. Jackson)

4.
"I haven't time to die while there are people oppressed, starving!"

—George Arliss making noble sounds in John Adolfi's *Voltaire*
(Screenplay by Paul Green and Maude T. Howell; based on the novel by George Gibbs and E. Lawrence Dudley)

5.
"I like persons better than principles. A person with no principles is better than anything else in the world."

—George Sanders preaching hedonism in Albert Lewin's *The Picture of Dorian Gray*
(Screenplay by Albert Lewin; based on the novel by Oscar Wilde)

6.
"Some of us prefer Austrian voices raised in song to ugly German threats."

—Christopher Plummer choosing to make music, not war, in Robert Wise's *The Sound of Music*
(Screenplay by Ernest Lehman; based on the musical play by Howard Lindsay and Russel Crouse and THE TRAPP FAMILY SINGERS, a book by Maria Augusta Trapp)

7.

"I'm more interested in 'The Rock of Ages' than I am in the age of rocks."

—Fredric March twisting Spencer Tracy's geological question into a religious declaration in Stanley Kramer's *Inherit the Wind*
(*Screenplay by Nathan E. Douglas and Harold Jacob Smith; based on the play by Jerome Lawrence and Robert E. Lee*)

8.

"People here are funny. They work so hard at living they forget how to live. Last night, after I left you, I was walking along and—and looking at the tall buildings, and I got to thinking about what Thoreau said. 'They created a lot of grand palaces here, but they forgot to create the noblemen to put in them.' I'd rather have Mandrake Falls."

—Gary Cooper giving Jean Arthur his reaction to New York in Frank Capra's *Mr. Deeds Goes to Town* (*Screenplay by Robert Riskin; based on "Opera Hat," a short story by Clarence Budington Kelland*)

ALSO SEE: Love Objects-3; Proposals-1.

PRISON

1.

"Big nose of yours been going over me like a sheep in a vegetable patch. Well, I ain't keepin' it a secret. I been in the penitentiary. Been there four years. Anything else you wanna know?"

—Henry Fonda saying good-bye to the ride he hitched in John Ford's *The Grapes of Wrath* (*Screenplay by Nunnally Johnson; based on the novel by John Steinbeck*)

2.

"Yeah, I've been a lot of places and no place. To tell you the truth, Danny, I've been sightseeing. I spent a year and a day on a sweet little island they call Blackwell's. And I took a little trip up the Hudson, too. Hey, there's a beautiful view up there from a certain window, and I ought to know because I looked at it for 36 months."

—Elia Kazan greeting James Cagney in Anatole Litvak's *City for Conquest*
(*Screenplay by John Wexley; based on the novel by Aben Kandel*)

3.

"You think you're not in prison now, living in a gray little room, going to a gray little job, leading a gray little life?"

—Zero Mostel talking Gene Wilder into risking a prison stretch in Mel Brooks's *The Producers* (*Original Screenplay by Mel Brooks*)

4.

"I always thought it was a ridiculous name for a prison—Sing Sing, I mean. Sounds more like it should be an opera house or something."

—Audrey Hepburn making a wry observation in Blake Edwards's *Breakfast at Tiffany's* (*Screenplay by George Axelrod; based on the novella by Truman Capote*)

5.

(a) "Gentlemen, Chicolini here may talk like an idiot and look like an idiot, but don't let that fool you. He really is an idiot. I implore you, send him back to his father and brothers who are waiting for him with open arms in the penitentiary. I suggest we give him ten years in Leavenworth or eleven years in Twelveworth."

(b) "I tell you what I'll do. I'll take five and ten in Woolworth."

—(a) Groucho Marx and (b) Chico Marx cutting up in court in Leo McCarey's *Duck Soup* (*Screenplay by Bert Kalmar and Harry Ruby; additional dialogue by Arthur Sheekman and Nat Perrin*)

6.

(a) "Well, I'll say one thing for prison. It's a better class of people."

(b) "There's a lot to be said for prison."

(c) "You always know where you are when you get up in the morning."

(b) "Yes. And I could do with sleep."

(c) "What do you say? Prison wasn't so bad. Let's all go back. Think of the welcome we'll get."

(a) "Well, if it don't work out right, we'll do it all over again next year."

—(a) Humphrey Bogart, (b) Peter Ustinov and (c) Aldo Ray talking themselves back into prison in the last lines of Michael Curtiz's *We're No Angels* *(Screenplay by Ranald MacDougall; based on* LA CUISINE DES ANGES, *a play by Albert Husson, and* MY THREE ANGELS, *a Broadway adaptation by Bella Spewack and Samuel Spewack)*

7.
"Jail is no place for a young fellow. There's no advancement."

—Groucho Marx cautioning Oscar Shaw in Joseph Santley and Robert Florey's *The Cocoanuts* *(Screenplay by Morrie Ryskind; based on the musical play by George S. Kaufman and Morrie Ryskind)*

ALSO SEE: Greetings-4; Help-4; Lies-16; Neck-2; Prayers-6; Trouble-9.

PRIVACY

1.
"When I finishes with my work, I wants my solitude and I wants my privitation."

—Hattie McDaniel explaining her one rule as a live-in maid to Claudette Colbert in John Cromwell's *Since You Went Away* *(Screenplay by David O. Selznick; adaptation by Margaret Buell Wilder; based on her book of letters)*

2.
"Life without a room to oneself is a barbarity."

—Edith Evans agreeing to a room for her granddaughter's governess-companion (Deborah Kerr) in Ronald Neame's *The Chalk Garden* *(Screenplay by John Michael Hayes; based on the play by Enid Bagnold)*

3.
"Murder victims have no claim to privacy."

—Dana Andrews telling Clifton Webb the cruel truth about Gene Tierney in Otto Preminger's *Laura* *(Screenplay by Jay Dratler, Samuel Hoffenstein and Betty Reinhardt; based on the novel by Vera Caspary)*

ALSO SEE: Chin-3; Nose-3; Progress-2.

PRODUCERS

1.
"Why do they always look like unhappy rabbits?"

—Marilyn Monroe asking George Sanders a not-so-dumb question in Joseph L. Mankiewicz's *All About Eve* *(Screenplay by Joseph L. Mankiewicz; based on "The Wisdom of Eve," a radio play and short story by Mary Orr)*

2.
"Meet Kirk Edwards. You're saying to yourself, 'So that's what he looks like. That's what a Wall Street wizard looks like, who came up from the streets of New York, who came up from the bottom but never really left it.' Don't feel sorry for Kirk Edwards—not unless you're a hungry psychiatrist. Kirk was producing a motion picture. His first. He had as much in common with anything creative as I have with nuclear physics."

—Humphrey Bogart providing the introductory notes on his producer-employer (Warren Stevens) in Joseph L. Mankiewicz's *The Barefoot Contessa* *(Original Screenplay by Joseph L. Mankiewicz)*

3.
"That's exactly why we want to produce this play: to show the world the true Hitler—the Hitler you loved, the Hitler you knew, the Hitler with a song in his heart."

—Zero Mostel enthusiastically conning the author of the worst play in the world (Kenneth Mars) in Mel Brooks's *The Producers* *(Original Screenplay by Mel Brooks)*

4.

"If you keep that door closed, you'll never know anything. You're a producer. You ought to see people. Why, the greatest actress in the world might be living out there, 50 feet away from you, and you'd never even give her a chance."

—Katharine Hepburn chewing out Adolphe Menjou in Gregory La Cava's *Stage Door*
(Screenplay by Morrie Ryskind and Anthony Veiller; based on the play by Edna Ferber and George S. Kaufman)

ALSO SEE: Plans-4; Star-5; Success-2; Wrong-1.

PROFESSIONS

1.

"I run a couple of newspapers. What do you do?"

—Orson Welles getting acquainted with Dorothy Comingore in Orson Welles's *Citizen Kane*
(Original Screenplay by Herman J. Mankiewicz and Orson Welles)

2.

"Well, I would describe myself as a contact man. I keep contact between Matuschek & Co. and the customers—on a bicycle."

—William Tracy inflating his errand-boy position in Ernst Lubitsch's *The Shop Around the Corner*
(Screenplay by Samson Raphaelson; based on PARFUMERIE, a play by Miklos Laszlo)

3.

"You know, what I was hoping was that you and your old man—between you—might be able to fix me up with a job. . . . Maybe something with a nice office where I can wear a tie and have a sweet little secretary and talk over the telephone about enterprises and things. I gotta get some place in this world. I just gotta."

—William Holden prevailing on his rich college buddy (Cliff Robertson) for a job in Joshua Logan's *Picnic*
(Screenplay by Daniel Taradash; based on the play by William Inge)

4.

"Well, I'm all fixed far as I'm concerned as a medicine man. I'll have three meals a day—five if I want 'em—roof over my head and a drink every now and then to warm me up. I'll be worshiped and fed and treated like a high priest for telling people things they want to hear. Good medicine men are born, not made. Come and see me sometime, my boy. Even you would take off your hat when you see how respected I am. Why, only day before yesterday, they wanted to make me the legislature. Their whole legislature! I don't know what that means, but it must be the highest honor they can bestow. Yeah, I'm all fixed for the rest of my natural life."

—Walter Huston explaining his sweet setup to Tim Holt in John Huston's *The Treasure of the Sierra Madre*
(Screenplay by John Huston; based on the novel by B. Traven)

5.

"I loaf—but in a decorative and highly charming manner."

—Zachary Scott doing his "idle rich" number on Joan Crawford in Michael Curtiz's *Mildred Pierce*
(Screenplay by Ranald MacDougall; based on the novel by James M. Cain)

6.

(a) "Tell me, is Mrs. Van Hopper a friend of yours or just a relation?"

(b) "No, she's my employer. I'm what is known as a paid companion."

(a) "I didn't know that companionship could be bought."

—(b) Joan Fontaine explaining to (a) Laurence Olivier that she's Florence Bates's friend-for-hire in Alfred Hitchcock's *Rebecca*
(Screenplay by Robert E. Sherwood and Joan Harrison; adaptation by Philip MacDonald and Michael Hogan; based on the novel by Daphne du Maurier)

7.

"Make it ten. I am only a poor corrupt official."

—Claude Rains lowering a 20,000-franc bet with Humphrey Bogart in Michael Curtiz's *Casablanca* (*Screenplay by Julius J. Epstein, Philip G. Epstein and Howard Koch; based on EVERYBODY COMES TO RICK'S, a play by Murray Burnett and Joan Alison*)

8.

"Simple phonetics. The science of speech. That's my profession, also my hobby. Anybody can spot an Irishman or a Yorkshireman by his brogue. I can place a man within six miles. I can place him within two miles in London, sometimes within two streets."

—Rex Harrison crowing a bit in George Cukor's *My Fair Lady* (*Screenplay by Alan Jay Lerner; based on his musical play and PYGMALION, a screenplay and play by George Bernard Shaw*) and (almost verbatim)

—Leslie Howard dittoing in the original, Anthony Asquith and Leslie Howard's *Pygmalion* (*Screenplay by George Bernard Shaw; adaptation by W. P. Lipscomb, Cecil Lewis and Ian Dalrymple; based on the play by George Bernard Shaw*)

9.

"My job is to teach these natives the meaning of democracy, and they're going to learn democracy if I have to shoot every one of them."

—Paul Ford threatening some learning on postwar Okinawans in Daniel Mann's *The Teahouse of the August Moon* (*Screenplay by John Patrick; based on his play and the book by Vern J. Sneider*)

10.

"Little girls, I am in the business of putting old heads on young shoulders, and all my pupils are the *crème de la crème*. Give me a girl of an impressionable age, and she is mine for life."

—Maggie Smith's teaching credo echoing in Pamela Franklin's mind in the last lines of Ronald Neame's *The Prime of Miss Jean Brodie*

(*Screenplay by Jay Presson Allen; based on her play and the novel by Muriel Spark*)

11.

"I'm going to tell you something, Miz Thornton —something you can teach your class some day. The minute they walk out that there door, they walk into a dog-eat-dog world. It's 'Crawl in front of the big dogs if you want to eat.' 'Get a job.' I won't do it! I *won't* do it! That—that's why I'm washing windows, scrubbing walls, emptying ashes."

—Arthur Kennedy telling Mildred Dunnock why he's a janitor in Mark Robson's *Peyton Place* (*Screenplay by John Michael Hayes; based on the novel by Grace Metalious*)

12.

"Well, that's a hopeful way of putting it. I'm really in the junk business—an occupation for which many people feel I'm well qualified by temperament and training. It's fascinating work."

—Dana Andrews exhibiting more than a trace of bitterness in telling Teresa Wright about his new job in William Wyler's *The Best Years of Our Lives* (*Screenplay by Robert E. Sherwood; based on GLORY FOR ME, a verse novel by MacKinlay Kantor*)

13.

(a) "I was reading a book the other day."

   (b) "Reading a book!"

   (a) "Yes. It's all about civilization or something—a nutty kind of a book. Do you know that the guy said that machinery is going to take the place of every profession?"

   (b) "Oh, my dear. That's something you need never worry about."

—(a) Jean Harlow and (b) Marie Dressler chitchatting on the way to the dinner table in George Cukor's *Dinner at Eight* (*Screenplay by Frances Marion and Herman J. Mankiewicz; based on the play by George S. Kaufman and Edna Ferber*)

14.

"As long as they've got sidewalks, you've got a job."

—Joan Blondell insulting Claire Dodd in Lloyd Bacon's *Footlight Parade*
(Original Screenplay by Manuel Seff and James Seymour)

ALSO SEE: Actors; Detectives; Directors; Doctors; Floozy; Gigolo; Nurses; Poets; Producers; Psychiatry; Public Relations; Star; Thieves; Writers; Friends-6; Genius-2, Money-2; Politics-2; Translations-4; Wives-10

PROGRESS

1.
"What is this progress? What is the good of all this progress onward and onward? We demand a halt. We demand a rest. . . . An end to progress! Make an end to this progress now! Let this be the last day of the scientific age!"

—Cedric Hardwicke playing false prophet of the future in William Cameron Menzies's *Things To Come*
(Screenplay by H. G. Wells; based on his novel, THE SHAPE OF THINGS TO COME)

2.
"Gentlemen, progress has never been a bargain. You have to pay for it. Sometimes, I think there's a man who sits behind the counter who says, 'All right, you can have a telephone, but you lose privacy and the charm of distance.' 'I know you may vote, but at a price: you lose the right to retreat behind the powder puff or your petticoat,' 'Mister, you may conquer the air, but the birds will lose their wonder and the clouds will smell of gasoline.' Darwin took us forward to a hilltop from where we could look back and see the way from which we came. But, for this insight and for this knowledge, we must abandon our faith in the pleasant poetry of Genesis."

—Spencer Tracy arguing his case in Stanley Kramer's *Inherit the Wind*
(Screenplay by Nathan E. Douglas and Harold Jacob Smith; based on the play by Jerome Lawrence and Robert E. Lee)

3.
"I'm not sure George is wrong about automobiles. With all their speed forward, they may be a step backward in civilization. It may be that they won't add to the beauty of the world, nor to the life of men's souls. I'm not sure. But automobiles have come, and almost all outward things are going to be different because of what they bring. They're going to alter war, and they're going to alter peace. I think men's minds are going to be changed in subtle ways because of automobiles, and it may be that George is right. It may be that in ten or twenty years from now, if we can see the inward change in men by that time, I shouldn't be able to defend the gasoline engine but would have to agree with George that automobiles had no business to be invented."

—Joseph Cotten questioning the kind of future that Tim Holt predicts the horseless carriage will bring in Orson Welles's *The Magnificent Ambersons*
(Screenplay by Orson Welles; based on the novel by Booth Tarkington)

4.
"The girls call me Pilgrim because every time I dance with one I make a little progress."

—Bob Hope coming on to Paulette Goddard in George Marshall's *The Ghost Breakers*
(Screenplay by Walter De Leon; based on THE GHOST BREAKER, a play by Paul Dickey and Charles W. Goddard)

ALSO SEE: Action-3; Defense-3; Doctors-3; Intelligence-1.

PROLOGUES

1.
"There was a land of Cavaliers and Cotton Fields called the Old South. Here in this patrician world the Age of Chivalry took its last bows. Here was the last ever seen of the Knights and their Ladies Fair, of Master and Slave. Look for it only in books, for it is no more than a dream remembered, a Civilization gone with the wind . . ."

—Victor Fleming's *Gone With the Wind*
(Screenplay by Sidney Howard; based on the novel by Margaret Mitchell; prologue written by an uncredited Ben Hecht)

2.
"Nobody with a dream should come to Italy. No matter how dead and buried the dream is thought to be, in Italy it will rise and walk again."

—Guy Green's *Light in the Piazza*
(Screenplay by Julius J. Epstein; based on the novel by Elizabeth Spencer; prologue written by an uncredited Arthur Freed)

3.
"This picture takes place in Paris in those wonderful days when a siren was a brunette and not an alarm—and if a Frenchman turned out the light it was not on account of an air raid!"

—Ernst Lubitsch's *Ninotchka*
(Screenplay by Charles Brackett, Billy Wilder and Walter Reisch; based on an original story by Melchior Lengyel)

4.
"This is the story of the unconquerable fortress—the American home, 1943."

—John Cromwell's *Since You Went Away*
(Screenplay by David O. Selznick; adaptation by Margaret Buell Wilder; based on her book of letters)

5.
"The love of a man for a woman waxes and wanes like the moon, but the love of brother for brother is steadfast as the stars and endures like the word of the prophet.
                              —Arabian Proverb"

—William A. Wellman's *Beau Geste*
(Screenplay by Robert Carson; based on the novel by Percival Christopher Wren)

6.
"I sent my soul through the invisible,
     Some letter of that after-life to spell:
And by and by my soul returned to me,

And answered, 'I myself am Heaven and Hell.'
                              —Rubaiyat of Omar Khayyam"

—Albert Lewin's *The Picture of Dorian Gray*
(Screenplay by Albert Lewin; based on the novel by Oscar Wilde)

7.
"For those who believe in God, no explanation is necessary. For those who do not believe in God, no explanation is possible."

—Henry King's *The Song of Bernadette*
(Screenplay by George Seaton; based on the novel by Franz Werfel)

PROMISCUITY

1.
"It took more than one man to change my name to Shanghai Lily."

—Marlene Dietrich telling Clive Brook that, no, she isn't married in Josef von Sternberg's *Shanghai Express*
(Screenplay by Jules Furthman; based on a story by Harry Hervey)

2.
"Not Anytime Annie! Say, who could forget her? She only said 'no' once—and then she couldn't hear the question."

—George E. Stone characterizing Ginger Rogers in Lloyd Bacon's *42nd Street*
(Screenplay by Rian James and James Seymour; based on the novel by Bradford Ropes)

3.
"I am the most virtuous man in Rome. I keep these women out of my respect for Roman morality—that morality which has made Rome strong enough to steal two-thirds of the world from its rightful owners, founded on the sanctity of Roman marriage and the Roman family. I happen to like women. I have a promiscuous nature, and, unlike these aristocrats, I will not take a marriage vow which I know that my nature will prevent me from keeping."

—Charles Laughton rationalizing his self-styled morality in Stanley Kubrick's *Spartacus*
(Screenplay by Dalton Trumbo; based on the novel by Howard Fast)

4.

(a) "I idealized them. Every woman I meet I put up there. Of course, the longer I know her —I mean, the better I know her . . ."

(b) "Un huh. Yes, it's hard to keep them up there."

(a) "Yes, isn't it?"

(b) "Pretty soon, the pedestal wobbles and then topples."

(a) "C'est la vie, et cetera."

—(a) Cary Grant telling (b) Deborah Kerr how he worships women (i.e., briefly) in Leo McCarey's *An Affair To Remember*
(Screenplay by Delmer Daves and Leo McCarey; based on an original story by Mildred Cram and Leo McCarey)

5.

"To those who find our hero's behavior startling, the answer is simple. Tom had always thought that any woman was better than none. While Molly never felt that one man was quite as good as two."

—Narrator Michael MacLiammoir explaining the easy passions of Albert Finney and Diane Cilento in Tony Richardson's *Tom Jones*
(Screenplay by John Osborne; based on the novel by Henry Fielding)

6.

(a) "She was a tramp."

(b) "She was a human being. Let me remind you that even the most unworthy of us has the right to life and the pursuit of happiness."

(a) "From what I hear, she pursued it in all directions."

—(a) Patricia Hitchcock and (b) Leo G. Carroll discussing the murdered Laura Elliot in Alfred Hitchcock's *Strangers on a Train*
(Screenplay by Raymond Chandler and Czenzi Ormonde; adaptation by Whitfield Cook; based on the novel by Patricia Highsmith)

ALSO SEE: Fidelity-2; Loneliness-10; Marriage-15; Static-9.

PROPOSALS

1.
"Better Wed Than Dead"

—Steve McQueen proposing to Natalie Wood with a picket sign in the closing shot of Robert Mulligan's *Love With the Proper Stranger*
(Original Screenplay by Arnold Schulman)

2.

(a) "I'm not going to marry anyone who says, 'You gotta marry me, Howard.' I mean, the thing is if a woman wants me to marry her, she can at least say 'please.' "

(b) "Please marry me, Howard. Please. Please."

—(b) Rosalind Russell saying "please" to (a) Arthur O'Connell in Joshua Logan's *Picnic*
(Screenplay by Daniel Taradash; based on the play by William Inge)

3.
"Marry me, and I'll never look at another horse."

—Groucho Marx proposing to Margaret Dumont in Sam Wood's *A Day at the Races*
(Screenplay by Robert Pirosh, George Seaton and George Oppenheimer; based on a story by Robert Pirosh and George Seaton)

4.

(a) "I repeat what I said: either you go to America with Mrs. Van Hopper or you come home to Manderley with me."

(b) "You mean you want a secretary or something?"

(a) "I'm asking you to marry me, you little fool."

—(a) Laurence Olivier making it perfectly clear to (b) Joan Fontaine in Alfred Hitchcock's *Rebecca*
(Screenplay by Robert E. Sherwood and Joan Harrison; adaptation by Philip MacDonald and

Michael Hogan; based on the novel by Daphne du Maurier)

5.

"Forgive me for startling you with the impetuosity of my sentiments, my dear Scarlett—I mean, my dear Mrs. Kennedy—but it cannot have escaped your notice that, for some time past, the friendship I have felt for you has ripened into a deeper feeling—a feeling more beautiful, more pure, more sacred—dare I name it? Can it be love?"

—Clark Gable doing a mock proposal, on bended knee, to win Vivien Leigh in Victor Fleming's *Gone With the Wind*
(Screenplay by Sidney Howard; based on the novel by Margaret Mitchell)

6.

"Who's asking you to be rational? Listen, when I courted your grandmother, it took me two years to propose. Know why? The moment she'd walk into the room, my knees would buckle, the blood would rush to my head and the walls would start dancing. Twice I keeled over in a dead faint. . . . Finally, she dragged it out of me when I was in bed with a 104 fever—and in a state of hysteria. The moment she accepted, the fever went down to normal—and I hopped out of bed. The case was written up in medical journals as the phenomena of the times. There was nothing phenomenal about it. I just had it bad, and I never got over it either."

—Lionel Barrymore reminiscing with his granddaughter (Jean Arthur) in Frank Capra's *You Can't Take It With You*
(Screenplay by Robert Riskin; based on the play by George S. Kaufman and Moss Hart)

7.

"Do you remember what you said when you asked me to marry you? You said, 'There's nothing about me to attract a young girl's fancy, but those who've known me very well have come to like me.' "

—Josephine Hutchinson reminding Paul Muni in William Dieterle's *The Story of Louis Pasteur*
(Screenplay by Sheridan Gibney and Pierre

Collings; based on an original story by Sheridan Gibney and Pierre Collings)

8.

"I will guarantee you the companionship you want. You've certainly had time to get used to me. There will be no surprises in store for you. You know me too well. I have enormous respect for you. You add greatly to my comfort. In fact, you're about the only woman I know to whom I would make such a rash offer."

—Clifton Webb popping the question, after 15 years, to his secretary (Dorothy McGuire) in Jean Negulesco's *Three Coins in the Fountain*
(Screenplay by John Patrick; based on the novel by John H. Secondari)

9.

"You'll never want for food, and you'll never worry about rent. I've worked since I was seven. . . . I'm 21. I'm not legitimate. I've got good teeth. I'm not tattooed."

—Richard Todd itemizing his strong points for Patricia Neal in Vincent Sherman's *The Hasty Heart*
(Screenplay by Ranald MacDougall; based on the play by John Patrick)

10.

"I don't owe a nickel in this town. I'll eat anything that's put down in front of me. I can fix anything electrical. I'm all right after—after I've had my first cup of coffee. I want that bad though. I got me a new job at the gas station. I'd turn over my paycheck the minute I get it—that's every Friday—and I come straight home from work, and I stay there. I got me and Alice, and we're alone. You got your two kids; you're alone. If you could help me, maybe I could help you."

—Beau Bridges itemizing his strong points for Sally Field in Martin Ritt's *Norma Rae*
(Original Screenplay by Irving Ravetch and Harriet Frank, Jr.)

11.

"You need somebody, and I need somebody, too. Can it be you and me, Blanche?"

—Karl Malden wondering aloud to Vivien Leigh in Elia Kazan's *A Streetcar Named Desire*
(Screenplay by Tennessee Williams; adaptation by Oscar Saul; based on the play by Tennessee Williams)

12.

"I believe that a man is fire and a woman, fuel. And she who is born beautiful is born married."

—Marlon Brando inventing amorous sayings for his formal courtship of Jean Peters in Elia Kazan's *Viva Zapata!*
(Original Screenplay by John Steinbeck)

13.

(a) "I must have your golden hair, fascinating eyes, alluring smile, your lovely arms, your form divine—"

    (b) "Wait a minute. Wait a minute! Is this a proposal, or are you taking an inventory?"

—(b) Mae West putting (a) John Miljan in his place in Leo McCarey's *Belle of the Nineties*
(Original Screenplay by Mae West)

14.

"All of which doesn't answer my question. Will you marry me? I'm aging visibly."

—Raymond Massey getting insistent with Joan Crawford in Curtis Bernhardt's *Possessed*
(Screenplay by Sylvia Richards and Ranald MacDougall; based on ONE MAN'S SECRET, a novelette by Rita Weiman)

ALSO SEE: Apology-2; Life-5; Timing-2; Toasts-17.

PROPOSITIONS

1.

"Why don't you come up sometime and see me? I'm home every evening."

—Mae West vamping Cary Grant in Lowell Sherman's *She Done Him Wrong*
(Screenplay by Harvey Thew and John Bright; based on DIAMOND LIL, a play by Mae West)

2.

"Come to my room in half an hour, and bring some rye bread."

—Jimmy Durante barking lustfully at Mary Wickes in William Keighley's *The Man Who Came to Dinner*
(Screenplay by Julius J. Epstein and Philip G. Epstein; based on the play by George S. Kaufman and Moss Hart)

3.

"Years from now, when you talk about this— and you will—be kind."

—Deborah Kerr seducing John Kerr in Vincente Minnelli's *Tea and Sympathy*
(Screenplay by Robert Anderson; based on his play)

4.

"Years from now, when they talk about this— and they will—remember to tell them that it was my idea."

—Faye Dunaway vamping Paul Newman in John Guillermin and Irwin Allen's *The Towering Inferno*
(Screenplay by Stirling Silliphant; based on two novels, THE TOWER by Richard Martin Stern and THE GLASS INFERNO by Thomas N. Scortia and Frank M. Robinson)

5.

"Used to have a boyfriend was a cowboy. Met him in Colorado. He was in love with me because I was a—an older woman and had some sense. . . . Took me up in the mountains one night and wanted to marry me, right there on the mountain top. He said the stars'd be our preacher and the moon our best man. Did you ever hear such talk?"

—Rosalind Russell trying to impress William Holden in Joshua Logan's *Picnic*
(Screenplay by Daniel Taradash; based on the play by William Inge)

6.

"It's a good night to be abroad and looking for game."

—Albert Finney punning around with Diane Cilento in Tony Richardson's *Tom Jones*

(Screenplay by John Osborne; based on the novel by Henry Fielding)

7.
"You know me. I'm just like you. It's two in the morning, and I don't know nobody."

—Robert Redford arriving on Dimitra Arliss's doorstep in George Roy Hill's *The Sting*
(Original Screenplay by David S. Ward)

8.
"You know, there are three things that we could do right now: you could call a taxi and go home, or we could go on walking and I could lecture you on the real dilemma of modern art, or we could go to my place and we could thoroughly enjoy each other."

—Alan Bates emphasizing the latter to Jill Clayburgh in Paul Mazursky's *An Unmarried Woman*
(Original Screenplay by Paul Mazursky)

9.
"Oh, why can't we break away from all this, just you and I, and lodge with my fleas in the hills—I mean, flee to my lodge in the hills."

—Groucho Marx encouraging Thelma Todd to reckless abandon in Norman Z. McLeod's *Monkey Business*
(Screenplay by S. J. Perelman and Will B. Johnstone; additional dialogue by Arthur Sheekman)

10.
"How about coming up to my place for a spot of heavy breathing?"

—Walter Matthau asking Carol Burnett a direct question in Martin Ritt's *Pete 'n' Tillie*
(Screenplay by Julius J. Epstein; based on WITCH'S MILK, a novella by Peter De Vries)

11.
"They flew in last night—knockouts! And one big blonde especially, see? Of course, she went for me right away, naturally, so I started to turn on the old personality, you know, and I said, 'Isn't there anything in the world that'll make you come out to the ship with me?' And she

said, 'Yes'—she said, 'Yes, there is, one thing and one thing only—a good stiff drink of Scotch.'"

—Jack Lemmon revealing Betsy Palmer's weakness to Henry Fonda and William Powell in John Ford and Mervyn LeRoy's *Mister Roberts*
(Screenplay by Frank S. Nugent and Joshua Logan; based on the play by Thomas Heggen and Joshua Logan and novel by Thomas Heggen)

12.
"Why don't you get out of that wet coat and into a dry martini?"

—Robert Benchley coming on to Ginger Rogers in Billy Wilder's *The Major and the Minor*
(Screenplay by Charles Brackett and Billy Wilder; based on CONNIE GOES HOME, a play by Edward Childs Carpenter, and "Sunny Goes Home," a short story by Fannie Kilbourne)

13.
(a) "I think he's upset. We didn't order enough."
   (b) "Shall we cheer him up? Waiter! Do you have any rooms?"

—(b) Jean-Louis Trintignant using a third party to proposition (a) Anouk Aimée in Claude Lelouch's *A Man and a Woman*
(Original Screenplay by Claude Lelouch and Pierre Uytterhoven)

14.
(a) "What would you like to have?"
   (b) "Sex."

—(a) George Segal and (b) Susan Anspach displaying at a bar the single-mindedness of young marrieds in Paul Mazursky's *Blume in Love*
(Original Screenplay by Paul Mazursky)

15.
"Oh, I don't know. I'm just a hack writer who drinks too much and falls in love with girls. You."

—Joseph Cotten admitting his feeling for Valli in Carol Reed's *The Third Man*
(Original Screenplay by Graham Greene)

16.

"You give me powders, pills, baths, injections, and enemas—when all I need is love."

—William Holden coming on to his nurse (Ann Sears) in David Lean's *The Bridge on the River Kwai* (*Screenplay by Pierre Boulle; based on his novel,* THE BRIDGE OVER THE RIVER KWAI)

17.

"All they have to do is to play eight bars of 'Come to Me, My Melancholy Baby,' and my spine turns to custard, I get goose pimply all over and I come to 'em."

—Marilyn Monroe explaining to Tony Curtis her weakness for tenor saxophone players in Billy Wilder's *Some Like It Hot* (*Screenplay by Billy Wilder and I. A. L. Diamond; suggested by a story by R. Thoeren and M. Logan*)

18.

"You're a very attractive girl. Got a great comic quality, yet you're very sensual. Audience response to you has been interesting. We think you're going to be very big. Got a nice part for you. Six weeks work. Your agent will tell you to jump at it. I'm sending the script. We'd like to have you under contract, young lady. We'll make very nice terms for you. Why don't you come to my house tonight, and we'll discuss the whole matter? I eat at eight o'clock. I'm sure you'll enjoy the food."

—Donald McKee luring Kim Stanley to his home with stardom promises in John Cromwell's *The Goddess* (*Original Screenplay by Paddy Chayefsky*)

19.

"I suppose you know you have a wonderful body. I'd like to do it in clay."

—Lola Albright admiring Kirk Douglas in Mark Robson's *Champion* (*Screenplay by Carl Foreman; based on the short story by Ring Lardner*)

20.

"There is only one way to deal with Rome, Antoninus. You must serve her. You must abase yourself before her. You must grovel at her feet. You must love her."

—Laurence Olivier coming on obliquely to Tony Curtis in Stanley Kubrick's *Spartacus* (*Screenplay by Dalton Trumbo; based on the novel by Howard Fast*)

21.

"Come on, darling. Why don't you kick off your spurs?"

—Elizabeth Taylor calling Rock Hudson to bed in George Stevens's *Giant* (*Screenplay by Fred Guiol and Ivan Moffat; based on the novel by Edna Ferber*)

22.

(a) "Well, speaking of horses, I like to play them myself—but I like to see them work out a little first, see if they're front-runners or come from behind, find out what their hole-card is, what makes them run."

(b) "Find out mine?"

(a) "I think so."

(b) "Go ahead."

(a) "I'd say you don't like to be rated. You like to get out in front, open up a lead, take a little breather in the backstretch and then come home free."

(b) "You don't like to be rated yourself."

(a) "I haven't met anyone yet that could do it. Any suggestions?"

(b) "Well, I can't tell till I've seen you over a distance of ground. You've got a touch of class, but I don't know how—how far you can go."

(a) "A lot depends on who's in the saddle. Go ahead, Marlowe. I like the way you work. In case you don't know it, you're doing all right."

—(a) Lauren Bacall and (b) Humphrey Bogart horsing around with double entendres in Howard Hawks's *The Big Sleep* (*Screenplay by William Faulkner, Leigh Brackett and Jules Furthman; based on the novel by Raymond Chandler*)

23.

"Aw, if we could find a little bungalow—eh?

Oh, of course, we could find one, but maybe the people wouldn't get out. But if we could find a nice little empty bungalow just for me and you where we could bill and cow—no, where we could bull and cow—"

—Groucho Marx romancing Margaret Dumont in Joseph Santley and Robert Florey's *The Cocoanuts*
(Screenplay by Morrie Ryskind; based on the musical play by George S. Kaufman and Morrie Ryskind)

24.

(a) "I was bored to death. I hadn't seen one attractive woman on this ship since we left. Now, isn't that terrible? I was alarmed. I said to myself, 'Don't beautiful women travel anymore?' And then I saw you, and I was saved— I hope."

(b) "Tell me, have you been getting results with a line like that, or would I be surprised?"

(a) "If you'd be surprised, I'd be surprised."

—(a) Cary Grant telling (b) Deborah Kerr that she is just as worldly as he in Leo McCarey's *An Affair To Remember*
(Screenplay by Delmer Daves and Leo McCarey; based on an original story by Mildred Cram and Leo McCarey)

and (almost verbatim)

—(a) Charles Boyer dittoing (b) Irene Dunne in the original, Leo McCarey's *Love Affair*
(Screenplay by Delmer Daves and Donald Ogden Stewart; based on an original screenplay by Mildred Cram and Leo McCarey)

ALSO SEE: Awakenings-3; Boredom-6; Firsts-3; Flowers-5; Hunger-7; Names-20; Run-3; Whistle-1.

PSYCHIATRY

1.

"There's nothing shameful about my work but frightening ideas. It's very simple really what I try to do. People walk along a road. They come to a fork in the road. They're confused. They don't know which way to take. I just put up a signpost: 'Not that way—this way.' "

—Claude Rains explaining his work to Gladys Cooper and Bette Davis in Irving Rapper's *Now, Voyager*
(Screenplay by Casey Robinson; based on the novel by Olive Higgins Prouty)

2.

"There's some mystery about Cassie herself. Dr. Tower said something once: 'Each of us live in multiple worlds.' It's like that with her, too."

—Robert Cummings characterizing Betty Field with a quote from her father (Claude Rains) in Sam Wood's *Kings Row*
(Screenplay by Casey Robinson; based on the novel by Henry Bellamann)

3.

"I wanted to be a dancer. Psychiatry showed me I was wrong."

—Fred Astaire admitting the error of his ways in Mark Sandrich's *Carefree*
(Screenplay by Ernest Pagano and Allan Scott; adaptation by Dudley Nichols and Hagar Wilde; based on a story by Marian Ainslee and Guy Endore)

4.

"I should have listened to my psychiatrist. He told me never to trust anyone but him."

—Tony Randall discovering his girlfriend (Doris Day) is getting the rush from his best friend (Rock Hudson) in Michael Gordon's *Pillow Talk*
(Screenplay by Stanley Shapiro and Maurice Richlin; based on a story by Russell Rouse and Clarence Greene)

5.

"I have to tell my psychiatrist everything that happens to me. We're down to the smaller, starker details."

—Elizabeth Taylor being glib with Laurence Harvey in Daniel Mann's *Butterfield 8*
(Screenplay by Charles Schnee and John Michael Hayes; based on the novel by John O'Hara)

6.

"I'm making excellent progress. Pretty soon, when I lie down on his couch, I won't have to wear the lobster bib."

—Woody Allen telling Colleen Dewhurst the result of 15 years in analysis in Woody Allen's *Annie Hall*
(Original Screenplay by Woody Allen and Marshall Brickman)

7.
"You are right. I'm not an analyst—not even a doctor—here. I'm not talking to you as one. But believe me—not what I say but what I feel. The mind isn't everything. The heart can see deeper sometimes."

—Ingrid Bergman assuring Michael Chekhov that her patient-lover (Gregory Peck) is not a murderer in Alfred Hitchcock's *Spellbound*
(Screenplay by Ben Hecht; adaptation by Angus MacPhail; based on THE HOUSE OF DR. EDWARDES, a novel by Francis Beeding)

8.
"At $50 an hour, *all* my cases interest me."

—Oscar Homolka admitting to playing no favorites in Billy Wilder's *The Seven Year Itch*
(Screenplay by Billy Wilder and George Axelrod; based on the play by George Axelrod)

ALSO SEE: Amateur-2; Mind-12; Mind-13; Suicide-4; Women-6.

PUBLIC RELATIONS

1.
"The man with the sweaty face and the frightened eyes was, and is, Oscar Muldoon. He is a public relations counselor, which can be many things—unrelated and not public at all."

—Humphrey Bogart introducing Edmond O'Brien in Joseph L. Mankiewicz's *The Barefoot Contessa*
(Original Screenplay by Joseph L. Mankiewicz)

2.
"I want to be a public relations man, not a pimp."

—Jack Lemmon boozing after a bad day in Blake Edwards's *Days of Wine and Roses*
(Screenplay by J. P. Miller; based on his teleplay)

3.
"And now I'm going to turn you over to our demon press agent, Libby. Don't let him frighten you. He has a heart of gold—only harder."

—Adolphe Menjou preparing Janet Gaynor for Lionel Stander in William A. Wellman's *A Star Is Born*
(Screenplay by Dorothy Parker, Alan Campbell and Robert Carson; based on an original story by William A. Wellman and Robert Carson)

4.
"Mr. Libby looks after me like a fond mother with a good sense of double-entry bookkeeping."

—James Mason characterizing his overly protective publicist (Jack Carson) in George Cukor's *A Star Is Born*
(Screenplay by Moss Hart; based on a screenplay by Dorothy Parker, Alan Campbell and Robert Carson and original story by William A. Wellman and Robert Carson)

5.
"A glorified doormat."

—Lionel Stander defining his press-agent role for Gary Cooper in Frank Capra's *Mr. Deeds Goes to Town*
(Screenplay by Robert Riskin; based on "Opera Hat," a short story by Clarence Budington Kelland)

6.
"You know, a dozen press agents working overtime can do terrible things to the human spirit."

—Cecil B. DeMille seeing the results in Gloria Swanson in Billy Wilder's *Sunset Boulevard*
(Original Screenplay by Charles Brackett, Billy Wilder and D. M. Marshman Jr.)

ALSO SEE: Parting Shots-7.

QUESTIONS

1.

"I agree with Alexandra: what *was* a man in a wheelchair doing on a staircase? I ask myself that."

—Charles Dingle suspecting Bette Davis of foul play in the death of her husband (Herbert Marshall) in William Wyler's *The Little Foxes*
(Screenplay by Lillian Hellman; additional scenes and dialogue by Arthur Kober, Dorothy Parker and Alan Campbell; based on the play by Lillian Hellman)

2.

"Where does it say that you can't kill a cop?"

—Al Pacino planning to avenge the near-murder of his father (Marlon Brando) in Francis Ford Coppola's *The Godfather*
(Screenplay by Mario Puzo and Francis Ford Coppola; based on the novel by Mario Puzo)

3.

"Is it really true, Dad, 'If you wanna know, ask Joe'?"

—Burt Lancaster probing a wartime crime by invoking the stock remark always made about his father (Edward G. Robinson) in Irving Reis's *All My Sons*
(Screenplay by Chester Erskine; based on the play by Arthur Miller)

4.

"How do you tell a six-year-old child his new daddy is a teenager?"

—Divorcée Linda Miller confessing the one question she has about her 19-year-old lover in Paul Mazursky's *An Unmarried Woman*
(Original Screenplay by Paul Mazursky)

5.

"How can they give you a medal for a war they don't even want you to fight?"

—Bruce Dern feeling more hollow than heroic after Vietnam in Hal Ashby's *Coming Home*
(Screenplay by Waldo Salt and Robert C. Jones; based on a story by Nancy Dowd)

6.

"Then how in perdition have you got the gall to whoop up this holy war about something that you don't know anything about? How can you be so cocksure that the body of scientific knowledge, systematized in the writings of Charles Darwin, is in any way irreconcilable with the book of Genesis?"

—Spencer Tracy responding to Fredric March's admitted ignorance of evolution in Stanley Kramer's *Inherit the Wind*
(Screenplay by Nathan E. Douglas and Harold Jacob Smith; based on the play by Jerome Lawrence and Robert E. Lee)

7.

"What in the name of Occupation do you mean by saying you built a teahouse instead of a schoolhouse?"

—Paul Ford discovering Glenn Ford's radical change in Army plans in Daniel Mann's *The Teahouse of the August Moon*
(Screenplay by John Patrick; based on his play and the book by Vern J. Sneider)

8.

"Here's a man that could have been President, who was as loved and hated and as talked about as any man in our time, but, when he comes to die, he's got something on his mind called Rosebud. Now, what does that mean?"

—Philip Van Zandt assigning a reporter (William Alland) to discover the meaning of Orson Welles's dying word in Orson Welles's *Citizen Kane*
(Original Screenplay by Herman J. Mankiewicz and Orson Welles)

9.

"I know we met just a couple of hours ago, but just what do I mean to you? I mean, am I just a passing train you want to board for the night, or are you attracted to my inner being and this night could be the start of a meaningful relationship?"

—Marian Hailey giving her date (Bob Dishy) a choice of responses in Cy Howard's *Lovers and Other Strangers*

(Screenplay by Renee Taylor, Joseph Bologna and David Z. Goodman; based on the play by Renee Taylor and Joseph Bologna)

10.

"Mrs. Robinson, you're trying to seduce me. Aren't you?"

—Dustin Hoffman checking to see if he's getting the right reading from Anne Bancroft in Mike Nichols's *The Graduate*
(Screenplay by Calder Willingham and Buck Henry; based on the novel by Charles Webb)

11.

"Would you try to seduce me?"

—Maggie McNamara clarifying William Holden's invitation to his pad in Otto Preminger's *The Moon Is Blue*
(Screenplay by F. Hugh Herbert; based on his play)

12.

"There can only be one winner, folks, but isn't that the American way?"

—Gig Young brandishing the bromides as he emcees a dance marathon in Sydney Pollack's *They Shoot Horses, Don't They?*
(Screenplay by James Poe and Robert E. Thompson; based on the novel by Horace McCoy)

13.

"Oh dear, *Yankees* in *Georgia!* How did they ever get in?"

—Laura Hope Crews scurrying dizzily out of Atlanta in Victor Fleming's *Gone With the Wind*
(Screenplay by Sidney Howard; based on the novel by Margaret Mitchell)

14.

"Does this boat go to Europe, France?"

—Marilyn Monroe making a wide-eyed inquiry in Howard Hawks's *Gentlemen Prefer Blondes*
(Screenplay by Charles Lederer; based on the musical play by Joseph Fields and Anita Loos and novel by Anita Loos)

15.

"Waiter, will you serve the nuts—I mean, would you serve the guests the nuts?"

—Myrna Loy hostessing a party for murder-suspects in W. S. Van Dyke's *The Thin Man*
(Screenplay by Albert Hackett and Frances Goodrich; based on the novel by Dashiell Hammett)

16.

"What happened at the office? Well, I shot Mr. Brady in the head, made violent love to Miss Morris and set fire to 300,000 copies of *Little Women.* That's what happened at the office."

—Tom Ewell fantasizing a response to the stock question of his wife (Evelyn Keyes) in Billy Wilder's *The Seven Year Itch*
(Screenplay by Billy Wilder and George Axelrod; based on the play by George Axelrod)

17.

"How many times have I told you I hated you and believed it in my heart? How many times have you said you were sick and tired of me and that we were all washed up? How many times have we had to fall in love all over again?"

—Myrna Loy reciting her blues with Fredric March when their daughter (Teresa Wright) accuses them of a trouble-free marriage in William Wyler's *The Best Years of Our Lives*
(Screenplay by Robert E. Sherwood; based on GLORY FOR ME, a verse novel by MacKinlay Kantor)

18.

"Oh, isn't it wonderful to see all our lives so settled, temporarily?"

—Mary Boland gushing with a qualifier in George Cukor's *The Women*
(Screenplay by Anita Loos and Jane Murfin; based on the play by Clare Boothe)

19.

"Now, just one more question. You see the judge here? He's a nice man, isn't he? . . . Do you think he's pixilated?"

—Gary Cooper winning his case with his cross-examination of a "pixilated" pair from his hometown (Margaret McWade and Margaret Seddon) in Frank Capra's *Mr. Deeds Goes to Town*
(Screenplay by Robert Riskin; based on "Opera

Hat," a short story by Clarence Budington Kelland)

ALSO SEE: Firsts-3; God-6; Guns-7; Sex-2; Sex-3; Smile-3; Sons-5; Telephone Scenes-3.

QUIET

1.
"Quiet? You can get a room here with an adjoining hole in your head."

—Bob Hope differing with Jane Russell's opinion of a ghost-town hotel in Frank Tashlin's *Son of Paleface*
(Original Screenplay by Frank Tashlin, Robert L. Welch and Joseph Quillan)

2.
"Now it isn't that I don't like you, Susan, because, after all, in moments of quiet, I'm strangely drawn toward you, but—well, there haven't been any quiet moments."

—Cary Grant being delicate about the chaos Katharine Hepburn incites in Howard Hawks's *Bringing Up Baby*
(Screenplay by Dudley Nichols and Hagar Wilde; based on a story by Hagar Wilde)

3.
"Martha, in my mind, you are buried in cement right up to the neck. Now, up to the nose, it's much quieter."

—Richard Burton suggesting Elizabeth Taylor shut up in Mike Nichols's *Who's Afraid of Virginia Woolf?*
(Screenplay by Ernest Lehman; based on the play by Edward Albee)

ALSO SEE: Lasts-1.

REALITIES

1.
"I've wrestled with reality for 35 years, and I'm happy, Doctor. I finally won out over it."

—James Stewart beaming about his victory in Henry Koster's *Harvey*

(Screenplay by Mary Chase and Oscar Brodney; based on the play by Mary Chase)

2.
"Oh, wake up, Norma. You'd be killing yourself to an empty house. The audience left 20 years ago. Now face it."

—William Holden telling Gloria Swanson to surrender her illusion of persistent fans in Billy Wilder's *Sunset Boulevard*
(Original Screenplay by Charles Brackett, Billy Wilder and D. M. Marshman Jr.)

3.
"Take a look at yourself here in a worn-out Mardi Gras outfit, rented for 50 cents from some rag-dealer, with a crazy crown on. Just what kind of a queen do you think you are? You know that I've been on to you from the start. And not once did you pull the wool over this boy's eyes. You come in here and you sprinkle the place with powder and you spray perfume and you stick a paper lantern over the light bulb—and, lo and behold, the place has turned to Egypt and you are the Queen of the Nile, sitting on your throne, swilling down my liquor. And do you know what I say? Ha ha! Do you hear me? Ha ha ha!"

—Marlon Brando confronting Vivien Leigh in Elia Kazan's *A Streetcar Named Desire*
(Screenplay by Tennessee Williams; adaptation by Oscar Saul; based on the play by Tennessee Williams)

4.
"Pinch me, Rosie. Here we are, going down the river like Antony and Cleopatra on that barge."

—Humphrey Bogart feeling euphoric with Katharine Hepburn in John Huston's *The African Queen*
(Screenplay by James Agee and John Huston; based on the novel by C. S. Forester)

5.
"No, I gotta be Lizzie. Melisande is a name for one night, but Lizzie can do me my whole life long."

—Katharine Hepburn choosing Wendell Corey instead of Burt Lancaster in Joseph Anthony's *The Rainmaker*
(Screenplay by N. Richard Nash; based on his play)

6.
"No matter what I ever do or say, Heathcliff, this is me—now—standing on this hill with you. This is me, forever."

—Merle Oberon managing a real moment with Laurence Olivier in William Wyler's *Wuthering Heights*
(Screenplay by Ben Hecht and Charles MacArthur; based on the novel by Emily Brontë)

ALSO SEE: Names-14; Night-4; Screenplays-2; Theater-4; Theater-5.

REGRETS

1.
"Most people get by on a sort of creepy common sense and discover too late that the only things one never regrets are one's mistakes."

—George Sanders preaching the hedonist party line in Albert Lewin's *The Picture of Dorian Gray*
(Screenplay by Albert Lewin; based on the novel by Oscar Wilde)

2.
"As you grow older, you'll find that the only things you regret are the things you didn't do."

—Zachary Scott moving in on Joan Crawford in Michael Curtiz's *Mildred Pierce*
(Screenplay by Ranald MacDougall; based on the novel by James M. Cain)

3.
" 'Mr. Elliott Templeton regrets he cannot accept Princess Novemali's kind invitation owing to a previous engagement with his Blessed Lord.' The old witch!"

—Clifton Webb declining Cobina Wright Sr.'s party invitation with his last gasps in Edmund Goulding's *The Razor's Edge*
(Screenplay by Lamar Trotti; based on the novel by W. Somerset Maugham)

4.
"He'll regret it to his dying day—if ever he lives that long."

—Victor McLaglen muttering to himself threats against John Wayne in John Ford's *The Quiet Man*
(Screenplay by Frank S. Nugent; based on "Green Rushes," a short story by Maurice Walsh)

ALSO SEE: Frigidity-3; Last Lines-13; Parting Shots-6; Pleasures-2; Self-Depreciation-4; Telegrams-3; Wants-4.

REJECTION

1.
"I just called up a girl this afternoon, and I got a real brush-off, boy! I figured I was past the point of being hurt, but that hurt. Some stupid woman who I didn't even want to call up. She gave me the brush. No, Ma, I don't want to go to the Stardust Ballroom because all that ever happened to me there was girls made me feel like a—a—a bug. I got feelings, you know. I—I had enough pain. No thanks, Ma!"

—Ernest Borgnine explaining pain-avoidance to his mother (Esther Minciotti) in Delbert Mann's *Marty*
(Screenplay by Paddy Chayefsky; based on his teleplay)

2.
"Thirty million fans have given her the brush. Isn't that enough?"

—Cecil B. DeMille showing sympathetic consideration for a one-time star (Gloria Swanson) in Billy Wilder's *Sunset Boulevard*
(Original Screenplay by Charles Brackett, Billy Wilder and D. M. Marshman Jr.)

3.
"You don't know what it means to know that people are—that a whole audience just doesn't want you."

—Dorothy Comingore explaining her suicide attempt to Orson Welles in Orson Welles's *Citizen Kane*

(Original Screenplay by Herman J. Mankiewicz and Orson Welles)

4.

"No, I'd never make it, and maybe it wouldn't make no difference even if I did. Maybe it's just the whole world is like Central Casting. They got it all rigged before you ever show up."

—Jane Fonda giving up on acting (and life in general) in Sydney Pollack's *They Shoot Horses, Don't They?* *(Screenplay by James Poe and Robert E. Thompson; based on the novel by Horace McCoy)*

5.

"Look, Pop, let's not beat around the bush. I know why you sent me to Sweetriver. Because Uncle Ned's got six boys. Three of them are old enough to get married, and so am I. Well, I'm sorry you went to all that expense—the railroad ticket and all those new clothes. Noah, you can write it in the books, in red ink, 'I'm sorry—the trip didn't work.'"

—Katharine Hepburn returning ringless to her father (Cameron Prud'homme) and brother (Lloyd Bridges) in Joseph Anthony's *The Rainmaker* *(Screenplay by N. Richard Nash; based on his play)*

6.

"If he'd been a lover—a real man—he'd have taken you in his arms. He'd have been tender. Instead of that, he stalked out of the room like the Reverend Henry Davidson in *Rain*."

—John Barrymore questioning Ralph Forbes's devotion to Carole Lombard in Howard Hawks's *Twentieth Century* *(Screenplay by Ben Hecht and Charles MacArthur; based on their play and NAPOLEON OF BROADWAY, a play by Charles Bruce Milholland)*

7.

(a) "Jeez, you're old-fashioned, aren't you?"
   (b) "From the waist up."

—(b) Robert Mitchum walking out on a more-than-willing (a) Charlotte Rampling in Dick Richards's *Farewell, My Lovely* *(Screenplay by David Zelag Goodman; based on the novel by Raymond Chandler)*

8.

(a) "Love isn't an opinion. It's, it's a chemical reaction. We've never even kissed—well, they didn't hit the moon with the first missile shot either."

   (b) "Oh, Jonathan. I guess that's what I want: to hit the moon."

—(a) Tony Randall kissing, and failing to convince, (b) Doris Day in Michael Gordon's *Pillow Talk* *(Screenplay by Stanley Shapiro and Maurice Richlin; based on a story by Russell Rouse and Clarence Greene)*

9.

"I'd make comic faces and stand on my head and grin at you between my legs and learn all sorts of jokes—I wouldn't stand a chance, would I? Hmmmm? Well, you *did* tell me I ought to find myself a girl."

—Joseph Cotten asking, and not receiving, Valli in Carol Reed's *The Third Man* *(Original Screenplay by Graham Greene)*

10.

"All right, but I'll look awfully silly some day making verbal passes at you when we're both in wheelchairs."

—Joseph Cotten gracefully accepting Claudette Colbert's "just friends" edict in John Cromwell's *Since You Went Away* *(Screenplay by David O. Selznick; adaptation by Margaret Buell Wilder; based on her book of letters)*

11.

"I wouldn't have you on a Christmas tree, Alvin York."

—Joan Leslie telling off Gary Cooper in Howard Hawks's *Sergeant York* *(Original Screenplay by Abem Finkel, Harry Chandlee, Howard Koch and John Huston; based on WAR DIARY OF SERGEANT YORK and SERGEANT YORK AND HIS PEOPLE, two books by Sam K. Cowan, and SERGEANT YORK—LAST OF THE LONG HUNTERS, a book by Tom Skeyhill)*

12.

"I wouldn't go on living with you if you were dipped in platinum."

—Irene Dunne telling off Cary Grant in Leo McCarey's *The Awful Truth*
(Screenplay by Vina Delmar; based on the play by Arthur Richman)

13.
"I wouldn't have you if you were hung with diamonds, upside down."

—Joan Crawford telling off Jeff Chandler in Joseph Pevney's *Female on the Beach*
(Screenplay by Robert Hill and Richard Alan Simmons; based on THE BESIEGED HEART, a play by Robert Hill)

14.
"Well, I really wouldn't care to scratch your surface, Mr. Kralik, because I know exactly what I'd find: instead of a heart, a handbag; instead of a soul, a suitcase; and instead of an intellect, a cigarette lighter which doesn't work."

—Margaret Sullavan telling off James Stewart in Ernst Lubitsch's *The Shop Around the Corner*
(Screenplay by Samson Raphaelson; based on PARFUMERIE, a play by Miklos Laszlo)
and (similarly)

—Judy Garland dittoing Van Johnson in the remake, Robert Z. Leonard's *In the Good Old Summertime*
(Screenplay by Albert Hackett, Frances Goodrich and Ivan Tors; based on THE SHOP AROUND THE CORNER, a screenplay by Samson Raphaelson, and PARFUMERIE, a play by Miklos Laszlo)

15.
"There'll be ice cream parlors in hell before I walk back into this place and listen to your jaw!"

—Robert Preston walking out on Dorothy McGuire in Delbert Mann's *The Dark at the Top of the Stairs*
(Screenplay by Irving Ravetch and Harriet Frank Jr.; based on the play by William Inge)

16.
"I'm sorry, Louise. You watch temperatures go down and then go up again. In love, there are no relapses. Once you're out of it, the fever never comes back again."

—Van Heflin cooling it with Joan Crawford in Curtis Bernhardt's *Possessed*
(Screenplay by Sylvia Richards and Ranald MacDougall; based on ONE MAN'S SECRET, a novelette by Rita Weiman)

ALSO SEE: Telephone Scenes-5.

RELATIVES

1.
"That's not fair, Vinnie. When I talk about *my* relatives, I *criticize* them."

—William Powell making a minor point to Irene Dunne in Michael Curtiz's *Life With Father*
(Screenplay by Donald Ogden Stewart; based on the play by Howard Lindsay and Russel Crouse and stories by Clarence Day Jr.)

2.
"My great-aunt Jennifer ate a whole box of candy every day of her life. She lived to be 102, and, when she had been dead three days, she looked better than you do now."

—Monty Woolley insulting his nurse (Mary Wickes) in William Keighley's *The Man Who Came to Dinner*
(Screenplay by Julius J. Epstein and Philip G. Epstein; based on the play by George S. Kaufman and Moss Hart)

3.
"I used to have a cousin who could open a bottle of beer with his teeth, and that was all he could do. He was just a human bottle-opener. Then—then one time at a wedding party, he broke his front teeth right off. And, after that, he was so ashamed of himself that he used to sneak outta the house when company came."

—Marlon Brando shaking his family tree in Elia Kazan's *A Streetcar Named Desire*
(Screenplay by Tennessee Williams; adaptation by Oscar Saul; based on the play by Tennessee Williams)

4.
"Some people are better off dead—like your wife and my father, for instance."

—Robert Walker proposing a murder-swapping arrangement to Farley Granger in Alfred Hitchcock's *Strangers on a Train*
(Screenplay by Raymond Chandler and Czenzi Ormonde; adaptation by Whitfield Cook; based on the novel by Patricia Highsmith)

5.
"You're a disgrace to our family name of Wagstaff, if such a thing is possible."

—Groucho Marx putting down his son (Zeppo Marx) in Norman Z. McLeod's *Horse Feathers*
(Screenplay by Bert Kalmar, Harry Ruby, S. J. Perelman and Will B. Johnstone)

6.
"Every family has curious little traits. What of it? My father raises orchids at $10,000 a bulb. Is that sensible? My mother believes in spiritualism. That's just as bad as your mother writing plays, isn't it?"

—James Stewart consoling Jean Arthur about her eccentric clan in Frank Capra's *You Can't Take It With You*
(Screenplay by Robert Riskin; based on the play by George S. Kaufman and Moss Hart)

7.
"Well, what family doesn't have its ups and downs?"

—Katharine Hepburn shrugging off the domestic warfare in her royal house in Anthony Harvey's *The Lion in Winter*
(Screenplay by James Goldman; based on his play)

ALSO SEE: Innocent-5; Neck-3; Run-1; Spinsters-1; Spinsters-2; Strangers-5.

RELIGIONS

1.
"My religion? My dear, I'm a millionaire. That's my religion."

—Robert Morley telling his daughter (Wendy Hiller) what he truly believes in in Gabriel Pascal's *Major Barbara*
(Screenplay by George Bernard Shaw; based on his play)

2.
"Strength is her religion, Mr. Connor. She finds human imperfection unforgivable."

—Cary Grant informing James Stewart about Katharine Hepburn in George Cukor's *The Philadelphia Story*
(Screenplay by Donald Ogden Stewart; based on the play by Philip Barry)

3.
"His name is Peter Gay. He's the apostle of a new religion, called swing."

—James Mason describing Hugh McDermott in Compton Bennett's *The Seventh Veil*
(Original Screenplay by Muriel Box and Sydney Box)

4.
(a) "What do you know about Yogi Berra, Miss Deverich?"
   (b) "I beg your pardon."
   (a) "Yogi Berra."
   (b) "Yogi? Well, it's a sort of religion, isn't it?"
   (a) "You bet it is! A belief in the New York Yankees!"

—(a) Kirk Douglas rattling a newspaper office co-worker (Edith Evanson) in Billy Wilder's *The Big Carnival*
(Original Screenplay by Billy Wilder, Lesser Samuels and Walter Newman)

5.
"It's my religion to play the winning streak."

—Omar Sharif telling Barbra Streisand his gambling credo in William Wyler's *Funny Girl*
(Screenplay by Isobel Lennart; based on her musical play)

6.
"I can't get with any religion that advertises in *Popular Mechanics.*"

—Woody Allen stating his position to Shelley Duvall in Woody Allen's *Annie Hall*

(Original Screenplay by Woody Allen and Marshall Brickman)

ALSO SEE: Ignorance-2; Talent-4.

REMEMBER

1.
" . . . but, first and foremost, I remember Mama."

—Barbara Bel Geddes recalling, among others, Irene Dunne at the beginning and at the end of George Stevens's *I Remember Mama*
(Screenplay by DeWitt Bodeen; based on the play by John Van Druten and "Mama's Bank Account," the stories by Kathryn Forbes)

2.
"I remember every detail. The Germans wore gray. You wore blue."

—Humphrey Bogart reminding Ingrid Bergman of their last meeting the day the Nazis marched into Paris in Michael Curtiz's *Casablanca*
(Screenplay by Julius J. Epstein, Philip G. Epstein and Howard Koch; based on EVERYBODY COMES TO RICK'S, a play by Murray Burnett and Joan Alison)

3.
"The wolf at my door? Why, I remember when he came right into my room and had pups!"

—Mae West admitting that she has known harder times in Lowell Sherman's *She Done Him Wrong*
(Screenplay by Harvey Thew and John Bright; based on DIAMOND LIL, a play by Mae West)

4.
"If I'd have forgotten myself with that girl, I'd remember it."

—Fred Astaire mooning over Ginger Rogers in Mark Sandrich's *Top Hat*
(Screenplay by Dwight Taylor and Allan Scott; adaptation by Karl Noti; based on THE GIRL WHO DARED, a play by Alexander Farago and Aladar Laszlo)

5.
"I'll never forget this village. And, on the other side of the world, in the autumn of my life, when an August moon rises in the East, I'll remember what was beautiful and what I was wise enough to leave beautiful."

—Glenn Ford making a heavy-hearted exit from Okinawa in Daniel Mann's *The Teahouse of the August Moon*
(Screenplay by John Patrick; based on his play and the book by Vern J. Sneider)

6.
"Millie remembers the same things I do. That's important. For one thing, she's the only one I know who remembers when I used to be called Chunky."

—Bette Davis acknowledging her long history with Miriam Hopkins in Vincent Sherman's *Old Acquaintance*
(Screenplay by John Van Druten and Lenore Coffee; based on the play by John Van Druten)

7.
(a) "Is it a crime to want to be remembered?"
      (b) "No. The pharaohs built the pyramids for that reason."

—(b) Deborah Kerr consoling (a) Edith Evans about Hayley Mills's departure in Ronald Neame's *The Chalk Garden*
(Screenplay by John Michael Hayes; based on the play by Enid Bagnold)

ALSO SEE: Memory; Heaven-7; Honor-2; Letters-3; Letters-10; Never-2; Pep Talks-3; Pride-1; Rules-4; Selfish-6; War-4.

REPETITIONS

1.
"Badges? We ain't got no badges. We don't need no badges. I don't have to show you any stinking badges."

—Alfonso Bedoya flaring up when Humphrey Bogart requests credentials in John Huston's *The Treasure of the Sierra Madre*
(Screenplay by John Huston; based on the novel by B. Traven)

2.

" 'Can't make it.' 'Can't make it.' That's all I ever hear from you. It used to be because my husband was your friend. Well, he's dead. He's been dead for six months. What's wrong with me now? Why can't you make it?"

—Ida Lupino pressuring George Raft for some attention in Raoul Walsh's *They Drive by Night*
(Screenplay by Jerry Wald and Richard Macaulay; based on LONG HAUL, a novel by A. I. Bezzerides)

3.

"Explain! Explain! That's all I've ever done is explain. I'm tired of explaining, sick and tired of it. I don't want to have to explain—not to you. You're my son. You're in with me. My flesh and blood. You wear my clothes, eat my food, live in my home. I don't have to explain to you. If I'm guilty, then you're guilty, too. You understand me? You're guilty, too."

—Edward G. Robinson resenting Burt Lancaster's questions about a wartime crime in Irving Reis's *All My Sons*
(Screenplay by Chester Erskine; based on the play by Arthur Miller)

ALSO SEE: Appearances-6; Stupid-1.

REPUBLICANS

1.

(a) "It's so spooky down here. Do you believe in reincarnation—you know that dead people come back?"

(b) "You mean like the Republicans?"

—(b) Bob Hope neutralizing the ominous question of (a) Nydia Westman in Elliott Nugent's *The Cat and the Canary*
(Screenplay by Walter De Leon and Lynn Starling; based on the play by John Willard)

2.

"Don't tell me it's subversive to kiss a Republican."

—John Lund romancing an Iowa congresswoman (Jean Arthur) in Billy Wilder's *A Foreign Affair*

(Screenplay by Charles Brackett, Billy Wilder and Richard L. Breen; adaptation by Robert Harari; based on an original story by David Shaw)

ALSO SEE: Indecision-3; Lies-4.

RESPECT

1.

"You know, on the—on the screen, I'm a—you know; in private life, I'm a—well, you know! But, whatever I do, I—I still respect lovely things. And you're lovely. You understand?"

—Fredric March leveling with Janet Gaynor in William A. Wellman's *A Star Is Born*
(Screenplay by Dorothy Parker, Alan Campbell and Robert Carson; based on an original story by William A. Wellman and Robert Carson)

2.

"Oh, you mistake me, my dear. I have the highest respect for your nerves. I have heard you mention them with consideration for the last 20 years."

—Edmund Gwenn calming his excitable wife (Mary Boland) in Robert Z. Leonard's *Pride and Prejudice*
(Screenplay by Aldous Huxley and Jane Murfin; based on the play by Helen Jerome and novel by Jane Austen)

3.

"Hello. I told you never to call me here; don't you know where I am? Now look, baby, I—I can't talk to you now, the—my President needs me. Of course, Bucky would rather be there with you. Of course, it isn't only physical. I deeply respect you as a human being. Someday I'm going to make you Mrs. Buck Turgidson. All right, now listen, hon, you can go back to sleep now—Bucky'll be back there just as soon as he can. All right. Listen, suge: don't forget to say your prayers."

—George C. Scott getting a less-than-pressing phone call from his girlfriend (Tracy Reed) during a War Room crisis in Stanley Kubrick's *Dr. Strangelove or: How I Learned To Stop Worrying and Love the Bomb*
(Screenplay by Stanley Kubrick, Terry Southern

and Peter George; based on RED ALERT, *a novel by Peter George)*

4.

"Four hours. You must have paid him an awful lot of respects."

—Shelley Winters complaining about Montgomery Clift's late arrival in George Stevens's *A Place in the Sun*
(Screenplay by Michael Wilson and Harry Brown; based on AN AMERICAN TRAGEDY, *a play by Patrick Kearney and novel by Theodore Dreiser)*

ALSO SEE: Adultery-3; Decency-4; Honest-4; Human-9; Innocent-3; Men-13; Professions-4; Promiscuity-3; Proposals-8.

RESPONSIBILITY

1.

"It's quite a responsibility, knowing every day you have 20 million stomachs to fill."

—Eugene Pallette playing the proud, loud meatpacker in Ernst Lubitsch's *Heaven Can Wait*
(Screenplay by Samson Raphaelson; based on BIRTHDAY, *a play by Lazlo Bus-Fekete)*

2.

"Gooper is your first-born. Why, he's always had to carry a bigger load of the responsibility than Brick. Brick never carried anything in his life but a football or a highball."

—Madeleine Sherwood telling Judith Anderson that Jack Carson is more responsible than Paul Newman in Richard Brooks's *Cat on a Hot Tin Roof*
(Screenplay by Richard Brooks and James Poe; based on the play by Tennessee Williams)

3.

"Where is the responsibility of the Soviet Union who signed in 1939 the pact with Hitler and enabled him to make war? Are we now to find Russia guilty? Where is the responsibility of the Vatican who signed in 1933 the Concordat with Hitler, giving him his first tremendous prestige? Are we now to find the Vatican guilty? Where is the responsibility of the world

leader, Winston Churchill, who said in an open letter to the *London Times* in 1938—*1938, Your Honor!*—'Were England to suffer a national disaster, I should pray to God to send a man of the strength of mind and will of an Adolf Hitler'? Are we now to find Winston Churchill guilty? Where is the responsibility of those American industrialists who helped Hitler to rebuild his armaments and profited by that rebuilding? Are we now to find the American industrialists guilty? No, Your Honor, no. Germany alone is not guilty. The whole world is as responsible for Hitler as Germany. It is an easy thing to condemn one man in the dock. It is easy to condemn the German people—to speak of the 'basic flaw' in the German character that allowed Hitler to rise to power—and at the same time comfortably ignore the 'basic flaw' of character that made the Russians sign pacts with him, Winston Churchill praise him, American industrialists profit by him. Ernst Janning said he is guilty. If he is, Ernst Janning's guilt is the world's guilt. No more and no less."

—Maximilian Schell stating his case in Stanley Kramer's *Judgment at Nuremberg*
(Screenplay by Abby Mann; based on his teleplay)

ALSO SEE: Defense-1; Detectives-1; Detectives-2; Differences-5; Hands-3; Laugh-3; Marriage-17; Men-13.

RIGHT

1.

"Look, I'm way ahead of the right doctor. I know the reason. The reason is me and what I am—or, rather, what I'm not—what I wanted to become and didn't."

—Ray Milland understanding why he drinks in Billy Wilder's *The Lost Weekend*
(Screenplay by Charles Brackett and Billy Wilder; based on the novel by Charles R. Jackson)

2.

"Oh, I'm eternally right. But what good does it do me?"

—Leslie Howard having a point there in Archie Mayo's *The Petrified Forest*
(Screenplay by Delmer Daves and Charles Kenyon; based on the play by Robert E. Sherwood)

3.
"The trouble about being on the side of right, as one sees it, is that one often finds oneself in the company of such very questionable allies."

—Felix Aylmer resenting his own participation in expelling David Niven from a seaside hotel in Delbert Mann's *Separate Tables*
(Screenplay by Terence Rattigan and John Gay; based on the play by Terence Rattigan)

4.
"Realizing that I may prejudice the case of my client, I must tell you that right has no meaning for me whatsoever—but truth has meaning, as a direction."

—Spencer Tracy arguing for evolution in Stanley Kramer's *Inherit the Wind*
(Screenplay by Nathan E. Douglas and Harold Jacob Smith; based on the play by Jerome Lawrence and Robert E. Lee)

5.
"You got no right to call me a murderer. You have a right to kill me—you have the right to do that—but you have no right to judge me."

—Marlon Brando informing Martin Sheen of rights in Francis Ford Coppola's *Apocalypse Now*
(Screenplay by John Milius and Francis Ford Coppola; narration written by Michael Herr)

ALSO SEE: Awakenings-3; Crazy-11; Curses-4; Defense-3; Fights-11; Good-6; Knowledge-3; Lies-9; Life and Death-3; Men-15; Murder-7; Peace-7; Pep Talks-8; Promiscuity-6; Similarities-5; Wrong-1; Wrong-2; Wrong-3.

ROME

1.
"Rome is an eternal thought in the mind of God."

—Laurence Olivier being more than chauvinistic about it to Julius Caesar (John Gavin) in Stanley Kubrick's *Spartacus*
(Screenplay by Dalton Trumbo; based on the novel by Howard Fast)

2.
"Rome is an affront to God. Rome is strangling my people and my country and the whole earth."

—Charlton Heston responding to the anti-Semitism of his boyhood friend (Stephen Boyd) in William Wyler's *Ben-Hur*
(Screenplay by Karl Tunberg; based on BEN-HUR, A TALE OF THE CHRIST, a novel by General Lew Wallace)

3.
"I am aware that I must compete with those who sang at the burning of Troy. My song must be greater, just as Rome is greater than Troy."

—Peter Ustinov pondering his ditty for Rome's burning in Mervyn LeRoy's *Quo Vadis*
(Screenplay by John Lee Mahin, S. N. Behrman and Sonya Levien; based on the novel by Henryk Sienkiewicz)

4.
"There's nothing rushed in Rome."

—Jean Peters advising newcomer Maggie McNamara in Jean Negulesco's *Three Coins in the Fountain*
(Screenplay by John Patrick; based on the novel by John H. Secondari)

ALSO SEE: Dignity-1; Mad Act-6; Promiscuity-3; Propositions-20; Rules-4; Wish-1.

ROSE

1.

"What goes to make a rose, ma'am, is breeding and budding and horse manure, if you'll pardon the expression."

—Henry Travers genteelly tipping the secret of his rose-growing success to Greer Garson in William Wyler's *Mrs. Miniver*
(Screenplay by Arthur Wimperis, George Froeschel, James Hilton and Claudine West; based on the novel by Jan Struther)

2.

"A rose. A poor little rose for your thoughts."

—Katharine Hepburn bribing her beau-to-be (Fred MacMurray) in George Stevens's *Alice Adams*
(Screenplay by Dorothy Yost and Mortimer Offner; based on the novel by Booth Tarkington)

3.

"When you brought the roses, I felt something stir in me that I thought was dead forever."

—Patricia Neal acknowledging a breath of life in her dead marriage to Jack Albertson in Ulu Grosbard's *The Subject Was Roses*
(Screenplay by Frank D. Gilroy; based on his play)

4.

"I bet when he leaves, it won't be without a pension. It'll be roses, roses all the way, cheers, cheers and good-bye Mr. Chips."

—Jean Kent forecasting Michael Redgrave's retirement in Anthony Asquith's *The Browning Version*
(Screenplay by Terence Rattigan; based on his play)

5.
(a) "Blue rose?"
    (b) "I've heard about that. That—that's the blue rose of forgetfulness. If she inhales its fragrance, she'll forget everything."

—(b) John Justin informing (a) Sabu of the fate that awaits June Duprez in Ludwig Berger, Tim Whelan and Michael Powell's *The Thief of Bagdad*
(Screenplay and dialogue by Miles Malleson; based on a scenario by Lajos Biro)

6.
(a) "Say, how did I ever get to call you Blue Roses?"
    (b) "I was absent from school for a while with pleurosis. And when I came back, you asked me what was the matter and I told you that I had pleurosis, and you thought I said Blue Roses."

—(a) Kirk Douglas learning the origin of his high-school nickname for (b) Jane Wyman in Irving Rapper's *The Glass Menagerie*
(Screenplay by Tennessee Williams and Peter Berneis; based on the play by Tennessee Williams)

ALSO SEE: Awards-4; Life-12; Names-4; Notes-3; Tattoo-2.

ROYALTY

1.
"Cathy, you're still my queen."

—Laurence Olivier declaring his love for his childhood sweetheart (Merle Oberon) in William Wyler's *Wuthering Heights*
(Screenplay by Ben Hecht and Charles MacArthur; based on the novel by Emily Brontë)

2.
"You know, looking back on it, I don't think Matt would have made a great President, but I would have voted for him for king—just to have you for queen."

—Spencer Tracy complimenting Florence Eldridge while putting down her husband (Fredric March) in Stanley Kramer's *Inherit the Wind*
(Screenplay by Nathan E. Douglas and Harold Jacob Smith; based on the play by Jerome Lawrence and Robert E. Lee)

3.
(a) "You are king of the Chapel, but I will be queen in my own kitchen."
    (b) "You will be queen wherever you walk."

—(b) Walter Pidgeon verbalizing his attraction to (a) Maureen O'Hara in John Ford's *How Green Was My Valley*

(Screenplay by Philip Dunne; based on the novel by Richard Llewellyn)

4.
"Yes, you squashed cabbage leaf, you disgrace to the noble architecture of these columns, you incarnate insult to the English language, I can pass you off as the queen of Sheba."

—Leslie Howard promising Wendy Hiller a radical transformation in Anthony Asquith and Leslie Howard's *Pygmalion*
(Screenplay by George Bernard Shaw; adaptation by W. P. Lipscomb, Cecil Lewis and Ian Dalrymple; based on the play by George Bernard Shaw)

and

—Rex Harrison dittoing Audrey Hepburn in the remake, George Cukor's *My Fair Lady*
(Screenplay by Alan Jay Lerner; based on his musical play and PYGMALION, a screenplay and play by George Bernard Shaw)

5.
"Don't you ever talk that way to me! 'Pig,' 'disgusting,' 'vulgar,' 'greasy'—those kind of words have been on your tongue and your sister's tongue too much around here. What do you think you are? A pair of queens? Now, just remember what Huey Long said—that every man's a king—and I'm the king around here, and don't you forget it."

—Marlon Brando telling off Kim Hunter in Elia Kazan's *A Streetcar Named Desire*
(Screenplay by Tennessee Williams; adaptation by Oscar Saul; based on the play by Tennessee Williams)

6.
"I shared a moment with kings."

—Richard Todd finally feeling the friendships around him in Vincent Sherman's *The Hasty Heart*
(Screenplay by Ranald MacDougall; based on the play by John Patrick)

7.
"Who is he? He's Gypo Nolan, and he's as strong as any bull. Hey, Gypo, am I right?

. . . He's a king, that's what he is. King Gypo. Am I right?"

—J. M. Kerrigan singing the praises of Victor McLaglen in John Ford's *The Informer*
(Screenplay by Dudley Nichols; based on the novel by Liam O'Flaherty)

8.
"How's it going? How are you getting on with King Junk?"

—Howard St. John asking journalist William Holden about junk tycoon Broderick Crawford in George Cukor's *Born Yesterday*
(Screenplay by Albert Mannheimer; based on the play by Garson Kanin)

9.
"I don't know who's to be congratulated—kings, queens, knights, everywhere you look, and I'm the only pawn. I haven't a thing to lose. That makes me dangerous."

—Jane Merrow describing her position in the royal power-play in Anthony Harvey's *The Lion in Winter*
(Screenplay by James Goldman; based on his play)

ALSO SEE: Choice-6; Dying Words-21; Eyes-14; Introductions-1; Names-17; Names-18; Realities-3; Youth-3; Youth-5.

RULES

1.
"Last year, it was Kill Japs. This year, it's Make Money."

—Fredric March characterizing the postwar times in William Wyler's *The Best Years of Our Lives*
(Screenplay by Robert E. Sherwood; based on GLORY FOR ME, a verse novel by MacKinlay Kantor)

2.
"You were extremely attractive. And, as for distant and forbidding, on the contrary. But you were also a little worse, or better, for wine —and there are rules about that."

—James Stewart informing Katharine Hepburn that he did not take advantage of her tipsiness in George Cukor's *The Philadelphia Story*
(Screenplay by Donald Ogden Stewart; based on the play by Philip Barry)
and (almost verbatim)

—Frank Sinatra dittoing Grace Kelly in the remake, Charles Walters's *High Society*
(Screenplay by John Patrick; based on THE PHILADELPHIA STORY, *a screenplay by Donald Ogden Stewart and play by Philip Barry)*

3.
"Course, we all grasp at happiness—but there are such things as rules."

—Clifton Webb pretending to console Louis Jourdan in Jean Negulesco's *Three Coins in the Fountain*
(Screenplay by John Patrick; based on the novel by John H. Secondari)

4.
"First rule: you get an instant kill on the red. Here, here. Always remember: go for the red first because if you don't your opponent will. The blue, you get a cripple. Here, here, here, and here. Second rule: go for the cripple before the slow kill. Here's the slow kill on the yellow. Here, here, and here. Remember: the slow kill may have enough left in him to kill you before he dies. With a cripple, you know you've got him. Keep your distance. Just wear him down. The rest is all right for a public spectacle in Rome. Here, at Padua, we expect more than simple butchery—and we get it."

—Charles McGraw painting up Kirk Douglas's body in gladiator school in Stanley Kubrick's *Spartacus*
(Screenplay by Dalton Trumbo; based on the novel by Howard Fast)

5.
"Oh, no, no, no, my little Volga Boatman. Have you forgotten our First Commandment? Never Complain, Never Explain. Now, it's worked so often and so perfectly in the past, let's not break the rule."

—Ina Claire hoping to resume her affair with Melvyn Douglas after Greta Garbo's exit in Ernst Lubitsch's *Ninotchka*

(Screenplay by Charles Brackett, Billy Wilder and Walter Reisch; based on an original story by Melchior Lengyel)

ALSO SEE: Crooked-1; Diamonds-1; Kindness-3; Legs-3; Manners-7; Never-2; Never-12; Orders-4; Politics-4.

RUN

1.
"Your brother is an old-fashioned man. He believes in his sister's honor. Me? I'm a modern man. The 20th-century type. I run."

—John Ireland being cynical with Joanne Dru in Robert Rossen's *All the King's Men*
(Screenplay by Robert Rossen; based on the novel by Robert Penn Warren)

2.
"I like a man who can run faster than I can."

—Jane Russell telling Marilyn Monroe her preference in Howard Hawks's *Gentlemen Prefer Blondes*
(Screenplay by Charles Lederer; based on the musical play by Joseph Fields and Anita Loos and novel by Anita Loos)

3.
"All right, then run, lady—and you keep on running. Buy yourself a bus ticket and disappear. Change your name. Dye your hair. Get lost. And then maybe—just maybe—you're gonna be safe from me."

—Paul Newman propositioning Joanne Woodward with words she later uses on him in Martin Ritt's *The Long, Hot Summer*
(Screenplay by Irving Ravetch and Harriet Frank Jr.; based on THE HAMLET, *a novel by William Faulkner, and "Barn Burning" and "The Spotted Horses," two short stories by William Faulkner)*

4.
(a) "Was it the Rose Bowl he made his famous run?"
(b) "It was the Punch Bowl, honey. The cut-glass Punch Bowl."

(a) "That's right. I always get that boy's bowls mixed up."

—(a) Jack Carson and (b) Madeleine Sherwood calling Paul Newman an alcoholic has-been in Richard Brooks's *Cat on a Hot Tin Roof*
(Screenplay by Richard Brooks and James Poe; based on the play by Tennessee Williams)

5.
"Go on, Heathcliff. Run away. Bring me back the world."

—Merle Oberon exhibiting romantic abandon with Laurence Olivier in William Wyler's *Wuthering Heights*
(Screenplay by Ben Hecht and Charles MacArthur; based on the novel by Emily Brontë)

6.
"Sonny, I think you're going to have to learn how to fight. Running's no good. You run now, you'll be doing it when you're a grown man."

—Robert Preston advising his son (Robert Eyer) in Delbert Mann's *The Dark at the Top of the Stairs*
(Screenplay by Irving Ravetch and Harriet Frank Jr.; based on the play by William Inge)

7.
"It's no good. I've got to go back. They're making me run. I've never run from anybody before."

—Gary Cooper telling Grace Kelly that their honeymoon will have to wait till after his 12 o'clock showdown in Fred Zinnemann's *High Noon*
(Screenplay by Carl Foreman; based on "The Tin Star," a short story by John W. Cunningham)

8.
"What am I running for? I got $30 million."

—Eugene Pallette catching himself rushing to meet Jack Carson's plane in William Keighley's *The Bride Came C.O.D.*
(Screenplay by Julius J. Epstein and Philip G. Epstein; based on a story by Kenneth Earl and M. M. Musselman)

ALSO SEE: Eulogies-14.

SAYINGS

1.
(a) "I must have a complete report of your negotiations and a detailed expense account."
  (b) "No, no, Ninotchka. Don't ask for it. There is an old Turkish proverb that says 'If something smells bad, why put your nose in it?' "
  (a) "And there is an old Russian saying: 'The cat who has cream on his whiskers had better find good excuses.' "

—(a) Greta Garbo bringing up, and (b) Felix Bressart ducking, government business in Ernst Lubitsch's *Ninotchka*
(Screenplay by Charles Brackett, Billy Wilder and Walter Reisch; based on an original story by Melchior Lengyel)

2.
"Yes, well, I come from a long line of Swedes. We have an old saying, too: 'When the cat's away, why should the mouse act like a rat?' "

—Celeste Holm restating her claim on Frank Sinatra in Charles Walters's *High Society*
(Screenplay by John Patrick; based on THE PHILADELPHIA STORY, a screenplay by Donald Ogden Stewart and play by Philip Barry)

3.
"You know, the Somalis have a proverb. Would you care to hear it? 'A brave man is afraid of a lion three times: when he first sees its track, when he first hears its roar and when he first looks it in the eye.' "

—Gregory Peck giving Robert Preston courage in Zoltan Korda's *The Macomber Affair*
(Screenplay by Casey Robinson and Seymour Bennett; adaptation by Seymour Bennett and Frank Arnold; based on "The Short Happy Life of Francis Macomber," a short story by Ernest Hemingway)

4.
(a) "Mark, there is an old Chinese proverb: 'Do not wake a sleeping tiger.' "
  (b) "Certainly not in a small boat."

—(a) Jennifer Jones responding to her first kiss from (b) William Holden as they sail home in Henry King's *Love Is a Many-Splendored Thing.*
(*Screenplay by John Patrick; based on A MANY-SPLENDORED THING, a novel by Han Suyin*)

5.
"We have a saying back in Texas, ma'am: 'Never drink anything stronger than you are—or older.'"

—Rock Hudson faking the Texas charm as he aids Doris Day's alcoholic date (Nick Adams) in Michael Gordon's *Pillow Talk*
(*Screenplay by Stanley Shapiro and Maurice Richlin; based on a story by Russell Rouse and Clarence Greene*)

6.
"That's what I always tell my drivers: 'No phone pole ever hit a truck unless it was in self-defense.'"

—Alan Hale boozily dispensing bromides at a party in Raoul Walsh's *They Drive by Night*
(*Screenplay by Jerry Wald and Richard Macaulay; based on LONG HAUL, a novel by A. I. Bezzerides*)

ALSO SEE: Never-10; Patience-2; Sin-1; Tears-4.

SCIENCE

1.
"Haven't you heard of science's newest triumph—the doorbell?"

—Clifton Webb resenting Dana Andrews walking in on a private talk with Gene Tierney in Otto Preminger's *Laura*
(*Screenplay by Jay Dratler, Samuel Hoffenstein and Betty Reinhardt; based on the novel by Vera Caspary*)

2.
"The benefits of science are not for scientists, Marie. They're for humanity."

—Paul Muni preaching in bed to his wife (Josephine Hutchinson) in William Dieterle's *The Story of Louis Pasteur*
(*Screenplay by Sheridan Gibney and Pierre*

Collings; based on an original story by Sheridan Gibney and Pierre Collings)

3.
"He was one of our greatest scientists. He has proved, beyond any question, that physical attraction is purely electrochemical."

—Cyd Charisse talking down love to Fred Astaire in Rouben Mamoulian's *Silk Stockings*
(*Screenplay by Leonard Gershe and Leonard Spigelgass; based on the musical play by George S. Kaufman, Leueen MacGrath and Abe Burrows and NINOTCHKA, a screenplay by Charles Brackett, Billy Wilder and Walter Reisch and original story by Melchior Lengyel*)

4.
"With me, loafing is a science."

—Zachary Scott taking pride in his idle-rich status in Michael Curtiz's *Mildred Pierce*
(*Screenplay by Ranald MacDougall; based on the novel by James M. Cain*)

ALSO SEE: Furnishings-3; Heart-19; Love-9; Professions-8; Questions-6.

SCREENPLAYS

1.
"The last one I wrote was about Okies in the dust bowl. You'd never know because, when it reached the screen, the whole thing played on a torpedo boat."

—William Holden commenting on the hazards of screenwriting in Billy Wilder's *Sunset Boulevard*
(*Original Screenplay by Charles Brackett, Billy Wilder and D. M. Marshman Jr.*)

2.
"The only reality she knows comes to her over the TV set. She's very carefully devised a number of scenarios for all of us to play, like Movie of the Week. My God! look at us, Louise. Here we are going through the obligatory middle-of-Act-Two scorned-wife-throws-peccant-husband-out scene. But don't worry. I'll come back to you in the end. All of her plot outlines have

me leaving her and coming back to you because the audience won't buy a rejection of the happy American family. She does have one script in which I kill myself—an adapted-for-television version of *Anna Karenina*—where she's Count Vronsky and I'm Anna."

—William Holden explaining Faye Dunaway to the wife he's leaving (Beatrice Straight) in Sidney Lumet's *Network*
(*Original Screenplay by Paddy Chayefsky*)

3.
"Kirk was wrong when he said I didn't know where movie scripts left off and life began. A script has to make sense, and life doesn't."

—Humphrey Bogart noting the big difference between life and the movies in Joseph L. Mankiewicz's *The Barefoot Contessa*
(*Original Screenplay by Joseph L. Mankiewicz*)

ALSO SEE: Movies.

SEA

1.
"Choose any path you please and tend to one that carries you down to water. There's a magic in water that draws all men away from the land, that leads them over the hills down creeks and streams and rivers to the sea—the sea where each man, as in a mirror, finds himself."

—Richard Basehart following his own calling as he begins the narration of John Huston's *Moby Dick*
(*Screenplay by Ray Bradbury and John Huston; based on the novel by Herman Melville*)

2.
"This is a story of the Battle of the Atlantic, a story of an ocean, two ships and a handful of men. The men are the heroes. The heroines are the ships. The only villain is the sea—the cruel sea—that man has made more cruel."

—Jack Hawkins establishing the essentials in the first words of Charles Frend's *The Cruel Sea*

(*Screenplay by Eric Ambler; based on the novel by Nicholas Monsarrat*)

3.
"Listen to that bitch—the sea—that maker of widows."

—Anthony Quinn cursing the sea in Michael Cacoyannis's *Zorba the Greek*
(*Screenplay by Michael Cacoyannis; based on the novel by Nikos Kazantzakis*)

4.
"You thought you could be Mrs. de Winter—live in her house—walk in her steps—take the things that were hers. But she's too strong for you. *You* can't fight her. No one ever got the better of her—never—never. She was beaten in the end. But it wasn't a man—it wasn't a woman—it was the sea!"

—Judith Anderson raging at Joan Fontaine about the late title character in Alfred Hitchcock's *Rebecca*
(*Screenplay by Robert E. Sherwood and Joan Harrison; adaptation by Philip MacDonald and Michael Hogan; based on the novel by Daphne du Maurier*)

ALSO SEE: Last Lines-25; Law-6.

SEASONS

1.
"We finally discovered that season of love. It is only found in someone else's heart. Right now, someone you know is looking everywhere for it —and it's in you."

—Diane Varsi concluding her narration with the last lines of Mark Robson's *Peyton Place*
(*Screenplay by John Michael Hayes; based on the novel by Grace Metalious*)

2.
"Love's Young Dream. What is it *The Rubaiyat* says:
'Yet Ah, that Spring should vanish with the Rose! That Youth's sweet-scented manuscript must close!'

Well, spring isn't everything, is it, Essie? There's a lot to be said for autumn. That has beauty, too. And winter—if you're together."

—Lionel Barrymore sweet-talking Spring Byington in the last lines of Clarence Brown's *Ah, Wilderness!* *(Screenplay by Albert Hackett and Frances Goodrich; based on the play by Eugene O'Neill)* and (almost verbatim)

—Walter Huston dittoing Selena Royle in the re-make, Rouben Mamoulian's *Summer Holiday* *(Screenplay by Irving Brecher and Jean Holloway; based on AH, WILDERNESS!, a screenplay by Albert Hackett and Frances Goodrich and play by Eugene O'Neill)*

3.
"Winter must be cold for those with no warm memories. We've already missed the spring."

—Deborah Kerr considering her middle-life romance with Cary Grant in Leo McCarey's *An Affair To Remember* *(Screenplay by Delmer Daves and Leo McCarey; based on an original story by Mildred Cram and Leo McCarey)*

4.
"You know, Mildred, in the spring a young man's fancy lightly turns to what he's been thinking about all winter."

—Zachary Scott coming on to Joan Crawford in Michael Curtiz's *Mildred Pierce* *(Screenplay by Ranald MacDougall; based on the novel by James M. Cain)*

5.
"In the spring, a young man's fancy turns pretty fancy."

—Burt Lancaster recalling his courting days in Daniel Mann's *Come Back, Little Sheba* *(Screenplay by Ketti Frings; based on the play by William Inge)*

6.
"Suddenly, last summer he wasn't young anymore."

—Elizabeth Taylor discussing her late cousin in Joseph L. Mankiewicz's *Suddenly, Last Summer*

(Screenplay by Gore Vidal and Tennessee Williams; based on the one-act play by Tennessee Williams)

ALSO SEE: Mad Act-11; Names-6; Paris-4; Remember-5.

SECRETS

1.
"The Thirty-Nine Steps is an organization of spies, collecting information on behalf of the foreign office of—"

—Wylie Watson stopping a bullet as he starts to spill spy secrets during his vaudeville act in Alfred Hitchcock's *The Thirty-Nine Steps* *(Screenplay by Charles Bennett; dialogue by Ian Hay; continuity by Alma Reville; based on the novel by John Buchan)*

2.
"There are few people who know the secret of making a heaven here on earth. You are one of those rare people."

—Cary Grant complimenting Loretta Young in Henry Koster's *The Bishop's Wife* *(Screenplay by Robert E. Sherwood and Leonardo Bercovici; based on the novel by Robert Nathan)*

3.
"The trouble is, you don't realize you're talking to two people. As Charles Foster Kane, who owns 82,364 shares of Public Transit Preferred —you see, I do have a general idea of my holdings—I sympathize with you. Charles Foster Kane is a scoundrel. His paper should be run out of town. A committee should be formed to boycott him. You may, if you can form such a committee, put me down for a contribution of $1,000. . . . On the other hand, I am the publisher of the *Inquirer*. As such, it is my duty— and I'll let you in on a little secret—it is also my pleasure to see to it that decent, hard-working people in this community aren't robbed blind by a pack of money-mad pirates just because they haven't anybody to look after their interests. I'll let you in on another little secret, Mr.

Thatcher. I think I'm the man to do it. You see, I have money and property. If I don't look after the interest of the underprivileged, maybe somebody else will—maybe somebody without any money or property."

—Orson Welles telling off his financial advisor (George Coulouris) in Orson Welles's *Citizen Kane* (Original Screenplay by Herman J. Mankiewicz and Orson Welles)

4.
"Oh, there's—there's one more thing, dear. I'd like to stay here until your father's on his way to California. He's funny about things, you know. He'd never believe that the home was a grand place. He's a little old-fashioned, your father is. Those places seem terrible to him. He must never know that I'm going, and you tell Cora and Nellie and the others that he must never know. This is one thing that has to be handled my way. . . . Let him go on thinking that I'm living with you and Anita. You can always forward my letters. It'll be the first secret I've ever had from him. It'll—it'll seem mighty funny. Ah, well. Here's another little secret, just between us two: You were always my favorite child."

—Beulah Bondi telling Thomas Mitchell to spare Victor Moore the news that she's going to a rest home in Leo McCarey's *Make Way for Tomorrow* (Screenplay by Vina Delmar; based on the play by Helen Leary and Nolan Leary and THE YEARS ARE SO LONG, a novel by Josephine Lawrence)

ALSO SEE: Betrayal-2; Men-7; Prison-1.

SELF-DEPRECIATION

1.
"It's typical of my career that in the great crises of life I should stand flanked by two incompetent alcoholics."

—John Barrymore counting his aides (Roscoe Karns and Walter Connolly) as more bad luck in Howard Hawks's *Twentieth Century*
(Screenplay by Ben Hecht and Charles MacArthur; based on their play and NAPOLEON OF BROADWAY, a play by Charles Bruce Milholland)

2.
"You wouldn't treat anyone in the world like this except Old Fanny. 'Old Fanny,' you say. 'It's nobody but Old Fanny so I'll kick her. Nobody'll resent it. I'll kick her all I want to.' And you're right. I haven't got anything in the world since my brother died. Nobody. Nothing."

—Agnes Moorehead railing at her nephew (Tim Holt) in Orson Welles's *The Magnificent Ambersons* (Screenplay by Orson Welles; based on the novel by Booth Tarkington)

3.
"You call that abuse? You don't know what I'm used to. With all your carrying on—to me, Jonathan, you're a gift."

—Ann-Margret crawling to Jack Nicholson in Mike Nichols's *Carnal Knowledge* (Original Screenplay by Jules Feiffer)

4.
"Maybe you're sorry you married me now, Doc. You didn't know I was going to get old and fat and sloppy."

—Shirley Booth whining to Burt Lancaster in Daniel Mann's *Come Back, Little Sheba* (Screenplay by Ketti Frings; based on the play by William Inge)

5.
"Some girls—when a fella comes to see 'em, he brings flowers. Orchids even. I'm the other type girl. Me, a fella brings four bottles of beer. What's the sense of kidding myself?"

—Pamela Britton being the Brooklyn broad about it in George Sidney's *Anchors Aweigh* (Screenplay by Isobel Lennart; based on "You Can't Fool a Marine," a short story by Natalie Marcin)

6.
"I'm filthy, period."

—Dorothy Malone beating her brother (Robert Stack) to the bottom line in Douglas Sirk's *Written on the Wind*
(Screenplay by George Zuckerman; based on the novel by Robert Wilder)

9.
"I used to—used to make obscene phone calls to her—collect—and she used to accept the charges all the time."

—Woody Allen recalling an old flame in Woody Allen's *Take the Money and Run*
(Original Screenplay by Woody Allen and Mickey Rose)

ALSO SEE: Arrogance-3; Fathers-9; Floozy-1; Mind-16.

SELF-PERCEPTION

1.
"The fates, the Destinies—whoever-they-are that decide what we do or don't get. They've been at me now nearly a quarter of a century. No letup. First they said, 'Let him do without parents. He'll get along.' Then they decided, 'He doesn't need any education—that's for sissies.' And, right at the beginning, they tossed a coin. Heads, he's poor; tails, he's rich. So they tossed a coin—with two heads. And when you put all this together you got Michael Bolgar."

—John Garfield singing his sad song for Priscilla Lane in Michael Curtiz's *Four Daughters*
(Screenplay by Julius J. Epstein and Lenore Coffee; based on "Sister Act," a short story by Fannie Hurst)

2.
"I do hateful things for which people love me, and I do lovable things for which they hate me. I'm admired for my detestability. Now don't worry, Little Eva. I may be rancid butter, but I'm on your side of the bread."

—Gene Kelly telling Donna Anderson his irascibility is an asset in Stanley Kramer's *Inherit the Wind*
(Screenplay by Nathan E. Douglas and Harold Jacob Smith; based on the play by Jerome Lawrence and Robert E. Lee)

3.
"I'm a bagel on a plate of onion rolls."

—Barbra Streisand arguing the advantage of not being a look-alike chorine in William Wyler's *Funny Girl*
(Screenplay by Isobel Lennart; based on her musical play)

4.
"I'm used to being top banana in the shock department."

—Audrey Hepburn being jaded with George Peppard in Blake Edwards's *Breakfast at Tiffany's*
(Screenplay by George Axelrod; based on the novella by Truman Capote)

5.
"I'm not the kind of man to take no answer for an answer."

—Paul Ford telling his aide (Harry Morgan) to keep trying to get through to Glenn Ford on the phone in Daniel Mann's *The Teahouse of the August Moon*
(Screenplay by John Patrick; based on his play and the book by Vern J. Sneider)

6.
"I'm more like the old horse the fella's trying to sell: sound of skin and skeleton, and free from faults and faculties."

—Henry Fonda underselling himself to Pauline Moore in John Ford's *Young Mr. Lincoln*
(Original Screenplay by Lamar Trotti)

7.
"I'm loud and I'm vulgar and I wear the pants in the house because somebody's got to, but I am not a monster."

—Elizabeth Taylor drawing the line in Mike Nichols's *Who's Afraid of Virginia Woolf?*
(Screenplay by Ernest Lehman; based on the play by Edward Albee)

8.
"I wear the pants, and she beats me with the belt."

—Edward G. Robinson using a half-joke to recover from being corrected by his wife (Mady Christians) in Irving Reis's *All My Sons*

(Screenplay by Chester Erskine; based on the play by Arthur Miller)

9.

"Who the hell do you think you're dealing with? In case you didn't happen to notice it, you big Texas longhorn bull, I'm one helluvah gorgeous chick!"

—Sylvia Miles acting indignant when Jon Voight asks to be paid for his sex service in John Schlesinger's *Midnight Cowboy*
(Screenplay by Waldo Salt; based on the novel by James Leo Herlihy)

10.

"I'm just a girl from the country. The theater and the people in it have always been a complete mystery to me. They still are."

—Grace Kelly admitting an outsider's perspective in George Seaton's *The Country Girl*
(Screenplay by George Seaton; based on the play by Clifford Odets)

11.

"Now what can I tell you? Last year, two or three—goes way back, I suppose—I can remember entertaining suicidal thoughts as a college student. At any rate, I've always found life demanding. I'm an only child of lower middle-class people. I was the glory of my parents. 'My son the doctor,' you know. I was always top in my class. Scholarship to Harvard. Boy genius. The brilliant eccentric. Terrified of women. Clumsy at sports. Doctor, how do I go about this?"

—George C. Scott unburdening himself to the staff psychiatrist (David Hooks) in Arthur Hiller's *The Hospital*
(Original Screenplay by Paddy Chayefsky)

ALSO SEE: Drunk-1; Drunk-2; Frigidity-2; Honest-3; Honest-4; Pride-7; Truth-6.

SELFISH

1.

"The whole history of the world is the story of the struggle between the selfish and the un-

selfish. . . . All that's bad around us is bred by selfishness. Sometimes, selfishness can even get to be a—a cause, a—an organized force, even a government. And then it's called fascism. Can you understand that?"

—William Holden simplifying politics for Judy Holliday in George Cukor's *Born Yesterday*
(Screenplay by Albert Mannheimer; based on the play by Garson Kanin)

2.

"Oh, yes, I was afraid, but that's not why I didn't pull the trigger. What do I care about Johnny Rocco, whether he lives or dies? I only care about me. Me and mine. If Rocco wants to come back to America, let him. Let him be President. I fight nobody's battles but my own."

—Humphrey Bogart explaining why he didn't stand up to Edward G. Robinson in John Huston's *Key Largo*
(Screenplay by Richard Brooks and John Huston; based on the play by Maxwell Anderson)

3.

"That's wonderful, sir, wonderful. I do like a man who tells you right out that he's looking out for himself. Don't we all? I don't trust a man who says he's not."

—Sydney Greenstreet commending Humphrey Bogart's directness in John Huston's *The Maltese Falcon*
(Screenplay by John Huston; based on the novel by Dashiell Hammett)

4.

"I'm glad you didn't get sore at me the way I took you over the hurdles, Mildred. I didn't mean to cut up your business the way I did. I just got started and couldn't stop. I can't help myself. I see an angle, and right away I start cutting myself a piece of throat."

—Jack Carson rationalizing his greed to Joan Crawford in Michael Curtiz's *Mildred Pierce*
(Screenplay by Ranald MacDougall; based on the novel by James M. Cain)

5.

"Oh, I'd love to, Frank, but I've only just volunteered for another important watching service: the Watch Over Walter Eckland Service."

—Cary Grant putting a beachcomber named Walter Eckland (i.e., himself) ahead of Trevor Howard's offer to be a wartime plane-spotter in Ralph Nelson's *Father Goose*
(*Screenplay by Peter Stone and Frank Tarloff; based on "A Place of Dragons," a short story by S. H. Barnett*)

6.
"Well, you argue with her, you argue with her. Otherwise, you're going on a honeymoon with blood on your hands. How can you have any happiness after that? All through the years, you'll remember that a man went to the gallows because she was too selfish to wait two hours. I tell you, Bruce, Earl Williams's face'll come between you on the train tonight and at the preacher tomorrow and all the rest of your lives."

—Cary Grant trying to win back his ex-wife and star reporter (Rosalind Russell) by appealing to her fiancé (Ralph Bellamy) in Howard Hawks's *His Girl Friday*
(*Screenplay by Charles Lederer; based on THE FRONT PAGE, a play by Ben Hecht and Charles MacArthur*)

ALSO SEE: Beliefs-2; Joke-2; Neck-1; Normal-1; Pleasures-6; Similarities-5.

SENSIBLE

1.
"You know, since I started taking lithium, I feel more sensible than this month's *Good Housekeeping*."

—Kelly Bishop explaining her calmness to Jill Clayburgh in Paul Mazursky's *An Unmarried Woman*
(*Original Screenplay by Paul Mazursky*)

2.
"Going to a man's apartment always ends in one of two ways: either a girl is willing to lose her virtue, or she fights for it. I don't want to lose mine, and I think it's vulgar to fight for it, so I always put my cards on the table. Don't you think that's sensible?"

—Maggie McNamara heading off William Holden's overtures in Otto Preminger's *The Moon Is Blue*
(*Screenplay by F. Hugh Herbert; based on his play*)

3.
(a) "Be sensible, Martins."
    (b) "Haven't got a sensible name, Calloway."

—(a) Trevor Howard trying to talk (b) Joseph Cotten out of saying good-bye to Valli in what indeed turns out to be the last lines of Carol Reed's *The Third Man*
(*Original Screenplay by Graham Greene*)

4.
"I am trying to be sensible. You are an American. In my heart, I am Chinese. You are married. I am a widow. You are a journalist, a front-row spectator not directly involved. I am a doctor deeply involved, with a duty toward my people."

—Jennifer Jones outlining the obstacles to William Holden in Henry King's *Love Is a Many-Splendored Thing*
(*Screenplay by John Patrick; based on A MANY-SPLENDORED THING, a novel by Han Suyin*)

ALSO SEE: Adultery-8; Names-25; Relatives-6.

SEX

1.
"That was the most fun I've had without laughing."

—Woody Allen complimenting Diane Keaton in Woody Allen's *Annie Hall*
(*Original Screenplay by Woody Allen and Marshall Brickman*)

2.
"Do you think it will ever take the place of night baseball?"

—Deborah Kerr teasing Cary Grant in Leo McCarey's *An Affair To Remember*
(*Screenplay by Delmer Daves and Leo McCarey; based on an original story by Mildred Cram and Leo McCarey*)
                    and (almost verbatim)

—Irene Dunne dittoing Charles Boyer in the original, Leo McCarey's *Love Affair*
(Screenplay by Delmer Daves and Donald Ogden Stewart; based on an original story by Mildred Cram and Leo McCarey)

3.

"Don't you think it's better for a girl to be preoccupied with sex than occupied?"

—Maggie McNamara making one of her wide-eyed inquiries in Otto Preminger's *The Moon Is Blue*
(Screenplay by F. Hugh Herbert; based on his play)

4.

"You would never have found him through his office, Mr. President. Our premier is a man of the people—but he is also a man, if you follow my meaning."

—Peter Bull explaining his leader's libido to Peter Sellers in Stanley Kubrick's *Dr. Strangelove or: How I Learned To Stop Worrying and Love the Bomb*
(Screenplay by Stanley Kubrick, Terry Southern and Peter George; based on RED ALERT, a novel by Peter George)

5.

"Then I shall have to use a word I've never used in your presence. It seems to be a book about—sex."

—Ronald Colman broaching a delicate subject with his wife (Edna Best) in Joseph L. Mankiewicz's *The Late George Apley*
(Screenplay by Philip Dunne; based on the play by John P. Marquand and George S. Kaufman and novel by John P. Marquand)

6.

(a) "When I married Frank, he was very handsome. Clean, so clean. Why, it came as a big shock to me on my wedding night to find out what a—physical person he was. You know what I'm talking about, Joan?
   (b) "Sex."
   (a) "You said it, not me. It's very hard for me to talk about these things. Well, I was so nauseous on my wedding night with you-know-who that I didn't say a word. I just ran into the bathroom and locked the door because I don't like to make a scene."

   (b) "You mean you never enjoyed sex?"
   (a) "What's to enjoy? Love isn't physical. Love is spiritual, like—like the great love that Ingrid Bergman had for Bing Crosby in *The Bells of St. Mary's* when she was a nun and he was a priest and they loved each other from afar. But Frank didn't want to know from that."

—Beatrice Arthur discussing her husband (Richard Castellano) with her daughter-in-law (Diane Keaton) in Cy Howard's *Lovers and Other Strangers*
(Screenplay by Renee Taylor, Joseph Bologna and David Z. Goodman; based on the play by Renee Taylor and Joseph Bologna)

7.

"Get him to take you out to dinner, and work around to the play. Good heavens, I don't have to tell you how to do these things. How did you get all those other parts?"

—Monty Woolley assuming Ann Sheridan vamped her way to stardom in William Keighley's *The Man Who Came to Dinner*
(Screenplay by Julius J. Epstein and Philip G. Epstein; based on the play by George S. Kaufman and Moss Hart)

8.

(a) "It's just that I don't like to become involved in other people's affairs."
   (b) "Oh, you'll get over that. Small college and all. Musical beds is the faculty sport around here."

—(b) Richard Burton putting (a) George Segal wise in Mike Nichols's *Who's Afraid of Virginia Woolf?*
(Screenplay by Ernest Lehman; based on the play by Edward Albee)

9.

"They was giving me 10,000 watts a day, and, you know, I'm hot to trot. The next woman takes me out is going to light up like a pinball machine and pay off in silver dollars."

—Jack Nicholson boasting about his shock treatment to his therapy group in Milos Forman's *One Flew Over the Cuckoo's Nest*
(Screenplay by Lawrence Hauben and Bo Goldman; based on the novel by Ken Kesey)

ALSO SEE: Sex Appeal; Available-3; Communication-4; Communication-5; Crazy-15; Dress-8; Feelings-8; Firsts-4; Furnishings-3; Guilty-5; Insults-9; Letters-13; Macho-2; Narcissism-1; Party-7; Propositions-14; Sensible-2; Similarities-2; Smile-4.

SEX APPEAL

1.

"What Lotus Blossom has, the government doesn't issue."

—Glenn Ford commenting on the sensuality of Machiko Kyo in Daniel Mann's *The Teahouse of the August Moon*
(Screenplay by John Patrick; based on his play and the book by Vern J. Sneider)

2.

"Ma, sooner or later, there comes a point in a man's life when he's got to face some facts. And one fact I got to face is that, whatever it is that women like, I ain't got it. I chased after enough girls in my life. I—I went to enough dances. I got hurt enough. I don't want to get hurt no more."

—Ernest Borgnine leveling with his mother (Esther Minciotti) in Delbert Mann's *Marty*
(Screenplay by Paddy Chayefsky; based on his teleplay)

3.

"What you don't realize, Helen, is this thing about women and me. I walk into a room, and they sense it instantly. I arouse something in 'em. I bother 'em. It's a kind of animal thing I've got. It's really quite extraordinary."

—Tom Ewell fantasizing a confrontation with his wife (Evelyn Keyes) in Billy Wilder's *The Seven Year Itch*
(Screenplay by Billy Wilder and George Axelrod; based on the play by George Axelrod)

ALSO SEE: Sex; Bottle-2; Callings-7; Help-4; Mothers-6; Prayers-4; Temptation-1; Walk-4; Walk-5.

SIGNS

1.

"There Is Still Time . . Brother"

—Sign from a religion meeting flapping in the wind in an empty town square after a nuclear accident in the last shot of Stanley Kramer's *On the Beach*
(Screenplay by John Paxton; based on the novel by Nevil Shute)

2.

"Closed on Account of a lot of death."

—Sign on the door posted by Pat Quinn in Arthur Penn's *Alice's Restaurant*
(Screenplay by Venable Herndon and Arthur Penn; based on "The Alice's Restaurant Massacree," a song by Arlo Guthrie)

3.

"Join the Army and See the Navy"

—Sign paraded by Harpo Marx in the heat of battle in Leo McCarey's *Duck Soup*
(Screenplay by Bert Kalmar and Harry Ruby; additional dialogue by Arthur Sheekman and Nat Perrin)

4.

"Sadie Thompson Slept Here"

—Sign posted in Bing Crosby and Bob Hope's bedroom in Hal Walker's *Road to Bali*
(Screenplay by Frank Butler, Hal Kanter and William Morrow; based on an original story by Frank Butler and Harry Tugend)

5.

"Welcome to Mandrake Falls
    Where the scenery enthralls
    Where no hardship e'er befalls
    Welcome to Mandrake Falls."

—City sign authored by poet-in-residence Gary Cooper and recited by Lionel Stander in Frank Capra's *Mr. Deeds Goes to Town*
(Screenplay by Robert Riskin; based on "Opera Hat," a short story by Clarence Budington Kelland)

6.

"Beware of
    the Children"

—Fair warning posted at the home of Percy Kilbride and Marjorie Main in Chester Erskine's *The Egg and I*
(Screenplay by Chester Erskine and Fred F. Finklehoffe; based on the book by Betty MacDonald)

SILENCE

1.
"There has never been such a silence."

—Elizabeth Taylor responding to the death of Richard Burton in Joseph L. Mankiewicz's *Cleopatra*
(Screenplay by Joseph L. Mankiewicz, Ranald MacDougall and Sidney Buchman; based upon histories by Plutarch, Suetonius and Appian and THE LIFE AND TIMES OF CLEOPATRA, a book by C. M. Franzero)

2.
"Some people think the Crucifixion only took place on Calvary. They better wise up. Taking Joey Doyle's life to stop him from testifying is a crucifixion. Dropping a sling on 'Kayo' Dugan because he was ready to spill his guts tomorrow —that's a crucifixion. And every time the mob puts the crusher on a good man, tries to stop him from doing his duty as a citizen—it's a crucifixion. And anybody who sits around and lets it happen—keeps silent about something he knows has happened—shares the guilt of it just as much as the Roman soldier who pierced the flesh of our Lord to see if He was dead."

—Karl Malden preaching against apathy in Elia Kazan's *On the Waterfront*
(Original Screenplay by Budd Schulberg; based on "Crime on the Waterfront," nonfiction articles by Malcolm Johnson)

3.
"Joey, this may be the last chance I'll ever have to tell you to do anything, so I'm telling you: shut up."

—Spencer Tracy hushing his about-to-be-married daughter (Katharine Houghton) in Stanley Kramer's *Guess Who's Coming to Dinner*
(Original Screenplay by William Rose)

4.
" 'Shut up'? You can't talk like that to me until after we've married."

—Bob Hope telling Jane Russell the rules in Frank Tashlin's *Son of Paleface*
(Original Screenplay by Frank Tashlin, Robert L. Welch and Joseph Quillan)

5.
"Not anything. Don't say anything—and especially not 'darling.' "

—Katharine Hepburn hushing a sudden suitor (James Stewart) in George Cukor's *The Philadelphia Story*
(Screenplay by Donald Ogden Stewart; based on the play by Philip Barry)
and

—Grace Kelly dittoing Frank Sinatra in the remake, Charles Walters's *High Society*
(Screenplay by John Patrick; based on THE PHILADELPHIA STORY, a screenplay by Donald Ogden Stewart and play by Philip Barry)

ALSO SEE: Compliments-9; Husbands-5; Last Lines-2; Talk-4; Talk-5.

SIMILARITIES

1.
"Nobody thinks in terms of human beings. Governments don't. Why should we? They talk about the people and the proletariat, and I talk about the slickers and the mugs. It's the same thing. They have their five-year plans. So have I."

—Orson Welles rationalizing his criminal activities to Joseph Cotten in Carol Reed's *The Third Man*
(Original Screenplay by Graham Greene)

2.
"I suppose it's because you're so scared of— well, shall we call it life? That sounds more respectable than that word I know you hate. We're awfully alike, you know—you and I—in many ways. I suppose that's why we drifted so much together in this place."

—David Niven confessing his affinity for another repressed soul (Deborah Kerr) in Delbert Mann's *Separate Tables*
(Screenplay by Terence Rattigan and John Gay; based on the play by Terence Rattigan)

3.

"That I should want you at all suddenly strikes me as the height of improbability, but that in itself is probably the reason. You're an improbable person, Eve, and so am I. We have that in common. Also a contempt for humanity, an inability to love or to be loved, insatiable ambition—and talent. We deserve each other."

—George Sanders settling for Anne Baxter in Joseph L. Mankiewicz's *All About Eve*
(Screenplay by Joseph L. Mankiewicz; based on "The Wisdom of Eve," a radio play and short story by Mary Orr)

4.

"I can afford him and understand him. He's no good, but he's what I want. I'm not a nice person, Laura. Neither is he. He knows I know he's just what he is. He also knows that I don't care. We belong together because we're both weak and can't seem to help it."

—Judith Anderson explaining why she's better for Vincent Price than Gene Tierney in Otto Preminger's *Laura*
(Screenplay by Jay Dratler, Samuel Hoffenstein and Betty Reinhardt; based on the novel by Vera Caspary)

5.

"There's one thing I *do* know, and that is that I love you, Scarlett. In spite of you and me and the whole silly world going to pieces around us, I love you. Because we're alike—bad lots both of us, selfish and shrewd, but able to look things in the eyes and call them by their right names."

—Clark Gable wooing Vivien Leigh in Victor Fleming's *Gone With the Wind*
(Screenplay by Sidney Howard; based on the novel by Margaret Mitchell)

ALSO SEE: Help-3; Hero-2; Murder-6; Propositions-7; Relatives-6; Remember-6; Sex-6.

SIN

1.
"If a woman sleeps alone, it puts a shame on all men. God has a very big heart, but there is one sin He will not forgive: if a woman calls a man to her bed and he will not go. I know, because a very wise old Turk told me."

—Anthony Quinn passing along some libertine advice to Alan Bates in Michael Cacoyannis's *Zorba the Greek*
(Screenplay by Michael Cacoyannis; based on the novel by Nikos Kazantzakis)

2.
"There's no such thing as a good influence, Mr. Gray. All influence is immoral."

—George Sanders debating the point with Hurd Hatfield in Albert Lewin's *The Picture of Dorian Gray*
(Screenplay by Albert Lewin; based on the novel by Oscar Wilde)

3.
"Why, yes, of course. Isn't that what we're all most concerned with? Sin."

—Jennifer Jones striking a spiritual pose for Robert Morley in John Huston's *Beat the Devil*
(Screenplay by John Huston and Truman Capote; based on the novel by James Helvick)

4.
"Jenny's daughter is still going with that actor. An actor? Fashions in sin change. In my day, it was Englishmen."

—Lucile Watson reflecting over the morning mail in Herman Shumlin's *Watch on the Rhine*
(Screenplay by Dashiell Hammett; additional scenes and dialogue by Lillian Hellman; based on her play)

5.
"20,000! The wages of sin are rising!"

—Burt Lancaster sneering at a bribe from the bad guys in John Sturges's *Gunfight at the O. K. Corral*
(Screenplay by Leon Uris; suggested by "The Killer," a short story by George Scullin)

6.

"El Paso and Amarillo ain't no different than Sodom and Gomorrah—on a smaller scale, of course."

—Walter Huston finding sinners aplenty in Texas in King Vidor's *Duel in the Sun*
(Screenplay by David O. Selznick; adaptation by Oliver H. P. Garrett; based on the novel by Niven Busch)

7.

"Well, sir, I suppose every train carries its cargo of sin, but this train is burdened with more than its share!"

—Lawrence Grant complaining to Clive Brook about some shady-lady passengers (Marlene Dietrich and Anna May Wong) in Josef von Sternberg's *Shanghai Express*
(Screenplay by Jules Furthman; based on a story by Harry Hervey)

ALSO SEE: Men-5; Pity-5.

SLEEP

1.

"May August moon bring gentle sleep. Sayonara."

—Marlon Brando addressing the audience in the last lines of Daniel Mann's *The Teahouse of the August Moon*
(Screenplay by John Patrick; based on his play and the book by Vern J. Sneider)

2.

"You get a good rest, too. Good night."

—Frank Craven addressing the audience in the last lines of Sam Wood's *Our Town*
(Screenplay by Thornton Wilder, Frank Craven and Harry Chandlee; based on the play by Thornton Wilder)

3.

"A good night's rest'll do you a lot of good. Besides, you got nothing to worry about: the walls of Jericho will protect you from the big bad wolf."

—Clark Gable teasingly reassuring Claudette Colbert about the blanket dividing their motel room in Frank Capra's *It Happened One Night*
(Screenplay by Robert Riskin; based on "Night Bus," a short story by Samuel Hopkins Adams)

4.

(a) "I am troubled with insomnia."
  (b) "Well, I know a good cure for it."
  (a) "Yeah?"
  (b) "Get plenty of sleep."

—(b) W. C. Fields advising (a) John Lipson in Edward Cline's *Never Give a Sucker an Even Break*
(Screenplay by John T. Neville and Prescott Chaplin; based on an original story by Otis Criblecoblis, a.k.a. W. C. Fields)

5.

"He's a genius, and he needs eight hours undisturbed sleep. He says so all the time."

—Larry Olsen dreading the idea of waking his baby-sitter-in-residence (Clifton Webb) in Walter Lang's *Sitting Pretty*
(Screenplay by F. Hugh Herbert; based on the novel by Gwen Davenport)

ALSO SEE: Advertising Slogans-1; Crazy-12; Crazy-17; Deals-3; Good-8; Greetings-3; Prison-6; Respect-3; Signs-4; Sex-1; Spiders-2; Telephone Scenes-7.

SMELL

1.

"I love the smell of napalm in the morning. . . . It smells like victory."

—Robert Duvall swaggering on the frontlines in Francis Ford Coppola's *Apocalypse Now*
(Screenplay by John Milius and Francis Ford Coppola; narration written by Michael Herr)

2.

"Evil's got a smell of its own. A child can spot it. I know, Joe. I know. . . . I lived with it. I learned it early and deep. My own father was one of them. Every day in my childhood, I saw that father of mine—with that criminal mind of his—abuse and torment my mother and drive her straight into a lunatic asylum. She died there. Yeah, I know it when I smell it. Every time I look at one of those 'babies,' I see my old man's face."

—Kirk Douglas explaining his passion for police work to Luis Van Rooten in William Wyler's *Detective Story*
(Screenplay by Philip Yordan and Robert Wyler; based on the play by Sidney Kingsley)

3.
"You stink! You stink from corruption. You're worse than a murderer. You're a graverobber."

—Arthur Kennedy telling off Kirk Douglas in Mark Robson's *Champion*
(Screenplay by Carl Foreman; based on the short story by Ring Lardner)

4.
"Don't say 'stinks,' darling. If absolutely necessary, 'smells'—but only if absolutely necessary."

—Mary Nash correcting Virginia Weidler in George Cukor's *The Philadelphia Story*
(Screenplay by Donald Ogden Stewart; based on the play by Philip Barry)
and

—Margalo Gillmore dittoing Lydia Reed in the remake, Charles Walters's *High Society*
(Screenplay by John Patrick; based on THE PHILADELPHIA STORY, a screenplay by Donald Ogden Stewart and play by Philip Barry)

5.
"Didn't anybody ever tell you before that you smell bad?"

—Anne Baxter dampening Gregory Peck's ardor in William A. Wellman's *Yellow Sky*
(Screenplay by Lamar Trotti; based on a story by W. R. Burnett)

6.
"If I smelled as bad as you, I wouldn't live near people."

—Kim Darby objecting to John Wayne's drinking in Henry Hathaway's *True Grit*
(Screenplay by Marguerite Roberts; based on the novel by Charles Portis)

7.
"And I'll tell you another thing: frankly, you're beginning to smell—and, for a stud in New York, that's a handicap."

—Dustin Hoffman advising Jon Voight in John Schlesinger's *Midnight Cowboy*
(Screenplay by Waldo Salt; based on the novel by James Leo Herlihy)

8.
"Do you know what I think, young fella? I think you're a newspaperman. I can smell 'em. I've always been able to smell 'em. Excuse me while I open the window."

—Charles Winninger greeting Fredric March in William A. Wellman's *Nothing Sacred*
(Screenplay by Ben Hecht; based on "Letter to the Editor," a short story by James H. Street)

9.
"Well, if you look at it, it's a barn. If you smell it, it's a stable."

—Groucho Marx explaining to Chico Marx that either noun is correct in Norman Z. McLeod's *Monkey Business*
(Screenplay by S. J. Perelman and Will B. Johnstone; additional dialogue by Arthur Sheekman)

10.
"What's that smell in this room? Didn't you notice it, Brick? Didn't you notice a powerful and obnoxious odor of mendacity in this room?"

—Burl Ives walking with Paul Newman among the family plotters in Richard Brooks's *Cat on a Hot Tin Roof*
(Screenplay by Richard Brooks and James Poe; based on the play by Tennessee Williams)

11.
"Yes, I take money from you, Mildred—but not enough to make me like kitchens or cooks. They smell of grease."

—Zachary Scott getting snooty about Joan Crawford's waitress past in Michael Curtiz's *Mildred Pierce*
(Screenplay by Ranald MacDougall; based on the novel by James M. Cain)

12.
"You're joking! Ask that common little woman to the house with that noisy, vulgar man? He smells Oklahoma!"

—Billie Burke resisting the suggestion of her husband (Lionel Barrymore) to have Jean Harlow and Wallace Beery over for dinner in George Cukor's *Dinner at Eight*
(Screenplay by Frances Marion and Herman J. Mankiewicz; based on the play by George S. Kaufman and Edna Ferber)

13.
"I can just tell the way it smells this is gonna be a great year for cotton."

—Charley Grapewin holding on to his unfounded optimism to the very end in John Ford's *Tobacco Road*
(Screenplay by Nunnally Johnson; based on the play by Jack Kirkland and novel by Erskine Caldwell)

14.
"Who wants perfume? Give me the fresh, wet smell of Iowa corn right after it rains."

—John Lund complimenting an Iowa congresswoman (Jean Arthur) in Billy Wilder's *A Foreign Affair*
(Screenplay by Charles Brackett, Billy Wilder and Richard L. Breen; adaptation by Robert Harari; based on an original story by David Shaw)

15.
"Smells wonderful! Why do they still make perfumes like 'Bouquet de Fleur' as if things still happened in flower gardens? Now if they turned out something like 'Wet Hair After Swimming,' you'd have something."

—Van Heflin romancing Joan Crawford in Curtis Bernhardt's *Possessed*
(Screenplay by Sylvia Richards and Ranald MacDougall; based on ONE MAN'S SECRET, a novelette by Rita Weiman)

16.
"I knew it was the real thing because I loved everything about him. I loved the way he moved. Sometimes, I just spent hours and hours of watching him move around. And his hair—oh, you're going to think I'm crazy, but I loved the way his hair smells like raisins. And when he kissed me—I never told him this—but the best part about being in his arms was that I could get a good whiff of his hair. Well, I don't know if it's me or Richie that changed, but it's just no big deal anymore to feel him or smell him."

—Diane Keaton explaining her estrangement with Joseph Hindy to her mother-in-law (Beatrice Arthur) in Cy Howard's *Lovers and Other Strangers*
(Screenplay by Renee Taylor, Joseph Bologna and David Z. Goodman; based on the play by Renee Taylor and Joseph Bologna)

ALSO SEE: Cigarette-5; New York-1; New York-2; Orchids-2; Pretense-2; Progress-2; Sayings-1; Soul-1.

SMILE

1.
"If you want to call me that, smile."

—Gary Cooper standing up to Walter Huston in Victor Fleming's *The Virginian*
(Screenplay by Howard Estabrook; based on the play by Kirk La Shelle and Owen Wister and novel by Owen Wister)

2.
"When you call me madam, smile."

—Ethel Merman warning Billy De Wolfe in Walter Lang's *Call Me Madam*
(Screenplay by Arthur Sheekman; based on the musical play by Howard Lindsay and Russel Crouse)

3.
"May I ask you a personal question: do you smile all the time?"

—Barbra Streisand rattling Robert Redford in Sydney Pollack's *The Way We Were*

(Screenplay by Arthur Laurents; based on his novel)

4.

"Yes sir, they're gonna say, 'There goes that poor old Clara Varner whose father married her off to a dirt-scratching, shiftless, no-good farmer who just happened by.' Well, let 'em talk. I'll tell you one thing: you're gonna wake up in the morning, smiling."

—Paul Newman moving in on Joanne Woodward in Martin Ritt's *The Long, Hot Summer*
(Screenplay by Irving Ravetch and Harriet Frank Jr.; based on THE HAMLET, a novel by William Faulkner, and "Barn Burning" and "The Spotted Horses," two short stories by William Faulkner)

5.

"Gotta make hay while she's still smiling at me."

—Richard Jaeckel being glib with Shirley Booth about Terry Moore in Daniel Mann's *Come Back, Little Sheba*
(Screenplay by Ketti Frings; based on the play by William Inge)

6.

"Once I tried to let a smile be my umbrella. I got awful wet."

—Celeste Holm finding lies in the old lyrics in Elia Kazan's *Gentleman's Agreement*
(Screenplay by Moss Hart; based on the novel by Laura Z. Hobson)

7.

"What a funny look on your face, dear. Smiling like that. You look so kind. So kind. What you going to do with that—"

—Dame May Whitty misreading Robert Montgomery's madness with her last words in Richard Thorpe's *Night Must Fall*
(Screenplay by John Van Druten; based on the play by Emlyn Williams)

8.

"No face on this one at all. Oh, look. There's another one smiling. It's monstrous of them to die smiling. It's inhuman!"

—Peter Ustinov inspecting the Christian corpses in his lions' arena in Mervyn LeRoy's *Quo Vadis*
(Screenplay by John Lee Mahin, S. N. Behrman and Sonya Levien; based on the novel by Henryk Sienkiewicz)

9.

"No mean Machiavellian is smiling, cynical Sidney Kidd. The world's his oyster, with an R in every month."

—Cary Grant characterizing Henry Daniell to James Stewart in George Cukor's *The Philadelphia Story*
(Screenplay by Donald Ogden Stewart; based on the play by Philip Barry)

ALSO SEE: Proposals-13; Stupid-6.

SNAKE

1.

"Would you take your clammy hand off my chair? You have the touch of a love-starved cobra."

—Monty Woolley crabbing to his nurse (Mary Wilkes) in William Keighley's *The Man Who Came to Dinner*
(Screenplay by Julius J. Epstein and Philip G. Epstein; based on the play by George S. Kaufman and Moss Hart)

2.

(a) "He's not the man for you. I can see that, but I sorta like him. He's got a lot of charm."

(b) "He comes by it naturally. His grandfather was a snake."

—(a) Ralph Bellamy and (b) Rosalind Russell discussing her ex (Cary Grant) in Howard Hawks's *His Girl Friday*
(Screenplay by Charles Lederer; based on THE FRONT PAGE, a play by Ben Hecht and Charles MacArthur)

3.

"I've never known a better seaman—but, as a man, he's a snake. He doesn't punish for discipline. He likes to see men crawl. Sometimes,

I'd like to push his poison down his own throat."

—Clark Gable describing Charles Laughton in Frank Lloyd's *Mutiny on the Bounty*
(Screenplay by Talbot Jennings, Jules Furthman and Carey Wilson; based on the novel by Charles Nordhoff and James Norman Hall)

4.
"You know the old story: when St. Patrick drove the snakes out of Ireland, they swam to New York and joined the police force."

—Fredric March insulting a policeman on his premises in John Frankenheimer's *The Iceman Cometh*
(Screenplay based on the play by Eugene O'Neill; text edited by Thomas Quinn Curtiss)

5.
"Cut off the head of the snake, and the body will die."

—Joseph Wiseman proposing Marlon Brando's assassination to stop the people's rebellion in Elia Kazan's *Viva Zapata!*
(Original Screenplay by John Steinbeck)

6.
"I remembered once reading in a book that long ago they used to put insane people into pits full of snakes. I think they figured that something which might drive a normal person insane might shock an insane person back into sanity."

—Olivia De Havilland explaining her vision to her doctor (Leo Genn) in Anatole Litvak's *The Snake Pit*
(Screenplay by Frank Partos and Millen Brand; based on the novel by Mary Jane Ward)

ALSO SEE: Strange-6.

SONS

1.
"He's a nice kid, really—in spite of his home-life. I mean, most kids would grow up neurotic, what with Martha here carrying on the way she does, sleeping till four in the p.m., climbing all over the poor bastard, trying to break down the bathroom door to wash him in the tub when he's 16, dragging strangers into the house at all hours."

—Richard Burton voting Elizabeth Taylor something less than Mother of the Year in Mike Nichols's *Who's Afraid of Virginia Woolf?*
(Screenplay by Ernest Lehman; based on the play by Edward Albee)

2.
"All my sons are bastards."

—Peter O'Toole raging at his estranged wife (Katharine Hepburn) in Anthony Harvey's *The Lion in Winter*
(Screenplay by James Goldman; based on his play)

3.
"Now I know why I have such a tribe of sons. It is you, Beth Morgan, is the cause."

—Donald Crisp commenting on Sara Allgood's fiery temper in John Ford's *How Green Was My Valley*
(Screenplay by Philip Dunne; based on the novel by Richard Llewellyn)

4.
"You got hellfire and damnation in you, Jody Varner, but you got redemption, too. When I think of the hate that put me in there and locked the door and set fire to it, and when I think of the love that wouldn't let me go—I got me a son again. I got me a good right arm. And a left."

—Orson Welles reconciling with Anthony Franciosa in Martin Ritt's *The Long, Hot Summer*
(Screenplay by Irving Ravetch and Harriet Frank Jr.; based on THE HAMLET, a novel by William Faulkner, and "Barn Burning" and "The Spotted Horses," two short stories by William Faulkner)

5.
"You gentlemen aren't *really* trying to kill my son, are you?"

—Jessie Royce Landis neutralizing Cary Grant's pursuers (Adam Williams and Robert Ellenstein) in a crowded elevator in Alfred Hitchcock's *North by Northwest*
(Original Screenplay by Ernest Lehman)

6.

"Well, Wilmer, I'm sorry indeed to lose you, but I want you to know I couldn't be fonder of you if you were my own son. Well, if you lose a son, it's possible to get another. There's only one Maltese falcon."

—Sydney Greenstreet selling out his gunsel (Elisha Cook Jr.) in John Huston's *The Maltese Falcon*
(Screenplay by John Huston; based on the novel by Dashiell Hammett)

7.

"My son, Sebastian, and I constructed our days. Each day we—we would carve each day like a piece of sculpture, leaving behind us a trail of days like a gallery of sculpture until suddenly last summer."

—Katharine Hepburn recalling happier times with her late son in Joseph L. Mankiewicz's *Suddenly, Last Summer*
(Screenplay by Gore Vidal and Tennessee Williams; based on the one-act play by Tennessee Williams)

8.

"A son is a poor substitute for a lover."

—Anthony Perkins telling Janet Leigh about the death of his mother's lover in Alfred Hitchcock's *Psycho*
(Screenplay by Joseph Stefano; based on the novel by Robert Bloch)

ALSO SEE: Betrayal-4; Children-5; Confessions-1; Dictation-6; Eyes-3; Free-2; Hypocrisy-6; Identity Crisis-3; Lies-1; Mad Act-12; Men-11; Names-10; Names-11; Never-15; Oops!-2; Repetitions-3; Responsibility-2; Secrets-4; Strange-2.

SOUL

1.

"A soul—a soul is nothing. Can you see it, smell it, touch it? No. Think of it—this soul—your soul—a nothing, against seven whole years of good luck! You will have money and all that money can buy."

—Walter Huston tempting James Craig with promises of prosperity in William Dieterle's *All That Money Can Buy*
(Screenplay by Dan Totheroh and Stephen Vincent Benét; based on "The Devil and Daniel Webster," a short story by Stephen Vincent Benét)

2.

"If only the picture could change and I could be always what I am now. For that, I would give everything. Yes, there's nothing in the whole world I would not give. I'd give my soul for that."

—Hurd Hatfield offering his soul for perpetual youth in Albert Lewin's *The Picture of Dorian Gray*
(Screenplay by Albert Lewin; based on the novel by Oscar Wilde)

3.

"One long ball hitter, that's what we need. I'd sell my soul for one long ball hitter—hey, where did you come from?"

—Robert Shafer accidentally summoning a devil (Ray Walston) in George Abbott and Stanley Donen's *Damn Yankees*
(Screenplay by George Abbott; based on the musical play by George Abbott and Douglass Wallop and THE YEAR THE YANKEES LOST THE PENNANT, a novel by Douglass Wallop)

4.

"I'd give my soul to take out my mind, hold it under the faucet and wash away the dirty pictures you put there today."

—Kirk Douglas failing to forgive his wife (Eleanor Parker) for her past in William Wyler's *Detective Story*
(Screenplay by Philip Yordan and Robert Wyler; based on the play by Sidney Kingsley)

5.

"Every morning when the hiring boss blows his whistle, Jesus stands alongside you in the shape-up. He sees why some of you get picked and some of you get passed over. He sees the family man worried about getting the rent and worried about getting food in the house for the wife and the kids. He sees you selling your souls to the mob for a day's pay."

—Karl Malden lecturing the longshoremen in Elia Kazan's *On the Waterfront*
(Original Screenplay by Budd Schulberg; based on "Crime on the Waterfront," nonfiction articles by Malcolm Johnson)

6.
"Oh, Richard, it profits a man nothing to give his soul for the whole world—but for Wales?"

—Paul Scofield accusing his betrayer (John Hurt) of selling short (committing perjury to become attorney general for Wales) in Fred Zinnemann's *A Man for All Seasons*
(Screenplay by Robert Bolt; based on his play)

7.
"Do you believe what that old man who was doing all the talking at the Oso Negro said the other night about gold changing a man's soul so that he ain't the same kind of guy as he was before finding it?"

—Humphrey Bogart pondering the ravages of greed as he quotes Walter Huston to Tim Holt in John Huston's *The Treasure of the Sierra Madre*
(Screenplay by John Huston; based on the novel by B. Traven)

8.
"Well, maybe it's like Casy says. A fella ain't got a soul of his own, just a little piece of a big soul —the one big soul that belongs to ever'body."

—Henry Fonda preaching a humanistic gospel as he quotes John Carradine to Jane Darwell in John Ford's *The Grapes of Wrath*
(Screenplay by Nunnally Johnson; based on the novel by John Steinbeck)

9.
"Good and evil are so close they are chained together in the soul."

—Spencer Tracy discussing man's duality in Victor Fleming's *Dr. Jekyll and Mr. Hyde*
(Screenplay by John Lee Mahin; based on the novel by Robert Louis Stevenson)

10.
(a) "One of them is yellow, and the other one is white—but both their souls are rotten!"
    (b) "You interest me, Mr. Carmichael. I'm

not exactly irreligious, and, being a physician, I sometimes wonder how a man like you can locate a soul and, having located it, diagnose its condition as rotten."

—(b) Clive Brook criticizing (a) Lawrence Grant for criticizing Anna May Wong and Marlene Dietrich in Josef von Sternberg's *Shanghai Express*
(Screenplay by Jules Furthman; based on a story by Harry Hervey)

11.
"I knew of course that I was not only not liked but now positively disliked. I had realized too that the boys—for many long years now—had ceased to laugh at me. I don't know why they no longer found me a joke. Perhaps it was my illness—no. I don't think it was that. Something deeper than that. Not a sickness of the body, but a sickness of the soul. At all events it didn't take much discernment on my part to realize I had become an utter failure as a schoolmaster. Still, stupidly enough, I had not realized I was also feared."

—Michael Redgrave acknowledging his failure in Anthony Asquith's *The Browning Version*
(Screenplay by Terence Rattigan; based on his play)

12.
"You can burn my body but never my soul: that is in the keeping of the people of France!"

—George Arliss grandstanding against injustice in John Adolfi's *Voltaire*
(Screenplay by Paul Green and Maude T. Howell; based on the novel by George Gibbs and E. Lawrence Dudley)

13.
"Yes, the soul. It's not shown on the anatomy chart, but it's there just the same. It's somewhere not seen but there. And it is that that I loved you with, John. Yes, *did* love you with, John. Did nearly die of when you hurt me."

—Geraldine Page displaying soulful insight in Peter Glenville's *Summer and Smoke*
(Screenplay by James Poe and Meade Roberts; based on the play by Tennessee Williams)

14.

"I'm going to find the soul that's there and release it so it will fly, soar up to the top gallery."

—John Barrymore directing Carole Lombard in Howard Hawks's *Twentieth Century*
(Screenplay by Ben Hecht and Charles MacArthur; based on their play and NAPOLEON OF BROADWAY, a play by Charles Bruce Milholland)

15.

"I thought I might get her once—just this once in the whole of her life—to publicly disagree with her mother. It'd save her soul if she ever did."

—Burt Lancaster hoping for some spunk from Deborah Kerr in Delbert Mann's *Separate Tables*
(Screenplay by Terence Rattigan and John Gay; based on the play by Terence Rattigan)

16.

"I know, Mrs. Beragon. Everybody thinks that detectives do nothing but ask questions, but detectives have souls same as anyone else."

—Moroni Olsen correcting Joan Crawford's misconception in Michael Curtiz's *Mildred Pierce*
(Screenplay by Ranald MacDougall; based on the novel by James M. Cain)

17.

"But I can see past their eyes into their souls. Leave us not forget little Donnie Dark and all that vision."

—Edward Albert trying to be bright about his blindness in Milton Katselas's *Butterflies Are Free*
(Screenplay by Leonard Gershe; based on his play)

18.

"I was thrown out of N.Y.U. my freshman year for cheating on my metaphysics final, you know. I looked into the soul of the boy sitting next to me."

—Woody Allen dispensing standup comedy to a college audience in Woody Allen's *Annie Hall*
(Original Screenplay by Woody Allen and Marshall Brickman)

ALSO SEE: Blood-1; Body-4; Church-1; Cruel-1; Empathy-4; Future-9; Goals-1; Guilty-5; Knowledge-2; Love-42; Macho-19; Prayers-1; Prayers-5; Progress-3; Prologues-6; Rejection-14; Wants-4.

SOUNDS

1.

"Think what you're trying to accomplish. Just think what you're dealing with. The majesty and grandeur of the English language. It's the greatest possession we have. The noblest thoughts that ever flowed through the hearts of men are contained in its extraordinary, imaginative and musical mixtures of sounds. And that's what you've set yourself out to conquer, Eliza. And conquer it you will!"

—Rex Harrison inspiring his speech student (Audrey Hepburn) in George Cukor's *My Fair Lady*
(Screenplay by Alan Jay Lerner; based on his musical play and PYGMALION, a screenplay and play by George Bernard Shaw)

2.

"Every time you hear a bell ring, it means that some angel's just got his wings."

—Henry Travers translating a heavenly tingle for James Stewart in Frank Capra's *It's a Wonderful Life*
(Screenplay by Albert Hackett, Frances Goodrich, and Frank Capra; based on "The Greatest Gift," a short story by Philip Van Doren Stern)

3.

"Did you ever hear a rhinoceros in labor?"

—Fred Astaire noting the foghorns in Frisco bay in George Seaton's *The Pleasure of His Company*
(Screenplay by Samuel A. Taylor; based on the play by Samuel A. Taylor and Cornelia Otis Skinner)

ALSO SEE: Good-10; Good and Bad-1; New York-2; Sayings-3; Sea-3; Stomach-1; Tired-4; Translations-1; Trumpet-2.

SPECIALIZATIONS

1.

"All right, Frank. Doug and I made the scotch. The nurse is your department."

—William Powell wishing Jack Lemmon luck with Betsy Palmer in John Ford and Mervyn LeRoy's *Mister Roberts*
(Screenplay by Frank S. Nugent and Joshua Logan; based on the play by Thomas Heggen and Joshua Logan and novel by Thomas Heggen)

2.

"Suicide attempts are Frank's department."

—Grace Kelly informing William Holden that Bing Crosby, not she, is suicidal in George Seaton's *The Country Girl*
(Screenplay by George Seaton; based on the play by Clifford Odets)

3.

"I'm not interested in politics. The problems of the world are not in my department. I'm a saloon keeper."

—Humphrey Bogart pretending neutrality to Paul Henreid in Michael Curtiz's *Casablanca*
(Screenplay by Julius J. Epstein, Philip G. Epstein and Howard Koch; based on EVERYBODY COMES TO RICK'S, a play by Murray Burnett and Joan Alison)

4.

"Now, I know you. No fields, no home, no wife, no woman, no friends, no loves. You only destroy—that is your love."

—Marlon Brando telling off Joseph Wiseman in Elia Kazan's *Viva Zapata!*
(Original Screenplay by John Steinbeck)

5.

"I expect that is to be your gift, Sandy—to kill without concern."

—Maggie Smith damning Pamela Franklin in Ronald Neame's *The Prime of Miss Jean Brodie*
(Screenplay by Jay Presson Allen; based on her play and the novel by Muriel Spark)

6.

"Getting me into heaven is your business, Vinnie. If there's anything wrong with my ticket when I get there, you can fix it up. Everybody loves you so much I'm sure God must too."

—William Powell trying to calm his fretful wife (Irene Dunne) in Michael Curtiz's *Life With Father*
(Screenplay by Donald Ogden Stewart; based on the play by Howard Lindsay and Russel Crouse and stories by Clarence Day Jr.)

7.

"How do you *know* I'm a liar? How do you *know* I'm a fake? Maybe I *can* bring rain. Maybe when I was born, God whispered a special word in my ear. Maybe He said, 'Bill Starbuck, you ain't gonna have much in this world. You ain't gonna have no money, no fancy spurs, no white horse with a golden feather—but, Bill Starbuck, wherever you go, you'll bring rain.' Maybe that's my one and only blessing."

—Burt Lancaster conning Katharine Hepburn in Joseph Anthony's *The Rainmaker*
(Screenplay by N. Richard Nash; based on his play)

8.

"Love and affection is what I've got to offer on hot or cold days in this lonely old world. I got nothing else. Mangiacavallo has nothing."

—Burt Lancaster wooing Anna Magnani in Daniel Mann's *The Rose Tattoo*
(Screenplay by Tennessee Williams; adaptation by Hal Kanter; based on the play by Tennessee Williams)

SPIDERS

1.

"I've been killing spiders since I was 30. Okay?"

—Woody Allen coming to the rescue of an insect-distressed hysteric (Diane Keaton) in Woody Allen's *Annie Hall*
(Original Screenplay by Woody Allen and Marshall Brickman)

2.

"You are looking, sir, at a very dull survival of a very gaudy life—crippled, paralyzed in both legs, very little I can eat, and my sleep is so near waking that it's hardly worth the name. I seem to exist largely on heat, like a newborn spider."

—Charles Waldron telling Humphrey Bogart about the dreariness of a dragged-out life in Howard Hawks's *The Big Sleep*
(Screenplay by William Faulkner, Leigh Brackett and Jules Furthman; based on the novel by Raymond Chandler)
and (similarly)

—James Stewart dittoing Robert Mitchum in the remake, Michael Winner's *The Big Sleep*
(Screenplay by Michael Winner; based on the novel by Raymond Chandler)

3.

"You sit around here and you spin your little webs and you think the whole world revolves around you and your money. Well, it doesn't, Mr. Potter. In the—in the whole vast configuration of things, I'd say you were nothing but a scurvy little spider."

—James Stewart telling off Lionel Barrymore in Frank Capra's *It's a Wonderful Life*
(Screenplay by Albert Hackett, Frances Goodrich and Frank Capra; based on "The Greatest Gift," a short story by Philip Van Doren Stern)

4.

"He's like a spider, and he expects me to redecorate his web."

—Doris Day dreading having to redecorate Rock Hudson's bachelor pad in Michael Gordon's *Pillow Talk*
(Screenplay by Stanley Shapiro and Maurice Richlin; based on a story by Russell Rouse and Clarence Greene)

5.

"I stayed at a hotel called the Tarantula Arms. . . . That's where I brought my victims."

—Vivien Leigh snarling at Karl Malden's questions about her past in Elia Kazan's *A Streetcar Named Desire*

(Screenplay by Tennessee Williams; adaptation by Oscar Saul; based on the play by Tennessee Williams)

6.

"You know what trouble I's talking about. I's talking about Mr. Ashley Wilkes. He'll be coming to Atlanta when he gets his leave—and you sittin' there waitin' for him jes' like a spider."

—Hattie McDaniel accusing Vivien Leigh of lying in wait for Leslie Howard in Victor Fleming's *Gone With the Wind*
(Screenplay by Sidney Howard; based on the novel by Margaret Mitchell)

SPINSTERS

1.

"I know so well what becomes of unmarried women who aren't prepared to occupy a position in life. I've seen such pitiful cases in the South—barely tolerated spinsters living on some brother's wife or sister's husband—stuck away in some little mousetrap of a room—encouraged by one in-law to visit another—little birdlike women without any nest—eating the crust of humility all their life. Is that the future we've mapped out for ourselves?"

—Gertrude Lawrence warning Jane Wyman in Irving Rapper's *The Glass Menagerie*
(Screenplay by Tennessee Williams and Peter Berneis; based on the play by Tennessee Williams)

2.

"I've got to see things the way they are and the way they will be. I've got to start thinking of myself as I am: old maid. Jim will get married, and one of these days even Noah will get married. I'll be the visiting aunt. I'll bring presents to their children to be sure I'm welcome. And Noah will say, 'Junior, be kind to your Aunt Lizzie. Her nerves aren't so good.' And Jim's wife will say, 'She's been visiting here a whole week. Why don't she ever go?' Go where? Go where?"

—Katharine Hepburn forecasting a bleak future for herself in Joseph Anthony's *The Rainmaker*

(Screenplay by N. Richard Nash; based on his play)

3.

"I'm no spring chicken, either. Maybe I'm a little older than you think. My ways are formed, too—but they can be changed. They *gotta* be changed. No good livin' like this, in rented rooms, meetin' a bunch of old maids for supper every night, then comin' back home alone. Each year I keep tellin' myself is the last. Something'll happen. Nothing ever does—except I get a little crazier all the time."

—Rosalind Russell cuing Arthur O'Connell to propose to her in Joshua Logan's *Picnic*
(Screenplay by Daniel Taradash; based on the play by William Inge)

4.

"Well, what's wrong with that? Unwedhood is a respectable institution. All women are not alike. Lina has intellect and fine, solid character."

—Cedric Hardwicke defending his spinster daughter (Joan Fontaine) in Alfred Hitchcock's *Suspicion*
(Screenplay by Samson Raphaelson, Joan Harrison and Alma Reville; based on BEFORE THE FACT, a novel by Francis Iles)

5.

"I want to be a Sadie. . . . That's a married lady."

—Barbra Streisand cuing Omar Sharif to propose to her in William Wyler's *Funny Girl*
(Screenplay by Isobel Lennart; based on her musical play)

6.

"I shall die a bachelor."

—Greta Garbo objecting to the term "old maid" in Rouben Mamoulian's *Queen Christina*
(Screenplay by H. M. Harwood and Salka Viertel; dialogue by S. N. Behrman; based on a story by Salka Viertel and Margaret P. Levino)

7.

"I'm a bachelor girl. My baby's going to be a little basta—"

—Jane Connell beaming to a scandalized Audrey Christie in Gene Saks's *Mame*
(Screenplay by Paul Zindel; based on the musical play by Jerome Lawrence, Robert E. Lee and Jerry Herman and AUNTIE MAME, a play by Jerome Lawrence and Robert E. Lee and novel by Patrick Dennis)

ALSO SEE: Marriage-11; Tears-8.

STAR

1.

"Sawyer, you listen to me, and you listen hard. Two hundred people, two hundred jobs, $200,-000, five weeks of grind and blood and sweat depend upon you. It's the lives of all these people who've worked with you. You got to go on, and you've got to give and give and give. They got to like you. Got to. Do you understand? You can't fall down. You can't because your future's in it, my future and everything all of us have is staked on you. All right, now I'm through, but you keep your feet on the ground and your head on those shoulders of yours and go out, and, Sawyer, you're going out a youngster, but you've *got* to come back a star."

—Warner Baxter pushing Ruby Keeler from the wings to instant stardom in Lloyd Bacon's *42nd Street*
(Screenplay by Rian James and James Seymour; based on the novel by Bradford Ropes)

2.

"You've got that little something extra that Ellen Terry talked about. Ellen Terry, a great actress long before you were born. She said that that was what star quality was—that little something extra. Well, you've got it."

—James Mason praising Judy Garland in George Cukor's *A Star Is Born*
(Screenplay by Moss Hart; based on a screenplay by Dorothy Parker, Alan Campbell and Robert Carson and original story by William A. Wellman and Robert Carson)

3.

"Whatever it is, you name it—whether you're

born with it or catch it from a public drinking cup—Maria had it. The people with the money in their hot little hands put her up there, and she could do no wrong."

—Edmond O'Brien characterizing the star quality of Ava Gardner in Joseph L. Mankiewicz's *The Barefoot Contessa*
(Original Screenplay by Joseph L. Mankiewicz)

4.
"If we bring a little joy into your humdrum lives, it makes us feel our work ain't been in vain for nothin'."

—Jean Hagen explaining why she's a movie star (and a silent one) in Gene Kelly and Stanley Donen's *Singin' in the Rain*
(Original Screenplay by Adolph Green and Betty Comden)

5.
"Oh, those idiot producers! Those imbeciles! Haven't they got any eyes? Have they forgotten what a star looks like? I'll show them! I'll be up there again! So help me!"

—Gloria Swanson vowing a screen return in Billy Wilder's *Sunset Boulevard*
(Original Screenplay by Charles Brackett, Billy Wilder and D. M. Marshman Jr.)

6.
"Margo Channing is a Star of the Theater. She made her first stage appearance, at the age of four, in *Midsummer Night's Dream*. She played a fairy and entered—quite unexpectedly—stark naked. She has been a Star ever since."

—George Sanders providing introductory notes on Bette Davis in Joseph L. Mankiewicz's *All About Eve*
(Screenplay by Joseph L. Mankiewicz; based on "The Wisdom of Eve," a radio play and short story by Mary Orr)

7.
"I wasn't only in the chorus. I spoke lines. . . . I could have been a star probably if I'd stuck to it."

—Judy Holliday telling Howard St. John of her showbiz past in George Cukor's *Born Yesterday*

(Screenplay by Albert Mannheimer; based on the play by Garson Kanin)

8.
"I'm on my way to town to become a country music singer or star."

—Barbara Harris heading for Nashville in Robert Altman's *Nashville*
(Original Screenplay by Joan Tewkesbury)

9.
"Ever daydream? I daydream sometimes, about going to Hollywood and being a movie star. I guess most girls daydream about that. Not that I think I'm so pretty or anything like that. But, you know, they have cosmeticians out there in Hollywood that—that make those Hollywood stars look a lot more beautiful than they really are. I mean, you ought to read some of those magazines. They tell the inside story on those movie stars. I mean, most of that's just cosmetics."

—Kim Stanley dishing the Hollywood dirt in John Cromwell's *The Goddess*
(Original Screenplay by Paddy Chayefsky)

ALSO SEE: Actors; Applause; Movies; Theater; First Lines-5; Firsts-9; Headlines-9; Loneliness-6; Newspapering-8; Pride-8; Telephone Scenes-11.

STATIC

1.
"Grand Hotel. Always the same. People come. People go. Nothing ever happens."

—Lewis Stone missing all the multi-charactered dramas in Edmund Goulding's *Grand Hotel*
(Screenplay by William A. Drake; based on the play and novel by Vicki Baum)

2.
"A relationship, I think, is—is like a shark. You know, it has to constantly move forward or it dies, and I think what we got on our hands is a dead shark."

—Woody Allen reaching the end of the affair with Diane Keaton in Woody Allen's *Annie Hall* (*Original Screenplay by Woody Allen and Marshall Brickman*)

3.
"Well, don't stand there, Miss Preen. You look like a frozen custard."

—Monty Woolley braying at his nurse (Mary Wickes) in William Keighley's *The Man Who Came to Dinner* (*Screenplay by Julius J. Epstein and Philip G. Epstein; based on the play by George S. Kaufman and Moss Hart*)

4.
(a) "Heathcliff, make the world stop right here. Make everything stop and stand still and never move again. Make the moors never change and you and I never change."
    (b) "The moors and I will never change— don't you, Cathy."

—(a) Merle Oberon and (b) Laurence Olivier hoping to hold on to a romantic moment in William Wyler's *Wuthering Heights* (*Screenplay by Ben Hecht and Charles MacArthur; based on the novel by Emily Brontë*)

5.
"I know I'm different from the others. I'm here out of principle. All my life I've lived according to principle, and I couldn't change even if I wanted to."

—Kirk Douglas defending his inflexibility as a police detective in William Wyler's *Detective Story* (*Screenplay by Philip Yordan and Robert Wyler; based on the play by Sidney Kingsley*)

6.
"If you come back to me, I shall treat you just the same as I have always treated you. I can't change my nature, and I don't intend to change my manners."

—Leslie Howard promising Wendy Hiller status quo in Anthony Asquith and Leslie Howard's *Pygmalion* (*Screenplay by George Bernard Shaw; adaptation by W. P. Lipscomb, Cecil Lewis and Ian Dalrymple; based on the play by George Bernard Shaw*)

and (almost verbatim)

—Rex Harrison dittoing Audrey Hepburn in the remake, George Cukor's *My Fair Lady* (*Screenplay by Alan Jay Lerner; based on his musical play and* PYGMALION, *a screenplay and play by George Bernard Shaw*)

7.
"I'm not a boy anymore. A person forms certain ways of living. Then, one day it's too late to change."

—Arthur O'Connell telling Rosalind Russell he's too old for marriage in Joshua Logan's *Picnic* (*Screenplay by Daniel Taradash; based on the play by William Inge*)

8.
"A man doesn't tell a woman what to do. She does it herself. You almost had me believing that little hokey-pokey miracle of yours—that a woman like you could ever change her spots."

—Cary Grant insulting Ingrid Bergman in Alfred Hitchcock's *Notorious* (*Original Screenplay by Ben Hecht*)

9.
"Well, I started at Amherst, and I worked my way through the alphabet to Yale. I'm stuck there."

—Elizabeth Taylor telling Laurence Harvey the order of her promiscuity in Daniel Mann's *Butterfield 8* (*Screenplay by Charles Schnee and John Michael Hayes; based on the novel by John O'Hara*)

10.
"George is bogged down in the history department. He's an old bog in the history department. That's what George is. A bog."

—Elizabeth Taylor berating Richard Burton in Mike Nichols's *Who's Afraid of Virginia Woolf?* (*Screenplay by Ernest Lehman; based on the play by Edward Albee*)

11.
"Now look at us. We went through college together. You worked your way through. You've become an important songwriter. You've had a

couple of big Broadway hits. You started out with nothing, and you've really made something out of yourself. Me? I started out in college with $8,000,000, and I've still got $8,000,000. I just can't seem to get ahead."

—Tony Randall crying over his status quo to Rock Hudson in Michael Gordon's *Pillow Talk* (*Screenplay by Stanley Shapiro and Maurice Richlin; based on a story by Russell Rouse and Clarence Greene*)

12.
"You think just because you made a little money you can get yourself a new hairdo and some expensive clothes and turn yourself into a lady, but you can't, because you'll never be anything but a common frump, whose father lived over a grocery store and whose mother took in washing."

—Ann Blyth telling off Joan Crawford in Michael Curtiz's *Mildred Pierce* (*Screenplay by Ranald MacDougall; based on the novel by James M. Cain*)

13.
"Little Sheba should have stayed young forever. Some things should never grow old."

—Burt Lancaster making a melancholy observation about Shirley Booth's dog in Daniel Mann's *Come Back, Little Sheba* (*Screenplay by Ketti Frings; based on the play by William Inge*)

14.
"You can be the heroes, the guys with fruit salad on your chest. Me? I'm staying put. I'm going to make myself as comfortable as I can, and, if it takes a little trading with the enemy to get me some food or a better mattress, that's okay by Sefton."

—William Holden stating his wartime position to his fellow POWs in Billy Wilder's *Stalag 17* (*Screenplay by Billy Wilder and Edwin Blum; based on the play by Donald Bevan and Edmund Trzcinski*)

15.
"When I came here, I thought this was going to be a 30-day stretch. Maybe 60. Now it's a year.

It looks like a life sentence. Where is it? Where's the loaf of bread with a file in it? Where's that big story to get me out of here? One year, and what's the hot news? A soapbox derby. A tornado that double-crossed us and went to Texas. An old goof who said he was the real Jesse James, until they found out he was a chicken-thief from Gallup by the name of Schimmelmacher. I'm stuck here, fans. Stuck for good."

—Kirk Douglas railing around the newspaper office in Billy Wilder's *The Big Carnival* (*Original Screenplay by Billy Wilder, Lesser Samuels and Walter Newman*)

16.
"You know what I think? I think that we're all in our private traps, clamped in them, and none of us can ever get out. We scratch and—and claw but only at the air, only at each other. And, for all of it, we never budge an inch."

—Anthony Perkins advancing his view to Janet Leigh in Alfred Hitchcock's *Psycho* (*Screenplay by Joseph Stefano; based on the novel by Robert Bloch*)

ALSO SEE: Army-1; Soul-2; Spinsters-3; Strangers-2.

STIMULATING

1.
"I never dreamed that any mere physical experience could be so stimulating. . . . I've only known such excitement a few times before—a few times in my dear brother's sermons when the spirit was really upon him."

—Katharine Hepburn gushing about shooting the rapids in John Huston's *The African Queen* (*Screenplay by James Agee and John Huston; based on the novel by C. S. Forester*)

2.
"I've never caught a jewel thief before. It's stimulating."

—Grace Kelly kidding on the square with Cary Grant in Alfred Hitchcock's *To Catch a Thief*

(Screenplay by John Michael Hayes; based on the novel by David Dodge)

3.

"I hate cold showers. They stimulate me, then I don't know what to do."

—Oscar Levant confessing a pet hate in Jean Negulesco's *Humoresque*
(Screenplay by Clifford Odets and Zachary Gold; based on a short story by Fannie Hurst)

4.

"Look, it happens to everybody. I mean, I love your mother, but, you know, sometimes you need a little stimulation, you know."

—Richard Castellano rationalizing his adultery to his son (Joseph Hindy) in Cy Howard's *Lovers and Other Strangers*
(Screenplay by Renee Taylor, Joseph Bologna and David Z. Goodman; based on the play by Renee Taylor and Joseph Bologna)

ALSO SEE: New York-1.

STOMACH

1.

"Just listen to this stomach of mine. Way it sounds, you'd think I had a hyena inside me."

—Humphrey Bogart apologizing for his stomach growls at the table of Katharine Hepburn and Robert Morley in John Huston's *The African Queen*
(Screenplay by James Agee and John Huston; based on the novel by C. S. Forester)

2.

"Thank *you* for giving me the chance to meet the man who feeds the nation. I hope this will be the beginning of a lifelong friendship. May you lie as solidly anchored in our hearts as you do in our stomachs."

—Charles Coburn pretending to appreciate meeting Eugene Pallette in Ernst Lubitsch's *Heaven Can Wait*
(Screenplay by Samson Raphaelson; based on BIRTHDAY, a play by Lazlo Bus-Fekete)

ALSO SEE: Betrayal-4; Body-6; Human-4; Laugh-4; Responsibility-1.

STRANGE

1.

"Oh, how strange that I should be called a destitute woman when I have all these treasures locked in my heart. I think of myself as a very, very rich woman! But I have been foolish—casting my pearls before swine."

—Vivien Leigh drifting into her fantasy world in Elia Kazan's *A Streetcar Named Desire*
(Screenplay by Tennessee Williams; adaptation by Oscar Saul; based on the play by Tennessee Williams)

2.

"I haven't been richly blessed with friends or with sons—my eldest, a penny-grubbing trickster; my second, a proud illiterate. Strange, Regina, you turned out to be my only son."

—Fredric March playing to his pet (Ann Blyth) in Michael Gordon's *Another Part of the Forest*
(Screenplay by Vladimir Pozner; based on the play by Lillian Hellman)

3.

"Mrs. Robinson, if you don't mind my saying so, this conversation is getting a little strange."

—Dustin Hoffman resisting Anne Bancroft's come-on in Mike Nichols's *The Graduate*
(Screenplay by Calder Willingham and Buck Henry; based on the novel by Charles Webb)

4.

"Jose brought up the blueprints for a new ranch house he's building, and I have the strange feeling that the blueprints and my knitting instructions got switched. I mean, it isn't impossible that I'm knitting a ranch house."

—Audrey Hepburn cracking wise to George Peppard in Blake Edwards's *Breakfast at Tiffany's*
(Screenplay by George Axelrod; based on the novella by Truman Capote)

5.

"It's an odd thing, but everyone who disappears is said to be seen in San Francisco. It must be a delightful city. It has all the attractions of the next world."

—George Sanders making an offbeat observation in Albert Lewin's *The Picture of Dorian Gray* *(Screenplay by Albert Lewin; based on the novel by Oscar Wilde)*

6.
"It was strange. Here I was, among all those people, and, at the same time, I felt as if I were looking at them from some place far away. The whole place seemed to me like a deep hole and the people down in it like strange animals, like —like snakes, and I'd been thrown into it. Yes, as though—as though I were in a snake pit."

—Olivia De Havilland telling her vision to her doctor (Leo Genn) in Anatole Litvak's *The Snake Pit* *(Screenplay by Frank Partos and Millen Brand; based on the novel by Mary Jane Ward)*

7.
"Strange? She's right out of The Hound of the Baskervilles."

—Monty Woolley commenting on the eccentric behavior of Ruth Vivian in William Keighley's *The Man Who Came to Dinner* *(Screenplay by Julius J. Epstein and Philip G. Epstein; based on the play by George S. Kaufman and Moss Hart)*

8.
"Strange how an unpleasant child can be a decent dog."

—Conrad Veidt beaming about the black magic that turned Sabu into a dog in Ludwig Berger, Tim Whelan, and Michael Powell's *The Thief of Bagdad* *(Screenplay and dialogue by Miles Malleson; based on a scenario by Lajos Biro)*

9.
"Strange that a man can live with a woman for ten years and not know the first thing about her."

—James Stephenson commenting on the marriage of Herbert Marshall and Bette Davis in William Wyler's *The Letter*

(Screenplay by Howard Koch; based on the play and short story by W. Somerset Maugham)

10.
"Strange, isn't it? Each man's life touches so many other lives—and, when he's not around, it leaves an awful hole, doesn't it?"

—Henry Travers giving James Stewart something to ponder in Frank Capra's *It's a Wonderful Life* *(Screenplay by Albert Hackett, Frances Goodrich and Frank Capra; based on "The Greatest Gift," a short story by Philip Van Doren Stern)*

11.
"Strange? Because I can feel for beaten, helpless people?"

—Errol Flynn finding nothing at all strange about his cause in Michael Curtiz and William Keighley's *The Adventures of Robin Hood* *(Original Screenplay by Norman Reilly Raine and Seton I. Miller; based on the ancient Robin Hood legends)*

ALSO SEE: Crazy-1; Future-2; Heaven-5; Introductions-1; Letters-12.

STRANGERS

1.
"Whoever you are, I have always depended on the kindness of strangers."

—Vivien Leigh exiting to a mental hospital in Elia Kazan's *A Streetcar Named Desire* *(Screenplay by Tennessee Williams; adaptation by Oscar Saul; based on the play by Tennessee Williams)*

2.
"I'm made in a certain way, and I can't change it. It had to be the dark, you see, and strangers because—"

—David Niven trying to tell Deborah Kerr about his movie-theater sex-life in Delbert Mann's *Separate Tables* *(Screenplay by Terence Rattigan and John Gay; based on the play by Terence Rattigan)*

3.

"Agnes, the last desperate resort is strangers. We haven't come to that yet."

—Joanne Woodward pep-talking a kindred spinster (Sarah Marshall) in Martin Ritt's *The Long, Hot Summer*
(Screenplay by Irving Ravetch and Harriet Frank Jr.; based on THE HAMLET, a novel by William Faulkner, and "Barn Burning" and "The Spotted Horses," two short stories by William Faulkner)

4.

"We're all strangers, but, after a while, you get used to it. You become deeper strangers. That's a sort of love."

—Richard Castellano explaining marriage to his son (Joseph Hindy) in Cy Howard's *Lovers and Other Strangers*
(Screenplay by Renee Taylor, Joseph Bologna, and David Z. Goodman; based on the play by Renee Taylor and Joseph Bologna)

5.

"Let me tell you something. I am not a father figure. I am not an uncle figure or a brother figure or a cousin figure. In fact, the only figure I intend being is a total-stranger figure."

—Cary Grant telling off Leslie Caron in Ralph Nelson's *Father Goose*
(Screenplay by Peter Stone and Frank Tarloff; based on "A Place of Dragons," a short story by S. H. Barnett)

ALSO SEE: Exchanges-1.

STRENGTH

1.

"We O'Learys are a strange tribe, but there's strength in us. And what we set out to do, we'll finish."

—Alice Brady showing some fighting Irish spirit in the last lines of Henry King's *In Old Chicago*
(Screenplay by Lamar Trotti and Sonya Levien; based on "We the O'Learys," a story by Niven Busch)

2.

"We will manage. I'm not put together with flour paste—and neither are you, I'm happy to learn."

—Lucile Watson discovering unsuspected strength in her son (Donald Woods) in Herman Shumlin's *Watch on the Rhine*
(Screenplay by Dashiell Hammett; additional scenes and dialogue by Lillian Hellman; based on her play)

3.

"You get your strength from this red earth of Tara, Scarlett. You're part of it, and it's part of you."

—Clark Gable recognizing his true rival for Vivien Leigh's love in Victor Fleming's *Gone With the Wind*
(Screenplay by Sidney Howard; based on the novel by Margaret Mitchell)

4.

"He's strong. Anyone who can get in front of an audience for 57 years has to be strong."

—George Burns giving Walter Matthau points for strength in Herbert Ross's *The Sunshine Boys*
(Screenplay by Neil Simon; based on his play)

5.

"Let me tell you all about making men strong: Einstein couldn't kick a football across this dance floor, but he changed the shape of the universe."

—Kirk Douglas arguing brains-over-brawn with Paul Douglas in Joseph L. Mankiewicz's *A Letter to Three Wives*
(Screenplay by Joseph L. Mankiewicz; adaptation by Vera Caspary; based on "One of Our Hearts," a short story by John Klempner)

6.

"Nothing is stronger than the law in the universe, but on earth nothing is stronger than love!"

—Roger Livesey resting his case for David Niven in Michael Powell and Emeric Pressburger's *Stairway to Heaven*

(Original Screenplay by Michael Powell and Emeric Pressburger)

7.
"My strength justifies me, Mr. Van Weyden—the fact that I can kill you or let you live as I choose, the fact that I control the destinies of all on board the ship, the fact that it is my will and my will alone that rules here. That's justification enough."

—Edward G. Robinson clarifying his position to Alexander Knox in Michael Curtiz's *The Sea Wolf* *(Screenplay by Robert Rossen; based on the novel by Jack London)*

8.
"You've always looked to leaders—strong men without faults. There aren't any. They're only men, like yourselves. They change. They desert. They die. There are no leaders but yourselves. A strong people is the only lasting strength."

—Marlon Brando addressing his people in Elia Kazan's *Viva Zapata!* *(Original Screenplay by John Steinbeck)*

ALSO SEE: Boredom-3; Gentle-3; Goodbyes-6; Hate-4; Love-15; Love-16; Love-18; People-5; Prayers-2; Religions-2; Threats-6.

STUPID

1.
(a) "I think you're a very stupid person. You look stupid. You're in a stupid business. And you're on a stupid case."
    (b) "I get it: I'm stupid."

—(b) Robert Mitchum following what (a) Kate Murtagh is driving at in Dick Richards's *Farewell, My Lovely* *(Screenplay by David Zelag Goodman; based on the novel by Raymond Chandler)*

2.
"The boy has a fine mind, but it's overtaxed. That's the trouble. It's too good a mind. A weak mind isn't strong enough to hurt itself. Stupidity has saved many a man from going mad."

—Roger Livesey regretting David Niven's intelligence in Michael Powell and Emeric Pressburger's *Stairway to Heaven* *(Original Screenplay by Michael Powell and Emeric Pressburger)*

3.
"His criticism of your plans didn't go that far to imagine that you are married to an American agent. We are protected by the enormity of your stupidity."

—Madame Konstantin finding one consolation about the mess that her son (Claude Rains) has gotten into in Alfred Hitchcock's *Notorious* *(Original Screenplay by Ben Hecht)*

4.
"Am I not a man? And is not a man stupid? I'm a man, so I married. Wife, children, house, everything, the full catastrophe."

—Anthony Quinn confessing a domestic blunder in his past in Michael Cacoyannis's *Zorba the Greek* *(Screenplay by Michael Cacoyannis; based on the novel by Nikos Kazantzakis)*

5.
"My first wife was clever. My second was ambitious. My third—Thomas, if you want to be happy, marry a girl like my sweet little Jane. Marry a stupid woman."

—Charles Laughton advising Robert Donat in Alexander Korda's *The Private Life of Henry VIII* *(Original Screenplay by Lajos Biro and Arthur Wimperis)*

6.
"Ben Hubbard wanted the cotton, and Oscar Hubbard married it for him. He was kind to me then. He used to smile at me. He hasn't smiled at me since. Well, everybody knew that's what he married me for—everybody but me. Stupid, stupid me."

—Patricia Collinge resenting being duped into marriage in William Wyler's *The Little Foxes* *(Screenplay by Lillian Hellman; additional scenes* and dialogue by Arthur Kober, Dorothy Parker, and Alan Campbell; based on the play by Lillian Hellman)

ALSO SEE: Ignorance-4; Jealous-3; Lies-19; Murder-12; Oops!-3; Rejection-1; Unfeeling-2.

STYLE

1.
"Well, it's a new style of courting a pretty girl, I must say, for a young fellow to go deliberately out of his way to try and make an enemy of her father by attacking his business! By Jove! That's a new way of winning a woman."

—Ray Collins "complimenting" Tim Holt's boorishness in Orson Welles's *The Magnificent Ambersons*
(Screenplay by Orson Welles; based on the novel by Booth Tarkington)

2.
"You're a very stylish girl. Can't we end this stylishly?"

—George Peppard trying to dump Patricia Neal in Blake Edwards's *Breakfast at Tiffany's*
(Screenplay by George Axelrod; based on the novella by Truman Capote)

SUCCESS

1.
"Success? That's a strange choice of word. Usually, newlyweds are wished happiness."

—Joan Crawford distrusting Jan Sterling in Joseph Pevney's *Female on the Beach*
(Screenplay by Robert Hill and Richard Alan Simmons; based on THE BESIEGED HEART, a play by Robert Hill)

2.
"Under the right circumstances, a producer could make more money with a flop than he could with a hit. . . . If he were certain that the show would fail, a man could make a fortune."

—Gene Wilder giving Zero Mostel an idea in Mel Brooks's *The Producers*
(Original Screenplay by Mel Brooks)

3.
"I used to think about $25,000, too, and what I'd do with it, that I'd be a failure if I didn't get a hold of it. And then one day I realized I was never going to have $25,000, Mr. MacDonald. And then another day, a little bit later, considerably later, I realized something else—something I'm imparting to you now, Mr. MacDonald: I'm not a failure. I'm a success. You see, ambition is all right if it works, but no system could be right where one half of one percent were successes and all the rest were failures. That wouldn't be right. I'm not a failure. I'm a success. And so are you if you earn your own living and pay your bills and look the world in the eye. I hope you win your $25,000, Mr. MacDonald, but, if you shouldn't happen to, don't worry about it."

—Harry Hayden counseling his daydreaming employee (Dick Powell) in Preston Sturges's *Christmas in July*
(Original Screenplay by Preston Sturges)

4.
"You're my kind of man, laddie. In this world, there is only one payoff window: Number One. The winner. Success. Now, that can be you. For the man who's going places, he needs a place where he can go climb, bust high—place like New York. Now, this here is a ticket that'll get you there. Train leaves at 9:40 tonight, this night. I'm betting this $100 on you, laddie, that you come back to St. Cloud Number One, riding high on the hog."

—Ed Begley pep-talking his daughter's boyfriend (Paul Newman) out of town in Richard Brooks's *Sweet Bird of Youth*
(Screenplay by Richard Brooks; based on the play by Tennessee Williams)

5.
"And then it happened: You wound up on the floor, on your back, in the middle of the salad,

and I said to myself, 'Well, after 100 years, the Benedict family is a real big success.' "

—Elizabeth Taylor praising Rock Hudson for losing a fight worth fighting in George Stevens's *Giant* (*Screenplay by Fred Guiol and Ivan Moffat; based on the novel by Edna Ferber*)

6.

"One more success like that, and I'll sell my body to a medical institute."

—Groucho Marx cracking wise in Joseph Santley and Robert Florey's *The Cocoanuts* (*Screenplay by Morrie Ryskind; based on the musical play by George S. Kaufman and Morrie Ryskind*)

ALSO SEE: Discipline-1; Failure-1; Failure-4; Laugh-5; Money-11; Trumpet-3.

SUICIDE

1.

"Look at it this way, Helen: this business is just a formality. Don Birnam is dead already. He died over this weekend."

—Ray Milland trying to justify his suicide attempt to Jane Wyman in Billy Wilder's *The Lost Weekend* (*Screenplay by Charles Brackett and Billy Wilder; based on the novel by Charles W. Jackson*)

2.

"Petronius? Dead? By his own hand? I don't believe it. . . . I shall never forgive him for this. Never. Without my permission? It's rebellion! It's blasphemy!"

—Peter Ustinov taking badly the news of Leo Genn's suicide in Mervyn LeRoy's *Quo Vadis* (*Screenplay by John Lee Mahin, S. N. Behrman, and Sonya Levien; based on the novel by Henryk Sienkiewicz*)

3.

"You should look upon this tragedy as an episode in the wonderful spectacle of life. What is it that has really happened? Someone has killed herself for love of you. I do wish that I had had

such an experience. The women who have admired me—and there have been some—have always insisted on living on long after I have ceased to care for them or they to care for me."

—George Sanders helping Hurd Hatfield look on the bright side of Angela Lansbury's suicide in Albert Lewin's *The Picture of Dorian Gray* (*Screenplay by Albert Lewin; based on the novel by Oscar Wilde*)

4.

"I was suicidal, as a matter of fact, and would have killed myself, but I was in analysis with a strict Freudian, and, if you kill yourself, they make you pay for the sessions you miss."

—Woody Allen dispensing standup comedy to a college audience in Woody Allen's *Annie Hall* (*Original Screenplay by Woody Allen and Marshall Brickman*)

5.

(a) "All right! Shall I kill myself?"
    (b) "Aw, don't minimize this."

—(b) Paul Ford chewing out (a) Glenn Ford in Daniel Mann's *The Teahouse of the August Moon* (*Screenplay by John Patrick; based on his play and the book by Vern J. Sneider*)

6.

"Ladies and gentlemen, I would like at this moment to announce that I will be retiring from this program in two weeks time because of poor ratings. Since this show was the only thing I had going for me in my life, I have decided to kill myself. I'm going to blow my brains out right on this program a week from today."

—Peter Finch going very public with his suicide promise in Sidney Lumet's *Network* (*Original Screenplay by Paddy Chayefsky*)

7.

"Billions of years it's taken to evolve human consciousness, and you want to wipe it out—wipe out the miracle of all existence, more important than anything in the whole universe. What can the stars do? Nothing. They can sit on their axis."

—Charles Chaplin pep-talking life into Claire Bloom in Charles Chaplin's *Limelight*
(Original Screenplay by Charles Chaplin)

8.

"You see, George, you've really had a wonderful life. Don't you see what a mistake it would be to throw it away?"

—Henry Travers talking James Stewart out of suicide in Frank Capra's *It's a Wonderful Life*
(Screenplay by Albert Hackett, Frances Goodrich, and Frank Capra; based on "The Greatest Gift," a short story by Philip Van Doren Stern)

9.
(a) "Where are you going?"
 (b) "To the river."
(a) "What for?"
 (b) "To make a hole in it."

—(b) Wendy Hiller telling (a) David Tree she's suicide-bound in Anthony Asquith and Leslie Howard's *Pygmalion*
(Screenplay by George Bernard Shaw; adaptation by W. P. Lipscomb, Cecil Lewis and Ian Dalrymple; based on the play by George Bernard Shaw)

and

—(b) Audrey Hepburn dittoing (a) Jeremy Brett in the remake, George Cukor's *My Fair Lady*
(Screenplay by Alan Jay Lerner; based on his musical play and PYGMALION, a screenplay and play by George Bernard Shaw)

10.

"We're coming to a tree in the middle of the road. We're taking it. If you're killed, I'll be free. If I'm killed, it really doesn't matter. If we both die, good riddance."

—Bette Davis racing herself and her husband (John Eldredge) toward highway deaths in Alfred E. Green's *Dangerous*
(Original Screenplay by Laird Doyle)

11.

"Living, I'm worth nothing to her. But dead, I can buy her the tallest cathedrals, golden vineyards and dancing in the streets. One well-directed bullet will accomplish all that. It'll earn a measure of reflected glory for him that fired it and him that stopped it. This document will be my ticket to immortality. It'll inspire people to say of me, 'There was an artist who died before his time!' Will you do it, Duke?"

—Leslie Howard asking Humphrey Bogart to kill him so Bette Davis will get the insurance money in Archie Mayo's *The Petrified Forest*
(Screenplay by Delmer Daves and Charles Kenyon; based on the play by Robert E. Sherwood)

12.
(a) "You think you'll ever get me out of your blood?"
 (b) "Maybe not, but love has got to stop some place short of suicide."

—(b) Walter Huston walking out on his wife, (a) Ruth Chatterton, in William Wyler's *Dodsworth*
(Screenplay by Sidney Howard; based on his play and the novel by Sinclair Lewis)

ALSO SEE: Boredom-3; Letters-12; Self-Perception-11; Specializations-2; Window-2.

SUN

1.

"I shall never forget the weekend Laura died. A silver sun burned through the sky like a huge magnifying glass. It was the hottest Sunday in my recollection. I felt as if I were the only human being left in New York. For, with Laura's horrible death, I was alone. I, Waldo Lydecker, was the only one who really knew her. And I had just begun to write Laura's story when another of those detectives came to see me. I had him wait."

—Clifton Webb wearing his mourning tones for the first lines of Otto Preminger's *Laura*
(Screenplay by Jay Dratler, Samuel Hoffenstein and Betty Reinhardt; based on the novel by Vera Caspary)

2.

"How I detest the dawn! The grass always looks like it's been left out all night."

—Clifton Webb making a brittle observation to Kurt Kreuger in Henry Hathaway's *The Dark Corner*
(Screenplay by Jay Dratler and Bernard C. Schoenfeld; based on the short story by Leo Rosten)

3.
"Every day, up at the crack of noon."

—Lucille Ball flicking off her daily routine to Joyce Van Patten in Gene Saks's *Mame*
(Screenplay by Paul Zindel; based on the musical play by Jerome Lawrence, Robert E. Lee and Jerry Herman and AUNTIE MAME, a play by Jerome Lawrence and Robert E. Lee and novel by Patrick Dennis)

4.
(a) "You presume to know me very well, don't you?"
    (b) "Sire, you stand in the sun."

—(a) Charles Boyer meeting his match, (b) Greta Garbo in Clarence Brown's *Conquest*
(Screenplay by Samuel Hoffenstein, Salka Viertel and S. N. Behrman; based on PANI WALEWSKA, a play by Helen Jerome and novel by Waclaw Gasiorowski)

5.
(a) "It doesn't seem a sad death."
    (b) "Oh, it's not, Sister. It happens in bright daylight, the sun flooding everything in a light of pure gold."

—(b) Kirk Douglas describing his vision of death to (a) nun Marion Ross in the last lines of Vincente Minnelli's *Lust for Life*
(Screenplay by Norman Corwin; based on the novel by Irving Stone)

ALSO SEE: Future-9; Home-11; Love-48; Night-6.

SWEAR

1.
"Kneel and swear this oath: That you, the free men of this forest, swear to despoil the rich only to give to the poor, to shelter the old and the helpless and to protect all women, rich or poor, Norman or Saxon. Swear to fight for a free England, to protect her loyally until the return of our king and sovereign, Richard the Lionhearted. And swear to fight to the death against our oppressors."

—Errol Flynn recruiting his merry men in Michael Curtiz and William Keighley's *The Adventures of Robin Hood*
(Original Screenplay by Norman Reilly Raine and Seton I. Miller; based on the ancient Robin Hood legends)

2.
"It's easy work for an informer to be swearing oaths."

—Victor McLaglen trying to pin his crime on Donald Meek in John Ford's *The Informer*
(Screenplay by Dudley Nichols; based on the novel by Liam O'Flaherty)

3.
"Oh, Judge, I never swear."

—Jane Russell being chorus-girl coy on the witness stand in Howard Hawks's *Gentlemen Prefer Blondes*
(Screenplay by Charles Lederer; based on the musical play by Joseph Fields and Anita Loos and novel by Anita Loos)

4.
"I don't swear just for the hell of it. Language is a poor enough means of communication. I think we should use all the words we've got. Besides, there are damn few words that anybody understands."

—Spencer Tracy defending his profanity to Fredric March in Stanley Kramer's *Inherit the Wind*
(Screenplay by Nathan E. Douglas and Harold Jacob Smith; based on the play by Jerome Lawrence and Robert E. Lee)

ALSO SEE: God-2; Hunger-1; Innocent-1; Lies-4.

TACT

1.

"Young man, as a—as a matter of curiosity, what made you become a priest?"

—Barry Fitzgerald trying to inquire casually about Bing Crosby's calling in Leo McCarey's *Going My Way*
(Screenplay by Frank Butler and Frank Cavett; based on an original story by Leo McCarey)

2.

"Did anyone ever tell you that you have a dishonest face—for a priest, I mean?"

—Ingrid Bergman being similarly suspicious about the same Bing Crosby in Leo McCarey's *The Bells of St. Mary's*
(Screenplay by Dudley Nichols; based on an original story by Leo McCarey)

3.

"Frank, were you on this religious kick at home, or did you crack up over here?"

—Donald Sutherland wondering about Robert Duvall's religious zeal in Robert Altman's *M*A*S*H*
(Screenplay by Ring Lardner Jr.; based on the novel by Richard Hooker)

4.

"Fraulein, is it to be at every meal or merely at dinner time that you intend leading us all through this rare and wonderful new world of indigestion?"

—Christopher Plummer attempting to silence Julie Andrews at the table in Robert Wise's *The Sound of Music*
(Screenplay by Ernest Lehman; based on the musical play by Howard Lindsay and Russel Crouse and THE TRAPP FAMILY SINGERS, a book by Maria Augusta Trapp)

5.

"But we mustn't underestimate American blundering. I was with them when they 'blundered' into Berlin in 1918."

—Claude Rains cautioning Conrad Veidt in Michael Curtiz's *Casablanca*
(Screenplay by Julius J. Epstein, Philip G. Epstein
and Howard Koch; based on EVERYBODY COMES TO RICK'S, a play by Murray Burnett and Joan Alison)*

6.

"Tell me, Scarlett, do you never shrink from marrying men you don't love?"

—Clark Gable criticizing Vivien Leigh's choice of husbands in Victor Fleming's *Gone With the Wind*
(Screenplay by Sidney Howard; based on the novel by Margaret Mitchell)

7.

"Tell me, Mrs. Wright, does your husband interfere with your marriage?"

—Oscar Levant making a snide aside to Joan Crawford in Jean Negulesco's *Humoresque*
(Screenplay by Clifford Odets and Zachary Gold; based on a short story by Fannie Hurst)

8.

"Among the gods, your humor is unique."

—Leo Genn ducking his true feelings about Peter Ustinov's wit in Mervyn LeRoy's *Quo Vadis*
(Screenplay by John Lee Mahin, S. N. Behrman, and Sonya Levien; based on the novel by Henryk Sienkiewicz)

TALENT

1.

"Do you not know that the great Peter Boroff may not come back from Paris, and, if he does not, he no longer has any talent?"

—George Tobias delivering the Red ruling on a possibly defecting composer (Wim Sonneveld) in Rouben Mamoulian's *Silk Stockings*
(Screenplay by Leonard Gershe and Leonard Spigelgass; based on the musical play by George S. Kaufman, Leueen MacGrath and Abe Burrows and NINOTCHKA, a screenplay by Charles Brackett, Billy Wilder and Walter Reisch and original story by Melchior Lengyel)

2.

"Back home everyone said I didn't have any talent. They might be saying the same thing over here, but it sounds better in French."

—Gene Kelly finding it easier to paint in Paris in Vincente Minnelli's *An American in Paris* (*Original Screenplay by Alan Jay Lerner*)

3.

"Oh, you should have seen me when I had stage fever. You know, every girl has a time in her life when she's positive she's divinely talented for the stage. I used to play Juliet all alone in my room."

—Katharine Hepburn rattling on in George Stevens's *Alice Adams* (*Screenplay by Dorothy Yost and Mortimer Offner; based on the novel by Booth Tarkington*)

4.

"We understand you got a lot of talent, and that's the one thing that could make Mr. Kirk Edwards fly all the way here from Rome, all the way from California you might say. *Talent!* Now where other men go for a pretty face or a pair of legs, *talent* is what Mr. Kirk Edwards worships. It's his religion, you might almost say."

—Edmond O'Brien selling Ava Gardner on his employer (Warren Stevens) in Joseph L. Mankiewicz's *The Barefoot Contessa* (*Original Screenplay by Joseph L. Mankiewicz*)

ALSO SEE: Available-4; Character-4; Diamonds-3; Fat-1; Genius-3; Similarities-3; Timing-4.

TALK

1.

"There was a time in this business when they had the eyes of the whole wide world. But that wasn't good enough for them. Oh, no. They had to have the ears of the world, too. So they opened their big mouths, and out came talk. Talk! Talk!"

—Gloria Swanson lamenting the demise of silent films in Billy Wilder's *Sunset Boulevard* (*Original Screenplay by Charles Brackett, Billy Wilder, and D. M. Marshman Jr.*)

2.

"I distrust a closed-mouth man. He generally picks the wrong time to talk and says the wrong things. Talking's something you can't do judiciously, unless you keep in practice. Now, sir, we'll talk if you like. I'll tell you right out, I'm a man who likes talking to a man who likes to talk."

—Sydney Greenstreet settling down to a black-bird discussion with Humphrey Bogart in John Huston's *The Maltese Falcon* (*Screenplay by John Huston; based on the novel by Dashiell Hammett*)

3.

"I call that bold talk for a one-eyed fat man."

—Robert Duvall provoking John Wayne into a gunfight in Henry Hathaway's *True Grit* (*Screenplay by Marguerite Roberts; based on the novel by Charles Portis*)

4.

"He *talked* like a Greek statue. I don't think he knew more than a dozen words—'scotch and soda,' and one or two more."

—Ingrid Bergman berating a recent beau to her sister (Phyllis Calvert) in Stanley Donen's *Indiscreet* (*Screenplay by Norman Krasna; based on his play, KIND SIR*)

5.

"There was never any talk while we were eating. I never met anybody whose talk was better than good food."

—Irving Pichel, as the never-seen narrator (a grown-up version of Roddy McDowall), recalling a rule of his boyhood home in John Ford's *How Green Was My Valley* (*Screenplay by Philip Dunne; based on the novel by Richard Llewellyn*)

6.

"Only time a woman doesn't care to talk is when she's dead."

—William Demarest disbelieving the sudden silence of his daughter (Betty Hutton) in Preston Sturges's *The Miracle of Morgan's Creek* (*Original Screenplay by Preston Sturges*)

7.

"Do not complete the sentence with the usual female contradictions. You grant me I know more than you, but, on the other hand, you know more than me. Women's talk!"

—Michael Chekhov correcting Ingrid Bergman in Alfred Hitchcock's *Spellbound*
(Screenplay by Ben Hecht; adaptation by Angus MacPhail; based on THE HOUSE OF DR. EDWARDES, a novel by Francis Beeding)

8.

"Why is it that sooner or later, no matter what we talk about, we wind up talking about Addie Ross?"

—Jeanne Crain objecting to the recurring topic of conversation for her, Ann Sothern, and Linda Darnell in Joseph L. Mankiewicz's *A Letter to Three Wives*
(Screenplay by Joseph L. Mankiewicz; adaptation by Vera Caspary; based on "One of Our Hearts," a short story by John Klempner)

9.

"George here doesn't cotton too much to body talk. 'Paunchy' here isn't too happy when the conversation moves to muscle."

—Elizabeth Taylor berating Richard Burton in Mike Nichols's *Who's Afraid of Virginia Woolf?*
(Screenplay by Ernest Lehman; based on the play by Edward Albee)

10.

"If thee talked as much to the Almighty as thee does to that horse, thee might stand more squarely in the light."

—Dorothy McGuire advising her husband (Gary Cooper) in William Wyler's *Friendly Persuasion*
(Screenplay by an uncredited Michael Wilson; based on stories by Jessamyn West)

11.

"Heavens, Laurel! Talk as a thoroughbred. One doesn't say 'go on' as if it were a donkey."

—Edith Evans correcting the conversation skills of her granddaughter (Hayley Mills) in Ronald Neame's *The Chalk Garden*
(Screenplay by John Michael Hayes; based on the play by Enid Bagnold)

12.

"I'm trying to imagine your—your half of this conversation. My feeling is I don't know that, if you could talk, we wouldn't be talking. That's pretty much the way that it got to be before I left. Are you all right? I don't know what to say. Partita suggested that we try to com—I don't know, I think that she—I think that she feels that we've got some understanding to reach. She totally denies the fact that we were never that comfortable with one another to begin with. The best that I can do is apologize. We both know that I was never really that good at it anyway. I'm sorry it didn't work out."

—Jack Nicholson struggling tearfully to communicate with his stroke-victim father (William Challee) in Bob Rafelson's *Five Easy Pieces*
(Screenplay by Adrien Joyce; based on a story by Bob Rafelson and Adrien Joyce)

ALSO SEE: Communication; Propositions-3; Propositions-4; Propositions-5.

TASTE

1.

"With Nixon in the White House, good health seemed to be in bad taste."

—Jane Fonda making her liberal position clear to Alan Alda in Herbert Ross's *California Suite*
(Screenplay by Neil Simon; based on his play)

2.

(a) "Ah, that woman has the taste of a water buffalo."
      (b) "Well, then why do business with her?"
      (a) "Because she happens to be a very rich water buffalo."

—(a) Marcel Dalio and (b) Doris Day discussing Lee Patrick in Michael Gordon's *Pillow Talk*
(Screenplay by Stanley Shapiro and Maurice Richlin; based on a story by Russell Rouse and Clarence Greene)

3.

"My dear, I have no taste for the abject."

—Claude Rains dismissing Bette Davis in Irving Rapper's *Deception*
(Screenplay by John Collier and Joseph Than; based on MONSIEUR LAMBERTHIER, a play by Louis Verneuil)

TATTOO

1.

(a) "What are those letters on your diaphragm?"

(b) "Love letters."

(a) "Oh, you believe in advertising. . . . Never could understand the quaint habit of making a billboard out of one's torso. . . . I must say, however, you've shown the most commendable delicacy in just tattooing the initials and not printing the names, addresses and telephone numbers. . . . How many are there? One, two, three, four, five—"

(b) "Remind me to show you the rest of them sometime."

—(a) Tallulah Bankhead wrangling (b) John Hodiak about his tattooed torso in Alfred Hitchcock's *Lifeboat*
(Screenplay by Jo Swerling; based on a story by John Steinbeck)

2.

"See for yourself. His rose tattooed on my chest."

—Virginia Grey confronting her lover's widow (Anna Magnani) in Daniel Mann's *The Rose Tattoo*
(Screenplay by Tennessee Williams; adaptation by Hal Kanter; based on the play by Tennessee Williams)

3.

"I wouldn't believe anything you said if you had it tattooed on your forehead."

—Jane Russell distrusting Elliott Reid in Howard Hawks's *Gentlemen Prefer Blondes*
(Screenplay by Charles Lederer; based on the musical play by Joseph Fields and Anita Loos and novel by Anita Loos)

TEARS

1.

"You know what I thought of him, and I know what you thought so let's leave the lamentations to the illiterate. What is this, Be Kind to Bigots week? Why should we weep for him? Because he's dead? Besides, he cried enough for himself during his lifetime. The national tear duct from Weeping Water, Nebraska. Ho, ho. He flooded the nation like a one-man Mississippi. You know what he was, that Bible-beating bunco artist."

—Gene Kelly eulogizing (in his cynical fashion) Fredric March in Stanley Kramer's *Inherit the Wind*
(Screenplay by Nathan E. Douglas and Harold Jacob Smith; based on the play by Jerome Lawrence and Robert E. Lee)

2.

"Who will listen to my songs now? Who will appreciate the true value of my verses? I weep for you, Petronius. One tear for you, one for me. Seal up these fruits of my sorrow so that posterity may know how Nero grieved for his dear little friend and truest critic."

—Peter Ustinov saving the tears he shed over Leo Genn's suicide in Mervyn LeRoy's *Quo Vadis*
(Screenplay by John Lee Mahin, S. N. Behrman and Sonya Levien; based on the novel by Henryk Sienkiewicz)

3.

"That's it. The only real bit of evidence we have."

—Roger Livesey using Kim Hunter's tear as Exhibit A in his argument for David Niven's life in Michael Powell and Emeric Pressburger's *Stairway to Heaven*
(Original Screenplay by Michael Powell and Emeric Pressburger)

4.

"Tears are good. You know what they say in Turkey? They say, 'Tears wash the eyes that one can see better.' "

—Heinz Ruehmann inventing a saying to console a tearful Gila Golan in Stanley Kramer's *Ship of Fools*

(Screenplay by Abby Mann; based on the novel by Katherine Anne Porter)

5.

"You can cry on my shoulder. I'm not going to bathe anyhow."

—Ginger Rogers consoling Andrea Leeds while waiting for a boarding-house bathroom to become unoccupied in Gregory La Cava's *Stage Door* *(Screenplay by Morrie Ryskind and Anthony Veiller; based on the play by Edna Ferber and George S. Kaufman)*

6.

"I will be very happy every moment that I have him. Every moment. If I must lose him, there'll be time enough for tears. There'll be a lifetime for tears."

—Teresa Wright facing the facts of wartime married-life in William Wyler's *Mrs. Miniver* *(Screenplay by Arthur Wimperis, George Froeschel, James Hilton, and Claudine West; based on the novel by Jan Struther)*

7.

"Joe, wasn't it absolutely the most wonderful wedding? Now we *really* do belong to each other, till death us do part—darling, you're crying. I believe you really are sentimental, after all."

—Heather Sears misreading the gloom of her trapped groom (Laurence Harvey) in the last lines of Jack Clayton's *Room at the Top* *(Screenplay by Neil Paterson; based on the novel by John Braine)*

8.

(a) "My darling, you're crying."

(b) "Oh, I'm such a fool—such an old fool. These are only tears of gratitude—an old maid's gratitude for the crumbs offered."

(a) "Don't talk like that."

(b) "You see, no one ever called me darling before."

—(a) Paul Henreid comforting (b) Bette Davis in Irving Rapper's *Now, Voyager* *(Screenplay by Casey Robinson; based on the novel by Olive Higgins Prouty)*

ALSO SEE: Beauty-2; Empathy-1; Empathy-2; Water-8.

TELEGRAMS

1.

" 'Come ahead stop stop being a sap stop you can even bring Alberto stop my husband is stopping at your hotel stop when do you start stop.' "

—Erik Rhodes reading Helen Broderick's cloudy message to Ginger Rogers in Mark Sandrich's *Top Hat* *(Screenplay by Dwight Taylor and Allan Scott; adaptation by Karl Noti; based on THE GIRL WHO DARED, a play by Alexander Farago and Aladar Laszlo)*

2.

(a) " 'Girls delightful in Cuba stop. Could send you prose poems about scenery but don't feel right spending your money stop. There is no war in Cuba. Signed, Wheeler.' Any answer?"

(b) "Yes. 'Dear Wheeler, you provide the prose poems. I'll provide the war.' "

—(b) Orson Welles responding jingoistically to a no-war correspondent's communiqué, read by (a) Everett Sloane, in Orson Welles's *Citizen Kane* *(Original Screenplay by Herman J. Mankiewicz and Orson Welles)*

3.

"Mrs. Kate Maccauley
    2226 Santa Clara Avenue
    Ithaca, California
    The Department of War regrets to inform you that your son Marcus—"

—Frank Morgan dying at his telegraph desk receiving the news of Van Johnson's death in Clarence Brown's *The Human Comedy* *(Screenplay by Howard Estabrook; based on an original story by William Saroyan)*

4.

"Hannah Eastman
    Bethel Independent Mission

Kansas City, Mo.
Mother I am convicted

George"

—Montgomery Clift wiring Anne Revere the bad news in George Stevens's *A Place in the Sun* *(Screenplay by Michael Wilson and Harry Brown; based on* AN AMERICAN TRAGEDY, *a play by Patrick Kearney and novel by Theodore Dreiser)*

TELEPHONE SCENES

1.

"Hello, Flo? Yes, it is Anna. I am so happy for you today. I could not help but calling you and congratulating you. Wonderful, Flo. Never better in my whole life. I am so excited about my new plans. I am going to Paris. Yes, for a few weeks, and then I can get back and then I am doing a musical, and I—oh, it's all so wonderful. And I'm so happy. Yes, and I hope you are happy, too. Yes. Oh, I am so glad for you, Flo. It sounds funny for exes, but every ex-wife could tell each other how happy they are, oui? Yes, Flo. Good-bye, Flo. Good-bye, my darling."

—Luise Rainer pretending happiness as she congratulates her ex (William Powell) on his marriage to Billie Burke (Myrna Loy) in Robert Z. Leonard's *The Great Ziegfeld*
(Original Screenplay by William Anthony McGuire)

2.

"Hello? Hello, hello, Dimitri. Listen, I—I can't hear too well. Do you suppose you could turn the music down just a little? Ah, ah, that's much better. Yes, huh, yes. Fine. I can hear you now, Dimitri, clear and plain and coming through fine. I'm coming through fine, too, eh? Good. Then—well, then, as you say, we're both coming through fine. Good. Well, it's good that you're fine then, and—and I'm fine. I agree with you, it's great to be fine. Ha, ha, ha, ha. Now then, Dimitri, you know how we've always talked about the possibility of something going wrong with the bomb. The bomb, Dimitri. The hydrogen bomb."

—Peter Sellers beating around the bush on the hot line to Moscow in Stanley Kubrick's *Dr. Strangelove or: How I Learned To Stop Worrying and Love the Bomb*
(Screenplay by Stanley Kubrick, Terry Southern and Peter George; based on RED ALERT, *a novel by Peter George)*

3.

"Hello? Hello? Yes, Jonathan. No, I can hear you perfectly. Yes, they're here. Uh huh, all three of them. I'll ask them. I'll ask them. Jonathan wants to know will you help him get started again? Will you work with him just this once? Will you do this picture with him? Georgia? Sorry, Jonathan. No, I can't. I'm sorry, Jonathan, but they're gone. Yeah, I'm sure it's a great idea, but, Jonathan—Jonathan, this is costing $4.80 a minute. Don't tell me your idea. Write me. Jonathan, please. Yeah, yeah. Uh huh. Yes. Yeah. What? Yeah, yeah, yeah, yeah, yeah, yeah. Go on. Sure, I'm listening. She does what?"

—Walter Pidgeon falling victim (along with Lana Turner, Dick Powell, and Barry Sullivan) to the persuasive powers of Kirk Douglas in the last lines of Vincente Minnelli's *The Bad and the Beautiful*
(Screenplay by Charles Schnee; based on "Memorial to a Bad Man" and "Of Good and Evil," two short stories by George Bradshaw)

4.

"One. Eight. Nine. Dr. Parry? Come. This is Helen."

—Dorothy McGuire speaking her first words (over the phone to Kent Smith) in the last lines of Robert Siodmak's *The Spiral Staircase*
(Screenplay by Mel Dinelli; based on SOME MUST WATCH, *a novel by Ethel Lina White)*

5.

"Oh, hello there. Is this Mary Feeney? Hello, there. This is Marty Pilletti. I—I wonder if you recall me. Well, I'm kind of a stocky guy. The last time we met was in the RKO Chester. You was with a friend of yours, and I—I was with a friend of mine, name of Angie. This was about a month ago. The RKO Chester on West Palm

Square. Yeah, you was sitting in front of us, and we was annoying you, and—and you got mad and—I'm the fella who works in a butcher shop. Oh, come on, you—you know who I am! That's right, and then—then afterwards we went to Howard Johnson's. We had hamburgers. You hadda milkshake. Yeah, that's right. Yeah, well, I'm the stocky one, the heavy-set fella. Yeah, well, I'm—I'm glad you recall me because I hadda pretty nice time that night, and I was wondering how everything was with you. How's everything? That's swell. Yeah, well, I tell you why I called. I was figuring on taking in a movie tonight, and I was wondering if you and your friend would care to see a movie tonight with me and my friend. Yeah, tonight. Well, I know it's a little late to call for a date, but I didn't know myself till—yeah, I know. Yeah, well, what about—well, how about next Saturday night? Are—are you free next Saturday night? Well, what about the Saturday after that? Yeah. Yeah, I know. Well, I mean, I understand that. Yeah. Yeah."

—Ernest Borgnine getting the brushoff in Delbert Mann's *Marty*
(Screenplay by Paddy Chayefsky; based on his teleplay)

6.
"What's that, Walter? They want me! They really want me!"

—Geraldine Page getting the word from Walter Winchell that her film career is far from finished in Richard Brooks's *Sweet Bird of Youth*
(Screenplay by Richard Brooks; based on the play by Tennessee Williams)

7.
"Hello, Ida Scott? It's Amanda Wingfield. Honey, how's that—how's that kidney condition of yours? Aw, honey, you're a martyr. That's what you are. You're just a martyr. Ida, I was just looking in my little book, and I discovered that your subscription to the *Companion's* running out, just when that wonderful new serial by Bessie Mae Harper is starting. It's the first thing she's written since 'Honeymoon

for Three,' and I believe it's going to be even lovelier. It's all about the horsy Long Island set, and the debutante gets thrown from a horse and her spine is injured. That's what the horse did. He just stepped right on her. Why do you sound so cross, honey? What's the matter? Eight o'clock! Why, so it is! I didn't realize it was so early. Am I a fool? You—you will renew. You—you will. Why, bless you, honey, bless you. You just go right back to sleep. Bless you, honey."

—Gertrude Lawrence hustling subscriptions at an ungodly hour in Irving Rapper's *The Glass Menagerie*
(Screenplay by Tennessee Williams and Peter Berneis; based on the play by Tennessee Williams)

8.
"Oh, Ed. It's Mrs. Delaney again. I hated to call you so early, but I just had to. Did you find Doc? No. No, nothing. He probably won't—won't come home until he's had all he can drink and wants to go to sleep. Well, I don't know what else to think, Ed. I'm scared. I'm awfully scared. If I need you later on, would you come over? Thanks."

—Shirley Booth calling an A.A. friend (Philip Ober) about her missing husband (Burt Lancaster) in Daniel Mann's *Come Back, Little Sheba*
(Screenplay by Ketti Frings; based on the play by William Inge)

9.
"Hello, Jack. Yeah. Listen, can Millie hear me? I don't want her to know, but I'm in a jam. I need your help, so don't let on. Make out like it's nothing. I'm at a police station. I took a bag. From a counter in a department store. I had to admit it, Jack. It was on my arm."

—Lee Grant confessing her shoplifting to her brother-in-law in William Wyler's *Detective Story*
(Screenplay by Philip Yordan and Robert Wyler; based on the play by Sidney Kingsley)

10.
"Hello. Is this someone with good news or money? No? Good-bye."

—Jason Robards getting down to basics in Fred Coe's *A Thousand Clowns*
(*Screenplay by Herb Gardner; based on his play*)

11.

"Times City Desk? Hedda Hopper speaking. I'm talking from the bedroom of Norma Desmond. Don't bother with a rewrite man. Take it direct. Ready? 'As day breaks over the murder house, Norma Desmond, famous star of yesteryear, is in a state of complete mental shock. . . .' "

—Hedda Hopper phoning in her story in Billy Wilder's *Sunset Boulevard*
(*Original Screenplay by Charles Brackett, Billy Wilder and D. M. Marshman Jr.*)

12.

" 'As you know, for all last night and today, the legion of the unwashed and holy have been rivering out of the rustic backways to listen to their pop messiah coo and bellow. The high priest of mumbo-jumbo, Matthew Harrison Brady, has alternately been stuffing himself with fried chicken and belching platitudes since his arrival here two days ago.' "

—Gene Kelly phoning in his story in Stanley Kramer's *Inherit the Wind*
(*Screenplay by Nathan E. Douglas and Harold Jacob Smith; based on the play by Jerome Lawrence and Robert E. Lee*)

13.

"Hello? Is that you? Well, this is Charlie. I just called you up *not* to wish you a merry Christmas."

—Alan Baxter drunkenly sending a seasonal insult in John Cromwell's *In Name Only*
(*Screenplay by Richard Sherman; based on MEMORY OF LOVE, a novel by Bessie Breuer*)

ALSO SEE: Dying Words-10; Last Lines-6; Respect-3.

TELEVISION

1.

"You're television incarnate, Diana, indifferent to suffering, insensitive to joy. All of life is reduced to the common rubble of banality. War, murder, death—all the same to you as bottles of beer, and the daily business of life is a corrupt comedy. You even shatter the sensations of time and space into split seconds and instant replays. You're madness, Diana."

—William Holden telling off Faye Dunaway in Sidney Lumet's *Network*
(*Original Screenplay by Paddy Chayefsky*)

2.

"That's all television is, my dear. Nothing but auditions."

—George Sanders pointing his protégé (Marilyn Monroe) in the direction of television in Joseph L. Mankiewicz's *All About Eve*
(*Screenplay by Joseph L. Mankiewicz; based on "The Wisdom of Eve," a radio play and short story by Mary Orr*)

3.

"And now that I have your attention, I want to warn all you girls and women of New York about an evil, dangerous, perfectly dreadful married man who lives downstairs in my building. His name is Sherman. Richard Sherman. S-h-e-r-m-a-n. While his lovely wife and son are in Maine for the summer, this monstrous man is terrorizing young girls in New York."

—Marilyn Monroe telling all on TV (or, at least, in Tom Ewell's imagination) in Billy Wilder's *The Seven Year Itch*
(*Screenplay by Billy Wilder and George Axelrod; based on the play by George Axelrod*)

ALSO SEE: Books-4; Business-5; Frigidity-5; Murder-4; Suicide-6; Truth-1.

TEMPTATION

1.

"Pearl, you're curved in the flesh of temptation. Resistance is going to be a darn sight harder for you than for females protected by the shape of sows."

—Walter Huston making a lustful observation to the sinner he's saving (Jennifer Jones) in King Vidor's *Duel in the Sun*
(Screenplay by David O. Selznick; adaptation by Oliver H. P. Garrett; based on the novel by Niven Busch)

2.

"Look, I can understand the temptation of a young man over here—but a grandfather! Really, Colonel Plummer, you should have your brakes relined."

—Jean Arthur accusing Millard Mitchell of hanky-panky in postwar Berlin in Billy Wilder's *A Foreign Affair*
(Screenplay by Charles Brackett, Billy Wilder and Richard L. Breen; adaptation by Robert Harari; based on an original story by David Shaw)

ALSO SEE: Goals-1; Youth-2.

THEATER

1.

"The theatuh, the theatuh—what book of rules says the theater exists only within some ugly buildings crowded into one square mile of New York City? Or London, Paris, or Vienna? Listen, junior. And learn. Want to know what the theater is? A flea circus. Also opera. Also rodeos, carnivals, ballets, Indian tribal dances, Punch and Judy, a one-man band—all theater. Wherever there's magic and make-believe and an audience—there's theater. Donald Duck, Ibsen, and The Lone Ranger. Sarah Bernhardt, Poodles Hanneford, Lunt and Fontanne, Betty Grable—Rex the Wild Horse and Eleanora Duse, you don't understand them all, you don't like them all—why should you? The theater's for everybody—you included, but not exclu-sively—so don't approve or disapprove. It may not be your theater, but it's theater for somebody, somewhere."

—Gary Merrill defining the word for Anne Baxter in Joseph L. Mankiewicz's *All About Eve*
(Screenplay by Joseph L. Mankiewicz; based on "The Wisdom of Eve," a radio play and short story by Mary Orr)

2.

(a) "I tell you if it moves, if it stimulates you, if it entertains you—it's theater. When the right combination gets together and it spells theater —well, I got to be right in there up to my armpits."

   (b) "That's higher than usual."

—(b) Oscar Levant deflating the hot air of (a) Jack Buchanan in Vincente Minnelli's *The Band Wagon*
(Original Screenplay by Betty Comden and Adolph Green)

3.

"Does someone have to die to create an actress? Is that what the theater's about?"

—Katharine Hepburn emerging triumphant on Broadway because of Andrea Leeds's suicide in Gregory La Cava's *Stage Door*
(Screenplay by Morrie Ryskind and Anthony Veiller; based on the play by Edna Ferber and George S. Kaufman)

4.

(a) "I could cut my throat."

   (b) "If you did, greasepaint would run out of it. That's the trouble with you, Oscar—with both of us. We're not people. We're lithographs. We don't know anything about love until it's written and rehearsed. We're only real in between curtains."

—(b) Carole Lombard analyzing herself and (a) John Barrymore in Howard Hawks's *Twentieth Century*
(Screenplay by Ben Hecht and Charles MacArthur; based on their play and NAPOLEON OF BROADWAY, a play by Charles Bruce Milholland)

5.

"It's that our theater cannot compete with life in these melodramatic times. Politicians have stolen all our tricks and blown them up into earth-sized, untidy productions and discarded the happy ending."

—Robert Montgomery doing his spiel for John Payne in Claude Binyon's *The Saxon Charm*
(*Screenplay by Claude Binyon; based on the novel by Frederic Wakeman*)

6.
"There's nothing quite so mysterious and silent as a dark theater. A night without a star."

—Grace Kelly making a moody observation in George Seaton's *The Country Girl*
(*Screenplay by George Seaton; based on the play by Clifford Odets*)

ALSO SEE: Actors; Applause; Star; Birthdays-4; Hunger-8; Narcissism-7; Plans-4; Self-Perception-10; Writers-4.

THIEVES

1.
"I'm Abu the thief, son of Abu the thief, grandson of Abu the thief, most unfortunate of ten sons with a hunger that yearns day and night."

—Sabu introducing himself to John Justin in Ludwig Berger, Tim Whelan and Michael Powell's *The Thief of Bagdad*
(*Screenplay and dialogue by Miles Malleson; based on a scenario by Lajos Biro*)

2.
"I steal."

—Paul Muni sinking into the shadows with the last line of Mervyn LeRoy's *I Am a Fugitive from a Chain Gang*
(*Screenplay by Howard J. Green and Brown Holmes; based on the story by Robert E. Burns*)

3.
"That son of a bitch stole my watch!"

—Adolphe Menjou telling a lie that will keep Pat O'Brien an unmarried newspaperman in the last (somewhat bleeped) line of Lewis Milestone's *The Front Page*

(*Screenplay by Bartlett Cormack and Charles Lederer; based on the play by Ben Hecht and Charles MacArthur*)

and

—Walter Matthau dittoing to Jack Lemmon in the remake, Billy Wilder's *The Front Page*
(*Screenplay by Billy Wilder and I. A. L. Diamond; based on the play by Ben Hecht and Charles MacArthur*)

4.
"Maybe he just wanted to steal our wire cutters. Did you ever think of that?"

—Robert Strauss developing second thoughts about William Holden's concentration-camp escape in the last lines of Billy Wilder's *Stalag 17*
(*Screenplay by Billy Wilder and Edwin Blum; based on the play by Donald Bevan and Edmund Trzcinski*)

5.
"Nobody calls me a thief but the man I steals from."

—Donald Crisp distinguishing between his victims and his captain (Charles Laughton) in Frank Lloyd's *Mutiny on the Bounty*
(*Screenplay by Talbot Jennings, Jules Furthman and Carey Wilson; based on the novel by Charles Nordhoff and James Norman Hall*)

6.
"Charlie, what are you hanging your head for? What do you got to be ashamed of? You wanted to be a burglar so be a good one. Be proud of your chosen profession. Hold up your head. There, that's better. You're a good thief, Charlie. You're no bum. They wear sweaters. Not you. You got a $100 suit on. You—wait a minute! Take it off, you bum. It's stolen. The name's still in it. 'Jerome Armstrong.' Where'd you get this, Charlie?"

—Kirk Douglas grilling Joseph Wiseman in William Wyler's *Detective Story*
(*Screenplay by Philip Yordan and Robert Wyler; based on the play by Sidney Kingsley*)

7.
"Oh, I did Shakespeare in the Park, Max. I got

mugged. I was playing 'Richard II,' and two guys with leather jackets stole my leotards."

—Tony Roberts relaying an actor's horror story in Woody Allen's *Annie Hall*
(Original Screenplay by Woody Allen and Marshall Brickman)

8.
"We rob banks."

—Warren Beatty being direct about the profession he and Faye Dunaway have chosen in Arthur Penn's *Bonnie and Clyde*
(Original Screenplay by David Newman and Robert Benton)

ALSO SEE: Cameras-1; Fools-6; Greed-3; Honor-6; Life-2; Love-41; Love-42; Stimulating-2; Telephone Scenes-9.

THREATS

1.
(a) "Well, when Johnny was first starting out, he signed this personal service contract with a big band leader, and, as his career got better and better, he wanted to get out of it. Now, Johnny is my father's godson, and my father went to see this band leader and offered him $10,000 to let Johnny go, and the band leader said no so the next day my father went to see him, only this time with Luca Brasi. Within an hour, he signed a release for a certified check of $1,000."
(b) "Why did he do that?"
(a) "My father made him an offer he couldn't refuse."
(b) "What was that?"
(a) "Luca Brasi held a gun to his head, and my father assured him that either his brains or his signature would be on the contract. It's a true story."

—(a) Al Pacino telling (b) Diane Keaton about Marlon Brando's powers of persuasion in Francis Ford Coppola's *The Godfather*
(Screenplay by Mario Puzo and Francis Ford Coppola; based on the novel by Mario Puzo)

2.
"Tough monkey. Guys like you end up in the stockade sooner or later. Some day you'll walk in. I'll be waiting. I'll show you a couple of things."

—Ernest Borgnine threatening Frank Sinatra in Fred Zinnemann's *From Here to Eternity*
(Screenplay by Daniel Taradash; based on the novel by James Jones)

3.
"I told you we'd meet up sometime when you didn't have no stripes on your sleeve, and here we are."

—Humphrey Bogart gunning down his former sergeant (Joe Sawyer) in Raoul Walsh's *The Roaring Twenties*
(Screenplay by Richard Macaulay, Jerry Wald and Robert Rossen; based on a story by Mark Hellinger)

4.
"You shoulda let 'em kill me 'cause I'm gonna kill you. I'll catch up with you. I don't know when, but I'll catch up. And every time you turn around, expect to see me, because one time you'll turn around and I'll be there. I'll kill you, Matt."

—John Wayne promising revenge on Montgomery Clift in Howard Hawks's *Red River*
(Screenplay by Borden Chase and Charles Schnee; based on THE CHISHOLM TRAIL, a novel by Borden Chase)

5.
"Well, my little pretty, I can cause accidents, too."

—Margaret Hamilton cackling wickedly to Judy Garland in Victor Fleming's *The Wizard of Oz*
(Screenplay by Noel Langley, Florence Ryerson and Edgar Allan Woolf; adaptation by Noel Langley; based on the novel by L. Frank Baum)

6.
"We have other prisoners, Captain. Must I remind you that a chain is only as strong as its weakest link?"

—Richard Loo threatening Dana Andrews in Lewis Milestone's *The Purple Heart*
(Screenplay by Jerome Cady; based on a story by Melville Crossman)

7.
"Casting me adrift 3,500 miles from a port of call! You're sending me to my doom, eh? Well, you're wrong, Christian. I'll take this boat, as she floats, to England if I must. I'll live to see you—all of you—hanging from the highest yardarm in the British fleet."

—Charles Laughton promising death to Clark Gable and the mutineers for a parting shot in Frank Lloyd's *Mutiny on the Bounty*
(Screenplay by Talbot Jennings, Jules Furthman and Carey Wilson; based on the novel by Charles Nordhoff and James Norman Hall)

8.
"You're dead on this waterfront and every waterfront from Boston to New Orleans. You don't drive a truck or a cab. You don't push a baggage rack. You don't work no place. You're dead."

—Lee J. Cobb promising unemployment to his betrayer (Marlon Brando) in Elia Kazan's *On the Waterfront*
(Original Screenplay by Budd Schulberg; based on "Crime on the Waterfront," nonfiction articles by Malcolm Johnson)

9.
"I caught this guy stealing our water. Next time you try that, I'll let it out of you through little round holes."

—Humphrey Bogart threatening to shoot a water-stealing guest (Bruce Bennett) in John Huston's *The Treasure of the Sierra Madre*
(Screenplay by John Huston; based on the novel by B. Traven)

10.
"One more crack, Queenie—just one—and I will not only spit in your eye, but I will punch it black and blue."

—Elizabeth Taylor threatening Madeleine Sherwood in Richard Brooks's *Cat on a Hot Tin Roof*
(Screenplay by Richard Brooks and James Poe; based on the play by Tennessee Williams)

11.
"Shall I spit in Crystal's eye for you? You're passing up a swell chance, honey. Where I spit, no grass grows ever."

—Paulette Goddard offering to battle Joan Crawford for Norma Shearer in George Cukor's *The Women*
(Screenplay by Anita Loos and Jane Murfin; based on the play by Clare Boothe)

ALSO SEE: Advice-5; Games-4; Good-6; Hands-1; Heart-10; Priorities-6; Professions-9; Regrets-4; Time-12; Tough-7.

TIME

1.
"Time. Time. What is time? Swiss manufacture it. French horde it. Italians want it. Americans say it is money. Hindus say it does not exist. Do you know what I say? I say time is a crook."

—Peter Lorre getting in his vote in John Huston's *Beat the Devil*
(Screenplay by John Huston and Truman Capote; based on the novel by James Helvick)

2.
"Time! Time is one thing to a lawmaker, but, to a farmer, there is a time to plant and a time to harvest—and you cannot plant and harvest time."

—Marlon Brando showing impatience with governmental red tape in Elia Kazan's *Viva Zapata!*
(Original Screenplay by John Steinbeck)

3.
"Time! Time happens, I suppose, to people. Everything becomes too late, finally. You know it's going on up on the hill. You can see the dust and hear the cries. But you wait. Time happens."

—Katharine Hepburn making a weary observation in Tony Richardson's *A Delicate Balance*
(Screenplay by Edward Albee; based on his play)

4.

"Time is never reasonable. Time is our enemy, Caesar."

—Elizabeth Taylor regretting the brevity of her affair with Rex Harrison in Joseph L. Mankiewicz's *Cleopatra*
(Screenplay by Joseph L. Mankiewicz, Ranald MacDougall and Sidney Buchman; based upon histories by Plutarch, Suetonius and Appian and THE LIFE AND TIMES OF CLEOPATRA, a book by C. M. Franzero)

5.

"Time. Lots of time. There are many things we're short of in state hospitals, time most of all."

—Leo Genn telling a patient's husband (Mark Stevens) about mental health's big need in Anatole Litvak's *The Snake Pit*
(Screenplay by Frank Partos and Millen Brand; based on the novel by Mary Jane Ward)

6.

"Aw, time ain't so important, Miss Belle. Seems like the longer I live, the more there is of it."

—George Brent getting philosophical with Fay Bainter in William Wyler's *Jezebel*
(Screenplay by Clements Ripley, Abem Finkel and John Huston; based on the play by Owen Davis Sr.)

7.

"My check-out time in any hotel in the world is when—when I check out."

—Geraldine Page rising imperiously to Rip Torn's "bum's rush" in Richard Brooks's *Sweet Bird of Youth*
(Screenplay by Richard Brooks; based on the play by Tennessee Williams)

8.

(a) "I wasn't thinking about time."
    (b) "Oh, how good it is to know a man who doesn't live his life measuring time in bits and pieces."

—(b) Jennifer Jones appreciating (a) William Holden in Henry King's *Love Is a Many-Splendored Thing*
(Screenplay by John Patrick; based on A MANY-SPLENDORED THING, a novel by Han Suyin)

9.

"Don't you ever think about time, Alec? It goes. That's the business of time."

—Bette Davis boozing it up about her imminent death with Ronald Reagan in Edmund Goulding's *Dark Victory*
(Screenplay by Casey Robinson; based on the play by George Brewer Jr. and Bertram Bloch)

10.

"You know what the trouble is? The trouble is that probably all the good things in life take place in no more than a minute—I mean, all added up. Especially at the end of 70 years, if you should live so long, you still haven't even figured it all out. You spent 35 years sleeping. You spent five years going to the bathroom. You spent 19 years doing some kind of work you absolutely hated. You spent 8,759 minutes blinking your eyes. And, after that, you got one minute of good things. So one day you wonder when your minute's up."

—Liza Minnelli philosophizing in Alan J. Pakula's *The Sterile Cuckoo*
(Screenplay by Alvin Sargent; based on the novel by John Nichols)

11.

"A man sentenced to life can always 'spare a few minutes.'"

—Humphrey Bogart being flip with his employer-away-from-prison (Joan Bennett) in Michael Curtiz's *We're No Angels*
(Screenplay by Ranald MacDougall; based on LA CUISINE DES ANGES, a play by Albert Husson, and MY THREE ANGELS, a Broadway adaptation by Bella Spewack and Samuel Spewack)

12.

(a) "Oliver, if you marry her now, I'll not give you the time of day."
    (b) "Father, you don't know the time of day."

—(a) Ray Milland and (b) Ryan O'Neal warring over Ali MacGraw in Arthur Hiller's *Love Story*
(Original Screenplay by Erich Segal)

13.

"Can you read what time it is by my brand new silver watch?"

—John Wayne making a recurring show of his new retirement watch in John Ford's *She Wore a Yellow Ribbon*
(Screenplay by Frank S. Nugent and Laurence Stallings; based on "The Big Hunt" and "War Party," two short stories by James Warner Bellah)

14.

"What's the bleeding time?"

—James Robertson-Justice asking a medical question that is answered as if it were a profane one in Ralph Thomas's *Doctor in the House*
(Screenplay by Nicholas Phipps; adaptation by Richard Gordon; based on the novel by Richard Gordon)

15.

(a) "It's midnight. Look at the clock. One hand has met the other hand. They kiss. Isn't that wonderful?"
 (b) "That's the way a clock works. What's wonderful about it?"
 (a) "But, Ninotchka, it's midnight. One half of Paris is making love to the other half."

—(a) Melvyn Douglas trying to bewitch (b) Greta Garbo in Ernst Lubitsch's *Ninotchka*
(Screenplay by Charles Brackett, Billy Wilder and Walter Reisch; based on an original story by Melchior Lengyel)

16.

"Now I have kissed you through two centuries."

—Laurence Olivier romancing Vivien Leigh into the 19th century in Alexander Korda's *That Hamilton Woman*
(Original Screenplay by Walter Reisch and R. C. Sherriff)

17.

"Even when I was making love to you, I felt you were wondering what time it was."

—Robert Montgomery criticizing Bette Davis in Bretaigne Windust's *June Bride*

(Screenplay by Ranald MacDougall; based on FEATURE FOR JUNE, a play by Eileen Tighe and Graeme Lorimer)

18.

"Somehow I knew it would work out that way. Time is the great author. Always writes the perfect ending."

—Charles Chaplin learning he has lost Claire Bloom to Sydney Chaplin in Charles Chaplin's *Limelight*
(Original Screenplay by Charles Chaplin)

19.

"Play it, Sam. Play 'As Time Goes By.'"

—Ingrid Bergman making a sentimental song request to Dooley Wilson in Michael Curtiz's *Casablanca*
(Screenplay by Julius J. Epstein, Philip G. Epstein and Howard Koch; based on EVERYBODY COMES TO RICK'S, a play by Murray Burnett and Joan Alison)

ALSO SEE: Aging-12; Awakenings-3; Live-3; Signs-1; Telephone Scenes-7.

TIMING

1.

"I've been waiting for a girl like you all my life. I just timed it wrong. Here's the plan: I'm definitely getting out. I just have to figure a way to let her down easy. It kinda complicates things, this being our honeymoon and everything."

—Charles Grodin switching allegiances from Jeannie Berlin to Cybill Shepherd in Elaine May's *The Heartbreak Kid*
(Screenplay by Neil Simon; based on "A Change of Plan," a story by Bruce Jay Friedman)

2.

"This is an honorable proposal of marriage, made at what I consider a most opportune moment. I can't go all my life waiting to catch you between husbands."

—Clark Gable popping the question to twice-widowed Vivien Leigh in Victor Fleming's *Gone With the Wind*

(Screenplay by Sidney Howard; based on the novel by Margaret Mitchell)

3.

"They say opportunity's only got one hair on its head and you got to grab it while it's going by."

—William Demarest advising Eddie Bracken in Preston Sturges's *Hail the Conquering Hero*
(Original Screenplay by Preston Sturges)

4.

"Listen to me, Esther, a career is a curious thing. Talent isn't always enough. You need a sense of timing—an eye for seeing the turning point or recognizing the big chance when it comes along and grabbing it. A career can rest on a trifle. Like—like us sitting here tonight. Or it can turn on somebody saying to you, 'You're better than that. You're better than you know.' Don't settle for the little dream. Go on to the big one."

—James Mason advising Judy Garland in George Cukor's *A Star Is Born*
(Screenplay by Moss Hart; based on a screenplay by Dorothy Parker, Alan Campbell and Robert Carson and original story by William A. Wellman and Robert Carson)

5.

"Sidney, I have just thrown up in front of the best people in Hollywood. Now is no time to be sensitive."

—Maggie Smith dismissing the delicacy of her husband (Michael Caine) in Herbert Ross's *California Suite*
(Screenplay by Neil Simon; based on his play)

ALSO SEE: Adultery-11; Life and Death-1; Prayers-6.

TIRED

1.

"This past spring was the first that I'd felt tired and realized I was growing old. Maybe it was the rotten weather we'd had in L.A. Maybe it was the rotten cases I'd had—mostly chasing a few missing husbands and then chasing their wives, once I'd found them, in order to get paid. Or maybe it was just the plain fact that I am tired and growing old."

—Robert Mitchum coming on as the world-weary detective in the first lines of Dick Richards's *Farewell, My Lovely*
(Screenplay by David Zelag Goodman; based on the novel by Raymond Chandler)
            and (almost verbatim)

—Dick Powell dittoing in the original, Edward Dmytryk's *Murder, My Sweet*
(Screenplay by John Patrick; based on FAREWELL, MY LOVELY, a novel by Raymond Chandler)

2.

"You're too tired. I know that feeling of exhaustion only too well. One must humor it, or it explodes."

—Leo G. Carroll advising Ingrid Bergman in Alfred Hitchcock's *Spellbound*
(Screenplay by Ben Hecht; adaptation by Angus MacPhail; based on THE HOUSE OF DR. EDWARDES, a novel by Francis Beeding)

3.

"When a man says he has exhausted life, you may be sure life has exhausted him."

—George Sanders giving his view in Albert Lewin's *The Picture of Dorian Gray*
(Screenplay by Albert Lewin; based on the novel by Oscar Wilde)

4.

"I *am* pretty sick and tired of the sound of her voice. Not that she isn't a good woman. I'm just sick and tired of the sound of her voice."

—Frank Overton discussing his talkative wife (Eve Arden) with Robert Preston in Delbert Mann's *The Dark at the Top of the Stairs*
(Screenplay by Irving Ravetch and Harriet Frank Jr.; based on the play by William Inge)

5.

"I get so tired of just being told I'm pretty."

—Kim Novak admitting to William Holden her boredom with superficial compliments in Joshua Logan's *Picnic*

(Screenplay by Daniel Taradash; based on the play by William Inge)

6.

"I'm tired of whipping you, year after year."

—Elizabeth Taylor arguing with Richard Burton in Mike Nichols's *Who's Afraid of Virginia Woolf?*
(Screenplay by Ernest Lehman; based on the play by Edward Albee)

7.

"And now you will never be tired again. Come, Lucia. Come, my dear."

—Rex Harrison welcoming Gene Tierney as a ghost in the last lines of Joseph L. Mankiewicz's *The Ghost and Mrs. Muir*
(Screenplay by Philip Dunne; based on THE GHOST OF CAPTAIN GREGG AND MRS. MUIR, a novel by R. A. Dick)

ALSO SEE: Looks-2; Marriage-12; Platonic Relationships-2; Priorities-1; Repetitions-3.

TOASTS

1.

"Here's looking at you, kid."

—Humphrey Bogart toasting Ingrid Bergman in Michael Curtiz's *Casablanca*
(Screenplay by Julius J. Epstein, Philip G. Epstein and Howard Koch; based on EVERYBODY COMES TO RICK'S, a play by Murray Burnett and Joan Alison)

2.

"Here's to plain speaking and clear understanding."

—Sydney Greenstreet beginning his black-bird pow-wow with Humphrey Bogart in John Huston's *The Maltese Falcon*
(Screenplay by John Huston; based on the novel by Dashiell Hammett)

3.

"Here's mud in my throat."

—Bob Hope doing his "saloon tough" in Frank Tashlin's *Son of Paleface*

(Original Screenplay by Frank Tashlin, Robert L. Welch and Joseph Quillan)

4.

"Here's to our house
   Through sunshine or showers,
   Be it ever so humble,
   By golly, it's ours."

—Ray Mayer proposing a toast to the home that his parents (Victor Moore and Beulah Bondi) are losing to the bank in Leo McCarey's *Make Way for Tomorrow*
(Screenplay by Vina Delmar; based on the play by Helen Leary and Nolan Leary and THE YEARS ARE SO LONG, a novel by Josephine Lawrence)

5.

"Here is my hope that Robert Conway will find his Shangri-La. Here is my hope that we all find our Shangri-La."

—Hugh Buckler saluting a missing Ronald Colman in the last lines of Frank Capra's *Lost Horizon*
(Screenplay by Robert Riskin; based on the novel by James Hilton)

6.

"To the Fountain of Trevi—to the lovely, romantic Fountain of Trevi where hope can be had for a penny."

—Dorothy McGuire singing the romantic blues when in Rome in Jean Negulesco's *Three Coins in the Fountain*
(Screenplay by John Patrick; based on the novel by John H. Secondari)

7.

(a) "To Reno, the biggest little city in the world, the American cradle of liberty!"
   (b) "Reno—beautiful emblem of the Great Divide."

—(a) Mary Boland and (b) Paulette Goddard toasting their divorce town in George Cukor's *The Women*
(Screenplay by Anita Loos and Jane Murfin; based on the play by Clare Boothe)

8.

"To all the dumb chumps and all the crazy broads—past, present and future—who thirst

for knowledge and search for truth, who fight
for justice and civilize each other and make it
so tough for crooks like you. And me."

—Howard St. John boozing with Broderick Crawford
over Judy Holliday's exit in George Cukor's *Born
Yesterday*
*(Screenplay by Albert Mannheimer; based on the
play by Garson Kanin)*

9.
"To new worlds of Gods and Monsters!"

—Ernest Thesiger drinking to evil doings in James
Whale's *The Bride of Frankenstein*
*(Screenplay by William Hurlbut and John L.
Balderston; suggested by FRANKENSTEIN, a novel
by Mary Wollstonecraft Shelley)*

10.
"To the voyage of the *Bounty!* Still waters and
the great golden sea. Flying fish like streaks of
silver, and mermaids that sing in the night. The
Southern Cross and all the stars on the other
side of the world."

—Franchot Tone voicing some unrealized optimism
before setting sail in Frank Lloyd's *Mutiny on the
Bounty*
*(Screenplay by Talbot Jennings, Jules Furthman
and Carey Wilson; based on the novel by Charles
Nordhoff and James Norman Hall)*

11.
"I love her—I love her with every fiber of my
being, ladies and gentlemen—*H.M.S. Torrin.*"

—Bernard Miles toasting his ship in Noel Coward
and David Lean's *In Which We Serve*
(Original Screenplay by Noel Coward)

12.
"I want to drink a toast to you, Mr. Keefer.
From the beginning, you hated the Navy. You
thought up the whole idea, and you kept your
skirts all starched and clean. Steve Maryk will
be remembered as a mutineer—but you! You'll
publish a novel, you'll make a million bucks,
you'll marry a big movie star, and, for the rest
of your life, you'll have to live with your conscience, if you have any. Now, here's to the real

author of 'The Caine Mutiny.' Here's to you,
Mr. Keefer."

—José Ferrer flinging his drink in Fred MacMurray's
face in Edward Dmytryk's *The Caine Mutiny*
*(Screenplay by Stanley Roberts; additional
dialogue by Michael Blankfort; based on the novel
by Herman Wouk)*

13.
"Now I want you to drink to him, to King Gypo,
as brave as a lion and as strong as a bull. I'd go
through fire and water for him—and he'd do
the same for me—and, from now on, from this
night, wherever you see one of us, you see the
other, or vice versa as the case may be. Am I
right, or am I wrong, Gypo?"

—J. M. Kerrigan toasting Victor McLaglen in John
Ford's *The Informer*
*(Screenplay by Dudley Nichols; based on the
novel by Liam O'Flaherty)*

14.
"A toast! A toast! A toast to Mother Dollar and
to Papa Dollar—and, if you want to keep this
old Building and Loan in business, you'd better
have a family real quick."

—James Stewart celebrating the halt of a run on his
loan company in Frank Capra's *It's a Wonderful Life*
*(Screenplay by Albert Hackett, Frances Goodrich
and Frank Capra; based on "The Greatest Gift," a
short story by Philip Van Doren Stern)*

15.
"A toast, Jedediah—to love on my terms. Those
are the only terms anybody ever knows, his
own."

—Orson Welles drinking with Joseph Cotten in
Orson Welles's *Citizen Kane*
*(Original Screenplay by Herman J. Mankiewicz
and Orson Welles)*

16.
"I'm going to propose a toast. Without wit.
With all my heart. To Margo. To my bride-to-
be."

—Gary Merrill announcing, with a toast, his engagement to Bette Davis in Joseph L. Mankiewicz's *All
About Eve*

(Screenplay by Joseph L. Mankiewicz; based on "The Wisdom of Eve," a radio play and short story by Mary Orr)

17.

"So, without further eloquence, I will give you a toast—to myself, who is soon to be wed. All she has to do is to say that little word. When's the happy day, Sarah darlin'?"

—Victor McLaglen proposing marriage (to a stunned Mildred Natwick) as well as a toast in John Ford's *The Quiet Man*
(Screenplay by Frank S. Nugent; based on "Green Rushes," a short story by Maurice Walsh)

18.

"There was an old fellow named Sidney,
    Who drank till he ruined a kidney.
    It shriveled and shrank,
    But he drank and he drank.
    He had his fun doing it, didn't he?"

—Marilyn Monroe getting Elliott Reid in a jolly mood in Howard Hawks's *Gentlemen Prefer Blondes*
(Screenplay by Charles Lederer; based on the musical play by Joseph Fields and Anita Loos and novel by Anita Loos)

19.

"I'm an old man. My life is almost over. Here, with the sunset in my face, it thrills me to see these young people marching on. Let us drink to youth—to innocent, joyous youth. To Angelo. To Robert, who will this day, unstained by the evils of the world, look to the future. Today I stood by Robert's side as he embraced his faith. May it please the Almighty, I stand by his side as he enters manhood."

—Charles Coburn toasting his great-grandson (Dean Stockwell) in Victor Saville's *The Green Years*
(Screenplay by Robert Ardrey and Sonya Levien; based on the novel by A. J. Cronin)

20.

"Early to rise
    And early to bed
    Makes a man healthy
    But socially dead."

—Alan Hale drinking to the contrary in Raoul Walsh's *They Drive by Night*
(Screenplay by Jerry Wald and Richard Macaulay; based on LONG HAUL, a novel by A. I. Bezzerides)

ALSO SEE: Dying Words-14.

TOGETHER

1.

"Look, I don't want somebody pointing to Joan and me in a couple of years, telling some miserable story ending with 'And they're still together.'"

—Joseph Hindy suggesting to his parents (Richard Castellano and Beatrice Arthur) that divorce is better than gossip in Cy Howard's *Lovers and Other Strangers*
(Screenplay by Renee Taylor, Joseph Bologna and David Z. Goodman; based on the play by Renee Taylor and Joseph Bologna)

2.

"Do not pity me, Master Judah. In fact, I'm twice the man I was. There's Malluch, my other half. We met in the dungeons at the citadel. We were released on the same day, Malluch without a tongue and I without life in my legs. Since then, I have been his tongue and he has been my legs. Together, we make a considerable man."

—Sam Jaffe introducing Adi Berber to Charlton Heston in William Wyler's *Ben-Hur*
(Screenplay by Karl Tunberg; based on BEN-HUR, A TALE OF THE CHRIST, a novel by General Lew Wallace)

3.

"That's the unholy pity of it! The one man, in all of your fantasy—and the one woman, in all of his—who could have made each other happy. And, once more, life louses up the script."

—Humphrey Bogart lamenting Ava Gardner's marital problems in Joseph L. Mankiewicz's *The Barefoot Contessa*
(Original Screenplay by Joseph L. Mankiewicz)

4.

"Well, Max, here we are: middle-aged man reaffirming his middle-aged manhood and a terrified young woman with a father complex. What sort of script do you think we can make out of this?"

—Faye Dunaway proposing an affair to William Holden in Sidney Lumet's *Network*
(Original Screenplay by Paddy Chayefsky)

5.

"Maybe we could do something else together. Mrs. Robinson, would you like to go to a movie?"

—Dustin Hoffman suggesting to Anne Bancroft an alternative to adultery in Mike Nichols's *The Graduate*
(Screenplay by Calder Willingham and Buck Henry; based on the novel by Charles Webb)

6.

"Let's get out of here together. No use staying here, letting the South come down around your ears. Too many nice places to go and visit. Mexico, London, Paris—"

—Clark Gable trying to woo Vivien Leigh away in Victor Fleming's *Gone With the Wind*
(Screenplay by Sidney Howard; based on the novel by Margaret Mitchell)

7.

"Listen, baby, when we first met—you and me—you thought I was common. Well, how right you was! I was common as dirt. You showed me a snapshot of the place with them columns, and I pulled you down off them columns, and you loved it! We were having them colored lights going! And wasn't we happy together? Wasn't it all okay till she showed here?"

—Marlon Brando reminding Kim Hunter of the good times before Vivien Leigh's arrival in Elia Kazan's *A Streetcar Named Desire*
(Screenplay by Tennessee Williams; adaptation by Oscar Saul; based on the play by Tennessee Williams)

8.

"You remember how it really was? You and me and booze—a threesome. . . . You and I were a couple of drunks on the sea of booze, and the boat sank. I got hold of something that kept me from going under, and I'm not going to let go of it. Not for you. Not for anyone. If you want to grab on, grab on. But there's just room for you and me—no threesome."

—Jack Lemmon establishing the rule for reconciliation with Lee Remick in Blake Edwards's *Days of Wine and Roses*
(Screenplay by J. P. Miller; based on his teleplay)

9.

"You know, I used to live like Robinson Crusoe—shipwrecked among eight million people. Then one day I saw a footprint in the sand, and there you were. It's a wonderful thing, dinner for two."

—Jack Lemmon sweet-talking Shirley MacLaine in Billy Wilder's *The Apartment*
(Original Screenplay by Billy Wilder and I. A. L. Diamond)

10.

"All right. It'll be you at the tiller and me at the engine, just like it was from the start."

—Humphrey Bogart deciding to let Katharine Hepburn help him knock off a 100-foot German gunboat in John Huston's *The African Queen*
(Screenplay by James Agee and John Huston; based on the novel by C. S. Forester)

11.

"We McDonalds—we're high-tempered. We fight amongst ourselves, but let trouble come from outside and we stick together."

—Agnes Moorehead vowing to help her pregnant niece (Jane Wyman) in Jean Negulesco's *Johnny Belinda*
(Screenplay by Irmgard Von Cube and Allen Vincent; based on the play by Elmer Harris)

12.

"Now an army is a team. It lives, eats, sleeps, fights as a team. This individuality stuff is a bunch of crap. The bilious bastards who wrote that stuff about individuality for the *Saturday Evening Post* don't know any more about real battle than they do about fornicating."

—George C. Scott preaching teamwork to the troops in Franklin Schaffner's *Patton*
(*Original Screenplay by Francis Ford Coppola and Edmund H. North; based on PATTON: ORDEAL AND TRIUMPH, a book by Ladislas Farago, and A SOLDIER'S STORY, a book by Omar N. Bradley*)

ALSO SEE: Choice-10; Fools-10; Future-2; Guns-11; Hanging-8; Hope-5; Lasts-4; Letters-12; Mad Act-11; Never-6; Parents-2; Poverty-4; Seasons-2; Similarities-4; Soul-9; Toasts-13; Wants-8.

TONGUE

1.
"I feel as though somebody stepped on my tongue with muddy feet."

—W. C. Fields making a liquid-refreshment stop in Edward Cline's *Never Give a Sucker an Even Break*
(*Screenplay by John T. Neville and Prescott Chaplin; based on an original story by Otis Criblecoblis, a.k.a. W. C. Fields*)

2.
"Are you remembering the time you wanted me to wear white? Are you? Well, until now, I never have. Cat got your tongue?"

—Bette Davis, contrite and dressed in white, stunning a newly married Henry Fonda in William Wyler's *Jezebel*
(*Screenplay by Clements Ripley, Abem Finkel and John Huston; based on the play by Owen Davis Sr.*)

3.
"What's the matter? Cathouse got your tongue?"

—Robert Mitchum interrogating a brothel madam (Kate Murtagh) in Dick Richards's *Farewell, My Lovely*
(*Screenplay by David Zelag Goodman; based on the novel by Raymond Chandler*)

4.
"I know you have a civil tongue in your head. I sewed it there myself."

—Whit Bissell reprimanding his creation (Gary Conway) in Herbert L. Strock's *I Was a Teenage Frankenstein*
(*Original Screenplay by Kenneth Langtry*)

ALSO SEE: Together-2.

TOUGH

1.
"When I get in a tight spot, I shoot my way out of it. Why, sure! Shoot first and argue afterwards. You know, this game ain't for guys that's soft."

—Edward G. Robinson snarling out his trigger-happy credo to Douglas Fairbanks Jr. in Mervyn LeRoy's *Little Caesar*
(*Screenplay by Francis Edwards Faragoh; based on the novel by W. R. Burnett*)

2.
"I met a lot of hard-boiled eggs in my life, but you—you're 20 minutes!"

—Jan Sterling giving Kirk Douglas a dubious compliment in Billy Wilder's *The Big Carnival*
(*Original Screenplay by Billy Wilder, Lesser Samuels and Walter Newman*)

3.
"We think you're the softest hard-boiled egg in the world."

—Charlie McCarthy giving W. C. Fields a dubious compliment in George Marshall's *You Can't Cheat an Honest Man*
(*Screenplay by George Marion Jr., Richard Mack and Everett Freeman; based on an original story by Charles Bogle, a.k.a. W. C. Fields*)

4.
"I'm not thin-skinned, Mr. Shannon."

—Deborah Kerr telling Richard Burton that her appearance is deceiving in John Huston's *The Night of the Iguana*

(Screenplay by Anthony Veiller and John Huston; based on the play by Tennessee Williams)

5.

"Now, don't you worry about me. I'm a tough 'Texian' now."

—Elizabeth Taylor telling her groom (Rock Hudson) that she can take a tiring day on the range in George Stevens's *Giant*
(Screenplay by Fred Guiol and Ivan Moffat; based on the novel by Edna Ferber)

6.

" 'Okay, Marlowe,' I said to myself. 'You're a tough guy. You've been sapped twice, choked, beaten silly with a gun, shot in the arm until you're as crazy as a couple of waltzing mice. Now, let's see you do something really tough— like putting your pants on.' "

—Dick Powell coming out of a drug-induced nightmare in Edward Dmytryk's *Murder, My Sweet*
(Screenplay by John Paxton; based on FAREWELL, MY LOVELY, a novel by Raymond Chandler)
and (similarly)

—Robert Mitchum dittoing in the remake, Dick Richards's *Farewell, My Lovely*
(Screenplay by David Zelag Goodman; based on the novel by Raymond Chandler)

7.

(a) "Is that what my father taught you? Be a great Marine! Be tough! Well, you can sit here and be tough if you want to, but I'm going out there and get that guy, and the only way you can stop me is to kill me."
(b) "That's just what I'll do!"

—(b) John Wayne preventing (a) John Agar from walking into a possible enemy trap in Allan Dwan's *Sands of Iwo Jima*
(Screenplay by Harry Brown and James Edward Grant; based on a story by Harry Brown)

8.

"Now, look, Whitey. In a pinch I can be tougher than you are, and I guess maybe this is the pinch. You're coming with me to Boys Town because that's the way your brother wants it and that's the way I want it."

—Spencer Tracy laying down the law to Mickey Rooney in Norman Taurog's *Boys Town*
(Screenplay by John Meehan and Dore Schary; based on an original story by Dore Schary and Eleanore Griffin)

TRANSITIONS

1.

"I understand the Christians say that death is but a transition to a better life. It will be interesting to discover."

—Leo Genn bracing for the next life in Mervyn LeRoy's *Quo Vadis*
(Screenplay by John Lee Mahin, S. N. Behrman and Sonya Levien; based on the novel by Henryk Sienkiewicz)

2.

(a) "Oh, Pop, I've got me a beau."
   (b) "Have you, honey?"
   (a) "Not an 'always' beau, but a beau for meanwhile until he goes."

—Katharine Hepburn telling Cameron Prud'homme about Burt Lancaster in Joseph Anthony's *The Rainmaker*
(Screenplay by N. Richard Nash; based on his play)

ALSO SEE: Communication-11; Flowers-2.

TRANSLATIONS

1.

"Republic. I like the sound of the word. It means people can live free, talk free, go or come, buy or sell, be drunk or sober, however they choose. Some words give you a feeling. Republic is one of those words that makes me tight in the throat—the same tightness a man gets when his baby takes his first step or his first baby shaves or makes his first sound like a man. Some words can give you a feeling that make your heart warm. Republic is one of those words."

—John Wayne grandstanding in John Wayne's *The Alamo*
(*Original Screenplay by James Edward Grant*)

2.
"That's a Sicilian message. It means 'Luca Brasi sleeps with the fishes.' "

—Richard Castellano reading the death of Lenny Montana into the delivery of a fish in Francis Ford Coppola's *The Godfather*
(*Screenplay by Mario Puzo and Francis Ford Coppola; based on the novel by Mario Puzo*)

3.
(a) "Wainwright."
    (b) "Hmmm?"
(a) "What does prognosis mean?"
    (b) "It means what the future of a case looks like."
(a) "What does negative mean?"
    (b) "That's not so good. It means hopeless."

—(a) Bette Davis accidentally discovering she's doomed from (b) Dorothy Peterson in Edmund Goulding's *Dark Victory*
(*Screenplay by Casey Robinson; based on the play by George Brewer Jr. and Bertram Bloch*)

4.
"Adam Cook is my name. I'm a concert pianist. That's a pretentious way of saying I'm unemployed at the moment."

—Oscar Levant introducing himself in Vincente Minnelli's *An American in Paris*
(*Original Screenplay by Alan Jay Lerner*)

5.
"That is a B, darling—the first letter of a seven-letter word that means your late father."

—Rosalind Russell name-calling in code in front of her young nephew (Jan Handzlik) in Morton Da Costa's *Auntie Mame*
(*Screenplay by Betty Comden and Adolph Green; based on the play by Jerome Lawrence and Robert E. Lee and novel by Patrick Dennis*)

6.
(a) "I always have liked redheads."

(b) "You shouldn't. Red means stop."
(a) "I'm color-blind."

—(a) George Raft making a play for (b) Ann Sheridan in Raoul Walsh's *They Drive by Night*
(*Screenplay by Jerry Wald and Richard Macaulay; based on LONG HAUL, a novel by A. I. Bezzerides*)

7.
"A lot of women say no when they mean yes."

—Paul Newman taking Joanne Woodward's aloofness lightly in Martin Ritt's *The Long, Hot Summer*
(*Screenplay by Irving Ravetch and Harriet Frank Jr.; based on THE HAMLET, a novel by William Faulkner, and "Barn Burning" and "The Spotted Horses," two short stories by William Faulkner*)

8.
(a) "What does P. S. stand for?"
    (b) "Please Sweetheart."

—(a) Danny Kaye and (b) Walter Slezak going over a love letter in Henry Koster's *The Inspector General*
(*Screenplay by Philip Rapp and Harry Kurnitz; based on the play by Nikolai Gogol*)

ALSO SEE: Amateur-1; Love-28; Money-12; Names-6; Names-7; Sounds-2; Talent-1; Talent-2.

TROUBLE

1.
"Boss, life is trouble. Only death is not. To be alive is to undo your belt and look for trouble."

—Anthony Quinn advising Alan Bates in Michael Cacoyannis's *Zorba the Greek*
(*Screenplay by Michael Cacoyannis; based on the novel by Nikos Kazantzakis*)

2.
"George, I'm in trouble—real trouble, I think."

—Shelley Winters telling Montgomery Clift that she thinks she's pregnant in George Stevens's *A Place in the Sun*
(*Screenplay by Michael Wilson and Harry Brown; based on AN AMERICAN TRAGEDY, a play by Patrick Kearney and novel by Theodore Dreiser*)

3.

"I'm in terrible trouble, Norval. Somehow I just naturally turned to you. Like you said that night, you remember, you almost wished I'd be in terrible trouble so you could help me out of it? . . . Well, you certainly got your wish."

—Betty Hutton telling Eddie Bracken that she is pregnant in Preston Sturges's *The Miracle of Morgan's Creek*
(Original Screenplay by Preston Sturges)

4.

"You know, it takes two to get one in trouble."

—Mae West advising Rochelle Hudson in Lowell Sherman's *She Done Him Wrong*
(Screenplay by Harvey Thew and John Bright; based on DIAMOND LIL, a play by Mae West)

5.

"You see, Evelyn loved me. And I loved her. And that was the trouble. Oh, it would have been easy to find a way out if she hadn't have loved me so much. Or if I hadn't loved her. But, as it was, there was only one possible way. I had to kill her."

—Lee Marvin admitting murder to his barroom cronies in John Frankenheimer's *The Iceman Cometh*
(Screenplay based on the play by Eugene O'Neill; text edited by Thomas Quinn Curtiss)

6.

"Everyone has trouble at home. The only ones who deny it have had too much of it. I denied it for five years with the former Mrs. Dodd."

—William Holden projecting his own bad marriage onto Bing Crosby and Grace Kelly in George Seaton's *The Country Girl*
(Screenplay by George Seaton; based on the play by Clifford Odets)

7.

"Well, every man has his own sack of rocks to carry."

—Robert Preston consoling an equally troubled Ken Lynch in Delbert Mann's *The Dark at the Top of the Stairs*

(Screenplay by Irving Ravetch and Harriet Frank Jr.; based on the play by William Inge)

8.

"As long as there's no find, the noble brotherhood will last, but when the piles of gold begin to grow, that's when the trouble starts."

—Walter Huston warning of the corruption of greed in John Huston's *The Treasure of the Sierra Madre*
(Screenplay by John Huston; based on the novel by B. Traven)

9.

"Blackmail is not so pure, nor so simple. It can bring a lot of trouble to a great many people, and the blackmailer sometimes finds himself in jail at the end of it."

—C. Aubrey Smith warning George Sanders in Alfred Hitchcock's *Rebecca*
(Screenplay by Robert E. Sherwood and Joan Harrison; adaptation by Philip MacDonald and Michael Hogan; based on the novel by Daphne du Maurier)

10.

"What the hell are you talking about a tumor? Do you know what your trouble is? You don't have enough to occupy your brain so you put a tumor there to fill up the space."

—Martin Balsam calming his fretful wife (Joanne Woodward) in Gilbert Cates's *Summer Wishes, Winter Dreams*
(Original Screenplay by Stewart Stern)

11.

"Trouble with England, it's all pomp and no circumstance. You're very wise to get out of it, escape while you can."

—Humphrey Bogart welcoming Jennifer Jones and Edward Underdown to the expatriate fold in John Huston's *Beat the Devil*
(Screenplay by John Huston and Truman Capote; based on the novel by James Helvick)

12.

"Until you stirred Him up, I had no trouble with God."

—William Powell butting heads with the Christian will of his wife (Irene Dunne) in Michael Curtiz's *Life With Father*
(Screenplay by Donald Ogden Stewart; based on the play by Howard Lindsay and Russel Crouse and stories by Clarence Day Jr.)

ALSO SEE: Good-byes-6; Hanging-2; Joke-5; Life and Death-15; Mind-11; Prayers-13; Prayers-14; Right-3; Secrets-3; Stupid-2; Theater-4; Together-11; Wives-1; Women-13.

TRUMPET

1.
"Behold the walls of Jericho! Maybe not as thick as the ones that Joshua blew down with his trumpet, but a lot safer. You see, I have no trumpet."

—Clark Gable giving proper fanfare to the blanket wall separating his bed and Claudette Colbert's in the motel scene from Frank Capra's *It Happened One Night*
(Screenplay by Robert Riskin; based on "Night Bus," a short story by Samuel Hopkins Adams)

2.
"Suddenly, all the pieces fitted together. I knew how the crime had been done. The high note on the trumpet that shattered the glass. The glass with the nitroglycerine!"

—Fred Astaire solving a crime as he narrates "The Girl Hunt" ballet from Vincente Minnelli's *The Band Wagon*
(Original Screenplay by Betty Comden and Adolph Green; narration for "The Girl Hunt" ballet, written by an uncredited Alan Jay Lerner)

3.
"You see, Rick was a pretty hard guy to understand—and, for a long time, he didn't understand himself—but the desire to live is a great teacher, and I think it taught Rick a lot of things. He learned that you can't say everything through the end of a trumpet and a man doesn't destroy himself just because he can't hit some high note that he dreamed up. Maybe that's why Rick went on to be a success as a

human being first and an artist second. And what an artist!"

—Hoagy Carmichael winding up his narration of Kirk Douglas's story in the last lines of Michael Curtiz's *Young Man With a Horn*
(Screenplay by Carl Foreman and Edmund H. North; based on the novel by Dorothy Baker)

TRUST AND DISTRUST

1.
"The first thing to do is to make sure that he's dead. I don't trust him."

—Leo G. Carroll hardly lamenting the loss of Basil Rathbone in Michael Curtiz's *We're No Angels*
(Screenplay by Ranald MacDougall; based on LA CUISINE DES ANGES, a play by Albert Husson, and MY THREE ANGELS, a Broadway adaptation by Bella Spewack and Samuel Spewack)

2.
"Trust! The word has always made me apprehensive. Like wine, whenever I've tried it, the after-effects have not been good. I've given up wine—and trusting."

—Rex Harrison preferring to be sober and suspicious in Joseph L. Mankiewicz's *Cleopatra*
(Screenplay by Joseph L. Mankiewicz, Ranald MacDougall and Sidney Buchman; based upon histories by Plutarch, Suetonius and Appian and THE LIFE AND TIMES OF CLEOPATRA, a book by C. M. Franzero)

3.
"I distrust a man who says 'when.' If he's got to be careful not to drink too much, it's because he's not to be trusted when he does."

—Sydney Greenstreet getting down to cases with Humphrey Bogart in John Huston's *The Maltese Falcon*
(Screenplay by John Huston; based on the novel by Dashiell Hammett)

4.
"You know, Rick, I have many friends in Casablanca, but somehow, just because you despise me, you're the only one I trust."

—Peter Lorre recognizing the irony in his compliment to Humphrey Bogart in Michael Curtiz's *Casablanca*
(Screenplay by Julius J. Epstein, Philip G. Epstein and Howard Koch; based on EVERYBODY COMES TO RICK'S, a play by Murray Burnett and Joan Alison)

5.
"When a Dillon gets polite, lock the henhouses and reach for the pitchfork."

—Walter Brennan perpetuating a long-standing feud in David Butler's *Kentucky*
(Screenplay by Lamar Trotti and John Taintor Foote; based on THE LOOK OF EAGLES, a novel by John Taintor Foote)

6.
"I won't let myself fall in love with a man who won't trust me no matter what I might do."

—Marilyn Monroe telling off her boyfriend (Tommy Noonan) in Howard Hawks's *Gentlemen Prefer Blondes*
(Screenplay by Charles Lederer; based on the musical play by Joseph Fields and Anita Loos and novel by Anita Loos)

7.
(a) "Hasn't your own experience taught you the human heart can't be trusted?"
    (b) "I think I know my own heart better than you can, Monsieur, and I can trust it not to change."

—(a) Lionel Barrymore and (b) Greta Garbo battling over his son and her lover (Robert Taylor) in George Cukor's *Camille*
(Screenplay by Zoë Akins, Frances Marion and James Hilton; based on LA DAME AUX CAMÉLIAS, a play and novel by Alexandre Dumas)

8.
"Never trust anyone who functions from noble motives because they're never sure, and, in the end, they'll let you down."

—Yul Brynner advising Ingrid Bergman in Anatole Litvak's *Anastasia*
(Screenplay by Arthur Laurents; based on the play by Marcelle Maurette and Broadway adaptation by Guy Bolton)

9.
"But you're a bishop. You, of all people, can trust the word of an angel."

—Cary Grant pleading with David Niven in Henry Koster's *The Bishop's Wife*
(Screenplay by Robert E. Sherwood and Leonardo Bercovici; based on the novel by Robert Nathan)

ALSO SEE: Changes-3; Choice-9; Lies-4; Never-3; Never-4; Politics-4; Psychiatry-4; Selfish-3; Talk-2.

TRUTH

1.
"The Voice said to me, 'I want you to tell the people the truth, not an easy thing to do; because the people don't want to know the truth.' And I said, 'You're kidding. What the hell should I know about the truth?' But the Voice said to me, 'Don't worry about the truth. I will put the words in your mouth.' And I said, 'What is this, the burning bush? For God's sake, I'm not Moses.' And the Voice said to me, 'And I'm not God. What has that got to do with it?' And the Voice said to me, 'We're not talking about eternal truth or absolute truth or ultimate truth! We're talking about impermanent, transient, human truth! I don't expect you people to be capable of truth, but, goddammit, at least you're capable of self-preservation!' And I said, 'Why me?' And the Voice said, 'Because you're on television, dummy!' "

—Peter Finch explaining, on television, his calling in Sidney Lumet's *Network*
(Original Screenplay by Paddy Chayefsky)

2.
"The truth is that I'm an ordinary man. You might have told me that, Brighton."

—Peter O'Toole acknowledging that he's less than a god in David Lean's *Lawrence of Arabia*
(Screenplay by Robert Bolt; based on THE SEVEN PILLARS OF WISDOM, the autobiography of T. E. Lawrence, and other works by and about T. E. Lawrence)

3.

"I thought when I was a young man that I would conquer the world with truth. Thought I would lead an army greater than Alexander ever dreamed of, not to conquer nations but to liberate mankind—with truth, with the golden sound of the word—but only a few of them heard. Only a few of you understood."

—Walter Pidgeon addressing his congregation in John Ford's *How Green Was My Valley* *(Screenplay by Philip Dunne; based on the novel by Richard Llewellyn)*

4.

"Ladies and gentlemen, in all the years that I have been unsuccessfully mixed into politics, this is the first and only time that I have ever seen a candidate for office given an opportunity to prove publicly, permanently and beyond peradventure of doubt, that he was honest, courageous and veracious at being truthful."

—Harry Hayden praising Eddie Bracken in Preston Sturges's *Hail the Conquering Hero* *(Original Screenplay by Preston Sturges)*

5.

"Let's have the truth for once. You think you're on the side of the angels. Well, you're not. You haven't a drop of ordinary human forgiveness in your whole nature. You're a cruel, vengeful man. You're everything you always said you hated in your own father."

—Eleanor Parker telling off Kirk Douglas in William Wyler's *Detective Story* *(Screenplay by Philip Yordan and Robert Wyler; based on the play by Sidney Kingsley)*

6.

(a) "If you had any compassion or love whatsoever for this man, you could never call him a cunning drunkard."

(b) "Maybe I have a greater love for the truth. That's what he is. And I'm a drunkard's wife. That's the truth, too. And I think it's high time you stopped looking at everything as if it were a musical comedy and faced a little bit of it yourself."

—(a) William Holden and (b) Grace Kelly having different views of Bing Crosby in George Seaton's *The Country Girl* *(Screenplay by George Seaton; based on the play by Clifford Odets)*

7.

"Truth is pain and sweat and paying bills and making love to a woman that you don't love anymore. Truth is dreams that don't come true and nobody prints your name in the paper till you die."

—Burl Ives defining the word for his son (Paul Newman) in Richard Brooks's *Cat on a Hot Tin Roof* *(Screenplay by Richard Brooks and James Poe; based on the play by Tennessee Williams)*

8.

"Sebastian said, 'Truth is the bottom of a bottomless well.' "

—Katharine Hepburn quoting her late son in Joseph L. Mankiewicz's *Suddenly, Last Summer* *(Screenplay by Gore Vidal and Tennessee Williams; based on the one-act play by Tennessee Williams)*

ALSO SEE: Choice-2; Confessions-6; Dark-3; Desperate-1; Differences-5; Differences-10; Flattery-2; Letters-11; Lies-15; Lies-18; Life and Death-3; Love-27; Manners-12; Memory-1; Prison-2; Right-4; Toasts-8.

UGLY

1.

"I'm just a fat little man. A fat ugly man. . . . I'm ugly, I'm ugly, I'm ugly!"

—Ernest Borgnine berating himself in Delbert Mann's *Marty* *(Screenplay by Paddy Chayefsky; based on his teleplay)*

2.

"I was born ugly! Do you know how an ugly woman feels? Do you know what it is to be ugly all your life and to feel in here that you are beautiful?"

—Katina Paxinou arguing the case of inner beauty in Sam Wood's *For Whom the Bell Tolls*
(Screenplay by Dudley Nichols; based on the novel by Ernest Hemingway)

3.
"The older I got, the uglier I got. When I was a kid, they said, 'He'll grow out it.' But I guess a face like mine you just can't grow out of so easy. It's like it's cast in iron."

—Eddie Bracken being direct with Betty Hutton in Preston Sturges's *The Miracle of Morgan's Creek*
(Original Screenplay by Preston Sturges)

ALSO SEE: Beautiful-4.

UNDERSTAND

1.
"I understand we understand each other."

—Henry Daniell greeting Cary Grant in George Cukor's *The Philadelphia Story*
(Screenplay by Donald Ogden Stewart; based on the play by Philip Barry)

2.
"What's there to understand? You went with him, a pig like that. You had a child by him. Then, you went to that butcher Schneider—everything I hate. What's left to understand?"

—Kirk Douglas being unforgiving about the past of his wife (Eleanor Parker) in William Wyler's *Detective Story*
(Screenplay by Philip Yordan and Robert Wyler; based on the play by Sidney Kingsley)

3.
"It's very hard for a man to understand how a woman feels inside, although I tried to understand Frank—not that there's that much there to understand. That's why I was so hurt when he strayed. But, you know me, Joan. I always try to look on the bright side. I said to myself, 'Well, at least she's the one who'll be nauseous now.'"

—Beatrice Arthur discussing her husband (Richard Castellano) with her daughter-in-law (Diane Keaton) in Cy Howard's *Lovers and Other Strangers*
(Screenplay by Renee Taylor, Joseph Bologna and David Z. Goodman; based on the play by Renee Taylor and Joseph Bologna)

4.
"In the event of drunkenness—mine, not yours—I shall ask of you a depth of understanding one may expect only from children."

—Frank Morgan leveling with his new telegraph-office assistant (Mickey Rooney) in Clarence Brown's *The Human Comedy*
(Screenplay by Howard Estabrook; based on an original story by William Saroyan)

5.
"Do you know what I like about your program? Even when I'm running the vacuum, I can understand it."

—Thelma Ritter passing a dubious compliment about the radio show that her employer (Ann Sothern) writes in Joseph L. Mankiewicz's *A Letter to Three Wives*
(Screenplay by Joseph L. Mankiewicz; adaptation by Vera Caspary; based on "One of Our Hearts," a short story by John Klempner)

6.
"Oh, dear me. I must be losing my finesse. If I'm not careful, I'll be understood by everybody."

—Ina Claire recognizing the sharpness of her romantic rival (Greta Garbo) in Ernst Lubitsch's *Ninotchka*
(Screenplay by Charles Brackett, Billy Wilder and Walter Reisch; based on an original story by Melchior Lengyel)

7.
"As many times as I'll be married, I'll never understand women."

—Tony Randall throwing his hands up over the gender in Michael Gordon's *Pillow Talk*
(Screenplay by Stanley Shapiro and Maurice Richlin; based on a story by Russell Rouse and Clarence Greene)

8.

"You want to know something, Leslie? If I live to be 90, I'm never going to be able to figure you out."

—Rock Hudson remaining mystified by Elizabeth Taylor to the very end in the last lines of George Stevens's *Giant*
(Screenplay by Fred Guiol and Ivan Moffat; based on the novel by Edna Ferber)

ALSO SEE: Fear-9; Heart-12; Human-9; Talk-12.

UNFEELING

1.

"Now that was impertinent of him—to die with his rent unpaid."

—Basil Rathbone grousing to H. B. Warner in Jack Conway's *A Tale of Two Cities*
(Screenplay by W. P. Lipscomb and S. N. Behrman; based on the novel by Charles Dickens)

2.

"Very stupid to kill the only servant in the house. Now we don't even know where to find the marmalade."

—Judith Anderson acting very inconvenienced by Richard Haydn's murder in René Clair's *And Then There Were None*
(Screenplay by Dudley Nichols; based on TEN LITTLE INDIANS, a play and novel by Agatha Christie)

3.

"Well, then, let the story ride. It'll be forgotten in the morning. Oh, you remember the awful things they printed about that what's-her-name before she jumped out of the window? There. You see? I can't even remember her name—so who cares, Edith?"

—Rosalind Russell telling Phyllis Povah not to feel bad about passing a lie along to a gossip columnist in George Cukor's *The Women*
(Screenplay by Anita Loos and Jane Murfin; based on the play by Clare Boothe)

VANITY

1.

"Is it faith or just habit that compels a woman to put on fresh makeup before boarding a life raft?"

—Paul Kelly watching Jan Sterling get all dolled up in William A. Wellman's *The High and the Mighty*
(Screenplay by Ernest K. Gann; based on his novel)

2.

"He's the only man I know who can strut sitting down."

—Gene Kelly puncturing Fredric March's pomposity in Stanley Kramer's *Inherit the Wind*
(Screenplay by Nathan E. Douglas and Harold Jacob Smith; based on the play by Jerome Lawrence and Robert E. Lee)

ALSO SEE: Husbands-2; Love-18.

VICTORY

1.

"And tomorrow morning, you will have won your beachhead on the shores of Immortality."

—George Sanders congratulating Anne Baxter on the eve of her D-Day in the theater in Joseph L. Mankiewicz's *All About Eve*
(Screenplay by Joseph L. Mankiewicz; based on "The Wisdom of Eve," a radio play and short story by Mary Orr)

2.

(a) "Win what? What is the—the victory of a cat on a hot tin roof?"

　　(b) "Just staying on it, I guess, as long as she can."

—(b) Elizabeth Taylor struggling to keep her marriage to (a) Paul Newman afloat in Richard Brooks's *Cat on a Hot Tin Roof*
(Screenplay by Richard Brooks and James Poe; based on the play by Tennessee Williams)

ALSO SEE: Dark-5; Eulogies-18; Letters-9; Smell-1.

VIOLENCE

1.

"I caught the blackjack right behind my ear. A black pool opened up at my feet. I dived in. It had no bottom."

—Dick Powell taking a hard knock in Edward Dmytryk's *Murder, My Sweet*
(Screenplay by John Paxton; based on FAREWELL, MY LOVELY, a novel by Raymond Chandler)

2.

"He pulled a knife on me. A kitchen knife. It was still dirty from breakfast."

—George Burns blowing the whistle on Walter Matthau in Herbert Ross's *The Sunshine Boys*
(Screenplay by Neil Simon; based on his play)

3.

"There was me, that is Alex, and my three droogs, that is Pete, Georgie, and Dim, and we sat in the Korova trying to make up our rassoodocks what to do with the evening. The Korova milkbar sold milk-plus—milk plus vellocet or synthemsc or drencrom—which is what we were drinking. This would sharpen you up and make you ready for a bit of the old ultra-violence."

—Malcolm McDowell juicing up for a rough night out with the boys in the first lines of Stanley Kubrick's *A Clockwork Orange*
(Screenplay by Stanley Kubrick; based on the novel by Anthony Burgess)

4.

"When you're slapped, you'll take it and like it."

—Humphrey Bogart slapping around Peter Lorre in John Huston's *The Maltese Falcon*
(Screenplay by John Huston; based on the novel by Dashiell Hammett)

5.

(a) "Ah, Vincent, why do I do it? Here I pride myself on my sense of logic and order, and inside I'm a savage. I have this—this attraction to violence."

(b) "Violence makes me sick. You know, I have too much inside me. I'm afraid of it."

(a) "Ah, that's why I let it out before it hurts me."

—(a) Anthony Quinn and (b) Kirk Douglas advancing opposite views on violence in Vincente Minnelli's *Lust for Life*
(Screenplay by Norman Corwin; based on the novel by Irving Stone)

6.

"I don't like violence, Tom. I'm a businessman. Murder's a big expense."

—Al Lettieri being practical about it in Francis Ford Coppola's *The Godfather*
(Screenplay by Mario Puzo and Francis Ford Coppola; based on the novel by Mario Puzo)

ALSO SEE: Dying Words-19; Loneliness-9; People-6; Rules-4.

VULTURE

1.

"Mister, the stork that brought you must have been a vulture."

—Ann Sheridan returning Pat O'Brien's hostile fire in William Keighley's *Torrid Zone*
(Original Screenplay by Richard Macaulay and Jerry Wald)

2.

"Congratulations, Karl. You're still a lucky man. You must have been kissed in your cradle by a vulture."

—Kirk Douglas informing the criminal in his custody (George Macready) that the star witness just died in William Wyler's *Detective Story*
(Screenplay by Philip Yordan and Robert Wyler; based on the play by Sidney Kingsley)

3.

"Well, I suppose we'll have to feed the duchess. Even vultures have to eat."

—Shirley MacLaine playing reluctant Samaritan to her aunt (Miriam Hopkins) in William Wyler's *The Children's Hour*

(Screenplay by John Michael Hayes; adaptation by Lillian Hellman; based on her play)

4.

"The Mountain of the Seven Vultures? It's got a sound to it. Get me a few shots, Herbie."

—Kirk Douglas sensing instantly a cave-in story he can exploit in Billy Wilder's *The Big Carnival* *(Original Screenplay by Billy Wilder, Lesser Samuels and Walter Newman)*

WALK

1.

"George Amberson Minafer walked homeward slowly through what seemed to be a strange street of a strange city, for the town was growing and changing. It was heaving up in the middle incredibly; it was spreading incredibly; and as it heaved and spread, it befouled itself and darkened its sky. This was the 'last walk' home he was ever to take up National Avenue to Amberson Addition and the big old home at the foot of Amberson Boulevard. Tomorrow, they were to 'move out.' Tomorrow, everything would be gone."

—Orson Welles narrating Tim Holt's long crawl to a once lofty perch at the end of Orson Welles's *The Magnificent Ambersons* *(Screenplay by Orson Welles; based on the novel by Booth Tarkington)*

2.

"Oh, darling. Don't—don't worry, darling. If—if you can paint, I can walk. Anything can happen."

—A crippled Deborah Kerr reuniting with her lover-turned-painter (Cary Grant) at the end of Leo McCarey's *An Affair To Remember* *(Screenplay by Delmer Daves and Leo McCarey; based on an original story by Mildred Cram and Leo McCarey)*

3.

"Mein Fuehrer! I can valk!"

—Peter Sellers rising out of his wheelchair at the end of Stanley Kubrick's *Dr. Strangelove or: How I Learned To Stop Worrying and Love the Bomb* *(Screenplay by Stanley Kubrick, Terry Southern and Peter George; based on RED ALERT, a novel by Peter George)*

4.

"She came at me in sections. More curves than the scenic railway."

—Fred Astaire characterizing Cyd Charisse as she slinks into "The Girl Hunt" ballet in Vincente Minnelli's *The Band Wagon* *(Original Screenplay by Betty Comden and Adolph Green; narration for "The Girl Hunt" ballet written by an uncredited Alan Jay Lerner)*

5.

"Look at that! Look how she moves! That's just like Jello on springs. She's got some sort of built-in motor or something, huh? I tell you it's a whole different sex."

—Jack Lemmon going ga-ga at his first sight of Marilyn Monroe in Billy Wilder's *Some Like It Hot* *(Screenplay by Billy Wilder and I. A. L. Diamond; suggested by a story by R. Thoeren and M. Logan)*

6.

"Hey, I'm walking here! I'm walking here!"

—Dustin Hoffman banging his hand assertively on the hood of a car intruding on the pedestrian crossing in John Schlesinger's *Midnight Cowboy* *(Screenplay by Waldo Salt; based on the novel by James Leo Herlihy)*

7.

"Morris is funny, Cora. Sometimes, he just gets up and goes out for a walk. I never know why. He says the walk helps his digestion. I think it's just because he wants to get away from me once in a while."

—Eve Arden thinking correctly about her passive hubby (Frank Overton) in Delbert Mann's *The Dark at the Top of the Stairs* *(Screenplay by Irving Ravetch and Harriet Frank Jr.; based on the play by William Inge)*

ALSO SEE: Compliments-1; Democrats-5; Mistakes-7.

WANTS

1.

"A happy and efficient ship. A very happy and very efficient ship. Some of you might think I'm a bit ambitious wanting both, but in my experience you can't have one without the other. A ship can't be happy unless she's efficient, and she certainly won't be efficient unless she's happy."

—Noel Coward greeting his crew with their first order of business in Noel Coward and David Lean's *In Which We Serve*
(Original Screenplay by Noel Coward)

2.

"All I want is to enter my house justified."

—Joel McCrea getting his life's goal in one sentence in Sam Peckinpah's *Ride the High Country*
(Original Screenplay by N. B. Stone Jr.)

3.

"No mob ever wants justice. They want vengeance."

—Peter Ustinov fretting about the masses storming his palace gates in Mervyn LeRoy's *Quo Vadis*
(Screenplay by John Lee Mahin, S. N. Behrman and Sonya Levien; based on the novel by Henryk Sienkiewicz)

4.

"There are lovely teahouses in the big cities, but the men of Tobiki have never been inside them. We are too poor. All of my life I have dreamed of visiting a teahouse where paper lanterns cast their light in the lotus pond and the bamboo bells hanging in the pines tinkle as the breezes brush them. But this picture is only in my heart. I may never see it. I am an old man, sir. I shall die soon. It is evil for the soul to depart this world laden with envy or regret. Give us our teahouse, sir. Free my soul for death."

—Raynum K. Tsukamoto making an eloquent pitch to Glenn Ford in Daniel Mann's *The Teahouse of the August Moon*
(Screenplay by John Patrick; based on his play and the book by Vern J. Sneider)

5.

"Don't want no money, Ethan. No money, Marty. Just a roof over Ol' Mose's head and a rocking chair by the fire. My own rocking chair by the fire, Marty."

—Hank Worden keeping it to the essentials in John Ford's *The Searchers*
(Screenplay by Frank S. Nugent; based on the novel by Alan LeMay)

6.

(a) "Don't start flirting with me. I'm not one of your plantation beaus. I want more than flirting from you."

(b) "What *do* you want?"

(a) "I'll tell you, Scarlett O'Hara, if you'll take that Southern-belle simper off your face. Someday I want you to say to me the words I heard you say to Ashley Wilkes: I love you."

—(a) Clark Gable being direct with (b) Vivien Leigh in Victor Fleming's *Gone With the Wind*
(Screenplay by Sidney Howard; based on the novel by Margaret Mitchell)

7.

"Listen, Baby, you're the only real thing I ever wanted. Ever. You're mine. I gotta claim what's mine, or I'll be nothing as long as I live. You love me. You know it. You love me. You love me. You love me."

—William Holden claiming Kim Novak while he races to catch a passing train in Joshua Logan's *Picnic*
(Screenplay by Daniel Taradash; based on the play by William Inge)

8.

"I want—I, er—I want to make somebody happy. I want somebody to be glad he found me the way I'll be glad I found him. I want him to be able to tell me who he is and to tell me who I am too because, heaven knows, I have no idea who I am. And I want to be able to do things for him—all kinds of things—and he never has to say thank you because thank you is our whole life together. I guess it comes down to one thing: to make somebody happy."

—Katharine Hepburn pining for that "somebody" in Joseph Anthony's *The Rainmaker*
(Screenplay by N. Richard Nash; based on his play)

9.

"I want you to be a merry widower."

—Ali MacGraw making a noble deathbed-request of Ryan O'Neal in Arthur Hiller's *Love Story*
(Original Screenplay by Erich Segal)

ALSO SEE: Goals; Alone-1; Alone-2; Birds-3; Daughters-2; Daughters-3; Drunken Rantings-2; Excuses-5; Fathers-8; Foolish-1; Gentleman-2; Good-4; Heart-23; Home-3; Illusions-3; Intelligence-2; Jewels-1; Kindness-1; Kiss-19; Last Lines-23; Money-13; Moon-2; Moon-4; Mothers-8; Orders-5; Politics-2; Pride-2; Public Relations-2; Rejection-8; Tough-8; Women-2; Women-3.

WAR

1.

"I've talked with the responsible leaders of the Great Powers—England, France, Germany, and Italy. They're too intelligent to embark on a project which would mean the end of civilization as we now know it. You can take my word for it: there'll be no war!"

—Orson Welles bluffing and blustering through a pre-war press conference in Orson Welles's *Citizen Kane*
(Original Screenplay by Herman J. Mankiewicz and Orson Welles)

2.

"Fiddle-dee-dee. War, war, war. This war talk's spoiling all the fun at every party this spring. I get so bored I could scream. Besides, there isn't going to be any war!"

—Vivien Leigh putting things in improper perspective with her first words in Victor Fleming's *Gone With the Wind*
(Screenplay by Sidney Howard; based on the novel by Margaret Mitchell)

3.

"War? That's torn it! Bang goes the French ambassador. Oh, dear—well, who can I get to sit between these two dreary old ladies?"

—Vivien Leigh finding her seating plans for dinner unbalanced by war in Alexander Korda's *That Hamilton Woman*
(Original Screenplay by Walter Reisch and R. C. Sherriff)

4.

"Be seated. Now, I want you to remember that no bastard ever won a war by dying for his country. He won it by making the other poor dumb bastard die for his country. Men, all this stuff you heard about America not wanting to fight, wanting to stay out of the war, is a lot of horse dung. Americans, traditionally, love to fight. All real Americans love the sting of battle. When you were kids, you all admired the champion marble shooter, the fastest runner, the big-league ballplayer, the toughest boxer. Americans love a winner and will not tolerate a loser. Americans play to win all the time. I wouldn't give a hoot in hell for a man who lost and laughed. That's why Americans have never lost—and will never lose—a war, because the very thought of losing is hateful to Americans."

—George C. Scott addressing the audience like troops with the first lines of Franklin Schaffner's *Patton*
(Original Screenplay by Francis Ford Coppola and Edmund H. North; based on PATTON: ORDEAL AND TRIUMPH, a book by Ladislas Farago, and A SOLDIER'S STORY, a book by Omar N. Bradley)

5.

"And now I'm here to tell you that I have killed for my country, or whatever, and I don't feel good about it 'cause there's not enough reason, man, to feel a person die in your hands or to see your best buddy get blown away. I'm here to tell you it's a lousy thing, man. I don't see any reason for it. And there's a lot of shit that I did over there that I find fucking hard to live with. And I don't want to see people like you, man, coming back and having to face the rest of your lives with that kind of shit. It's as simple as that. I don't feel sorry for myself. I'm a lot fucking smarter now than when I went. And I'm just telling you there's a choice to be made here."

—Jon Voight deglamorizing the Vietnam War for American high-school students in the last lines of Hal Ashby's *Coming Home*
(Screenplay by Waldo Salt and Robert C. Jones; based on a story by Nancy Dowd)

6.
"We live in the trenches out there. We fight. We try not to be killed, but sometimes we are —that's all."

—Lew Ayres deglamorizing World War I for German high-school students in Lewis Milestone's *All Quiet on the Western Front*
(Screenplay by Dell Andrews, Maxwell Anderson and George Abbott; based on the novel by Erich Maria Remarque)

7.
"For us, the Battle of the Atlantic was becoming a private war. If you were in it, you knew all about it. You knew how to keep watch on filthy nights, and how to go without sleep; and how to bury the dead and how to die without wasting anyone's time."

—Jack Hawkins characterizing life and death aboard his ship in Charles Frend's *The Cruel Sea*
(Screenplay by Eric Ambler; based on the novel by Nicholas Monsarrat)

8.
"Well, boys, I guess this is it: nuclear combat, toe to toe, with the Rooskies!"

—Slim Pickens mounting his bomb as if it were a bronc in Stanley Kubrick's *Dr. Strangelove or: How I Learned To Stop Worrying and Love the Bomb*
(Screenplay by Stanley Kubrick, Terry Southern and Peter George; based on RED ALERT, a novel by Peter George)

9.
"Fried Jap coming down!"

—George Tobias indelicately noting an enemy plane in flames in Howard Hawks's *Air Force*
(Original Screenplay by Dudley Nichols)

10.
"This is not only a war of soldiers in uniforms. It is a war of the people—of all the people—and it must be fought not only on the battlefield but in the cities and in the villages, in the factories and on the farms, in the home and in the heart of every man, woman and child who loves freedom. Well, we have buried our dead, but we shall not forget them. Instead, they will inspire us with an unbreakable determination to free ourselves and those who come after us from the tyranny and terror that threaten to strike us down. This is the people's war. It is our war. We are the fighters. Fight it then. Fight it with all that is in us. And may God defend the right."

—Henry Wilcoxon preaching war from the pulpit in the last lines of William Wyler's *Mrs. Miniver*
(Screenplay by Arthur Wimperis, George Froeschel, James Hilton and Claudine West; based on the novel by Jan Struther)

11.
"Regina, don't speak of pleading. I'm no good for you. I was only good once—in a war. Some men should never come back from war."

—John Dall preferring battle to Ann Blyth in Michael Gordon's *Another Part of the Forest*
(Screenplay by Vladimir Pozner; based on the play by Lillian Hellman)

12.
"The duty officer asked General Ripper to confirm the fact that he had issued the go-code, and he said, 'Yes, gentlemen. They are on their way in, and no one can bring them back. For the sake of our country and our way of life, I suggest you get the rest of SAC in after them; otherwise, we will be totally destroyed by Red retaliation. Uh, my boys will give you the best kind of start: 1,400 megatons worth. And you sure as hell won't stop them now. So let's get going. There's no other choice. God willing, we will prevail in peace and freedom from fear and in true health through the purity and essence of our natural fluid. God bless you all.' Then he hung up. We—we're still trying to figure out the meaning of that last phrase, sir."

—George C. Scott relaying Sterling Hayden's message to the President (Peter Sellers) in Stanley Kubrick's *Dr. Strangelove or: How I Learned To Stop Worrying and Love the Bomb*
(Screenplay by Stanley Kubrick, Terry Southern and Peter George; based on RED ALERT, a novel by Peter George)

13.
"Madness! Madness!"

—James Donald summing up the insane turn of last-reel events in the last lines of David Lean's *The Bridge on the River Kwai*
(Screenplay by Pierre Boulle; based on his novel THE BRIDGE OVER THE RIVER KWAI)

ALSO SEE: Crazy-19; Fights-1; Fights-2; Hair-7; Letters-7; Money-11; Narcissism-7; Passion-4; Peace-1; Peace-2; Peace-3; Pep Talks-3; Progress-3; Questions-5; Responsibility-3; Telegrams-2.

WATER

1.
"Robbie, I've just had a most shattering experience. Did you ever look at a drop of water? All my life, I've had an instinct about that stuff. My instincts were: look at it."

—Charles Coburn, a drinking man, playing with the microscope of his great-grandson (Dean Stockwell) in Victor Saville's *The Green Years*
(Screenplay by Robert Ardrey and Sonya Levien; based on the novel by A. J. Cronin)

2.
"First drink of water he had in 20 years, and then he had to get it by accident. Bud, how do you wire congratulations to the Pacific Ocean?"

—Lionel Stander drinking to the drowning of an alcoholic actor (Fredric March) in William A. Wellman's *A Star Is Born*
(Screenplay by Dorothy Parker, Alan Campbell and Robert Carson; based on an original story by William A. Wellman and Robert Carson)

3.
"Of course, you all know who de Soto was? He discovered a body of water. You've all heard of the water that they named after him: de Soto water."

—Groucho Marx cracking wise in Joseph Santley and Robert Florey's *The Cocoanuts*
(Screenplay by Morrie Ryskind; based on the musical play by George S. Kaufman and Morrie Ryskind)

4.
(a) "I came to Casablanca for the waters."
    (b) "The waters? What waters? We're in the desert."
    (a) "I was misinformed."

—(a) Humphrey Bogart drily dodging the questions of (b) Claude Rains in Michael Curtiz's *Casablanca*
(Screenplay by Julius J. Epstein, Philip G. Epstein and Howard Koch; based on EVERYBODY COMES TO RICK'S, a play by Murray Burnett and Joan Alison)

5.
"Next time you fellas 'strike it rich,' holler for me, will you, before you start splashing water around? Water's precious. Sometimes it can be more precious than gold."

—Walter Huston cautioning Humphrey Bogart and Tim Holt about wasting water on "fool's gold" in John Huston's *The Treasure of the Sierra Madre*
(Screenplay by John Huston; based on the novel by B. Traven)

6.
"I'll give you water. Mr. Morrison, keel haul this man."

—Charles Laughton sadistically overfilling a seaman's request for a drink of water in Frank Lloyd's *Mutiny on the Bounty*
(Screenplay by Talbot Jennings, Jules Furthman and Carey Wilson; based on the novel by Charles Nordhoff and James Norman Hall)

7.
"You see, Mr. Scott, in the water I'm a very skinny lady."

—A very heavy Shelley Winters bragging to Gene Hackman after bringing off a difficult swimming feat in Ronald Neame's *The Poseidon Adventure*
(Screenplay by Stirling Silliphant and Wendell Mayes; based on the novel by Paul Gallico)

8.
(a) "If I remember rightly, tears are water, with a trace of sodium chloride. Isn't that so, Willie?"
(b) "Ya."
(c) "What about sweat? What's the chemical composition of sweat?"
(a) "Water, with a trace of something or other."
(d) "Now I remember. Gus said Willie had some water."
(e) "Yeah. Right under his shirt."
(b) "Quite so. I took the precaution of filling the flask from the water breakers before the storm just in case of emergency."

—(a) Tallulah Bankhead, (c) John Hodiak, (d) Hume Cronyn and (e) Canada Lee turning on the waterhoarder aboard, (b) Walter Slezak, in Alfred Hitchcock's *Lifeboat*
(Screenplay by Jo Swerling; based on the story by John Steinbeck)

9.
"*Cry?* I never knew a woman that size had that much water in her."

—Tony Randall informing Rock Hudson that Doris Day was indeed upset in Michael Gordon's *Pillow Talk*
(Screenplay by Stanley Shapiro and Maurice Richlin; based on a story by Russell Rouse and Clarence Greene)

10.
"I don't hold with too much water, anyhow. Rusts the bones."

—Percy Kilbride volunteering one of his idiotic opinions in Chester Erskine's *The Egg and I*
(Screenplay by Chester Erskine and Fred F. Finklehoffe; based on the book by Betty MacDonald)

ALSO SEE: Drink Excuses-5; Dying Words-15; Fear-1; Honor-7; Movies-2; Sea-1; Threats-9; Wine-3.

WEAKNESS

1.
"If you ever looked at me once with what I know is in you, I'd be your slave. Cathy, if your heart were only stronger than your dull fear of God and the world, I would live silently contented in your shadow. But no—you must destroy us both with that weakness you call virtue."

—Laurence Olivier damning Merle Oberon for betraying their love in William Wyler's *Wuthering Heights*
(Screenplay by Ben Hecht and Charles MacArthur; based on the novel by Emily Brontë)

2.
"I assure you it's finished. It's dead. For three years they couldn't talk me out of you. I was the only one that really understood you. I never knew there was a core of something. Well, there is a core, and now I know what it is: a sponge."

—Jane Wyman confronting Ray Milland in Billy Wilder's *The Lost Weekend*
(Screenplay by Charles Brackett and Billy Wilder; based on the novel by Charles R. Jackson)

3.
"Kittredge is no great tower of strength, you know, Tracy. He's just a tower."

—Cary Grant berating Katharine Hepburn's fiancé (John Howard) in George Cukor's *The Philadelphia Story*
(Screenplay by Donald Ogden Stewart; based on the play by Philip Barry)

4.
"Whether you like it or not, Frank's weak. He's a leaner, and I happen to be the one he leans on."

—Grace Kelly defining to William Holden her role as Bing Crosby's wife in George Seaton's *The Country Girl*
(Screenplay by George Seaton; based on the play by Clifford Odets)

5.

"Don't apologize. It's a sign of weakness."

—John Wayne dispensing his favorite piece of advice in John Ford's *She Wore a Yellow Ribbon*
(Screenplay by Frank S. Nugent and Laurence Stallings; based on "The Big Hunt" and "War Party," two short stories by James Warner Bellah)

ALSO SEE: Gin-6; Men-8; People-5; Prayers-7; Similarities-4; Threats-6.

WEALTH

1.

"That's it, baby! When you got it, flaunt it! Flaunt it!"

—Zero Mostel yelling from his shabby office to a conspicuous big-spender in Mel Brooks's *The Producers*
(Original Screenplay by Mel Brooks)

2.

"Bick, you should have shot that fella a long time ago. Now, he's too rich to kill."

—Chill Wills cracking wise to Rock Hudson about James Dean's sudden wealth in George Stevens's *Giant*
(Screenplay by Fred Guiol and Ivan Moffat; based on the novel by Edna Ferber)

3.

"Are you mountainously rich?"

—Vanessa Redgrave being direct with Jason Robards in Karel Reisz's *Isadora*
(Screenplay by Melvyn Bragg and Clive Exton; additional dialogue by Margaret Drabble; adaptation by Melvyn Bragg; based on the books MY LIFE by Isadora Duncan and ISADORA DUNCAN, AN INTIMATE PORTRAIT by Sewell Stokes)

4.

"With all the unrest in the world, I don't think anybody should have a yacht that sleeps more than 12."

—Tony Curtis impressing Marilyn Monroe with his "wealth" and "humanity" in Billy Wilder's *Some Like It Hot*
(Screenplay by Billy Wilder and I. A. L. Diamond; suggested by a story by R. Thoeren and M. Logan)

5.

"It was a nice little front yard. Cozy. Okay for the average family. Only you'd need a compass to go to the mailbox. The house was all right, too. But it wasn't as big as Buckingham Palace."

—Dick Powell drinking in the estate of Miles Mander in Edward Dmytryk's *Murder, My Sweet*
(Screenplay by John Paxton; based on FAREWELL, MY LOVELY, a novel by Raymond Chandler)
and (similarly)

—Robert Mitchum dittoing the estate of Jim Thompson in the remake, Dick Richards's *Farewell, My Lovely*
(Screenplay by David Zelag Goodman; based on the novel by Raymond Chandler)

6.

"Well, don't look at me. I got so many maids some of the maids are taking care of the maids. Can't say I blame the poor fellow. I just haven't got the kind of face that goes with a bankroll."

—Thelma Ritter bristling about being mistaken for a maid in Jean Negulesco's *Titanic*
(Original Screenplay by Charles Brackett, Walter Reisch and Richard L. Breen)

7.

"The dashing Kyle Hadley! I saw him dash through the office recently. It seems he misplaced his money belt."

—Lauren Bacall telling Rock Hudson about her first encounter with Robert Stack in Douglas Sirk's *Written on the Wind*
(Screenplay by George Zuckerman; based on the novel by Robert Wilder)

8.

"And while I'm on the broad subject of what I can't figure, I give you that phenomenon of this day and age called the international set. Once a year on the French Riviera, one of the most beautiful seashores on God's earth, the international set gather the way an annual fungus gathers on a beautiful tree. It's quite a set. It's as if ordinary human beings living ordinary lives had suddenly vanished from the earth, and the world was suddenly full of butterflies shaped like people. They are all happy all the time. Some of them are happy because they are beautiful, and some of them have to be happy because they are nothing but rich."

—Edmond O'Brien narrating a shift of scenery in Joseph L. Mankiewicz's *The Barefoot Contessa* *(Original Screenplay by Joseph L. Mankiewicz)*

ALSO SEE: Money; Always-3; Boredom-2; Pleasures-3; Pretense-6; Producers-2; Run-8; Static-11.

WEDDING

1.

"Stand still, Godfrey. It'll all be over in a minute."

—Carole Lombard calming a fidgety William Powell in the last lines of Gregory La Cava's *My Man Godfrey* *(Screenplay by Morrie Ryskind, Eric Hatch and Gregory La Cava; based on TEN ELEVEN FIFTH, a novel by Eric Hatch)*

2.

"You're going to have a wedding whether you like it or not!"

—Bette Davis threatening Debbie Reynolds in Richard Brooks's *The Catered Affair* *(Screenplay by Gore Vidal; based on the teleplay by Paddy Chayefsky)*

3.

"Marry? Oh, wouldn't it be marvelous if we could—have a real wedding and be given away

—church bells and champagne and a white frock and orange blossoms and a wedding cake. That's one thing I won't have missed, and you're giving it to me. I can never love you enough."

—Bette Davis accepting George Brent's offer in Edmund Goulding's *Dark Victory* *(Screenplay by Casey Robinson; based on the play by George Brewer Jr. and Bertram Bloch)*

4.

"We've decided on a white wedding, in spite of the circumstances."

—Ambrosine Philpotts planning the wedding of her pregnant daughter (Heather Sears) in Jack Clayton's *Room at the Top* *(Screenplay by Neil Paterson; based on the novel by John Braine)*

ALSO SEE: Dress-5; Last Lines-16; Tears-7; Why-4.

WHISTLE

1.

"You know you don't have to act with me, Steve. You don't have to say anything, and you don't have to do anything. Not a thing. Oh, maybe just whistle. You know how to whistle, don't you, Steve? You just put your lips together and blow."

—Lauren Bacall slinking out of Humphrey Bogart's room, dangling a proposition, in Howard Hawks's *To Have and Have Not* *(Screenplay by Jules Furthman and William Faulkner; based on the novel by Ernest Hemingway)*

2.

"I'm sorry, sir. I could never answer to a whistle. Whistles are for dogs and cats and other animals but not for children and definitely not for me. It would be too humiliating."

—Julie Andrews getting indignant with Christopher Plummer in Robert Wise's *The Sound of Music* *(Screenplay by Ernest Lehman; based on the*

musical play by Howard Lindsay and Russel
Crouse and THE TRAPP FAMILY SINGERS, *a book*
by Maria Augusta Trapp)

WHY

1.

"Then why did God plague us with the power
to think, Mr. Brady? Why do you deny the one
faculty of man that raises him above the other
creatures of the earth, the power of his brain to
reason?"

—Spencer Tracy cross-examining Fredric March in
Stanley Kramer's *Inherit the Wind*
(Screenplay by Nathan E. Douglas and Harold
Jacob Smith; based on the play by Jerome
Lawrence and Robert E. Lee)

2.

"Why don't you stop imitating a gorilla and
imitate a man?"

—Eugene Pallette asking too much of Mischa Auer in
Gregory La Cava's *My Man Godfrey*
(Screenplay by Morrie Ryskind, Eric Hatch and
Gregory La Cava; based on TEN ELEVEN FIFTH, *a*
novel by Eric Hatch)

3.

"Why don't you bore a hole in yourself and let
the sap run out?"

—Groucho Marx cracking wise in Norman Z.
McLeod's *Horse Feathers*
(Screenplay by Bert Kalmar and Harry Ruby, S. J.
Perelman and Will B. Johnstone)

4.

"By the way, when the minister asks if
there's any reason why these two should not
be joined together in holy matrimony, don't
be surprised if somebody in the back of the
room mentions a reason—loud and clear and
unpleasant."

—Jan Sterling getting off a parting shot at Joan Crawford in Joseph Pevney's *Female on the Beach*
(Screenplay by Robert Hill and Richard Alan
Simmons; based on THE BESIEGED HEART, *a play*
by Robert Hill)

5.

" 'As fit as a fiddle and ready for love,' though
why being as fit as a fiddle should make one
ready for love I never understood. How did
they decide that a fiddle was fit?"

—James Mason struggling to be lighthearted with
Judy Garland in George Cukor's *A Star Is Born*
(Screenplay by Moss Hart; based on a screenplay
by Dorothy Parker, Alan Campbell and Robert
Carson and original story by William A. Wellman
and Robert Carson)

6.

"Tell me why it is that every man who seems
attractive these days is either married or
barred on a technicality."

—Celeste Holm asking herself that in Elia Kazan's
Gentleman's Agreement
(Screenplay by Moss Hart; based on the novel by
Laura Z. Hobson)

7.

(a) "Why is it that women always think they
understand men better than men do?"
      (b) "Maybe because they live with them."

—(a) William Holden and (b) Grace Kelly arguing
over Bing Crosby in George Seaton's *The Country*
Girl
(Screenplay by George Seaton; based on the play
by Clifford Odets)

8.

"Why is it that a woman always thinks that the
most savage thing she can say to a man is to
impugn his cocksmanship?"

—William Holden counterattacking Faye Dunaway
in Sidney Lumet's *Network*
(Original Screenplay by Paddy Chayefsky)

9.

"Why me? Because I'm handy and know how
to use a gun or just because I wear pants?"

—Dick Powell responding to Claire Trevor's mur-
derous suggestion in Edward Dmytryk's *Murder, My*
Sweet
(Screenplay by John Paxton; based on FAREWELL,
MY LOVELY, *a novel by Raymond Chandler)*

10.

"You see, Mrs. Beragon, we start out with nothing. Just a corpse, if you'll pardon the expression. Okay. We look at the corpse, and we say, 'Why? What was the reason?' And when we find the reason, we find the man that made the corpse."

—Moroni Olsen explaining detective work to Joan Crawford in Michael Curtiz's *Mildred Pierce*
(Screenplay by Ranald MacDougall; based on the novel by James M. Cain)

11.

"Just this once, Kirk, why don't you empty your own ashtrays?"

—Edmond O'Brien finally walking out on his abusive employer (Warren Stevens) in Joseph L. Mankiewicz's *The Barefoot Contessa*
(Original Screenplay by Joseph L. Mankiewicz)

12.

"You know, I've never been able to understand why, when there's so much space in the world, people should deliberately choose to live in the Middle West."

—Clifton Webb making a snooty observation in Edmund Goulding's *The Razor's Edge*
(Screenplay by Lamar Trotti; based on the novel by W. Somerset Maugham)

13.

"Why anyone would want to live anywhere but Hong Kong I can't understand. Where else in the world could you get ten servants for the price of one?"

—Isobel Elsom doing cut-rate elitism in Henry King's *Love Is a Many-Splendored Thing*
(Screenplay by John Patrick; based on A MANY-SPLENDORED THING, a novel by Han Suyin)

14.

" 'Why'? Will no man ever do something without a 'why'? Just like that, for the hell of it?"

—Anthony Quinn preaching spontaneity to Alan Bates in Michael Cacoyannis's *Zorba the Greek*
(Screenplay by Michael Cacoyannis; based on the novel by Nikos Kazantzakis)

ALSO SEE: Death-4; Democrats-1; Hands-9; Mind-8; Pretense-9; Producers-1; Propositions-1; Propositions-9; Propositions-12; Truth-1; Worry-1.

WINDOW

1.

"For nine years I've tried to open some windows in his life, and now all you want to do is shut him up in some—in some safe-deposit box. Well, I won't let you do that to my little one! He's not little anymore—and he's not mine. But he's not yours, Mr. Babcock! Patrick won't allow you to settle him down in some dry-veined, restricted community, make him a—an Aryan from Darien and marry him off to some girl with braces on her brains."

—Rosalind Russell warring with Fred Clark over her nephew (Roger Smith) in Morton DaCosta's *Auntie Mame*
(Screenplay by Betty Comden and Adolph Green; based on the play by Jerome Lawrence and Robert E. Lee and novel by Patrick Dennis)

2.

"You're overwrought, Madam. I've opened a window for you. A little air will do you good. Why don't you go? Why don't you leave Manderley? He doesn't need you. He's got his memories. He doesn't love you—he wants to be alone again with *her*. You've nothing to stay for. You've nothing to live for, really, have you? Look down there. It's easy, isn't it? Why don't you? Why don't you? Go on. Go on. Don't be afraid!"

—Judith Anderson encouraging Joan Fontaine to jump in Alfred Hitchcock's *Rebecca*
(Screenplay by Robert E. Sherwood and Joan Harrison; adaptation by Philip MacDonald and Michael Hogan; based on the novel by Daphne du Maurier)

3.

"Take me to the window. Let me look at the moors with you once more, my darling. Once more."

—Merle Oberon making a deathbed request of Laurence Olivier in William Wyler's *Wuthering Heights*
(Screenplay by Ben Hecht and Charles MacArthur; based on the novel by Emily Brontë)

4.

"The Reverend Mother always says when the Lord closes a door somewhere He opens a window."

—Julie Andrews quoting Peggy Wood in Robert Wise's *The Sound of Music*
(Screenplay by Ernest Lehman; based on the musical play by Howard Lindsay and Russel Crouse and THE TRAPP FAMILY SINGERS, a book by Maria Augusta Trapp)

5.

"I opened a new window."

—Jane Connell explaining her pregnancy in Gene Saks's *Mame*
(Screenplay by Paul Zindel; based on the musical play by Jerome Lawrence, Robert E. Lee and Jerry Herman and AUNTIE MAME, a play by Jerome Lawrence and Robert E. Lee and novel by Patrick Dennis)

6.

"That's what I always say. Love flies out the door when money comes innuendo."

—Groucho Marx punning around with Maxine Castle in Norman Z. McLeod's *Monkey Business*
(Screenplay by S. J. Perelman and Will B. Johnstone; additional dialogue by Arthur Sheekman)

7.

"Through the window? That's a funny way for a cousin to leave."

—Humphrey Bogart noting the exit of Ava Gardner's amorous "cousin" in Joseph L. Mankiewicz's *The Barefoot Contessa*
(Original Screenplay by Joseph L. Mankiewicz)

ALSO SEE: Prison-2; Smell-8.

WINE

1.

"I never drink—wine."

—Bela Lugosi declining wine in Tod Browning's *Dracula*
(Screenplay by Garrett Fort; based on the play by Hamilton Deane and John L. Balderston and novel by Bram Stoker)

and

—Frank Langella dittoing in the remake, John Badham's *Dracula*
(Screenplay by W. D. Richter; based on the play by Hamilton Deane and John L. Balderston and novel by Bram Stoker)

2.

"It is widely held that too much wine will dull a man's desire. Indeed, it will—in a dull man."

—Narrator Michael MacLiammoir plainly making an exception of Albert Finney in Tony Richardson's *Tom Jones*
(Screenplay by John Osborne; based on the novel by Henry Fielding)

3.

"She insisted upon diving into the pool. And, when she hit the water, the wine hit her."

—Frank Sinatra explaining the soaked and soused Grace Kelly in his arms in Charles Walters's *High Society*
(Screenplay by John Patrick; based on THE PHILADELPHIA STORY, a screenplay by Donald Ogden Stewart and play by Philip Barry)
and (almost verbatim)

—James Stewart dittoing Katharine Hepburn in the original, George Cukor's *The Philadelphia Story*
(Screenplay by Donald Ogden Stewart; based on the play by Philip Barry)

ALSO SEE: Aging-14; Rules-2; Trust and Distrust-2.

WISDOM

1.
"Little story now concluded, but history of world unfinished. Lovely ladies, kind gentlemen: go home to ponder. What was true at beginning remains true. Play make man think. Thought make man wise. And wisdom make life endurable."

—Marlon Brando delivering the closing remarks in Daniel Mann's *The Teahouse of the August Moon* (*Screenplay by John Patrick; based on his play and the book by Vern J. Sneider*)

2.
"For one who has not lived even a single lifetime, you are a wise man, Van Helsing."

—Bela Lugosi complimenting his adversary (Edward Van Sloan) in Tod Browning's *Dracula* (*Screenplay by Garrett Fort; based on the play by Hamilton Deane and John L. Balderston and novel by Bram Stoker*)

and

—Frank Langella dittoing Laurence Olivier in the remake, John Badham's *Dracula* (*Screenplay by W. D. Richter; based on the play by Hamilton Deane and John L. Balderston and novel by Bram Stoker*)

3.
"If I ever acquire wisdom, I suppose I'll be wise enough to know what to do with it."

—Tyrone Power making sense in Edmund Goulding's *The Razor's Edge* (*Screenplay by Lamar Trotti; based on the novel by W. Somerset Maugham*)

ALSO SEE: Drink Excuses-9; God-3; Peace-7; Prayers-3; Prayers-11; Remember-5.

WISH

1.
"If you throw a coin into the pool, you're supposed to get your wish—only the wish must always be the same thing: that you return again to Rome."

—Jean Peters apprising Maggie McNamara of an old Roman custom in Jean Negulesco's *Three Coins in the Fountain* (*Screenplay by John Patrick; based on the novel by John H. Secondari*)

2.
"If I ever go looking for my heart's desire again, I won't look any further than my own back yard because, if it isn't there, I never really lost it to begin with."

—Judy Garland learning a lot from a trip to Oz in Victor Fleming's *The Wizard of Oz* (*Screenplay by Noel Langley, Florence Ryerson and Edgar Allan Woolf; adaptation by Noel Langley; based on the novel by L. Frank Baum*)

3.
"Oh brilliant, merciful master, let me out and I'll grant you three wishes!"

—Rex Ingram deal-making (from inside a bottle!) with Sabu in Ludwig Berger, Tim Whelan and Michael Powell's *The Thief of Bagdad* (*Screenplay and dialogue by Miles Malleson; based on a scenario by Lajos Biro*)

4.
"Now, wait a minute, Susie. Just because every child can't get its wish, that doesn't mean there isn't a Santa Claus."

—Edmund Gwenn clarifying things for Natalie Wood in George Seaton's *Miracle on 34th Street* (*Screenplay by George Seaton; based on an original story by Valentine Davis*)

5.
"As I grow old, this picture will remain always young. If it were only the other way! If it were I who was always to be young and the picture was to grow old."

—Hurd Hatfield wishing himself a horrible fate in Albert Lewin's *The Picture of Dorian Gray* (*Screenplay by Albert Lewin; based on the novel by Oscar Wilde*)

6.
"Oh, let me alone. I wish I really could die, go

someplace by myself and—and die alone, like an elephant."

—Carole Lombard regretting her doomed public image in William A. Wellman's *Nothing Sacred* *(Screenplay by Ben Hecht; based on "Letter to the Editor," a short story by James H. Street)*

7.
"You've got your wish: you've never been born."

—Henry Travers granting James Stewart an unusual perspective in Frank Capra's *It's a Wonderful Life* *(Screenplay by Albert Hackett, Frances Goodrich and Frank Capra; based on "The Greatest Gift," a short story by Philip Van Doren Stern)*

ALSO SEE: Suicide-3; Trouble-3.

WIVES

1.
"They cause me more trouble than the Methodist Church."

—Ray Walston cursing the lot as the Devil in George Abbott and Stanley Donen's *Damn Yankees* *(Screenplay by George Abbott; based on the musical play by George Abbott and Douglass Wallop and THE YEAR THE YANKEES LOST THE PENNANT, a novel by Douglass Wallop)*

2.
"They all start out as Juliets and end up as Lady Macbeths."

—William Holden generalizing from his own bad marriage in George Seaton's *The Country Girl* *(Screenplay by George Seaton; based on the play by Clifford Odets)*

3.
"Do you Alice, Ruth, Martha, Liza, Sarah, Dorcas, take these men to be your lawfully married husbands?"

—Ian Wolfe performing the finale wedding in Stanley Donen's *Seven Brides for Seven Brothers* *(Screenplay by Albert Hackett, Frances Goodrich and Dorothy Kingsley; based on "The Sobbin' Women," a short story by Stephen Vincent Benét)*

4.
"Six wives—and the best of them was the worst."

—Charles Laughton coming up with an irony from his many marriages in the last line of Alexander Korda's *The Private Life of Henry VIII* *(Original Screenplay by Lajos Biro and Arthur Wimperis)*

5.
"I've had five wives already. One more or less makes no difference to me."

—Charles Chaplin suggesting a "pretend marriage" to Claire Bloom in Charles Chaplin's *Limelight* *(Original Screenplay by Charles Chaplin)*

6.
"Buried three of 'em. Good women, bad diets."

—Arthur Hunnicutt discussing his wives with Art Carney in Paul Mazursky's *Harry and Tonto* *(Original Screenplay by Paul Mazursky and Josh Greenfeld)*

7.
"One wife? One god, that I can understand—but one wife! That is not civilized. It is not generous."

—Hugh Griffith becoming dismayed with Charlton Heston's objective in William Wyler's *Ben-Hur* *(Screenplay by Karl Tunberg; based on BEN-HUR, A TALE OF THE CHRIST, a novel by General Lew Wallace)*

8.
"You thought I loved Rebecca? You thought that? I *hated* her. Oh, I was carried away by her—enchanted by her, as everyone was—and, when I was married, I was told I was the luckiest man in the world. She was so lovely—so accomplished—so amusing. 'She's got the three things that really matter in a wife,' everyone said—'breeding, brains and beauty.' And I believed them completely. But I never had a moment's happiness with her. She was incapable of love, or tenderness, or decency."

—Laurence Olivier discussing his first wife with Joan Fontaine in Alfred Hitchcock's *Rebecca*

(Screenplay by Robert E. Sherwood and Joan Harrison; adaptation by Philip MacDonald and Michael Hogan; based on the novel by Daphne du Maurier)

9.

"A man wants his wife to be more than just a companion, Kathy—more than his beloved girl, more than even the mother of his children. He wants a sidekick, a buddy to go through the rough spots with, and—well, she has to feel the same things are the rough spots."

—John Garfield advising Dorothy McGuire in Elia Kazan's *Gentleman's Agreement*
(Screenplay by Moss Hart; based on the novel by Laura Z. Hobson)

10.

(a) "Now, that's it! I mean, you can shove aside all the older men you can find, but until you start plowing pertinent wives, you're really not working. That's the way to power. Plow 'em all!"

(b) "Yeah!"

(a) "The way to a man's heart—the wide, inviting avenue to his job—is through his wife, and don't you forget it."

(b) "And I'll bet you your wife has got the widest, most inviting avenue of the whole damn campus. I mean, her father being president and all."

—(a) Richard Burton and (b) George Segal kidding on the square about ambition and adultery in Mike Nichols's *Who's Afraid of Virginia Woolf?*
(Screenplay by Ernest Lehman; based on the play by Edward Albee)

11.

"Listen, honey, don't you know that we dames have got to be a lot more to the guy we marry than a schoolgirl sweetheart? We got to be a *wife*—a real wife! And a mother, too, and a pal. Yeah, and a nursemaid. Sometimes, when it comes to the point, we've even got to be a 'cutie.' You should have licked that girl where she licked you: in his arms. That's where you win in the first round. And, if I know men, it's still Custer's Last Stand."

—Paulette Goddard advising Norma Shearer in George Cukor's *The Women*
(Screenplay by Anita Loos and Jane Murfin; based on the play by Clare Boothe)

ALSO SEE: Actors-1; Adultery-3; Adultery-4; Choice-7; Dictation-6; Differences-5; Eat-6; Failure-5; Foolish-2; Good-byes-2; Love-39; Pep Talks-5; Pretense-6; Pretense-7; Stupid-5; Telephone Scenes-1; Tired-1.

WOMEN

1.

"Women, as so many Frenchmen put it, inspire us with the desire to do masterpieces and always prevent us from carrying them out."

—George Sanders popping off in Albert Lewin's *The Picture of Dorian Gray*
(Screenplay by Albert Lewin; based on the novel by Oscar Wilde)

2.

"I thought you were sexless, but you've suddenly turned into a woman. Do you know how I know that? Because you, not me, are taking pleasure in my being tied up. All women, whether they want to face it or not, want to see a man in a tied-up situation. They spend their lives trying to get a man into a tied-up situation. Their lives are fulfilled when they can get a man—or as many men as they can—into a tied-up situation."

—Richard Burton lashing out at Deborah Kerr in John Huston's *The Night of the Iguana*
(Screenplay by Anthony Veiller and John Huston; based on the play by Tennessee Williams)

3.

"I told you this sponsoring business was complicated. See what happens today? Women act like men and want to be treated like women."

—Oscar Levant counseling Gene Kelly about Nina Foch in Vincente Minnelli's *An American in Paris*
(Original Screenplay by Alan Jay Lerner)

4.

"Funny business, a woman's career. The things you drop on your way up the ladder so you can move faster. You forget you'll need them again when you go back to being a woman. That's one career all females have in common, whether we like it or not: being a woman. Sooner or later we've got to work at it, no matter what other careers we've had or wanted. And, in the last analysis, nothing is any good unless you can look up or turn around in bed—and there he is. Without that, you're not a woman. You're something with a French provincial office or a book full of clippings, but you're not a woman."

—Bette Davis putting her career in second place in Joseph L. Mankiewicz's *All About Eve*
(Screenplay by Joseph L. Mankiewicz; based on "The Wisdom of Eve," a radio play and short story by Mary Orr)

5.

"Now look, all I've been trying to say is this. Lots of things a man can do, and in society's eyes it's all hunky-dory. A woman does the same things—the same, mind you—and she's an outcast. . . . All I say is why let this deplorable system seep into our courts of law, where women are supposed to be equal?"

—Katharine Hepburn pointing out the inequality of it all to her lawyer-husband (Spencer Tracy) in George Cukor's *Adam's Rib*
(Original Screenplay by Ruth Gordon and Garson Kanin)

6.

"As my old friend Zannebaum used to say, 'Women make the best psychoanalysts till they fall in love. After that, they make the best patients.' "

—Michael Chekhov teasing his newly married ex-associate (Ingrid Bergman) in Alfred Hitchcock's *Spellbound*
(Screenplay by Ben Hecht; adaptation by Angus MacPhail; based on THE HOUSE OF DR. EDWARDES, a novel by Francis Beeding)

7.

"Well, Pa, women can change better 'n a man. Man lives—well, in jerks. Baby born or somebody dies, that's a jerk. Gets a farm or loses one, an' that's a jerk. With a woman, it's all one flow, like a stream—little eddies, little waterfalls—but the river, it goes right on. Woman looks at it that way."

—Jane Darwell explaining her gender to Russell Simpson in John Ford's *The Grapes of Wrath*
(Screenplay by Nunnally Johnson; based on the novel by John Steinbeck)

8.

"Dignity? I'm talking about women, man, women! I like 'em fat and vicious and not too smart. Nothing spiritual, either. To have to say 'I love you' would break my teeth. I don't want to be loved."

—Anthony Quinn advancing a different view of women from Kirk Douglas's in Vincente Minnelli's *Lust for Life*
(Screenplay by Norman Corwin; based on the novel by Irving Stone)

9.

"I have loved, with all my heart, 100 women I never want to see again—and he's still after this one. It escapes me."

—Anthony Quinn advancing a different view of women from Marlon Brando's in Elia Kazan's *Viva Zapata!*
(Original Screenplay by John Steinbeck)

10.

"And, as for women, you make fun of me that I love them. How can I not love them? They are such poor, weak creatures. They think so little. A man's hand on their breast, and they give you all they got."

—Anthony Quinn advancing a different view of women from Alan Bates's in Michael Cacoyannis's *Zorba the Greek*
(Screenplay by Michael Cacoyannis; based on the novel by Nikos Kazantzakis)

11.

"How extravagant you are, throwing away

women like that. Someday they may be scarce."

—Claude Rains observing Humphrey Bogart dispatch an alcoholic mistress (Madeleine LeBeau) in Michael Curtiz's *Casablanca*
(Screenplay by Julius J. Epstein, Philip G. Epstein and Howard Koch; based on EVERYBODY COMES TO RICK'S, a play by Murray Burnett and Joan Alison)

12.
"Do you know what he calls women? Dames! A dame in Washington Heights got a fox fur out of him. His very words."

—Clifton Webb questioning Gene Tierney's taste in beaus in Otto Preminger's *Laura*
(Screenplay by Jay Dratler, Samuel Hoffenstein and Betty Reinhardt; based on the novel by Vera Caspary)

13.
"Women sometimes make trouble. A woman can muck up a hunt plenty. They get bored. They don't like killing. They get lazy. Still, they want their money's worth."

—Gregory Peck trying to talk Robert Preston out of bringing Joan Bennett along in Zoltan Korda's *The Macomber Affair*
(Screenplay by Casey Robinson and Seymour Bennett; adaptation by Seymour Bennett and Frank Arnold; based on "The Short Happy Life of Francis Macomber," a short story by Ernest Hemingway)

14.
"There are two kinds of women: those who pay too much attention to themselves and those who don't pay enough."

—William Holden blocking them out for Grace Kelly in George Seaton's *The Country Girl*
(Screenplay by George Seaton; based on the play by Clifford Odets)

15.
"I'm an old woman, my dear. I know my own sex."

—Lucile Watson advising Norma Shearer in George Cukor's *The Women*

(Screenplay by Anita Loos and Jane Murfin; based on the play by Clare Boothe)

ALSO SEE: Always-1; Beautiful-6; Character-5; Compliments-2; Compliments-9; Courtroom Lines-5; Democrats-3; Don't-8; Don't-9; Honest-5; Honor-4; Jewels-3; Kiss-9; Kiss-10; Love-9; Love-32; Macho-2; Macho-5; Macho-10; Macho-11; Macho-13; Macho-14; Macho-16; Macho-18; Macho-19; Macho-21; Manners-7; Marriage-9; Marriage-17; Mind-11; Narcissism-2; Orchids-1; Pep Talks-5; Pride-2; Pride-3; Promiscuity-3; Promiscuity-4; Promiscuity-5; Proposals-2; Proposals-12; Sex Appeal-2; Sex Appeal-3; Spinsters-4; Suicide-3; Talk-6; Talk-7; Translations-7; Understand-7; Water-9; Why-7; Why-8; Wrong-4.

WORK

1.
"Work never hurt anyone. It's good for them. But if you're going to work, work hard. King Solomon had the right idea about work. 'Whatever thy hand findeth to do,' Solomon said, 'do thy doggonedest.' "

—William Powell inventing a Biblical flourish for the work lecture he's giving his eldest (James Lydon) in Michael Curtiz's *Life With Father*
(Screenplay by Donald Ogden Stewart; based on the play by Howard Lindsay and Russel Crouse and stories by Clarence Day Jr.)

2.
"You look down on me because I work for a living, don't you? You always have. All right, I work. I cook food and sell it and make a profit on it—which, I might point out, you're not too proud to share with me."

—Joan Crawford defending her waitress roots to a highborn lowlife (Zachary Scott) in Michael Curtiz's *Mildred Pierce*
(Screenplay by Ranald MacDougall; based on the novel by James M. Cain)

3.
"I haven't looked for work since I was a night watchman at Vassar."

—Bob Hope priding himself on unemployment in Hal Walker's *Road to Bali*
(Screenplay by Frank Butler, Hal Kanter and William Morrow; based on an original story by Frank Butler and Harry Tugend)

4.
(a) "I just happened to think of something. I got a job you can take a crack at. Of course, it isn't much, and I'm not begging you to take it, but it's a job."
(b) "Yeah. Well, that's all I wanted."
(a) "I mean, it'll keep you in coffee cakes, bottle every day, a place to sleep it off in. Whaddaya say? Anyway, it's only temporary—just until we can get a real geek."
(b) "Geek?"
(a) "You know what a geek is, don't you?"
(b) "Yeah. Sure, I—I know what a geek is."
(a) "Do you think you can handle it?"
(b) "Mister, I was made for it."

—(a) Roy Roberts giving (b) Tyrone Power a chance to be a sideshow freak in Edmund Goulding's *Nightmare Alley*
(Screenplay by Jules Furthman; based on the novel by William Lindsay Gresham)

5.
"I'm adamant. I will not have an officer from my battalion working as a coolie."

—Alec Guinness stubbornly insisting that only enlisted men do physical labor on the title bridge in David Lean's *The Bridge on the River Kwai*
(Screenplay by Pierre Boulle; based on his novel THE BRIDGE OVER THE RIVER KWAI)

6.
"On Nov. 1, 1959, the population of New York City was 8,042,783. If you laid all these people end to end, figuring an average height of five feet six and a half inches, they would reach from Times Square to the outskirts of Karachi, Pakistan. I know facts like this because I work for an insurance company—Consolidated Life of New York. We are one of the top five companies in the country. Last year we wrote nine-point-three billion dollars worth of policies. Our home office has 31,259 employees—which is more than the entire population of Natchez, Mississippi, or Gallup, New Mexico. I work on the 19th floor—Ordinary Policy Department—Premium Accounting Division—Section W—desk number 861."

—Jack Lemmon establishing his nebbish character with the first lines of Billy Wilder's *The Apartment*
(Original Screenplay by Billy Wilder and I. A. L. Diamond)

7.
"All right, everybody. Quiet and listen to me. Tomorrow morning, we're going to start a show. We're going to rehearse for five weeks, and we're going to open on scheduled time—and I mean scheduled time. You're going to work and sweat and work some more. You're going to work days, and you're going to work nights, and you're going to work between time when I think you need it. You're going to dance until your feet fall off and you're not able to stand up any longer. But five weeks from now, we're going to have a show."

—Warner Baxter greeting his chorus line in Lloyd Bacon's *42nd Street*
(Screenplay by Rian James and James Seymour; based on the novel by Bradford Ropes)

8.
"It is very sad. To love—and lose somebody. But in a while, you will forget. And you will take up the threads of your life where you left off—not so long ago. And you will work hard. There is lots of happiness in working hard. Maybe the most."

—Michael Chekhov comforting Ingrid Bergman in Alfred Hitchcock's *Spellbound*
(Screenplay by Ben Hecht; adaptation by Angus MacPhail; based on THE HOUSE OF DR. EDWARDES, a novel by Francis Beeding)

ALSO SEE: Professions; Men-10; Poets-1.

WORRY

1.

"Somewhere, sometime, there may be the right bullet or the wrong bottle waiting for Josiah Boone. Why worry when or where?"

—Thomas Mitchell showing the proper spirit(s) in John Ford's *Stagecoach*
(Screenplay by Dudley Nichols; based on "Stage to Lordsburg," a short story by Ernest Haycox)

2.

"Now what's the use of worrying? It's silly to worry, isn't it? You're gone today and here tomorrow."

—Groucho Marx advising Oscar Shaw in Joseph Santley and Robert Florey's *The Cocoanuts*
(Screenplay by Morrie Ryskind; based on the musical play by George S. Kaufman and Morrie Ryskind)

3.

"Oh, I ain't worried, Miss. Gave myself up for dead back where we started."

—Humphrey Bogart being chipper about the dangers ahead for him and Katharine Hepburn in John Huston's *The African Queen*
(Screenplay by James Agee and John Huston; based on the novel by C. S. Forester)

ALSO SEE: Adolescence-1; Crazy-14; Lasts-1; Never-5; Past-10; Plans-2; Professions-13; Sleep-3; Soul-5; Success-3; Tough-5; Truth-1; Walk-2.

WRITERS

1.

"All that inwardly-downwardly-pulsating-back-with-the-hair-across-the-pillow malarkey! No woman is safe around a guy who writes stuff like that—especially not on a hayride."

—Tom Ewell fretting about his wife (Evelyn Keyes) on the same hayride with Sonny Tufts in Billy Wilder's *The Seven Year Itch*
(Screenplay by Billy Wilder and George Axelrod; based on the play by George Axelrod)

2.

"I have no sceptre, but I have a pen."

—George Arliss choosing words over swords in John Adolfi's *Voltaire*
(Screenplay by Paul Green and Maude T. Howell; based on the novel by George Gibbs and E. Lawrence Dudley)

3.

"I don't use a pen. I write with a goose quill dipped in venom."

—Clifton Webb priding himself on being an acrid columnist in Otto Preminger's *Laura*
(Screenplay by Jay Dratler, Samuel Hoffenstein and Betty Reinhardt; based on the novel by Vera Caspary)

4.

"My native habitat is the theater. In it I toil not, neither do I spin. I am a critic and commentator. I am essential to the theater—as ants to a picnic, as the boll weevil to a cotton field."

—George Sanders characterizing his line of work in Joseph L. Mankiewicz's *All About Eve*
(Screenplay by Joseph L. Mankiewicz; based on "The Wisdom of Eve," a radio play and short story by Mary Orr)

5.

"Golly, to think you can put words down on paper like that and all I can do is hem brassieres!"

—Shirley MacLaine registering awe for Frank Sinatra's writing skill in Vincente Minnelli's *Some Came Running*
(Screenplay by John Patrick and Arthur Sheekman; based on the novel by James Jones)

ALSO SEE: Advice-8; Exchanges-14; First Lines-5; Headlines-4; Money-16; Narcissism-7; Newspapering-1; Propositions-15; Relatives-6; Sensible-4.

WRONG

1.

"How could this happen? I was so careful. I picked the wrong play, the wrong director, the wrong cast. Where did I go right?"

—Zero Mostel groaning over the hit on his hands in Mel Brooks's *The Producers*
(Original Screenplay by Mel Brooks)

2.

"Democracy is a system of self-determination. It's the—it's the right to make the wrong choice."

—Glenn Ford instructing the Okinawans in American values in Daniel Mann's *The Teahouse of the August Moon*
(Screenplay by John Patrick; based on his play and the book by Vern J. Sneider)

3.

"When women go wrong, men go right after them."

—Mae West counseling Rochelle Hudson in Lowell Sherman's *She Done Him Wrong*
(Screenplay by Harvey Thew and John Bright; based on DIAMOND LIL, a play by Mae West)

4.

"Even as a kid, I always went for the wrong women. I feel that's my problem. When my mother took me to see *Snow White*, everyone fell in love with Snow White. I immediately fell for the wicked queen."

—Woody Allen getting his signals crossed early in Woody Allen's *Annie Hall*
(Original Screenplay by Woody Allen and Marshall Brickman)

5.

"I certainly had him pegged wrong, didn't I? I thought he was just a rat, but he was a superrat all along—a superrat in rat's clothing."

—Audrey Hepburn grieving over a beau's marriage in Blake Edwards's *Breakfast at Tiffany's*
(Screenplay by George Axelrod; based on the novella by Truman Capote)

6.

"I chose the wrong man. How many times have you heard that said, I wonder? Oh, he was the most promising, the most handsome. He had the most glorious facade. The facade was all there was. He made me the best-known wife of the best-known skirt-chaser in the community. I made life hell for him. It ended in the divorce courts. We met one day in the corridor outside the courtroom. He struck me. I took every penny he had."

—Vivien Leigh relaying her bitter brush with love in Stanley Kramer's *Ship of Fools*
(Screenplay by Abby Mann; based on the novel by Katherine Anne Porter)

7.

"I hope I'm not saying the wrong thing, but I love you."

—Joan Fontaine saying the right thing to Cary Grant in Alfred Hitchcock's *Suspicion*
(Screenplay by Samson Raphaelson, Joan Harrison and Alma Reville; based on BEFORE THE FACT, a novel by Francis Iles)

8.

"No, I don't think I will kiss you—although you need kissing badly. That's what's wrong with you. You should be kissed and often and by someone who knows how."

—Clark Gable telling off Vivien Leigh in Victor Fleming's *Gone With the Wind*
(Screenplay by Sidney Howard; based on the novel by Margaret Mitchell)

9.

"You know what's wrong with you, Lewis? You've been sitting on a New Jersey porch for too long. You're out of touch. From my window here, I see everything that's going on in the world. Here I see old people, I see young people, nice people, bad people. I see holdups. I see drug addicts, ambulances, car crashes, jumpings from buildings. I see everything. You see a lawn mower and a milkman."

—Walter Matthau presenting himself as "current" to his former vaudeville partner (George Burns) in Herbert Ross's *The Sunshine Boys*
(Screenplay by Neil Simon; based on his play)

ALSO SEE: Mistakes; Beliefs; Defense-3; Genius-4; Life and Death-3; Love-38; Love Objects-3; Spinsters-4; Threats-7; Timing-1.

YOUTH

1.

"Youth! Stay close to the young, and a little rubs off."

—Maurice Chevalier advising Louis Jourdan in Vincente Minnelli's *Gigi*
(Screenplay by Alan Jay Lerner; based on the novel by Colette)

2.

"As we grow older, our memories are haunted by the exquisite temptations we haven't the courage to yield to. The world is yours for a season. It would be tragic if you realized too late, as so many others do, there's only one thing in the world worth having—and that is youth."

—George Sanders advising Hurd Hatfield in Albert Lewin's *The Picture of Dorian Gray*
(Screenplay by Albert Lewin; based on the novel by Oscar Wilde)

3.

"A pretty girl doesn't have long—just a few years. Then, she's the equal of kings. She can walk out of a shanty like this and live in a palace. If she loses her chance when she's young, she might as well throw all of her prettiness away."

—Betty Field advising Kim Novak in Joshua Logan's *Picnic*
(Screenplay by Daniel Taradash; based on the play by William Inge)

4.

"This is the Land of Legend where everything is possible when seen through the eyes of youth."

—Morton Selten welcoming Sabu in Ludwig Berger, Tim Whelan and Michael Powell's *The Thief of Bagdad*
(Screenplay by Miles Malleson; based on a scenario by Lajos Biro)

5.

"Young man. Young, young, young man. Did anyone ever tell you you look like a prince out of the Arabian Nights?"

—Vivien Leigh drifting toward a bewildered young bill-collector (Wright King) in Elia Kazan's *A Streetcar Named Desire*
(Screenplay by Tennessee Williams; adaptation by Oscar Saul; based on the play by Tennessee Williams)

6.

"Too young. I had a very young week last week. It's not worth it."

—James Mason cruising for just the right pickup in George Cukor's *A Star Is Born*
(Screenplay by Moss Hart; based on a screenplay by Dorothy Parker, Alan Campbell and Robert Carson and original story by William A. Wellman and Robert Carson)

7.

"We older men supply the champagne—but, when youth sings, the old fool stays home and pays the piper."

—Lionel Barrymore questioning Greta Garbo's commitment in George Fitzmaurice's *Mata Hari*
(Original Screenplay by Benjamin Glazer and Leo Birinski; dialogue by Doris Anderson and Gilbert Emery)

ALSO SEE: Disease-2; Flowers-2; Help-4; Hope-1; If-1; Live-3; Mistakes-4; Money-6; Toasts-19.

FILMS

A

ABBOTT AND COSTELLO MEET FRANKENSTEIN (Universal, 1948). Original Screenplay by Robert Lees, Frederic I. Rinaldo and John Grant. Directed by Charles T. Barton. Moon-7.

ADAM'S RIB (Metro-Goldwyn-Mayer, 1949). Original Screenplay by Ruth Gordon and Garson Kanin. Directed by George Cukor. Courtroom Lines-5; Differences-2; Women-5.

THE ADVENTURES OF MARK TWAIN (Warner Bros., 1944). Screenplay by Alan LeMay; additional dialogue by Harry Chandlee; adaptation by Alan LeMay and Harold M. Sherman; based on *Mark Twain,* a play by Harold M. Sherman, and works owned or controlled by the Mark Twain Company. Directed by Irving Rapper. Men-6.

THE ADVENTURES OF ROBIN HOOD (Warner Bros., 1938). Original Screenplay by Norman Reilly Raine and Seton I. Miller; based on the ancient Robin Hood legends. Directed by Michael Curtiz and William Keighley. Hanging-4; Hate-2; Pep Talks-4; Strange-11; Swear-1.

AN AFFAIR TO REMEMBER (20th Century-Fox, 1957). Screenplay by Delmer Daves and Leo McCarey; based on an original story by Mildred Cram and Leo McCarey. Directed by Leo McCarey. Advice-7; Beauty-2; Champagne-2; Heaven-9; Likes and Dislikes-3; Mood-Breakers-3; Promiscuity-4; Propositions-24; Seasons-3; Sex-2; Walk-2.

THE AFRICAN QUEEN (United Artists, 1951). Screenplay by James Agee and John Huston; based on the novel by C. S. Forester. Directed by John Huston. Clean-1; Firsts-12; Gin-4; Hanging-8; Hate-1; Idea-9; Joke-6; Nature-1; Never-16; Pity-4; Prayers-7; Realities-4; Stimulating-1; Stomach-1; Together-10; Worry-3.

AH, WILDERNESS! (Metro-Goldwyn-Mayer, 1935). Screenplay by Albert Hackett and Frances Goodrich; based on the play by Eugene O'Neill. Directed by Clarence Brown. Birth-5; Drunken Rantings-7; Eat-5; Eyes-16; Laugh-3; Seasons-2.

AIR FORCE (Warner Bros., 1943). Original Screenplay by Dudley Nichols. Directed by Howard Hawks. War-9.

THE ALAMO (United Artists, 1960). Original Screenplay by James Edward Grant. Directed by John Wayne. Life and Death-3; Translations-1.

ALGIERS (United Artists, 1938). Screenplay by John Howard Lawson and James M. Cain; based on *Pepe le Moko,* a novel by Detective Ashelbe. Directed by John Cromwell. Dying Words-18; Hypocrisy-1; Paris-4.

ALICE ADAMS (RKO Radio, 1935). Screenplay by Dorothy Yost and Mortimer Offner; based on the novel by Booth Tarkington. Directed by George Stevens. Feelings-3; Pretense-1; Roses-2; Talent-3.

ALICE'S RESTAURANT (United Artists, 1969). Screenplay by Venable Herndon and Arthur Penn; based on "The Alice's Restaurant Massacree," a song by Arlo Guthrie. Directed by Arthur Penn. Dogs-3; Signs-2.

ALL ABOUT EVE (20th Century-Fox, 1950). Screenplay by Joseph L. Mankiewicz; based on "The Wisdom of Eve," a radio play and short story by Mary Orr. Directed by Joseph L. Mankiewicz. Actors-3; Applause-1; Awards-1; Champion-3; Fools-13; Heart-14; Human-9; Humility-1; Introductions-3; Mood-Breakers-1; Night-1; Oops!-3; Piano-2; Producers-1; Similarities-3;

Star-6; Television-2; Theater-1; Toasts-16; Victory-1; Women-4; Writers-4.

ALL MY SONS (Universal, 1948). Screenplay by Chester Erskine; based on the play by Arthur Miller. Directed by Irving Reis. Questions-3; Repetitions-3; Self-Perception-8.

ALL QUIET ON THE WESTERN FRONT (Universal, 1930). Screenplay by Dell Andrews, Maxwell Anderson, and George Abbott; based on the novel by Erich Maria Remarque. Directed by Lewis Milestone. Death-2; Enemy-3; Fights-1; War-6.

ALL THAT MONEY CAN BUY (RKO Radio, 1941). Screenplay by Dan Totheroh and Stephen Vincent Benét; based on "The Devil and Daniel Webster," a short story by Stephen Vincent Benét. Directed by William Dieterle. Soul-1.

ALL THE KING'S MEN (Columbia, 1949). Screenplay by Robert Rossen; based on the novel by Robert Penn Warren. Directed by Robert Rossen. Men-3; Run-1.

ALL THIS AND HEAVEN, TOO (Warner Bros., 1940). Screenplay by Casey Robinson. Based on the novel by Rachel Field. Directed by Anatole Litvak. Friends-2.

AN AMERICAN IN PARIS (Metro-Goldwyn-Mayer, 1951). Original Screenplay by Alan Jay Lerner. Directed by Vincente Minnelli. Compliments-7; Dress-1; Faces-5; Feelings-9; Gigolo-2; Painting-1; Paris-3; Talent-2; Translations-4; Women-3.

ANASTASIA (20th Century-Fox, 1956). Screenplay by Arthur Laurents; based on the play by Marcelle Maurette and Broadway adaptation by Guy Bolton. Directed by Anatole Litvak. Fear-4; Identity Crisis-1; Joke-2; Last Lines-26; Life-4; Memory-5; Mind-6; Names-14; Past-9; Trust and Distrust-8.

ANCHORS AWEIGH (Metro-Goldwyn-Mayer, 1945). Screenplay by Isobel Lennart; based on "You Can't Fool a Marine," a short story by Natalie Marcin. Directed by George Sidney. Self-Depreciation-5.

AND THEN THERE WERE NONE (20th Century-Fox, 1945). Screenplay by Dudley Nichols; based on Ten Little Indians, a play and novel by Agatha Christie. Directed by René Clair. Dying Words-14; Never-4; Unfeeling-2.

ANGELS WITH DIRTY FACES (Warner Bros., 1938). Screenplay by John Wexley and Warren Duff; based on an original story by Rowland Brown. Directed by Michael Curtiz. Coward-1; Electric Chairs-2; Eulogies-14; Headlines-5; Heart-11; Hero-3; Pet Expressions-5.

ANIMAL CRACKERS (Paramount, 1930). Screenplay by Morrie Ryskind; based on the musical play by George S. Kaufman and Morrie Ryskind. Directed by Victor Heerman. Beautiful-8; Elephants-1.

ANNA AND THE KING OF SIAM (20th Century-Fox, 1946). Screenplay by Talbot Jennings and Sally Benson; based on the book by Margaret Landon. Directed by John Cromwell. Dictation-7.

ANNA CHRISTIE (Metro-Goldwyn-Mayer, 1930). Screenplay by Frances Marion; based on the play by Eugene O'Neill. Directed by Clarence Brown. Drink Orders-1.

ANNIE HALL (United Artists, 1977). Original Screenplay by Woody Allen and Marshall Brickman. Directed by Woody Allen. Books-2; Life-11; Los Angeles-1; Mellow-1; Narcissism-1; Psychiatry-6; Religions-6; Sex-1; Soul-18; Spiders-1; Static-2; Suicide-4; Thieves-7; Wrong-4.

THE ANNIVERSARY (20th Century-Fox, 1968). Screenplay by Jimmy Sangster; based on the play by Bill MacIlwraith. Directed by Roy Ward Baker. Eyes-2.

ANOTHER PART OF THE FOREST (Universal, 1948). Screenplay by Vladimir Pozner; based on the play by Lillian Hellman. Directed by Michael Gordon. Coward-2; Democrats-4; Don't-14; Hanging-3; Loneliness-13; Manners-10; Parents-3; Pity-2; Strange-2; War-11.

THE APARTMENT (United Artists, 1960). Original Screenplay by Billy Wilder and I. A. L. Diamond. Directed by Billy Wilder. Adultery-1; Decency-1; Divorce-3; Last Lines-2; Together-9; Work-6.

APOCALYPSE NOW (United Artists, 1979). Screenplay by John Milius and Francis Ford Coppola; narration written by Michael Herr. Directed by Francis Ford Coppola. Friends-10; Right-5; Smell-1.

ARSENIC AND OLD LACE (Warner Bros., 1944). Screenplay by Julius J. Epstein and Philip G. Epstein; based on the play by Joseph Kesselring. Directed by Frank Capra. Crazy-6; Dying Words-16.

AUNTIE MAME (Warner Bros., 1958). Screenplay by Betty Comden and Adolph Green; based on the play by Jerome Lawrence and Robert E. Lee and novel by Patrick Dennis. Directed by Morton DaCosta. Breasts-3; Dictation-1; Fingers-1; Flattery-3; Games-7; Greetings-9; Hair-2; Hangover-2; Heart-16; If-4; Indecision-4; Knowledge-4; Last Lines-10; Live-1; Party-4; Pittsburgh-2; Translations-5; Window-1.

THE AWFUL TRUTH (Columbia, 1937). Screenplay by Vina Delmar; based on the play by Arthur Richman. Directed by Leo McCarey. Rejection-12.

B

THE BACHELOR AND THE BOBBY-SOXER (RKO Radio, 1947). Original Screenplay by Sidney Sheldon. Directed by Irving Reis. Adolescence-2; Coward-5; Mind-9.

THE BACHELOR PARTY (United Artists, 1957). Screenplay by Paddy Chayefsky; based on his teleplay. Directed by Delbert Mann. Love-44.

THE BAD AND THE BEAUTIFUL (Metro-Goldwyn-Mayer, 1952). Screenplay by Charles Schnee; based on "Memorial to a Bad Man" and "Of Good and Evil," two short stories by George Bradshaw. Directed by Vincente Minnelli. Alone-9; Bottle-3; Directors-2; Exchanges-14; Feelings-2; Humility-2; Imagination-2; Love-12; Men-1; Party-1; Telephone Scenes-3.

THE BAD SEED (Warner Bros., 1956). Screenplay by John Lee Mahin; based on the play by Maxwell Anderson and novel by William March. Directed by Mervyn LeRoy. Drunken Rantings-4; Electric Chairs-1; Kiss-17; Lies-22; Names-26.

BALL OF FIRE (RKO Radio, 1941). Screenplay by Charles Brackett and Billy Wilder; based on "From A to Z," an original story by Thomas Monroe and Billy Wilder. Directed by Howard Hawks. Appearances-6; Life-5.

THE BAND WAGON (Metro-Goldwyn-Mayer, 1953). Original Screenplay by Betty Comden and Adolph Green; Narration for "The Girl Hunt" ballet written by an uncredited Alan Jay Lerner. Directed by Vincente Minnelli. Hate-7; Pain-2; Theater-2; Trumpet-2; Walk-4.

BANG THE DRUM SLOWLY (Paramount, 1973). Screenplay by Mark Harris; based on his novel. Directed by John Hancock. Death-9.

THE BAREFOOT CONTESSA (United Artists, 1954). Original Screenplay by Joseph L. Mankiewicz. Directed by Joseph L. Mankiewicz. Floozy-5; Hate-9; Heart-1; Life-7; Parting Shots-7; Producers-2; Public Relations-1; Screenplays-3; Star-3; Talent-4; Together-3; Wealth-8; Why-11; Window-7.

BAREFOOT IN THE PARK (Paramount, 1967). Screenplay by Neil Simon; based on his play. Directed by Gene Saks. Heart-1; Heaven-2; Marriage-7.

BEAT THE DEVIL (United Artists, 1954). Screenplay by John Huston and Truman Capote; based on the novel by James Helvick. Directed by John Huston. Laugh-4; Legs-2; Names-22; Sin-3; Time-1; Trouble-11.

BEAU GESTE (Paramount, 1939). Screenplay by Robert Carson; based on the novel by Percival Christopher Wren. Directed by William A. Wellman. Prologues-5.

BEAU JAMES (Paramount, 1957). Screenplay by Jack Rose and Melville Shavelson; based on the biography by Gene Fowler. Directed by Melville Shavelson. Marriage-4.

BELLE OF THE NINETIES (Paramount, 1934). Original Screenplay by Mae West. Directed by Leo McCarey. Proposals-13.

THE BELLS OF ST. MARY'S (RKO Radio, 1945). Screenplay by Dudley Nichols; based on an original story by Leo McCarey. Directed by Leo McCarey. Boxing-2; Goodbyes-5; Macho-4; Tact-2.

BEN-HUR (Metro-Goldwyn-Mayer, 1959). Screenplay by Karl Tunberg; based on *Ben-Hur (A Tale of the Christ)*, a novel by General Lew Wallace. Directed by William Wyler. Hate-4; Horses-3; Rome-2; Together-2; Wives-7.

THE BEST MAN (United Artists, 1964). Screenplay by Gore Vidal; based on his play. Directed by Franklin Schaffner. Dogs-6; Fools-12.

THE BEST YEARS OF OUR LIVES (RKO Radio, 1946). Screenplay by Robert E. Sherwood; based on *Glory for Me*, a verse novel by MacKinlay Kantor. Directed by William Wyler. Conflicts-4; Daughters-5; Drunken Rantings-1; Future-3; Love Objects-4; Money-11; Professions-12; Questions-17; Rules-1.

BEYOND THE FOREST (Warner Bros., 1949). Screenplay by Lenore Coffee; based on the novel by Stuart Engstrand. Directed by King Vidor. Boredom-1; Home-5.

THE BIG CARNIVAL, a.k.a. ACE IN THE HOLE (Paramount, 1951). Original Screenplay by Billy Wilder, Lesser Samuels, and Walter Newman. Directed by Billy Wilder. Church-2; Dying Words-5; Lies-19; New York-2; Newspapering-6; Religions-4; Static-15; Tough-2; Vulture-4.

THE BIG HEAT (Columbia, 1953). Screenplay by Sydney Boehm; based on a story by William P. McGivern. Directed by Fritz Lang. Furnishings-1.

BIG JIM McLAIN (Warner Bros., 1952). Screenplay by James Edward Grant, Richard English, and Eric Taylor; based on a story by Richard English. Directed by Edward Ludwig. Don't-10.

THE BIG KNIFE (United Artists, 1955). Screenplay by James Poe; based on the play by Clifford Odets. Directed by Robert Aldrich. Floozy-4.

THE BIG SLEEP (Warner Bros., 1946). Screenplay by William Faulkner, Leigh Brackett, and Jules Furthman; based on the novel by Raymond Chandler. Directed by Howard Hawks. Business-2; Cigarette-5; Detectives-4; Floozy-6; Guns-2; Manners-8; Orchids-2; Parents-4; Propositions-22; Spiders-2.

THE BIG SLEEP (United Artists, 1978). Screenplay by Michael Winner; based on the novel by Raymond Chandler. Directed by Michael Winner. Spiders-2.

THE BISHOP'S WIFE (RKO Radio, 1947). Screenplay by Robert E. Sherwood and Leonardo Bercovici; based on the novel by Robert Nathan. Directed by Henry Koster. Dictation-4; Differences-9; Fights-9; Secrets-2; Trust and Distrust-9.

BLUE MURDER AT ST. TRINIAN'S (Continental Distributing, 1957). Screenplay by Frank Launder, Val Valentine, and Sidney Gilliat; inspired by the cartoon drawings of Ronald Searle. Directed by Frank Launder. Callings-2.

BLUME IN LOVE (Warner Bros., 1973). Original Screenplay by Paul Mazursky. Directed by Paul Mazursky. Love-3; Propositions-14.

BONNIE AND CLYDE (Warner Bros., 1967). Original Screenplay by David Newman and Robert Benton. Directed by Arthur Penn. First Lines-6; Thieves-8.

BORDERTOWN (Warner Bros., 1935). Screenplay by Laird Doyle and Wallace Smith; adaptation by Robert Lord; based on the novel by Carroll Graham. Directed by Archie Mayo. Fun-5; Heart-15; Murder-6.

BORN YESTERDAY (Columbia, 1950). Screenplay by Albert Mannheimer; based on the play by Garson Kanin. Directed by George Cukor. Birds-3; Dismissals-3; Gin-1; Greetings-11; Ignorance-4; Intelligence-2; Life and Death-5; Manners-4; Royalty-8; Selfish-1; Star-7; Toasts-8.

THE BOY WITH GREEN HAIR (RKO Radio, 1948). Screenplay by Ben Barzman and Alfred Lewis Levitt; based on a short story by Betsy Beaton. Directed by Joseph Losey. Hair-5.

BOYS TOWN (Metro-Goldwyn-Mayer, 1938). Screenplay by John Meehan and Dore Schary; based on an original story by Dore Schary and Eleanore Griffin. Directed by Norman Taurog. Home-3; Tough-8.

BREAKFAST AT TIFFANY'S (Paramount, 1961). Screenplay by George Axelrod; based on the novella by Truman Capote. Directed by Blake Edwards. Bathroom-5; Callings-8; Diamonds-6; Dismissals-2; Faces-10; Fake-2; Fear-5; Feelings-1; Gigolo-5; Headlines-7; Honest-7; Idea-1; Love-25; Pet Expressions-11; Prison-4; Self-Perception-4; Strange-4; Style-2; Wrong-5.

THE BRIDE CAME C.O.D. (Warner Bros., 1941). Screenplay by Julius J. Epstein and Philip G. Epstein; based on a story by Kenneth Earl and M. M. Musselman. Directed by William Keighley. Differences-6; Kiss-13; Run-8.

THE BRIDE OF FRANKENSTEIN (Universal, 1935). Screenplay by William Hurlbut and John L. Balderston; suggested by *Frankenstein*, a novel by Mary Wollstonecraft Shelley. Directed by James Whale. Gin-6; Toasts-9.

THE BRIDE WALKS OUT (RKO Radio, 1936). Screenplay by P. J. Wolfson and Philip G. Epstein; based on a story by Howard Emmett Rogers. Directed by Leigh Jason. Pittsburgh-1.

THE BRIDGE ON THE RIVER KWAI (Columbia, 1957). Screenplay by Pierre Boulle; based on his novel, *The Bridge Over the River Kwai*. Directed by David Lean. Crazy-18; Pet Expressions-4; Propositions-16; War-13; Work-5.

BRIEF ENCOUNTER (Universal, 1946). Screenplay by David Lean, Anthony Havelock-Allan, and Ronald Neame; based on *Still Life*, a one-act play by Noel Coward. Directed by David Lean. Lasts-4; Loneliness-9.

BRINGING UP BABY (RKO Radio, 1938). Screenplay by Dudley Nichols and Hagar Wilde; based on a story by Hagar Wilde. Directed by Howard Hawks. Butterflies-2; Conflict-1; Crazy-1; Quiet-2.

BROADWAY MELODY OF 1938 (Metro-Goldwyn-Mayer, 1937). Screenplay by Jack McGowan; based on a story by Jack McGowan and Sid Silvers; special lyrics for the song, "You Made Me Love You," by Roger Edens. Directed by Roy Del Ruth. Letters-5.

THE BROWNING VERSION (Universal, 1951). Screenplay by Terence Rattigan; based on his play. Directed by Anthony Asquith. Epitaphs-2; Incompatibility-1; Laugh-5; Life and Death-11; Love-36; Roses-4; Soul-11.

BUS STOP (20th Century-Fox, 1956). Screenplay by George Axelrod; based on the play by William Inge. Directed by Joshua Logan. Angel-1.

BUTTERFIELD 8 (Metro-Goldwyn-Mayer, 1960). Screenplay by Charles Schnee and John Michael Hayes; based on the novel by John O'Hara. Directed by Daniel Mann. Apology-2; Eulogies-15; Floozy-1; Frigidity-4; Joke-4; Live-4; Past-7; Pride-4; Psychiatry-5; Static-9.

BUTTERFLIES ARE FREE (Columbia, 1972). Screenplay by Leonard Gershe; based on his play. Directed by Milton Katselas. Soul-17.

C

CABIN IN THE COTTON (Warner Bros., 1932). Screenplay by Paul Green; based on the novel by Harry Harrison Kroll. Directed by Michael Curtiz. Hair-1.

CACTUS FLOWER (Columbia, 1969). Screenplay by I. A. L. Diamond; based on *Fleur de Cactus,* a French play by Pierre Barillet and Jean-Pierre Gredy and Broadway adaptation by Abe Burrows. Directed by Gene Saks. Lies-7.

THE CAINE MUTINY (Columbia, 1954). Screenplay by Stanley Roberts; additional dialogue by Michael Blankfort; based on the novel by Herman Wouk. Directed by Edward Dmytryk. Insults-3; Mad Act-3; Names-2; Orders-7; Toasts-12.

CALIFORNIA SUITE (Columbia, 1978). Screenplay by Neil Simon; based on his play. Directed by Herbert Ross. Aging-7; Callings-10; Dress-8; Drunk-5; Excuses-6; Hope-4; Life-9; Los Angeles-2; Mind-5; New York-1; Pretense-9; Taste-1; Timing-5.

CALL ME MADAM (20th Century-Fox, 1953). Screenplay by Arthur Sheekman; based on the musical play by Howard Lindsay and Russel Crouse. Directed by Walter Lang. Smile-2.

CAMILLE (Metro-Goldwyn-Mayer, 1936). Screenplay by Zoë Akins, Frances Marion, and James Hilton; based on *La Dame aux Camelias,* a play and novel by Alexandre Dumas. Directed by George Cukor. Always-2; Boredom-4; Dying Words-3; Fidelity-3; Love-19; Trust and Distrust-7.

CAREFREE (RKO Radio, 1938). Screenplay by Ernest Pagano and Allan Scott; adaptation by Dudley Nichols and Hagar Wilde; based on a story by Marian Ainslee and Guy Endore. Directed by Mark Sandrich. Psychiatry-3.

CARNAL KNOWLEDGE (Avco Embassy, 1971). Original Screenplay by Jules Feiffer. Directed by Mike Nichols. Love-31; Self-Depreciation-3.

CASABLANCA (Warner Bros., 1942). Screenplay by Julius J. Epstein, Philip G. Epstein and Howard Koch; based on *Everybody Comes to Rick's,* a play by Murray Burnett and Joan Alison. Directed by Michael Curtiz. Business-3; Convictions-3; Democrats-3; Friends-1; Good-byes-1; Heart-20; Insults-5; Neck-1; Orders-2; Paris-2; Professions-7; Remember-2; Specializations-3; Tact-5; Time-19; Toasts-1; Trust and Distrust-4; Water-4; Women-11.

THE CAT AND THE CANARY (Paramount, 1939). Screenplay by Walter De Leon and Lynn Starling; based on the play by John Willard. Directed by Elliott Nugent. Bravado-2; Crooked-2; Fear-2; Republicans-1.

CAT ON A HOT TIN ROOF (Metro-Goldwyn-Mayer, 1958). Screenplay by Richard Brooks and James Poe; based on the play by Tennessee Williams. Directed by Richard Brooks. Bed-1; Big-3; Birth-4; Birthdays-5; Children-3; Conflict-3; Desperate-1; Drink Excuses-11; Fathers-8; Feelings-4; Football-1; Hero-5; Hypocrisy-4; Illusions-5; Lies-17; Lock-1; Love-28; Money-6; Neck-3; Responsibility-2; Run-3; Smell-10; Threats-10; Truth-7; Victory-2.

CATCH-22. (Paramount, 1970). Screenplay by Buck Henry; based on the novel by Joseph Heller. Directed by Mike Nichols. Crazy-19.

THE CATERED AFFAIR (Metro-Goldwyn-Mayer, 1956). Screenplay by Gore Vidal; based on the teleplay by Paddy Chayefsky. Directed by Richard Brooks. Wedding-2.

THE CHALK GARDEN (Universal, 1964). Screenplay by John Michael Hayes; based on the play by Enid Bagnold. Directed by Ronald Neame. Aging-14; Appearances-1; Convictions-1; Curses-3; Drink-7; Empa-

thy-6; Flowers-4; God-6; Help-3; Kindness-4; Lock-4; Mothers-6; Murder-9; Privacy-2; Remember-7; Talk-11.

CHAMPION (United Artists, 1949). Screenplay by Carl Foreman; based on the short story by Ring Lardner. Directed by Mark Robson. Applause-3; Blood-3; Body-6; Boxing-1; Callings-6; Champion-2; Eulogies-8; Fathers-4; Lady-3; Love-20; Propositions-19; Smell-3.

THE CHILDREN'S HOUR (United Artists, 1962). Screenplay by John Michael Hayes; adaptation by Lillian Hellman; based on her play. Directed by William Wyler. Apology-3; Honest-1; Human-8; Lies-18; Vulture-3.

CHRISTMAS IN JULY (Paramount, 1940). Original Screenplay by Preston Sturges. Directed by Preston Sturges. Advertising Slogans-1; Success-3.

THE CITADEL (Metro-Goldwyn-Mayer, 1938). Screenplay by Ian Dalrymple, Frank Wead, and Elizabeth Hill; additional dialogue by Emlyn Williams; based on the novel by A. J. Cronin. Directed by King Vidor. Defense-3; Doctors-3; Drink Excuses-2; Murder-10; Notes-2.

CITIZEN KANE (RKO Radio, 1941). Original Screenplay by Herman J. Mankiewicz and Orson Welles. Directed by Orson Welles. Always-3; Amateur-3; Death-6; Disease-1; Drunken Rantings-5; Eulogies-10; Firings-1; First Lines-2; Friends-5; Fun-1; Headlines-4; History-3; Idea-6; Loneliness-1; Love-40; Memory-3; Money-18; Newspapering-5; Professions-1; Questions-8; Rejection-3; Secrets-3; Telegrams-2; Toasts-15; War-1.

CITY FOR CONQUEST (Warner Bros., 1940). Screenplay by John Wexley; based on the novel by Aben Kandel. Directed by Anatole Litvak. Applause-2; Curtain Speeches-5; Hair-3; Prison-2.

CLAUDINE (20th Century-Fox, 1974). Original Screenplay by Tina Pine and Lester Pine. Directed by John Berry. Home-7.

CLEOPATRA (20th Century-Fox, 1963). Screenplay by Joseph L. Mankiewicz, Ranald MacDougall, and Sidney Buchman; based upon histories by Plutarch, Suetonius and Appian and *The Life and Times of Cleopatra,* a book by C. M. Franzero. Directed by Joseph L. Mankiewicz. Beautiful-7; Dying Words-31; Fear-3; God-3; Head-4; Insults-1; Life and Death-18; Love-24; Macho-10; Past-5; Silence-1; Time-4; Trust and Distrust-2.

A CLOCKWORK ORANGE (Warner Bros., 1971). Screenplay by Stanley Kubrick; based on the novel by Anthony Burgess. Directed by Stanley Kubrick. Violence-3.

THE COCOANUTS (Paramount, 1929). Screenplay by Morrie Ryskind; based on the musical play by George S. Kaufman and Morrie Ryskind. Directed by Joseph Santley and Robert Florey. Eyes-12; Firings-8; Heart-7; Home-13; Identity Crisis-2; Introductions-9; Moon-8; Prison-7; Propositions-23; Success-6; Water-3; Worry-2.

COME BACK, LITTLE SHEBA (Paramount, 1952). Screenplay by Ketti Frings; based on the play by William Inge. Directed by Daniel Mann. Dogs-4; Dreams-4; Innocent-2; Prayers-11; Seasons-5; Self-Depreciation-4; Smile-5; Static-13; Telephone Scenes-8.

COME FILL THE CUP (Warner Bros., 1951). Screenplay by Ivan Goff and Ben Roberts; based on the novel by Harlan Ware. Directed by Gordon Douglas. Drink Excuses-1; Newspapering-4.

COMING HOME (United Artists, 1978). Screenplay by Waldo Salt and Robert C. Jones; based on a story by Nancy Dowd. Directed by Hal Ashby. Peace-8; Pity-7; Questions-5; War-5.

COMMAND DECISION (Metro-Goldwyn-Mayer, 1948). Screenplay by William B. Laidlaw and George Froeschel; based on an idea by William Wister Haines. Directed by Sam Wood. Idea-3.

CONQUEST (Metro-Goldwyn-Mayer, 1937). Screenplay by Samuel Hoffenstein, Salka Viertel, and S. N. Behrman; based on *Pani Walewska,* a play by Helen Jerome and novel by Waclaw Gasiorowski. Directed by Clarence Brown. Loneliness-2; Sun-4.

COOL HAND LUKE (Warner Bros., 1967). Screenplay by Donn Pearce and Frank Pierson; based on the novel by Donn Pearce. Directed by Stuart Rosenberg. Eulogies-19; Failure-2; Good-10; Prayers-12.

THE COUNTRY GIRL (Paramount, 1954). Screenplay by George Seaton; based on the play by Clifford Odets. Directed by George Seaton. Actors-1; Choice-7; Cigarette-4; Differences-5; Disease-7; Drink Excuses-7; Elephants-4; Failure-5; Flattery-2; Hands-3; Idea-5; Indecision-3; Love-26; Pride-11; Self-Perception-10; Specializations-2; Theater-6; Trouble-6; Truth-6; Weakness-4; Why-7; Wives-2; Women-14.

THE CRUEL SEA (Universal, 1953). Screenplay by Eric Ambler; based on the novel by Nicholas Monsarrat. Directed by Charles Frend. Sea-2; War-7.

D

DAMN YANKEES (Warner Bros., 1958). Screenplay by George Abbott; based on the musical play by George Abbott and Douglass Wallop and *The Year the Yankees Lost the Pennant,* a novel by Douglass Wallop. Directed by George Abbott and Stanley Donen. Soul-3; Wives-1.

DANGEROUS (Warner Bros., 1935). Original Screenplay by Laird Doyle. Directed by Alfred E. Green. Suicide-10.

THE DARK AT THE TOP OF THE STAIRS (Warner Bros., 1960). Screenplay by Irving Ravetch and Harriet Frank Jr.; based on the play by William Inge. Directed by Delbert Mann. Awakenings-3; Children-4; Dying Words-10; Fights-6; Heart-8; Mothers-7; Prejudice-3; Rejection-15; Run-6; Tired-4; Trouble-7; Walk-4.

THE DARK CORNER (20th Century-Fox, 1946). Screenplay by Jay Dratler and Bernard C. Schoenfeld; based on the short story by Leo Rosten. Directed by Henry Hathaway. Appearances-3; Dark-4; Games-4; Gigolo-7; Love-13; Painting-7; Party-5; Pleasures-5; Sun-2.

DARK VICTORY (Warner Bros., 1939). Screenplay by Casey Robinson; based on the play by George Brewer Jr. and Bertram Bloch. Directed by Edmund Goulding. Awakenings-2; Dark-5; Death-1; Dying Words-30; Fools-9; Orders-3; Time-9; Translations-3; Wedding-3.

DARLING (Embassy, 1965). Original Screenplay by Frederic Raphael. Directed by John Schlesinger. Fidelity-2.

A DAY AT THE RACES (Metro-Goldwyn-Mayer, 1937). Screenplay by Robert Pirosh, George Seaton, and George Oppenheimer; based on a story by Robert Pirosh and George Seaton. Directed by Sam Wood. Crooked-4; If-2; Love-1; Proposals-3.

DAYS OF WINE AND ROSES (Warner Bros., 1962). Screenplay by J. P. Miller; based on his teleplay. Directed by Blake Edwards. Appearances-5; Bums-1; Drink Excuses-5; Drunk-1; Idea-2; Loneliness-10; Public Relations-2; Together-8.

DEAD END (United Artists, 1937). Screenplay by Lillian Hellman; based on the play by Sidney Kingsley. Directed by William Wyler. Looks-2.

DEATH OF A SALESMAN (Columbia, 1951). Screenplay by Stanley Roberts; based on the play by Arthur Miller. Directed by Laslo Benedek. Dreams-10; Eulogies-11.

DEATH TAKES A HOLIDAY (Paramount, 1934). Screenplay by Maxwell Anderson and Gladys Lehman; based on the play by Alberto Casella. Directed by Mitchell Leisen. Love-22.

DECEPTION (Warner Bros., 1946). Screenplay by John Collier and Joseph Than; based on *Monsieur Lamberthier,* a play by Louis Verneuil. Directed by Irving Rapper. Fools-8; Future-4; Lies-20; Loneliness-4; Taste-3.

A DELICATE BALANCE (American Film Theater, 1973). Screenplay by Edward Albee; based on his play. Directed by Tony Richardson. Gin-5; Men-17; Time-3.

DESIGNING WOMAN (Metro-Goldwyn-Mayer, 1957). Original Screenplay by George Wells; based on a suggestion by Helen Rose. Directed by Vincente Minnelli. Blood-2; Comeback-2; Eat-4; Never-6.

DESK SET (20th Century-Fox, 1957). Screenplay by Phoebe Ephron and Henry Ephron; based on *The Desk Set,* a play by William Marchant. Directed by Walter Lang. Available-1.

THE DESPERATE HOURS (Paramount, 1955). Screenplay by Joseph Hayes; based on his play and novel. Directed by William Wyler. Mind-7.

DETECTIVE STORY (Paramount, 1951). Screenplay by Philip Yordan and Robert Wyler; based on the play by Sidney Kingsley. Directed by William Wyler. Advice-5; Compromise-2; Conscience-4; Dismissals-4; Marriage-11; Mistakes-1; Smell-2; Soul-4; Static-5; Telephone Scenes-9; Thieves-6; Truth-5; Understand-2; Vulture-2.

THE DEVIL AND MISS JONES (RKO Radio, 1941). Original Screenplay by Norman Krasna. Directed by Sam Wood. Betrayal-8; Elephants-3; Looks-12; Love-9.

DIAL M FOR MURDER (Warner Bros., 1954). Screenplay by Frederick Knott; based on his play. Directed by Alfred Hitchcock. Amateur-2; Murder-8.

THE DIARY OF ANNE FRANK (20th Century-Fox, 1959). Screenplay by Albert Hackett and Frances Goodrich; based on their play and the book *Anne Frank, the Diary of a Young Girl*. Directed by George Stevens. Good-1.

DINNER AT EIGHT (Metro-Goldwyn-Mayer, 1933). Screenplay by Frances Marion and Herman J. Mankiewicz; based on the play by George S. Kaufman and Edna Ferber. Directed by George Cukor. Aging-4; Chins-3; Dictation-8; Lady-2; Life and Death-14; Men-10; Movies-4; Politics-3; Professions-13; Smell-12.

DIRTY HARRY (Warner Bros., 1971). Screenplay by Harry Julian Fink, R. M. Fink, and Dean Riesner; based on a story by Harry Julian Fink and R. M. Fink. Directed by Don Siegel. Guns-7.

DOCTOR IN THE HOUSE (Republic, 1954). Screenplay by Nicholas Phipps; adaptation by Richard Gordon; based on the novel by Richard Gordon. Directed by Ralph Thomas. Time-14.

DR. JEKYLL AND MR. HYDE (Metro-Goldwyn-Mayer, 1941). Screenplay by John Lee Mahin; based on the novel by Robert Louis Stevenson. Directed by Victor Fleming. Soul-9.

DR. STRANGELOVE OR: HOW I LEARNED TO STOP WORRYING AND LOVE THE BOMB (Columbia, 1964). Screenplay by Stanley Kubrick, Terry Southern, and Peter George; based on *Red Alert,* a novel by Peter George. Directed by Stanley Kubrick. Choice-2; Fights-2; Hair-7; Mad Act-8; Respect-3; Sex-4; Telephone Scenes-2; Walk-3; War-8; War-12.

DODSWORTH (United Artists, 1936). Screenplay by Sidney Howard; based on his play and the novel by Sinclair Lewis. Directed by William Wyler. Aging-2; Suicide-12.

DOG DAY AFTERNOON (Warner Bros., 1975). Original Screenplay by Frank Pierson. Directed by Sidney Lumet. Crazy-12; Dictation-6; Hope-6; Parents-2.

DOUBLE INDEMNITY (Paramount, 1944). Screenplay by Billy Wilder and Raymond Chandler; based on the novel by James M. Cain. Directed by Billy Wilder. Dictation-5; Husbands-7.

DRACULA (Universal, 1931). Screenplay by Garrett Fort; based on the play by Hamilton Deane and John L. Balderston and novel by Bram Stoker. Directed by Tod Browning. Greetings-13; Music-8; Wine-1; Wisdom-2.

DRACULA (Universal, 1979). Screenplay by W. D. Richter; based on the play by Hamilton Deane and John L. Balderston and novel by Bram Stoker. Directed by John Badham. Greetings-13; Music-8; Wine-1; Wisdom-2.

DRAGON SEED (Metro-Goldwyn-Mayer, 1944). Screenplay by Marguerite Roberts and Jane Murfin; based on the novel by Pearl S. Buck. Directed by Jack Conway and Harold S. Bucquet. Macho-8.

DRUMS ALONG THE MOHAWK (20th Century-Fox, 1939). Screenplay by Lamar Trotti and Sonya Levien; based on the novel by Walter D. Edmonds. Directed by John Ford. Faces-9; Kiss-12.

DUCK SOUP (Paramount, 1933). Screenplay by Bert Kalmar and Harry Ruby; additional dialogue by Arthur Sheekman and Nat Perrin. Directed by Leo McCarey. Communication-13; Compliments-4; Dance-3; Dismissals-1; Dogs-5; Greetings-2; Honor-2; Music-2; Never-8; Prison-5; Signs-3.

DUEL IN THE SUN (Selznick Releasing Organization, 1946). Screenplay by David O. Selznick; adaptation by Oliver H. P. Garrett; based on the novel by Niven Busch. Directed by King Vidor. Callings-7; Good-4; Life and Death-12; Prayer-4; Sin-6; Temptation-1.

DUST BE MY DESTINY (Warner Bros., 1939). Screenplay by Robert Rossen; based on the novel by Jerome Odlum. Directed by Lewis Seiler. Defense-2.

E

EAST OF EDEN (Warner Bros., 1955). Screenplay by Paul Osborn; based on the novel by John Steinbeck. Directed by Elia Kazan. Life-10; Man-12.

THE EGG AND I (Universal, 1947). Screenplay by Chester Erskine and Fred F. Finklehoffe; based on the book by Betty MacDonald. Directed by Chester Erskine. Signs-6; Water-10.

THE ELECTRIC HORSEMAN (Columbia, 1979). Screenplay by Robert Garland; based on a screen story by Paul Gaer and Robert Garland and story by Shelly Burton. Directed by Sydney Pollack. Life and Death-4.

ELMER GANTRY (United Artists, 1960). Screenplay by Richard Brooks; based on the novel by Sinclair Lewis. Directed by Richard Brooks. Drink-3; Fathers-3; Love-5; Pep Talks-2.

F

FAME (Metro-Goldwyn-Mayer, 1980). Original Screenplay by Christopher Gore. Directed by Alan Parker. Pain-1.

FAREWELL, MY LOVELY (Avco Embassy, 1975). Screenplay by David Zelag Goodman; based on the novel by Raymond Chandler. Directed by Dick Richards. Confessions-3; Guns-10; Hands-10; Insults-4; Looks-10; Rejection-7; Stupid-1; Tired-1; Tongue-3; Tough-6; Wealth-5.

THE FARMER'S DAUGHTER (RKO Radio, 1947). Screenplay by Allen Rivkin and Laura Kerr; based on *Hulda, Daughter of Parliament,* a play by Juhni Tervataa. Directed by H. C. Potter. Drink-6; Headlines-3.

FATHER GOOSE (Universal, 1964). Screenplay by Peter Stone and Frank Tarloff; based on "A Place of Dragons," a short story by S. H. Barnett. Directed by Ralph Nelson. Selfish-5; Strangers-5.

FEMALE ON THE BEACH (Universal, 1955). Screenplay by Robert Hill and Richard Alan Simmons; based on *The Besieged Heart,* a play by Robert Hill. Directed by Joseph Pevney. Apology-5; Decency-2; Exchanges-8; Likes and Dislikes-1; Mistakes-6; Rejection-13; Success-1; Why-4.

FIVE EASY PIECES (Columbia, 1970). Screenplay by Adrien Joyce; based on a story by Bob Rafelson and Adrien Joyce. Directed by Bob Rafelson. Animals-2; Orders-4; People-6; Talk-12.

THE FIVE PENNIES (Paramount, 1959). Screenplay by Jack Rose and Melville Shavelson; based on a story by Robert Smith; suggested by the life of Loring "Red" Nichols. Directed by Melville Shavelson. Drink-8.

FOOTLIGHT PARADE (Warner Bros., 1933). Original Screenplay by Manuel Seff and James Seymour. Directed by Lloyd Bacon. Professions-14.

FOR WHOM THE BELL TOLLS (Paramount, 1943). Screenplay by Dudley Nichols; based on the novel by Ernest Hemingway. Directed by Sam Wood. Beliefs-7; Courage-3; Don't-7; Drink Excuses-9; Dying Words-32; Empathy-7; Kiss-2; Never-10; Ugly-2.

A FOREIGN AFFAIR (Paramount, 1948). Screenplay by Charles Brackett, Billy Wilder, and Richard L. Breen; adaptation by Robert Harari; based on an original story by David Shaw. Directed by Billy Wilder. Angel-4; Excuses-3; Good-byes-9; Hunger-4; Republicans-2; Smell-14; Temptation-2.

FORT APACHE (RKO Radio, 1948). Screenplay by Frank S. Nugent; based on "Massacre," a story by James Warner Bellah. Directed by John Ford. Army-3; Honor-5; Pride-11.

THE FORTUNE COOKIE (United Artists, 1966). Original Screenplay by Billy Wilder and I. A. L. Diamond. Directed by Billy Wilder. Greed-1.

42ND STREET (Warner Bros., 1933). Screenplay by Rian James and James Seymour; based on the novel by Bradford Ropes. Directed by Lloyd Bacon. Faces-11; Promiscuity-2; Star-1; Work-7.

FOUR DAUGHTERS (Warner Bros., 1938). Screenplay by Julius J. Epstein and Lenore Coffee; based on "Sister Act," a short story by Fannie Hurst. Directed by Michael Curtiz. Hair-4; Looks-4; Self-Perception-1.

FRIENDLY PERSUASION (Allied Artists, 1956). Screenplay by an uncredited Michael Wilson; based on stories by Jessamyn West. Directed by William Wyler. Talk-10.

FROM HERE TO ETERNITY (Columbia, 1953). Screenplay by Daniel Taradash; based on the novel by James Jones. Directed by Fred Zinnemann. Army-2; Boxing-3; Dying Words-19; Floozy-2; Friends-9; Loneliness-5; Love Objects-1; Men-14; Names-5; Names-24; Threats-2.

THE FRONT PAGE (United Artists, 1931). Screenplay by Bartlett Cormack and Charles Lederer; based on the play by Ben Hecht and Charles MacArthur. Directed by Lewis Milestone. Thieves-3.

THE FRONT PAGE (Universal, 1974). Screenplay by Billy Wilder and I. A. L. Diamond; based on the play by Ben Hecht and Charles MacArthur. Directed by Billy Wilder. Thieves-3.

FUNNY FACE (Paramount, 1957). Original Screenplay by Leonard Gershe. Directed by Stanley Donen. Beautiful-5; Dictation-3.

FUNNY GIRL (Columbia, 1968). Screenplay by Isobel Lennart; based on her musical play. Directed by William Wyler. Eyes-8; First Lines-1; Live-6; Names-11; Religions-5; Self-Perception-3; Spinsters-5.

THE FURIES (Paramount, 1950). Screenplay by Charles Schnee; based on the novel by Niven Busch. Directed by Anthony Mann. Dying Words-29.

FURY (Metro-Goldwyn-Mayer, 1936). Screenplay by Bartlett Cormack and Fritz Lang; based on an original story by Norman Krasna. Directed by Fritz Lang. Conscience-5; Letters-10; Life and Death-13.

G

GASLIGHT (Metro-Goldwyn-Mayer, 1944). Screenplay by John Van Druten, Walter Reisch, and John L. Balderston; based on *Angel Street*, a play by Patrick Hamilton. Directed by George Cukor. Crazy-8; Jewels-1; Night-6.

GENTLEMAN'S AGREEMENT (20th Century-Fox, 1947). Screenplay by Moss Hart; based on the novel by Laura Z. Hobson. Directed by Elia Kazan. Action-2; Future-2; Hypocrisy-2; Looks-3; Manners-9; People-3; Prejudice-2; Smile-6; Why-6; Wives-9.

GENTLEMEN PREFER BLONDES (20th Century-Fox, 1953). Screenplay by Charles Lederer; based on the musical play by Joseph Fields and Anita Loos and novel by Anita Loos. Directed by Howard Hawks. Diamonds-1; Flattery-1; Help-4; Questions-14; Run-2; Swear-3; Tattoo-3; Toasts-18; Trust and Distrust-6.

THE GHOST AND MRS. MUIR (20th Century-Fox, 1947). Screenplay by Philip Dunne; based on *The Ghost of Captain Gregg and Mrs. Muir*, a novel by R. A. Dick. Directed by Joseph L. Mankiewicz. Jealous-1; Names-17; Poets-4; Tired-7.

THE GHOST BREAKERS (Paramount, 1940). Screenplay by Walter De Leon; based on "The Ghost Breaker," a play by Paul Dickey and Charles W. Goddard. Directed by George Marshall. Democrats-5; Fear-1; Progress-4.

GIANT (Warner Bros., 1956). Screenplay by Fred Guiol and Ivan Moffat; based on the novel by Edna Ferber. Directed by George Stevens. Children-6; Conflict-2; Drink-4; Greed-4; Hero-1; Land-3; Macho-16; Mind-4; Money-7; Moon-5; Parting Shots-4; Propositions-21; Success-5; Tough-5; Understand-8; Wealth-2.

GIGI (Metro-Goldwyn-Mayer, 1958). Screenplay by Alan Jay Lerner; based on the novel by Colette. Directed by Vincente Minnelli. Boredom-2; Class-7; Diamonds-5; Don't-13; Fingers-3; Honor-4; Jewels-3; Lies-8; Love-4; Manners-5; Marriage-13; Pleasures-3; Youth-1.

THE GLASS MENAGERIE (Warner Bros., 1950). Screenplay by Tennessee Williams and Peter Berneis; based on the play by Tennessee Williams. Directed by Irving Rapper. Awakenings-4; Dance-6; Eat-1; Fathers-5; Memory-2; Roses-6; Spinsters-1; Telephone Scenes-7.

GO WEST, YOUNG MAN (Paramount, 1936). Screenplay by Mae West; based on *Personal Appearance*, a play by Lawrence Riley. Directed by Henry Hathaway. Feelings-7; Hair-6.

THE GO-BETWEEN (Columbia, 1971). Screenplay by Harold Pinter; based on the novel by L. P. Hartley. Directed by Joseph Losey. Past-1.

THE GODDESS (Columbia, 1958). Original Screenplay by Paddy Chayefsky. Directed by John Cromwell. Available-3; Loneliness-11; Love-6; Propositions-18; Star-9.

THE GODFATHER (Paramount, 1972). Screenplay by Mario Puzo and Francis Ford Coppola; based on the novel by Mario Puzo. Directed by Francis Ford Coppola. Changes-3; Don't-11; Innocent-5; Questions-2; Threats-1; Translations-2; Violence-6.

GOING MY WAY (Paramount, 1944). Screenplay by Frank Butler and Frank Cavett; based on an original story by Leo McCarey. Directed by Leo McCarey. Firsts-8; Golf-1; Hope-1; Indecision-6; Money-10; Pleasures-4; Tact-1.

GONE WITH THE WIND (Metro-Goldwyn-Mayer, 1939). Screenplay by Sidney Howard; based on the novel by Margaret Mitchell; prologue written by an uncredited Ben Hecht. Directed by Victor Fleming. Beliefs-2; Birth-1; Breasts-1; Children-1; Conflict-5; Courage-4; Eat-3; Exchanges-16; Fools-5; Hands-1; Happiness-2; Heart-6; History-5; Home-1; Honor-3; Hunger-1; Indecision-2; Jealous-2; Kiss-1; Lady-4; Land-2; Lock-2; Looks-11; Love-35; Love Objects-2; Macho-17; Marriage-14; Murder-2; Never-7; Parting Shots-2; Past-6; Peace-2; Pet Expressions-1; Prologues-1; Proposals-5; Questions-13; Similarities-5; Spiders-6; Strength-3; Tact-6; Timing-2; Together-6; Wants-6; War-2; Wrong-8.

THE GOOD EARTH (Metro-Goldwyn-Mayer, 1937). Screenplay by Talbot Jennings, Tess Slesinger, and Claudine West; based on the novel by Pearl S. Buck. Directed by Sidney Franklin. Dying Words-12; Eulogies-5; Land-1.

THE GRADUATE (Embassy, 1967). Screenplay by Calder Willingham and Buck Henry; based on the novel by Charles Webb. Directed by Mike Nichols. Advice-1; Communication-7; Questions-10; Strange-3; Together-5.

GRAND HOTEL (Metro-Goldwyn-Mayer, 1932). Screenplay by William A. Drake; based on the play and novel by Vicki Baum. Directed by Edmund Goulding. Alone-1; Firings-2; Firsts-10; Life-13; Life and Death-17; Static-1.

THE GRAPES OF WRATH (20th Century-Fox, 1940). Screenplay by Nunnally Johnson; based on the novel by John Steinbeck. Directed by John Ford. Empathy-8; Epitaphs-1; Goals-2; Kiss-22; People-1; Prayers-13; Prison-1; Soul-8; Women-7.

THE GRASSHOPPER (National General Pictures, 1970). Screenplay by Jerry Belson and Garry Marshall; based on *The Passing of Evil,* a novel by Mark McShane. Directed by Jerry Paris. Choice-11.

THE GREAT DICTATOR (United Artists, 1940). Original Screenplay by Charles Chaplin. Directed by Charles Chaplin. Action-3; Future-9.

THE GREAT LIE (Warner Bros., 1941). Screenplay by Lenore Coffee; based on *January Heights,* a novel by Polan Banks. Directed by Edmund Goulding. Lies-2; Pride-10.

THE GREAT ZIEGFELD (Metro-Goldwyn-Mayer, 1936). Original Screenplay by William Anthony McGuire. Directed by Robert Z. Leonard. Divorce-1; Dying Words-6; Telephone Scenes-1.

THE GREEN BERETS (Warner Bros., 1968). Screenplay by James Lee Barrett; based on the novel by Robin Moore. Directed by John Wayne and Ray Kellogg. Guns-4.

THE GREEN PASTURES (Warner Bros., 1936). Screenplay by Marc Connelly and Sheridan Gibney; based on the play by Marc Connelly and suggested by the sketches in *Ol' Man Adam an' His Chillun,* a novel by Roark Bradford. Directed by Marc Connelly and William Keighley. Orders-5.

THE GREEN YEARS (Metro-Goldwyn-Mayer, 1946). Screenplay by Robert Ardrey and Sonya Levien; based on the novel by A. J. Cronin. Directed by Victor Saville. Disease-2; Dying Words-22; Eulogies-13; If-3; Toasts-19; Water-1.

GUESS WHO'S COMING TO DINNER (Columbia, 1967). Original Screenplay by William Rose. Directed by Stanley Kramer. Eat-7; Firings-3; Love-38; Marriage-6; Men-11; Silence-3.

GUNFIGHT AT THE O.K. CORRAL (Paramount, 1957). Screenplay by Leon Uris; suggested by "The Killer," a short story by George Scullin. Directed by John Sturges. Games-9; Never-11; Sin-2.

GYPSY (Warner Bros., 1962). Screenplay by Leonard Spigelgass; based on the musical play by Arthur Laurents and the memoirs of Gypsy Rose Lee. Directed by Mervyn LeRoy. Advice-6; Firsts-9; Letters-6.

H

HAIL THE CONQUERING HERO (Paramount, 1944). Original Screenplay by Preston Sturges. Directed by Preston Sturges. Crazy-5; Excuses-5; Hanging-6; Hero-2; Lies-3; Politics-2; Timing-3; Truth-4.

HAROLD AND MAUDE (Paramount, 1971). Original Screenplay by Colin Higgins. Directed by Hal Ashby. Live-2.

HARRY AND TONTO (20th Century-Fox, 1974). Original Screenplay by Paul Mazursky and Josh Greenfeld. Directed by Paul Mazursky. Automobiles-3; Feelings-6; Home-12; Wives-6.

HARVEY (Universal, 1950). Screenplay by Mary Chase and Oscar Brodney; based on the play by Mary Chase. Directed by Henry Koster. Hope-3; Illusions-2; Realities-1.

THE HASTY HEART (Warner Bros., 1949). Screenplay by Ranald MacDougall; based on the play by John Patrick. Directed by Vincent Sherman. Alone-4; Birthdays-2; Character-3; Friends-3; Health-2; Lies-5; Pity-6; Pride-6; Proposals-9; Royalty-6.

THE HEARTBREAK KID (20th Century-Fox, 1972). Screenplay by Neil Simon; based on "A Change of Plan," a story by Bruce Jay Friedman. Directed by Elaine May. Daughters-6; Timing-1.

THE HEAT'S ON (Columbia, 1943). Original Screenplay by Fitzroy Davis, George S. George, and Fred Schiller. Directed by Gregory Ratoff. Lucky-6.

HEAVEN CAN WAIT (20th Century-Fox, 1943). Screenplay by Samson Raphaelson; based on Birthday, a play by Lazlo Bus-Fekete. Directed by Ernst Lubitsch. Chin-4; Responsibility-1; Stomach-2.

THE HEIRESS (Paramount, 1949). Screenplay by Ruth Goetz and Augustus Goetz; based on their play and Washington Square, a novel by Henry James. Directed by William Wyler. Cruel-2; Greed-2; Last Lines-8.

HERE COMES MR. JORDAN (Columbia, 1941). Screenplay by Sidney Buchman and Seton I. Miller; based on Heaven Can Wait, a play by Harry Segall. Directed by Alexander Hall. Body-2; Headlines-12; Life and Death-1; Lucky-5; Memory-7.

THE HIGH AND THE MIGHTY (Warner Bros., 1954). Screenplay by Ernest K. Gann; based on his novel. Directed by William A. Wellman. Aging-11; Good-byes-7; Heart-26; Home-4; Looks-1; Vanity-1.

HIGH NOON (United Artists, 1952). Screenplay by Carl Foreman; based on "The Tin Star," a short story by John W. Cunningham. Directed by Fred Zinnemann. Run-7.

HIGH SOCIETY (Metro-Goldwyn-Mayer, 1956). Screenplay by John Patrick; based on The Philadelphia Story, a screenplay by Donald Ogden Stewart and play by Philip Barry. Directed by Charles Walters. Adultery-4; Champagne-4; Class-2; Compliments-1; Exchanges-6; Gentleman-1; Heart-12; History-1; Human-1; Looks-9; Love-33; Patience-2; Rules-2; Sayings-2; Silence-5; Smell-4; Wine-3.

HIS GIRL FRIDAY (Columbia, 1940). Screenplay by Charles Lederer; based on *The Front Page*, a play by Ben Hecht and Charles MacArthur. Directed by Howard Hawks. Husbands-3; Selfish-6; Snake-2.

HOLD BACK THE DAWN (Paramount, 1941). Screenplay by Charles Brackett and Billy Wilder; based on the novel by Ketti Frings. Directed by Mitchell Leisen. Marriage-5.

HOLIDAY (RKO Pathé, 1930). Screenplay by Horace Jackson; based on the play by Philip Barry. Directed by Edward H. Griffith. Faith-2.

HOLIDAY (Columbia, 1938). Screenplay by Donald Ogden Stewart and Sidney Buchman; based on the play by Philip Barry. Directed by George Cukor. Faith-2.

HONDO (Warner Bros., 1953). Screenplay by James Edward Grant; based on "The Gift of Cochise," a short story by Louis L'Amour. Directed by John Farrow. Men-15.

HORSE FEATHERS (Paramount, 1932). Screenplay by Bert Kalmar, Harry Ruby, S. J. Perelman, and Will B. Johnstone. Directed by Norman Z. McLeod. Fathers-7; Heart-22; Relatives-5; Why-3.

THE HOSPITAL (United Artists, 1971). Original Screenplay by Paddy Chayefsky. Directed by Arthur Hiller. Children-5; Doctors-1; Hypocrisy-6; Self-Perception-11.

HOUSE OF STRANGERS (20th Century-Fox, 1949). Screenplay by Philip Yordan; based on the novel by Jerome Weidman. Directed by Joseph L. Mankiewicz. Epitaphs-4; Men-9.

HOW GREEN WAS MY VALLEY (20th Century-Fox, 1941). Screenplay by Philip Dunne; based on the novel by Richard Llewellyn. Directed by John Ford. Coward-7; Drink Orders-6; Excuses-7; Fathers-1; Fear-8; Honor-7; Legs-6; Life and Death-20; Manners-12; Memory-1; Mind-8; Mothers-4; Music-7; Prayers-2; Royalty-3; Sons-3; Talk-5; Truth-3.

THE HUMAN COMEDY (Metro-Goldwyn-Mayer, 1943). Screenplay by Howard Estabrook; based on an original story by William Saroyan. Directed by Clarence Brown. First Lines-4; Human-7; Nose-1; Telegrams-3; Understand-4.

HUMORESQUE (Warner Bros., 1946). Screenplay by Clifford Odets and Zachary Gold; based on a short story by Fannie Hurst. Directed by Jean Negulesco. Drink Excuses-3; Priorities-1; Stimulating-3; Tact-7.

THE HUSTLER (20th Century-Fox, 1961). Screenplay by Sidney Carroll and Robert Rossen; based on the novel by Walter Tevis. Directed by Robert Rossen. Birth-7; Character-4; Church-3; Drink Excuses-13; Games-8; Idea-7; Illusions-3; Knowledge-3; Looks-8; Night-3.

I

I AM A FUGITIVE FROM A CHAIN GANG (Warner Bros., 1932). Screenplay by Howard J. Green and Brown Holmes; based on the story by Robert E. Burns. Directed by Mervyn LeRoy. Lies-16; Thieves-2.

I NEVER SANG FOR MY FATHER (Columbia, 1970). Screenplay by Robert Anderson; based on his play. Directed by Gilbert Cates. Death-7.

I REMEMBER MAMA (RKO Radio, 1948). Screenplay by DeWitt Bodeen; based on the play by John Van Druten and "Mama's Bank Account," the stories by Kathryn Forbes. Directed by George Stevens. Dying Words-15; Laugh-7; Remember-1.

I WAS A TEENAGE FRANKENSTEIN (American International, 1958). Original Screenplay by Kenneth Langtry. Directed by Herbert L. Strock. Tongue-4.

I'D CLIMB THE HIGHEST MOUNTAIN (20th Century-Fox, 1951). Screenplay by Lamar Trotti; based on the novel by Corra Harris. Directed by Henry King. Kiss-20.

I'M NO ANGEL (Paramount, 1933). Screenplay and dialogue by Mae West; story suggestions by Lowell Brentano; continuity by Harlan Thompson. Directed by Wesley Ruggles. Men-19; Orders-1.

THE ICEMAN COMETH (American Film Theater, 1973). Screenplay based on the play by Eugene O'Neill; text edited by Thomas Quinn Curtiss. Directed by John Frankenheimer. Apathy-1; Birthdays-3; Drink Excuses-12; Empathy-5; Fools-11; Goals-4; Lasts-1; Lies-24; Mellow-2; Peace-5; Pity-1; Pretense-4; Snakes-4; Trouble-5.

IMITATION OF LIFE (Universal, 1934). Screenplay by William Hurlbut; based on the novel by Fannie Hurst. Directed by John Stahl. Advice-2.

IN A LONELY PLACE (Columbia, 1950). Screenplay by Andrew Solt; adaptation by Edmund H. North; based on the novel by Dorothy B. Hughes. Directed by Nicholas Ray. Life and Death-9.

IN NAME ONLY (RKO Radio, 1939). Screenplay by Richard Sherman; based on *Memory of Love*, a novel by Bessie Breuer. Directed by John Cromwell. Illusions-4; Telephone Scenes-13.

IN OLD CHICAGO (20th Century-Fox, 1937). Screenplay by Lamar Trotti and Sonya Levien; based on "W the O'Learys," a short story by Niven Busch. Directed by Henry King. Strength-1.

IN THE GOOD OLD SUMMERTIME (Metro-Goldwyn-Mayer, 1949). Screenplay by Albert Hackett, Frances Goodrich, and Ivan Tors; based on *The Shop Around the Corner*, a screenplay by Samson Raphaelson, and *Parfumerie*, a play by Miklos Laszlo. Directed by Robert Z. Leonard. Letters-4; Rejection-14.

IN WHICH WE SERVE (United Artists, 1942). Original Screenplay by Noel Coward. Directed by Noel Coward and David Lean. Pep Talks-3; Toasts-11; Wants-1.

INDISCREET (Warner Bros., 1958). Screenplay by Norman Krasna; based on his play, *Kind Sir*. Directed by Stanley Donen. Adultery-5; Lies-10; Pretense-8; Talk-4.

THE INFORMER (RKO Radio, 1935). Screenplay by Dudley Nichols; based on the novel by Liam O'Flaherty. Directed by John Ford. Confessions-1; Dying Words-9; Heaven-5; Parting Shots-5; Royalty-7; Swear-2; Toasts-13.

INHERIT THE WIND (United Artists, 1960). Screenplay by Nathan E. Douglas and Harold Jacob Smith; based on the play by Jerome Lawrence and Robert E. Lee. Directed by Stanley Kramer. Alone-3; Beliefs-1; Courtroom Lines-4; Duty-3; Eulogies-12; Friends-8; Future-1; God-1; Greetings-10; Headlines-8; Hero-7; Ignorance-2; Intelligence-1; Law-4; Loneliness-12; Love-30; Mad Act-4; Newspapering-1; Priorities-7; Progress-2; Questions-6; Right-1; Royalty-2; Self-Perception-2; Swear-4; Tears-1; Telephone Scenes-12; Vanity-2; Why-1.

THE INN OF THE SIXTH HAPPINESS (20th Century-Fox, 1958). Screenplay by Isobel Lennart; based on *The Small Woman*, a book by Alan Burgess. Directed by Mark Robson. Beautiful-1; Courage-2; Good-byes-6; Happiness-6; Help-2; Live-4; Newspapering-11.

THE INSPECTOR GENERAL (Warner Bros., 1949). Screenplay by Philip Rapp and Harry Kurnitz; based on the play by Nikolai Gogol. Directed by Henry Koster. Translations-8.

THE INVISIBLE MAN (Universal, 1933). Screenplay by R. C. Sherriff; based on the novel by H. G. Wells. Directed by James Whale. Murder-3.

ISADORA (Universal, 1968). Screenplay by Melvyn Bragg and Clive Exton; additional dialogue by Margaret Drabble; adaptation by Melvyn Bragg; based on the books, *My Life* by Isadora Duncan and *Isadora Duncan, an Intimate Portrait* by Sewell Stokes. Directed by Karel Reisz. Dance-8; Diamonds-3; Live-8; Nature-5; Wealth-3.

IT HAPPENED ONE NIGHT (Columbia, 1934). Screenplay by Robert Riskin; based on "Night Bus," a short story by Samuel Hopkins Adams. Directed by Frank Capra. Automobiles-1; Books-5; Class-3; Greetings-3; Hot-1; Humility-4; Legs-1; Men-7; Names-20; Newspapering-12; Nose-4; Sleep-3; Trumpet-1.

IT'S A WONDERFUL LIFE (RKO Radio, 1946). Screenplay by Albert Hackett, Frances Goodrich, and Frank Capra; based on "The Greatest Gift," a short story by Philip Van Doren Stern. Directed by Frank Capra. Angel-2; Birth-9; Moon-2; Prayers-10; Sounds-2; Spiders-3; Strange-10; Suicide-8; Toasts-14; Wish-7.

J

JEZEBEL (Warner Bros., 1938). Screenplay by Clements Ripley, Abem Finkel, and John Huston; based on the play by Owen Davis Sr. Directed by William Wyler. Apology-1; Convictions-2; Dress-6; Time-6; Tongue-2.

JOE (Cannon, 1970). Original Screenplay by Norman Wexler. Directed by John Avildsen. Democrats-2.

JOHNNY BELINDA (Warner Bros., 1948). Screenplay by Irmgard Von Cube and Allen Vincent; based on the play by Elmer Harris. Directed by Jean Negulesco. Mothers-9; Oops!-2; Together-11.

JOHNNY EAGER (Metro-Goldwyn-Mayer, 1941). Screenplay by John Lee Mahin and James Edward Grant; based on a story by James Edward Grant. Directed by Mervyn LeRoy. Betrayal-5; Books-8; Communication-10; Drunken Rantings-6; Dying Words-7; Eulogies-4; Friends-4.

JUDGMENT AT NUREMBERG (United Artists, 1961). Screenplay by Abby Mann; based on his teleplay. Directed by Stanley Kramer. Defense-1; Fear-9; Mothers-5; Music-5; Responsibility-3.

JUNE BRIDE (Warner Bros., 1948). Screenplay by Ranald MacDougall; based on *Feature for June,* a play by Eileen Tighe and Graeme Lorimer. Frigidity-1; Macho-14; Time-17.

K

KENTUCKY (20th Century-Fox, 1938). Screenplay by Lamar Trotti and John Taintor Foote; based on *The Look of Eagles,* a novel by John Taintor Foote. Directed by David Butler. Eulogies-18; Eyes-18; Trust and Distrust-5.

KEY LARGO (Warner Bros., 1948). Screenplay by Richard Brooks and John Huston; based on the play by Maxwell Anderson. Directed by John Huston. Deals-2; Drunk-4; Exchanges-2; Firsts-7; Head-2; Selfish-2.

THE KEYS OF THE KINGDOM (20th Century-Fox, 1944). Screenplay by Joseph L. Mankiewicz and Nunnally Johnson; based on the novel by A. J. Cronin. Directed by John M. Stahl. God-5.

KID GALAHAD (Warner Bros., 1937). Screenplay by Seton I. Miller; based on the novel by Francis Wallace. Directed by Michael Curtiz. Champion-1.

THE KING AND I (20th Century-Fox, 1956). Screenplay by Ernest Lehman; based on the musical play by Oscar Hammerstein II and *Anna and the King of Siam,* a book by Margaret Landon. Directed by Walter Lang. Dictation-7; Pet Expressions-9.

KING KONG (RKO Radio, 1933). Screenplay by James Creelman and Ruth Rose; based on an original story by Merian C. Cooper and Edgar Wallace. Directed by Merian C. Cooper and Ernest B. Schoedsack. Cameras-2; Eulogies-1; Introductions-1.

KINGS ROW (Warner Bros., 1941). Screenplay by Casey Robinson; based on the novel by Henry Bellamann. Directed by Sam Wood. Crazy-14; Hate-3; Legs-4; Psychiatry-2.

KISS OF DEATH (20th Century-Fox, 1947). Screenplay by Ben Hecht and Charles Lederer; based on a story by Eleazar Lipsky. Directed by Henry Hathaway. Betrayal-4; Big-2.

KLONDIKE ANNIE (Paramount, 1936). Screenplay and dialogue by Mae West; additional material suggested by Frank Mitchell Dazey; story ingredients by Marion Morgan and George B. Dowell; based on an original story by Mae West. Directed by Raoul Walsh. Good-5; Men-18.

KLUTE (Warner Bros., 1971). Original Screenplay by Andy Lewis and Dave Lewis. Directed by Alan J. Pakula. Floozy-3.

KNUTE ROCKNE—ALL AMERICAN (Warner Bros., 1940). Original Screenplay by Robert Buckner; based on the private papers of Mrs. Knute Rockne and reports of Knute Rockne's associates and intimate friends. Directed by Lloyd Bacon. Pep Talks-1.

L

THE L-SHAPED ROOM (Davis-Royal Films, 1962). Screenplay by Bryan Forbes; based on the novel by Lynne Reid Banks. Directed by Bryan Forbes. Notes-8.

THE LADY EVE (Paramount, 1941). Screenplay by Preston Sturges; based on a story by Monckton Hoffe. Directed by Preston Sturges. Crooked-1; Head-5.

LADY IN THE DARK (Paramount, 1944). Screenplay by Albert Hackett and Frances Goodrich; based on the play by Moss Hart. Directed by Mitchell Leisen. Macho-12.

THE LADY VANISHES (Gainsborough, 1938). Screenplay by Sidney Gilliat and Frank Launder; based on *The Wheel Spins,* a novel by Ethel Lina White. Directed by Alfred Hitchcock. Mind-16; Murder-11.

THE LAST OF SHEILA (Warner Bros., 1973). Original Screenplay by Anthony Perkins and Stephen Sondheim. Directed by Herbert Ross. Drink Orders-4.

LAST TANGO IN PARIS (United Artists, 1972). Original Screenplay by Bernardo Bertolucci and Franco Arcalli. Directed by Bernardo Bertolucci. Eulogies-16.

THE LATE GEORGE APLEY (20th Century-Fox, 1947). Screenplay by Philip Dunne; based on the play by John P. Marquand and George S. Kaufman and novel by John P. Marquand. Directed by Joseph L. Mankiewicz. Love-11; Mind-3; Sex-5.

LAURA (20th Century-Fox, 1944). Screenplay by Jay Dratler, Samuel Hoffenstein, and Betty Reinhardt; based on the novel by Vera Caspary. Directed by Otto Preminger. Accuracy-1; Changes-5; Character-6; Faces-3; Home-9; Insults-7; Love-15; Mad Act-9; Manners-7; Men-8; Mistakes-2; Money-16; Narcissism-4; Parting Shots-6; Privacy-3; Science-1; Similarities-4; Sun-1; Women-12; Writers-3.

LAWRENCE OF ARABIA (Columbia, 1962). Screenplay by Robert Bolt; based on *The Seven Pillars of Wisdom,* the autobiography of T. E. Lawrence, and other works by and about T. E. Lawrence. Directed by David Lean. Cameras-1; Discipline-3; Eulogies-9; Fools-3; Fun-2; Honor-6; Hunger-9; Lies-15; Manners-11; Truth-2.

LET'S FACE IT (Paramount, 1943). Screenplay by Harry Tugend; based on the musical play by Dorothy Fields and Herbert Fields and suggested by the play by Norma Mitchell and Russell G. Medcraft. Directed by Sidney Lanfield. Eyes-4.

THE LETTER (Warner Bros., 1940). Screenplay by Howard Koch; based on the play and short story by W. Somerset Maugham. Directed by William Wyler. Duty-4; Guns-6; Heart-17; Honest-3; Letters-2; Love-23; Strange-9.

A LETTER TO THREE WIVES (20th Century-Fox, 1949). Screenplay by Joseph L. Mankiewicz; adaptation by Vera Caspary; based on "One of Our Hearts," a short story by John Klempner. Directed by Joseph L. Mankiewicz. Champagne-3; Changes-4; Class-5; Communication-12; Ignorance-1; Intelligence-4; Introductions-6; Letters-1; Macho-5; Strength-5; Talk-8; Understand-5.

THE LIFE OF EMILE ZOLA (Warner Bros., 1937). Screenplay by Heinz Herald, Geza Herczeg, and Norman Reilly Raine; based on a story by Heinz Herald and Geza Herczeg. Directed by William Dieterle. Conscience-1; Courtroom Lines-3; Innocent-1.

LIFE WITH FATHER (Warner Bros., 1947). Screenplay by Donald Ogden Stewart; based on the play by Howard Lindsay and Russel Crouse and stories by Clarence Day Jr. Directed by Michael Curtiz. Business-1; Character-1; Church-1; Democrats-1; Don't-8; Heaven-1; Last Lines-15; Loneliness-8; Love-37; Macho-7; Pet Expressions-14; Relatives-1; Specializations-6; Trouble-12; Work-1.

LIFEBOAT (20th Century-Fox, 1944). Screenplay by Jo Swerling; based on the story by John Steinbeck. Directed by Alfred Hitchcock. Diamonds-7; Enemy-5; Epitaphs-3; Heart-4; Hunger-2; Law-7; Legs-5; Narcissism-7; Peace-4; Pet Expressions-8; Plans-2; Prayers-9; Tattoo-1; Water-8.

LIGHT IN THE PIAZZA (Metro-Goldwyn-Mayer, 1962). Screenplay by Julius J. Epstein; based on the novel by Elizabeth Spencer; prologue written by an uncredited Arthur Freed. Directed by Guy Green. Prologues-2.

LIMELIGHT (United Artists, 1952). Original Screenplay by Charles Chaplin. Directed by Charles Chaplin. Drink Excuses-6; Fights-8; Hunger-5; Life-12; Life and Death-15; Likes and Dislikes-4; Platonic Relationships-1; Suicide-7; Time-18; Wives-5.

THE LION IN WINTER (Embassy, 1968). Screenplay by James Goldman; based on his play. Directed by Anthony Harvey. Greetings-4; Knowledge-1; Relatives-7; Royalty-9; Sons-2.

LITTLE CAESAR (Warner Bros., 1930). Screenplay by Francis Edwards Faragoh; based on the novel by W. R. Burnett. Directed by Mervyn LeRoy. Dying Words-1; Guns-11; Tough-1.

THE LITTLE FOXES (RKO Radio, 1941). Screenplay by Lillian Hellman; additional scenes and dialogue by Arthur Kober, Dorothy Parker, and Alan Campbell; based on the play by Lillian Hellman. Directed by William Wyler. Apathy-2; Daughters-3; Honest-8; Lies-23; Questions-1; Stupid-6.

THE LITTLE PRINCE (Paramount, 1974). Screenplay by Alan Jay Lerner; based on the story by Antoine de Saint Exupery. Directed by Stanley Donen. Heart-9.

LIVING IT UP (Paramount, 1954). Screenplay by Jack Rose and Melville Shavelson; based on *Hazel Flagg,* a musical play by Ben Hecht, *Nothing Sacred,* a screenplay by Ben Hecht, and "Letter to the Editor," a short story by James H. Street. Directed by Norman Taurog. Heart-10; Letters-12.

LOLITA   (Metro-Goldwyn-Mayer,   1962). Screenplay by Vladimir Nabokov; based on his novel. Directed by Stanley Kubrick. Games-6.

THE LONG, HOT SUMMER (20th Century-Fox, 1958). Screenplay by Irving Ravetch and Harriet Frank Jr.; based on *The Hamlet,* a novel by William Faulkner, and "Barn Burning" and "The Spotted Horses," two short stories by William Faulkner. Directed by Martin Ritt. Life-6; Names-7; Nature-2; Never-17; Run-3; Smile-4; Sons-4; Strangers-3; Translations-7.

LOST HORIZON (Columbia, 1937). Screenplay by Robert Riskin; based on the novel by James Hilton. Directed by Frank Capra. Toasts-5.

THE LOST WEEKEND (Paramount, 1945). Screenplay by Charles Brackett and Billy Wilder; based on the novel by Charles W. Jackson. Directed by Billy Wilder. Callings-9; Desperate-2; Disease-3; Dreams-9; Drink-1; Drink Excuses-14; Drink Orders-5; Drunk-2; Last Lines-3; Mind-2; Priorities-3; Right-1; Suicide-1; Weakness-2.

LOVE AFFAIR (RKO Radio, 1939). Screenplay by Delmer Daves and Donald Ogden Stewart; based on an original story by Mildred Cram and Leo McCarey. Directed by Leo McCarey. Advice-7; Champagne-2; Heaven-9; Likes and Dislikes-3; Propositions-24; Sex-2.

LOVE FINDS ANDY HARDY (Metro-Goldwyn-Mayer, 1938). Screenplay by William Ludwig; based on the stories by Vivien R. Bretherton and characters created by Aurania Rouverol. Directed by George B. Seitz. Kiss-19.

LOVE IS A MANY-SPLENDORED THING (20th Century-Fox, 1955). Screenplay by John Patrick; based on *A Many-Splendored Thing,* a novel by Han Suyin. Directed by Henry King. Beautiful-4; Beliefs-4; Gentle-3; Good-byes-11; Heaven-7; Knowledge-7; Loneliness-15; Love-51; Sayings-4; Sensible-4; Time-8; Why-13.

LOVE STORY (Paramount, 1970). Original Screenplay by Erich Segal. Directed by Arthur Hiller. Eulogies-7; Love-2; Names-10; Time-12; Wants-9.

LOVE WITH THE PROPER STRANGER (Paramount, 1963). Original Screenplay by Arnold Schulman. Directed by Robert Mulligan. Proposals-1.

LOVERS AND OTHER STRANGERS (Cinerama Releasing Corporation, 1970). Screenplay by Renee Taylor, Joseph Bologna, and David Z. Goodman; based on the play by Renee Taylor and Joseph Bologna. Directed by Cy Howard. Adultery-6; Books-1; Happiness-1; Macho-20; Marriage-15; Past-3; Pet Expressions-3; Questions-9; Sex-6; Smell-16; Stimulating-4; Strangers-4; Together-1; Understand-3.

LUST FOR LIFE (Metro-Goldwyn-Mayer, 1956). Screenplay by Norman Corwin; based on the novel by Irving Stone. Directed by Vincente Minnelli. Loneliness-7; Painting-3; Sun-5; Violence-5; Women-8.

M

M*A*S*H (20th Century-Fox, 1970). Screenplay by Ring Lardner Jr.; based on the novel by Richard Hooker. Directed by Robert Altman. Football-2; Tact-3.

THE MACOMBER AFFAIR (United Artists, 1947). Screenplay by Casey Robinson and Seymour Bennett; adaptation by Seymour Bennett and Frank Arnold; based on "The Short Happy Life of Francis Macomber," a short story by Ernest Hemingway. Directed by Zoltan Korda. Eulogies-20; Feelings-8; Heart-18; Incompatibility-3; Macho-15; Sayings-3; Women-13.

THE MAGNIFICENT AMBERSONS (RKO Radio, 1942). Screenplay by Orson Welles; based on the novel by Booth Tarkington. Directed by Orson Welles. Aging-15; Automobiles-2; Heaven-3; Justice-3; Law-1; Life-1; Memory-4; Names-23; Progress-3; Self-Depreciation-2; Style-1; Walk-1.

MAGNIFICENT OBSESSION (Universal, 1954). Screenplay by Robert Blees; adaptation by Wells Root; based on a screenplay by George O'Neill, Sarah Y. Mason, and Victor Heerman and novel by Lloyd C. Douglas. Directed by Douglas Sirk. Painting-2.

THE MAGNIFICENT YANKEE (Metro-Goldwyn-Mayer, 1950). Screenplay by Emmett Lavery; based on his play and *Mr. Justice Holmes,* the biography by Francis Biddle. Directed by John Sturges. Aging-16.

THE MAJOR AND THE MINOR (Paramount, 1942). Screenplay by Charles Brackett and Billy Wilder; based on *Connie Goes Home,* a play by Edward Childs Carpenter, and "Sunny Goes Home," a short story by Fannie Kilbourne. Directed by Billy Wilder. Propositions-12.

MAJOR BARBARA (United Artists, 1941). Screenplay by George Bernard Shaw; based on his play. Directed by Gabriel Pascal. Beliefs-8; Macho-21; Poverty-4; Religions-1.

MAKE WAY FOR TOMORROW (Paramount, 1937). Screenplay by Vina Delmar; based on the play by Helen Leary and Nolan Leary and *The Years Are So Long,* a novel by Josephine Lawrence. Directed by Leo McCarey. Don't-12; Drink Orders-3; Good-byes-2; Happiness-4; Pretense-5; Secrets-4; Toasts-4.

THE MALE ANIMAL (Warner Bros., 1942). Screenplay by Julius J. Epstein, Philip G. Epstein and Stephen Morehouse Avery; based on the play by James Thurber and Elliott Nugent. Directed by Elliott Nugent. Letters-8.

THE MALTESE FALCON (Warner Bros., 1941). Screenplay by John Huston; based on the novel by Dashiell Hammett. Directed by John Huston. Always-5; Angel-3; Beliefs-3; Birds-2; Choice-9; Crooked-3; Detectives-2; Dreams-2; Fake-1; Good-2; Hanging-5; Neck-2; Pretense-3; Selfish-3; Sons-6; Talk-2; Toasts-2; Trust and Distrust-3; Violence-4.

MAME (Warner Bros., 1974). Screenplay by Paul Zindel; based on the musical play by Jerome Lawrence, Robert E. Lee, and Jerry Herman and *Auntie Mame,* a play by Jerome Lawrence and Robert E. Lee, and novel by Patrick Dennis. Directed by Gene Saks. Awakenings-1; Breasts-3; Drink Orders-7; Greetings-7; Hair-2; Hangover-2; If-4; Live-1; Money-9; Never-13; Pittsburgh-2; Spinsters-7; Sun-3; Window-5.

A MAN AND A WOMAN (Allied Artists, 1966). Original Screenplay by Claude Lelouch and Pierre Uytterhoven. Directed by Claude Lelouch. Propositions-13.

A MAN FOR ALL SEASONS (Columbia, 1966). Screenplay by Robert Bolt; based on his play. Directed by Fred Zinnemann. Dying Words-21; Marriage-3; Soul-6.

THE MAN WHO CAME TO DINNER (Warner Bros., 1941). Screenplay by Julius J. Epstein and Philip G. Epstein; based on the play by George S. Kaufman and Moss Hart. Directed by William Keighley. Appearances-4; Books-7; Changes-1; Dismissals-6; Doctors-5; Introductions-8; Kindness-6; Narcissism-6; Never-1; Nurses-2; Parents-1; Parting Shots-7; Passion-1; Propositions-2; Relatives-2; Sex-7; Snake-1; Static-3; Strange-7.

THE MAN WHO SHOT LIBERTY VALANCE (Paramount, 1962). Screenplay by James Warner Bellah and Willis Goldbeck; based on the short story by Dorothy M. Johnson. Directed by John Ford. Newspapering-2.

MARTY (United Artists, 1955). Screenplay by Paddy Chayefsky; based on his teleplay. Directed by Delbert Mann. Aging-3; Available-2; Dogs-1; Eat-6; Empathy-1; Faces-7; Fear-6; Good-7; Heart-25; Indecision-1; Kindness-1; Last Lines-6; Marriage-12; Pain-1; Pet Expressions-2; Rejection-1; Sex Appeal-2; Telephone Scenes-5; Ugly-1.

MARY, MARY (Warner Bros., 1963). Screenplay by Richard L. Breen; based on the play by Jean Kerr. Directed by Mervyn LeRoy. Eyes-1.

THE MASK OF DIMITRIOS (Warner Bros., 1944). Screenplay by Frank Gruber; based on A Coffin for Dimitrios, a novel by Eric Ambler. Directed by Jean Negulesco. Intelligence-5; Kindness-5; Money-5.

MATA HARI (Metro-Goldwyn-Mayer, 1931). Original Screenplay by Benjamin Glazer and Leo Birinski; dialogue by Doris Anderson and Gilbert Emery. Directed by George Fitzmaurice. Youth-7.

THE MATCHMAKER (Paramount, 1958). Screenplay by John Michael Hayes; based on the play by Thornton Wilder. Directed by Joseph Anthony. Life-8.

THE MATING SEASON (Paramount, 1951). Screenplay by Charles Brackett, Walter Reisch, and Richard L. Breen; suggested by Maggie, a play by Caesar Dunn. Directed by Mitchell Leisen. Hunger-6; Nose-2.

MEET JOHN DOE (Warner Bros., 1941). Screenplay by Robert Riskin; based on a story by Richard Connell and Robert Presnell Sr. Directed by Frank Capra. People-2.

MEET ME IN ST. LOUIS (Metro-Goldwyn-Mayer, 1944). Screenplay by Irving Brecher and Fred F. Finklehoffe; based on the stories and novel by Sally Benson. Directed by Vincente Minnelli. Disease-4; Lies-14.

THE MERRY WIDOW (Metro-Goldwyn-Mayer, 1934). Screenplay by Ernest Vajda and Samson Raphaelson; based on Franz Lehar's operetta, libretto by Victor Leon and Leo Stern. Directed by Ernst Lubitsch. Eyes-7.

MIDNIGHT (Paramount, 1939). Screenplay by Charles Brackett and Billy Wilder; based on a story by Edwin Justus Mayer and Franz Schulz. Directed by Mitchell Leisen. Chin-1; Crazy-7.

MIDNIGHT COWBOY (United Artists, 1969). Screenplay by Waldo Salt; based on the novel by James Leo Herlihy. Directed by John Schlesinger. Bathroom-4; Fathers-2;

Gigolo-3; Laugh-6; Self-Perception-9; Smell-7; Walk-6.

MILDRED PIERCE (Warner Bros., 1945). Screenplay by Ranald MacDougall; based on the novel by James M. Cain. Directed by Michael Curtiz. Advice-4; Children-2; Compliments-2; Daughters-2; Detectives-3; Disease-5; Dismissals-5; Exchanges-13; First Lines-3; Firsts-2; Gigolo-6; Heart-21; Last Lines-13; Laziness-2; Men-2; Mothers-1; Murder-1; Parting Shots-3; Platonic Relationships-2; Pretense-2; Pride-9; Professions-5; Regrets-2; Science-4; Seasons-4; Selfish-4; Smell-11; Soul-16; Static-12; Why-10; Work-2.

THE MIRACLE OF MORGAN'S CREEK (Paramount, 1944). Original Screenplay by Preston Sturges. Directed by Preston Sturges. Daughters-1; Firings-7; Gentleman-2; Good and Bad-4; Headlines-2; Marriage-17; Mind-10; Talk-6; Trouble-3; Ugly-3.

MIRACLE ON 34TH STREET (20th Century-Fox, 1947). Screenplay by George Seaton; based on an original story by Valentine Davis. Directed by George Seaton. Amateur-4; Choice-5; Christmas-1; Courtroom Lines-1; Faith-3; Headlines-1; Imagination-1; Normal-1; Wish-4.

THE MISFITS (United Artists, 1961). Screenplay by Arthur Miller; Based on his story. Directed by John Huston. Dark-1; Eyes-11.

MR. BLANDINGS BUILDS HIS DREAM HOUSE (RKO Radio, 1948). Screenplay by Norman Panama and Melvin Frank; based on the novel by Eric Hodgins. Directed by H. C. Potter. Advertising Slogans-2; Home-8; Money-4.

MR. DEEDS GOES TO TOWN (Columbia, 1936). Screenplay by Robert Riskin; based on "Opera Hat," a short story by Clarence Budington Kelland. Directed by Frank Capra. Courtroom Lines-2; Crazy-10; Firings-4; Help-1; Names-21; Newspapering-9; Priorities-8; Public Relations-5; Questions-19; Signs-5.

MR. PEABODY AND THE MERMAID (Universal, 1948). Screenplay by Nunnally Johnson; based on *Peabody's Mermaid,* a novel by Guy Jones and Constance Jones. Directed by Irving Pichel. Aging-10; Headlines-11.

MISTER ROBERTS (Warner Bros., 1955). Screenplay by Frank S. Nugent and Joshua Logan; based on the play by Thomas Heggen and Joshua Logan and novel by Thomas Heggen. Directed by John Ford and Mervyn LeRoy. Awards-5; Awards-6; Books-9; Boredom-3; Courage-1; Crazy-3; Disease-8; Fights-3; Firsts-3; Last Lines-1; Laziness-1; Letters-7; Men-13; Orders-8; Plans-1; Propositions-11; Specializations-1.

MR. SKEFFINGTON (Warner Bros., 1944). Screenplay by Julius J. Epstein and Philip G. Epstein; based on the story by "Elizabeth." Directed by Vincent Sherman. Adultery-2; Beautiful-2; Live-5; Looks-7.

MR. SMITH GOES TO WASHINGTON (Columbia, 1939). Screenplay by Sidney Buchman; based on "The Gentleman From Montana," a story by Lewis R. Foster. Directed by Frank Capra. Compromise-1; Confessions-6; Crazy-11; Eyes-9; Free-3; Guilty-4; Kindness-3; Politics-4.

MRS. MINIVER (Metro-Goldwyn-Mayer, 1942). Screenplay by Arthur Wimperis, George Froeschel, James Hilton, and Claudine West; based on the novel by Jan Struther. Directed by William Wyler. Awards-4; Macho-6; Roses-1; Tears-6; War-10.

MOBY DICK (Warner Bros., 1956). Screenplay by Ray Bradbury and John Huston; based on the novel by Herman Melville. Directed by John Huston. Blood-1; Callings-1; God-4; Last Lines-25; Orders-9; Sea-1.

MONKEY BUSINESS (Paramount, 1931). Screenplay by S. J. Perelman and Will B. Johnstone; additional dialogue by Arthur Sheekman. Directed by Norman Z. McLeod. Law-2; Loneliness-16; Party-2; Poverty-2; Propositions-9; Smell-9; Window-6.

THE MOON AND SIXPENCE (United Artists, 1942). Screenplay by Albert Lewin; based on the novel by W. Somerset Maugham. Directed by Albert Lewin. Macho-19.

THE MOON IS BLUE (United Artists, 1953). Screenplay by F. Hugh Herbert; based on his play. Directed by Otto Preminger. Boredom-7; Communication-4; Kiss-16; Money-17; Questions-11; Sensible-2; Sex-3.

THE MORE THE MERRIER (Columbia, 1943). Screenplay by Richard Flournoy and Lewis R. Foster; based on a story by Robert Russell and Frank Ross. Directed by George Stevens. Action-1; Birth-6; Don't-5; Nose-3; Pet Expressions-6; Plans-3.

MORNING GLORY (RKO Radio, 1933). Screenplay by Howard J. Green; based on the play by Zoë Akins. Directed by Lowell Sherman. Flowers-2; Foolish-1; Names-27.

MOULIN ROUGE (United Artists, 1952). Screenplay by Anthony Veiller and John Huston; based on the novel by Pierre La Mure. Directed by John Huston. Loneliness-14; Marriage-1.

MOURNING BECOMES ELECTRA (RKO Radio, 1947). Screenplay by Dudley Nichols; based on the play by Eugene O'Neill. Directed by Dudley Nichols. Don't-3.

MURDER, MY SWEET (RKO Radio, 1944). Screenplay by John Paxton; based on *Farewell, My Lovely,* a novel by Raymond Chandler. Directed by Edward Dmytryk. Always-6; Amateur-1; Communication-11; Detectives-1; Faces-8; Guns-1; Insults-4; Lady-5; Money-13; Names-18; Pretense-6;

Tired-1; Tough-6; Violence-1; Wealth-5; Why-9.

MURDER ON THE ORIENT EXPRESS (Paramount, 1974). Screenplay by Paul Dehn; based on the novel by Agatha Christie. Directed by Sidney Lumet Birth-2.

MUTINY ON THE BOUNTY (Metro-Goldwyn-Mayer, 1935). Screenplay by Talbot Jennings, Jules Furthman, and Carey Wilson; based on the novel by Charles Nordhoff and James Norman Hall. Directed by Frank Lloyd. Duty-2; Dying Words-20; Law-6; Names-1; Orders-6; Snake-3; Thieves-5; Threats-7; Toasts-10; Water-6.

MY DARLING CLEMENTINE (20th Century-Fox, 1946). Screenplay by Samuel G. Engel and Winston Miller; based on a story by Sam Hellman and *Wyatt Earp, Frontier Marshal,* a book by Stuart N. Lake. Directed by John Ford. Love-29; Names-19.

MY FAIR LADY (Warner Bros., 1964). Screenplay by Alan Jay Lerner; based on his musical play and *Pygmalion,* a screenplay and play by George Bernard Shaw. Directed by George Cukor. Character-5; Clean-2; Daughters-4; Gin-3; Good-3; Greetings-8; Lady-1; Last Lines-5; Parting Shots-1; Pet Expressions-14; Poverty-3; Professions-8; Royalty-4; Sounds-1; Static-6; Suicide-9.

MY FAVORITE WIFE (RKO Radio, 1940). Screenplay by Bella Spewack and Samuel Spewack; based on a story by Bella Spewack, Samuel Spewack, and Leo McCarey. Directed by Garson Kanin. Communication-8; Courtroom Lines-7; Life and Death-21.

MY MAN GODFREY (Universal, 1936). Screenplay by Morrie Ryskind, Eric Hatch and Gregory La Cava; based on *Ten Eleven Fifth,* a novel by Eric Hatch. Directed by Gregory La Cava. Discipline-2; Money-3; Nature-4; Wedding-1; Why-2.

MY REPUTATION (Warner Bros., 1946). Screenplay by Catherine Turney; based on *Instruct My Sorrows,* a novel by Clare Jaynes. Directed by Curtis Bernhardt. Innocent-4.

N

NASHVILLE (Paramount, 1975). Original Screenplay by Joan Tewkesbury. Directed by Robert Altman. Star-8.

NETWORK (United Artists, 1976). Original Screenplay by Paddy Chayefsky. Directed by Sidney Lumet. Adultery-3; Books-4; Business-5; Crazy-9; Death-5; Decency-3; Firings-5; Frigidity-5; Good-byes-10; Greetings-1; Hypocrisy-5; Life-3; Love-43; Mad Act-1; Movies-3; Murder-4; Screenplays-2; Suicide-6; Television-1; Together-4; Truth-1; Why-8.

NEVER GIVE A SUCKER AN EVEN BREAK (Universal, 1941). Screenplay by John T. Neville and Prescott Chaplin; based on an original story by Otis Criblecoblis, a.k.a. W. C. Fields. Directed by Edward Cline. Ignorance-6; Sleep-4; Tongue-1.

NIGHT AFTER NIGHT (Paramount, 1932). Screenplay by Vincent Lawrence; additional dialogue by Mae West; based on "Single Night," an original story by Louis Bromfield. Directed by Archie Mayo. Good-13.

A NIGHT IN CASABLANCA (United Artists, 1946). Original Screenplay by Joseph Fields and Roland Kibbee. Directed by Archie Mayo. Head-3.

NIGHT MUST FALL (Metro-Goldwyn-Mayer, 1937). Screenplay by John Van Druten; based on the play by Emlyn Williams. Directed by Richard Thorpe. Hanging-7; Mad Act-7; Night-4; Smile-7.

THE NIGHT OF THE HUNTER (United Artists, 1955). Screenplay by James Agee; based on the novel by Davis Grubb. Directed by Charles Laughton. Prayers-6.

THE NIGHT OF THE IGUANA (Metro-Goldwyn-Mayer, 1964). Screenplay by Anthony Veiller and John Huston; based on the play by Tennessee Williams. Directed by John Huston. Decency-4; Home-10; Human-5; Priorities-2; Tough-4; Women-2.

NIGHTMARE ALLEY (20th Century-Fox, 1947). Screenplay by Jules Furthman; based on the novel by William Lindsay Gresham. Directed by Edmund Goulding. Birth-8; God-2; Headlines-10; Heart-5; Joke-3; Last Lines-11; Love-41; Work-4.

NINOTCHKA (Metro-Goldwyn-Mayer, 1939). Screenplay by Charles Brackett, Billy Wilder, and Walter Reisch; based on an original story by Melchior Lengyel. Directed by Ernst Lubitsch. Alone-2; Business-4; Confessions-4; Discipline-1; Don't-9; Eyes-10; Kiss-4; Love-10; Memory-6; Paris-1; Passion-2; Past-10; Pity-3; Prologues-3; Rules-5; Sayings-1; Time-15; Understand-6.

NONE BUT THE LONELY HEART (RKO Radio, 1944). Screenplay by Clifford Odets; based on the novel by Richard Llewellyn. Directed by Clifford Odets. Money-8.

NORMA RAE (20th Century-Fox, 1979). Original Screenplay by Irving Ravetch and Harriet Frank Jr. Directed by Martin Ritt. Proposals-10.

NORTH BY NORTHWEST (Metro-Goldwyn-Mayer, 1959). Original Screenplay by Ernest Lehman. Directed by Alfred Hitchcock. Sons-5.

NOTHING SACRED (United Artists, 1937). Screenplay by Ben Hecht; based on "Letter to the Editor," a short story by James H. Street. Directed by William A. Wellman. Elephants-2; Hangover-1; Heart-10; If-5;

Letters-12; Life and Death-7; Newspapering-3; Smell-8; Wish-6.

NOTORIOUS (RKO Radio, 1946). Original Screenplay by Ben Hecht. Directed by Alfred Hitchcock. Confessions-5; Last Lines-19; Static-8; Stupid-3.

NOW, VOYAGER (Warner Bros., 1942). Screenplay by Casey Robinson; based on the novel by Olive Higgins Prouty. Directed by Irving Rapper. Cigarette-2; Fools-10; Love-16; Moon-1; Psychiatry-1; Tears-8.

O

THE ODD COUPLE (Paramount, 1968). Screenplay by Neil Simon; based on his play. Directed by Gene Saks. Chin-2; Choice-12; Don't-4; Fingers-2; Fun-4; Good and Bad-1; Notes-1.

ODD MAN OUT (General Film Distributors/ Universal, 1947). Screenplay by F. L. Green and R. C. Sherriff; based on the novel by F. L. Green. Directed by Carol Reed. Eyes-15.

OF HUMAN BONDAGE (RKO Radio, 1934). Screenplay by Lester Cohen; based on the novel by W. Somerset Maugham. Directed by John Cromwell. Kiss-14.

OF HUMAN HEARTS (Metro-Goldwyn-Mayer, 1938). Screenplay by Bradbury Foote; based on "Benefits Forgot," a story by Honore Morrow. Directed by Clarence Brown. Prayers-3.

OKLAHOMA! (Magna Corp., 1955). Screenplay by Sonya Levien and William Ludwig; based on the musical play by Oscar Hammerstein II and Green Grow the Lilacs, a play by Lynn Riggs. Directed by Fred Zinnemann. Kiss-23; Moon-4.

OLD ACQUAINTANCE (Warner Bros., 1943). Screenplay by John Van Druten and Lenore Coffee; based on the play by John Van Druten. Directed by Vincent Sherman. Champagne-1; Remember-6.

THE OLD DARK HOUSE (Universal, 1932). Screenplay by Benn W. Levy; additional dialogue by R. C. Sherriff; based on Benighted, a novel by J. B. Priestley. Directed by James Whale. Gin-6.

THE OLD MAID (Warner Bros., 1939). Screenplay by Casey Robinson; based on the play by Zoë Akins and novel by Edith Wharton. Directed by Edmund Goulding. Mothers-8.

THE OLD MAN AND THE SEA (Warner Bros., 1958). Screenplay by Peter Viertel; based on the novel by Ernest Hemingway. Directed by John Sturges. Dreams-3; Men-16.

ON THE BEACH (United Artists, 1959). Screenplay by John Paxton; based on the novel by Nevil Shute. Directed by Stanley Kramer. Signs-1.

ON THE WATERFRONT (Columbia, 1954). Original Screenplay by Budd Schulberg; based on "Crime on the Waterfront," nonfiction articles by Malcolm Johnson. Directed by Elia Kazan. Betrayal-1; Boxing-5; Bums-2; Love Objects-3; Silence-2; Soul-5; Threats-8.

ONCE UPON A HONEYMOON (RKO Radio, 1942). Screenplay by Sheridan Gibney; based on an original story by Leo McCarey. Directed by Leo McCarey. Mind-1.

ONE FLEW OVER THE CUCKOO'S NEST (United Artists, 1975). Screenplay by Lawrence Hauben and Bo Goldman; based on the novel by Ken Kesey. Directed by Milos Forman. Crazy-15; Sex-9.

THE ONION FIELD (Avco Embassy, 1979). Screenplay by Joseph Wambaugh; based on his book. Directed by Harold Becker. Guilty-1.

OUR TOWN (United Artists, 1940). Screenplay by Thornton Wilder, Frank Craven, and Harry Chandlee; based on the play by Thornton Wilder. Directed by Sam Wood. Compliments-8; Sleep-2.

OUT OF THE PAST (RKO Radio, 1947). Screenplay by Geoffrey Homes; based on his novel, *Build My Gallows High*. Directed by Jacques Tourneur. Love-8.

THE OX-BOW INCIDENT (20th Century-Fox, 1943). Screenplay by Lamar Trotti; based on the novel by Walter Van Tilburg Clark. Directed by William A. Wellman. Fights-11; Hanging-1; Last Lines-20; Letters-9.

P

THE PALM BEACH STORY (Paramount, 1942). Original Screenplay by Preston Sturges. Directed by Preston Sturges. Aging-12; Coward-6; Husbands-5; Manners-2; Men-3.

PAPER MOON (Paramount, 1973). Screenplay by Alvin Sargent; based on *Addie Pray*, a novel by Joe David Brown. Directed by Peter Bogdanovich. Bathroom-3.

THE PARADINE CASE (Selznick Releasing Organization, 1947). Screenplay by David O. Selznick; adaptation by Alma Reville and James Bridie; based on the novel by Robert Hichens. Directed by Alfred Hitchcock. Aging-13; Bad-2; Confessions-2; Likes and Dislikes-5; People-4; Pity-5.

PAT AND MIKE (Metro-Goldwyn-Mayer, 1952). Original Screenplay by Ruth Gordon and Garson Kanin. Directed by George Cukor. Choice-1; Dress-3; Faces-6; Names-9.

PATTON (20th Century-Fox, 1970). Original Screenplay by Francis Ford Coppola and Edmund H. North; based on *Patton: Ordeal and Triumph*, a book by Ladislas Farago, and *A Soldier's Story*, a book by Omar N. Bradley. Directed by Franklin Schaffner. Duty-1; Enemy-2; Together-12; War-4.

PERSONAL AFFAIR (United Artists, 1954). Screenplay by Lesley Storm; based on *The Day's Mischief*, a play by Lesley Storm. Directed by Anthony Pelissier. Love-45.

PETE KELLY'S BLUES (Warner Bros., 1955). Original Screenplay by Richard L. Breen. Directed by Jack Webb. Children-8; Drink Excuses-4.

PETE 'N' TILLIE (Universal, 1972). Screenplay by Julius J. Epstein; Based on *Witch's Milk*, a novella by Peter De Vries. Directed by Martin Ritt. Propositions-10.

THE PETRIFIED FOREST (Warner Bros., 1936). Screenplay by Delmer Daves and Charles Kenyon; based on the play by Robert E. Sherwood. Directed by Archie Mayo. Dying Words-13; Feelings-5; Future-6; Introductions-7; Lasts-3; Life and Death-6; Love-34; Right-2; Suicide-11.

PEYTON PLACE (20th Century-Fox, 1957). Screenplay by John Michael Hayes; based on the novel by Grace Metalious. Directed by Mark Robson. Games-3; Hypocrisy-3; Kiss-3; Professions-11; Seasons-1.

THE PHILADELPHIA STORY (Metro-Goldwyn-Mayer, 1940). Screenplay by Donald Ogden Stewart; based on the play by Philip Barry. Directed by George Cukor. Adultery-4; Champagne-4; Class-2; Compliments-1; Crazy-16; Differences-7; Drink-5; Exchanges-6; Hangover-4; Hate-10; Heart-12; History-1; Human-1; Husbands-2; Knowledge-6; Looks-9; Love-33; Narcissism-3; Patience-2; Religions-2; Rules-2; Silence-5; Smell-4; Smile-9; Understand-1; Weakness-3; Wine-3.

PHONE CALL FROM A STRANGER (20th Century-Fox, 1952). Screenplay by Nunnally Johnson; based on a novella by I. A. R. Wylie. Directed by Jean Negulesco. Love-18.

PICNIC (Columbia, 1955). Screenplay by Daniel Taradash; based on the play by William Inge. Directed by Joshua Logan. Advice-8; Books-3; Bums-3; Dance-5; Domesticity-1; Fake-3; Flowers-5; Kiss-10; Legs-3; Macho-3; Night-5; Party-7; Patience-3; Professions-3; Proposals-2; Propositions-5; Spinsters-3; Static-7; Tired-5; Wants-7; Youth-3.

THE PICTURE OF DORIAN GRAY (Metro-Goldwyn-Mayer, 1945). Screenplay by Albert Lewin; based on the novel by Oscar Wilde. Directed by Albert Lewin. Always-1; Differences-3; Empathy-3; Enemy-1; Exchanges-17; Faces-4; Friends-11; Goals-1; If-1; Intelligence-3; Lasts-2; Live-3; Love-32; Macho-13; Mistakes-4; Painting-5; Pleasures-2; Priorities-5; Prologues-6; Regrets-1; Sin-2; Soul-2; Strange-5; Suicide-3; Tired-3; Wish-5; Women-1; Youth-2.

PILLOW TALK (Universal, 1959). Screenplay by Stanley Shapiro and Maurice Richlin; based on a story by Russell Rouse and Clarence Greene. Directed by Michael Gordon. Alone-10; Birds-4; Communication-2; Drunk-3; Furnishings-3; Hangover-3; Marriage-16; Money-14; New York-3; Psychiatry-4; Rejection-8; Sayings-5; Spiders-4; Static-11; Taste-2; Understand-7; Water-9.

A PLACE IN THE SUN (Paramount, 1951). Screenplay by Michael Wilson and Harry Brown; based on *An American Tragedy*, a play by Patrick Kearney and novel by Theodore Dreiser. Directed by George Stevens. Differences-10; Good-byes-12; Heart-13; Kiss-9; Love-47; Respect-4; Telegrams-4; Trouble-2.

THE PLEASURE OF HIS COMPANY (Paramount, 1961). Screenplay by Samuel A. Taylor; based on the play by Samuel A. Taylor and Cornelia Otis Skinner. Directed by George Seaton. Birth-3; Husbands-1; Sounds-3.

THE POSEIDON ADVENTURE (20th Century-Fox, 1972). Screenplay by Stirling Silliphant and Wendell Mayes; based on the novel by Paul Gallico. Directed by Ronald Neame. Water-7.

POSSESSED (Warner Bros., 1947). Screenplay by Sylvia Richards and Ranald MacDougall; based on *One Man's Secret*, a novelette by Rita Weiman. Directed by Curtis Bernhardt. Crazy-13; Excuses-4; Fidelity-4; Kiss-6; Looks-5; Narcissism-8; Piano-1; Proposals-14; Rejection-16; Smell-15.

PRIDE AND PREJUDICE (Metro-Goldwyn-Mayer, 1940). Screenplay by Aldous Huxley and Jane Murfin; based on the play by Helen Jerome and novel by Jane Austen. Directed by Robert Z. Leonard. Class-4; Dance-7; Dignity-2; Fashion-5; Games-5; Pride-5; Respect-2.

THE PRIDE OF THE YANKEES (RKO Radio, 1942). Screenplay by Herman J. Mankiewicz and Jo Swerling; based on an original story by Paul Gallico. Directed by Sam Wood. Lucky-1.

THE PRIME OF MISS JEAN BRODIE (20th Century-Fox, 1969). Screenplay by Jay Presson Allen; based on her play and the novel by Muriel Spark. Directed by Ronald Neame. Beliefs-6; Betrayal-7; Choice-8; Letters-13; Love-46; Professions-10; Specializations-5.

THE PRINCE AND THE PAUPER (Warner Bros., 1937). Screenplay by Laird Doyle; based on the novel by Mark Twain. Directed by William Keighley. Never-3.

THE PRISONER OF ZENDA (United Artists, 1937). Screenplay by Donald Ogden Stewart, John L. Balderston, and Wells Root; based on the novel by Anthony Hope. Directed by John Cromwell. Eyes-14.

THE PRIVATE LIFE OF HENRY VIII (London Films/United Artists, 1933). Original Screenplay by Lajos Biro and Arthur Wimperis. Directed by Alexander Korda. Choice-6; Stupid-5; Wives-4.

PRIVATE LIVES (Metro-Goldwyn-Mayer, 1931). Screenplay by Hans Kraly, Richard Schayer, and Claudine West; based on the play by Noel Coward. Directed by Sidney Franklin. Don't-1; Macho-18.

THE PRIVATE LIVES OF ELIZABETH AND ESSEX (Warner Bros., 1939). Screenplay by Norman Reilly Raine and Aeneas MacKenzie; based on *Elizabeth the Queen*, a play by Maxwell Anderson. Directed by Michael Curtiz. Alone-5.

PRIVATE WORLDS (Paramount, 1935). Screenplay by Lynn Starling; based on the novel by Phyllis Bottome. Directed by Gregory La Cava. Hate-6.

THE PRODUCERS (Embassy, 1968). Original Screenplay by Mel Brooks. Directed by Mel Brooks. Actors-6; Bad-1; Birds-1; Butterflies-1; Directors-3; Dishonest-2; Failure-4; Fashion-3; Games-2; Greetings-6; Guilty-3; Mad Act-10; Money-2; Plans-4; Poverty-5; Prison-3; Producers-3; Success-2; Wealth-1; Wrong-1.

PSYCHO (Paramount, 1960). Screenplay by Joseph Stefano; based on the novel by Robert Bloch. Directed by Alfred Hitchcock. Hate-8; Identity Crisis-3; Mad Act-12; Mind-12; Mothers-10; Sons-8; Static-16.

THE PUMPKIN EATER (Royal Films/Columbia, 1964). Screenplay by Harold Pinter; based on the novel by Penelope Mortimer. Directed by Jack Clayton. Honest-4.

THE PURPLE HEART (20th Century-Fox, 1944). Screenplay by Jerome Cady; based on a story by Melville Crossman. Directed by Lewis Milestone. Threats-6.

PYGMALION (Metro-Goldwyn-Mayer, 1938). Screenplay by George Bernard Shaw; adaptation by W. P. Lipscomb, Cecil Lewis, and Ian Dalrymple; based on the play by George Bernard Shaw. Directed by Anthony Asquith and Leslie Howard. Character-5; Clean-2; Daughters-4; Gin-3; Good-3; Lady-1; Last Lines-5; Parting Shots-1; Poverty-3; Professions-8; Royalty-4; Static-6; Suicide-9.

Q

QUEEN CHRISTINA (Metro-Goldwyn-Mayer, 1933). Screenplay by H. M. Harwood and Salka Viertel; dialogue by S. N. Behrman; based on a story by Salka Viertel and Margaret P. Levino. Directed by Rouben Mamoulian. Human-2; Lies-12; Love-48; Memory-8; Spinsters-6.

THE QUIET MAN (Republic, 1952). Screenplay by Frank S. Nugent; based on "Green Rushes," a short story by Maurice Walsh. Directed by John Ford. Applause-4; Dreams-6; Lock-3; Manners-6; Regrets-4; Toasts-17.

QUO VADIS (Metro-Goldwyn-Mayer, 1951). Screenplay by John Lee Mahin, S. N. Behrman, and Sonya Levien; based on the novel by Henryk Sienkiewicz. Directed by Mervyn LeRoy. Callings-5; Compliments-3; Cruel-1; Exchanges-4; Genius-1; History-6; Honest-5; Justice-1; Lies-13; Macho-11; Mad Act-6; Men-4; Music-1; Poets-3; Rome-3; Smile-8; Suicide-2; Tact-8; Tears-2; Transitions-1; Wants-3.

R

THE RAINMAKER (Paramount, 1956). Screenplay by N. Richard Nash; based on his play. Directed by Joseph Anthony. Appearances-7; Beautiful-3; Beliefs-5; Deals-1; Dreams-5; Faith-1; Firsts-1; Good-6; Hope-2; Last Lines-14; Names-8; Pride-2; Realities-5; Rejection-5; Specializations-7; Spinsters-2; Transitions-2; Wants-8.

THE RAZOR'S EDGE (20th Century-Fox, 1946). Screenplay by Lamar Trotti; based on the novel by W. Somerset Maugham. Directed by Edmund Goulding. Arrogance-2; Bad-3; Compliments-5; Exchanges-11; Fashion-1; Good-12; Heaven-4; Kiss-15; Likes and Dislikes-2; Manners-1; Party-6; Regrets-3; Why-12; Wisdom-3.

REBECCA (United Artists, 1940). Screenplay by Robert E. Sherwood and Joan Harrison; adaptation by Philip MacDonald and Michael Hogan; based on the novel by Daphne du Maurier. Directed by Alfred Hitchcock. Bed-2; Crazy-4; Dreams-1; Eyes-5; Foolish-2; Happiness-5; Kindness-2; Looks-6; Names-15; Never-14; New York-4; Professions-6; Proposals-4; Sea-4; Trouble-9; Window-2; Wives-8.

REBEL WITHOUT A CAUSE (Warner Bros., 1955). Screenplay by Stewart Stern; adaptation by Irving Shulman; based on an original story by Nicholas Ray. Directed by Nicholas Ray. Honor-8; Night-2.

RED RIVER (United Artists, 1948). Screenplay by Borden Chase and Charles Schnee; based on *The Chisholm Trail,* a novel by Borden Chase. Directed by Howard Hawks. Threats-4.

THE RED SHOES (Eagle-Lion, 1948). Original Screenplay by Emeric Pressburger; additional dialogue by Keith Winter. Directed by Michael Powell and Emeric Pressburger. Curtain Speeches-2; Dance-2; Dying Words-23.

REFLECTIONS IN A GOLDEN EYE (Warner Bros., 1967). Screenplay by Chapman Mortimer and Gladys Hill; based on the novel by Carson McCullers. Directed by John Huston. Normal-2.

RIDE THE HIGH COUNTRY (Metro-Goldwyn-Mayer, 1962). Original Screenplay by N. B. Stone Jr. Directed by Sam Peckinpah. Wants-2.

ROAD TO BALI (Paramount, 1952). Screenplay by Frank Butler, Hal Kanter, and William Morrow; based on an original story by Frank Butler and Harry Tugend. Directed by Hal Walker. Pain-3; Signs-4; Work-3.

ROAD TO RIO (Paramount, 1947). Original Screenplay by Edmund Beloin and Jack Rose. Directed by Norman Z. McLeod. Dress-2.

ROAD TO UTOPIA (Paramount, 1945). Original Screenplay by Norman Panama and Melvin Frank. Directed by Hal Walker. Drink Orders-2.

THE ROARING TWENTIES (Warner Bros., 1939). Screenplay by Richard Macaulay, Jerry Wald, and Robert Rossen; based on a story by Mark Hellinger. Directed by Raoul Walsh. Eulogies-2; Threats-3.

ROBERTA (RKO Radio, 1935). Screenplay by Jane Murfin and Sam Mintz; additional dialogue by Glenn Tryon and Allan Scott; based on the musical play by Otto Harbach and *Gowns by Roberta,* a novel by Alice Duer Miller. Directed by William A. Seiter. Fashion-2; Introductions-5.

ROMAN HOLIDAY (Paramount, 1953). Screenplay by Ian McLellan Hunter and John Dighton; based on an original story by Ian McLellan Hunter. Directed by William Wyler. Dress-7; Home-6.

THE ROMAN SPRING OF MRS. STONE (Warner Bros., 1961). Screenplay by Gavin Lambert; based on the novel by Tennessee Williams. Directed by Jose Quintero. Beautiful-9; Beauty-1; Lady-6.

ROOM AT THE TOP (Continental Distributing, 1959). Screenplay by Neil Paterson; based on the novel by John Braine. Directed by Jack Clayton. Tears-7; Wedding-4.

THE ROSE TATTOO (Paramount, 1955). Screenplay by Tennessee Williams; adaptation by Hal Kanter; based on the play by Tennessee Williams. Directed by Daniel Mann. Empathy-2; Innocent-3; Names-4; Specializations-8; Tattoo-2.

A ROYAL SCANDAL (20th Century-Fox, 1945). Screenplay by Edwin Justus Mayer; adaptation by Bruno Frank; Based on *The Czarina*, a play by Lajos Biro and Melchior Lengyel. Directed by Otto Preminger. Loneliness-3.

THE RUSSIANS ARE COMING THE RUSSIANS ARE COMING (United Artists, 1966). Screenplay by William Rose; based on *The Off-Islanders*, a novel by Nathaniel Benchley. Directed by Norman Jewison. Last Lines-18.

S

SABOTEUR (Universal, 1942). Original Screenplay by Peter Viertel, Joan Harrison, and Dorothy Parker. Directed by Alfred Hitchcock. Boredom-5; Innocent-6.

SAMSON AND DELILAH (Paramount, 1949). Screenplay by Jesse Lasky Jr. and Fredric M. Frank from original treatments by Harold Lamb and Vladimir Jabotinsky; based on the history of Samson and Delilah in the *Holy Bible*, Judges 13–16. Directed by Cecil B. DeMille. Macho-1.

SANDS OF IWO JIMA (Republic, 1949). Screenplay by Harry Brown and James Edward Grant; based on a story by Harry Brown.

Directed by Allan Dwan. Bravado-1; Cigarette-1; Mistakes-7; Tough-7.

THE SAXON CHARM (Universal, 1948). Screenplay by Claude Binyon; based on the novel by Frederic Wakeman. Directed by Claude Binyon. Arrogance-3; Theater-5.

SAYONARA (Warner Bros., 1957). Screenplay by Paul Osborn; based on the novel by James A. Michener. Directed by Joshua Logan. Last Lines-27.

THE SCOUNDREL (Paramount, 1935). Original Screenplay by Ben Hecht and Charles MacArthur. Directed by Ben Hecht and Charles MacArthur. Differences-8.

THE SEA WOLF (Warner Bros., 1941). Screenplay by Robert Rossen; based on the novel by Jack London. Directed by Michael Curtiz. Strength-7.

THE SEARCHERS (Warner Bros., 1956). Screenplay by Frank S. Nugent; based on the novel by Alan LeMay. Directed by John Ford. Wants-5.

SEPARATE TABLES (United Artists, 1958). Screenplay by Terence Rattigan and John Gay; based on the play by Terence Rattigan. Directed by Delbert Mann. Aging-8; Alone-6; Choice-10; Class-6; Coward-3; Dark-3; Excuses-1; Fear-7; Good-byes-3; Headlines-6; Hope-5; Horses-1; Husbands-6; Identity Crisis-4; Lies-11; Love-27; Pet Expressions-15; Right-3; Similarities-2; Soul-15; Strangers-2.

SERGEANT YORK (Warner Bros., 1941). Original Screenplay by Abem Finkel, Harry Chandlee, Howard Koch, and John Huston; based on *War Diary of Sergeant York* and *Sergeant York and His People*, two books by Sam K. Cowan, and *Sergeant York—Last of the Long Hunters*, a book by Tom Skeyhill. Directed by Howard Hawks. Dying Words-24; Guns-5; Law-5; Rejection-11.

SEVEN BRIDES FOR SEVEN BROTHERS (Metro-Goldwyn-Mayer, 1954). Screenplay by Albert Hackett, Frances Goodrich, and Dorothy Kingsley; based on "The Sobbin' Women," a short story by Stephen Vincent Benét. Directed by Stanley Donen. Last Lines-16; Love-14; Wives-3.

THE SEVEN YEAR ITCH (20th Century-Fox, 1955). Screenplay by Billy Wilder and George Axelrod; based on the play by George Axelrod. Directed by Billy Wilder. Hot-2; Imagination-3; Kiss-21; Pity-8; Psychiatry-8; Questions-16; Sex Appeal-3; Television-3; Writers-1.

THE SEVENTH VEIL (General Film Distributors/Universal, 1945). Original Screenplay by Muriel Box and Sydney Box. Directed by Compton Bennett. Hands-2; Mind-13; Painting-6; Religions-3.

SHANGHAI EXPRESS (Paramount, 1932). Screenplay by Jules Furthman; based on a story by Harry Hervey. Directed by Josef von Sternberg. Future-8; Promiscuity-1; Sin-7; Soul-10.

SHE DONE HIM WRONG (Paramount, 1933). Screenplay by Harvey Thew and John Bright; based on *Diamond Lil*, a play by Mae West. Directed by Lowell Sherman. History-2; Poverty-6; Propositions-1; Remember-3; Trouble-4; Wrong-3.

SHE WORE A YELLOW RIBBON (RKO Radio, 1949). Screenplay by Frank S. Nugent and Laurence Stallings; based on "The Big Hunt" and "War Party," two short stories by James Warner Bellah. Directed by John Ford. Army-1; Never-9; Notes-6; Pride-12; Time-13; Weakness-5.

SHIP OF FOOLS (Columbia, 1965). Screenplay by Abby Mann; based on the novel by Katherine Anne Porter. Directed by Stanley Kramer. Adolescence-1; Aging-6; Alone-7; Conscience-3; Dreams-8; Fools-1;

Future-5; Goals-3; Last Lines-22; Love-21; Music-6; Tears-4; Wrong-6.

THE SHOP AROUND THE CORNER (Metro-Goldwyn-Mayer, 1940). Screenplay by Samson Raphaelson; based on *Parfumerie*, a play by Miklos Laszlo. Directed by Ernst Lubitsch. Communication-3; Dictation-2; Fools-4; Letters-4; Professions-2; Rejection-14.

SILK STOCKINGS (Metro-Goldwyn-Mayer, 1957). Screenplay by Leonard Gershe and Leonard Spigelgass; based on the musical play by George S. Kaufman, Leueen MacGrath, and Abe Burrows and *Ninotchka*, a screenplay by Charles Brackett, Billy Wilder, and Walter Reisch, and original story by Melchior Lengyel. Directed by Rouben Mamoulian. Bathroom-1; Books-6; Business-4; Champagne-5; Don't-9; Faces-2; Fingernails-2; Happiness-3; Kiss-4; Memory-6; Movies-2; Music-4; Pity-3; Pleasures-6; Science-3; Talent-1.

SINCE YOU WENT AWAY (United Artists, 1944). Screenplay by David O. Selznick; adaptation by Margaret Buell Wilder; based on her book of letters. Directed by John Cromwell. Aging-1; Body-1; Compliments-6; Privacy-1; Prologues-4; Rejection-10.

SINGIN' IN THE RAIN (Metro-Goldwyn-Mayer, 1952). Original Screenplay by Adolph Green and Betty Comden. Directed by Gene Kelly and Stanley Donen. Loneliness-6; Star-4.

SITTING PRETTY (20th Century-Fox, 1948). Screenplay by F. Hugh Herbert; based on the novel by Gwen Davenport. Directed by Walter Lang. Callings-4; Eat-2; Fights-10; Genius-2; Insults-6; Jealous-3; Never-15; Sleep-5.

THE SNAKE PIT (20th Century-Fox, 1948). Screenplay by Frank Partos and Millen

Brand; based on the novel by Mary Jane Ward. Directed by Anatole Litvak. Accuracy-3; Crazy-2; Health-1; Jewels-2; Notes-4; Snake-6; Strange-6; Time-5.

SOME CAME RUNNING (Metro-Goldwyn-Mayer, 1958). Screenplay by John Patrick and Arthur Sheekman; based on the novel by James Jones. Directed by Vincente Minnelli. Writers-5.

SOME LIKE IT HOT (United Artists, 1959). Screenplay by Billy Wilder and I.A.L. Diamond; suggested by a story by R. Thoeren and M. Logan. Directed by Billy Wilder. Always-4; Breasts-2; Diamonds-2; Dress-5; Eyes-17; Good-byes-4; Horses-4; Kiss-11; Last Lines-4; Names-16; Propositions-17; Walk-5; Wealth-4.

SON OF PALEFACE (Paramount, 1952). Original Screenplay by Frank Tashlin, Robert L. Welch, and Joseph Quillan. Directed by Frank Tashlin. Blood-5; Bottle-2; Coward-4; Fathers-6; Greetings-12; Narcissism-5; Questions-1; Silence-4; Toasts-3.

THE SONG OF BERNADETTE (20th Century-Fox, 1943). Screenplay by George Seaton; based on the novel by Franz Werfel. Directed by Henry King. Eulogies-6; Heaven-8; Prayers-5; Prologues-7.

THE SOUND OF MUSIC (20th Century-Fox, 1965). Screenplay by Ernest Lehman; based on the musical play by Howard Lindsay and Russel Crouse and *The Trapp Family Singers,* a book by Maria Augusta Trapp. Directed by Robert Wise. Children-7; Music-3; Priorities-6; Tact-4; Whistle-2; Window-4.

THE SOUTHERNER (United Artists, 1945). Screenplay by Jean Renoir; adaptation by Hugo Butler; based on *Hold Autumn in Your Hand,* a novel by George Sessions Perry. Directed by Jean Renoir. Prayers-15.

SPARTACUS (Universal, 1960). Screenplay by Dalton Trumbo; based on the novel by Howard Fast. Directed by Stanley Kubrick. Body-3; Death-4; Dignity-1; Fat-1; Fools-7; Free-2; Narcissism-2; Politics-2; Promiscuity-3; Propositions-20; Rome-1; Rules-4.

SPELLBOUND (United Artists, 1945). Screenplay by Ben Hecht; adaptation by Angus MacPhail; based on *The House of Dr. Edwardes,* a novel by Francis Beeding. Directed by Alfred Hitchcock. Firsts-11; Guilty-6; Heart-19; Husbands-4; Marriage-8; Mind-11; Murder-12; Oops!-1; Poets-2; Psychiatry-7; Talk-7; Tired-2; Women-6; Work-8.

THE SPIRAL STAIRCASE (RKO Radio, 1946). Screenplay by Mel Dinelli; based on *Some Must Watch,* a novel by Ethel Lina White. Directed by Robert Siodmak. Telephone Scenes-4.

STAGE DOOR (RKO Radio, 1937). Screenplay by Morrie Ryskind and Anthony Veiller; based on the play by Edna Ferber and George S. Kaufman. Directed by Gregory La Cava. Actors-4; Birthdays-4; Curtain Speeches-3; Fake-5; Fashion-4; Flowers-1; Hearts-24; Insults-9; Mind-15; Notes-3; Pep Talks-6; Pretense-7; Producers-4; Tears-5; Theater-3.

STAGE STRUCK (RKO Radio-Buena Vista, 1958). Screenplay by Ruth Goetz and Augustus Goetz; based on *Morning Glory,* a play by Zoë Akins. Directed by Sidney Lumet. Hunger-8.

STAGECOACH (United Artists, 1939). Screenplay by Dudley Nichols; based on "Stage to Lordsburg," a short story by Ernest Haycox. Directed by John Ford. Prejudice-1; Worry-1.

STAIRWAY TO HEAVEN (Universal, 1946). Original Screenplay by Michael Powell and

Emeric Pressburger. Directed by Michael Powell and Emeric Pressburger. Life and Death-10; Strength-6; Stupid-2; Tears-3.

STALAG 17 (Paramount, 1953). Screenplay by Billy Wilder and Edwin Blum; based on the play by Donald Bevan and Edmund Trzcinski. Directed by Billy Wilder. Betrayal-2; Bums-4; Christmas-2; Exchanges-12; Firsts-5; Static-14; Thieves-4.

A STAR IS BORN (United Artists, 1937). Screenplay by Dorothy Parker, Alan Campbell, and Robert Carson; based on an original story by William A. Wellman and Robert Carson. Directed by William A. Wellman. Betrayal-6; Communication-6; Curtain Speeches-1; Drunken Rantings-2; Exchanges-9; Excuses-2; Friends-6; Heart-23; Looks-13; Pep Talks-8; Public Relations-3; Respect-1; Water-5.

A STAR IS BORN (Warner Bros., 1954). Screenplay by Moss Hart; based on a screenplay by Dorothy Parker, Alan Campbell and Robert Carson and original story by William A. Wellman and Robert Carson. Directed by George Cukor. Betrayal-6; Communication-6; Curtain Speeches-1; Drunken Rantings-3; Friends-6; Genius-4; Good and Bad-3; Live-7; Looks-13; Names-13; Pain-4; Pep Talks-7; Pleasures-1; Public Relations-4; Star-2; Timing-4; Why-5; Youth-6.

STATE OF THE UNION (Metro-Goldwyn-Mayer, 1948). Screenplay by Anthony Veiller and Myles Connolly; based on the play by Howard Lindsay and Russel Crouse. Directed by Frank Capra. Beautiful-6.

THE STERILE CUCKOO (Paramount, 1969). Screenplay by Alvin Sargent; based on the novel by John Nichols. Directed by Alan J. Pakula. Time-10.

THE STING (Universal, 1973). Original Screenplay by David S. Ward. Directed by George Roy Hill. Propositions-7.

STORM CENTER (Columbia, 1956). Original Screenplay by Daniel Taradash and Elick Moll. Directed by Daniel Taradash. Books-10.

THE STORY OF DR. WASSELL (Paramount, 1944). Screenplay by Alan LeMay and Charles Bennett; based on the short story by James Hilton and nonfiction account by Commander Corydon M. Wassell. Directed by Cecil B. DeMille. Prayers-8.

THE STORY OF LOUIS PASTEUR (Warner Bros., 1936). Screenplay by Sheridan Gibney and Pierre Collings; based on an original story by Sheridan Gibney and Pierre Collings. Directed by William Dieterle. Doctors-2; Goals-5; Humility-3; Nature-3; Proposals-7; Science-2.

STRANGERS ON A TRAIN (Warner Bros., 1951). Screenplay by Raymond Chandler and Czenzi Ormonde; adaptation by Whitfield Cook; based on the novel by Patricia Highsmith. Directed by Alfred Hitchcock. Exchanges-1; Hands-11; Murder-5; Promiscuity-6; Relatives-4.

A STREETCAR NAMED DESIRE (Warner Bros., 1951). Screenplay by Tennessee Williams; adaptation by Oscar Saul; based on the play by Tennessee Williams. Directed by Elia Kazan. Aging-5; Animals-1; Compliments-9; Dark-2; Drink-2; Exchanges-7; Hands-5; Heart-2; Last Lines-7; Lies-6; Likes and Dislikes-6; Lucky-4; Names-6; Proposal-11; Realities-3; Relatives-3; Royalty-5; Spiders-5; Strange-1; Strangers-1; Together-7; Youth-5.

THE SUBJECT WAS ROSES (Metro-Goldwyn-Mayer, 1968). Screenplay by Frank D. Gilroy; based on his play. Directed by Ulu Grosbard. Dreams-7; Roses-3.

SUDDENLY, LAST SUMMER (Columbia, 1959). Screenplay by Gore Vidal and Tennessee Williams; based on the one-act play by Tennessee Williams. Directed by Joseph

L. Mankiewicz. Disease-6; Gentle-2; Last Lines-9; Life-2; Love-7; Mad Act-11; Names-3; Poets-1; Seasons-6; Sons-7; Truth-8.

SULLIVAN'S TRAVELS (Paramount, 1941). Original Screenplay by Preston Sturges. Directed by Preston Sturges. Laugh-2.

SUMMER AND SMOKE (Paramount, 1961). Screenplay by James Poe and Meade Roberts; based on the play by Tennessee Williams. Directed by Peter Glenville. Guilty-5; Pride-1; Soul-13.

SUMMER HOLIDAY (Metro-Goldwyn-Mayer, 1948). Screenplay by Irving Brecher and Jean Holloway; based on *Ah, Wilderness!*, a screenplay by Albert Hackett and Frances Goodrich and play by Eugene O'-Neill. Directed by Rouben Mamoulian. Drink Excuses-8; Drunken Rantings-7; Eat-5; Laugh-3; Seasons-2.

SUMMER OF '42 (Warner Bros., 1971). Original Screenplay by Herman Raucher. Directed by Robert Mulligan. Adolescence-3; Letters-3.

SUMMER WISHES, WINTER DREAMS (Columbia, 1973). Original Screenplay by Stewart Stern. Directed by Gilbert Cates. Dying Words-4; Exchanges-15; Frigidity-3; Manners-3; Past-2; Trouble-10.

SUMMERTIME (United Artists, 1955). Screenplay by David Lean and H. E. Bates; based on *The Time of the Cuckoo,* a play by Arthur Laurents. Directed by David Lean. Hunger-7.

SUNDAY BLOODY SUNDAY (United Artists, 1971). Original Screenplay by Penelope Gilliatt. Directed by John Schlesinger. Last Lines-23.

THE SUNDOWNERS (Warner Bros., 1960). Screenplay by Isobel Lennart; based on

the novel by Jon Cleary. Directed by Fred Zinnemann. Home-11.

SUNSET BOULEVARD (Paramount, 1950). Original Screenplay by Charles Brackett, Billy Wilder, and D. M. Marshman Jr. Directed by Billy Wilder. Aging-9; Big-1; Cameras-3; Comeback-1; Crazy-17; Dance-10; Faces-1; First Lines-5; Gentle-1; Gigolo-8; Headlines-9; Mad Act-2; Newspapering-8; Past-4; Pride-8; Public Relations-6; Realities-2; Rejection-2; Screenplays-1; Star-5; Talk-1; Telephone Scenes-11.

THE SUNSHINE BOYS (Metro-Goldwyn-Mayer, 1975). Screenplay by Neil Simon; based on his play. Directed by Herbert Ross. Actors-5; Apology-4; Blood-4; Insults-2; Joke-5; Nurses-1; Past-8; Strength-4; Violence-2; Wrong-9.

SUSPICION (RKO Radio, 1941). Screenplay by Samson Raphaelson, Joan Harrison, and Alma Reville; based on *Before the Fact,* a novel by Francis Iles. Directed by Alfred Hitchcock. Greetings-5; Hero-4; Honest-2; Lies-21; Spinsters-4; Wrong-7.

SWEET BIRD OF YOUTH (Metro-Goldwyn-Mayer, 1962). Screenplay by Richard Brooks; based on the play by Tennessee Williams. Directed by Richard Brooks. Differences-1; Failure-3; Free-4; Gigolo-9; Success-4; Telephone Scenes-6; Time-7.

T

TAKE THE MONEY AND RUN (Cinerama Releasing Corporation, 1969). Original Screenplay by Woody Allen and Mickey Rose. Directed by Woody Allen. Beauty-3; Notes-7; Self-Depreciation-9.

A TALE OF TWO CITIES (Metro-Goldwyn-Mayer, 1935). Screenplay by W. P. Lipscomb and S. N. Behrman; based on the novel by Charles Dickens. Directed by Jack Conway. Appearances-2; Drink Excuses-10; Dying Words-2; Hands-4; Human-6; Hunger-3; Unfeeling-1.

A TALE OF TWO CITIES (J. Arthur Rank, 1958). Screenplay by T. E. B. Clarke; based on the novel by Charles Dickens. Directed by Ralph Thomas. Dying Words-2.

A TASTE OF HONEY (Continental Distributing, 1961). Screenplay by Shelagh Delaney and Tony Richardson; based on the play by Shelagh Delaney. Directed by Tony Richardson. Firsts-4; Genius-3; Mistakes-3.

TEA AND SYMPATHY (Metro-Goldwyn-Mayer, 1956). Screenplay by Robert Anderson; based on his play. Directed by Vincente Minnelli. Propositions-3.

THE TEAHOUSE OF THE AUGUST MOON (Metro-Goldwyn-Mayer, 1956). Screenplay by John Patrick; based on his play and the book by Vern J. Sneider. Directed by Daniel Mann. Introductions-2; Money-12; Peace-7; Professions-9; Questions-7; Remember-5; Self-Perception-5; Sex Appeal-1; Sleep-1; Suicide-5; Wants-4; Wisdom-1; Wrong-2.

THAT CERTAIN FEELING (Paramount, 1956). Screenplay by Norman Panama, Melvin Frank, I. A. L. Diamond, and William Altman; based on The King of Hearts, a play by Jean Kerr and Eleanor Brooke. Directed by Norman Panama and Melvin Frank. Furnishings-2.

THAT HAMILTON WOMAN (United Artists, 1941). Original Screenplay by Walter Reisch and R. C. Sherriff. Directed by Alexander Korda. Adultery-7; Honor-1; Time-16; War-3.

THESE THREE (United Artists, 1936). Screenplay by Lillian Hellman; based on her play, The Children's Hour. Directed by William Wyler. Apology-3; Honest-1; Human-8; Lies-18.

THEY DRIVE BY NIGHT (Warner Bros., 1940). Screenplay by Jerry Wald and Richard Macaulay; based on Long Haul, a novel by A. I. Bezzerides. Directed by Raoul Walsh. Drunk-6; Hands-6; Mad Act-5; Murder-7; Repetitions-2; Sayings-6; Toasts-20; Translations-6.

THEY KNEW WHAT THEY WANTED (RKO Radio, 1940). Screenplay by Robert Ardrey; based on the play by Sidney Howard. Directed by Garson Kanin. Marriage-2.

THEY SHOOT HORSES, DON'T THEY? (Cinerama Releasing Corporation, 1969). Screenplay by James Poe and Robert E. Thompson; based on the novel by Horace McCoy. Directed by Sydney Pollack. Eulogies-17; Good-byes-8; Last Lines-21; Pet Expressions-13; Questions-12; Rejection-4.

THE THIEF OF BAGDAD (United Artists, 1940). Screenplay and dialogue by Miles Malleson; based on a scenario by Lajos Biro. Directed by Ludwig Berger, Tim Whelan, and Michael Powell. Bottle-1; Curses-2; Human-4; Knowledge-5; Roses-5; Strange-8; Thieves-1; Wish-3; Youth-4.

THE THIN MAN (Metro-Goldwyn-Mayer, 1934). Screenplay by Albert Hackett and Frances Goodrich; based on the novel by Dashiell Hammett. Directed by W. S. Van Dyke. Questions-15.

THINGS TO COME (London Films/United Artists, 1936). Screenplay by H. G. Wells; based on his novel The Shape of Things To Come. Directed by William Cameron Menzies. Choice-3; Death-3; Life and Death-16; Progress-1.

THE THIRD MAN (Selznick-London Films, 1949). Original Screenplay by Graham Greene. Directed by Carol Reed. Betrayal-3; Death-8; Fools-2; Hero-6; Life and Death-2; Money-1; Names-25; Peace-1;

Propositions-15; Rejection-9; Sensible-3; Similarities-1.

THE THIRTY-NINE STEPS (Gaumont British, 1935). Screenplay by Charles Bennett; dialogue by Ian Hay; continuity by Alma Reville; based on the novel by John Buchan. Directed by Alfred Hitchcock. Fingers-4; Head-1; Mind-17; Secrets-1.

A THOUSAND CLOWNS (United Artists, 1965). Screenplay by Herb Gardner; based on his play. Directed by Fred Coe. Arrogance-1; Available-4; Birthdays-1; Cigarette-3; Class-1; Communication-9; Failure-1; Frigidity-2; Last Lines-24; Mood-Breakers-2; Names-12; Never-12; Pride-7; Telephone Scenes-10.

THREE COINS IN THE FOUNTAIN (20th Century-Fox, 1954). Screenplay by John Patrick; based on the novel by John H. Secondari. Directed by Jean Negulesco. Dishonest-1; Help-5; Idea-4; Lies-9; Passion-3; Proposals-8; Rome-4; Rules-3; Toasts-6; Wish-1.

TITANIC (20th Century-Fox, 1953). Original Screenplay by Charles Brackett, Walter Reisch, and Richard L. Breen. Directed by Jean Negulesco. Incompatibility-5; Mistakes-5; Mothers-2; Wealth-6.

TO BE OR NOT TO BE (United Artists, 1942). Screenplay by Edwin Justus Mayer; based on an original story by Ernst Lubitsch and Melchior Lengyel. Directed by Ernst Lubitsch. Actors-2; Callings-3.

TO CATCH A THIEF (Paramount, 1955). Screenplay by John Michael Hayes; based on the novel by David Dodge. Directed by Alfred Hitchcock. Communication-1; Stimulating-2.

TO EACH HIS OWN (Paramount, 1946). Screenplay by Charles Brackett and Jacques Thery; based on an original story by

Charles Brackett. Directed by Mitchell Leisen. Dance-1.

TO HAVE AND HAVE NOT (Warner Bros., 1944). Screenplay by Jules Furthman and William Faulkner; based on the novel by Ernest Hemingway. Directed by Howard Hawks. Kiss-5; Pet Expressions-12; Whistle-1.

TO KILL A MOCKINGBIRD (Universal, 1962). Screenplay by Horton Foote; based on the novel by Harper Lee. Directed by Robert Mulligan. Last Lines-12.

TOBACCO ROAD (20th Century-Fox, 1941). Screenplay by Nunnally Johnson; based on the play by Jack Kirkland and novel by Erskine Caldwell. Directed by John Ford. Smell-13.

TOM JONES (United Artists, 1963). Screenplay by John Osborne; based on the novel by Henry Fielding. Directed by Tony Richardson. Awakenings-5; Body-5; Daughters-7; Fools-6; Gigolo-4; Human-3; Ignorance-3; Live-10; Love-49; Pep Talks-5; Pet Expressions-5; Promiscuity-5; Propositions-6; Wine-2.

TOP HAT (RKO Radio, 1935). Screenplay by Dwight Taylor and Allan Scott; adaptation by Karl Noti; based on *The Girl Who Dared,* a play by Alexander Farago and Aladar Laszlo. Directed by Mark Sandrich. Differences-4; Kiss-18; Remember-4; Telegrams-1.

TOPKAPI (United Artists, 1964). Screenplay by Monja Danischewsky; based on *The Light of Day,* a novel by Eric Ambler. Directed by Jules Dassin. Fathers-9.

TOPPER (Metro-Goldwyn-Mayer, 1937). Screenplay by Jack Jevne, Eric Hatch, and Eddie Moran; based on the novel by Thorne Smith. Directed by Norman Z. McLeod. Changes-2; Don't-2.

TORRID ZONE (Warner Bros., 1940). Original Screenplay by Richard Macaulay and Jerry Wald. Directed by William Keighley. Vulture-1.

A TOUCH OF CLASS (Avco Embassy, 1973). Original Screenplay by Melvin Frank and Jack Rose. Directed by Melvin Frank. Communication-5.

TOUCH OF EVIL (Universal, 1958). Screenplay by Orson Welles; based on *Badge of Evil,* a novel by Whit Masterson. Directed by Orson Welles. Eulogies-21.

THE TOWERING INFERNO (20th Century-Fox/Warner Bros., 1974). Screenplay by Stirling Silliphant; based on two novels, *The Tower* by Richard Martin Stern and *The Glass Inferno* by Thomas N. Scortia and Frank M. Robinson. Directed by John Guillermin and Irwin Allen. Propositions-3.

THE TREASURE OF THE SIERRA MADRE (Warner Bros., 1948). Screenplay by John Huston; based on the novel by B. Traven. Directed by John Huston. Accuracy-2; Curses-4; Deals-3; Greed-3; Ignorance-5; Joke-1; Justice-2; Knowledge-2; Professions-4; Repetitions-1; Soul-7; Threats-9; Trouble-8; Water-5.

TRIAL (Metro-Goldwyn-Mayer, 1955). Screenplay by Don M. Mankiewicz; based on his novel. Directed by Mark Robson. Lies-4; Prejudice-3.

TROUBLE IN PARADISE (Paramount, 1932). Screenplay by Grover Jones and Samson Raphaelson; based on *The Honest Finder,* a play by Laszlo Aladar. Directed by Ernst Lubitsch. Moon-3.

TRUE GRIT (Paramount, 1969). Screenplay by Marguerite Roberts; based on the novel by Charles Portis. Directed by Henry Hathaway. Choice-4; Fat-2; Guns-8; Hands-12; Lucky-2; Smell-6; Talk-3.

TWELVE ANGRY MEN (United Artists, 1957). Screenplay by Reginald Rose; based on his teleplay. Directed by Sidney Lumet. Guilty-2.

TWENTIETH CENTURY (Columbia, 1934). Screenplay by Ben Hecht and Charles MacArthur; based on their play and *Napoleon of Broadway,* a play by Charles Bruce Milholland. Directed by Howard Hawks. Diamonds-4; Directors-1; Don't-15; Fake-4; Firings-6; Guns-9; Incompatibility-2; Love-17; Movies-1; Rejection-6; Self-Depreciation-1; Soul-14; Theater-4.

U

AN UNMARRIED WOMAN (20th Century-Fox, 1978). Original Screenplay by Paul Mazursky. Directed by Paul Mazursky. Domesticity-2; Fights-4; Guilty-7; Honest-6; Macho-2; Normal-3; Party-3; Passion-4; Propositions-8; Questions-4; Sensible-1.

V

THE V.I.P.'S (Metro-Goldwyn-Mayer, 1963). Original Screenplay by Terence Rattigan. Directed by Anthony Asquith. Firsts-6; Gigolo-1.

THE VIRGINIAN (Paramount, 1929). Screenplay by Howard Estabrook; based on the play by Kirk La Shelle and Owen Wister and novel by Owen Wister. Directed by Victor Fleming. Smile-1.

VIVA VILLA! (Metro-Goldwyn-Mayer, 1934). Screenplay by Ben Hecht; based on the book by Edgcumb Pinchon and O. B. Stade. Directed by Jack Conway. Dying Words-33; History-4; Law-3; Newspapering-10; Notes-5.

VIVA ZAPATA! (20th Century-Fox, 1952). Original Screenplay by John Steinbeck. Directed by Elia Kazan. Body-4; Conscience-2; Enemy-4; Friends-7; Good-11; Horses-2; Land-4; Love-39; Patience-1; Peace-3; People-5; Poverty-1; Proposals-12; Snake-5; Specializations-4; Strength-8; Time-2; Women-9.

VOLTAIRE (Warner Bros., 1933). Screenplay by Paul Green and Maude T. Howell; based on the novel by George Gibbs and E. Lawrence Dudley. Directed by John Adolfi. Priorities-4; Soul-12; Writers-2.

W

WAKE OF THE RED WITCH (Republic, 1948). Screenplay by Harry Brown and Kenneth Gamet; based on the novel by Garland Roark. Directed by Edward Ludwig. Eyes-6.

WATCH ON THE RHINE (Warner Bros., 1943). Screenplay by Dashiell Hammett; additional scenes and dialogue by Lillian Hellman; based on her play. Directed by Herman Shumlin. Alone-8; Fights-7; Flowers-3; Future-7; Sin-4; Strength-2.

THE WAY WE WERE (Columbia, 1973). Screenplay by Arthur Laurents; based on his novel. Directed by Sydney Pollack. Smile-3.

WE'RE NO ANGELS (Paramount, 1955). Screenplay by Ranald MacDougall; based on *La Cuisine des Anges,* a play by Albert Husson, and *My Three Angels,* a Broadway adaptation by Bella Spewack and Samuel Spewack. Directed by Michael Curtiz. Dying Words-17; Money-15; Prison-6; Time-11; Trust and Distrust-1.

THE WESTERNER (United Artists, 1940). Screenplay by Jo Swerling and Niven Busch; based on a story by Stuart N. Lake.

Directed by William Wyler. Courtroom Lines-6; Horses-5; Pet Expressions-10.

WHAT'S UP, DOC? (Warner Bros., 1972). Screenplay by Buck Henry, David Newman and Robert Benton; based on a story by Peter Bogdanovich. Directed by Peter Bogdanovich. Last Lines-28; Love-2.

WHITE CARGO (Metro-Goldwyn-Mayer, 1942). Screenplay by Leon Gordon; based on his play and *Hell's Playground,* a novel by Ida Vera Simonton. Directed by Richard Thorpe. Introductions-4.

WHITE HEAT (Warner Bros., 1949). Screenplay by Ivan Goff and Ben Roberts; based on a story by Virginia Kellogg. Directed by Raoul Walsh. Dying Words-8; Eulogies-3.

WHO'S AFRAID OF VIRGINIA WOOLF? (Warner Bros., 1966). Screenplay by Ernest Lehman; based on the play by Edward Albee. Directed by Mike Nichols. Awards-3; Bathroom-2; Boxing-4; Confessions-7; Dance-9; Divorce-4; Don't-6; Drink Orders-8; Eyes-3; Failure-6; Fear-10; Fights-5; Fun-3; Games-1; Good-9; Hands-7; Home-5; Illusions-1; Kiss-8; Lies-1; Life and Death-19; Never-5; Painting-4; Quiet-3; Self-Perception-7; Sex-8; Sons-1; Static-10; Tired-6; Talk-9; Wives-10.

THE WILD BUNCH (Warner Bros., 1969). Screenplay by Walon Green and Sam Peckinpah; based on a story by Walon Green and Roy N. Sickner. Directed by Sam Peckinpah. Exchanges-3; Guns-3.

WILSON (20th Century-Fox, 1944). Original Screenplay by Lamar Trotti. Directed by Henry King. Orchids-1.

WITNESS FOR THE PROSECUTION (United Artists, 1957). Screenplay by Billy Wilder and Harry Kurnitz; adaptation by Larry Marcus; based on the play and story by Agatha

Christie. Directed by Billy Wilder. Kiss-7; Letters-11.

THE WIZARD OF OZ (Metro-Goldwyn-Mayer, 1939). Screenplay by Noel Langley, Florence Ryerson, and Edgar Allan Woolf; adaptation by Noel Langley; based on the novel by L. Frank Baum. Directed by Victor Fleming. Heart-3; Home-2; Lucky-3; Never-2; Orders-10; Threats-5; Wish-2.

THE WOLF MAN (Universal, 1941). Screenplay by Kurt Siodmak and Gordon Kahn; based on a story by Kurt Siodmak. Directed by George Waggner. Moon-6.

WOMAN OF THE YEAR (Metro-Goldwyn-Mayer, 1942). Original Screenplay by Ring Lardner Jr. and Michael Kanin. Directed by George Stevens. Last Lines-17; Macho-9; Marriage-9; Newspapering-7.

THE WOMEN (Metro-Goldwyn-Mayer, 1939). Screenplay by Anita Loos and Jane Murfin; based on the play by Clare Boothe. Directed by George Cukor. Adultery-8; Advice-9; Awards-2; Bathroom-6; Divorce-2; Dogs-2; Dress-4; Exchanges-5; Eyes-13; Fidelity-1; Fingernails-1; Gin-7; Good-8; Husbands-8; Idea-8; Love-52; Marriage-10; Mothers-3; Pride-3; Questions-18; Threats-11; Toasts-7; Unfeeling-3; Wives-11; Women-15.

WORD IS OUT (Mariposa Film Group, 1978). A documentary directed by Peter Adair, Nancy Adair, Veronica Selver, Andrew Brown, Robert Epstein, and Lucy Massie Phenix. Love-50.

WRITTEN ON THE WIND (Universal, 1956). Screenplay by George Zuckerman; based on the novel by Robert Wilder. Directed by Douglas Sirk. Automobiles-4; Boredom-6; Self-Depreciation-6; Wealth-7.

WUTHERING HEIGHTS (United Artists, 1939). Screenplay by Ben Hecht and Charles

MacArthur; based on the novel by Emily Brontë. Directed by William Wyler. Advice-3; Curses-1; Doctors-4; Dying Words-11; Empathy-4; Exchanges-10; Hands-8; Hate-5; Heaven-6; Laugh-1; Life and Death-8; Love-42; Prayer-1; Realities-6; Royalty-1; Run-5; Static-4; Weakness-1; Window-3.

WUTHERING HEIGHTS (American International, 1971). Screenplay by Patrick Tilley; based on the novel by Emily Brontë. Directed by Robert Fuest. Exchanges-10; Prayers-1.

Y

YANKEE DOODLE DANDY (Warner Bros., 1942). Screenplay by Robert Buckner and Edmund Joseph; based on an original story by Robert Buckner. Directed by Michael Curtiz. Curtain Speeches-4.

YELLOW SKY (20th Century-Fox, 1948). Screenplay by Lamar Trotti; based on a story by W. R. Burnett. Directed by William A. Wellman. Smell-5.

YOU CAN'T CHEAT AN HONEST MAN (Universal, 1939). Screenplay by George Marion Jr., Richard Mack, and Everett Freeman; based on an original story by Charles Bogle, a.k.a. W. C. Fields. Directed by George Marshall. Insults-8; Tough-3.

YOU CAN'T TAKE IT WITH YOU (Columbia, 1938). Screenplay by Robert Riskin; based on the play by George S. Kaufman and Moss Hart. Directed by Frank Capra. Prayers-14; Proposals-6; Relatives-6.

YOUNG MAN WITH A HORN (Warner Bros., 1950). Screenplay by Carl Foreman and Edmund H. North; based on the novel by Dorothy Baker. Directed by Michael Curtiz. Incompatibility-4; Trumpet-3.

YOUNG MR. LINCOLN (20th Century-Fox, 1939). Original Screenplay by Lamar Trotti. Directed by John Ford. Dance-4; Hanging-2; Indecision-5; Mind-14; Politics-1; Self-Perception-6.

Z

ZIEGFELD FOLLIES (Metro-Goldwyn-Mayer, 1946). Sketch "When Television Comes" by Harry Tugend; based on "Gulper's Gin," a sketch by Red Skelton and Edna Skelton, and directed by George Sidney. Directed by Vincente Minnelli. Gin-2.

ZORBA THE GREEK (20th Century-Fox, 1964). Screenplay by Michael Cacoyannis; based on the novel by Nikos Kazantzakis. Directed by Michael Cacoyannis. Free-1; Good and Bad-2; Hands-9; Sea-3; Sin-1; Stupid-4; Trouble-1; Why-14; Women-10.